Insights from
Accounting History

Routledge Historical Perspectives in Accounting

EDITED BY STEPHEN A. ZEFF, *RICE UNIVERSITY, USA*

1. Profitability, Accounting Theory and Methodology
The Selected Essays of Geoffrey Whittington
Geoffrey Whittington

2. Financial Reporting in the UK
A History of the Accounting Standards Committee, 1969–1990
Brian A. Rutherford

3. Insights from Accounting History
Selected Writings of Stephen Zeff
Stephen A. Zeff

Insights from Accounting History
Selected Writings of Stephen Zeff

Stephen A. Zeff

Rice University

Routledge
Taylor & Francis Group
New York   London

First published 2010
by Routledge
270 Madison Avenue, New York, NY 10016

Simultaneously published in the UK
by Routledge
2 Park Square, Milton Park, Abingdon, Oxon OX14 4RN

Routledge is an imprint of the Taylor & Francis Group, an informa business

Typeset in Sabon by IBT Global.

Library of Congress Cataloging-in-Publication Data
Zeff, Stephen A.
  Insights from accounting history : selected writings of Stephen Zeff / by Stephen A. Zeff. — 1st ed.
    p. cm. — (Routledge historical perspectives in accounting ; 3)
  Includes bibliographical references and index.
  ISBN 978-0-415-55429-9
  1. Accounting—History. I. Title.
  HF5611.Z44 2010
  657.09—dc22
  2009048976

ISBN13: 978-0-415-55429-9 (hbk)
ISBN13: 978-0-203-85129-6 (ebk)

Contents

Foreword

I first became aware of the existence of Steve Zeff in 1973. I had left the London office of Cooper Brothers (now PricewaterhouseCoopers) in 1971 to join the Economics Department of Cardiff University. In those days, in Britain, it was not unusual for newly qualified accountants to move into academe. With no PhD, no research training and little research leadership available, I spent much of the next two years floundering, while attempting to locate an area of study where I imagined I might make a contribution. In the summer of 1973, I read Littleton and Zimmerman's *Accounting Theory: Continuity and Change* (1962) and Zeff's *Forging Accounting Principles in Five Countries: a History and an Analysis of Trends* (1972). Together, they contain a fascinating treatment of the inter-relationship between history, environment, regulation and accounting. Of more immediate importance for me was the fact that they stimulated my interest in the study of accounting history and, having studied accounting and law at university, indicated that I might have some of the skills required to take forward a career in academe.

I first met Steve at the Second Congress of the European Accounting Association held in Köln, Germany, in the spring of 1979. At the end of the first day of papers, a number of us were meandering around the Congress foyer wondering what to do about dinner. Perhaps because he was already a leading academic, or perhaps because he was taller than the rest of us, he led the way. And it was a good dinner.

Zeff's twin areas of accounting research embrace the international and the historical, with the latter specialisation the focus of this anthology and preface. We can be sure that Zeff's belief in the importance of history dates from when he was a student, with his doctoral dissertation, completed 1961, entitled 'A critical examination of the orientation postulate in accounting, with particular attention to its historical development' (Zeff 1978a). An early feature of Zeff's work was the search for origins and influences, perhaps based on the conviction, attributed to Aristotle, that 'If you would understand anything, observe its beginning and its development'. A related significant focus has been the implications of past events within the accounting arena.

Zeff publicly announced himself to the accounting history community, in 1962, with a paper reproduced as part of the current collection of essays entitled 'Replacement cost: member of the family, welcome guest, or intruder?' (Zeff 1962). My purpose in writing this preface is not to review the content of the publications reproduced in this anthology; their availability here enables readers to judge Zeff's scholarship for themselves. However, it is worth noting that 'Replacement cost' appeared in the premier accounting journal, *The Accounting Review*. The leading north American accounting and finance journals were then a little more accessible to accounting history researchers than is now the case, given their present preoccupation with empirical, capital market-based research, but not that much. So it was an impressive 'hit' for a young academic.

Zeff's second paper reproduced in this volume is equally significant, but in a different way. It is an academic analysis of the growing recognition among regulators of the economic consequences of accounting standards. It is significant in terms of what it says. But also to whom it is said. Throughout his career, Zeff has undertaken historical research not just for its own sake but to contribute towards making a difference. He has always shown a willingness, even keenness, to engage with the business community. The chosen arena for the publication of 'The rise of "economic consequences"' (1978b) was *Journal of Accountancy*—the periodical published for practitioners by the American Institute of Certified Public Accountants. Zeff's continuing commitment to maintaining a dialogue between academe and the accounting profession, three decades later, is demonstrated in a pair of publications in the *CPA Journal*, with the both focusing on 'The political forces behind professional accounting standards' (Zeff 2005a, 2005b). It is one unfortunate consequence of the research assessment exercises mounted by governments during the last twenty years or so that they privilege publications in academic journals as a measure of research excellence. One outcome is that academics increasingly speak more and more to one another, and very little to the outside world despite the fact that their research often has potential relevance for business and policy makers.

The status of accounting history as an academic discipline has risen dramatically during the time Zeff has been an active researcher. Signals of its rising star include the creation of world-wide and national disciplinary organisations for accounting historians, the increasing numbers of congresses and conferences devoted to the subject, and growth in the extent and often the quality of the accounting history literature (Walker 2008). The recent past has also witnessed successful endeavours to broaden our understanding of accounting's past through application of a growing range of intellectual paradigms (Napier 2008).

It is perhaps 1970 that can be identified as the year when accounting historians revealed a determination to make their mark, publicly, on the intellectual landscape. An International Accounting History Symposium, now recognised as the first World Congress on Accounting History, was held in Belgium in the autumn of that year. It was also the year when the American Accounting Association became sufficiently aware of accounting history to establish a committee to:

> propose objectives for research in accounting history, develop guidelines for the teaching of accounting history in undergraduate and graduate courses, and provide a forum . . . through which those interested in the teaching or research of accounting history can hear papers and exchange ideas. (American Accounting Association 1970)

Zeff was appointed chair and, acknowledging the fact that the subject was by no means as advanced as the histories of other disciplines, but convinced of the role it could and should play, the committee's report provided a blueprint for accounting history's future development (Walker 2008, 15).

An anthology naturally allows insufficient space to reproduce any of the numerous books authored and edited by Zeff. A contemporary of Zeff, Richard P. Brief, who is now Professor Emeritus of Statistics and Accounting at New York University, made an important contribution to the study of accounting history through editorial work, first for Arno Press and then for Garland Publishing. Over nearly 25 years, from 1976 to 2000, Brief monitored the publication of about 500 works in accounting history, many published for the first time. Zeff strongly supported this endeavour by contributing a series of authored and edited works (Zeff 1976, 1978a, 1978c, 1982a, 1982b, 1988; Zeff and Moonitz 1984; Parker and Zeff 1996; Solomons and Zeff 1996). He also encouraged others to do so.

Zeff's research has had a significant biographical focus, reflecting a desire to help redress underinvestment 'in the intellectual history of our field' (Zeff 2002b, 8). Subjects include Kenneth MacNeal, John B. Canning, David Solomons, Ray Chambers and, one of his teachers when an undergraduate at the University of Michigan, William Paton. The first two of these proved particularly 'satisfying studies' for Zeff, because they were 'important contributors to our literature [MacNeal was a practising CPA and Canning an economist] whom few accounting academics ever met' (Zeff 2002b, 8). Another of Zeff's book-length contributions to accounting's historiography is his authoritative biography of the leading 'accounting educator' of the first half of the twentieth century, Henry Rand Hatfield (Zeff 2000). Zeff places Hatfield's story within 'developments in academic and professional accounting that paralleled his career' (Zeff 2000, xix) and, in common with all Zeff's writings, the readers' interest is captured from the outset and maintained throughout the work.

There has been a growing recognition, in recent years, of the need not to overlook oral evidence in the endeavour to enrich our understanding of accounting's past. The value of undertaking research, where possible face to face, was recognised early on by Zeff, who estimates that he conducted 200

interviews (Zeff 1972, vi) when collecting material for *Forging Accounting Principles in Five Countries.*[1] While acknowledging the valuable role
of committee minutes, internal reports, correspondence and other publicly
available material, he later observed:

> these documents will seldom yield useful insights into the *real factors*
> that influenced the course of standard-setting. It becomes necessary to
> conduct interviews with the principal policy makers and others who
> were close observers of the standard-setting process. (Zeff 1980, 14,
> emphasis added)

Zeff's fruitful collaboration with the Dutch academic Kees Camfferman
has also made significant use of oral testimony to compile a regulatory-
based study of financial reporting in Holland (also with F. Wel, Zeff et al.
1992) and to compose the history of the International Accounting Standards Committee (Camfferman and Zeff 2007).

Zeff has been a first-class ambassador for accounting and accounting
history. A leading US academic who engages with accounting in many
parts of the world, he has been a particular supporter of the European
arena, where accounting history has flourished over the last thirty years.
In 1997, the British Accounting Association (initially titled the Association of University Teachers in Accounting) celebrated the fiftieth anniversary of its formation. To commemorate this milestone, a special issue of
The British Accounting Review contained three papers which together
gave the story of the Association's first half-century. It is strong testament
to the esteem enjoyed by Zeff among British academics, and his engagement with them, that he was invited to write the piece entitled 'The early
years of the Association of University Teachers of Accounting: 1947–1959'
(Zeff 1997).

Five years later was published a special issue of *The European Accounting Review* to celebrate twenty-five years of Anthony Hopwood's brain-
child—the European Accounting Association. Among the 10 invited
contributions to this special issue, the single non-European author was
described by the editors as 'someone who has been a tireless supporter
and friend of the EAA throughout almost its entire history'. A signal
also of the affection for Zeff is indicated by their further reference to
'*our* "man from the US"' (Lukka and Loft 2002, 4, emphasis added).
Zeff's involvement with the European Accounting Association has been
at all levels. He has been a member of the editorial advisory board—the
only one from outside of Europe—of the Association's journal since the
outset. He has made three plenary addresses as well as presenting numerous papers at parallel sessions. Zeff has been co-opted on the executive

---

[1] Corresponding studies focused on Australia (Zeff 1973) and New Zealand (Zeff 1979).

committee of the EAA every year since the Barcelona conference in 1981 and, as he puts it:

> All of these involvements on the Continent, including the receipt of an honorary degree in Turku, emerged out of my activities in the EAA, and in this respect, as an American who had previously had few professional contacts in Europe, the EAA has enabled me to feel more like a European with every passing year. (Zeff 2002a, 95)

Zeff's world-wide interest in accounting, its institutions and its practitioners has not caused him to neglect his homeland. As well as serving on numerous committees of the American Accounting Association, he has occupied the following leading offices: Director of Education 1969–71, President 1985–86, and editor of *The Accounting Review* for three terms stretching from 1977 to 1982. Indeed, such is his standing in the US that he was inducted as the 70th member of the Accounting Hall of Fame, founded in 1950, in 2002.

Zeff is international in his outlook on accounting and on life generally—an American who even developed an interest in the quintessential British and Colonial pastime of cricket! He was inculcated in its mysteries in November 1972 when a Fulbright Lecturer at Monash University, Melbourne, Australia. The biennial challenge to win 'The Ashes' has as extensive a public following in Australia as in England. This aroused Zeff's awareness of the sport and his interest was increased when he attributed the good turnout to one of his lectures, that coincided with the last day of the second test, primarily to the fact that Australia quickly bowled out England. Responding to an invitation from Anthony Hopwood, Zeff spent several weeks in the summer of 1981 as a Deering research fellow at the London Business School. The sponsors of the fellowship, the accountants Arthur Young & Company, arranged for him to speak at a conference of its managers held at the Birmingham Convention Centre. There, a dinner companion was the cricket journalist and commentator Christopher Martin Jenkins who was surprised that an American should have any interest in cricket, let alone possess some knowledge of the sport. Responding to Jenkins' invitation, Zeff was soon afterwards a welcome guest in the commentary box at Lords during the drawn second Test of the 1981 Ashes series. The Test Match team also included Brian Johnston, Richie Benaud and Trevor Bailey, and there unexpectedly took place an intra-overs interview which enabled Zeff to recount the story of how he had become interested in cricket nine years earlier.

Steve Zeff's career has been marked by numerous honours from all over the world. He has responded to invitations to lecture and take up visiting professorships beyond the United States in Australia, Canada, Italy, Kuwait, Mexico, The Netherlands, New Zealand, Scotland and Wales. Again confining attention to when he has 'played away from home', the number and range of professional awards and distinctions is quite staggering. Focusing only on the most recent—in 2009 he was elected to honorary membership of both CPA Australia and the Institute of Chartered Accountants in England and Wales—in both cases the first American to receive such recognition. Also that year he was the recipient of the Anthony G. Hopwood Award for Academic Leadership presented by the European Accounting Association.

Steve has had a long and distinguished career. I see no sign of him slowing down and see no reason why he should.

John Richard Edwards

Cardiff University

REFERENCES

American Accounting Association. 1970. Committee on Accounting History. *Accounting Review* 45, no. 4 (supplement): 53–64.

Camfferman, K. and S. A. Zeff. 2007. *Financial Reporting and Global Capital Markets: a History of the International Accounting Standards Committee, 1973–2000*. Oxford: Oxford University Press.

Littleton, A. C. and V. K. Zimmerman. 1962. *Accounting Theory: Continuity and Change*. Englewood Cliffs, NJ: Prentice-Hall.

Lukka, K. and A. Loft. 2002. Special issue to celebrate the twenty-fifth anniversary of the European Accounting Association: Introduction. *European Accounting Review* 11, no. 1: 3–7.

Napier, C. J. 2008. Historiography. In *Companion to Accounting History*, eds. J. R. Edwards and S. P. Walker, 30–49. London: Routledge.

Parker, R. H. and S. A. Zeff, eds. 1996. *Milestones in the British Accounting Literature*. New York & London: Garland Publishing.

Solomons, D. and S. A. Zeff, eds. 1996. *Accounting Research 1948–1958*, 2 volumes. New York & London: Garland Publishing.

Walker, S. P. 2008. Structures, territories and tribes. In *Companion to Accounting History*, eds. J. R. Edwards and S. P. Walker, 9–29. London: Routledge.

Zeff, S. A. 1962. Replacement cost: member of the family, welcome guest, or intruder? *Accounting Review* 37, no. 4: 611–625.

Zeff, S. A. 1972. *Forging Accounting Principles in Five Countries: a History and an Analysis of Trends*. Champaign, IL: Stipes Publishing.

Zeff, S. A. 1973. *Forging Accounting Principles in Australia*. Melbourne: Australian Society of Accountants.

Zeff, S. A., ed. 1976. *Asset Appreciation, Business Income and Price-Level Accounting: 1918–1935*. New York: Arno Press.

Zeff, S. A. 1978a. A critical examination of the orientation postulate in accounting, with particular attention to its historical development. Doctoral dissertation, University of Michigan, 1961. New York: Arno Press.

Zeff, S. A. 1978b. The rise of 'economic consequences'. *Journal of Accountancy* 146, no. 6: 56–63.

Zeff, S. A., ed. 1978c. *Selected Dickinson Lectures in Accounting*. New York: Arno Press.

Zeff, S. A. 1979. *Forging Accounting Principles in New Zealand*. Wellington: Victoria University Press.

Zeff, S. A. 1980. The promise of historical research in accounting: some personal experiences. In *Perspectives on Research*, eds. R. D. Nair and T. H. Williams, 13–25. Madison, WI: University of Wisconsin.

Zeff, S. A., ed. 1982a. *Accounting Principles Through the Years: the Views of Professional and Academic Leaders 1938–1954*. New York & London: Garland Publishing.

Zeff, S. A., ed. 1982b. *The Accounting Postulates and Principles Controversy of the 1960s*. New York & London: Garland Publishing.

Zeff, S. A., ed. 1988. *The US Accounting Profession in the 1890s and Early 1900s*. New York & London: Garland Publishing.

Zeff, S. A. 1997. The early years of the Association of University Teachers of Accounting: 1947–1959. *British Accounting Review* 29, no. 1–2 (supplement): 3–39.

Zeff, S. A. 2000. *Henry Rand Hatfield: Humanist, Scholar and Accounting Educator*. Stamford, CT: JAI Press.

Zeff, S. A. 2002a. The first twenty-five years of the European Accounting Association: an American view. *European Accounting Review* 11, no. 1: 93–97.

Zeff, S. A. 2002b. Response. In *Accounting Hall of Fame 2002*. San Antonio, TX.

Zeff, S. A. 2005a. The evolution of U.S. GAAP. *CPA Journal* 75, no. 1: 18–27.

Zeff, S. A. 2005b. The evolution of U.S. GAAP: The political forces behind professional standards. *CPA Journal* 75, no. 2: 18–29.

Zeff, S. A. and M. Moonitz, eds. 1984. *Sourcebook on Accounting Principles and Auditing Procedures: 1917–1953*, 2 volumes. New York & London: Garland Publishing.

Zeff, S. A., F. Wel, and K. Camfferman. 1992. *Company Financial Reporting: a Historical and Comparative Study of the Dutch Regulatory Process*. North-Holland: Elsevier Science Publishers.

Acknowledgements

To the American Accounting Association for permission to reproduce the articles from *The Accounting Review* and *Accounting Horizons*.

To Professor Richard Fleischman for permission to reproduce the articles from *The Accounting Historians Journal*.

To the Taylor and Foster Group for permission to reproduce the article from *Accounting, Business & Financial History*.

To the Graduate School of Business, Stanford University for the following permission: Permission is hereby granted for Routledge Publishing to include Stephen A. Zeff's "The Rise of 'Economic Consequences'" from Stanford Lectures in Accounting 1978, in an anthology of Professor Zeff's work.

To CCH for permission to reproduce the article from *Accounting and Business Research*, with the following stipulation: Copyright: Wolters Kluwer (UK) Ltd.

To Wiley-Blackwell for permission to reproduce the article from *Abacus*.

To the Canadian Academic Accounting Association for permission to reproduce the articles from *Contemporary Accounting Research* and *Accounting Perspectives*.

To the Kresge Business Administration Library, Ross School of Business, The University of Michigan for permission to reproduce "Paton on the Effects of Changing Prices on Accounting, 1916–55" from *Essays in Honor of William A. Paton: Pioneer Accounting Theorist*.

To Elsevier and Rightslink © by Copyright Clearance Center, Inc. for permission to reproduce the articles from *The British Accounting Review* and the *Journal of Accounting and Public Policy*.

To Greenwood Publishing Group for the following permission: "Big Eight Firms and the Accounting Literature: The Falloff in Advocacy Writing," by Stephen A. Zeff. Copyright © 1986. Reproduced with permission of Greenwood Publishing Group, Inc., Westport, CT.

Introduction

Stephen A. Zeff

My interest in history was always there, but I didn't detect it until my second year as an assistant professor of accounting at Tulane University, in 1962. As an undergraduate at the University of Colorado, I had majored in accounting, yet I did take four elective courses in the history department. For a while, inspired by a graduate seminar on labor relations with Dallas L. Jones in 1955, I gave thought to entering the academic field of labor and industrial relations. To explore that idea, I took an M.S. degree in management at Colorado. For my thesis, I did an interview study on why workers moved to Denver. Still keeping my options open, I selected the fields of accounting and industrial relations for my PhD program at the University of Michigan. In the end, I chose a career in accounting, and William A. Paton's stimulating courses at Michigan were probably a factor.

Once at Tulane, as the academic year 1962–63 dawned, I looked back at my previous writings to see if there was a common thread in my approach to research. My undergraduate honors paper at Colorado was entitled, "Collective Bargaining vs. the Conspiracy Doctrine and the Injunction in the United States: Until 1932." Both it and my doctoral thesis, "A Critical Examination of the Orientation Postulate in Accounting, with Particular Attention to Its Historical Development,"[1] were historical studies. Two articles I had published—one in 1959 on standard costs, and another in 1961 on the dividend provisions in state corporation laws—were partly historical, and an article I was about to have published in the October 1962 issue of *The Accounting Review*, "Replacement Cost: Member of the Family, Welcome Guest, or Intruder?" which is included in this collection, was almost entirely historical. It was not difficult for me to discern that I looked at accounting issues through a historical prism.

Others seemed to reach the same conclusion about my research interests. In 1963, Professor Maurice Moonitz, at the University of California, Berkeley, encouraged me to spend a year there to inspect the late Professor Henry Rand Hatfield's many papers with a view towards writing a book on

---

[1] The dissertation was published in 1978 by Arno Press.

his contributions to the field of accounting. Hatfield was the first full-time accounting academic with a professorial title in a US university, and he was one of the most respected accounting academics during the first half of the twentieth century. The project was instantly attractive. I spent the summer terms of 1964 and 1965 and the fall semester of 1964 as a visiting associate professor at Berkeley to launch the project. The eventual book, *Henry Rand Hatfield: Humanist, Scholar, and Accounting Educator*, was not published until 36 years later, in 2000, because the Hatfield research began to compete with a steady stream of other research projects and significant assignments in the American Accounting Association (AAA), especially as Director of Education (1969–71), chairman of the arrangements committee for the 1974 annual meeting, editor of *The Accounting Review* (1977–82), and President-elect and President (1984–86). Yet, of all of my publications, the Hatfield biography is the one of which I am the most proud. It virtually became my life's work, and it drew on a great many interviews and letters exchanged with Hatfield's family, his former students, and former academic colleagues, as well as a review of his published and unpublished writings, voluminous correspondence, and many scrapbooks reflecting his personal and professional interests. The book covered a broad canvas: a study of Hatfield's career and contributions set against the backdrop of the early evolution of US accounting academe and the accounting literature.

The Hatfield study marked the first of many research projects in which I have relied heavily on interviews and correspondence. One of the attractions in doing recent contemporary historical research, that is, research focusing on developments during the past forty or so years, is that one can generate data through interviews and correspondence with the principals, and thus not be obliged to rely solely on accessible documents. During my career, I have conducted hundreds of interviews, most of which were transcribed, and have engaged in extensive correspondence with accounting academics, accounting professionals, preparers and users of financial statements, and regulators, and these have provided data that have been integral to much of my research.

Another invitation to embark on a historical study, which dove-tailed nicely with the Hatfield project, came my way at the AAA annual meeting in August/September 1964, when President-elect Robert K. Mautz, on behalf of the executive committee, approached me to conduct research and write a history of the AAA's first 50 years, from 1916 to 1966. Hatfield was the AAA's third President, in 1919. I felt honored and agreed to the request. Given that the history was to be published in time for the AAA's 50th anniversary meeting two years hence, I had to proceed with alacrity. The research entailed interviewing past Presidents and other officers, and reviewing minutes and committee reports in the AAA's large archive of historical documents. But then I learned from Herbert E. Miller, the AAA's 1965–66 President, that the published history had to be limited to 100 printed pages. Miller, the coauthor of the widely adopted Finney-Miller series of accounting textbooks, had persuaded his publisher, Prentice-Hall, Inc., to publish the AAA's history gratis and anonymously, but only if it were no longer than 100 printed pages. In the end, the published history ran to exactly 100 pages, including the paper covers. The title of the history was *The American Accounting Association: Its First 50 Years*, and the AAA reprinted it 25 years later, in 1991.

The first article in this collection, which is organized by chronology and consists mostly of reproductions of the originals so as to preserve the original pagination, is "Replacement Cost: Member of the Family, Welcome Guest, or Intruder?" which was published in the October 1962 issue of *The Accounting Review*. It was the outgrowth of my presentation at the annual meeting in April 1962 of the AAA's Southwestern Regional Group, in Dallas.[2] I was intrigued with the differences between general price-level accounting and relative price change accounting, as exemplified by replacement cost accounting, as well as with the disagreement among replacement cost advocates over how to account for the unrealized gains and losses—the "disposable income" v. "earning power" views, as I labeled them. Should they be included in income or be taken directly to shareholders' equity? I felt that there was much confusion in the literature on this contentious point, and my purpose was to dig back into history to classify theorists according to which view they espoused and to try to explain why they differed. At the time, I thought that this was a pioneering attempt at bringing out the treatments by the two schools of thought on the treatment of unrealized gains and losses, but years later I learned that Henry W. Sweeney had admirably performed the same analysis in "Maintenance of Capital," which appeared in the December 1930 issue of *The Accounting Review*. Even though I was familiar with Sweeney's work, I had somehow missed this article. Although my analysis was therefore not new to the literature, my historical arraying of authors on both sides of the issue was new, and the article probably served to acquaint many accounting academics in the early 1960s with this vital distinction between different theorists' approaches to replacement cost accounting: financial v. physical maintenance of capital, as it soon came to be known. As far as I know, Sweeney was the first to use that terminology.

There is a 16-year gap between this 1962 article and the next article in this collection, "The Rise of 'Economic Consequences,'" which was published in 1978 in the series of *Stanford Lectures in Accounting*, sponsored by the Price Waterhouse Foundation. The major reason for this long absence in articles worthy of republishing is that most of my research efforts during that span were destined for publication in books and monographs, including

---

[2] In those days, the *Review* editor did not conduct a formal peer review. If he liked a manuscript, he accepted it for publication. He liked my manuscript, and it was promptly processed for publication.

the Hatfield biography and the AAA history, mentioned above, and the *Forging Accounting Principles* series, mentioned below.

In 1969, my interest turned towards the history of committees tasked with establishing accounting principles or, as this activity came to be known in the early 1970s, the standard-setting process.[3] The "political" lobbying and divergent and shifting positions taken by members of the Accounting Principles Board (APB) during its deliberations on the vexed accounting for business combinations and goodwill from 1968 to 1970, as well as on the earlier controversies that erupted during the APB's efforts to resolve the accounting for the investment tax credit and income tax allocation, vividly suggested a fascinating new field of study: the process by which norms of practice become recommended in official pronouncements. It seemed fruitful to attempt to compare the US experience with those in other countries. My interest matured into a major research project during the August 1969 AAA annual meeting, when I met Professor Edward Stamp, of the University of Edinburgh. During a dinner conversation, he invited me to give the annual Arthur Andersen Lecture at his university in November 1970, and I learned that he, as I, was gripped by the process of establishing accounting principles. I proposed to deliver my lecture on the historical evolution of the approaches used in the United States, Canada, Mexico, England, and Scotland, and he liked the idea instantly.

It very soon became evident that I had given myself a much more daunting assignment than I had imagined. What I had not realized was that there was very little written evidence, apart from exposure drafts (but not in the UK) and final pronouncements, on how the decisions were reached and about how a range of factors impinged on the decision-making process. In the US, partners in audit firms, financial executives, and the Chief Accountant of the Securities and Exchange Commission (SEC) gave speeches and wrote articles on the accounting principles controversies, but they did not help one understand the dynamic of the APB's decision-making process. For the US, my task was to reconstruct the series of initiatives taken by the American Institute of Accountants from the 1910s onwards, leading up to the pronouncements issued by its Committee on Accounting Procedure (CAP) from 1939 to 1959 and by its APB since 1959. Beginning in the 1960s there were frequent news articles in *The Wall Street Journal* and sometimes elsewhere in the financial press, but the internal communications within the CAP and APB were confidential and thus were not available to a researcher. The same degree of secrecy prevailed in the four other countries. This was a time when professional accountancy bodies—which were the sponsors of all of the five countries' programs to provide guidance on accounting principles—and their committees were much more secretive

---

[3] The *Report of the Study on Establishment of Accounting Principles* (AICPA, 1972), known as the Wheat Study, brought the term, standard setting, into general use in accounting circles.

than they are today. There was no way to gather the necessary insights and to reconstruct the settings in which the decisions were taken other than by conducting interviews of the principals, but this meant traveling to Mexico City, New York, Chicago, Toronto, Montreal, London, Edinburgh, and Glasgow. Fortunately, Arthur Andersen & Co., which sponsored the Lecture, offered to reimburse me for travel costs, and Ian Hay Davison, the managing partner of the firm's UK firm, provided me with an office and other assistance. The firm also gave me access to CAP and APB files from its encyclopedic Subject File on microfilm. An important dimension of the US research was to come to understand the SEC's role and especially that played by its Chief Accountant. Andrew Barr, who had been the SEC's Chief Accountant since 1956, provided me with considerable documentation, including letters he had written to the APB on its research studies and exposure drafts.

I conducted numerous interviews during 1969 and 1970 in all of those cities, and I delivered the Lecture in two evenings in Edinburgh in November 1970. I decided to continue the research throughout 1971 and published a 332-page monograph, *Forging Accounting Principles in Five Countries: A History and an Analysis of Trends*, in 1972. Even though the length of this monograph was much greater than Andersen had expected from a two-day lecture, it generously subsidized the publication cost so as to keep the purchase price at $5.

I wanted to continue my comparative research in other countries. During the 1972 academic year in the southern hemisphere, I was a visiting Fulbright professor at Monash University, in Melbourne. I financed interview research in all of the capital cities by giving research seminars at eight universities. The resulting 67-page monograph, *Forging Accounting Principles in Australia*, was published in 1973 by the Australian Society of Accountants (known today as CPA Australia). I was fortunate to be able to gain access to the internal files of the two major accountancy bodies and to those of their jointly run research foundation, because Alan W. Graham, a New Zealander who was the general registrar of the Institute of Chartered Accountants in Australia, was a good friend. He trusted my discretion, and once it was learned that the Institute had allowed me to use its files, the Society did likewise, as did the Accountancy Research Foundation (later known as the Australian Accounting Research Foundation).

Then I moved on to New Zealand. During the southern winter of 1976, while a visiting professor at Victoria University of Wellington facilitated by Professor Don Trow, I did comparable research in the five major cities in New Zealand, and my resulting monograph, *Forging Accounting Principles in New Zealand*, published by Victoria University Press, came out three years later. The *Forging* series constituted, I believe, the first reports of historical research into the accounting standard-setting process, and through them I developed a deep appreciation of the self-interested lobbying of standard setters by companies and governments, as well as by other affected parties.

Hence, in 1977, when Charles T. Horngren, of Stanford University, invited me to deliver one of the two Stanford Lectures in Accounting the following June, I decided to speak on "The Rise of 'Economic Consequences.'" My purpose was to provide a framework for thinking about self-interested lobbying activity in standard setting and to relate a series of such interventions in the work of the CAP, the APB, and the Financial Accounting Standards Board (FASB), which succeeded the APB in 1973. An abridged version of the lecture was published in the December 1978 issue of the *Journal of Accountancy*, and this has been, by far, my most frequently reprinted and widely cited article. Especially with the emergence of the positive theorists' interest in standard setting at about the same time, as well as the controversy during the 1970s over the FASB's initiatives on accounting for troubled debt restructurings, inflation accounting, and accounting for oil and gas exploration, the subject of the "political" influences on, or the "economic consequences" of, standard setting had begun to captivate accounting researchers. In this collection, it is the unabridged version of "The Rise of 'Economic Consequences'" which is reproduced. This version was published in a slender monograph entitled *Stanford Lectures in Accounting 1978* (Graduate School of Business, Stanford University).[4]

At around the same time, I resumed my interest in studying the historical development of the accounting thought of important theorists. In 1979, I co-edited a *Festschrift* to honor William A. Paton, one of my teachers at Michigan and one of the most respected and influential US accounting academics, on the occasion of his 90th birthday.[5] As none of the invited contributors to the *Festschrift* wrote about Paton's body of work, I decided do a paper on the evolution of his views on accounting for changing general and relative prices, entitled "Paton on the Effects of Changing Prices on Accounting, 1916–55." This has not been a widely noticed paper, because the volume in which it appears came to the attention of few accounting academics. I wrote the paper because I had seen where academics had, unwittingly, cited a particular writing by Paton on current value accounting as if this had been his unaltered view during the entirety of his long career. Readers were unaware that he modified his position a number of times. He began in the 1910s with a strong advocacy of current value accounting, but by the 1930s he retreated because of the "questionable booking of write-ups in the 1920s and write-downs in the 1930s, the special problems wrought by the economic stagnation of the Great Depresssion" (page 110), and the

---

[4] The other Stanford Lecture given in June 1978 and included in the monograph was "Reflections of a Former Member of the FASB," by Walter Schuetze.

[5] Stephen A. Zeff, Joel Demski, and Nicholas Dopuch (editors), *Essays in Honor of William A. Paton: Pioneer Accounting Theorist* (Ann Arbor, MI: Division of Research, Graduate School of Business Administration, The University of Michigan, 1979).

importance of preserving recorded costs for federal income tax purposes and for complying with the provisions of state corporation laws. By 1940, when he coauthored *An Introduction to Corporate Accounting Standards* with the arch historical coster A. C. Littleton, Paton had become a supporter of historical cost in the basic financial statements, but with supplementary disclosures of replacement costs. Henry Sweeney's celebrated 1936 book, *Stabilized Accounting*, led Paton to recommend, for the rest of his career, a supplementary disclosure of general price-level effects—"common dollar accounting," as he called it. But on current value accounting, in the 1940s he began looking for ways of bringing current costs into the basic financial statements without totally supplanting historical costs. One device he created was his "compromise procedure" for recording depreciation at replacement cost, while determining net income based on historical cost depreciation, the difference being taken directly to a shareholders' equity adjustment account. In the 1950s, he began looking for ways of bringing current costs to the fore. A cunning example was his "even deal" accounting, under which a company would restate its recorded values if it were to purchase a substantial fraction of its common shares at a price significantly at variance from the book value per share, where the difference was believed to be indicative of a conscious revaluation of the company's net assets. Paton always regarded himself as a "value man," but in 1940, when he coauthored the famous monograph with Littleton, he was at the nadir of his advocacy for "value" in the basic financial statements.

My article, "*Truth in Accounting*: The Ordeal of Kenneth MacNeal," published in the July 1982 issue of *The Accounting Review*, had an unusual genesis. In 1962, I acquired an interest in learning why Kenneth MacNeal wrote his passionately argued advocacy of market value accounting, *Truth in Accounting*, published in 1939 by the University of Pennsylvania Press. He was not an academic and had published nothing previously, and then he disappeared from the literature almost as abruptly as he had entered. This was his only published work on accounting, apart from four short articles in 1939 and 1941, largely derived from the book. Nothing was known about the man apart from his listing in the membership directory of the American Institute of Certified Public Accountants (AICPA), which gave a mailing address for him in Philadelphia. I proceeded to correspond with him to obtain particulars. As I have written elsewhere, "He replied that the publication of his book had provoked such a torrent of unrelenting criticism that he had decided in the early 1940s to forget the subject altogether. I persisted. Would he tell me something of the criticisms and why he had undertaken to write the book? Finally, persuaded by my earnestness and eager to be rid of my prying questions, he sent me a thick scrapbook in which he kept correspondence, book reviews, and copies of his speeches and articles. The contents of the scrapbook told an interesting story about an article that MacNeal had been invited to write for a leading magazine, critical of the accounting profession [in the wake of the McKesson-Robbins fraud], and which apparently had been suppressed by forces within the profession."[6] In correspondence, MacNeal made it clear that he did not want to discuss the book or its aftermath ever again. Sensitive to MacNeal's desire to preserve his privacy, I postponed writing an article based on the contents of the scrapbook until his death, which, in the latter 1970s, I learned (with some difficulty) had occurred in March 1972. After composing a paper, I corresponded with MacNeal's son, who said his family had no objection to publication of the draft which I sent him. Indeed, he said that the family was pleased with the attention being given to MacNeal's book and its contribution to the accounting literature. This article thus finally told the story of the circumstances surrounding the work of this obscure author of one of the more widely cited books in the literature on current value accounting. It also shows how thin-skinned the accountancy profession can be at handling published criticism of its performance.

"Some Junctures in the Evolution of the Process of Establishing Accounting Principles in the U.S.A.: 1917–1972," published in *The Accounting Review* in July 1984, resulted from my plenary address to the AAA's 1983 annual meeting at the invitation of AAA President Yuji Ijiri. The aim of the article was to explain (1) the factors leading up to the American Institute of Accountants' decision in 1938 to endow its Committee on Accounting Procedure (CAP) with authority to establish accounting principles on a programmatic basis, (2) the factors attending the transition from the CAP to the APB in 1958–59, and (3) the issues prompting the transition in 1970–73 from the APB to the newly created independent body, the FASB. One can see in these "junctures" the repeated concern that, unless a better way was found within the private sector, accounting principles might instead be established by an organ of the federal government.

"Big Eight Firms and the Accounting Literature: The Falloff in Advocacy Writing," published in the Spring 1986 issue of the *Journal of Accounting, Auditing & Finance* (*JAAF*), was based on a presentation at the AAA's 1985 annual meeting, following which Hector R. Anton, *JAAF*'s editor, encouraged me to send a paper on the subject to his journal for editorial consideration. The article was intended to document and explain the precipitate decline in writing and speaking by partners in the major audit firms, and by the firms themselves in their house organs and informational booklets, on issues relating to the setting of accounting standards. It would surprise many of today's readers that, until the early 1970s, the Big Eight audit firms professed principled views on what constituted proper accounting practice, and their leading partners wrote and spoke about them. As part of my research, I wrote letters to numerous leading partners, active

---

[6] Stephen A. Zeff, "The Promise of Historical Research in Accounting: Some Personal Experiences," in Raghavan D. Nair and Thomas H. Williams (editors), *Perspectives on Research: 1980 Beyer Consortium* (Madison, WI: Graduate School of Business, University of Wisconsin-Madison, 1980), pp. 20–21.

and retired, in the major audit firms for their views on this dropoff in advocacy writing and speaking. In the article, I quoted responses which I found to be insightful. This was a time when the major firms were replacing their professional values by commercial values, and they had come to believe that their partners should not be taking public positions on controversial accounting issues if the expression of such views might offend even one of their important clients.

The story behind "Arthur Andersen & Co. and the Two-Part Opinion in the Auditor's Report: 1946–1962," which was published in the Spring 1992 issue of *Contemporary Accounting Research*, is worth telling. Since the early 1960s, I was impressed with the outspokenness of Leonard Spacek and other leading partners in Arthur Andersen & Co. on the need for sound accounting principles to serve the public interest. I wanted to be closer to a firm that took such inspired positions, and it was evident that Andersen wanted to be close to the academic community. I had grown up in Chicago and its suburbs, and my parents continued to live there. During the summer and winter holidays, I would return to the Chicago area for visits and would pay calls on the firm's home office, first on South LaSalle Street and then on West Washington and West Monroe Streets. I befriended Spacek, George Catlett, Norman Olson, Richard Claire, Walter Oliphant, Harvey Kapnick, Claude Rodgers, and most of the partners who were members of the firm's committee on accounting principles and auditing procedures, and I continued and nurtured those contacts over succeeding years. During the summers of 1982 and 1983, Arthur R. Wyatt, who then headed the committee, allowed me to occupy an office for the purpose of reading and photocopying large batches of the firm's massive files of correspondence, drafts, and other internal documents relating to the work of the APB, covering the period from 1959 to 1973. Included in the firm's APB files were correspondence with and about clients, but Art trusted my discretion. Neither the AICPA nor any of the other Big Eight audit firms, as far as I then knew, had retained their APB files. It was then my hope to write a history of the APB. Art also permitted me to make copies of earlier years' correspondence relating to the work of the CAP from the firm's Subject File. In the course of examining many of these files, I learned that the firm had, in 1946, rephrased the opinion in its auditor's report from the financial statements "present fairly in conformity with generally accepted accounting principles," to "present fairly and were prepared in conformity with generally accepted accounting principles," thus recasting a single opinion into a pair of opinions: "present fairly" and "conformity with generally accepted accounting principles." The firm believed that it had a professional obligation to give its opinion on whether the financial statements present fairly without regard to whether they complied with generally accepted accounting principles, i.e., the rules of accepted practice. This belief was motivated in part because the firm took issue with some of these rules. This change in wording had apparently gone unnoticed by academics and by most others in the accountancy profession. I used the Andersen files I had copied to explain the firm's reasons for departing from the standard form of the auditor's opinion in 1946 and then for reverting to the standard form in 1962. In addition, I introduced the experience in Canada, where, for a period of eight years, from 1968 to 1976, the profession's official guidance seemed to support the requirement of a "two-part opinion," as Andersen had once used. Andersen's "two-part opinion" experiment vividly illustrated its posture as an independent thinker when deciding how the firm should carry out its professional responsibilites.

"The Early Years of the Association of University Teachers of Accounting: 1947–1959," published in the June 1997 special issue of *The British Accounting Review*, was a work attributable entirely to the generosity of David Solomons. I had been a friend of David's for many years, but especially since 1985, when, as AAA President, I enlisted him to chair and coordinate the first conference ever held to bring national standard setters together to discuss common problems. The conference was held in August 1986 in Princeton, New Jersey and was co-sponsored by the AAA and Klynveld Main Goerdeler, the forerunner of KPMG Peat Marwick,[7] and David made it a great success. We became close friends and exchanged confidences via frequent telephone conversations during the ensuing years, but, sadly, David contracted cancer in 1994 and died in February 1995. In January 1995, he invited me to his home in Swarthmore, Pennsylvania for a farewell visit, and he urged me to take any of his extensive correspondence files or any of his books which interested me. Several thick files I brought home contained the correspondence and other documents relating to the formation and first dozen years of the Association of University Teachers in Accounting (AUTA), which is today known as The British Accounting Association (BAA). Some months later, when I began to examine the contents of the AUTA files, I learned that it was founded in December 1947. I thereupon wrote the Chairman of the BAA to inform him that the BAA will complete its first 50 years in 1997, and did he know that? He said no. Because the 1960s were a decade in which the AUTA almost died out, those who reinvigorated it in the 1970s, and in the 1980s under its new name, knew nothing of its early history. Once the American had informed the Brit of this historical fact, the BAA began trumpeting "50 Years/British Accounting Association/1947–1997," and it put out a special historical issue of *The British Accounting Review* in June 1997 which carried my article, together with very informative articles by Robert H. Parker and Keith Maunders covering the later installments of the AUTA/BAA history. My article was based mostly on the contents of the files retrieved from David's cabinet. Yet the historical discovery which I most enjoyed

---

[7] For the conference proceedings, see *Standard Setting for Financial Reporting* (Peat Marwick Main & Co., 1987).

relating was, based on other sources, that the first full-time professorship with Accounting or Accountancy in its title in the UK was established in, of all places, University College Galway in 1914. Prior to 1922, what is today the Republic of Ireland was a part of the UK. Thus, Ireland can claim the first full-time UK Chair of Accountancy. Of course, I dedicated the article to the memory of David Solomons, who, together with William T. Baxter and Harold C. Edey, all at the London School of Economics, played leading roles in the early going of AUTA.

"The Evolution of the Conceptual Framework for Business Enterprises in the United States," published in the December 1999 issue of *The Accounting Historians Journal*, undertook to trace the evolution of attempts at formulating what is today called the conceptual framework, beginning with the books written by William A. Paton and John B. Canning in the 1920s to the FASB's framework promulgated in stages between 1978 and 2000. My research was based solely on published writings and was my attempt to draw together the many threads of individual and institutional efforts to provide a theoretical foundation for accounting principles and practices. Most of the article dealt with the FASB's conceptual framework, which included assessments of its contribution.

"John B. Canning: A View of His Academic Career," which was published in the February 2000 issue of *Abacus*, was based on interviews, correspondence, and archival sources as well as on published writings. I conducted most of the interviews in 1964–65, when I was visiting Berkeley to begin my research on a biographical study of Henry Rand Hatfield. Several times, I drove the 40 miles to Palo Alto to interview Canning's widow and senior members of the economics department about Canning, as well as to study the Stanford University course catalogues and to use the archive in the Stanford Library. Other research was conducted by correspondence, telephone interviews, and a visit to the archive of the Regenstein Library of the University of Chicago, where Canning had taken all of his degrees and played on the varsity football team. Unfortunately, I missed the opportunity to talk to Canning himself by only two years: he died in July 1962 at age 77. I devoted the front part of the article to tracing Canning's evident intellectual influence on subsequent accounting theorists, a demonstration of impact of which we have all too few in the accounting literature. Canning was an economist and statistician of high standing who, during most of his career, took a large interest in what accountants do and in how best to prepare them for their careers. One can think of other economists who greatly influenced the accounting literature, but none of them compares to Canning in his dedication to developing a curriculum for aspiring accountancy professionals which was grounded not only in accounting but also in mathematics and statistics, economics, and law. He was not an inspiring classroom teacher, but he would devote endless time to expanding students' minds in one-to-one conversations. Like Hatfield at Berkeley, Canning taught students how to think, not how to solve practical problems. A former Canning doctoral student recalled him saying "that the only aspects of accounting definite enough to make good problems were not important enough to occupy the student's time."

"The Work of the Special Committee on Research Program," published in the December 2001 issue of *The Accounting Historians Journal*, is another article that was researched almost entirely in the files of Arthur Andersen & Co.[8] But these were not files that I copied during the summers of 1982 and 1983, when I was tapping the firm's immense archive of documents relating to the APB. They were given to me by Leonard Spacek in the 1960s. Spacek always believed that the documentary record of the deliberations of AICPA committees dealing with accounting principles should be made publicly available for use by scholars and other interested parties. Under his leadership, from 1960 to 1976 Andersen published 13 volumes entitled *Cases in Public Accounting Practice*. These volumes could be obtained free of charge, and they reproduced the transcripts, correspondence, and other documentation relating to court cases, public hearings, regulatory proceedings, and other areas of controversy where accounting principles were at issue. He and his firm advocated an "accounting court," which would make the "briefs" of contending positions and all supporting documentation publicly available. In the 1950s and into the 1960s, Andersen published booklets containing Spacek's speeches as well as the firm's positions on contested accounting principles, years before other major audit firms began doing likewise. The other firms claimed that such publications violated the ban on advertising. To be sure, they did serve to promote the firm's name, yet Spacek believed that his firm had an obligation to challenge the "dead hand" of conventional thinking on accounting principles. This article expanded upon "Some Junctures in the Evolution of the Process of Establishing Accounting Principles in the U.S.A.: 1917–1972," and it related the intense exchanges of views within the AICPA's Special Committee on Research Program, on which Spacek served, which produced a recommendation in 1958 that the CAP be succeeded by a newly created and better resourced Accounting Principles Board—the emphasis in its name being on accounting Principles, not on accounting Procedure. One of the charges given to the APB was to publish research studies on basic accounting postulates and broad accounting principles so that its future pronouncements would be predicated on sound theory. This charge echoed one of Spacek's criticisms of the CAP's performance during the 1950s, namely, that its pronouncements were not shown to be based on the objectives of financial statements.

"Du Pont's Early Policy on the Rotation of Audit Firms," published in the January/February 2003 issue of the *Journal of Accounting and Public*

---

[8] Yet another article which drew on the Andersen files, but which is not included in this collection, is "The Membership of the Accounting Principles Board," *Research in Accounting Regulation*, Vol. 19 (2007).

Policy, is another article researched mainly in archival sources, chiefly in the Hagley Museum and Library, in Wilmington, Delaware, where the Du Pont papers are housed. I had been aware since the 1960s that Du Pont once subscribed to the unique policy of rotating its external audit firm every year. Yet nothing had ever been written about the policy, let alone why the company adopted it, and then, after the passage of time, eventually modified and then abandoned it. The post-Enron debate over corporate governance, which included assertions that companies should rotate their audit firms on a regular basis, led me to look into the Du Pont policy, which dated from 1910. The article brings out evidence of the suspicions held by senior members of the Du Pont family, who ran the company until the 1950s, about possible collusion between middle-level managers and the audit firm, which could be facilitated by appointing the same firm to conduct the audit year after year. In a small point made in the article, I was able to make use of a letter I had received from Du Pont's Treasurer in 1965 to explain the company's curious practice of displaying its reserve for depreciation and obsolescence on the liabilities side of its balance sheet.

"'The Apotheosis of Holding Company Accounting': Unilever's Financial Reporting Innovations from the 1920s to the 1940s," written with Kees Camfferman, was published in the July 2003 issue of *Accounting, Business & Financial History.* The idea for this article arose during our research for the book, *Company Financial Reporting: A Historical and Comparative Study of the Dutch Regulatory Process* (Amsterdam: North-Holland, 1992). During our review of Dutch company annual reports during the 1940s, we stumbled on the fact that Unilever, in its 1945 annual report, provided a breakdown of sales turnover by nine product lines and a services sector. Then, in its 1947 annual report, the company added a segmental breakdown of sales according to five major geographical regions. In the 1940s, few European companies disclosed their sales turnover in the aggregate, let alone its breakdown into segments. We were astounded by the discovery, and we resolved to investigate Unilever's financial reporting during that era after our book was published. Because of the press of other research commitments, we could not get round to Unilever for several years, but, once into it, we discovered that the story was even more interesting than we had thought. We made extensive use of the Unilever archives in London and Rotterdam, as well as the financial press and the archive of company annual reports held by the Guildhall Library, London, and the papers given to it by the Institute of Chartered Accountants in England and Wales. Clearly, it was not just after the Second World War that Unilever became one of the most progressive of major listed companies in financial reporting transparency. As early as the 1930s, in his address to the annual general meeting in London, the Unilever Chairman disclosed sales and profit breakdowns by segments. Much has been made of the Unilever Chairman's assertion to the Greene Committee on Company Law Amendment in 1926 that consolidated balance sheets would not provide meaningful information. By this statement, it was thought that he and Unilever were against progress in financial reporting. Yet we concluded that Unilever was willing to experiment with innovative disclosures. We also concluded that, at that time, an unusually diversified and complex conglomerate such as Unilever had good reasons to believe that a consolidated balance sheet was less useful to shareholders than the disaggregation of sales and profits, apportioned to segments of the company's main lines of business activity, which it disclosed outside its audited financial statements.

My two-part article, "How the U.S. Accounting Profession Got Where It Is Today," which appeared in the September and December 2003 issues of *Accounting Horizons*, was a post-Enron study of the historical evolution of the evident values and thinking of the major audit firms and of the leaders of the accountancy profession. PricewaterhouseCoopers (PwC) had invited me to make a 15-minute presentation during an invitation-only conference preceding the AAA annual meeting in August 2002, at which I was asked to summarize the historical developments that, collectively, got the accountancy profession into its sad state by the end of the century. Fifteen minutes! I developed a historical time line and condensed it several times until it finally fit within 15 minutes, somehow. The presentation precipitated an active dialogue among the several dozen accounting academics and PwC partners in attendance. James A. Largay, the editor of *Accounting Horizons*, who was in the audience, encouraged me to compose an article to expand on what I said, for submission to his journal. Although I had a heavy teaching load from August to December, I nonetheless researched and wrote an article that was too long for one issue of *Horizons*. Jim's anonymous reviewers, as well as Jim himself as editor, helped me improve the article significantly. The essential story was that, as an earlier writer had observed, a profession that also happened to be a business gradually became a business that also happened to be a profession. Commercial values began to overwhelm professional values, and the profession, *qua* profession, lost its way. As greed had come to obsess so many financial firms on Wall Street, as well as many corporate managements, it had also come to roost in the big audit firms.

"The Primacy of 'Present Fairly' in the Auditor's Report," which appeared in Vol. 6, No. 1 (2007) of *Accounting Perspectives*, was a review of the historical evolution of the use and meaning of the term, "present fairly," in the opinion paragraph of the standard form of the US auditor's report. The article drew on my "two-part opinion" article mentioned above, and it concluded with a proposed framework for thinking about how to induce auditors to make subjective judgments on fair presentation without relying on a mechanical compliance with generally accepted accounting principles—in effect, decoupling the auditor's unitary opinion into two. The article was drawn from the Emanuel Saxe Lecture which I delivered in April 2006 at the Baruch College of the City University of New York.

A personal anecdote may serve to illustrate how even small changes in the preferred wording of the opinion in the auditor's report can spark controversy. In the latter 1980s, the AICPA's Auditing Standards Board, as part of its work on the "expectation gap" standards, proposed to recommend that the auditor affirm that the financial statements "are fairly presented," without affirming *what* they fairly present. Separately, Douglas Carmichael and I wrote letters to the Board, arguing that the verb "present" must have an object. The auditor must say *what* the financial statements "fairly present." As it turned out, the arguments contained in just the letters from the two of us were sufficient to persuade the Board to withdraw its proposal and reinstate the object of the verb.[9]

Even though "The SEC Preempts the Accounting Principles Board in 1965: The Classification of the Deferred Tax Credit Relating to Installment Sales," published in the June 2007 issue of *The Accounting Historians Journal*, deals with a narrow issue of balance-sheet classification, it brought to light a serious weakness in the effectiveness of the APB in 1964–65: the apparent inclination of some Board members who were partners in major audit firms to vote the preferences of their important and influential clients. Again I drew on the papers which I had obtained from the APB files of Arthur Andersen & Co., and these included the transcript of a unique and little-known hearing on accounting held by the SEC in November 1965. The debate and shifting positions on the balance-sheet classification issue in the APB, which is explored in this article, set the stage for bringing to light the decisive action which the SEC took after losing patience with the slothfulness of the APB in resolving controversial issues. Manuel F. Cohen, the SEC's activist Chairman and a former longtime SEC staff member, had been outspoken in speeches about the APB's slow pace of progress during the 1960s, and he used the hearing—at which the leaders of the APB were called before him to be upbraided—and the promulgation of a rule in an Accounting Series Release immediately thereafter to goad the Board into taking principled and prompt action on difficult issues. The reclassification issue was a concern to retailers that did not want the deferred tax liability arising from the different tax than accounting treatment of their installment receivables to reduce their working capital. They wanted it classified as a noncurrent liability, not as a current liability. Arthur Andersen & Co., which was represented on the Board first by Leonard Spacek and then by George Catlett, believed that the liability should be in the current section if the corresponding receivables themselves were current assets, and Spacek had persuaded the Board to issue an exposure draft to that effect. But then, at a subsequent meeting, after the retail companies had made known their antipathy towards the proposed classification to their audit firms, the Board reversed itself and deleted the paragraph on the classification as current from the final *Opinion*. Andersen thereupon petitioned the SEC, whose

[9] See Marshall A. Geiger, *Setting the Standard for the New Auditor's Report: An Analysis of Attempts to Influence the Auditing Standards Board* (Greenwich, CT: JAI Press Inc., 1993), p. 173.

accounting staff was known to be sympathetic with the firm's position, to overrule the Board, and Cohen seized the opportunity to convene a hearing and issue the Release, which mandated that companies classify the liability in the current section in circumstances where the receivable was a current asset. It was a unique occurrence: the SEC's use of rulemaking to implement a portion of an exposure draft which did not make it into the final pronouncement.

"The SEC Rules Historical Cost Accounting: 1934 to the 1970s," which appeared in a special issue of *Accounting and Business Research* in 2007, was an article idea I had had in mind for many years. It was brought to the fore when Robert Hodgkinson, the Executive Director, Technical of the Institute of Chartered Accountants in England and Wales, invited me to make a 15-minute presentation during a buffet dinner at the Institute's annual conference on "Information for Better Markets" in December 2006. The theme of the conference was "measurement in financial reporting," and I decided to focus my brief remarks on the role that the SEC had resolutely played from its founding in 1934 to the 1970s in preventing publicly traded companies in the United States from revaluing property, plant and equipment above historical cost. My brief presentation was so well received that I decided to expand it into an article. One of those in attendance paid me the highest compliment: that my 15-minute oration reminded him of the late Alistair Cooke's quarter-hour "Letter from America," which was broadcast weekly by the BBC for 58 years. The article was intended to help those interested in the evolution of generally accepted accounting principles in the United States to understand why historical cost accounting for fixed assets dominates US financial reporting. It also provides convincing evidence that the SEC regularly intervened potently during the CAP and APB eras in the establishment of accounting principles.

There are three broad themes represented in this collection: the historical development of the process of setting accounting standards, the evolution of accounting thought, and the evolution of the accountancy profession and of audit practice. The motivation behind my articles (as well as the *Forging* series) on standard setting has been to provide evidence that the process is not a dispassionate fashioning of recommendations in a cloistered environment. From the 1940s to the 1970s, there was a collision of philosophical differences between leading figures in the accountancy profession. In addition, the SEC, including its accounting staff, has exercised a proactive and at times intrusive oversight over the standard-setting process. And also since the 1940s, the preferences of preparers, government, and other self-interested parties have been pressed on the standard setter, sometimes powerfully, and any attempt to understand the evolving body of standards must take account of these influences. My aim has been to try to understand this dynamic through historical research.

My biographical interest, as reflected in the articles on Paton, MacNeal, and Canning (as well as by the Hatfield book), help us trace and illuminate the efforts by early, major writers to place their mark on the accounting literature and on accounting education, and to advance the quest for improved financial reporting.

Articles in this collection testify that the vitality and dedication to the public interest by the US accountancy profession began to weaken in the 1970s, and these qualities continued to deteriorate in the 1980s and 1990s.

On the subject of the evolution of audit practice, it is interesting to note that even the selection of wording in the auditor's opinion can be controversial.

Historical research can perform a valuable service by documenting and explaining the evolution of such change.

REPLACEMENT COST: MEMBER OF THE FAMILY, WELCOME GUEST, OR INTRUDER?

STEPHEN A. ZEFF*

FINANCIAL accounting in this country, apparently since its first appearance on these shores, has been anchored by the notion of historical cost. Net income for the great majority of firms has been determined to be the excess of (realized) revenues over historical costs that can reasonably be said to have "expired" as a proximate result of the generating of those revenues.[1] Necessarily, numerous conventions have been developed to effectuate the application of this income-determination process. One of the several assumptions that underlie the process provides that historical costs are not to be reinterpreted in the light of subsequent changes in the economy-wide exchange value of the monetary unit.

The historical cost-revenue realization concept of accounting net income is traceable to medieval days, when "sporadic" was descriptive of commercial activity. Continually available markets (as opposed to, say, the periodic great trade fairs in the Levant) were uncommon. Owners were also managers, and financial reckonings were derived mainly for the benefit of these owner-managers—although the figures might be shown to creditors and (except where it could be avoided) to tax assessors. Financial statements, as such, were unknown.

Record-keeping naturally followed the organization plan of each commercial undertaking. Venture accounting was the predictable outgrowth of this age. The initial commitment for a caravan or voyage was set down in the Ledger for ultimate comparison with the fruits attained upon completion of the venture. Historical cost was in effect matched with revenues upon termination of the venture.[2] If prices changed during the interim, owner-managers were either unaware (because of poor transportation and communication between distant markets) or unconcerned about them—for record-keeping purposes. The occasion for observing a change in their recorded capital was the return of the caravan or ship (or the closing of their filled-up Ledgers). Presumably, for sedentary merchants who were previously travelers it was a reasonable extension of the venture principle to define a venture in

---

* Stephen A. Zeff is Assistant Professor of Accounting, Tulane University. This manuscript was the basis of a presentation given before the annual meeeting of the Southwestern Section of the American Accounting Association, in Dallas, on April 21, 1962. The writer is indebted to Professors W. David Maxwell, James T. Murphy, and Peter A. Firmin, all of Tulane University, who provided numerous helpful suggestions.

[1] The authoritative expository statement on this "matching process" is in W. A. Paton and A. C. Littleton, *An Introduction to Corporate Accounting Standards*, Monograph No. 3 (Chicago: American Accounting Association, 1940).

[2] Admittedly, income-determination as such was probably not then prevalent. Bookkeeping activity led more directly to a reconciliation of beginning and ending capital balances, which would reflect, among other things, net income. The Profit and Loss account was a repository of "refuse and dregs."

their more continuing form of enterprise as comprehending the acquisition and sale of a particular unit of product. Long-lived assets were rarely significant factors in early accounts, and what there were of them were presumably viewed as enduring, for depreciation as we know it today was not recorded.

Suffice it to say that no writer of that day explained the evolution of venture accounting in this manner. Nevertheless, this explanation appears to be a reasonable inference from the several historical accounts.[3]

The essential outline of the venture approach survives today. This remarkable record of longevity may attest as easily to its adaptability to changing economic conditions as to the unresponsiveness of accountants to these same changing conditions. Which is the valid inference?

Many twentieth-century writers have attempted to demonstrate that venture accounting is either (1) imperfectly conceived, or (2) altogether inappropriate as a measure *apropos* of modern business enterprise. The basis for most criticism is the non-recognition by the conventional venture approach of price fluctuations that occur during the course of a venture. An alternative approach called "price-level accounting" is urged. Sometimes it is called "replacement cost accounting," although many writers contend that these are separate and distinct concepts. It is the objective of this paper to review these arguments and suggest what they mean to the conventional venture approach. The literature on this subject is rather large, and no attempt is made to be comprehensive.

Definition of Terms. Terms must first be demarcated carefully. Price changes are fundamentally of two kinds: general and specific. They reflect markedly different economic phenomena, and although it is often well-nigh impossible to measure precisely one apart from the other, they must nonetheless be kept separate at the conceptual level.

A general price level change is a shifting in the economy-wide exchange value of the monetary unit. It is not restricted to the potency of the monetary unit in buying only one article or even a group of articles. Instead, it mirrors the change in the purchasing power of the monetary unit as regards *all* goods and services that might be bought. A general price change is undesirable because, at the very least, of the misunderstanding it causes among buyers and sellers who are unable to discern general from specific price movements. As contrasted with a governmental edict to revalue the monetary unit, the usual kind of general price level change occurs subtly. Buyers and sellers (as well as investors, lenders, borrowers, etc.) only imperfectly perceive its presence. It is an unwanted phenomenon that can have pernicious effects on the smooth working of an economy.

"Price *level* [i.e., general] stability, however, should in no sense be identified with the stabilization of any *particular* [i.e., specific] price. It is the very essence of a free enterprise economy that the prices of *individual* products and services be free to adjust to changing market conditions."[4]

As a limiting case, if the prices of *all* commodities and services were to rise (or fall) by a uniform per cent, an illustration

---

[3] One thorough investigation of the historical roots of bookkeeping and accounting is in A. C. Littleton, *Accounting Evolution to 1900* (New York: The American Institute Publishing Co. Inc., 1933). Extracts from this hard-to-find book, which, by the way, is derived from the author's doctoral dissertation, are in A. C. Littleton, *Essay on Accountancy* (Urbana: University of Illinois Press, 1961). Others who have written extensively on historical matters are Henry Rand Hatfield, Raymond De Roover, Basil Yamey, Edward Peragallo, and Richard Brown. Of particular interest is Yamey's "Scientific Bookkeeping and the Rise of Capitalism," originally published in *The Economic History Review*, June, 1949, and reproduced in W. T. Baxter (editor), *Studies in Accounting* (London: Sweet & Maxwell, Limited, 1950), pp. 13–30.

[4] *Staff Report on Employment, Growth, and Price Levels*, Prepared for Consideration by the Joint Economic Committee; 86th Congress, 1st Session, December 24, 1959, p. 114.

of unequivocal *general* price change is at hand. It would be called "inflation" (or "deflation"). It might also be referred to as a "general price level" change or "general purchasing power" change. The terms "purchasing power" and "price level" would not be sufficiently descriptive unless the word "general" is attached thereto. Confusion in price-level discussions is caused by utilizing terms without the necessary adjectives, "general" and "specific," or their equivalents.[5]

In the absence of the aforementioned limiting case of general price level change, precise measurement in practice of this kind of price movement is probably impossible. To be sure, it seems impossible to *conceive* of a precise measure of changing general prices. For in the garden-variety of inflation (or deflation), weights must be assigned to different purchasable articles; such is not a problem where the price of every article moves in one direction by the same percent. Because these weights would need to be changed as buying habits alter over time, the development of a general price index for temporal comparisons can hardly yield precise and true results. Despite conceptual and methodological impediments, approximations of general price level change are nonetheless valuable indices of the trend in the economy-wide exchange value of the monetary unit. Available indices today are the Consumers Price Index, Wholesale Price Index (both developed by the Bureau of Labor Statistics, Department of Labor), and the Implicit Price Deflator used by the Office of Business Economics, Department of Commerce, in measuring changes in the Gross National Product. Each is more suitable for some purposes than for others. Each has weaknesses.[6] But each is used. Hereafter in this paper, a general price level change is denoted also as "Type A price movement."

Specific, or individual, price level changes refer to the movement in the prices of single, particular assets—presumably in response to shifting demand and supply functions. Clearly, the price movement of individual assets or even of groups of similar assets may vary significantly from Type A price movement. The average of the individual price movements of all articles (or assets), properly weighted, will necessarily be identical to the Type A price movement. Hereafter in this paper, specific price level changes are denoted also as "Type B price movements."

If an article is acquired for $40 at the beginning of a time period and there follows a Type A price movement upward of 10% during the time period, the acquisition cost of the article *in terms of end-of-the-period dollars* is $44. It is important to note that $44 does not represent (except coincidentally) the article's replacement cost as of the end of the time period, for it was observed above that Type B price movement—the price change of a specific article—may be quite different from Type A price movement. Type B price movements for a great many articles are each likely to be more volatile than is Type A price movement during the same period. Hence, in no sense will the $44 necessarily represent the "current price" or "current cost" of the article as of the end of the time period, because both of these terms imply replacement cost. (It is unfortunate that "current price" and "current cost" are

---

[5] It matters not whether the general price level change is caused by demand-pull, cost-push, or Schultze's structural influences.

[6] For the most comprehensive theoretical discussion and empirical testing of different indices and their apparent comparative effects on accounting data to which the indices are applied, see Eldon S. Hendriksen, *Price-Level Adjustments of Financial Statements— An Evaluation and Case Study of Two Public Utility Firms* (Washington State University Press, 1961), Chaps. 3–6. For technical material on the Consumers Price Index, see *Government Price Statistics*, Hearings before the Subcommittee on Economic Statistics of the Joint Economic Committee; 87th Congress, 1st Session, January 24, 1961 (Part 1) and May 1–5, 1961 (Part 2).

often used to describe historical costs that have been restated by an index of Type A price movement.)

Suppose, however, an investigation of suppliers' price lists for the article discloses that the replacement cost is $48.40 as of the end of the period. The increase in replacement cost—as typically represented—is then said to be $48.40 – $40.00/ $40.00, or 21% since the beginning of the period. Assuming for the moment that Type A price movement during the period had been nil, 21% would be the increase in *pure* replacement cost (i.e., a Type B price movement). If, on the other hand, the Type A price movement during the period had been 10% upward, the 21%, now viewed as a hybrid type of increase, is composed of two kinds of price movements, Type A and Type B. Of the $8.40 increase, $4.00, or 10% of $40.00, is the result of Type A price movement. This $4.00 is not a real change, but is merely the result of an alteration in the "length of the ruler." In a sense, the $4.00 is a fictitious price change. The additional $4.40, however, stands for the increase in pure replacement cost, for once the historical cost and replacement cost are stated in terms of a common monetary unit, the amount of the real increase, $4.40 (in terms of end-of-the-period dollars), may be ascertained. The increase in *hybrid* replacement cost is hereafter denoted as "Type C price movement," 21% in the latter situation. It should be evident that a measured Type C price movement, if accompanied by *both* Type A and Type B price movements, is in reality a mixed, or hybrid, calculation. It would reflect the combined effect of Type A and Type B price movements. Alternatively, where Type A price movement is nil, Type B and Type C price movements are equal. Where Type B price movement is nil, it is similarly true that Type A and Type C price movements are equal.

Evidence of Recognition of Type C Price Movement in Conventional Accounting. So long as the venture approach is accepted as the appropriate model, replacement costs are irrelevant to income determination. They reflect events that occur after the close of the "venture." Nonetheless, accountants' concern about price fluctuations during the course of a "venture" have been manifested by occasional resort to replacement costs. The deluge of unsystematic write-ups and write-downs of the 1920s and 1930s still lingers as a nightmare to many.[7] "Lower of cost or market" has a history of several hundred years.[8] LIFO is in many cases a *de facto* recognition of replacement cost. But these are exceptions, and rather than being consistently-applied, carefully worked out reinterpretations of the whole conventional income-determination process, they have been largely *ad hoc* expedients brought on by contemporaneous economic (including tax) problems. In each instance, the adjustment is for Type C price movements, showing no recognition of the important distinction between general and specific price movements, and, hence, between fictitious and real price changes.

Recent Attempts at Recognizing Type A Price Movement. It is here contended that the restatement of dated historical costs to homogeneous historical costs is not a departure from the venture approach.[9] The restatement merely corrects for a traditional accounting assumption, usually implicit, that the economy-wide exchange value of the monetary unit is stable. Inasmuch as all available Type A indices unequivocally contradict this assumption, it seems only appropriate to adopt the contrary assumption and alter accounting principles accordingly.

---

[7] For data on the magnitude of such adjustments, see Solomon Fabricant, *Capital Consumption and Adjustment* (New York: National Bureau of Economic Research, 1938), p. 213 ff.

[8] See A. C. Littleton, "Genealogy for 'Cost or Market,' " THE ACCOUNTING REVIEW (June, 1941), pp. 161–67.

[9] This point has been made repeatedly by William A. Paton and others.

Such methods as LIFO, which is really a Type C adjustment and thus a departure from historical cost, are only a patch when the pants need a reweaving. LIFO is a gimmick, and its presence in financial statements tends to defeat attempts at evolving a cohesive theory of asset valuation-income determination for a dynamic economy. "Base-stock" is no less reprehensible.

If an article is bought for $20 when an accepted Type A index is 100, and is sold for $33 when the same index is 110, the difference of $13—which is the net income that would be obtained by conventional accounting, under the stable-monetary-unit assumption—is meaningless. The dollar of 110 is not the same as the dollar of 100. No common denominator was used. Net income is either $10 in terms of index = 100

$$\left(\text{i.e., } \frac{\$33}{1.10} - \$20\right),$$

or $11 in terms of index = 110 [i.e., $33 − (1.10×$20)]. By either of the latter two approaches, the net income is calculated to be a 50% return on inventory investment.

Application of an appropriate Type A index to long-lived assets, in contrast to inventories, is the more pressing need today, however. It cannot be repeated too often that a Type A index adjustment has nothing to do with replacement cost. In the preceding example, replacement cost at the time of sale might have been $18, $20, $23, or any other amount. Whatever it is, it is ignored.

Indiana Telephone Corporation has, since 1955, used Type C and Type A indices concurrently. With the assistance of a consulting engineer, the company classifies "gross plant additions" on a FIFO basis by years of acquisition, selects an appropriate Type C index for each plant category, and then applies the derived multiplier to each year's cost of acquisition. Since this plant-account analysis is undertaken only once every three or four years, as needed, financial-statement amounts for interim years are found by applying a final multiplier to the Type C-adjusted figures. This final multiplier is based on the "all commodities other than farm and foods" component of the Wholesale Price Index.

Beginning in 1957, the Sacramento Municipal Utility District and Ayrshire Collieries Corporation recorded "supplementary" depreciation charges. Sacramento uses the term "fair value depreciation," while Ayrshire calls it "price level depreciation." Iowa-Illinois Gas and Electric Company, in response to a 1957 Iowa Supreme Court decision that allowed the company's rate base to reflect "fair value depreciation," began to record in 1958 a supplementary "fair value depreciation" charge on property located in Iowa districts in which the court decision had been implemented.

None of these latter three companies discloses the manner by which the supplementary depreciation charged is computed. Although they occasionally refer in their annual reports to "current purchasing power of the dollar" and "inflation," they uniformly contend that the new basis of accounting replaces "historical cost." Further, the key adjectives "general" and "specific" as well as equivalents thereto are not used. "Fair value" is hardly a definitive term.

All of the latter three companies retain the same firm of independent auditors. The certificate in the annual report of each company notes with approval the supplementary depreciation charge. These same certificates, either expressly or by implication, indicate that a substitute for "historical cost" is being used. Such is not true if in fact the adjustments are the result of applying an index that is reflective only of Type A price movement. Better communication is needed of the true nature of these adjustments.

None of these four companies exhibits adjustments for other than long-lived assets. Admittedly, these assets are by far the ones most seriously in need of attention. A complete recognition of Type A price movement, however, would require a restatement of all historical costs, together with a recognition of gains and losses as a result of holding cash and maintaining debtor or creditor positions during a period of such price movement.[10] Preferably, the complete restatement should be made.

Summary on Recognition of Type A Price Movement. That no index can measure precisely Type A price movement is insufficient justification for adhering to an assumption that is contrary to the results that have been produced by accepted measures of price-level experience.[11] The results of several practical applications have been published.[12] Although some U. S. companies complain in their annual reports that income taxes based on conventional historical costs are "unfair," "unsound," or "uneconomic," these same adjectives may be used to describe the manner in which they report their own affairs to stockholders. One can only conjecture whether companies would be quick to restate historical costs in a period of sustained *deflation* and hence show that conventionally-reported profits are understated, when, in a period of sustained *inflation* they do not even acknowledge the same fundamental deficiency in their published financial statements. U. S. industry has dallied far too long in taking action to restate their heterogeneous historical costs. It is to be hoped that the new Accounting Principles Board will take positive steps toward such a restatement.

Relevance of Replacement Cost to Income Determination. Wholly unrelated to any restatement as a result of Type A price movement is the question of whether historical cost—restated or not—is the appropriate frame of reference for asset

valuation-income determination. Consider these three charges.

Chambers contends that conventional financial statements, based on "price" data, are likely to mislead external decision-makers.[13] He advocates the use of "value"-based accounting determinations.

According to MacNeal, who agrees with Chambers' recommendation,

"The real difficulty lies in the sophistry, illogic, and untruth of present accounting principles, which produce figures deceiving accountants, business men, and the public alike."[14]

Edwards and Bell, in a book that should be read by all accountants, maintain that accounting determinations are valid raw data for decision-makers only if the economic environment possesses the charac-

---

[10] For a lucid exposition of the nature of such adjustments, see Perry Mason, *Price-Level Changes and Financial Statements: Basic Concepts and Methods* (Columbus, O.: American Accounting Association, 1956). An excellent discussion, together with a complete illustration, may be found in William A. Paton and Robert L. Dixon, *Essentials of Accounting* (New York: The Macmillan Company, 1958), Chap. 36.

[11] For agreement, see *Changing Concepts of Business Income*, Report of Study Group on Business Income (New York: The Macmillan Company, 1952), pp. 73–78. See also Ralph Coughenour Jones, *Effects of Price Level Changes on Business Income, Capital, and Taxes* (American Accounting Association, 1956), pp. 1–3.

[12] See Ralph Coughenour Jones, "Effect of Inflation on Capital and Profits: The Record of Nine Steel Companies," *The Journal of Accountancy* (January, 1949), pp. 9–27; Donald A. Corbin, "The Impact of Changing Prices on a Department Store," *The Journal of Accountancy* (April, 1954), pp. 430–40; Ralph Coughenour Jones, *Price-Level Changes and Financial Statements: Case Studies of Four Companies* (American Accounting Association, 1955); and Eldon S. Hendriksen, *op. cit.*

[13] R. J. Chambers, "Measurement and Misrepresentation," *Management Science* (January, 1960), pp. 141–48. Chambers argues that present-day "price" accounting is a throwback to horse-and-buggy days. *Ibid.*, at pp. 146–47.

[14] Kenneth MacNeal, "What's Wrong With Accounting?" originally published in *The Nation*, October 7–14, 1939, and reproduced in W. T. Baxter (editor), *op. cit.*, pp. 213–26, at p. 226. For a fuller statement of MacNeal's position, see his *Truth in Accounting* (Philadelphia: University of Pennsylvania Press, 1939). Among the leading pro-replacement cost statements in England and Canada are, respectively: K. Lacey, "Commodity Stocks and the Trade Cycle," *Economica* N.S. (February, 1944), pp. 12–18; and Alphonse Riverin, *Le profit comptable: fiction ou réalité* (Québec: Les Presses de l'Université Laval, 1961). See also Lacey's *Profit Measurement and Price Changes* (London: Sir Isaac Pitman & Sons, Ltd., 1952).

teristics of the "stationary state"—admittedly an improbable circumstance.[15]

These and other arguments, which derive from the major premise that current costs and not historical costs are appropriate to asset valuation-income determination, are not to be sidestepped by such neutral but empty replies as Louis Bromfield's "There may be something in what you say" or George Bernard Shaw's "You may be right." Nor are they to be rejected out of hand. Those who would defend historical cost should not be satisfied until the reasoning behind such arguments can be successfully rebutted.

Indeed, prominent foreign companies utilize replacement cost in the determination of their net income. N. V. Philips' Gloeilampenfabrieken, of The Netherlands, employs replacement cost for valuing long-lived assets and inventories.[16] Imperial Tobacco Co. of Canada, Ltd., converted in its 1961 annual report to a full-fledged replacement-cost accounting for long-lived assets. Previously, it had not revalued long-lived assets, but since 1955 had shown a supplementary replacement-cost depreciation charge. The one-shot revaluation of its long-lived assets did not, however, affect the carrying value of the company's total assets. Conveniently, the $25-million write-up in long-lived assets was more than offset by a concurrent write-down in goodwill. Imperial had charged operations with an inventory-replacement increment, but this practice was apparently abandoned in 1961.

A replacement cost adjustment should hardly be viewed as an alternative to a Type A restatement. Both the Philips and Imperial adjustments, for example, are recognition of Type C price movement, implying that these companies fail to disclose the important distinction between the fictitious (i.e., general) and real (i.e., specific) price changes.

"Disposable Income" Concept. Proponents of replacement-cost adjustments

contend variously that the conventional venture approach does not "preserve real capital," that it includes in net income an element of price appreciation that is not within the control of management and therefore does not contribute to an understanding of management's effectiveness, that it produces results that are not sufficiently forward looking, that it leads to a balance sheet that is not at all expressive of the firm's current position, that it yields figures that are not comparable over time, among others. The recommendations for change may be roughly classed into two groups. Both groups would restate historical costs by Type A indices, but there is no unanimity as to whether the company should disclose the general and specific price effects separately.

One group, the "disposable income proponents," would reduce accounting net income (after Type A restatement) by the upward Type B price movement that has occurred currently or in the past with respect to currently-sold inventories and currently-consumed long-lived assets. Hence, the reduction would be solely for "realized" increments in pure replacement cost. (This group would also reflect increases in net income if the Type B price movement has been downward.)

The second group, "earning power proponents," would reflect as net *income* (or *loss*) the enhancement (or decrement) during the period of the current value of assets, after giving effect to investments and withdrawals. The realized-unrealized dichotomy would be irrelevant in the determination of net income; the increase

---

[15] Edgar O. Edwards and Philip W. Bell, *The Theory and Measurement of Business Income* (Berkeley: University of California Press, 1961), esp. Chap. 1.
[16] A. Goudeket, "An Application of Replacement Value Theory," *The Journal of Accountancy* (July, 1960), pp. 37–47. The Philips practice is not, as Goudeket occasionally contends, a general purchasing power adjustment. *Ibid.*, at pp. 40, 44, 45. It is more than that; it is a Type C price movement adjustment. Willard J. Graham, in a letter to the editor, points this out. *The Journal of Accountancy* (August, 1960), pp. 28–31.

(decrease) in pure replacement cost during the period would be classed as income (loss). Clearly, the two groups differ on at least one fundamental question: Are increases in pure replacement cost properly described as income? The underpinnings of the two concepts are presented below.

Members of the first group, Schmidt,[17] Castenholz,[18] Blackie,[19] and Graham,[20] contend that accounting net income should reflect a charge at *current* replacement cost for "goods sold" and the currently-consumed portion of long-lived assets. It matters not that actual replacement is not contemplated. The following example should illustrate their proposal (assuming that Type A and Type B effects are kept separate):

Merchandise:
1. Cash expenditure at date of acquisition, $60
2. Type A index on acquisition date, 100
3. Type A index on sale date, 120
4. Replacement cost on sale date, $86

Long-lived asset:
1. Cash expenditure at date of acquisition, $10,000
2. Type A index on acquisition date, 80
3. Type A index at end of current period, 120
4. Depreciation rate per period, 4%
5. Replacement cost at end of period, $17,000

First, the historical costs would be restated:

Merchandise: $60 × (120/100) = $72
Long-lived asset: $10,000 × (120/80) = $15,000

Second, the "cost of goods sold" and current depreciation charge would be reinforced by pure replacement-cost charges:

Cost of Goods Sold:
Historical cost (restated) . . . . $ 72
Add excess of replacement cost
   over restated historical cost 14
                                                           ———
                                                           $ 86
                                                           ====

Depreciation Expense:
At restated historical cost, 4% × $15,000. . . . $600
Add excess of replacement cost over
   restated historical cost,
   4% × ($17,000 − $15,000) 80
                                                           ———
                                                           $680
                                                           ====

Evidently, this is a short-run[21] notion of net income. It answers very well the question, "What is the largest dividend that is consistent with permitting the enterprise to continue operating at no less than the same scale as before?" In brief, what is the disposable income, after allowing for replacement needs? Its results are quite similar to what would be yielded by a generalized application of LIFO to all non-monetary assets.

Technically, this approach departs from venture accounting, for the venture has fixed bounds and no inquiry is made into the subsequent disposition of new assets. The accounting cycle according to the proposed approach proceeds from non-monetary asset to monetary asset to (in effect) non-monetary asset instead of the venture ideal of monetary asset to non-monetary asset to monetary asset. But this

[17] Fritz Schmidt, "Is Appreciation Profits?" THE ACCOUNTING REVIEW (December, 1931), pp. 289–93. See also his "The Basis of Depreciation Charges," *Harvard Business Review* (April, 1930), pp. 257–64.

[18] William B. Castenholz, "The Accountant and Changing Monetary Values," THE ACCOUNTING REVIEW (December, 1931), pp. 282–88. Castenholz incorrectly maintains that he and Sweeney are in agreement. *Ibid.*, at p. 288; and Henry W. Sweeney, "Stabilized Depreciation," THE ACCOUNTING REVIEW (September, 1931), pp. 165–78, esp. pp. 172–73. For a fuller statement of Castenholz' position, see his *A Solution to the Appreciation Problem* (Chicago: LaSalle Extension University, 1931).

[19] William Blackie, "What is Accounting Accounting For—Now?" *Conference Proceedings, 1948* (New York: National Association of Cost Accountants, 1948), pp. 26–54 and discussion thereof, pp. 54–59. Blackie, then vice president of Caterpillar Tractor Co., was made president in early 1962. Although he contends that his is not a "replacement cost" theory because the adjustment does not presume actual replacement, the effect is the same. *Ibid.*, pp. 37–38. For support of Blackie's general proposition, see F. Sewell Bray, "English Accountant Agrees with Proposal to State Current Costs," *The Journal of Accountancy* (December, 1948), pp. 478–81.

[20] Willard J. Graham, "The Effect of Changing Price Levels Upon the Determination, Reporting, and Interpretation of Income," THE ACCOUNTING REVIEW (January, 1949), pp. 15–26. See also his letter to *The Journal of Accountancy*, cited in footnote 16. For contrast, see Carl Thomas Devine, "Depreciation and Income Measurement," THE ACCOUNTING REVIEW (January, 1944), pp. 39–47.

[21] This is not "short-run" in the Marshallian or micro-economic sense.

observation is merely technical, and is of little moment if the proposed approach is both feasible and productive of more useful information for stockholders.

That it is feasible is evidenced by the Philips and Imperial experience. But what new and unique information, other than that regarding current dividend-paying capacity, does it provide? Writes Graham:

"Only profits so defined are of any significance in an attempt to forecast the probable future course of the profits of the company or of the industry."[22]

On the contrary, there seems to be nothing in the proposed method that would enable stockholders to forecast future realized results more effectively than they can now with conventional (but Type A-restated) accounting data. Managerial needs, especially for pricing, would seem to be well served thereby, however. But we are concerned with external reports, not internal reporting.

Graham also argues that the proposed method separates "management profits" (which is the net income that would be reported by his method) from "price profits" (i.e., the excess of replacement cost over Type A-restated historical cost).[23] That it does, and the distinction is certainly worth making. But, as Edwards and Bell point out, the separation can be effected within the conventional framework.[24] After achieving the separation and thus arriving at Graham's net income ("management profits"), they would add back these realized increments ("price profits") in pure replacement cost to arrive at a net income that is fully consistent with the venture approach.

The Schmidt-Castenholz-Blackie-Graham conception of net income may well warrant the attention of state legislators as a proper current legal limitation on permissible dividends for a going concern. But it is not to be recommended as *the* accounting net income for reporting to stockholders. That is, it is not to be recommended unless stockholders can be assumed to be interested almost exclusively in current dividend matters. The proposed conception would better serve readers of a funds statement than of an income statement.

To be sure, the "current disposability" view has probably exerted too strong an influence on the development of accounting principles via emerging dividend law (both in Great Britain during the nineteenth century and in the U. S. during the present century)[25] and U. S. income tax law.[26] If these laws have not had the effect of making the realization criterion (i.e., the sale test) more ubiquitous in accounting, they at the least have helped defeat any movements in accounting *away* from the realization test.

[22] Graham, "The Effect of Changing Price Levels upon the Determination, Reporting, and Interpretation of Income," p. 19.
[23] *Ibid.*
[24] Edwards and Bell, *op. cit.*, Chap. 4 and pp. 153–55. Accounting net income would nonetheless be restated to reflect Type A price movement.
[25] See, for example, Prosper Reiter, *Profit, Dividend and the Law* (New York: The Ronald Press Co., 1926); Henry Rand Hatfield, *Accounting—Its Principles and Problems* (New York: D. Appleton and Company, 1927), Chap. 12; and A. C. Littleton, *Accounting Evolution to 1900*, Chap. 13. For a study of the trend of important court decisions in Great Britain and the U. S., stressing the realization criterion: Joseph L. Weiner and James C. Bonbright, "Theory of Anglo-American Dividend Law: Surplus and Profits," *Columbia Law Review* (March, 1930), pp. 330–58, at pp. 337–45. For the current status of the various state laws, see this writer's "Legal Dividend Sources—A National Survey and Critique" (concluding instalment), *The New York Certified Public Accountant* (December, 1961), pp. 802–16, at pp. 807–09. For comments on the early influence of dividend law on the auditor's view of net income, see Lawrence R. Dicksee, *Auditing* (7th ed.; London: Gee & Co., 1907), Chap. 8. A movement away from dependence on dividend law is evidenced in Montgomery's first edition. Robert H. Montgomery, *Auditing Theory and Practice* (New York: The Ronald Press Company, 1912), Chap. 13, esp. p. 194. His later criticisms of U. S. dividend law are well known.
[26] See, for example, the landmark cases of *Eisner v. Macomber*, 252 U. S. 189 (1920) and *La Belle Iron Works v. U. S.*, 256 U. S. 377 (1921), esp. Mr. Justice Pitney's oft-quoted dictum at 393–94. For discussion, see Floyd W. Windal, *The Accounting Concept of Realization*, Occasional Paper No. 5 (East Lansing, Mich.: Bureau of Business Research, Michigan State University, 1961), Chap. 3.

The concept of accounting net income should transcend the matter of current capacity (however that be defined) to pay dividends. Accounting net income is needed by stockholders as a basis for buy-sell decisions. It is submitted that more than just current dividend questions are relevant to such decisions. The time-shape of *future* dividends, together with the future trend of stock prices, would seem to be more controlling. Hence, a longer-run conception of net income would be preferable.

"Earning Power" Concept. "Income" has its roots in economics. Regrettably, however, economists do not agree on one meaning of this term. Irving Fisher, who was interested in the income of a consumer, expresses the futility that is evident from even a cursory examination of the literature:

"It is no exaggeration to say that at present the state of economic opinion on this important subject [i.e., the meaning of 'income'] is deplorably confused and conflicting."[27]

A quarter of a century later, Frank Knight wrote:

"Perhaps no term or concept in economic discussion is used with a more bewildering variety of well established meanings than profit."[28]

Despite this professed gap in economic theory, one definition recurs with remarkable frequency in economic and (especially) accounting writings. It is Hicks', which states that a man's income is " . . . the maximum value which he can consume during a week, and still expect to be as well off at the end of the week as he was at the beginning."[29] While Hicks seems at first to balk at the usefulness of this definition for the firm, particularly in a dynamic economy,[30] he nonetheless appears to accord it some status as an analytical tool.[31] "Well-offness" for the firm is defined with reference to the discounted value of future net receipts.[32] Since assets are *valu*able to the extent of

their presumed (subjectively determined) ability to produce future net receipts, their *present* significance to the firm would be the *present* equivalent of this future stream of net receipts.

It is here contended that the enhancement in this present (or discounted) value from one point in time to another, after adjusting for investments and withdrawals, is the appropriate net income to appear in corporate annual reports.

Presumably, members of the "disposable income" school would label this enhancement as a change in "capital," or "savings"—but not income. This was Fisher's view as well. At the turn of the century, he and Frank Fetter (and others) debated the issue; the reader is urged to examine Sweeney's excellent account of the disputants' arguments.[33] An increase in this present value would seem to be a change in capital. Yet at the same time it would be income; when ultimate realization occurs, that capital merely changes in composition. Those who prefer to defer recognition of income until the point of realization would emphasize the identification of "income" with current enjoyment of an increment to capital. Those who take the opposite view would emphasize the *prospect* of future enjoyment. The choice is essentially between short-run and long-

---

[27] Irving Fisher, *The Nature of Capital and Income* (New York: The Macmillan Company, 1906), p. 101.

[28] Frank H. Knight, "Profit," in *Encyclopaedia of the Social Sciences*, vol. 12 (1934), pp. 480–86, reproduced in *Readings in the Theory of Income Distribution* (Philadelphia: The Blakiston Company, 1946), pp. 533–46, at p. 533.

[29] J. R. Hicks, *Value and Capital* (Oxford, at the Clarendon Press, 1939), p. 172.

[30] *Ibid.*, pp. 171–77. Moonitz recommends against an uncritical application of the Hicksian concept to the firm. Maurice Moonitz, "Should We Discard the Income Concept?" THE ACCOUNTING REVIEW (April, 1962), pp. 175–80, at p. 178.

[31] Hicks, *op. cit.*, p. 196.

[32] E.g., see Edwards and Bell, *op. cit.*, p. 24.

[33] Henry W. Sweeney, "Income," THE ACCOUNTING REVIEW (December, 1933), pp. 323–35. Sweeney argues effectively that the increment is income. See also his *Stabilized Accounting* (New York: Harper & Brothers, 1936), esp. pp. 16–23 and Chap. 3.

run notions. That income is better defined in a long-run context is the position of Sweeney,[34] Buchanan,[35] Moonitz-Staehling,[36] and Alexander.[37]

The fact that accountants generally put off formal recognition of net income until the point of realization is not necessarily evidence that they disagree with the idea that net income may be said to emerge prior to realization.[38] Expectations cannot be audited. Were accountants to depend solely on subjective estimates of managers, not only would manipulation of accounting results be easily accomplished but also it would be impossible to tell whether there was manipulation in a given situation. No, the realization test is used because it is workable; criteria employed in the conventional recognition of revenue are objectively verifiable. (Notwithstanding the emphasis on objectivity in conventional accounting, it is noteworthy that so much subjectivity surrounds the important and material valuations of inventories and long-lived assets.)

It cannot be stressed too much that there is nothing sacrosanct about either conventional accounting net income or the process by which it is determined. That a procedure has been followed for many years is not sufficient reason for its indefinite continuance. Conventional accounting net income would seem to be what it is because of practical departures from some harder-to-measure ideal. An instance of a deviation from even the realization test is the accrual of interest revenue. This exception, writes Hatfield,

" . . . probably rests upon the idea that it is definitely calculable. . . . But if this is a satisfactory basis for differentiation, the rule for recognizing profits should be expressed in terms of calculability or certainty rather than made dependent upon the existence of a contract."[39]

What is there about the obtaining of a sale contract (or the delivering of product) that all associated income should be as-cribed to the occurring of that one event? After all, the getting of the contract (or the delivering of product) is only one of several economically important events that are necessary for a sale to be consummated. As George O. May writes, expediency is used to justify present practice:

"Manifestly, when a laborious process of manufacture and sale culminates in the delivery of the product at a profit, that profit is not attributable, except conventionally, to the moment when the sale or delivery occurred. The accounting convention which makes such an attribution is justified only by its demonstrated practical utility."[40]

Might not some other approach to determining net income produce more useful results without too great a sacrifice in "practical utility"? As a basis for uncovering such a substitute, the nature of what the income statement purports to disclose—the economic progress of the firm—should be combed for possible clues.

What is the most meaningful measure of economic progress of a firm? Should real increments in capital value (that presumably foreshadow concomitant changes in the stream of future net receipts) provide the occasion for recognizing progress or accomplishment? In short, should the net receipts-determining forces that have

---

[34] Sweeney, "Income." Sweeney quotes Fetter as concurring on this point.
[35] Norman S. Buchanan, *The Economics of Corporate Enterprise* (New York: Henry Holt and Company, 1940), pp. 211–12.
[36] Maurice Moonitz and Charles C. Staehling, *Accounting—An Analysis of Its Problems*, Volume I (Brooklyn: The Foundation Press, Inc., 1952), Chaps. 5 and 6.
[37] Sidney S. Alexander, "Income Measurement in a Dynamic Economy," in *Five Monographs on Business Income* (New York: Study Group on Business Income, American Institute of Accountants, 1950), pp. 1–95; see the interesting panel discussion on pp. 195–260. Boulding seems to lean in the direction of agreeing that unrealized "capital gains" are includible in income. Kenneth E. Boulding, *Economic Analysis* (3rd. ed.; New York: Harper & Brothers, 1955), p. 269.
[38] Some would disagree. See Russell Bowers, "Tests of Income Realization," THE ACCOUNTING REVIEW (June, 1941), pp. 139–55.
[39] Hatfield, *op. cit.*, p. 257.
[40] George O. May, *Financial Accounting* (New York: The Macmillan Company, 1943), p. 30.

worked to effect a change in capital value be given immediate acknowledgment as current net income? Or should the recognition of net income await the realized results—receipts and expenditures? As noted above, economists disagree.

It would seem, however, that the enhancement in a firm's ability to command future net receipts is sufficiently indicative of economic achievement, that awaiting the actual receipts and expenditures is tantamount to exalting form over substance. Investors, in valuing the prospects of different firms, should not be content with awaiting the moment at which the results of economic activity become obvious to all. Hence, a measure that supplies a basis for the informed projection of financial success would seem to be the most useful to investors.

Historical costs were values at different times in the past. At those times, costs represented jointly-agreed profitability projections of buyers and sellers. There is no reason, however, to believe that the exchange-value of a single transaction involving the acquisition of a commodity that a firm uses will continue to have this predictive quality throughout the interval that precedes the point at which that commodity yields its final productive service. Market values, opportunities, and expectations will change. That the firm chooses not to dispose of the asset at subsequently prevailing market values might provide the basis for inferring that the managers impute to the asset a pattern of net receipts such that their present value (at an assumed interest rate) is equal to or greater than the aforementioned prevailing market value. Naturally, assets are not perfectly divisible, and operations cannot conveniently be curtailed because, say, one key machine can be sold to an outsider at an attractive price.

Compared with medieval days, today the readers of financial summaries can acquire and dispose of ownership shares with ease and dispatch. Historical cost is justified in a situation in which all parties at interest have made irrevocable commitments to the venture. The examination of financial statements would be limited in the latter instance to the tracing of the success of *that* venture. Presumably, today's stockholder would want to know the magnitude of the impact on the firm of changing economic conditions.

If "market value" is to be used, what is its measure? Should it be the disposal price of the existing individual assets? The replacement cost of the entire firm? The sum of the replacement costs of the firm's individual assets? And how might each be calculated?

Vance criticizes individual replacement cost for this purpose as being (1) not necessarily indicative of potential realized income, and (2) inconclusive evidence that the net receipts stream will ever be realized.[41] Neither of these points can be rejected. To be sure, current selling price might be used as the basis (or one of the bases[42]) of imputing a current value to merchandise, but the same cannot be done for long-lived assets. At this juncture, it must be decided whether the accountant is to be satified with deferring the recognition of economic phenomena until he can take comfort that his figures are verifiable by final sales transactions, or whether he desires to acknowledge these changing economic forces as they occur, albeit sacrificing some finality and certainty in

---

[41] Lawrence L. Vance, "Earning-Power Valuation of Inventory," THE ACCOUNTING REVIEW (October, 1942), pp. 376–84, esp. pp. 378–80. For other reactions to the use of replacement cost for valuing inventories, see Carl Thomas Devine, *Inventory Valuation and Periodic Income* (New York: The Ronald Press Company, 1942), Chap. 6.

[42] Vance argues that both replacement cost and current selling price of inventory must change in the same direction before recognizing a new inventory carrying value. Vance, *op. cit.*, pp. 379–80. In computing "market" for purposes of "lower of cost or market," the AICPA has a loose requirement that changes in selling price must validate changes in replacement cost.

the raw data themselves. The accountant might put off the preparation of an income statement until the firm expires; figures as of that point would be unequivocally certain and final. Much of this certainty has been sacrificed, however, in the process of segmenting the life of a firm into "fiscal periods." Query: Is the present conception of the income-determination process, i.e., historical cost-revenue realization, the best balancing between a measure of economic progress (on the one hand) and relative certainty of obtained results (on the other)? It is argued here that further concessions should be made in operational precision in order to achieve greater conceptual precision.

Edwards and Bell, in their provocative volume, propound a measure called "business profit," which is predicated on what might be termed "factor replacement cost."[43] "Business profit" is the sum of (1) the excess of current revenues over the factor replacement cost of that portion of assets that can be said to have expired currently, and (2) the enhancement during the current period of the factor replacement cost of assets.

Component (1), which Edwards and Bell call "current operating profit," is presumably equivalent to Graham's "management profits." Whereas Graham would not give recognition to "price profits," realized or unrealized,[44] Edwards and Bell disclose as their component (2) a current increment labeled "realizable cost savings." Like Graham, Edwards and Bell contend that the merging of such cost savings with operating profit (as is done in conventional accounting) obscures the important distinction between efficiency in transforming inputs and marketing outputs (on the one hand) and effectiveness in acquiring inputs (on the other). Both Graham and Edwards-Bell retain the realization test for finding the former.

To Edwards and Bell, "business profit"

has little analytical value in itself, it being merely an amalgam of two more significant amounts. But it can be argued that "business profit" is not too bad an approximation of the current increment in the present value of future net receipts. (Edwards and Bell would most likely dissent from this view.)

Consistent with the notion of income that is shared by Buchanan *et al.*, it would be desirable to break away from the sale test of recognizing revenue in favor of acknowledging currently the effect of net receipts-determining forces. For inventories, valuation at current selling price would ascribe net income to the period in which the product acquires the potency to command this price. Long-lived assets, which are not subject to such a direct approach, might best be valued at the current acquisition cost (properly depreciated) of facilities that could most effectively perform the same expected flow of future services. Assuming that the entity does not intend to alter its production plan materially, fluctuations in such replacement cost could be interpreted as reflecting movement in the interest rate at which future net receipts should be discounted. This approach to asset valuation would seem to yield the most practicable approximation to a net income that would mirror the current enhancement in net receipts-generating potency. (In this as well as in the preceding discussion under "replacement cost," accounting data are assumed to have been restated, with

---

[43] "Factor replacement cost" is the current cost of acquiring the inputs that were necessary to produce an asset that is being valued, rather than the current cost of acquiring the asset itself. Edwards and Bell, *op. cit.*, Chaps. 3 and 4, esp. pp. 79–80 and 90–94. The purpose of this distinction is to avoid taking up prior to sale what Edwards and Bell call "current operating profit" on the transformation of inputs into the final product. See the discussion below.

[44] In an interview with the writer on May 14, 1962, Graham indicated that he had come to the view that (realized) price profits as well as management profits should be displayed in the financial statements.

appropriate disclosure thereof, by application of a Type A index.)

In a rapidly-adjusting economy, a good case can be made for the use of current factor replacement cost, properly depreciated, as an approximation of the market's evaluation of the asset's net-receipts-generating potency. If the entrepreneur in question has good reason to expect more from his asset than the market, by the prevailing price, would suggest, and if others demanding the same return agree with the entrepreneur, competitive entry will occur. Such entry would presumably push the asset price up toward (but probably not "to") the more "informed" subjective value. (In the process of entry, the first entrepreneur's subjective estimate would in all likelihood diminish as a result of the appearance of his new competitors.) Likewise, exit from the industry may be the consequence of too high an asset price in the face of projected sales receipts.

An evaluation of asset prices is being made continually by potential entrants. Where entry (and exit) is nil, and it is assumed that there is no monopoly on knowledge, it could be argued that the prevailing asset price of assets already owned by an entrepreneur agrees largely with his own subjective value.[45] Admittedly, this brief analysis is fitted to special conditions, and it will require more thorough investigation to test its applicability to the existing economic setting.

It is not consistent with the objective of this paper to develop an extended argument for any of the aforementioned applications of replacement cost. Suffice it to say that numerous possibilities have been advanced, signifying the need for a more intensified examination of the role of replacement cost in financial accounting. The goal of such a study is not necessarily the selection of the one best measure of net income. There is room in the income statement for the embodiment of several

approaches to the measurement of economic progress.

Whatever substitute along these lines that is found for historical cost-revenue realization, substantial problems will at the first surround the data-gathering and data-classifying processes. No perfect solution will present itself, however, and accountants should not put off a decision on such a revised approach in the hope that it will. It will take time before an adequate storehouse of replacement-cost information becomes available. The use of Type B index numbers for small groups of related assets might be quite feasible, and, as noted above, the more generally-found Type C indices even for single assets would need to be broken down into their Type A and Type B parts before meaningful calculations can result.[46] But it is not the purpose of this paper to inquire into the new problems that would be presented. It is first necessary to agree on the new theoretical framework.

Concluding Comments. If there is one overriding conclusion from this extended discussion, it is that serious consideration should be given to developing an operational substitute for historical cost-revenue

---

[45] The relevant future net receipts would be the *marginal* net receipts associable with the asset in question—not the total net receipts attributable to the single asset as though it were bereaved of the firm. Perfect certainty is not a requisite; probability distributions would be a desirable statistical tool for forecasting purposes. Compare with Arthur L. Thomas, "Precision and Discounted Services," THE ACCOUNTING REVIEW (January, 1962), pp. 67–72.

[46] Hendriksen explores the efficacy of a (weighted) composite replacement-cost index derived from the Handy-Whitman and Marshall-Stevens series for electric-power companies. He rejects this composite index as well as replacement-cost indices that firms themselves might keep; the latter type is viewed as too conducive to manipulation, as productive of non-comparable results among firms, and as too costly. An additional reason he gives, that this specific index might tend to overstate the magnitude of an adjustment as compared with a *general* (i.e., Type A) index, would seem to be invalid because of the different nature of the two adjustments. He recommends use of the Implicit Price Deflator for the construction and equipment components of the GNP. Hendriksen, *op. cit.*, pp. 56–76 and 117–21.

realization. No ideal solution will be found. Data having a lower order of empirical finality and certainty would need to be accepted.

For all its certainty at the data-gathering level, conventional accounting has glaring weaknesses. The accountant is continually faced with problems of inventory valuation and long-lived-asset valuation that seem no less difficult than would be the problem of finding individual replacement costs. With the present-day capacity of computers, obtaining the latter should not seem as overpowering a task as it once might have been. Indeed, it was because of a computer installation that Imperial Tobacco finally converted to full-fledged replacement-cost accounting for long-lived assets.

It was pointed out that Type A restatements have nothing to do with "current costs." Indeed, such restatements would improve the usefulness of historical costs. But a more equally basic question has been impliedly asked throughout the latter discussion: How relevant is "replacement cost"?

Accountants complain of the non-uniformity of inventory valuation methods. But a proper selection of a method requires a look toward the future—toward that stream of net receipts. For assets owe their value to an ability to generate such a stream. Any attempt by accountants to impose one inventory method (or one depreciation method) on all firms would create artificialities, because such a solution would ignore the differences in the time-shapes of future net receipts streams of different companies. A refurbishing more fundamental than a mere narrowing of inventory-valuation methods is needed. Introduction of replacement cost may not be the answer, but it is a candidate.

Without question, conventional accounting should continue to be studied for possible improvements within the existing framework. Too often overlooked, however, is the larger question of alternatives to historical cost. We are now at the threshold of probably the most important period in the history of public accounting (and financial reporting) in this country. An organizational overhaul has been accomplished, and we are about to re-evaluate the entire structure of accounting theory and applications. We must keep our minds open.

Reprinted from
The Accounting Review
Vol. XXXVII, No. 4, October, 1962

The Rise of "Economic Consequences"

Stephen A. Zeff

In the late 1960s, a literature began to build on the two related subjects of (a) the growing interest by third parties in the establishment of accounting standards, and (b) the impact of accounting standards, and especially changes in those standards, on the behavior of affected parties. In 1968, Moonitz wrote that

> The stake of nonprofessionals in the consequences of any given set of [accounting] principles is too great for them to accept the decisions of a body of technical experts on a voluntary basis, no matter how eminent those experts or how persuasive the research support for their findings [1968, p. 631].

He later urged the standard-setting bodies to cultivate allies, such as the Securities and Exchange Commission (SEC), in order to secure the enforcement of their pronouncements in the face of political action by "nonprofessionals" [1974, Chap. 7]. In 1969, Hawkins argued that "the time has come . . . to pay greater attention to the possible impact of accounting practices on people's actions" [1969, p. 21]. He referred not only to the possible dysfunctional effect of reported accounting figures on the behavior of managers, but also to the creation of an illusion of managerial performance when none exists [1969, p. 13].

By the mid-1970s, the literature on the politics of the standard-setting process, once a neglected subject, was growing apace [see, e.g., Stamp and Marley, 1970; Gerboth, 1973; Horngren, 1973; Moonitz, 1974; and Chatov, 1975], and the number of articles dealing with various phases of the social and economic consequences of accounting standards was also very much on the rise. Such terms as "feedback effects" [Prakash and Rappaport, 1976], "information inductance" [Prakash and Rappaport, 1977],

I gratefully acknowledge the suggestions of Alfred Rappaport, Lawrence Revsine, George J. Staubus, and Joseph G. San Miguel during the planning stage of writing this paper. Responsibility for what has emerged, however, is mine.

"economic impact" [Buckley, 1976; Horngren, 1976; Rappaport, 1977; and FAF, 1977], and finally "economic consequences" [FASB, 1977a and FASB, 1978] began to populate the literature. At the same time, and not entirely by coincidence, articles began to appear on the

> fundamental questions of resource allocation and social choice [which] appear to underlie the question of choice among financial reporting alternatives [Demski, 1974, p. 232].

As suggested above, these two developing strains in the literature—the increasing involvement of "nonprofessionals" in the standard-setting process, and the economic (and social) consequences of the accounting standards themselves—are inextricably related. The very intervention by outside parties in the setting of standards appears to be due, in large measure, to their belief in the fact of economic consequences. The two themes were novel in the accounting literature, and it would not be an exaggeration to label the suggestion that standard-setting bodies take account of economic consequences as nothing less than revolutionary. Judging from accounting textbooks, treatises, articles, and earlier statements emitted from standard-setting bodies and committees of the American Accounting Association, one would have fairly concluded that conventional accounting wisdom supported a resolution of accounting controversies exclusively by reference to some combination of accounting theory, "accounting principles," and "fair presentation." To suggest that accounting policy makers should seriously consider the impact of proposed accounting standards on the micro- and macro-economic welfare of affected parties would have been, only a few years ago, a heresy. Until recently accounting policy making was either assumed to be neutral in its effects or, if not neutral, it was not responsible for those effects. Today neither assumption is unquestioningly accepted as valid, and the subject of social and economic consequences "has become *the* central contemporary issue in accounting" [AAA, 1977b, p. 4]. That the Financial Accounting Standards Board (FASB) has commissioned research papers on the economic consequences of selected standards [see, e.g., FASB, 1977b and c] and has held a conference devoted entirely to the subject [FASB, 1978] underscores the current importance of this mode of inquiry.

In these discussions, the terms "professional" and "nonprofessional" are troublesome. The phrase "accounting profession" is used in a variety of senses. In the United States, it is confined in the strictest sense to independent certified public accountants. But some might include controllers, internal auditors, management accountants, and government accountants. In Great Britain, the term typically refers to a broader array of qualified accountants than in the United States. In the Institute of Chartered Accountants in England and Wales, nonpracticing accountants played leadership roles in the development of accounting principles as long ago as the early 1940s, nonpracticing members have been members of the Council since 1943, and the first nonpracticing president was elected in 1968 [Zeff, 1972, pp. 7–9], while it was not until 1978 that the American Institute of Certified Public Accountants (AICPA) changed its by-laws to permit nonpractitioners to become officers. It is not my intention to endeavor to resolve this problem of definition, but only to suggest that the terms are open to ambiguity. In the ensuing discussion, I will use "third party" or "outside party" in place of "nonprofessional."

Accounting policy makers have been aware since at least the 1960s of the third-party intervention issue,[1] while the issue of economic consequences has surfaced only in the 1970s. Indeed, much of the history of the Accounting Principles Board (APB) during the 1960s was one of endeavoring to understand and cope with the third-party forces which were intervening in the standard-setting process. In the end, the inability of the APB to deal effectively with these forces led to its demise and the establishment in 1973 of the FASB.

The true preoccupations of the intervening third parties have not always been made clear. When endeavoring to understand the third-party arguments, one must remember that prior to the 1970s the accounting model employed by the Committee on Accounting Procedure (CAP) and the APB was, formally at least, confined to technical accounting considerations (sometimes called "accounting principles" or "conceptual questions"), such as the measurement of assets, liabilities, and income, and the "fair presentation" of financial position and operations. The policy makers' sole concern was with the communication of financial information to actual and potential investors, for, indeed, their charter had been "granted" by the SEC, which itself had been charged by Congress to assure "full and fair disclosure" in reports to investors. Third-party intervenors, therefore, would have had an obvious incentive to appeal to the accounting model being used by the policy makers, rather than implicitly suggest that the policy makers should adopt an economic consequences model preferred by the third parties.

When management intervened in the standard-setting process, therefore, its true position may well have been disguised. The following three-part classification of management arguments suggests the range of tactical rhetoric employed over the years:

1. Arguments couched in terms of the traditional accounting model, where management is genuinely concerned about unbiased and "theoretically sound" accounting measurements.

---

[1] In this paper, I am chiefly concerned with third-party intervention in the standard setting for unregulated industries. Accounting policy makers in this country have been alive for several decades to the accounting implications of the rules and regulations of rate-making agencies in the energy, transportation, and communication industries. See, e.g., May [1943, Chaps. 7–8], Paton [1944], and Davidson [1952].

2. Arguments couched in terms of the traditional accounting model, where management is really seeking to advance its self-interest in the economic consequences of the contents of published reports.
3. Arguments couched in terms of the economic consequences in which management is self-interested.

If one accepts Johnson's dictum that it requires a "lively imagination" to believe that management is genuinely concerned with fair presentation when choosing between accounting alternatives [1966, p. 91; also see Moonitz, 1968, pp. 628–30], it could be concluded that Argument 1 has seldom been employed in third-party interventions. In recent years, particularly since the early 1970s, management appears to have become increasingly more candid, by electing Argument 3 in discussions with accounting policy makers. That the economic consequences issue was not scrutinized earlier than the 1970s was probably due, at least in part, to the habit of the APB to resolve, and to be seen to resolve, each controversy in the context of the traditional accounting model. Another possible explanation is the predominance of instances of Argument 2, which would have encouraged the Board to confine itself to the traditional model.

THE U.S. HISTORY OF THIRD-PARTY INTERVENTIONS OF THE "ECONOMIC CONSEQUENCES" VARIETY (CAP, APB, FASB)

It may be believed by some that third-party intervention coupled with the intrusion into accounting policy debates of economic-consequences considerations are of recent origin. Indeed, if one overlooks the unwitting support which a committee of the American Institute of [Certified Public] Accountants (AIA) gave to Congress as a pretext to impose LIFO inventory accounting on financial reporting [AIA, 1936, p. 465], the first evidence of economic-consequences reasoning in the pronouncements of American policy makers occurred as long ago as 1941. In Accounting Research Bulletin No. 11, "Corporate Accounting for Ordinary Stock Dividends," the CAP, in accordance with "proper accounting and corporate policy," required that fair market value be used to record the issuance of stock dividends where such market value was substantially in excess of book value [AIA, 1941, pp. 102–03]. George O. May, the *de facto* chairman of the CAP at that time, later wrote:

> The phrase 'proper accounting and corporate policy' indicates that the committee went beyond consideration of purely accounting questions. In the early stage of discussion such a step was not contemplated but as the study progressed, the committee came to feel strongly that it had an opportunity, in conjunction with the [New York] Stock Exchange, to take a step in the interest of *financial morality* and to safeguard against

recurrence of abuses such as took place in and immediately prior to 1929 in connection with the issue of periodical stock dividends [May, 1952, p. 1; emphasis mine].

Evidently, both the New York Stock Exchange and a majority of the Committee on Accounting Procedure regarded periodic stock dividends as "objectionable" [May, 1941, p. 1], and the CAP acted to make it more difficult for corporations to sustain a series of such stock dividends out of their accumulated earnings. As far as I know, the United States is still the only country in which an accounting pronouncement requires that stock dividends be capitalized at the fair market value of the issued shares [see, e.g., *Price Waterhouse International*, 1975, Table 145], and this position was originally adopted in this country, at least in part, in order to produce an impact on the stock dividend policies of corporations.

A second evidence of economic consequences entering into the debates surrounding the establishment of accounting standards, this time involving management representations, occurred in 1947–48. It was the height of the postwar inflation, and several corporations had adopted replacement cost depreciation in their published financial statements [*Depreciation Policy When Price Levels Change*, 1948, Chap. 14]. Among the arguments employed in the debate involving the CAP were the possible implications for tax reform, the possible impact on wage bargaining, and the need to counteract criticisms of profiteering by big business [see, e.g., "Dual Accounting System Suggested for Depreciation," 1948; "Institute Committee Holds to Depreciation on Cost," 1948; *Changing Concepts of Business Income*, 1952, p. 64; *Depreciation Policy When Price Levels Change*, 1948, Chap. 13; Storey, 1964, pp. 34–38; and Paton, 1948].[2] Notwithstanding the pressures for accounting reform, the CAP reaffirmed its support of historical cost accounting for depreciation in Accounting Research Bulletin No. 33 and in a letter issued in October, 1948.

A clear use of economic consequences occurred in 1958, when three subsidiaries of American Electric Power Company sued in the Federal courts to enjoin the AICPA from allowing the CAP to issue a letter saying that the Deferred Tax Credit account, as employed in the recently issued Accounting Research Bulletin No. 44 (Revised), should be classified as a liability [see *The AICPA Injunction Case*, 1960]. The three public utility companies were concerned that the SEC, under authority granted by the Public Utility Holding Company Act, would not permit them to issue debt securities in view of the unfavorable debt-to-equity ratios which the proposed

---

[2] In a survey conducted by the American Institute of [Certified Public] Accountants in 1948, the business executives who replied divided 31–22 in favor of reporting net income after subtracting cost of goods sold and depreciation expense on a current-cost basis if that were accepted for tax purposes. The executives divided 31–22 against such financial reporting if it were not accepted for tax purposes [AIA, 1948, pp. 1, 10].

reclassification would produce. The case reached the Supreme Court, where *certiorari* was denied. In the end, the clarifying letter was issued. Nonetheless, the SEC accommodated the public utility companies by consenting to exclude the Deferred Tax Credit from both liabilities and stockholders' equity for purposes of decisions taken under the Public Utility Holding Company Act [*SEC Administrative Policy . . .*, 1961, pp. 35–39].

Shortly after the creation of the APB, the accounting treatment of the investment tax credit exploded upon the scene. The three confrontations between the APB and the combined forces of industry and the administrations of Presidents Kennedy, Johnson, and Nixon have already been amply discussed in the literature [see Moonitz, 1966; Carey, 1970, pp. 98–104; and Zeff, 1972, pp. 178–80, 201–02, 219–21, and 326–27]. The Government's argument was not that the accounting deferral of the investment tax credit was bad accounting, but that it diluted the incentive effect of an instrument of fiscal policy.

In 1965, the subject of segmental reporting emerged from a hearing of the Senate Subcommittee on Antitrust and Monopoly on the economic effects of conglomerate mergers. The aim of the Senatorial inquiry was not to promote better accounting practices for investor use, but to provide the Subcommittee and other government policy makers with accounting data that would facilitate their assessment of the economic efficacy of conglomerate mergers. Company managements naturally looked upon such disclosures as potentially detrimental to their merger ambitions. Pressure applied by this powerful Subcommittee eventually forced the hand of the SEC to call for product-line disclosures in published financial reports. The repercussions of this initiative which had its origin in a Senate hearing room are still being felt [see, e.g., Plum and Collins, 1976].

In 1967–69, the APB responded to an anguished objection by the startled Investment Bankers Association of America (IBA) (known today as the Securities Industry Association) to a provision, once thought to be innocuous, in APB Opinion No. 10 which imputed a debt discount to convertible debt and debt issued with stock warrants. The IBA was concerned about the impact of the accounting procedure on the market for such securities. In APB Opinion No. 14, the Board rescinded its action in regard to convertible debt, while retaining the rest [see Zeff, 1972, pp. 202, 211].

During 1968–71, the banking industry opposed the inclusion of bad-debt provisions and losses on the sales of securities in the net income of commercial banks. Bankers believed that the new measure would reflect unfavorably on the performance of banks. Eventually, through a concerted effort by the APB, SEC, and the bank regulatory agencies, generally accepted accounting principles were made applicable to banks [see Cary, 1970, p. 134; Moonitz, 1974, pp. 38–39; and Zeff, 1972, pp. 210–11].

In 1968–70, the APB struggled with the accounting for business combinations. It was flanked on the one side by the Federal Trade Commission and the Department of Justice, who favored the elimination of "pooling of interests" accounting in order to produce a slowing effect on the merger movement, and on the other side by merger-minded corporations who were fervent supporters of "pooling of interests" accounting. The APB, appearing to behave as if it were a pawn in a game of political chess, disenchanted many of its supporters, as it abandoned positions of principle in favor of an embarrassing series of pressure-induced compromises [see Chatov, 1975, pp. 212–22; and Zeff, 1972, pp. 212–16].

In 1971, the APB held public hearings on accounting for marketable equity securities, leases, and the exploration and drilling costs of companies in the petroleum industry. In all three areas, powerful industry pressures thwarted the Board from acting. The insurance industry was intensely concerned about the possible effects on its companies' stock prices of including the unrealized gains and losses on portfolio holdings in their income statements [see Horngren, 1973, pp. 63–64]. The leasing question was squelched after senators, representatives, and even the secretary of transportation responded to a letter-writing campaign by making pointed inquiries of the SEC and APB. The letter-writers raised the specter of injury which the Board's proposed action would cause to consumers and to the viability of companies in several key industries [see Savoie, 1974, p. 326].[3] The petroleum industry was unable to unite on a solution to the controversy over full costing v. successful-efforts costing, as it was alleged that a general imposition of the latter would adversely affect the fortunes of the small, independent exploration companies [see the testimony and submissions in *APB Public Hearing on Accounting and Reporting Practices in the Petroleum Industry*, 1972]. Using its considerable political might, the industry succeeded in persuading the Board to postpone consideration of the sensitive subject [see Savoie, 1974, p. 326].

On each of the occasions enumerated above, outside parties intervened in the standard-setting process by an appeal to criteria which transcended the traditional questions of accounting measurement and fair presentation. They were concerned instead with the economic consequences of the accounting pronouncements.

---

[3] Several of the letters sent to congressmen and senators were in all material respects identical, and although the addresses of those whose names appeared at the bottoms of the letters were in different states, the secretary's initials (kh) and the type face used were all the same. These letter-writers uniformly claimed the following economic consequences of requiring lessees to capitalize leases:

1. Raise the cost of electric power to the public by an estimated $550 million yearly towards the end of the decade.
2. Raise the cost of freight transportation to industry and the public.
3. Reduce the inventory of railroad cars and locomotives.
4. Increase the costs of air fares to the public.
5. Damage the aerospace industry.
6. Raise the costs of all goods and services to the public.
7. Prevent many small and growing businesses from acquiring modern cost-cutting machinery and equipment.
8. Negatively affect our present adverse international balance of trade.

Economic consequences have been invoked with even greater intensity in the short life of the FASB. Such questions as accounting for research and development costs, self-insurance and catastrophe reserves, development stage companies, foreign currency fluctuations, leases, the restructuring of troubled debt,[4] domestic inflation and relative price changes, and the exploration and drilling costs of companies in the petroleum industry have provoked widespread interest in their economic consequences [see, e.g., Burns, 1976; AAA, 1977b, pp. 9–12; Rappaport, 1977, pp. 90, 92; FASB, 1978; U.S. Department of Energy, 1978].[5] The list is both extensive and impressive, and accounting academics are busily investigating the validity of claims that these and other accounting standards are empirically linked with the specified economic consequences.

RESPONSE OF STANDARD-SETTING BODIES TO THIRD-PARTY INTERVENTION AND "ECONOMIC CONSEQUENCES"

What have been the reactions of standard-setting bodies to (a) the intervention by outside parties, and (b) the claim that accounting standards should or should not be changed in order to avoid unhealthy economic consequences? The reactions have been of three kinds: procedural alone, procedural with apparent substantive effects, and explicitly substantive. The first two kinds of reactions predominated until the early 1970s [Zeff, 1972, pp. 167–208]:

---

[4] At the Board's public hearing, some bankers warned of the dire economic consequences of requiring banks to write down their receivables following restructuring. Walter B. Wriston, chairman of Citicorp, said:

> If the banks that held the New York City obligations had been required to record an immediate write-off of say, 25 percent of principal as a result of restructuring, that restructuring just might not have happened. Several of the banks whose cooperation was essential might not have been able to afford it, not from an economic point of view, but in terms of the way that readers of financial statements would interpret such charged earnings. Some New York banks were at that time under severe earning pressure and the prospect of a significant additional charge with a corresponding reduction in capital would have been totally unacceptable [Wriston, 1977, pp. 69–70].

Yet the FASB, in its lengthy "Basis for Conclusions" in Statement No. 15 (in which the feared write-downs were not required), did not refer to bankers' claims about the economic consequences of requiring significant write-downs. Does that omission imply that the Board paid no attention to those assertions? Did the Board conduct any empirical research (as it did concerning the economic consequences claims raised in connection with Statement No. 7, on development stage enterprises) to determine whether there was adequate ground to sustain such claims?

[5] Evidence attesting to the attention given by the FASB to economic consequences issues may be found in the "Basis of Conclusions" sections of the applicable statements. In addition to companies and industry groups, government departments (such as the Department of Commerce, in Statement No. 7, and the Departments of Energy and Justice, in Statement No. 19) were actively involved in the discussion of economic consequences.

1940s   The CAP improved liaison with outside parties and expanded the circulation of early drafts and subcommittee reports.

1950s   The CAP greatly enlarged the list of individuals and organizations to whom exposure drafts were sent.

1957–58   The AICPA appointed a prominent member of the Controllers Institute of America (now known as the Financial Executives Institute (FEI)) to the AICPA's Special Committee on Research Programs. (The Controllers Institute had complained about its small role in the standard-setting process, and the appointment of a controller to this important AICPA committee was perhaps the first instance in which an individual who was not a practitioner or academic was named to a policy-level AICPA committee.)

1959   The AICPA appointed two financial executives to the first APB. (This was evidently the first appointment of accountants in industry to an AICPA policy-making committee.)

1959–60   The APB began to appoint to the project advisory committees of its research studies some persons who were not members of the Board.

1964–65   For the first time, the APB employed subject-area committees to prepare drafts of proposed pronouncements, and non-Board members began to be appointed to the committees.

1964–65   The Board chairman and AICPA president urged interested organizations to collaborate more intensively with the Board, and several important bodies reorganized their liaison activities.

1960s   The Board intensified the exposure process, increasing the number of organizations and individuals to whom exposure drafts were routinely sent. During one period it published exposure drafts in *The Journal of Accountancy*, and later sent drafts to all members of the Institute by separate mail. In the deliberations leading up to Opinions 16 and 17, the Board sent some 20,000 exposure drafts to a wide range of interested organizations and individuals, in addition to sending copies to all AICPA members.

mid-1960s The Board began to issue "mini-exposure" drafts to interested organizations in order to obtain their views before publishing its formal exposure drafts.

1965–66   The Board's subject-area committees began to hold informal meetings with the representatives of interested organizations.

1966–67   The AICPA created the position of executive vice president who was to be a spokesman to the press and at meetings of interested organizations.

1968   At the initiative of the AICPA, a two-day symposium was held to exchange ideas between the preparers and users of accounting information; representatives attended from the four co-sponsors:

AICPA, FEI, Financial Analysts Federation, and Robert Morris Associates.

1969   In order to fortify the liaison with interested organizations, the Board began to hold symposia on the drafts of proposed pronouncements; attendance was by invitation and the proceedings were closed.

1971   In an effort to meet criticisms of its symposia (e.g., not all interested groups were invited), the Board began to hold public hearings, for which the subject-area committees prepared brief discussion memoranda.

It is evident from the series of steps taken by the AICPA and the APB that they endeavored to bring interested organizations more closely into the standard-setting process, hoping, one supposes, that these organizations would be satisfied that their opinions were given full consideration before the final issuance of opinions. These accommodations were, however, of a procedural sort, although it is possible that these outside opinions did have an impact on the substantive content of some of the resulting opinions. It would appear that the APB was at least somewhat influenced by economic consequences in its prolonged deliberations leading to the issuance of Opinions 16 and 17 [Wyatt, 1977, pp. 92–93]. Yet it is interesting that during the public hearings in 1971 on marketable equity securities and the accounting practices of companies in the petroleum industry, in which management representatives on several occasions asserted economic consequences as relevant considerations, none of the members of the Board's subject-area committees asked questions about the empirical basis for those assertions or, indeed, inquired about their relevance to the setting of accounting standards [see *Proceedings*, 1971; and *APB Public Hearing . . .* , 1972].

In view of the fact that it was the APB's inability to cope with the pressures brought by outside organizations which led to its demise, it is noteworthy that the FASB includes the Financial Executives Institute among its co-sponsors. In my opinion, the incorporation of the FEI in the formal structure of the FASB is one of the most significant advantages which the FASB possesses in relation to its predecessor.[6] Horngren, an APB member in its final years, has said,

> The FEI as an institutional body representing management, by the large, was opposed to the Board, particularly in the latter years, on almost every issue. . . . [T]he FEI seemed in favor of scrapping the APB; to the extent that it could be an institutional force it helped in its termination.

---

[6] The inclusion of the FEI could conceivably become the undoing of the Board. If the FEI were to lose confidence in the Board, it is possible that many of the companies which now contribute to the Financial Accounting Foundation might decline to continue doing so, provoking a financial crisis that could threaten the Board's viability.

> They felt . . . that they should have more of a direct voice in the forma-
> tion of accounting principles [Horngren, 1974, p. 95].

The procedural machinery established for the FASB is even more elaborate than that which existed in the final years of the APB. The object of these additional procedures has been to expand and intensify the interaction between the Board and interested outside parties, notably companies, industry associations, and government departments and agencies. Task forces drawn from a broad spectrum of interested groups are appointed prior to the preparation of each discussion memorandum. The memorandum itself is much bulkier than the modest document which the APB had issued prior to its public hearings; it contains a neutral discussion of the entire gamut of policy issues which bear on the resolution of the controversy before the Board. A Financial Accounting Standards Advisory Council (FASAC), composed of representatives of a wide array of interested groups, was appointed to be a sounding board for the FASB. The Board itself has been composed of members drawn from accounting practice, the universities, companies, and government—again, so that it would be responsive—and would appear to be responsive—to the concerns of those "constituencies." In an effort to persuade skeptics of the merit of its recommendations, the Board includes in its statements a lengthy explanation of the criteria, arguments, and empirical considerations which it used to fashion the recommended standards.

Following criticism from within the profession of the Board's operations and procedures, the Financial Accounting Foundation (FAF), the Board's parent, conducted a study in 1977 of the entire Board operation. Among its many recommendations were proposals that the Board expand its formal and informal contacts with interested groups and that it include an economic impact analysis in important exposure drafts [FAF, 1977, pp. 51, 52]. On this latter point, the FAF's Structure Committee concluded:

> The Board need not be unduly influenced by the possibility of an economic impact, but it should consider both the possible costs and the expected benefits of a proposal [FAF, 1977, p. 51].

In addition, the Structure Committee recommended actions that would strengthen the roles of the task forces and FASAC [FAF, 1977, pp. 23–25]. In 1978, under pressure from Congress, the Board began to conduct virtually all of its formal meetings (including those of FASAC) "in the sunshine."

The history of the APB and FASB is one of a succession of procedural steps taken to bring the Board's deliberations into closer proximity to the opinions and concerns of interested third parties. As in the case of the APB, it is possible that an effect of these more elaborate procedures has been a change in the substance of the FASB's conclusions and recommendations.

By the middle 1970s, however, it was decided that the FASB should add economic (and social) consequences to the substantive issues which it normally addresses. The inclusion of "Probable Economic or Social Impact" among the "other qualities of useful information" in the Board's Conceptual Framework discussion memorandum [FASB, 1976, paras. 367–71], coupled with the Board's announcement of its interest in empirical studies of economic consequences [FASB, 1977a] and the recommendation of the FAF Structure Committee that the Board inform itself adequately on the "various impacts its pronouncements might have" [FAF, 1977, p. 31] collectively confirm this new direction. The issue of economic consequences has, therefore, changed from one having only procedural implications for the standard-setting process to one which is now firmly a part of the standard setters' substantive policy framework.

WHAT FACTORS HAVE CONTRIBUTED TO THE EMERGENCE OF "ECONOMIC CONSEQUENCES" AS A SUBSTANTIVE ISSUE?

Economic consequences has finally become accepted as a valid substantive policy issue for a number of reasons:

- The tenor of the times. The decade of the 1970s is clearly one in which American society is holding its institutions responsible for the social, environmental, and economic consequences of their actions, and the crystallized public opinion on this subject eventually became evident (and relevant) to those interested in the accounting standard-setting activity.
- The sheer intractability of the accounting problems being addressed. Since the mid-1960s, the APB and FASB have been taking up difficult accounting questions on which industry positions have been well entrenched. To some degree, companies which are sensitive to the way their performance is evaluated through the medium of reported earnings, have permitted their decision-making behavior to be influenced by their perceptions of how such behavior will be seen through the prism of accounting earnings. Still other such companies have tailored their accounting practices to reflect their economic performance in the best light—and the managers are evidently loathe to change their decision-making behavior in order to

accommodate newly imposed accounting standards. This would also be a concern to managers who are being paid under incentive compensation plans [see Rappaport, 1978].

- The enormity of the impact. Several of the issues which have been facing the APB and FASB in recent years have portended such a high degree of impact on either the volatility or level of earnings and other key financial figures and ratios that the Board can no longer discuss the proposed accounting treatments without encountering incessant arguments over the probable economic consequences. Particularly apt examples are accounting for foreign exchange fluctuations, domestic inflation and relative price changes, and the explorations and drilling costs of companies in the petroleum industry.

- The growth in the information economics/social choice, behavioral, income smoothing, and decision usefulness literatures in accounting. Recent writings in the information economics/social choice literature have provided a broad analytical framework within which the problems or economic consequences may be conceptualized. Beginning with Stedry [1959], the literature on the behavioral implications of accounting numbers has grown significantly, drawing the attention of researchers and policy makers to the importance of considering the effects of accounting information. The literature on income smoothing has suggested the presence of a managerial motive for influencing the measurement of earnings trends. Finally, the decision usefulness literature, although it is confined to the direct users of accounting information, has served to lessen the inclination of accountants to argue over the inherent "truth" of different accounting incomes, and instead to focus on the use of information by those who receive accounting reports [AAA, 1977a, pp. 5–29].

- The insufficiency of the procedural reforms adopted by the APB and FASB. Notwithstanding the succession of procedural steps which both Boards have taken to provide outside parties with a forum for expressing their views, the claims of economic consequences—and the resulting criticisms of the Boards' pronouncements—continue unabated. The conclusion has evidently been reached that procedural remedies alone will not meet the problem.

- The Moss and Metcalf investigations. By the middle of 1976, it was known that Rep. John E. Moss and Senator Lee Metcalf were conducting investigations of the performance of the accounting profession, including their standard-setting activities, and it could have reasonably been inferred that the responsiveness of the standard-setting bodies to the economic and social effects of their decisions would be an issue.

- The increasing importance to corporate managers of the earnings figure in capital-market transactions. Especially in the 1960s, when capital markets were intensely competitive and the merger movement was fast-paced, the earnings figure came to be viewed as an important element of managerial strategy and tactics.

- Accounting figures came to be viewed as an instrument of social control. The social control of American enterprise has been well known in the rate-regulated energy, transportation, and communications fields, but in recent years the earnings figure has, to an increasing degree, been employed as a control device on a broader scale.[7] Examples are fiscal incentives (such as the investment tax credit and redefinitions of taxable income which diverge from accounting income) which have an influence on debates surrounding financial reporting,[8] the price-control mechanism of Phase II [Lanzillotti *et al.*, 1975, pp. 73–77; and Grayson and Neeb, 1974, pp. 71–76], and the data base which is contemplated by the Energy Policy and Conservation Act of 1975.

- The realization that outsiders could influence the outcome of accounting debates. Prior to the 1960s, accounting controversies were rarely reported in the financial press, and it was widely believed that accounting was a constant, if not a parameter, in the management of business operations. With the publicity given to the accounting for the investment credit in 1962–63, to the fractious dialogue within the AICPA in 1963–64 over the authority of the APB, and to other accounting disagreements involving the APB, managers and other outside parties came to realize that accounting may be a variable after all—that the rules of accounting were not unyielding or even unbending.

- The growing use of Argument 3 (see above) in accounting debates. Mostly for the reasons enumerated above, outside parties began to discard the pretense that their objections to proposed changes in accounting standards were solely, or even primarily, a function of differences over the proper interpretation of accounting principles. True reasons came out into the open, and accounting policy makers could no longer ignore their implications.

It is interesting that economic consequences have become an important issue at a time when accounting and finance academics have been arguing that the American capital markets are efficient with respect to publicly available information and, moreover, that the market cannot be

---

[7] D. R. Scott, though writing in a different context, nonetheless was prophetic in his prediction that accounting would increasingly be used as a means of social control [1931, esp. Chap. 14].

[8] The "required tax conformity" issue of the early 1970s [see Zeff, 1972, pp. 218–19] is another instance.

"fooled" by the use of different accounting methods to reflect the same economic reality [see, e.g., Beaver, 1973].

IMPLICATIONS FOR THE FASB

What are the implications of the "economic consequences" movement for the FASB? It has become clear that political agencies (such as government departments and congressional committees) expect accounting standard setters to take explicitly into consideration the possible adverse consequences of proposed accounting standards. This expectation appears to be strongest where the consequences are thought to be significant and widespread—and especially where they might impinge on economic and social policies being pursued by the government. In these instances, the FASB must show that it has studied the possible consequences and that its recommended standards either are innocent of such consequences or that the benefits from implementing the standards outweigh the possible adverse consequences. Where the claimed consequences have implications for economic or social policies of national importance, the FASB should not be surprised if a political resolution is imposed by outside forces.

But to say that any significant economic consequences should be studied by the Board does not imply that the accounting model—accounting principles and fair presentation—should be dismissed as the principal guiding factor in the Board's determination. The FASB is respected as a body of accounting experts, and it should focus its attention primarily on matters on which its expertise will be acknowledged. While some may suggest that accounting standards should be determined only with regard to their consequences for economic and social welfare, the FASB would assure the termination of its existence if it were to begin to make decisions primarily on other than accounting grounds.

The Board is thus faced with a dilemma which requires a delicate balancing of accounting and nonaccounting variables. Although its decisions should rest—and be seen to rest—chiefly on accounting considerations, it must also study—and be seen to study—the possible adverse economic and social consequences of its proposed actions. As in all micro- and macro-economic policy making, the identification and measurement of possible economic and social repercussions will be exceedingly difficult tasks.[9] In order to deal adequately with the consequences issue, the Board would be wise to develop a staff of competent analysts from allied disciplines, notably economics.

---

[9] For a discussion of some of these problems of implementation, see Swieringa [1976, pp. 31–35].

Economic consequences bid fair to be the most challenging accounting issue of the 1970s. We have entered an era in which economic and social consequences may no longer be ignored as a substantive issue in the setting of accounting standards.

REFERENCES

The AICPA Injunction Case: Re: ARB No. 44 (Revised), Cases in Public Accounting Practice No. 1 (Chicago: Arthur Andersen & Co., 1960).

APB Public Hearing on Accounting and Reporting Practices in the Petroleum Industry, Cases in Public Accounting Practice No. 10 (Chicago: Arthur Andersen & Co., 1972).

American Accounting Association, Committee on Concepts and Standards for External Financial Reports, *Statement on Accounting Theory and Theory Acceptance* (Sarasota, Florida: AAA, 1977a).

American Accounting Association, *Report of the Committee on the Social Consequences of Accounting Information* (Sarasota, Florida: AAA, 1977b).

American Institute of Accountants, *1936 Year Book of the American Institute of Accountants* (New York: AIA, 1937).

American Institute of Accountants, *Accounting Research Bulletins*, No. 11, "Corporate Accounting for Ordinary Stock Dividends" (New York: AIA, 1941), pp. 99–106.

American Institute of Accountants, "Accounting and Changing Price Levels," unpublished preliminary report, September 1, 1948, 48 pages.

Beaver, William H., "What Should Be the FASB's Objectives," *Journal of Accountancy*, August 1973, pp. 49–56.

Buckley, John W., "The FASB and Impact Analysis," *Management Accounting* (U.S.), April 1976, pp. 13–17.

Burns, Joseph M., *Accounting Standards and International Finance, with Special Reference to Multinationals* (Washington, D.C.: American Enterprise Institute for Public Policy Research, 1976).

Carey, John L., *The Rise of the Accounting Profession: To Responsibility and Authority 1937–1969* (New York: American Institute of Certified Public Accountants, 1970).

Changing Concepts of Business Income, Report of Study Group on Business Income (New York: The Macmillan Company, 1952).

Chatov, Robert, *Corporate Financial Reporting: Public or Private Control?* (New York: The Free Press, 1975).

Davidson, Sidney, *The Plant Accounting Regulations of the Federal Power Commission* (Ann Arbor: University of Michigan Press, 1952).

Demski, Joel S., "Choice among Financial Reporting Alternatives," *The Accounting Review*, April 1974, pp. 221–32.

Depreciation Policy When Price Levels Change (New York: Controllership Foundation, Inc., 1948).

"Dual Accounting System Suggested for Depreciation," *The Journal of Accountancy*, February 1948, p. 103.

Financial Accounting Foundation, Structure Committee, *The Structure of Establishing Financial Accounting Standards* (1977).

Financial Accounting Standards Board, *Conceptual Framework for Financial Accounting and Reporting: Elements of Financial Statements and Their Measurement*, Discussion Memorandum (Stamford, Connecticut: FASB, 1976).

———, *Status Report*, No. 45 (February 7, 1977a).

————, *Status Report*, No. 47 (April 19, 1977b).

————, *Status Report*, No. 50 (July 7, 1977c).

————, *Conference on the Economic Consequences of Financial Accounting Standards* (Stamford, Connecticut: FASB, 1978).

Gerboth, Dale L., "Research, Intuition, and Politics in Accounting Inquiry," *The Accounting Review*, July 1973, pp. 475–82.

Grayson, C. Jackson, Jr., and Louis Neeb, *Confessions of a Price Controller* (Homewood, Illinois: Dow Jones-Irwin, Inc., 1974).

Hawkins, David F., "Behavioral Implications of Generally Accepted Accounting Principles," *California Management Review*, Winter 1969, pp. 13–21.

Horngren, Charles T., "The Marketing of Accounting Standards," *Journal of Accountancy*, October 1973, pp. 61–66.

————, edited dialogue, in Thomas J. Burns (ed.), *Accounting in Transition: Oral Histories of Recent U.S. Experience* (Columbus: College of Administrative Science, The Ohio State University, 1974), pp. 82–100.

————, "Will the FASB Be Here in the 1980s?," *Journal of Accountancy*, November 1976, pp. 90–96.

"Institute Committee Holds to Depreciation on Cost," Editorial, *The Journal of Accountancy*, November 1948, pp. 353–54.

Johnson, Charles E., "Management's Role in External Accounting Measurements," in Robert K. Jaedicke, Yuji Ijiri, and Oswald Nielsen (eds.), *Research in Accounting Measurement* (American Accounting Association, 1966), pp. 88–100.

Lanzillotti, Robert F., Mary T. Hamilton, and R. Blaine Roberts, *Phase II in Review: The Price Commission Experience* (Washington, D.C.: The Brookings Institution, 1975).

May, George O., letter to J. S. Seidman, July 14, 1941 (Deposited in National Office Library, Price Waterhouse & Co., New York), 2 pages.

————, *Financial Accounting: A Distillation of Experience* (New York: The Macmillan Company, 1943).

————, letter to John B. Inglis, August 5, 1952 (Deposited in the National Office Library, Price Waterhouse & Co., New York), 2 pages.

Moonitz, Maurice, "Some Reflections on the Investment Credit Experience," *Journal of Accounting Research*, Spring 1966, pp. 47–61.

————, "Why Is It So Difficult to Agree upon a Set of Accounting Principles?," *The Australian Accountant*, November 1968, pp. 621–31.

————, *Obtaining Agreement on Standards in the Accounting Profession*, Studies in Accounting Research No. 8 (Sarasota, Florida: American Accounting Association, 1974).

Paton, William A., "Accounting Policies of the Federal Power Commission—A Critique," *Journal of Accountancy*, June 1944, pp. 432–60.

————, "Accounting Procedures and Private Enterprise," *The Journal of Accountancy*, April 1948, pp. 278–91.

Plum, Charles W., and Daniel W. Collins, "Business Segment Reporting," in James Don Edwards and Homer A. Black (eds.), *The Modern Accountant's Handbook* (Homewood, Illinois: Dow Jones-Irwin, Inc., 1976), pp. 469–511.

Prakash, Prem, and Alfred Rappaport, "The Feedback Effects of Accounting," *Business Week*, January 12, 1976, p. 12.

————, "Information Inductance and Its Significance for Accounting," *Accounting, Organizations and Society* (1977, No. 1), pp. 29–38.

Price Waterhouse International, A Survey in 46 Countries: Accounting Principles and Reporting Practices ([n.p.], PWI, 1975).

Proceedings of Hearing on Accounting for Equity Securities, Accounting Principles Board (New York: American Institute of Certified Public Accountants, 1971), Section A—Transcript.

Rappaport, Alfred, "Economic Impact of Accounting Standards—Implications for the FASB," *The Journal of Accountancy*, May 1977, pp. 89–98.

———, "Executive Incentives vs. Corporate Growth," *Harvard Business Review*, July-August 1978, pp. 81–88.

SEC Administrative Policy Re: Balance-Sheet Treatment of Deferred Income-Tax Credits, Cases in Public Accounting Practice Nos. 5 and 6 (Chicago: Arthur Andersen & Co., 1961), 2 vols.

Savoie, Leonard M., "Accounting Attitudes," in Robert R. Sterling (ed.), *Institutional Issues in Public Accounting* (Lawrence, Kansas: Scholars Book Co., 1974), pp. 317–27.

Scott, D R, *The Cultural Significance of Accounts* (New York: Henry Holt & Company, 1931).

Stamp, Edward, and Christopher Marley, *Accounting Principles and the City Code* (London: Butterworths, 1970).

Stedry, Andrew C., *Budget Control and Cost Behavior* (Englewood Cliffs, New Jersey: Prentice-Hall, Inc., 1959).

Storey, Reed K., *The Search for Accounting Principles* (New York: American Institute of Certified Public Accountants, 1964).

Swieringa, Robert J., "Consequences of Financial Accounting Standards," *The Accounting Forum*, May 1976, pp. 25–39.

U.S. Department of Energy, Comments before the Securities and Exchange Commission, "Accounting Practices—Oil and Gas Producers—Financial Accounting Standards," unpublished memorandum, April 3, 1978, 53 pages.

Wriston, Walter B., Transcript of Public Hearing on FASB Discussion Memorandum on Accounting by Debtors and Creditors When Debt Is Restructured (1977, Volume 1, Part 2), pp. 57–76.

Wyatt, Arthur R., "The Economic Impact of Financial Accounting Standards," *Journal of Accountancy*, October 1977, pp. 92–94.

Zeff, Stephen A., *Forging Accounting Principles in Five Countries: A History and an Analysis of Trends* (Champaign, Illinois: Stipes Publishing Company, 1972).

Paton on the Effects of Changing Prices on Accounting 1916–55

Stephen A. Zeff

From 1916, when he first contributed to the accounting literature, to 1955, when he published the last major textbook of which he was sole author, William A. Paton wrote frequently and with feeling on the vexing subject of the impact on accounting of changing prices. His writings have been widely quoted by both academics and practitioners, and one may confidently conclude that Paton was among the most influential American writers on accounting in this period.

Unfortunately the accounting literature in the English language contains very few historical studies showing how the thought of major contributors has evolved. For this reason, it may not be generally noticed when important normative writers alter their theoretical constructs or, in the light of particular economic and political conditions, introduce variables which affect their conclusions and policy recommendations. That Paton has done so in his writings on the impact of changing prices on accounting is my belief, and in this essay I propose to examine his contributions over a period of four decades in order to test this hypothesis.

More than most accounting writers, Paton has been acutely sensitive to shifting currents in the socioeconomic context in which accounting is performed. Over the period of this study, Paton seemed to accommodate his vision of accounting to his changing perceptions of the economic, legal, and political forces in the accounting environment.

It is no surprise that in the first significant period of his writings,

Note: I am grateful to Harold Bierman, Jr., William W. Cooper, Maurice Moonitz, William A. Paton, Jr., Edward Stamp, Herbert F. Taggart, and Roman L. Weil for their useful comments on an earlier draft, but the responsibility for errors is solely mine.

91

1917–18, Paton emerged as an idealist. Accounting writers are inclined to cite his 1918 textbook, *Principles of Accounting*, which he wrote with Russell A. Stevenson, as his most uncompromising challenge to accounting orthodoxy. And it was. But beginning in the 1920s, and continuing to the end of the 1930s, Paton gradually retreated from his enthusiastic and optimistic advocacy of 1917–18, as preoccupations over the post-World War I inflation, companies' questionable revaluation practices during the 1920s and early 1930s, the economic stagnation of the Depression, and the growing influence of the law in business operation collectively persuaded Paton to become more circumspect and constrained in his avowal of accounting reform. By the early 1940s, his penchant for innovation again became evident, and he began to employ his effective debating style to gain support for his measures among the accounting and legal authorities to whom deviation from precedent and convention was anathema. Following World War II, the accelerating pace of inflation, coupled with the persistent attacks on business and the free enterprise system, rekindled Paton's fire and enthusiasm of 1917–18, this time to persuade accountants, the Securities and Exchange Commission, Congress, and federal wage tribunals that corporate profits were being vastly overstated.

Paton was profoundly influenced by Sweeney's "stabilized accounting," and he frequently cited Sweeney's opus *Stabilized Accounting* in articles and speeches.[1] While he never preferred "stabilized accounting" to the booking of replacement costs, he regularly recommended that reckonings on a "common-dollar" basis be provided in supplementary disclosures. His enthusiasm for including unrealized appreciation in net income faded entirely in the 1920s and 1930s, and during these same two decades he showed growing reluctance even to reflect replacement costs formally in the accounts and financial statements. By the early 1940s, he had devised several techniques—the upward quasi-reorganization, the "compromise procedure" for supplementing plant costs and depreciation on a replacement cost basis without altering reported income, and the revaluation of assets upon the reacquisition of a corporation's own shares at a cost different from their book value—by which current costs or values might gain admission to the accounts and financial statements. Following the war, his advocacy of these and other reforms (including "common-dollar" accounting) assumed an intensity not before seen in his writings.

1. Henry W. Sweeney, *Stabilized Accounting* (New York: Harper & Bros., 1936).

This historical essay is organized on chronological lines, and at various stages the evolution of Paton's thought is explicitly examined. It is not my objective to argue with Paton, but instead to endeavor to understand and explain the development of his writings on this controversial subject. A more ambitious study would have included extensive references to the contemporaneous writings of other authors, both in the United States and in other countries. A complete examination of Paton's contribution to the literature would require the development of these links with the works of other writers, but the reader will appreciate that even my more limited undertaking is a large assignment. It is to be hoped that future studies will supply the missing dimension and that we might finally have a definitive study of Paton's impact on the literature of changing prices and accounting.

PRINCIPLES OF ACCOUNTING (1916)

The years 1916–18 were, following an uncertain start, the years of Unbridled Advocacy, since they produced Paton's most enthusiastic avowal of current-cost accounting. Idealism governed. Paton was a graduate student in economics at the University of Michigan when he and Russell A. Stevenson collaborated on a textbook entitled *Principles of Accounting*. The book appeared in three versions, published in 1916, 1917, and 1918. The 1917 and 1918 versions are not designated as second and third editions, although the titles are identical. Of the three versions, the one published in 1918 is by far the best known—indeed, few citations to its predecessors may be found in the literature. The successive versions grew steadily from 222 pages to 373 and finally 685 pages, reflecting, among other things, the authors' expansiveness and increasing conviction of the rightness of their controversial conclusions.

The 1916 version of *Principles of Accounting*, containing Paton's first published utterances on accounting measurement, bespeaks a degree of irresolution, as if the authors had not fully grasped their conception of accounting. While they endorse the principle of booking appreciation in the accounts, they hedge on its specific application. Paton and Stevenson emphasize that "accounting is concerned with the value representation of things," not with physical facts.[2]

---

2. William A. Paton and Russell A. Stevenson, *Principles of Accounting* (Ann Arbor: [no publisher], 1916), pp. 14, 101.

They add,

> The accounts should always show the present value of the property being used by an enterprise in producing its product, if accounting statistics are to furnish the entrepreneur with the information which shall enable him to make rational use of the economic resources at his disposal.[3]

The authors' underlying philosophy is taken from Wesley C. Mitchell's *Business Cycles:*[4]

> Prices render possible the rational direction of economic activity by accounting, for accounting is based upon the principle of representing all the heterogeneous commodities, services, and rights with which a business enterprise is concerned in terms of money price.

Their general principle is stated as follows: "The accounts, if they are to be scientifically accurate, should record *all* [value] changes, and immediately. That is, the accounts should be as sensitive as possible to all price and value changes."[5] It is nowhere stated, however, that revenues, or even net income, might in principle be credited for appreciation. Paton and Stevenson leave the inference that credits in respect of appreciation should be made to Surplus (a term which, in those days, implied an amalgam composed of the excess of total stockholders' equity over legal capital). When land appreciation is discussed, the authors worry over "a tendency to credit these increases to current revenue in lean years, which is illegitimate." "Increases in land value," they conclude, "should not be used [to] inflate current income, but should be credited to accumulated surplus." An equivocal qualification is added: "If, however, increases in land value are conservative estimates, and are not used to juggle the current Income sheet, there is no valid reason for keeping such items out of the accounts."[6] In the best light, the authors' discussion of the impact on net income of recorded appreciation is sketchy and incomplete.

To what extent should appreciation be recorded at all—as a practical matter? For merchandise, raw materials, etc., which move quickly through enterprise, it is not "expedient" to keep a continu-

3. *Ibid.*, p. 101. Although the authors do not define "present value," it is understood to mean any soundly based contemporary price or valuation.
4. Wesley C. Mitchell, *Business Cycles*, as quoted in Paton and Stevenson, *Principles of Accounting* (1916), pp. 31–32.
5. Paton and Stevenson, *Principles of Accounting* (1916), p. 103.
6. *Ibid.*, p. 105. Out of the accounts, or out of the Income sheet? The passage is unclear.

ing accounting record of changing prices. Only when "market prices fall or rise considerably or a long interval is involved," should market prices be entered in the accounts. A lower-of-cost-or-market solution is rejected as "unreasonable." For securities, "the reasonable course is to use cost prices unless market prices are widely divergent and for a long period, in which case securities should be valued at the market."

The authors' preoccupation with railroad property (numerous examples are chosen from this industry) evidently prompts a judgment that appreciation on land is the principal concern. Permanent changes in the value of buildings and machinery are asserted to be decreases more often than not, and any actual appreciation in such properties is said to be ordinarily offset by depreciation. Only land is left, and even here the authors are troubled by the booking of "unwarranted estimates."

The authors' 1916 position, therefore, is to recommend that the accounts continually reflect price and value changes; as a practical matter, however, valuations of land are open to suspicion, any appreciation in buildings and land is "normally more than offset by depreciation," and short-term assets should be kept at cost unless the price changes are pronounced over a long period.

"The Theory of Accounts" (1917)

By 1917 Paton, writing alone, achieves a clearer integration of his theory and policy recommendations. In his doctoral dissertation, "The Theory of Accounts," Paton unqualifiedly endorses the booking of appreciation as part of "net revenue" (a term he often used between 1917 and 1924 in place of net income).[7] He continues to espouse the accounting recognition of appreciation, but with the same exceptions for merchandise, raw materials, and securities, in virtually the identical language, as in the 1916 edition of *Principles of Accounting*. But the credit in respect of currently accrued appreciation is to be made to "net revenue."[8] He adds that "if an item of appreciation covers several accounting periods before it is recognized in the accounts [it] should be credited, not to net revenue,

7. William A. Paton, "The Theory of Accounts," unpublished doctoral dissertation, University of Michigan, 1917. The preface is dated May 1, 1917, and the manuscript extends to 144 pages, double-spaced, including bibliography.
8. *Ibid.*, pp. 119–20, 126–27.

but to surplus." The argument that a "net revenue" which includes appreciation might obscure the results of "actual operation" is met by the recommendation of a two-tier income statement, which would contain the calculation of "net revenue from operation, so-called, and total net revenue as well."[9] Paton shrewdly observes that conventional net income already includes a speculative price change, as, for example, when products purchased in a falling market are sold in a rising market. But his proposal would include unrealized effects as well.

In the dissertation, Paton repeats the idealistic conceptual statements about appreciation from the 1916 version of *Principles*, but he no longer harbors doubts about the practical implementation. In characteristic Paton debating style, he confidently dismisses the standard objections to booking appreciation and including appreciation in net income. As to the argument that appreciation is too subjective an estimate to appear in the accounts, Paton glibly replies, "As a matter of fact the appreciation of fixed property can be more accurately estimated than the depreciation." To those (such as Paton and Stevenson, in the 1916 version of *Principles*) who might be concerned about possible manipulation by management of appreciation estimates, the Paton of 1917 responds, "It is no more likely that illegitimate use will be made of appreciation than of depreciation."[10] In dealing with "that long-exploded notion that profits must be available in liquid assets in order to be considered as profits," Paton contends that stockholders can sell some shares and thus realize on the enhanced value of their equity interests whether "net revenue" is available in liquid form or not. Moreover, a dividend could be paid in respect of appreciation on fixed assets by borrowing "on short-term notes or otherwise." He concludes with the firm opinion that "all decreases in the values of assets constitute expense, and all increases represent revenue." "The net revenue figure for the accounting period," he adds, "is not accurately discovered until *all* these changes have been taken into consideration."[11] A stronger endorsement of current-value accounting could hardly be imagined.

The object of accounting is succinctly expressed: "From the standpoint of either the private enterprise or of the industrial community the accounts should answer the question: what economic resources

9. *Ibid.*, pp. 126–27.
10. *Ibid.*, p. 125.
11. *Ibid.*, pp. 128–29.

are being devoted to this or that particular end?"[12] Accounting is seen as an essential element in the free enterprise system, so as "to make effective the direction of economic activity by the system of market prices." Paton suggests that the severity of business cycles may be diminished by an accounting that reflects current price trends.[13] Perhaps the factor that led Paton to alter his position on the inclusion of appreciation in "net revenue" was a concern for the temporal impact on creditors and stockholders of "net revenue" measures that ignore appreciation. He notes that "the personnel of the owners is usually changing from day to day due to the ease with which securities can be transferred from one person to another."

> Thus [he continues] if an error in stating net revenue is made in one period it is probable that the rights of some of the individuals whose equities have been misstated cannot be restored by the correction of the error in a later period, because these rights are then in other hands. . . . The income bondholder, for example, has a right to income only when net revenue exists. . . . In the modern enterprise the constant shifting of the investors and the variety of property-rights as regards the aspects of ownership render imperative the *accurate* determination of [net revenue].[14]

The exigencies of a fluid market for equity interests, therefore, argue for current valuation in the accounts notwithstanding the absence of distributable funds corresponding to increments in net income. According to Paton of 1917, the prompt reflection of appreciation in the prices of equity shares was of paramount importance.

In the dissertation, Paton's meaning of the term "appreciation" is not always clear. At one point, it is described as "present value." A footnote explains that present value "may be based upon liquidating value, cost of reproduction, or going value to the specific enterprise. The cost of reproduction basis is the most significant—certainly in competitive enterprise."[15] A few pages later Paton also seems to include in appreciation the changes in the general level of prices, although this suggestion may have been developed mainly for the benefit of the Interstate Commerce Commission, whose property accounting rules were frequently the object of Patonian disdain.

12. *Ibid.*, p. 118.
13. *Ibid.*, pp. 6–8.
14. *Ibid.*, pp. 14–16.
15. *Ibid.*, p. 117.

PRINCIPLES OF ACCOUNTING (1917)

In their second version of *Principles of Accounting*, Paton and Stevenson include a seven-page section on "Appreciation and Depreciation," which is taken almost verbatim from Paton's dissertation.[16] Appreciation is to be credited to "net revenue," and all of the standard arguments (save one) against the booking of appreciation and the inclusion of appreciation in net income are rejected with the same aplomb as in the dissertation.[17] Two arguments in the dissertation, however, are omitted from the book. Nowhere in the book is Paton's argument against the view "that profits must be available in liquid assets in order to be considered as profits." His suggestions that short-term borrowings can be used to pay dividends and that stockholders can realize on the appreciation by selling off some of their stockholdings are not to be found in the book.

Also omitted from *Principles* is Paton's closing judgment in the dissertation that "all decreases in the values of assets constitute expense, and all increases represent revenue."[18] It is possible that these omitted items were too controversial for Stevenson's taste. But in other respects, the 1917 edition of *Principles* is entirely faithful to the contents of Paton's dissertation.

PRINCIPLES OF ACCOUNTING (1918)

In the third version of *Principles*, the substance of the authors' position on appreciation is unchanged from 1917, although their discussion is more expansive and confidently expressed than before.[19] That Paton was evidently the principal author of the well-known Chapter XX, "The Basis for Revaluation," is confirmed by his article published in the same year, "The Significance and Treatment of Appreciation in the Accounts," which closely corresponds to the chapter in *Principles*.[20]

16. William A. Paton and Russell A. Stevenson, *Principles of Accounting* (Ann Arbor: George Wahr, 1917).

17. *Ibid.*, pp. 213–19.

18. Paton, "Theory of Accounts," pp. 128–29.

19. William Andrew Paton and Russell Alger Stevenson, *Principles of Accounting* (New York: Macmillan Co., 1918).

20. William A. Paton, "The Significance and Treatment of Appreciation in the Accounts," in G.H. Coons, ed., *Twentieth Annual Report of the Michigan Academy of Science*, 1918, pp. 35–49. Reprinted in Herbert F. Taggart, ed., *Paton on Accounting* (Ann Arbor: Bureau of Business Research, University of Michigan, 1964), pp. 21–35; and in Stephen A. Zeff, ed., *Asset Appreciation, Business Income and Price-Level Accounting: 1918–1935* (New York: Arno Press, 1976), second article.

For the first time, Paton and Stevenson distinguish clearly between the booking of appreciation based on changes in replacement cost and the "illegitimate practice of forecasting profits in the accounts."[21] They write:

> To use selling prices in taking inventories—in other words to capitalize the services of the firm before those services are performed—is to anticipate profits. To recognize changing capital costs and equity changes due to the appreciation of working or fixed assets is an entirely different thing.[22]

The authors argue that an efficient management must be cognizant of replacement cost—that is, "the present significances of all assets as nearly as these facts may be ascertained"—in order to achieve "a wise utilization of available resources." But is it necessary that these figures appear in the actual accounts? Yes, reply Paton and Stevenson, "since it is generally admitted that it is an important function of the financial accounts to furnish information which will assist the management in making rational decisions regarding the employment of the investor's capital." In 1940, Paton retreated from this view, contending that management could be supplied with this information without disturbing the accounts. But in 1917, Paton and Stevenson claimed that "it is the function of the accounts to show economic facts."[23]

The authors cite Middleditch's path-breaking 1918 article when discussing the possibility of explicitly showing "changes in the significance of the money unit in the accounts."[24] They believe that such changes should not be displayed in the accounts, supporting their conclusion as follows:

> It has been argued thus far that costs of replacement should form the basis for the revaluation of assets for accounting purposes; and actual sacrifice and cost of replacement are not likely to coincide. The change in the value of the dollar reflects *general* price changes. But it is not values in general but *specific* values which the accounts should show.

In later years, Paton continued to avow that specific price changes, not the effects of general price trends, should be used if any modifications were to be made in the accounts or in the body of the financial statements.

21. Paton and Stevenson, *Principles of Accounting* (1918), p. 242.
22. *Ibid.*, p. 464.
23. *Ibid.*, pp. 456–57, 459 *n*.
24. *Ibid.*, p. 461. Livingston Middleditch, Jr., "Should Accounts Reflect the Changing Value of the Dollar?" *Journal of Accountancy* (Feb. 1918), pp. 114–20.

Most of the objections raised in the 1917 dissertation against the booking of appreciation and its inclusion in net income are again unqualifiedly rejected in this version of *Principles*. Even the argument that "profits must be available in liquid assets in order to be considered as profits," on which the 1917 version of *Principles* was silent, is rehearsed here, and the authors dismiss it with the same disdain displayed by Paton in his dissertation.[25]

Paton and Stevenson mention a new objection to the recording of appreciation: "that such a practice savors of non-conservatism. . . . A clear distinction should be made between conservatism and downright concealment." They argue vigorously against this objection:

> Ignoring the appreciation of unsold assets which results in an understatement of assets and a corresponding misstatement of equities—is simply another method of building up secret reserves; and it is essentially as misleading a practice as the charging of capital outlays to expense. . . .
>
> To insist that inventories in certain cases must be taken at a figure far below the actual values in order to prevent a general overstatement of assets is from the accountant an admission of incompetence.

Paton and Stevenson were willing to devise modes of presentation in order to meet part-way the defenders of historical cost. Appreciation "need not obscure cost figures" and "might [even] be kept out of the operating accounts." Supplementary statements might be used to maintain the record of appreciation. But the authors persisted in the belief that "accounts and statements which take into account *all* value changes would surely seem to be of more practical use to all parties concerned than records prepared on any other basis."[26]

Paton and Stevenson continue to defend the practice of crediting currently accrued appreciation to net income, although they confess at one point that "in general it is desirable to use the Surplus account to reflect all speculative changes in the equities."[27]

Finally worth noting: the recommendation in the 1916 and 1917 versions of *Principles* that appreciation not be recorded on most short-term assets, except when significant and over long periods, appears not to be repeated in the 1918 edition.

This third version of *Principles* was, as Hatfield later suggested, a bold argument for the "consistent treatment of fluctuations in

25. Paton and Stevenson, *Principles of Accounting* (1918), pp. 243, 467.
26. *Ibid.*, pp. 467, 469.
27. *Ibid.*, pp. 108, 238–42.

value."[28] In all of Paton's writings, it was his most inspired defense of current-cost accounting.

"Depreciation, Appreciation and Productive Capacity" (1920)

In a 1920 article entitled "Depreciation, Appreciation and Productive Capacity," Paton abruptly revises his stance on current-cost accounting.[29] No longer does he unreservedly favor crediting appreciation to net income. Indeed, his entire position on the booking of appreciation is less than clear, for he fails to reply to criticisms which he had calmly brushed aside in 1918. The tenor of this article is in stark contrast to his earlier writings. While his 1918 book with Stevenson brims with self-confidence and idealism, the 1920 article is tainted with doubt and pragmatic skepticism.

The excuse for the article is a reply to Bauer and Rastall,[30] chiefly to argue that replacement-cost depreciation should not be charged to operations unless the gross appreciation in the depreciable assets is also accorded accounting recognition. Paton's evident retreat from the view that appreciation credits should be made to net income seems to be explained, at least in part, by the persistent inflation of 1914–20, during which the consumer price index doubled. Paton writes,

> Is the proprietary credit, which should be made when a fixed asset is charged with the increment necessary to bring the book value up to the effective current cost, in any sense an index of income? So far as its expressing improved economic condition is concerned this depends . . . upon whether the price change in any particular instance involved is more or less acute than the general movement. In the average case it would no doubt be true that such appreciation would represent pretty largely not income but the application of the new measuring unit to the proprietary accounts.[31]

His discussion of the general price-level implications for accounting is more fully developed than in 1918. He again refers to Middleditch and cites a recent article by Scovill, and while he concludes that "it

28. Henry Rand Hatfield, "Book Reviews," *Journal of Accountancy* (Nov. 1925), p. 390.

29. W.A. Paton, "Depreciation, Appreciation and Productive Capacity," *Journal of Accountancy* (July 1920), pp. 1–11.

30. John Bauer, "Renewal Costs and Business Profits in Relation to Rising Prices," *Journal of Accountancy* (Dec. 1919), pp. 413–19; Ernest A. Rastall, "Depreciation Reserves and Rising Prices," *Journal of Accountancy* (Feb. 1920), pp. 123–26.

31. Paton, "Depreciation," p. 10.

is perhaps not unreasonable to argue that the accountant should prepare supplementary statements at the end of each period designed to show—by making proper allowances for the change in the value of money—the true comparative economic status of the enterprise," in the end he reaffirms his conclusion of 1918 that accounting should have regard to changes in specific prices, not general prices.[32]

But the principal point of interest in this article is Paton's less ardent support, expressed in the final two pages, of the accounting recognition of appreciation in any form. When Paton is sure of his ground, he does not fail to reply energetically to opposing arguments. Here he leaves them unanswered. In a remarkable modification of his 1918 stand, perhaps induced by the cumulative effect of an apparently unrelenting inflation coupled with the postwar economic uncertainty of 1919–20, Paton gives credence to arguments which he had enthusiastically rejected two years earlier:

> At any rate [an appreciation] credit in a practical case would not measure an amount which could conveniently or safely be turned over to the stockholders. . . .

> In view . . . of the conjectural character of asset values at best and the consequent importance of conservatism [sic], the difficulties in the way of determining effective replacement costs in the case of complex assets, the constant fluctuation of such costs and the fact that having once made an investment the management is often thereby committed to a policy for a considerable period regardless of the movement of prices, probably most accountants would feel that original cost is the best basis upon which to value fixed assets.[33]

Does Paton include himself among "most accountants"? Is he abandoning entirely the accounting recognition of appreciation, or is he limiting this reply to Bauer and Rastall to the points raised in their articles? However one might interpret this article, something has taken the wind out of Paton's sails.

A comparison of the 1918 and 1920 positions vividly demonstrates how much Paton was affected by the swirl of economic events. For all of his life, he has been a firm believer in the market system; it was, in effect, the text from which he read.

Evidently Paton's article had an impact. More than forty years later, Sweeney wrote,

32. *Ibid.*, p. 4.
33. *Ibid.*, pp. 10–11.

That excellent article, far in advance of its time, entitled "Depreciation, Appreciation and Productive Capacity" . . . was the first exposition I had seen of how accounting figures, representing depreciation, could be revised to show the changing purchasing power of money. It stimulated and encouraged me to try to develop all the great possibilities that this new subject in the United States seemed to offer.[34]

ACCOUNTING THEORY (1922)

Paton's celebrated *Accounting Theory—With Special Reference to the Corporate Enterprise*, published in 1922, reaffirms his position on fixed assets as set out in the 1920 article and discloses his qualified approval of showing appreciation on current assets.[35] *Accounting Theory* has erroneously been said to be the publication of Paton's doctoral dissertation.[36] In fact, *Accounting Theory* is four times the length of the dissertation, and while Chapters I through VII and X through XI of *Accounting Theory* largely correspond to material in the dissertation, the remaining chapters (including four which, Paton reported, were adapted in part from previously published articles) either did not appear in the dissertation or were lightly treated there.

Of particular importance is Paton's major change in posture on appreciation between the 1917 dissertation and *Accounting Theory*, published five years later. Where he concluded in the dissertation that it would be inexpedient to record appreciation in most instances on current assets, in *Accounting Theory* (as, apparently, in the 1918 version of *Principles of Accounting*) he actually espouses the normal booking of appreciation on certain kinds of current assets, and he would even credit such accruals to income.[37] Where, in the dissertation, he would credit the currently accrued appreciation of

34. Henry W. Sweeney, "Forty Years After: Or Stabilized Accounting Revisited," in the reissue of his *Stabilized Accounting* (New York: Holt, Rinehart and Winston, Inc., 1964), p. xx.

35. William Andrew Paton, *Accounting Theory—With Special Reference to the Corporate Enterprise* (New York: Ronald Press, 1922). Reprinted in 1962 by A.S.P. Accounting Studies Press, Ltd., Chicago, and in 1973 by Scholars Book Co., Houston.

36. This writer is among those who have erred. In the publisher's preface to the 1962 reprint of *Accounting Theory*, signed by this writer and three others, it is said that *Accounting Theory* "was [Paton's] doctoral dissertation at the University of Michigan." In many respects, *Accounting Theory* was based on the dissertation, but it went beyond the dissertation and departed from it in significant points (chiefly in the treatment of appreciation).

37. Paton, *Accounting Theory*, pp. 466–68.

fixed assets, notably land, to "net revenue," in *Accounting Theory*, following the inconclusive discussion in the 1920 article, Paton reviews the pros and cons, and appears to conclude that the appreciation on fixed assets is best not even entered in the accounts. If such appreciation is recorded, however, he is exceedingly reluctant to classify it as income. On one point he is decisive: the portion of recorded appreciation which coincides with the general movement of prices should be credited to capital.[38]

In *Accounting Theory*, not all current assets would qualify for the booking of appreciation. "The consistent valuation of standard materials and marketable securities on the basis of replacement cost," he counsels, "is a thoroughly sound procedure. . . . Goods in process and finished stock furnish a more dubious case." Moreover: "With respect to plant and equipment and other classes of fixed assets the propriety of cost-of-replacement valuations is still more questionable . . . " As in the dissertation, where he recommended that the appreciation credit on fixed assets be classified as "net revenue" from other than operations, in *Accounting Theory* he denominates the appreciation credit on eligible current assets as "non-operating income." Paton's mild support for crediting income with the currently accrued appreciation of current assets evaporated by the 1930s, and he has never again argued for the inclusion in income of appreciation accruals. In *Accounting Theory* he continues to argue, as did Paton and Stevenson in 1918, that recorded appreciation should not be based on the selling prices of merchandise, because its inclusion in income "may mean the [improper] recognition of a fraction of the normal income margin in advance of sale."[39]

Paton's principal reason for rejecting the inclusion in income of appreciation of fixed assets may be traced to his desire, first given expression in the 1920 article, to assist management in maintaining its physical capital. To achieve this end, depreciation should be based on appreciation, but the appreciation accrual itself should not be credited to income. "To revalue assets and base depreciation upon replacement costs," he writes, "would be an entirely futile policy unless the appreciation credit were excluded from the income account—at least as far as disposable income is concerned."[40] Beginning with his 1920 article, therefore, Paton left the ranks of those who would endeavor to approximate economic income in the

38. *Ibid.*, pp. 441–42.
39. *Ibid.*, pp. 466–68.
40. *Ibid.*, p. 441.

income statement, and became a member of what I have called the "disposable income school."[41]

Paton's discussion of the accounting effects of general price movements is more extensive in *Accounting Theory* than in his previous writings. In somewhat more than seven pages, he concludes that accountants should be interested primarily in "*specific* price and value changes," not "*general* price movements"; yet he grudgingly concedes:

> It would perhaps not be unreasonable to urge that the accountant should be held responsible for the preparation of supplementary statements at the end of each period designed to show—by making proper allowance for the change in the value of money—the true relation between the current statement and the one immediately preceding (or a series of earlier statements).[42]

This suggestion was also contained in the 1920 article, expressed in the same cautious language.[43]

He also proposes (in more positive terms) that the accountant prepare supplementary statements which reflect *individual* price movements—in the event, one supposes, that appreciation is not deemed proper for inclusion in the formal financial statements.

Accounting Theory is characterized by indecision and contradiction, as Paton was evidently passing through a period of profound reassessment of the theories which he had propounded so confidently in 1917–18.

ACCOUNTING (1924)

Paton's first textbook, *Accounting*, after the publication in 1918 of the third version of *Principles of Accounting* invites comparisons between the two.[44] The differences are instantly noticeable. Nowhere in *Accounting* does one find the idealistic formulations about the valuation of assets in relation to income that are evident in *Principles*. In this respect, *Accounting* is the more pragmatic and down-to-earth of the two volumes.

After persuasively arguing that appreciation of readily marketable securities has a strong claim as a credit to income, and offering the generalization that "wherever appreciation consists in a bona fide

41. See Stephen A. Zeff, "Replacement Cost: Member of the Family, Welcome Guest, or Intruder?" *Accounting Review* (Oct. 1962), pp. 617–20.

42. Paton, *Accounting Theory*, pp. 428–29.

43. Paton, "Depreciation," p. 4.

44. W.A. Paton, *Accounting* (New York: Macmillan Co., 1924).

increase in value in reasonably liquid assets there is ground fo
urging that such appreciation is quite as substantial a basis for tht
recognition of income as an increase in value brought abou
through the sale of original assets," Paton hastens to point out tha
since the Treasury Department "does not permit the ordinary inves·
tor in securities to treat appreciation as taxable income . . . it is
probably advisable in most cases for the investor not to set up
appreciated values in his regular accounts."[45] Thus enters the Law,
which plays a major role in Paton's writings in the 1930s.

The appreciation of plant assets is of "dubious significance as fai
as the asset accounts are concerned, and is of still more doubtful
character as an income determinant," and only with respect to land
which is highly marketable does "genuine appreciation [have] some
significance as true income."[46]

Elsewhere Paton mentions several objections to crediting appreciation to income:

> . . . appreciation is not in general viewed as income from the legal point
> of view, . . . enhancement does not measure liquid assets which may be
> disbursed as dividends, and . . . appraisal values may be used illegiti-
> mately to conceal operating deficits and other losses.[47]

He does not undertake to dispute these objections—which are, in
company with similar statements in his 1920 article and *Accounting
Theory*, difficult to associate with the Paton of 1917–18.

Paton is still willing to countenance the upward revaluation of
fixed assets and inventories so long as the credit is made to Surplus,
not income.[48] But his support for the practice falls well short of
advocacy, and when objections and limitations are raised, they are
seldom rebutted.

In *Accounting*, Paton does not discuss the accounting effects of
changing general prices. Nor does he make an issue of the preservation of physical capacity during periods of advancing prices, which
was a pivotal concern in his 1920 article and *Accounting Theory*.
Allowing for the fact that *Accounting* is an introductory text and
Accounting Theory is a major treatise, the tenor of Paton's remarks
on appreciation is in most respects similar in both. Perhaps the
noteworthy difference is the somewhat greater attention accorded to
legal prescriptions in *Accounting* than in *Accounting Theory*. The

45. *Ibid.*, pp. 624–25.
46. *Ibid.*, p. 625.
47. *Ibid.*, p. 367.
48. *Ibid.*, pp. 352–53, 368, 373–74.

differences between *Accounting* and the 1917–18 *Principles of Accounting* are, of course, graphic.

Four Articles and the AAA Statement in the Early to Mid-1930s

By the 1930s, Paton's enthusiasm for replacement cost accounting had diminished still further, and he began to warm to the recommendation that supplementary disclosures should report the effect of changing prices on the firm. The reasons were several. One, he was disturbed by the haphazard and unsubstantiated upward revaluations in the 1920s and downward revaluations in the early 1930s. He writes in 1934,

> One of the things which tends to discourage hopes of the possibility of improving accounting via the route of revaluation of fixed assets is observation of the way in which revaluations are handled in actual practice. The revaluations downward in recent years, for example, have in most cases been entirely unscientific and often arbitrary in the extreme.[49]

In 1932 he writes,

> And it is equally apparent that the [write-down] procedures being followed [in the early 1930s] are in many cases just as unsystematic and improper as were the procedures followed in many of the earlier write-ups.[50]

Also in the early 1930s, Paton began to be preoccupied with the legal boundaries within which the formal accounting system must operate. Paton's awareness of the growing importance of the federal income tax law coupled with the intense interest being shown during the Depression years in the legal definitions of income, capital, surplus, and dividends may have contributed to this concern.[51] The relative interests of different classes of investors in troubled corporations appear to have been a live issue in the early 1930s. Paton may also have been thinking of references to accounting figures in bond contracts. He reserved some of his most picturesque writing to describe the heavy hand of the law:

49. William A. Paton, "Aspects of Asset Valuations," *Accounting Review* (June 1934), p. 127.
50. W.A. Paton, "Accounting Problems of the Depression," *Accounting Review* (Dec. 1932), p. 264.
51. The attention being given to such questions may be discerned from reading issues of the *Accounting Review* during the early and middle 1930s.

It must also not be forgotten that our legal institutions care nothing fc purchasing power and treat all dollars, regardless of changing price lev els, as equivalents. And the accountant, called upon to report and trac the effects of a maze of specific legal relationships and contracts, cannc ignore the legal structure, and hence is circumscribed and harassed in hi efforts to become a statistical economist.[52]

In a 1931 article, Paton reveals the philosophical underpinning fo the use of current costs in financial statements. He argues that

to be an effective cost a cost factor must be significant in the competitiv price-making process, or, to put the matter more definitely from th standpoint of accounting valuation, to constitute a legitimate asset in th balance sheet an element of cost incurred must be of such a character tha the presence of the factor or condition represented by such cost makes : possible for the enterprise to avoid incurring another similar cost whic would otherwise be required in the production of revenue.[53]

He concludes that by "effective cost" the economist means "the po tential cost of replacement."[54] (In this period, Paton's references t replacement cost were to eventual replacement, not to simulated im mediate replacement.) And "It is only in the case of a continuou flow of standard units that replacement cost can be held to have an marked influence on value."[55] The same article is one of the rela tively few places in Paton's writings where he discusses in som depth a combination of replacement costs and general price-leve changes, the change in the former in relation to the latter yielding th "real" (or "true") enhancement or decrement in economic status.[5]

But experiences during the Depression convinced Paton that thi philosophy did not deal adequately with the times. By the end c 1932, he writes,

In fact in a time [of overcapacity, replacement cost] has been temporaril eclipsed as a price-determining factor, for the individual concern or fc business in general. . . .

In the first place cost of replacement means very little if anything i the case of obsolete or semi-obsolete property which is not being reprc duced in the form of a constant flow of new plants and new machines Second, the complex plant property of modern times is so specialize

52. Paton, "Aspects," p. 126.

53. W.A. Paton, "Economic Theory in Relation to Accounting Valuations," Ac counting Review (June 1931), p. 91. Compare the later article, David Green, Jr., "Mc ral to the Direct Costing Controversy?" Journal of Business (July 1960), pp. 218–26.

54. Paton, "Economic Theory," p. 94.

55. Ibid., ҏ. 95.

56. Ibid.

that much of it, even in the case of the newest and best types, will never be reproduced in precisely the same form.[57]

In 1934, he seemed to question the principle still further:

> Nevertheless it must be remembered, first that the operating expenses of the particular concern in which the accountant is interested will not as a rule be the focal point in price determination, and, second, that the influence of the depreciation charge upon price is obscure and not susceptible of statistical isolation.[58]

Only in the long run, or in periods of capacity operation, apparently, might the depreciation charge be price-determining, and Paton did not believe that the prospect of such a remote future effect was worth recording in the accounts.[59]

Paton was deeply troubled throughout the period. On the one hand, he wanted to argue on principle that historical costs constitute obsolete information, but on the other hand he felt constrained by institutional and economic considerations. It must have been painful for him to admit in 1934 that "barring exceptional circumstances the cost basis of valuation, with all its limitations, is not seriously defective for accounting purposes."[60] But then he adds his clarion call of the 1930s:

> These days of monetary tinkering, however, may be the "exceptional circumstances" which justify our giving more attention to devices and methods designed to *supplement*, in a useful way, our present types of records.[61]

He favored supplementary disclosures of the effects of changes in both replacement costs and general price levels,[62] and in a second 1934 article, he criticized accountants for being so "sluggish" in following the lead of Sweeney and others toward the preparation of supplementary analyses of the impact of inflation on enterprise affairs.[63]

By 1936, therefore, when he joined such arch historical costers as Eric L. Kohler, A.C. Littleton, and Howard C. Greer in the drafting of an accounting principles statement on behalf of the newly

57. Paton, "Depression," p. 266.
58. Paton, "Aspects," p. 126.
59. *Ibid.* See also p. 123.
60. *Ibid.*, p. 128.
61. *Ibid.* Emphasis added.
62. *Ibid.*
63. William A. Paton, "Shortcomings of Present-Day Financial Statements," *Journal of Accountancy* (Feb. 1934), p. 130.

reorganized American Accounting Association, Paton could fairly be said to be a historical coster himself in the basic financial statements. Nonetheless, the committee's assertion that "accounting is thus not essentially a process of valuation, but the allocation of historical costs and revenues to the current and succeeding fiscal periods" may not have been a genuine reflection of Paton's fundamental view of accounting.[64]

The committee's statement was a thoroughgoing paean to historical costs, although it conceded that "interpretation [of financial statements] is often impossible without extensive supplemental data, including the provision of common denominators through which comparisons may be effected."[65]

Elsewhere in the statement, the committee writes, "An extreme change in the value of money might vitiate the usefulness of cost records but there seems to be no sound reason for repeated adjustments of asset values for the ordinary changes in price levels commonly experienced from one generation to another."[66] This assertion is in line with Paton's separate writings on the desirability of preserving the record of cost in the accounts. Finally, the committee criticizes the "uncoordinated" appraisals of fixed assets in language that could well have been Paton's.[67]

Thus, by the middle of the 1930s, Paton had transformed his radical call for financial-statement reform of 1917–18 to a recommendation that corporations supplement their financial statements with informative disclosures. The questionable booking of write-ups in the 1920s and write-downs in the 1930s, the special problems wrought by the economic stagnation of the Great Depression, and his growing concern over the legal constraints within which accounting must be performed, collectively persuaded Paton that the formal accounting records and resulting financial statements were better kept on a cost footing than on a replacement-cost basis. When reporting to managers, Paton continued to prefer revaluations based on replacement cost to restatements in line with changing general price levels—a position from which he has never

64. "A Tentative Statement of Accounting Principles Affecting Corporate Reports," *Accounting Review* (June 1936), p. 188. Under the title, "A Tentative Statement of Accounting Principles Underlying Corporate Financial Statements," it was widely distributed as a reprint.
65. *Ibid.*
66. *Ibid.*, p. 189.
67. *Ibid.*

wavered.[68] Indeed, while he has recommended at different times that replacement costs might be reflected in the accounts and in the financial statements, he has never proposed that the effects of changes in general price levels be shown anywhere but in supplementary presentations. But in the 1930s, when economic conditions failed to substantiate the belief that replacement costs were price-influencing, Paton declined even to recommend that replacement costs be entered in the accounts. His conclusion during that era was that either replacement costs or general price-level effects should be displayed in supplementary disclosures.

ESSENTIALS OF ACCOUNTING (1938)

Essentials of Accounting was Paton's first textbook after *Accounting* (1924). In *Essentials,* Paton continues to espouse a cautious policy toward valuations other than historical cost. In the majority of instances, the financial statements should be based on historical cost, but Paton encourages supplementary disclosures to inform management of the impact of price fluctuations.[69] Nonetheless, in "periods of sharply changing prices," a departure from cost valuation of inventory "has some merit where the period of production is sufficiently long, and the selling market is sufficiently sensitive, to make possible modifications of policy based on observation of the changing costs of goods on hand." Paton adds, however, without rebutting the point, "The most common objection offered to the consistent use of replacement cost in pricing inventory is that such valuation will result in effect in the recognition of unrealized profit where replacement cost is higher than actual cost."[70]

In *Principles of Accounting* (1918), Paton and Stevenson were opposed to the inclusion in income of the margin between the net realizable value and replacement cost of merchandise inventories. In *Accounting,* published in 1924, Paton objected to crediting income with the spread between the replacement cost and historical cost of plant assets, but he seemed to countenance the inclusion in income of this spread in regard to "reasonably liquid assets," which excluded merchandise inventories. In 1938, he reaffirmed this position.

68. Paton, "Aspects," p. 126.
69. W.A. Paton, *Essentials of Accounting* (New York: Macmillan Co., 1938), pp. 482, 813.
70. *Ibid.,* pp. 482–83.

By 1938, Paton was prepared to consider a formal recognition in the accounts of the replacement cost of fixed assets. It is in *Essentials* that he reveals his new tactic. After stipulating that "the cost of replacement is truly significant [for business managements] only in the case of standard plant units which will presumably be replaced upon retirement substantially in kind," Paton recites "numerous difficulties in the way of achieving results which are worthwhile by attempting to shift the measure of depreciation from cost to replacement cost":

> Continuous revaluation is a costly process; appraisal results at the best are estimates; current costs of a particular date are not likely to measure the actual cost of replacement upon retirement; depreciation is only one cost and a modification of this element will not change the operating picture materially except where the movement of costs has been very sharp; [and] in general replacement cost is not recognized as a basis of depreciation for income-tax purposes or in other legal connections. [71]

If revaluations are nonetheless entered in the accounts, the "recorded cost figures [should not be] obscured." The gross revaluation of plant should be shown in a "distinct" account, the corresponding credit should be "segregated" from the ordinary capital and proprietary accounts, and as subsequent depreciation accruals are recorded on the basis of the revalued assets, a transfer should be made from the proprietorship account originally credited with the revaluation "to the income or [earned] surplus account as a correction." Thus, Earned Surplus, if not Net Income, would be shown as if the revaluations had not been recorded. "It is universally agreed," Paton asserts, incorrectly, "that no part of the unrealized appreciation or declination should be reflected in the income statement." [72] His recommended treatment of plant revaluations, including the "washout" of subsequent depreciation accruals in the income statement, was later labeled by Paton a "compromise procedure."

71. *Ibid.*, pp. 542–43.
72. *Ibid.*, p. 543. In 1939, Kenneth MacNeal published his controversial *Truth in Accounting* (Philadelphia: University of Pennsylvania Press) in which he advocated the inclusion of unrealized appreciation or declination of fixed assets in the income statement, but said these amounts should be carried to Capital Surplus, not Earned Surplus. He would, however, transfer the unrealized price appreciations and declinations on inventory to Earned Surplus (see chap. XIV). Sweeney recommended that each year's installment of real unrealized appreciation (the amount of unrealized appreciation which remains after allowing for changes in the general price level) be shown in the income statement as "unrealized net income," which would be transferred to "Unrealized Surplus," rather than the Retained Earnings-like account, "Realized Surplus." Henry W. Sweeney, *Stabilized Accounting* (1936), pp. 18–19, 50–52.

Finally, although *Essentials* was an introductory textbook, Paton devotes the last six pages to the impact of inflation on the accounts. He returns to earlier arguments:

> In attempting to deal with this problem the accountant is embarrassed by the fact that the law in general entirely fails to acknowledge the phenomenon of a variable unit of monetary measure. The accountant, in other words, is coerced in some measure by the framework of contracts and legal institutions by which the business enterprise—his immediate field of activity—is surrounded and sustained; he must report contractual earnings, amount subject to income tax, amount available for dividends, capital stock, accumulated surplus, etc., in the first instance at any rate, in accordance with impinging legal requirements. At the same time the accountant is coming to be depended upon more and more as an interpreter of the essential economic conditions of the enterprise for the purposes in particular of assisting in advising investors and framing managerial policies. And in these connections it is plain that he cannot fulfill his function adequately and remain blind to the limitations of the conventional accounts and reports in the face of a varying dollar.[73]

He discusses the impact of inflation on an enterprise's working capital and long-term liabilities, and illustrates in numerical format (for the first time) the conversion of a comparative balance sheet into dollars of a common index. "What is needed in most situations is a special report supplementing the periodic statements, [but] except in periods where the change in dollar value is sharp and prolonged as a result of emergency conditions and accompanying monetary tinkering the case for giving explicit attention to the problem is not very strong."[74] Here he uses, for the first time, the expression "common-dollar basis" to describe the method employed.[75] *Essentials* may well have been the first American accounting textbook to discuss and numerically illustrate general price-level accounting.

"Recent and Prospective Developments in Accounting Theory" (1940)

In April, 1940, Paton delivered the third Dickinson Lecture at the Harvard Graduate School of Business Administration.[76] Entitled "Recent and Prospective Developments in Accounting Theory," it

---

73. Paton, *Essentials*, p. 813.

74. *Ibid.*

75. *Ibid.*, p. 817.

76. *Dickinson Lectures in Accounting* (Cambridge, Mass.: Harvard University Press, 1943), pp. 85–131.

contains only a few pages on the effects of changing prices on accounting. Paton observes that the trends of specific and general prices "are regularly in the same direction," following which he offers a sly dictum which he became fond of repeating in later years,

It is this fact which affords some justification for the paradoxical statement that "the proponents of replacement cost valuations are in effect defending adherence to the original cost basis." Interpreting cost incurred in the sense of economic power committed to the enterprise, there is a measure of truth in this observation.[77]

Whatever the validity of this statement, it was undeniably a clever debating tactic.

He continues to argue that the replacement-cost approach is more useful than the purchasing-power approach to managers and owners of enterprise. In a statement which is prophetic of the American accounting literature of the 1960s and 1970s, Paton writes, "Business management is concerned in some degree with the maintenance of the integrity of investment measured in purchasing power but is perhaps even more devoted to the protection of productive capacity and scope of activity."[78]

He nonetheless persists in his opposition to any role for plant valuations in the determination of income. Among the reasons given, he contends that the use of replacement cost is "of marked significance only in the case of standard, up-to-date facilities, which will presumably be replaced substantially in kind." Returning to a theme in his "Aspects" (1932) and "Depression" (1934) articles, Paton adds, "Neither the original cost nor the replacement cost of facilities of an obsolescent character are potent factors in the economic process." Another reason given, which elaborates on a point made briefly in *Essentials of Accounting* two years before, is Paton's belief that depreciation is in most cases a relatively small fraction of total operating costs, and thus the effect of a change from original cost to replacement cost would be of little practical consequence. Following World War II, however, Paton cited the size of depreciation in relation to *net income* as justification for a change in the basis of depreciation accounting.

In Paton's view, the most important argument against the use of replacement costs in the determination of net income is its "conflict with the legal point of view." In language reminiscent of his

77. *Ibid.*, p. 126.
78. *Ibid.*, pp. 126–27.

"Aspects" (1934) article and *Essentials*, he writes that "the accountant is inevitably coerced in considerable measure by the legal framework, and in his search for ways of improving the reporting of operating data for managerial purposes he should not lose sight of the legal criteria of the general income statement."[79]

The legal impediments to changing the way in which net income is determined have continued to be an influential factor in Paton's thinking. In his Dickinson Lecture, Paton unveils his adaptation of the quasi-reorganization to deal with *under*valued fixed assets, an accounting adjustment which he urged on numerous occasions in the 1940s and 1950s as a means of supplanting historical cost records by infrequent upward revaluations of nonmonetary assets.[80] That quasi-reorganizations were acceptable under certain conditions for downward revaluations persuaded Paton that, by analogous reasoning, the same accounting device could be extended to upward revaluations. Even if upward quasi-reorganizations were not available to a company, it might, according to Paton, book replacement costs without obscuring recorded costs, with the proviso that the subsequent depreciation based on the appraisal increments would appear in the income statement as information only, without reducing the reported net income below what would have been shown by the use of historical cost. This is the same method that he introduced and discussed in *Essentials*.

An Introduction to Corporate Accounting Standards (1940)

Paton's posture on the accounting response to changing prices was faithfully reflected in his celebrated 1940 monograph with A.C. Littleton, *An Introduction to Corporate Accounting Standards*.[81] The monograph was an outgrowth of the tentative "Statement of Accounting Principles Underlying Corporate Financial Statements," issued by the executive committee (of which Paton was a member) of the American Accounting Association in 1936.

At several places in the monograph, the authors draw attention to the importance of legal considerations, thus obliging the accountant to employ traditional historical costs in the reckoning of income.[82]

---

79. *Ibid.*, pp. 127–29.

80. *Ibid.*, p. 129.

81. W.A. Paton and A.C. Littleton, *An Introduction to Corporate Accounting Standards* (Chicago: American Accounting Association, 1940).

82. *Ibid.*, pp. 4, 9, 62, 123, 135, 136, and 141; but see pp. 10–11.

Indeed, they categorically exclude appreciation on nonmonetary assets from income:

> Appreciation, in general, does not reflect or measure the progress ot operating activity; appreciation is not the result of any transaction or any act of conversion; appreciation makes available no additional liquid resources which may be used to meet obligations or make disbursements to investors; appreciation has little or no legal standing as income.[83]

A monograph in which "verifiable, objective evidence" is proposed as a basic concept is not a place where one would expect to find an argument for replacement costs in the principal financial statements.[84] Paton and Littleton acknowledge that managers should be made aware of the impact of changing replacement costs where such costs might affect business decisions, but they suggest that this information can be made available to management without altering the accounts. They enumerate several limitations of the replacement-cost approach, all of which would have been well known to readers of Paton's previous writings.[85] The set of entries by which historical-cost measurements of plant cost and depreciation would be accompanied by appraisal increments or decrements, but without altering the historical-cost net income, is discussed at length (the same approach was proposed in *Essentials of Accounting* and in the Dickinson Lecture). Paton's increasing interest in Sweeney's "stabilized accounting" is further evident in the monograph, where extensive discussion is devoted to a means by which recorded costs might be converted to "common dollars."[86] In regard to both replacement costs and common-dollar accounting, the authors conclude that supplementary disclosures would suffice to adapt the formal accounts to conditions of changing prices. It would appear that the imperative of "verifiable, objective evidence" together with the authors' pervasive preoccupation with legal considerations serves to defeat any argument which might displace historical costs in the formal financial statements. Replacement costs would perhaps be allowed in the financial statements only as bits of information, so long as they do not affect the measurement of net income.

Of interest, however, is the authors' reference (doubtless a Patonian initiative) to the possibility, albeit mildly suggested, that the

83. *Ibid.*, p. 62.
84. *Ibid.*, pp. 18–21.
85. *Ibid.*, pp. 131–34.
86. *Ibid.*, pp. 139–41.

difference between the incurred cost and book value of a corporation's reacquired shares might serve as a basis for the revaluation of the corporate assets.[87] The suggestion is mentioned in the most inoffensive terms, and the authors seem content not to carry out its implications.

ADVANCED ACCOUNTING (1941)

Advanced Accounting was Paton's first textbook designed for students above the introductory level. It may be distinguished from most other intermediate and advanced texts by Paton's determination to discuss and debate virtually all of the controversial issues of the day. *Advanced Accounting* was hardly a compendium of mechanics.

For inventories, Paton peremptorily rejects valuation at net selling prices and shows little enthusiasm even for the use of replacement costs.[88] Both of these alternatives to historical cost, he argues, would give rise to the recognition of unrealized profit. He does not discuss the alternative of crediting stockholders' equity instead of income for the amount of any such appreciation, perhaps because "for most trading concerns, it is fair to say, there is little to be gained [in the income statement] in the way of useful reporting by a shift from recorded cost to current buying price, particularly when cost is estimated by the first-in, first-out method." Moreover, "replacement cost as an independent valuation base is not generally approved by the income-tax authorities, and is viewed as nonconservative by many accountants, bankers, and business managers." When he is not disposed to criticize extant practice, Paton takes refuge in the word of other authorities.

In regard to the valuation of plant, Paton rejects valuation based on a discounting of the prospective earning power of the assets.[89] Two principal reasons are that such estimates "are none too dependable under the most favorable conditions" and that the income streams are not uniquely linked to particular assets, but to a composite of assets. In discussing valuation at replacement cost, Paton argues once again that "the influential costs in the economic process are those that are reflected in the immediate level of prices."

87. *Ibid.*, p. 116.
88. W.A. Paton, *Advanced Accounting* (New York: Macmillan Co., 1941), pp. 151–52, 160–61.
89. *Ibid.*, pp. 323–24.

But he cautions that the adoption of this view does not lead inexorably to "a continuous process of plant appraisal and a continuous revision of plant accounts." It would be "inexpedient" to embark on such a "systematic program" in the absence of a "major and persistent change" in prices. Furthermore,

> it must not be forgotten . . . that the price system is not uniformly sensitive throughout, and that for considerable periods selling prices may not move in harmony with changing costs of production. Selling prices, moreover, are not in general fixed by cost to the particular concern—whatever the basis on which such cost may be computed.

Finally (as in the 1940 monograph), he suggests that business management can take into consideration such price movements without necessarily "revamping the plant accounts." He concludes by striking a familiar chord:

> Particularly in view of income-tax regulations and other aspects of the legal framework within which a business enterprise must operate, the original cost of plant and the depreciation charges based on such cost are data which the accountant must continue to make available. From an accounting standpoint, that is, replacement costs are not a substitute for recorded costs, although they may represent significant supplementary facts.

Later in the same chapter, he claims that the failure of recorded cost to reflect replacement cost "is not the most serious weakness of the cost basis." Of greater consequence is that "the original dollar cost [of nonmonetary assets] is not a dependable expression of actual cost in the sense of economic sacrifice or committed purchasing power." Paton argues forcefully for an accounting recognition of changes in the value of the monetary unit and blames "the legal framework within which business transactions are conducted" for the lack of progress in this direction.[90] An entire chapter is devoted to "Common-Dollar Reporting," constituting (up to that time) the most extensive discussion of general price-level accounting in any American accounting textbook. In this 18-page chapter, he illustrates the conversion of the balance sheet and income statement and discusses the accounting treatment to be given to purchasing power gains and losses. Like Sweeney, Paton contends that the gains and losses on monetary items are unrealized so long as the monetary assets are held or the monetary liabilities are unpaid.[91] By 1955,

90. *Ibid.*, p. 329.
91. Sweeney, *Stabilized Accounting*, pp. 20–22, 33; Paton, *Advanced Accounting*, pp. 739, 748.

Paton modified this stance in regard to current monetary assets and liabilities.

Paton illustrates alternative accounting treatments for booked appreciation or "declination." His preference is to credit a special stockholders' equity account for the amount of the net appreciation (i.e., after allowing for accumulated depreciation on the appreciation) and then to "reserve" an amount of Surplus (Retained Earnings in today's parlance) equal to the accumulated depreciation on the appreciation. The object of the latter transfer is to "provide" for the understated depreciation of prior years. When depreciation is later recorded on the appreciated plant, an amount equal to the depreciation on appreciation is transferred to the income statement from the special stockholders' equity account. In this manner, the net income is undisturbed by the revaluation of the plant. At the end of the year, an amount equal to the year's depreciation on appreciation is transferred from the Surplus account to a surplus reserve. The effect of these entries is to display the revaluation in the balance sheet (while not erasing the historical costs) and to confine the revaluation in the income statement to disclosure of the year's depreciation on appreciation without thereby affecting net income. The unreserved Surplus account is nonetheless reduced as if net income had been lower by the amount of the depreciation on appreciation. "Declinations" would be treated, in a similar manner but with opposite effects, as appreciations. In later years, Paton came to call this treatment "a compromise procedure," as it recognized revaluations without obscuring historical costs or affecting the amount of the net income.[92] Paton defended this compromise as follows:

> Adoption of a policy of charging appreciation to operations, with no accompanying adjustment of profit and surplus figures, [would result] in a record of earnings that fails to satisfy legal requirements and may cause misunderstanding and definite impairment of the rights of particular classes of investors.[93]

Paton also apportioned the appreciation as between the real unrealized gain and the nominal unrealized gain. The latter was treated as a restatement of the Capital and Surplus accounts, while the former (being the residue after reducing the aggregate change in cost by the movement in the general price level) was denominated

92. Paton, *Advanced Accounting*, pp. 343–47.
93. *Ibid.*, p. 349.

as unrealized gain—and was credited to the special stockholders' equity account.[94]

Paton likewise argued against the inclusion of land appreciation in income, "as the enhancement does not represent realized or disposable income."[95] Here the role of income as a dividend base intrudes.

In a discussion of "Appreciation and Income" in the chapter on "Income Determination—Revenue," Paton rehearses the general arguments against booking unrealized appreciation as income. He summarizes his position as follows:

> Many accountants agree that where enhancement in value is unmistakable and is present in large amount it is not objectionable to give recognition thereto in the accounts and statements, although there is no consensus of opinion as to the details of how this should be done. Very few, however, are willing to view unrealized appreciation as genuine business income, no matter how apparent and fully validated the increase in value may be.
>
> The legal attitude is of decided consequence, if not controlling. The accountant is under obligation to report income in a manner that is acceptable in the eyes of the law, although this obligation does not prevent the disclosure of other significant figures.[96]

In *Advanced Accounting*, Paton repeats a suggestion which first appeared in the 1940 monograph, that a reacquisition by a corporation of a significant slice of its outstanding stock at a price different from its book value might be an occasion for recognizing an implied undervaluation or overvaluation of the corporation's assets.[97] This procedure would be parallel to a recommendation routinely made in leading textbooks in regard to partnerships, when the ownership interest of one of the partners is purchased by the partnership at a price above or below its book value—justifying in some circumstances the accounting recognition of an increase or decrease in the partnership goodwill. Thus, if a corporation reacquires a portion of its outstanding stock at a price lower than its book value, rather than recognizing a "profit from retirement," it would make an entry to remove the implied overvaluation of the company's assets. If 10 percent of the company's stock were purchased for $10,000 less than its book value, the overvaluation of ten times the discrepancy, or $100,000, would be eradicated as follows:

94. *Ibid.*, pp. 332–33.
95. *Ibid.*, p. 377.
96. *Ibid.*, p. 452.
97. *Ibid.*, pp. 543–45.

Estimated Loss of Capital and Surplus	$100,000
Allowance for General Revaluation	
of Resources	$100,000

Although individual asset accounts may be found to be overvalued, the Allowance account may be retained as "a blanket contra to resources."

Paton would confine such revaluations to reacquisitions "carried out on terms which are equally fair to both parties—the corporation representing the remaining stockholders on the one hand and the retiring stockholders on the other." Paton continues:

> Assuming good accounting and ignoring wild swings in security prices it may be said that the excess of the price of shares over book values rests primarily on two factors: one, the amount of goodwill and other intangibles which reflect the existence of superior earning power; two, appreciation of existing assets which have not been traced in the accounts. Similarly, where book value exceeds market price under the assumed conditions the difference may largely be explained by reference to lack of earning power and declinations in asset value due to price movements not covered by depreciation accruals and other offsets.

Notwithstanding the evident appeal of this revaluation procedure to one whose deeper sympathies were with the expression in the accounts of current prices, Paton, plagued by doubts so evident in his writings throughout the 1930s and early 1940s, recoiled from a recommendation that the idea actually be implemented:

> While [this revaluation of the stock equity] has intrinsic merit it can hardly be explicitly employed in accounting for stock retirements. Ignoring considerations of law and assuming that a practicable procedure could be worked out—without impairing the usefulness of accounts in other directions—the fact remains that the retirement of a portion of the outstanding stock could seldom be rated as a compelling reason for a complete revaluation of the equity. Certainly the acquisition of a few shares, at what may be a very temporary price, would not be controlling, and even the purchase of a substantial block at an established market or negotiated price would scarcely justify revaluation, particularly where the accounting of the corporation has been on an acceptable basis.

His reasons for declining to recommend the procedure, especially the vague reference to "an acceptable basis" of corporation accounting, seem reluctant and unconvincing.

Paton has advised me that this revaluation procedure occurred to him after reading Warner H. Hord's "The Flow of Property as a Basis of Internal Control" in the *Accounting Review* of September 1939.

Finally, Paton carries forward the upward quasi-reorganization, which he first exposed to view in his Dickinson Lecture a year earlier. Journal entries are proposed for the "fresh start," but Paton's support for the procedure is restrained, owing to the omnipresent legal factors:

> On the score of simplicity the procedure under consideration is all to the good. From the standpoint of adequate recognition of the cost basis and full disclosure of pertinent data, on the other hand, the immediate capitalization of appreciation is not satisfactory. Adoption of a policy of charging appreciation to operations, with no accompanying adjustment of profit and surplus figures, results in a record of earnings that fails to satisfy legal requirements and may cause misunderstanding and definite impairment of the rights of particular classes of investors.[98]

Advanced Accounting may be seen as the most important and complete statement of Paton's views on the impact of changing prices on accounting since the publication in 1924 of *Accounting*. It reflects, on the whole, a caution induced by Paton's continuing preoccupation with the legal confines of accounting. By 1941, he had developed several innovations by which changing prices might find their way into the accounts, but it was not until the postwar period that he became their full-throated advocate.

Response to the Postwar Inflation

Paton was a member of the Committee on Accounting Procedure of the American Institute of Accountants (as it was then known) between 1939, when it began issuing *Accounting Research Bulletins*, and 1950. In 1945, the Committee unanimously recommended that quasi-reorganizations be reflected when asset values were understated as well as overstated. Quasi-reorganizations had been accepted practice for many years when corporations were facing severe financial difficulties and their assets were significantly overvalued. But the Securities and Exchange Commission (SEC) firmly registered its opposition to write-ups under quasi-reorganizations, and the Institute's Committee declined to press the matter further.[99]

In 1947, the Committee issued *Accounting Research Bulletin No. 33*, in which it opposed the incipient practice of recording depreciation based on replacement cost. Paton did not vote on that bulletin, but in 1948, when the Committee issued a letter reaffirming *Bulletin No.*

98. *Ibid.*, p. 349.
99. Stephen A. Zeff, *Forging Accounting Principles in Five Countries: A History and an Analysis of Trends* (Champaign, Ill.: Stipes Publishing Co., 1972), p. 156.

33 in the face of criticism from within the profession, Paton dissented. It was reported that Paton and the three other dissenters

> believe . . . that inflation has proceeded to a point where original dollar costs have already lost their practical significance and that where depreciation is an important element of cost the advantages which would result from a basic change in accounting treatment outweigh the possible disadvantage against it. [100]

The postwar inflation convinced Paton that measures had to be taken—within the legal framework—to restore the financial statements as meaningful economic indicators.

In "Cost and Value in Accounting," a March 1946 article, [101] Paton briefly refers to the (two-way) quasi-reorganization as "the necessary safety valve in a structure of accounting generally based on cost. It furnishes a means under which a corporation may restate its accounts, and provide a new basis of income measurement, without undergoing an actual legal reorganization." [102] In the article, Paton emphasizes that historical costs are not to be treasured in themselves, but are merely the initial indications of value, later subject to revision as conditions change. He writes,

> In fact cost is significant primarily because it approximates fair value at date of acquisition. Cost is not of basic importance because it represents an amount paid; it is important as a measure of the value of what is acquired. . . . The problem in accounting is primarily the question of how cost figures should be dealt with, and when and how they should be revised in view of changing conditions. [103]

Here Paton begins to diverge from the Paton-Littleton devotion to the *fundamental* importance of price-aggregates in accounting reckonings.

In a March 1948 note entitled "What Is Actual Cost in Depreciation Accounting?" Paton criticizes *Bulletin No. 33* for discouraging efforts at dealing with the kinds of changed conditions to which he referred in his March 1946 article. [104] He proposes two possible reforms: (1)

100. "Institute Committee Rejects Change in Basis for Depreciation Charges," *Journal of Accountancy* (Nov. 1948), p. 381.

101. William A. Paton, "Cost and Value in Accounting," *Journal of Accountancy* (March 1946), pp. 192–99. An earlier, but similar, version of this article was drafted by Paton in 1944 for a possible accounting research bulletin to be issued by the Institute's Committee on Accounting Procedure. The proposed bulletin underwent revision within the Committee but did not survive final scrutiny.

102. *Ibid.*, p. 199.

103. *Ibid.*, p. 193.

104. W.A. Paton, "What Is Actual Cost in Depreciation Accounting?" *Journal of Accountancy* (March 1948), pp. 206–7.

supplementary disclosures to financial statements "designed to show the limitations of the conventional, legalistic presentation, in which—erroneously—all dollars are assumed to be homogeneous," and (2) a "fresh start" or quasi-reorganization which "should be defined in such terms as to permit application to all situations in which recorded cost data are so far from economic realities that the resulting reports are misleading, regardless of the arithmetical direction of the adjustment." Ever the skillful debater, Paton, who railed in the 1940s against the infamous "original cost" of the utility regulatory agencies and against federal income taxation based solely on unmodified historical cost, argues that "those who support replacement-cost depreciation are supporting *actual cost* more effectively than those who advocate continued adherence to depreciation based on the so-called 'actual cost.' " He and others hoped that an argument by analogy (a favorite Patonian ploy) would persuade accounting authorities, chiefly the SEC, that quasi-reorganizations could be extended to cover upward revaluations. In that endeavor the Institute's Committee on Accounting Procedure failed in 1945 and failed again in 1950. [105] From its inception in 1934 until the early 1970s, the SEC was an unyielding foe of departures from traditional historical cost in the measurement of income. Only the long-accepted use of downward quasi-reorganizations was countenanced by the SEC when corporations were in financial straits.

In "Accounting Procedures and Private Enterprise," an April 1948 article, Paton suggested three alternative approaches to dealing with the impact on accounting of changing prices:[106] (1) Supplementary disclosure of the pertinent data. (2) A "compromise procedure" for the booking of replacement cost of plant, the recording of depreciation based on the replacement cost, but determination of net income based on conventional, historical cost principles after the depreciation on appreciation was washed out against a stockholders' equity adjustment account. (This alternative was first exposed in *Essentials of Accounting* and was also discussed on pages 815–16 in the third edition of the *Accountants' Handbook*, which Paton edited and largely wrote in 1943.)[107] (3) A quasi-reorganization. [108] He insisted that any

105. Zeff, *Forging Accounting Principles*, pp. 156–57.

106. W.A. Paton, "Accounting Procedures and Private Enterprise," *Journal of Accountancy* (April 1948), pp. 278–91.

107. W.A. Paton, ed., *Accountants' Handbook* (3d ed.; New York: Ronald Press, 1943). It is evident from the editor's preface on p. x that Paton himself wrote the section on "Plant Appraisals," pp. 787–833.

108. Paton, "Accounting Procedures and Private Enterprise," pp. 289–90.

accounting adjustments should "be handled in an orderly, systematic manner and with complete disclosure. Arbitrary increasing or decreasing of the depreciation charge, with no concurrent revision of the basic figures on which depreciation is computed, cannot be supported by the accountant." Here he evidently refers to the efforts in the late 1940s of several large companies (notably United States Steel Corporation, E.I. du Pont de Nemours & Company, and Allied Chemical & Dye Corporation) to record replacement-cost depreciation in their published reports. In this respect, Paton reiterates the view he expressed in "Depreciation, Appreciation and Productive Capacity," published in 1920.

In urging accounting reform, Paton was alarmed by what he regarded as a growing trend toward socialism. American industry was being accused of profiteering and earning excessive rates of return, and Paton feared a crumbling away of the free enterprise system in the wake of such criticism. He foresaw "a great confiscation of private property if the state were to take over business concerns at present book values."[109] He was worried that accountants would concentrate their reform on the income statement, ignoring an understated balance sheet and the resulting overstated measures of earning power. He believed that sound accounting procedures were essential to a preservation of private enterprise. On several occasions, Paton criticized his brethren for playing into the hands of the socialists. In an address given in June 1949, he said,

What is important is that the aggregate of the earnings of American stockholders are being seriously overstated at a time when private property—particularly venture capital in the corporate field—is under attack and undergoing inequitable treatment tax-wise, as features of a strong current in the direction of state socialism. This is certainly a bad time in which to be lending aid and succor to those who are trying to hamstring and destroy private enterprise and our market economy by means— among other things—of accounting records and reports that seriously overstate the actual earnings of venture capital. This is a sad state of affairs and accountants should hang their heads as a result of their part in the process of encouraging misunderstanding and the unwarranted attack on the stake that the millions of common stockholders have in American business.[110]

109. *Ibid.*, p. 290.
110. William A. Paton, "Measuring Profits under Inflation Conditions: A Serious Problem for Accountants," *Journal of Accountancy* (Jan. 1950), p. 21.

Paton's great concern over the impact of overstated profits on decisions involving dividends, wages, prices (including especially those determined by utility regulatory commissions on the basis of "original cost"), and income taxes, evidently convinced him that informative disclosures accompanying a reckoning based on unmodified historical cost were not an adequate solution in most instances.[111] The figures in the financial statements themselves would need to be modified—either by means of his "compromise procedure" or a full-fledged "fresh start."

Paton spoke out frequently during the late 1940s and early 1950s on the dire effects of overstating companies' reported profits.[112] Although he evidently favored the quasi-reorganization approach when current replacement costs differed significantly from historical costs, he also complained of the confusion wrought by changes in the general price level.[113] He attacked on two fronts: relative price changes and economy-wide inflation. The tactical advantage of a general price-level reform would have been its evident objectivity and the commonsense appreciation of the diminishing purchasing power of the dollar. In testimony before the Subcommittee on Profits of the Joint Committee (of the U.S. Congress) on the Economic Report, in late 1948, Paton suggested that "we might call the 1948 unit the zollar, and this would encourage clear thinking when we were comparing the present value of money with, say the 1940 dollar."[114] Paton believed that the illusion that different years' dollars could meaningfully be added or subtracted was fortified by a continuing use of the same term to describe the monetary unit. He was later fond of saying that while accountants would carefully allow for a spread of 2 or 3 percentage points between the American and Canadian dollars, they would ignore altogether changes of 5 and 10 percentage points in successive

111. For Paton's views on the controversy over "original cost," see William A. Paton, "Accounting Policies of the Federal Power Commission—A Critique," *Journal of Accountancy* (June 1944), pp. 432–60.

112. In *Shirtsleeve Economics: A Commonsense Survey* (New York: Appleton-Century-Crofts, Inc., 1952), Paton makes many of his points in nontechnical terms. See pp. 232–58.

113. See, for example, the address by W.A. Paton in *Accounting Problems Relating to the Reporting of Profits* (New Wilmington, Pa.: Economic and Business Foundation, 1949), pp. 10–11.

114. U.S., Congress, *Corporate Profits, Hearings* before the Sub-Committee on Profits of the Joint Committee on the Economic Report, 80th Cong., 2d sess., 1948, p. 62.

American dollars.[115] In pressing his general price-level case, Paton repeatedly cited Henry W. Sweeney's path-breaking 1936 book, *Stabilized Accounting*.

In his congressional testimony in December 1948, Paton also modified his view of the late 1930s that depreciation was, after all, but a relatively small fraction of total expenses—implying that an adjustment of depreciation would not have a material effect on net income. In 1948, he said, "It must not be forgotten that although in many industrial companies the reported depreciation cost figure is not a large fraction of total expenses it may be an important figure when compared with net income."[116]

The base against which materiality should be judged was now net income, not total expenses.

Paton was greatly disturbed over the misuse of accounting information. In his speeches, monographs, and testimony, he dealt in particular with the need to reform the tax base (he recommended replacement-cost depreciation) and to predicate wage increases on sound measures of profit.[117]

ESSENTIALS OF ACCOUNTING (1949)

In the discussion of the valuation of plant, the principal difference between this second edition of *Essentials* and its predecessor of 1938 is the inclusion in the former of a reference to the upward quasi-reorganization. In the two editions, the treatments of general price-level-adjusted financial statements are virtually identical. But in 1949 Paton includes for the first time in *Essentials* a "fresh start" revaluation of assets arising from the reacquisition by the corporation of a significant block of its own shares. Carrying forward his discussion in *Advanced Accounting* (1941) and a commentary in the third edition of the *Accountants' Handbook* (1943) (where, on page 1010, Paton discloses his debt to Hord), Paton writes in *Essentials*:

115. See, for example, William A. Paton, with the assistance of William A. Paton, Jr., *Corporation Accounts and Statements: An Advanced Course* (New York: Macmillan Co., 1955), p. 531.

116. U.S., Congress, *Corporate Profits*, p. 63.

117. Regarding the latter, see his testimony before the Presidential Steel Board, *In the Matter of the United Steelworkers of America—CIO and Republic Steel Corporation et al.* (Aug. 19, 1949) and before the Steel Panel of the Wage Stabilization Board, *In the Matter of the United Steelworkers of America—CIO and Various Steel and Iron Ore Companies* (Feb. 14, 1952).

Assuming that corporation and stockholder are fully informed and acting intelligently on a commercial basis acquisition at a figure materially below book value implies that such value is overstated from the standpoint of going-concern value. . . . Similarly acquisition of shares at a figure materially above book value implies that the going-concern values of specific assets are in excess of book amounts or that unrecognized intangibles, reflecting superior earning power, are present.[118]

This view, which is compared above with a parallel procedure in partnership accounting, also may be shown to be analogous to the allocation of the excess of acquisition cost of a corporation's interest in a subsidiary over the underlying book values of the subsidiary's net assets. Paton's recommended revaluation of assets on the occasion of reacquisition of shares under certain conditions seems to have been generally ignored by his academic colleagues as well as by corporations and practicing accountants. I am aware of only a single comment by other writers on this Patonian innovation.[119] Nonetheless, Paton contends that this version of an accounting "fresh start" should serve to indicate the unreasonableness of the common assumption that a gain to the corporation emerges when shares are acquired at less than book value, or that a loss is suffered when shares are acquired at more than book value.[120]

It is curious that *Essentials* is largely devoid of the enthusiastic advocacy of accounting reform which typified Paton's every speech and article of the period. The reforms are indeed mentioned and in some instances illustrated in the book, but the passionate argument which one finds in Paton's other writings, including some of his later textbooks, is missing here.

ASSET ACCOUNTING (1952)

Asset Accounting was the first of two volumes (the other was *Corporation Accounts and Statements* [1955]) which collectively constituted the revision of *Advanced Accounting* (1941). Here one finds Paton the advocate and debater in full cry. Fresh from the battles of

118. William A. Paton, *Essentials of Accounting* (New York: Macmillan Co., 1949), pp. 710–11.

119. The lone comment appears in the finance literature. See Charles D. Ellis and Allan E. Young, *The Repurchase of Common Stock* (New York: Ronald Press Co., 1971), pp. 128–32. I am grateful to William A. Paton, Jr. for this reference.

120. *Ibid.*, p. 712.

the late 1940s and early 1950s, Paton carries the fight into this intermediate-level textbook.[121]

For internal managerial accounting, Paton recommends that all calculations be based on current prices, not historical costs.[122] In regard to published financial statements, Paton admits that it was "very discouraging" that corporations were doing so little to explain the limitations of conventional, unadjusted figures.

> Corporate earnings have been overstated by many billions in recent years, and such figures have been widely used to fan the fire of misrepresentation of the facts of business operation, but neither accountants nor business managements have done much of anything to put the figures being issued in proper perspective. Public accountants continue to certify financial statements, and insist that they fairly present the picture of earnings and financial position, when they are in fact downright misleading.[123]

This is a bold indictment to appear in a primer on financial accounting.

In a 25-page chapter on "Adjusting Plant Costs and Depreciation," Paton presents and illustrates his three alternative approaches to dealing with the impact of changing prices: supplementary statements showing plant cost, depreciation charges, and stockholders' equity on a current basis; the "compromise procedure"; and the "fresh start." For the first time, Paton illustrates the income statement which would result from adoption of the "compromise procedure" (although on page 816 of the *Accountants' Handbook* (1943) Paton suggests how the statement might appear). His two subtotals would seem to be parallel to Edwards' and Bell's "current operating profit" and "realized profit";[124] Paton, however, would credit Edwards' and Bell's "realizable gains" directly to stockholders' equity. Paton's "compromise procedure" income statement would appear as follows:[125]

---

121. William A. Paton, with the assistance of William A. Paton, Jr., *Asset Accounting: An Intermediate Course* (New York: Macmillan Co., 1952). Internal evidence strongly suggests, and correspondence with William A. Paton, Jr. confirms, that Paton the elder was the de facto author of this book and of *Corporation Accounts and Statements* (see below). Accordingly, Paton, Sr. will be cited as the author of these works.

122. Paton, *Asset Accounting*, pp. 333–34.

123. *Ibid.*, p. 334.

124. Edgar O. Edwards and Philip W. Bell, *The Theory and Measurement of Business Income* (Berkeley, Calif.: University of California Press, 1961), esp. chaps. 4–6.

125. Paton, *Asset Accounting*, p. 343.

Sales and other revenues	$500,000
Expenses, taxes, and other charges (including depreciation on a current cost basis, $12,500)	465,000
Net earnings [Edwards' and Bell's "current operating profit"]	$ 35,000
Increase in plant cost absorbed in year's expenses	7,500
Net earnings on unadjusted basis [Edwards' and Bell's "realized profit"]	$ 42,500

In the course of discussing the "compromise" and "fresh-start" procedures, Paton offers the following criterion for their use: "Only where a major change [in prices] has occurred, that bids fair to be quite persistent, should restatement be undertaken, and this happens only during periods of serious inflation and deflation."[126]

Asset Accounting is rich in colorful expression and is a vintage example of vigorous Patonian argument.[127] In this chapter alone, we are advised, for example, that the "fresh-start" procedure is "simpler than the compromise approach, which involves riding two horses at once."[128] The efforts by several large corporations in the late 1940s to record replacement-cost depreciation are derided as "not very well thought out," "incomplete," "somewhat slipshod," and "half-hearted tinkering with the income statement alone, with no systematic, well-grounded adjustment across the board."[129] The reader is informed that "in the depression days of the early '30s, for example, one of the favored indoor sports in financial management was that of writing down plant." Paton was unflinching in his criticism of those who would applaud writedowns in the early 1930s "no matter how sloppy the procedure and questionable the amount," but who would oppose postwar write-ups which were "carefully substantiated and well worked out on the procedural side."[130] Paton's thinly veiled denunciation

126. *Ibid.*, pp. 349–50.
127. Doubtless one of the more graphic characterizations in accounting textbooks of managerial misunderstanding of accounting information occurs in Paton's discussion of the interpretation sometimes placed on fully amortized fixed assets: "Of course the owner of the amortized facilities can shut his eyes to their economic significance, if he doesn't know any better, but so can the owner of similar assets recently purchased, if he is determined to make an ass of himself." *Ibid.*, p. 309.
128. *Ibid.*, p. 346.
129. *Ibid.*, p. 351.
130. *Ibid.*, p. 354.

of the SEC's undeviating opposition to departures from conventional practice leaps from the page:

> Here is a conspicuous example of the fatuous worship of "decrease" and the indiscriminate condemnation of "increase" long characteristic of many people in financial and accounting circles. It's a ridiculous attitude, with no redeeming savor of professional integrity or competence, and deserves thoroughgoing repudiation by all who are interested in accounting as a means of providing useful and valid compilations and interpretations of the facts of business operation. [131]

Paton declined to recommend any of the three alternative approaches as possessing the greatest merit, although he was already on record in favor of the "fresh-start" procedure. [132]

In a separate chapter, Paton discusses the problems which must be solved in the valuation of plant. For going-concern purposes, he prefers replacement cost to a capitalization of future earnings, as the latter is seldom practicable. [133]

Finally, Paton continues to espouse the accounting recognition of "marked appreciation" in the price of shares, although the reader is encouraged to infer that the credit would be to a special stockholders' equity account, and not to income or to Retained Earnings. [134] This position is unchanged from that in *Advanced Accounting* (1941).

On the whole, *Asset Accounting* shows a clear preference for modifying conventional accounting for plant costs and depreciation charges. Paton was greatly disturbed by allegedly misleading inferences being drawn from conventional financial reports, and he had launched a vigorous campaign for reform.

CORPORATION ACCOUNTS AND STATEMENTS (1955)

As the Patons observe in the preface of *Corporation Accounts and Statements*, "It would not have been altogether inappropriate to have adopted the title 'Equity Accounting' " for the book, as it deals with "the array of problems having to do with the rights of common stockholders, senior investors, and other interested parties. [135]

---

131. *Ibid.*
132. In addition to his remark in *Accounting Problems Relating to the Reporting of Profits* (see above), he took this position in "Measuring Profits Under Inflation Conditions," p. 25.
133. Paton, *Asset Accounting*, p. 360.
134. *Ibid.*, p. 130.
135. Paton, *Corporation Accounts and Statements*, p. v.

Paton's discussion of the accounting recognition of asset value appreciation or declination based on a divergence between the book value and acquisition price of treasury shares is treated more elaborately and with greater enthusiasm than in *Advanced Accounting* (1941). Such acquisitions are divided into two types: those based on an "uneven-deal" assumption and those supported by an "even-deal" assumption. Acquisitions of the uneven-deal type represent bargains or are otherwise "onesided and unfair" and would not yield sound inferences about undervalued or overvalued assets. [136] Where, however, "the terms of the acquisition transaction are fair to both parties"—the "even-deal" assumption, which Paton regards as the much more reasonable interpretation—a revaluation of assets could be defended and would be followed, Paton suggests, by a "fresh-start" accounting for any subsequent depreciation charges. [137] Paton's argument for a revaluation based on the "even-deal" interpretation is energetically advanced:

> Where . . . a substantial fraction of the outstanding shares is acquired (say 5% or more), and the amount paid has been carefully determined in the light of prevailing conditions, and, moreover, there is a substantial difference between book value and the determined market value, it can be urged that a restatement of recorded values, in harmony with the settlement made for the acquired shares, would be fully justified. [138]

Paton continues to oppose the inclusion in income of unrealized appreciation, although his reasoning has changed from that in *Advanced Accounting*. In both books, he cites six "usual arguments" against this practice. As recited in *Corporation Accounts and Statements*, they are:

1. Appreciation of existing assets does not bring about any increase in liquid funds and hence cannot be made a basis for dividend disbursements or payments for any other purpose.

2. An increase in the market value of property intended for sale may be offset by a later decline and hence may never be realized; an increase in the value of property held for use in the business, even if persistent, will be realized only through the process of consumption in production or unexpected liquidation.

3. Appreciation is based on estimate and hence the amount of the enhancement is uncertain.

4. Reporting of appreciation in the income statement, even if the item

---

136. *Ibid.*, p. 191.
137. *Ibid.*, pp. 198, 202.
138. *Ibid.*, p. 204.

were clearly labeled and excluded from operating results, would not be conservative practice.

5. Appreciation is likely to be largely a reflection of a change in the general level of prices, and thus represents an adjustment of capital rather than true income.

6. Appreciation has no legal standing as income.[139]

In both books, Paton regards the first argument as "decisive" for fixed assets but possessing "less force" for current assets. Yet even in the case of current assets, Paton continues, the appreciation may not be in the form of disposable funds. Also in both books, the second point is said to have merit. "Obviously," he writes, "appreciation of asset value is not on a level with accounts receivable, resulting from delivery of product, as evidence of the presence of revenue. Aside from the possibility of failure to collect, usually of minor importance, revenue is conclusively and finally determined by sale of product, whereas realization of appreciation depends on future events." In both books, Paton views the third and fourth arguments as "less serious," since "no one has ever advocated booking appreciation except where the evidence is convincing [sic!]," and accountants have, in his opinion, placed undue reliance on conservatism.[140]

In regard to the fifth and sixth arguments, however, Paton takes different positions in the two books. In *Advanced Accounting*, Paton observes that the argument is "important" when the change in specific prices is matched by movements in the general level of prices, but this point "is offset somewhat by the fact that conventional earned income likewise may not represent an increase in effective purchasing power."[141] In the 1955 book, however, Paton says that the fifth argument "has special importance in view of the inflationary condition which has prevailed in recent years," but after repeating the countervailing point of 1941, he concludes that "it would not improve matters to adopt the policy of regarding nominal unrealized appreciation as a form of income."[142] By "matters," Paton could well be referring to the many misleading interpretations that he had been attributing to grossly overstated corporate profits. Thus, Paton's new stance on the fifth argument may be traced to changed economic conditions and especially to Paton's

139. *Ibid.*, p. 298.
140. *Ibid.*, pp. 298–99.
141. Paton, *Advanced Accounting*, p. 452.
142. Paton, *Corporation Accounts*, p. 299.

great concern over the consequences of overstated profits. His altered view of the sixth argument reflects a lesser preoccupation with legal arguments which tended to dominate his thinking in the 1930s and early 1940s. In *Advanced Accounting*, Paton writes, "The legal attitude is of decided consequence, if not controlling."[143] Fourteen years later, in *Corporation Accounts and Statements*, he says, "The legal attitude . . . is of consequence, although not necessarily controlling."[144]

Finally, Paton devotes an entire chapter to what he now calls "Uniform-Dollar Accounting." It is by far his most extensive treatment, in textbooks or articles, of general price-level accounting, and is twice the length of the comparable chapter in *Advanced Accounting*. He again exhibits his desire not to be confined to what the law requires. He writes:

> There is more involved [in accounting] than prevailing legal rules and concepts. More and more the accounting process is being relied upon as the major means of compiling and interpreting the economic data of business enterprise, for operating management, for current and prospective investors, for legislative bodies interested in basic problems of policy, and in other connections. And accounting cannot possibly fulfill its obligations in these directions by remaining blind to the limitations of raw accounting data in the face of a major and sustained decline in the purchasing power of the dollar. Moreover, there is no reason why accounting should not lead the way to changes in the legal structure as it relates to business enterprise in so far as new conditions provide a valid basis for such changes.[145]

Paton's chapter on "uniform-dollar reporting" is not a neutral, bland presentation. It is vigorous, undiluted advocacy, drawing on Paton's considerable skills as a debater. All of the color found in the best examples of Patonian rhetoric is present here in abundance. He marshals arguments of diverse kinds—from intrinsic deficiencies in accounting measurement to the necessity of replying effectively to "the enemies of private enterprise"—in order to fortify the conclusion that unconverted historical costs, in periods of significant inflation, yield misleading information.[146] Paton concedes that figures expressed in specific current costs would be more useful to internal management than historical costs which are expressed in converted dollars. But as a "year-by-year appraisal of all the assets of the

143. Paton, *Advanced Accounting*, p. 452.
144. Paton, *Corporation Accounts*, p. 299.
145. *Ibid.*, pp. 526–27.
146. *Ibid.*, p. 540.

enterprise [is] ordinarily impracticable," converted historical cost "can be strongly defended."[147] Since his first utterances on the impact of changing prices in *Principles of Accounting* (1916), Paton has preferred the specific cost solution. For tactical and pragmatic reasons, however, he has often proposed the conversion of historical cost into dollars of current purchasing power, but only in supplementary statements. But there was another argument for "uniform-dollar reporting": to place multi-earnings summaries and other inter-year financial presentations on a comparable basis. As corporations began to point to trends in earnings and other financial statistics, Paton believed that the "raw figures of the successive years are literally not comparable, and showing them in juxtaposition without explanation [or conversion] is almost sure to lead to misinterpretation."[148]

In *Corporation Accounts and Statements*, Paton abandons his support of Sweeney's view that the gains and losses on monetary items should be treated as realized only to the extent that the monetary assets are utilized or the monetary liabilities are settled. Paton now regards the gains and losses on *current* monetary items as being realized when the relevant index changes, but the gain or loss on long-term debt is still unrealized until it is paid. His logic is as follows:

> The recognition of a current liability has long been regarded as having substantially the same force as an expenditure, and the current receivables have long been regarded as providing an adequate foundation for the booking of revenue. And when it comes to cash on hand—purchasing power as such—it is hard to see justification for the contention that a change in value is not realized until there is an actual disbursement.[149]

One finds, therefore, that Paton incorporated in *Asset Accounting* and *Corporation Accounts and Statements* the essence and full force of the arguments he made during the late 1940s and early 1950s in speeches, congressional testimony, submissions to government panels, and articles. Both books are faithful to the view that positive action must be taken to accommodate accounting to an environment of changing prices. In a sense, Paton came full circle from his undiluted idealism of 1917–18, through a long period of doubt and reassessment of his position in the face of changing economic conditions, to a renewed call for accounting reform. To be sure, the

147. *Ibid.*, p. 537.
148. *Ibid.*, p. 554.
149. *Ibid.*, p. 550.

latter-day Paton was much influenced by his fundamental belief in the efficacy of the free enterprise system and in the role which he believed that accounting must play to counter the misguided critics of private enterprise. This is not to suggest that Paton's specific policy recommendations of the late 1940s and 1950s were identical to those of the 1910s. They were not. Following the 1910s, he never again embraced the general proposition that income should be credited with unrealized appreciation. Furthermore, the Paton of the 1940s and 1950s was more alive to the tactics of devising a *form* of revised accounting that might appeal to the authorities and the accounting establishment. An apt example would be his tailoring of the quasi-reorganization, a device originally intended to deal exclusively with overvalued assets, to the circumstance of undervalued assets. Doubtless his twelve years of service on the Committee on Accounting Procedure heightened his sensitivity to the tactics of accounting reform. The Paton of the 1940s and 1950s was a more clever and resourceful advocate than was the idealist of the 1910s.

Conclusion

One is able to discern four periods in the evolution of Paton's writings on the impact of changing prices on accounting. The first period, 1916–18, is typified by youthful idealism. Paton is confident of his position and confidently dismisses most criticisms. He sees an integral role in the financial statements for replacement costs, but by the end of this period he only dimly perceives the possibilities of general price-level disclosures.

The years from 1920 to near the end of the 1930s were ones of reassessment and reconsideration of the place of replacement costs in financial accounting. At the outset of the period, he began to retreat from his earlier advocacy of crediting appreciation to income. By the mid-1930s, he seemed to conclude that replacement costs are better reported in supplementary disclosures than in the body of the financial statements. Concerns over the unscientific appraisals during the 1920s, the economic stagnation of the early 1930s, and the growing importance of legal considerations in business operation seem to have been influential. During this period, however, the possible role of general price-level disclosures appeared to grow in importance, and the publication in 1936 of Sweeney's *Stabilized Accounting* was doubtless a significant event.

From the late 1930s to the end of World War II, Paton devised a number of accounting stratagems by which replacement costs might find their way into the financial statements without doing violence to accounting conventions. That this period coincided with the first six years of Paton's service on the Institute's Committee on Accounting Procedure may not have been altogether an accident. He proposed upward quasi-reorganizations, revaluations based on the discrepancy between the book value and reacquisition price of large blocks of treasury shares, and a "compromise procedure" for booking replacement costs without passing their effects through net income. During the same period, his advocacy of the supplemental disclosure of general price-level effects accelerated, and by the end of the war, the positions which he had espoused in his famous 1940 monograph with A.C. Littleton, *An Introduction to Corporate Accounting Standards*, evidently were undergoing a change.

Following the war, his arguments in favor of an accounting recognition of replacement costs or of supplementary general price-level disclosures, or of a combination of the two, veritably reached the fever pitch of a campaign, and in his articles, speeches, and even textbooks, he passionately called for accounting reform. The postwar attack on the excessive profits of large American corporations, coupled with the trend which he detected toward socialism, galvanized his energies to defend the free enterprise system and to urge accountants, Congress, the SEC, and government wage tribunals to recognize that conventional accounting practices did not accurately reflect profits during inflationary times.

Through all of his active career, Paton has been highly attuned to the economic circumstances in which corporations find themselves. Although historical analysis does not admit of rigorously defensible interpretations of the factors which might have motivated a writer at different points in his career, the evidence adduced in this paper strongly suggests that some kind of accounting reform to deal with the effects of changing prices was never far from Paton's mind even in the 1930s. Prior to the post-World War II period, his was a lonely crusade, and his writings show that he was sensitive both to the problems wrought by changing economic times as well as to criticisms by others of a replacement-cost solution (e.g., that the questionable appraisals of the 1920s might reappear). Without sacrificing his basic belief that historical cost accounting per se does not deal adequately with changing prices, he retreated in the 1930s until he had devised procedures that could give effect to his beliefs while overcoming the earlier criticisms. In this light therefore, Paton's succession of changed positions on the accounting response to changing prices reflects more his attempt to develop defensible procedures to achieve his fundamental objectives than a rethinking or recanting of his objectives and basic beliefs.

March 1978

THE ACCOUNTING REVIEW
Vol. LVII, No. 3
July 1982

Truth in Accounting: The Ordeal of Kenneth MacNeal

Stephen A. Zeff

ABSTRACT: Kenneth MacNeal was the author of *Truth in Accounting*, a 1939 book known for its undiluted advocacy of "economic value" accounting. Thus far, MacNeal's book and other writings, though cited, have not been subjected to in-depth analysis. Nothing is publicly known about MacNeal's background, how he came to write the book, how it was received, and why he ceased contributing to the accounting literature a scant two years after the appearance of the book. In this article, MacNeal's work is placed in an historical frame, and the principal arguments in his book are critically examined. Finally, an incident, hitherto unreported in the accounting literature, in which MacNeal was commissioned by *Fortune* to write an article critical of the accounting profession in the wake of the McKesson & Robbins scandal, only to be told, under suspicious circumstances, that the commission had been rescinded, is related.

K ENNETH MacNeal is widely known as author of a vigorous advocacy of market-based valuations in financial statements. His magnum opus, *Truth in Accounting*, was published in 1939 by the University of Pennsylvania Press and was reprinted in 1970 by Scholars Book Co. His book continues to be cited and discussed in accounting theory seminars more than 40 years after its initial appearance. MacNeal wrote three articles in *The Nation* [1939b, c; 1941a][1] and one in *The Accounting Forum* [1941b].[2] Thus, his entire published output occurred between 1939 and 1941.

Virtually nothing can be found in the accounting literature about MacNeal. What was his trade or profession? What motivated him to break into print with a book that defied the conventional wisdom of his day? How was the book received in the literature? And, finally, what became of MacNeal—and why did his published writings reach an abrupt end in 1941? This article throws some light on these questions and evaluates MacNeal's contribution to the accounting literature.

This article consists of eight parts. First, some biographical data on Mac-Neal are presented, followed by a brief

[1] MacNeal's "What's Wrong with Accounting?" [1939b, c] became known to readers of the accounting literature when it was reprinted in Baxter [1950] and Baxter and Davidson [1962; 1977].

[2] MacNeal is also shown as author of "Shortcomings of Some Accepted Accounting Principles Under Modern Conditions," *The Annalist* (July 13, 1939), pp. 38–39, but this article is omitted here as it appears to consist of a straight reprinting of a few pages of *Truth in Accounting*.

The author gratefully acknowledges the useful comments and suggestions of R. J. Chambers, William W. Cooper, Roman L. Weil, G. Edward Philips, Loyd Heath, Robert J. Coombes, Frank L. Clarke, Geoffrey Whittington, and especially George Foster and Philip W. Bell.

Stephen A. Zeff is Herbert S. Autrey Professor of Accounting, Rice University.

Manuscript received September 1981.
Accepted (by the Editor-elect) October 1981.

The editorial review process for this article was conducted by the Editor-elect, Gary L. Sundem.

528

discussion of the reason why he wrote *Truth in Accounting*. The longest section is an examination of the main points of the argument presented in his book, and this is followed by a discussion of the major published criticism of the book. Then the source of MacNeal's well-known article, "What's Wrong With Accounting?", is traced, including the controversy attending its publication in *The Nation* instead of *Fortune*, whose editors had originally commissioned the article. Following a brief treatment of the contributions of early valuation theorists, the influence of MacNeal's writings among professionals, policy makers, and academics is reviewed. In the final section, a few concluding remarks are offered.

PERSONAL DATA

Kenneth Forsythe MacNeal (he never used his middle name) was born in Berwyn, Illinois on December 20, 1895. His father, Arthur W. MacNeal, was a physician and later founded what is today known as the MacNeal Memorial Hospital in Berwyn. He was educated in J. Sterling Morton High School in suburban Chicago and entered the University of Chicago in September, 1912, majoring in commerce and administration. He took but three courses in accounting, all taught by Jay Dunne (A.B., Michigan), an Instructor in Accounting: Introductory (B-), Intermediate (B), and Cost (C). Overall, his grades were a mixture of B's, C's, D's, and, finally, a quarter of F's. In January, 1916, he was dismissed, formally, for "poor work," but he explained to friends that the real reason was an excess of absences from class. It was said that this brush with University authorities was a source of pride, as it was the first evidence of his independent thinking.[3] While MacNeal was at the University of Chicago, John B.

Canning was taking courses and lecturing, but I have found no evidence that the two ever met. On the social side, MacNeal was active in Phi Gamma Delta fraternity.

In 1915–1916, he took three accounting courses in Northwestern University's School of Commerce, receiving a grade in only one. His courses were Accounting II and III (taught by David Himmelblau) and CPA Quiz (taught by Arthur E. Andersen, founder of Arthur Andersen & Co.), in which he received a grade of C. After two years of service with the U.S. Army in France during the World War (1917–1919), MacNeal enrolled for a brief period in the Université de Montpellier. He then returned to the United States and took the Uniform CPA Examination in November, 1919. His performance on the examination earned him the Gold Medal from the State of Illinois. He received Certificate No. 234 in April, 1920. He received a reciprocal certificate from Pennsylvania in 1944.

He married Marguerite Giroud on March 19, 1921, and they later had three children: Richard Henri, Edward Arthur, and Marguerite Louise.

MacNeal began his professional career in 1916 (at the age of 20), while attending Northwestern University. In January of that year, he joined the staff of Price, Waterhouse & Co., in Chicago, and in the Preface of *Truth* he mentions his early exposure to the conventional accounting wisdom and proceeds to state the premise of his book:

I was warned [at Price, Waterhouse] that accounting was, after all, "only common sense." Perhaps this warning was meant as an

[3] Related in introductory comments by Harold C. Stott, in "Remarks by Kenneth MacNeal, C.P.A. (Illinois), copied from Stenotype Operator's Report of Annual Meeting of Pennsylvania Institute of Certified Public Accountants—June 19, 1939" (Kenneth MacNeal Scrapbook).

antidote for undigested economic theories, acquired from two universities, in which I had much faith. Be that as it may, the intervening years of experience, in both public and private work, have not tended to confirm in me the idea that accounting is only common sense. . . . Yet . . . the vital defect in present accounting practice is its disharmony with the simpler principles of economics and logic, commonly called common sense [p. xi].

He remained with Price, Waterhouse & Co. until February, 1917, and then he left for France. Beginning in the 1920s, MacNeal occupied a series of accounting and financial positions in a number of Philadelphia enterprises which embraced manufacturing, building construction, and hotel, real estate, and financial projects. In 1929–1930, as a treasurer in an investment trust, he was immediate and directing head of a staff of five other CPAs which conducted an extensive five-year analysis of the published financial statements of all companies listed on the New York Stock Exchange. In 1944, he founded a small firm of CPAs in Philadelphia, known as MacNeal & Co., and later as MacNeal, Keetz & Allen.

MacNeal retired in the early 1960s, and he died on March 16, 1972.

BACKGROUND TO THE BOOK

According to MacNeal, the stimulus for his book arose in a dispute with Price, Waterhouse & Co. in 1930. In a long letter written on May 17, 1940 to Henry Rand Hatfield, MacNeal related that "P.W. & Co. were at that time auditing an investment trust which we controlled, and had refused to show the portfolio at market values and to exhibit the unrealized profits in the income statement." MacNeal drafted the "Fable of the Two Investment Trusts," which later appeared in the first chapter of *Truth*, in an effort to persuade the auditors to his view. The "Fable" shows how

the managers of two portfolios of securities, each of which has risen in value, can elect the fiscal period in which to recognize the gain as accounting profit merely by the decision of when to dispose of the portfolio. MacNeal says in the letter that PW evidently was impressed with his argument, although George O. May, then the PW senior partner, was reported as saying that it might be some time before practice would be likely to accept MacNeal's treatment of unrealized profits. Nonetheless, MacNeal writes, PW consented to have "the statements . . . prepared on a strictly present value basis, with unrealized profits shown in the body of the income account and included in the total profits earned." "At the time," MacNeal writes, "I can remember thinking that perhaps this was the first time a reputable firm of C.P.A.'s had ever done such a thing, and I remember feeling quite proud of myself."[4]

The victory in his bout with PW led MacNeal to undertake a "holy crusade" to bring about a change in accounting practice. It took seven years for MacNeal to complete the manuscript for the book that was eventually to be published under the provocative title, *Truth in Accounting*. MacNeal sent the typescript to several friends in CPA firms for their opinions, and he also sent copies to a number of publishers. It was rejected by McGraw-Hill Book Company, The Ronald Press Company, and Prentice-Hall, Inc. MacNeal then approached the University of Pennsylvania Press. (He was a resident of Philadelphia, where the Press was located.) Before reaching a decision, the Press obtained the views of an economist and an accounting academic. Both con-

---

[4] I found MacNeal's letter to Hatfield both in the Kenneth MacNeal Scrapbook and in the Hatfield Papers, Accounting Area, Schools of Business Administration, University of California, Berkeley.

sultants reported favorably, and the Press offered to publish MacNeal's manuscript.[5]

The book was dedicated to Lawrence E. Jones. In correspondence, MacNeal explained Jones's role in the project as follows:

Lawrence E. Jones was a Phi Gam brother with whom I was associated, off and on, for a great many years, starting with a partnership in Chicago in 1915.

[He] was quite a guy. Without putting them into words, he made the "Three Fables" [related in the first chapter of MacNeal's book] work for him all his life. I was younger than he and his contempt for accountants' figures and his understanding of their shortcomings could not fail to leave its mark on me. Eventually this resulted in my effort to explain a situation that few accountants would admit existed.[6]

Jones died a millionaire in 1961 at the age of 73. He was a successful inventor, although most of his career was spent in real estate development. For a number of years, he was president and MacNeal was secretary-treasurer of various building corporations associated with the Alden Park complex, in Philadelphia.

An Examination of *Truth in Accounting*

MacNeal's overriding concern in his writings is with the small investor. His argument is that small investors are deceived by financial statements that are predicated on the accountant's notions of "realization" and "conservatism."

In the first quarter of the book, he states the problem, examines some contradictions in a sample of major accounting treatises, endeavors to understand the reasons behind the realization and conservatism concepts, and traces the historical evolution of accounting practice—during all of which he reiterates his main contention, *viz.*, that small investors are being misled by financial statements that are not based on economic values.

In his first chapter, MacNeal presents three "Fables." Each "Fable" illustrates how the notions of realization and conservatism can be misleading. In the first "Fable," a small investor, relying totally on conventional financial statements, misjudges the worth of an investment. In the second, two flour mills are being compared. One had invested most of its funds in wheat, and the other had invested a like amount in interest-bearing securities. At the end of one period, by which time the price of wheat had doubled, the second mill liquidated its holding of securities, reported interest income in its certified financial statements, and used its proceeds from the sale of the securities to purchase wheat at the higher price. Thus, the second mill had half as much wheat as the first mill. The first mill continued to hold its wheat, and no gain owing to the increase in market price was reported in its certified financial statements. A banker, noting that both companies had an identical number of *dollars* invested in wheat but that only the second mill had reported any profit for the period, advised a small investor to invest in the second mill. The moral is that the accountant's realization test can mislead bankers and small investors.

In the third, MacNeal's well-known "Fable of the Two Investment Trusts," the financiers of two trusts which hold securities that are appreciating in price succeed in "fooling" the market by

[5] The Press's consultants were Professors Ernest Minor Patterson, the economist, and Edward Needles Wright, the accounting academic, both of the Wharton School, University of Pennsylvania. MacNeal proposed that he defray the costs of manufacture, and the Press accepted his manuscript on those terms.

[6] Letters dated August 2, 1963 and September 3, 1963 from MacNeal to the writer.

alternating the years in which each trust realizes its gain. The securities market is assumed to bid up the price of the trust that has realized its gains, and to bid down the price of the trust showing no such accounting gains during the period. MacNeal characterizes the market reaction as follows:

> ... as soon as the certified financial statements of the American Trust and of the National Trust were mailed to stockholders and printed in the newspapers, everybody learned that the American Trust had earned 23% on its capital stock during the year whereas the National Trust had earned only 3% on its capital stock. The price of the American Trust stock therefore rose sharply as many investors rushed to buy it, and the price of the National Trust stock dropped sharply due to selling by disappointed stockholders [p. 12].

The financiers of the two trusts sell a portion of their shares in the American Trust and buy more shares in the National Trust. In the following year, gains accrue on the investment holdings of both trusts, and the National Trust is instructed to sell its holdings, thus recognizing two years of gains in its profit and loss statement. The market reacts in like manner as in the first year, and the financiers dispose of a block of their shares in the National Trust and buy shares in the American Trust.[7]

Following the second "Fable," MacNeal does not tell his readers why a banker would regard financial statements as representing the worth of a company's assets. In the third "Fable," MacNeal does not explain why the aggregate securities market would be "fooled" by financial statements known to embody the realization and conservatism concepts, particularly when, as MacNeal indicates in this "Fable," the market values of the investments held by the two trusts were disclosed by each in a footnote.[8] He simply asserts that "most of the public did not pay much attention"

to the footnotes and, moreover, "[t]he few people who did see and understand the footnote disregarded it" because they knew that the unrealized gain would be wiped out prior to sale if the prices of the investments were soon to fall [pp. 11–12].[9] Except in his discussion of the third "Fable," MacNeal confines his argument to the supposed impact on the small investor and his advisers. MacNeal offers no defense of the view that the aggregate market could be deceived, indeed systematically deceived period after period, by financial statements known to reflect the notions of realization and conservatism, even when public disclosure were made of market prices on the balance-sheet date. It was not until the 1960s that researchers began to study the impact of accounting information on the aggregate market as opposed to the individual investor (see, e.g., Beaver [1981]).

In Chapters II and III, MacNeal skillfully exposes accounting authorities[10]

[7] In 1973, a committee of the American Institute of Certified Public Accountants recommended that the current market values of portfolio holdings and the resulting unrealized gains and losses be presented in the audited financial statements of investment companies [AICPA, 1973, Chap. 2]. This was, I believe, the first official acceptance of this position by the American accounting profession. Several works are cited in the AICPA Audit Guide, but MacNeal's book is not among them.

[8] MacNeal evidently did not regard footnote disclosure as an issue, for, in his rendering of this "Fable" in "What's Wrong with Accounting?" [MacNeal, 1939c, pp. 410–411], he omits mention of any footnotes.

[9] Page numbers shown alone refer to MacNeal [1939a].

[10] In Chapter II, MacNeal quotes at length from Hatfield [1909 (1913 printing)], Montgomery [1912 (1913 printing)], Dickinson [1913 (1914 printing)], and Esquerré [1914 (1915 printing)]. Why did he choose these particular works? Hatfield had revised his 1909 book in 1927, and Montgomery had since published three revisions of his 1912 volume. MacNeal is sensitive to the question. He writes:

> The four accounting works quoted in this chapter may be mistakenly assumed by some to be out of date inasmuch as the first edition of each was pub-

who, on the one hand, contend that financial statements should figure importantly in the making of economic decisions but, on the other, prescribe rules such as realization and conservatism which would generate information of little use for economic decision making. MacNeal writes,

> ... although accounting authorities do at times seem to give lip service to the idea that balance sheets should exhibit real values as of the date of the balance sheet, they advocate methods which make the exhibition of such values almost impossible [p. 32].

In Chapter II, MacNeal reviews the theoretical justifications for the realization and conservatism notions, and finds them wanting. He writes, "Conservatism will not appeal to intelligent individuals as a valid argument when it is used in defense of untruths which may cause widespread injustice" [p. 52]. He believes that, while the notion of "going value" (i.e., the use of original cost for assets) made sense when financial statements were of interest only to owner-managers, its use "ignores all consideration of creditors and inactive stockholders" [p. 48]. He adds that "uninformed, temporary stockholders are hopelessly deceived, not only as to the value of the assets behind their stock, but also as to the earnings of their company" [p. 48]. Finally, he rejects May's proposal (though he does not name May, who was then the powerful senior partner of Price, Waterhouse & Co., anywhere in the book) that listed companies should publish a summary of the accounting principles and practices used in their financial statements. May believed that investors, provided with such a summary, would be in a much better position to appreciate what financial statements do and do not report about a company.[11] MacNeal saw it as "a hopeless task to attempt to educate millions of stock-

holders regarding present accounting principles" [p. 56]. A more feasible answer, argued MacNeal, was to bring accounting principles into line with "simple truth as it is instinctively understood by laymen everywhere" [p. 57].

In Chapter IV, the last chapter before MacNeal begins to present his preferred concept of economic-value accounting, he lapses into an unfortunate 12-page digression on early bookkeeping techniques and treatises—unfortunate because, first, the great majority of readers would have found it to be of no interest or relevance, and, second, at least according to Hatfield, it contains numerous errors.[12] He follows this section with

---

lished over twenty years ago. In the writer's opinion, these books still constitute the most representative works on accounting in this country [and they have] exerted a dominating influence on the formation of current American accounting thought [p. 25, n. 2].

I think it is more likely that MacNeal selected books that had become known to him during his studies at the University of Chicago and Northwestern University in 1912–1916 and perhaps during his brief employment with Price, Waterhouse & Co. in 1916–1917. Since the period 1913–1915 (the printing dates of his cited works), major treatises had been written by Kester, Paton, Finney, Saliers, Canning, Rorem, and Scott, among others, and MacNeal cites none of their writings. One is therefore dubious that the four cited works could have been said to "constitute the most representative works on accounting" by the close of the 1930s. MacNeal does, however, discuss Sweeney [1936], as is brought out below.

[11] May was the principal author of the letter dated September 22, 1932 from the Special Committee on Co-operation with Stock Exchanges of the American Institute of Accountants, to the New York Stock Exchange, in which the proposal was first formulated (see *Audits of Corporate Accounts* [1934])

[12] In a letter dated November 17, 1939, Hatfield sent MacNeal a three-page, single-spaced corrigenda, dealing chiefly with MacNeal's pages 61 to 72 (the bookkeeping history). It became evident that MacNeal had relied heavily on Green [1930], one of three historical works cited in a footnote on page 58, which is a book that Hatfield had found to be "crudely inaccurate" [Hatfield, 1940, p. 15]. (Hatfield reviewed the Green book in *The Journal of Accountancy* [Hatfield, 1931]). In a letter to Hatfield dated November 30, 1939, MacNeal admitted a number of proofreading errors and misstatements, and regretted his naive reliance on Green [1930]. Hatfield Papers, Accounting Area, Schools of Business Administration, University of California, Berkeley.

a more pertinent discussion of the historical development of accounting practices against the background of the evolution of business enterprise. As MacNeal's available sources provided only thin support for this more germane historical foray,

> it seems necessary to endeavor to reconstruct conditions as they existed from medieval times and to attempt to deduce therefrom the probable development of these principles in the light of those conditions [p. 70].

In doing so, MacNeal interpolates liberally and with an occasional dash of cynicism. He identifies the eras of (1) the owner-manager, (2) the creditor, and (3) the "small uninformed security holder" [p. 82], and concludes that the accounting practices still in use in 1939 were those suited mainly to the first two eras—and that they are woefully anachronistic in the era of broad equity capital markets. Warming to his passionate sense of mission, and perhaps remembering the successes of Lawrence E. Jones, MacNeal assailed accountants for their ineptitude in serving small investors:

> In other words, the millions of small investors who own the great industries of this country, and of other countries, are unable to learn the truth about their own properties and are left at the mercy of individuals with inside information who may care to prey on them, largely because the accounting profession sees fit to turn out reports which, in many cases, are misleading and untrue, and whose preparation is in accordance with principles suited only to conditions existing many years ago. The simple truth of the matter is that an accountant's present knowledge and training do not wholly qualify him to prepare correct financial statements. If accountants would complete their educations, to the end that they might adopt sound accounting principles and might be fitted to value those assets whose economic values are not immediately apparent, they would be so qualified. Accountants must either become valuers, or must employ valuers, if they are to prepare truthful financial statements. Financial statements purport

to deal with present economic values, and they are apt to be useful only to the extent that they do. They are extremely apt to be mischievous to the extent that they do not do so [p. 84].

This is only one of many places in the book where MacNeal "lectures" accountants, and the effect was doubtless to rankle most of those upon whom he had hoped to make a favorable impact.

In the remaining three-quarters of his book, MacNeal methodically builds a case for accounting in terms of economic values. He devotes Chapter V to a primer on demand, supply, and the nature of value, and in Chapter VI he discourses on the nature of money as a medium of pricing and exchange. Half of the chapter on money is taken up with a critical discussion of Sweeney's "stabilized accounting" [1936]. He praises Sweeney (whose name he consistently misspells as "Sweeny") for having "clearly seen the glaring faults of accepted accounting principles" [p. 123]. In like vein, MacNeal adds:

> The result is, within the limits of accuracy of the data available an exhaustive and mathematically impregnable system for displaying changes in purchasing power. Whether or not one approves the concept employed by Stabilized Accounting, he must admit that it completely achieves its announced purpose [p. 123].

But MacNeal objects to Sweeney's general price-level concept on two grounds. First, the "stabilized" profit and loss statement, which would be expressed in purchasing power as of the balance-sheet date and not as of the dates of the several transactions, "may be far beyond the comprehension of the ordinary man or woman who would have to depend for financial information upon the figures presented" [pp. 123–124]. Further: "Such data would not inform the ordinary stockholder or the ordinary director. It would merely make him doubt the accountant's sanity" [p. 124]. MacNeal thus reiterates his theme that accountants should present financial statements that would be readily understood by stockholders, rather than expect stockholders to learn special accounting meanings, e.g., original cost/realization results, or purchasing-power-adjusted results. MacNeal's second objection is that stockholders and businessmen already understand intuitively that today's dollars are worth less than the dollars of a year or years ago, and it is unlikely that Sweeney's "stabilized accounting" would, therefore, tell them any more than they already know. That MacNeal may have less than fully understood the phenomenon for which Sweeney was endeavoring to account, is suggested by the following passage:

> If the general commodity index doubled during a year, [Sweeney's] Stabilized Accounting would show both the original capital account and surplus account at twice their former amounts and would omit the amount of this increase from earnings, whereas the writer would exhibit the capital account and surplus account unchanged and would show the entire increase in net worth as earnings [p. 116].

According to MacNeal, accounting must meet the common-sense expectations of the readers:

> A balance sheet and a profit and loss statement purport to state values. In order to fulfill their purpose, they must state values according to economic concepts, commonly called economic values, because these are the only values that anyone knows how to state [p. 86].

"Economic value" is "its 'power in exchange' which, measured in money, is its market price. The market price of a thing is the price at which it *is actually being bought and sold*" [p. 87; emphasis in original]. MacNeal makes it abundantly clear that he is not interested in "future improbabilities, probabilities, or

even certainties" [p. 146]. He would reject Canning's "direct valuation" [1929, Chap. XI], although nowhere in the book does MacNeal actually discuss the possible use of discounted present values of future cash flows. "It is an accountant's duty to deal with the facts as he find them, not to alter them to conform to some imaginary action on the part of his client" [p. 44].

In Chapter VI, "Market Prices," MacNeal describes at some length the circumstances in which acceptable market prices could be obtained. His ideal is to have free, competitive, broad, and active markets. The key terms are defined as follows:

> "A free market is one in which no constituted authority interferes with the free functioning of supply and demand" [p. 129].

> "A competitive market is one where buyers and sellers compete not only with each other but among themselves" [p. 129].

> "A market is broad to the extent that its prices represent the counteraction of world supply and demand" [p. 131].

> An active market is one in which transactions occur frequently or in which bid and offered quotations are available [p. 133].

MacNeal acknowledges that ideal conditions seldom obtain, and he advises accountants how they should proceed when imperfections exist. Of particular interest is his insistence that acceptable market prices are to be used strictly and without modification to value a company's assets. If a company holds a large block of securities, for example, the prevailing market price should not be modified downward (for asset-valuation purposes) on the assumption that it would be depressed if such a large block of shares were immediately sold.[13] Nor

---

[13] It is interesting to note that this position is consistent with the "substitution hypothesis" discussed by Scholes [1972] in relation to the impact of a block sale on the price of a security. Scholes examined the price

should an estimated broker's commission be deducted from the valuation, or should a liability for estimated income taxes be reflected [p. 144]. "[T]he value of a thing is not what it *could* be sold for *if* it were offered for sale. Its value is what it *is being bought and sold for* or, if it is not being bought and sold, its logical price under the ratio of supply and demand that *actually exists*" [p. 143]. This advice would not have been gladly received by a profession which employed "net realizable value"—i.e., estimated selling prices less expected cost of carrying, selling, and delivering—in its computation of "lower of cost or market" for inventories (see, e.g., Montgomery [1934, pp. 209–210]). MacNeal adjures the accountant not to make predictions of the unknowable future:

Many things may happen in the future to prevent a sale, a broker's commission, or an income tax. An accountant should not act as a prophet. Creditors and stockholders can do that as well as he can [p. 145].

As indicated above, MacNeal imposes strict conditions on what constitutes an acceptable market, and it soon becomes evident that not many assets are traded in such markets. Thus, where acceptable markets are not available for particular assets, surrogate measures must be found, and in Chapters VIII and IX MacNeal recommends candidates. Assets are classified into three kinds:

marketable,
nonmarketable and reproducible, and
nonmarketable and nonreproducible.

Surrogates apply to the second and third kinds. For nonmarketable and reproducible assets, MacNeal recommends replacement cost, which is defined as

the cost of reproducing a thing plus a profit sufficient to provide a motive for so doing. In this definition any two things are assumed to be alike if their utilities or serviceableness are

identical, regardless of differences in their structural form. The cost of matching the precise physical structure of a given asset is known as its reproduction cost. The cost of matching the utility or serviceableness of a given asset is known as its replacement cost [p. 161].

Owing to technological progress, the replacement cost of an asset may be less than the cost to reproduce it, in which event its reproduction would not be economically justified. For nonmarketable and nonreproducible assets (such as patents, copyrights, mines, and oil wells), MacNeal makes "a big concession to expediency" [p. 188] by recommending original cost. It is a last resort, and he sees original cost as a better alternative than a zero valuation [p. 188]. Here, however, MacNeal forgets his earlier logic and opens himself to avoidable criticism. He defends the use of original cost in such instances in the belief that "the public could be educated to understand the true nature of these assets" "and be put on notice that this part of the balance sheet, and that part of the profit and loss statement relating to the depreciation or depletion of these assets, was not to be trusted and was merely a concession to expediency" [p. 189]. Practitioner critics might add the refrain that, by the same token, the public could be educated that the entire balance sheet and profit and loss statement are based on original costs, and that readers should color their inferences accordingly. Why does MacNeal believe that education of the public might succeed for some assets (which, in some companies, constitute the lion's share) while not for all assets?

Aware that a recommendation in favor of original cost in certain cases places

reaction to a sample of "the largest block distributions of securities" (secondary distributions) and concluded that "the data give consistent and strong support to the assumptions of the substitution hypothesis" [p. 207].

him on a weakened foundation, he is seen in this chapter (Chapter IX) to soften his "lectures" to accountants. He nonetheless distinguishes his system of economic values from the practices used by accountants, by contending, perhaps a bit self-righteously, that he starts with an ideal and introduces concessions to expediency as necessary, while accountants "start from a basis of expediency and . . . work toward the ideal only as expediency might dictate" [p. 175]. These asides would not have endeared him to the very readers whom he sought to influence.

The next 125 pages are used to explain and defend how particular accounts in the balance sheet and profit and loss statement would be treated under his system. He goes into considerable detail, and some matters are discussed at length. Yet the section would have been shorter and more palatable if NacNeal had not continued to administer stern admonitions to accountants for their accounting practices—and the frequency of these reproofs seems to increase in the second half of the book.

MacNeal includes in profit all changes in economic value during the period, whether realized or unrealized, as the following, rather blunt passage affirms:

> There is one correct definition of profits in an accounting sense. A profit is an increase in net wealth. A loss is a decrease in net wealth. This is the economist's definition. It is terse, obvious, and mathematically demonstrable [p. 295].

MacNeal recommends against separating "speculative profits" from "processing profits" on inventories solely on pragmatic grounds [pp. 309–311]. He refers, without naming them, to practicing accountants who have suggested that a company's purchasing operation should be assessed apart from its ability in processing operations [p. 309], a view which he seems to favor, but the difficulty

of achieving the separation in practice leads him to merge both elements of profit in Cost of Sales in the "current" section of his profit and loss statement. The final result in his "current" section (Sales less the sum of Cost of Sales (at market price or replacement cost, as applicable) and period expenses) is called Net Profit from Business Operations, and is credited to Earned Surplus. Net Profit from Business Operations, by MacNeal's definition, would include the unrealized increases and decreases during the period in the market price or replacement cost of the company's inventories of raw materials, work in progress, and finished goods. The second section of his two-part profit and loss statement gathers the profits and losses on non-current assets; its final result is called Net Capital Profit and is credited to Capital Surplus. MacNeal dislikes making the "current"/"capital" separation at all, and does so only for "legal and historical considerations" [p. 289]. His reference is evidently to the definitions of Earned Surplus (Retained Earnings in today's jargon) and other surpluses propounded by committees of the American Institute of Accountants in the late 1920s and early 1930s. These committees excluded from Earned Surplus the revaluations arising from the appraisal of fixed assets (which MacNeal called "capital") but were silent on the treatment of the revaluation of inventories (which MacNeal called "current").[14]

In principle, MacNeal prefers not to separate realized from unrealized profits.

[14] In 1929, the Institute's Special Committee on Definition of Earned Surplus rendered a report in which it favored the exclusion of fixed-asset revaluations from Earned Surplus (see Heckert [1930, pp. 168–169]). Although the committee's report failed to gain acceptance at the Institute's annual membership meeting the following year, its proposed definition was nonetheless adopted by the Institute's Special Committee on Terminology "for purposes of [its] tentative report" in 1931 [AIA, 1931, pp. 119–120].

"Under modern conditions," he argues, "the term 'realized' applied to profits means literally nothing, for such profits are continually being 'derealized' by reinvestment in other assets" [p. 296].

MacNeal's position on goodwill is compatible with his view that the economic values in the balance sheet should represent "present facts":

> The books of a business are intended to record the transactions and the possessions of a business. They are not designed to record the present speculative value of its future expectations or probabilities. Men and corporations may pay money for such expectations and probabilities, but this does not cause them to become balance sheet assets. The simple truth is that such men and corporations undergo a present sacrifice, or a present loss of capital, for the expected benefit of a future gain. A balance sheet, being merely a statement of present condition, can only exhibit things as they stand after such a sacrifice has been made [p. 236].

When one corporation buys another at a price that would indicate the existence of goodwill, MacNeal's solution is to treat this amount as a reduction in stockholders' equity.[15] Even where, in rare instances, accountants are able to value the goodwill of a business, such goodwill should not be allowed to appear on the company's balance sheet, for

> such inclusion would be very apt to confuse or deceive many stockholders when they attempted to compare such a company with one whose goodwill was not susceptible to valuation [p. 234].

MacNeal adopts a similar view of organization costs. He looks upon the practice of capitalizing such costs as a subterfuge to conceal what should properly be shown as losses incurred by companies during their formative years [p. 242].

MacNeal's position on liabilities is unexpected. He would record all discounts and premiums as capital losses or gains, respectively, and long-term liabilities would be carried at face value. He looks upon the amortization of discounts and premiums as a "theoretical" averaging process which results in a misrepresentation of the amount of actual interest which the corporation is legally obligated to pay [pp. 283–285]. As to liabilities in general, he makes the following statement (after having disqualified goodwill and organization costs as assets):

> Since the asset side of the balance sheet does not exhibit the total value of a business, but merely exhibits the total wealth owned by that business, neither can the liability side of a balance sheet exhibit the total value of the liabilities of that business, but can merely exhibit the status of these liabilities as legal claims on the undivided [owned] wealth of the business [p. 274].

He adds:

> Furthermore, in many cases, the market values of existing liabilities and capital stock may be completely unknown. When such market values are known they are usually as available to stockholders and creditors as they are to accountants, and little additional information would be supplied by using them [pp. 274–275].

(From this last quotation, one evidently is to conclude that MacNeal's basis for not attempting to show liabilities at economic value is one of practicability, not principle.)

As in the cases of goodwill and organization costs, MacNeal has interposed some arbitrary (and undefended) definitions of the role of the balance sheet, and he has also made some empirical observations that may or may not be true. He talks about creditors and stockholders as if they were the class of readers to

---

[15] Dicksee and Tillyard [1906, pp. 82–83] had recommended that goodwill be written off against capital "at the earliest possible stage." An immediate write-off against capital was later advocated by Spacek [1964] and Chambers [1966, pp. 209–212].

whom financial statements are directed. Yet he asserts, *pace* Paton, that "Universal custom decrees that the profit and loss statement of a business be drawn from the standpoint of its owners, namely, its stockholders, its partners, or its sole proprietor" [p. 297]. If that were so, why shouldn't the liabilities be valued (as best one can, using market prices) for the benefit of the owners?

One concludes, therefore, that MacNeal's "truth" consists of a balance sheet showing a company's possessions at their respective economic values (or at surrogates where necessary), its liabilities at their legally owing amounts, and its stockholders' equity as the residuum; and a profit and loss statement reflecting both realized and unrealized profits and losses classified into "current" and "capital" sections. The "truthful" information is intended to place small investors (and, perhaps, creditors) on a plane with insiders regarding the "true" valuation of the company's assets. The economic valuations are to be based on actual or estimated "facts," but not on speculations about future events.

MacNeal says nothing about footnotes or other forms of supplementary disclosure. Since the early to mid-1930s, probably owing to the passage of the Securities Acts of 1933–1934 and the regulatory activities of the Securities and Exchange Commission, footnotes and other explanatory information had become commonplace in the financial statements published by listed American companies (see McLaren [1947, Chap. 18], "Footnotes" [1939], and Daniels [1939, pp. 109–110]). Other authors (e.g., Paton and Littleton [1940, Chap. VII]) argued for the disclosure of some kinds of accounting information, such as replacement-cost data or purchasing-power restatements, in supplementary reports. MacNeal, however, insisted that his

"truth" be embodied in the financial statements themselves. He was impatient for reform, and he makes no reference to a possible period of transition from then-extant practice to "truthful" financial statements.[16]

Was MacNeal an advocate of exit-price accounting? As indicated below, several authors associate MacNeal with exit-price accounting, i.e., the use of resale prices in the valuation of assets.[17] A close reading of *Truth in Accounting* does not justify such a conclusion.

In his specific discussion of the treatment of different classes of assets, MacNeal applies market prices only to marketable securities and raw materials. It was evidently his belief that the other classes of assets could not normally be found to trade in acceptable markets; therefore, he proceeds immediately to a discussion of a surrogate for these assets. He would employ a surrogate even for finished goods:

> . . . many inventories will be found to contain items such as goods in process, or finished goods, which have no acceptable market and which must therefore be valued at the best remaining index of value, namely, present replacement cost [p. 226].

Only perhaps in his choice of surrogates can one infer how MacNeal might have stood in the later controversy over entry prices and exit prices. Could

---

, [16] Although nothing is said in *Truth* about a possible transition, MacNeal is on record as favoring parallel money columns in the financial statements during any such transition. He would show conventional figures in one column and the figures resulting from his recommendations in the other. His views on this transitional procedure were given in reply to a question from M. C. Conick, partner in the Philadelphia office of Main and Company, at a meeting in 1939. "Remarks by Kenneth MacNeal, C.P.A. (Illinois), copied from Stenotype Operator's Report of Annual Meeting of Pennsylvania Institute of Certified Public Accountants—June 19, 1939" (Kenneth MacNeal Scrapbook).

[17] The terms "exit price" and "entry price" were coined by Edwards and Bell [1961, p. 75].

MacNeal's preference for replacement cost, and his failure to suggest resale price as another option (in markets where differences between entry prices and exit prices could be expected to exist), suggest that he had more in common with the advocates of entry-price accounting? No definitive answer may be given. Since MacNeal recommends that realizable cost savings on both inventories and fixed assets be included in income, he would be regarded today as an advocate of financial capital maintenance.[18]

CRITICISM FROM REVIEWERS

In view of the strength of MacNeal's convictions, and the almost sanctimonious tone of the argument, it is perhaps not surprising that MacNeal's academic and professional critics were quick to find fault. The words "the truth," "the simple truth," "the truth of the matter," "truthful," and "truthfully" are the standard-bearers of MacNeal's argument, and they are repeated on and on throughout the book. Such terms, when used in excess (as they are here), can offend both academic and professional alike, for different reasons. To suggest that one know the truth may imply that others do not.

MacNeal was stung by the ferocity of the published criticism, and in an address delivered in January, 1940, he catalogued some of the "more expressive words put in print by my brother accountants to denote their appreciation of me and my ideas":

audacious	combative	foolish
antiquated	crackpotty	inadequate
academic	disturbing	impractical
accusatory	dubious	illogical
bold	drastic	ineffective
controversial	extreme	light
unnecessarily	excited	mistaken
critical	exaggerated	nebulous[19]
cocky	unorthodox	
not plausible	unmerciful	
pugnacious		

rambling	unbalanced
revolutionary	vicious
sensational	worse than naive
thin	

As he indicates, this criticism was directed not only at MacNeal's ideas but also at MacNeal himself. Yet the invective suffered by MacNeal was caused, in some measure, by the strong and vivid language used in his book. MacNeal employs the following adjectives to describe accounting practices with which he took issue:

untruthful	faulty	fraudulent
deceptive	seriously false and	indefensible
misleading	misleading	
morally indefensible	misleading and untrue	
fallacious	unjust and pernicious	
false and pernicious	false	
false and misleading	untenable	
childish	disgraceful	
demonstrably	flagrant	
absurd	wholly misleading	
deplorable	maliciously misleading	

Non-adjectival characterizations by MacNeal are as follows:

sheerest nonsense
illogic and fundamental unsoundness
grotesque humor
sophistry and specious reasoning
defraud
a tool of knaves
misrepresented facts
exhibiting a meaningless figure
deception
falsify
erroneous ideas
evils
fraud

In the Preface, MacNeal writes,

I particularly wish that I had the ability to write without the occasional appearance of ill temper and sweeping denunciation which

[18] For a discussion of "financial capital maintenance" v. "physical capital maintenance," see FASB [1976, paras. 283–312]. The term "realizable cost savings" is defined in Edwards and Bell [1961, p. 93].

[19] Taken from "Address delivered January 11, 1940 by Kenneth MacNeal to Controllers' Institute of America, at The Penn Athletic Club, Philadelphia, Pa.," p. 1 (typescript). Hatfield Papers, Accounting Area, Schools of Business Administration, University of California, Berkeley.

my friends tell me is my greatest fault. Apparently, I have, in a literary sense, a low boiling point of which I am scarcely aware [p. xii].

It is unfortunate that MacNeal could not have avoided the frequent use of intemperate language, for his argument was developed with great care and considerable thought. It is clearly and simply expounded, easily suited to a wide audience. Several of the chapters reflect extensive library research. Attention is given both to broad economic and philosophical questions and to the details of financial-statement presentation. Technical terms are chosen judiciously and are used consistently and with good effect. Scholars may complain that MacNeal did not relate his ideas to those of others who had written in like vein. But MacNeal was not a trained researcher, and his book—unlike Paton [1922], Canning [1929], and Sweeney [1936], with which it is often compared—was not developed from a doctoral dissertation completed under the supervision of university dons. All things considered, it was indeed an admirable work.

The major reviewers of *Truth* were John B. Canning, William A. Paton, J. Hugh Jackson, Norman J. Lenhart, Henry Rand Hatfield, and Pearson Hunt. Paton and Hatfield were accounting professors at the Universities of Michigan and California, respectively. Jackson was an accounting professor and dean of the Graduate School of Business at Stanford University. Canning was an economics professor at Stanford University, and Lenhart was a partner in the public accounting firm of Lybrand, Ross Bros. & Montgomery (and was later to become a co-author of *Montgomery's Auditing*). Hunt was an economics instructor at Yale University (and later served on the faculty of the Harvard Graduate School of Business Administration).

Canning and Paton had themselves been major advocates of current-cost or current-value accounting. In his laconic review of *Truth*, Canning confines his remarks to MacNeal's view of product markets. After summarizing MacNeal's criteria for the identification of actual or imputed market prices, Canning writes:

[MacNeal] seems to regard such a procedure as uniquely correct regardless of the erratic and extreme amplitudes of price fluctuation to which such markets are subject . . . [Canning, 1939, p. 757].

He adds:

In price imputation the author gives much space to replacement cost but gives scant attention to the cost analysis necessary to a determination of usefulness equivalent to that of substitutes. Moreover, truth may be both expensive and useless. One may pay too much for estimates of present replacement costs, especially if no early replacements are contemplated [Canning, 1939, p. 758].

Canning thus raises an important point which MacNeal (and most accounting authors prior to the 1970s) ignored: the cost of producing the information. By his reference to "useless," Canning suggests that MacNeal did not undertake to show in a rigorous manner how the "truthful" information would actually lead to better economic decisions.

Paton, himself an uncompromising advocate of replacement-cost measures in 1917–1918, is seen to be offended by MacNeal's facile appeal to "truth," his "sweeping" assertions, and his heavy-handed criticism of the accounting profession [1940]. This was Paton at the most "conservative" moment of his career, having just completed, as senior author, *An Introduction to Corporate Accounting Standards* [Paton and Littleton, 1940], which was to become the definitive explication (and, in large measure, defense) of conventional financial accounting (see Zeff [1979]). Paton was, at best, a cautious reformer in 1939–1940, and although he was in sympathy with the general direction in which MacNeal was heading, he disagreed with a number of MacNeal's specific recommendations (e.g., the treatment of organization costs and of bond discounts and premiums) and was irritated by MacNeal's writing style.

Jackson, never the revolutionary, has nothing positive to say about the book. The closest he comes to praise is: "There is just enough truth in some of the author's contentions to make the book dangerous" [Jackson, 1939, p. 855]. In view of Jackson's rather traditional position on accounting matters, that statement should have been welcomed by MacNeal! There is little in Jackson's review to indicate that he read the book carefully, and there is no doubt that he was opposed to MacNeal's argument from the start.

Lenhart's is a sarcastic and derisive review [1939]. He questions some of MacNeal's facts about recent changes in the standard form of the auditor's report, and severely challenges the practicability of making annual revaluations of fixed assets. Lenhart shows no inclination to give MacNeal a hearing.

Hatfield's review is the most restrained and considerate [1940]. As usual in Hatfield's writings, his views are stated with caution and are clothed in understatement. He refers to the "three clever fables" [1940, p. 14] and avers that MacNeal "contributes some good arguments" to the "much-debated question" of the valuation of assets. Hatfield adds:

But [MacNeal] is somewhat ungenerous to those who hold the other view in that he repeatedly speaks of their statements as being untrue. It is just as truthful (whether as serviceable or not) to present a statement which professedly shows unamortized costs as it is to state estimated present value. One may prefer present value to original, or cost, value,

but one is as much a fact as the other. And, as in all accounting discussion, much depends on the debater's use of terms [1940, p. 14].

Hatfield questions some of MacNeal's specific recommendations, e.g., his zero valuation of goodwill, treatment of bond discounts and premiums as losses and gains, and

that amortizing discount on debentures payable falsifies the accounts; that, in this case, the effective rate of interest is "theoretical" interest, and the nominal rate is "actual" interest [1940, p. 15].

He praises MacNeal for his explanation of goodwill, his criticism of the cost method of carrying investments in wholly-owned subsidiaries ("By this method, a holding company may show virtually any earnings desired, whether earned or not" [MacNeal, 1939a, p. 213]), and his recommendation that companies not show all "reserves" in one place in the balance sheet. As indicated above, Hatfield mentions the presence of errors in MacNeal's rendering of bookkeeping history. Hatfield sent MacNeal a draft of his review of *Truth*, and the two exchanged friendly letters for the next few years. They both were possessed of large curiosities, and they quickly discovered this mutual quality in correspondence.

Hunt's assignment was to discuss *Truth* and Gilman [1939] in the same review. He finds MacNeal to be a "pamphleteer," while Gilman is "ever the cautious, thorough, academician" [p. 168].[20] On the subject of the use of appraisals in the accounts, Hunt writes,

---

[20] It is unfortunate that *Truth* was arrayed against Gilman [1939] in Hunt's review. The outstanding characteristic of Gilman was his comprehensive review of the accounting literature, as if it had been done as a doctoral dissertation. MacNeal's work of full-throated advocacy would have seemed to be shallow by comparison, and it should have been reviewed on its own ground.

Lawyers and economists who have struggled over some matter of valuation will find Mac-Neal's confidence in appraisals and appraisers worse than naive [p. 169].

He concludes that "MacNeal's work is too light to do more than to stimulate controversy" [p. 170]. As will be suggested below, the controversy stirred by *Truth* seems to have been principally in its published reviews. Subsequent references to the book, and to MacNeal's few articles, have largely been perfunctory, even though (or perhaps because) other writers have, in their own treatises, taken up his cause.

On the whole, the major reviews were less than encouraging. THE ACCOUNTING REVIEW did not even review MacNeal's book, and the reason can only be guessed.[21] MacNeal's style of argument and exposition would probably have offended most academics and accounting professionals, and his undisguised contempt for the hallowed doctrines of conservatism and realization would have won acceptance only among the very small number of other renegades of the day. The known antipathy of the Securities and Exchange Commission to current valuation, and the recollection of corporate abuses of appraisal valuations of assets during the 1920s, hardly provided a climate in which to challenge the primacy of original cost. MacNeal was a courageous figure in his day, but if his writings succeeded in converting any of the heathen, they kept it to themselves.

Evidently, MacNeal was not prepared for the torrent of negative criticism provoked by his book. After his talks at professional meetings in Philadelphia, the opposition was sometimes bitter. He heard rumors of how he was regarded by some members of the Accounting Establishment, and he was not pleased. In the end, MacNeal decided irrevocably to abandon the crusade. He withdrew from

the literature two years after he had entered, a disappointed man. He refused to be drawn into controversy on the subject in later years.[22]

MACNEAL WRITES AN ARTICLE FOR *Fortune*

In December, 1938, less than six months before *Truth in Accounting* was to be published, the McKesson & Robbins scandal broke.[23] *Fortune* magazine had got wind of MacNeal's forthcoming book and approached him about writing a critical article on the accounting profession in the light of charges stemming from the Securities and Exchange Commission's inquiry into the manipulated accounts of the large drug firm. MacNeal accepted the assignment,[24] and in a matter of weeks the *Fortune* editors were reviewing a 9,000-word manuscript that was cut from the same cloth as *Truth in Accounting*. In their journalistic style, the *Fortune* editors led off the article with the following title and prefatory remarks:

> *Accountants Are Honest, But—*
>
> . . . their ways are hopelessly archaic. So says an author who calls upon his profession to adopt new methods which he feels would more truly portray the conditions of a business.

In a note to the article, *Fortune* introduced MacNeal as "long a severe critic of his own profession."

MacNeal's manuscript was a stern

[21] See footnote 26.
[22] Telephone conversation with MacNeal, December, 1963.
[23] For a popular account, see Shaplen [1955]. A summary of the final report of the Securities and Exchange Commission appears in its Accounting Series Release No. 19 [SEC, 1940a]. See SEC [1940b] for the full report.
[24] By a coincidence worth noting, the auditor of McKesson & Robbins was Price, Waterhouse & Co., which was the firm for which MacNeal worked in 1916–1917 and with which he jousted in 1929 (as a client) over the accounting treatment of the unrealized gains and losses on securities held by an investment trust.

indictment of the profession's conception of its role. In the opening paragraphs, which were a preview of the lines of argument to be developed later in the manuscript, MacNeal veritably seizes the reader's attention with the assertion that "The principles of accounting ... are obsolete conventions which are inaccurate, misleading, and untruthful." He then describes the nature of an independent audit and traces the changes in wording of the audit opinion from the use of "correct" to "present fairly." He cites the five "broad principles" enumerated in *Audits of Corporate Accounts* [1934, pp. 10–11] which underlie the "accepted principles of accounting" referred to in the standard form of the auditor's opinion, and proceeds to criticize accounting practice for its nonrecognition of unrealized gains on the holding of assets. After presenting several simplified examples in which marketable securities are carried at "lower of cost or market" and land and buildings are shown at "going concern value" (original cost), notwithstanding major swings in the market prices of both, MacNeal writes,

> Behind these theories lies the fact that too many certified public accountants today are likely to be little more than highly-trained experts in the mechanics of bookkeeping.

He then sketches the historical development of accounting, from service to the sole owner alone, to providing information for the creditor ("when public accounting came into existence"), and finally to serving smaller investors. He argues that the practice of understating, even grossly understating, asset values emerged during the creditor period in order to provide the banker with additional "security." MacNeal claims that this bias toward conservatism, which continued unabated in the 1930s, works

against the interest of the small investor. After presenting an abridged version of his "Fable of the Two Investment Trusts," where the securities market is assumed to react only to the reporting of realized profits, MacNeal concludes that "Contemporary financial statements ... allow insiders to enrich themselves at the expense of stock-holders in a most comfortable manner." And:

> ... thanks to the principles of accounting, balance sheets and profit-and-loss statements are *not* statements of fact; they are statements of bookkeeping fact. To you as a shareholder, unless you are a fortunate insider knowing the real values behind the items reported, they offer little information upon which sound judgment can be based, even though they are certified with no qualifications.

MacNeal suggests that the same mentality that leads accountants to prefer original costs over current valuations also is responsible for deficiencies in auditing practices:

> For the most part [the public accountant] satisfies himself that the bookkeeping has been properly done, and he then uses book figures with an almost total disregard of how they may fail to reflect indisputable facts. It is this emphasis on book figures rather than on present facts that lies at the bottom of such occurrences as the McKesson and Robbins situation.

And:

> If these accountants [i.e., the auditors of McKesson & Robbins] had been concerned more with the assets and less with the books, if they had been concerned more with physical facts and less with documentary evidence, they would hardly have been deceived by such simple expedients as false book entries and supporting vouchers.

He was careful to point out that his criticisms of accountants referred to their actions, not their motives:

> The main problem is intellectual, not moral. The accounting profession is not corrupt. Its individual members are, on the whole, as

honorable as any group of men in the country. The real difficulty lies in the sophistry, illogic, and untruth of present accounting principles, which produce figures deceiving accountants, business men, and the public alike.[25]

MacNeal's manuscript was edited by the *Fortune* staff, and independent reviews were secured from outside parties. It was set in page proofs, and MacNeal was told that it would run in the June, 1939 issue. But the article never appeared. At the eleventh hour, the article was canceled. MacNeal believed that the reason was pressure brought by Price, Waterhouse & Co. (the auditors of McKesson & Robbins) and the American Institute of Accountants.

Four months later, an abridged version of MacNeal's article was published in two parts in *The Nation* under the title, "What's Wrong with Accounting?" [MacNeal, 1939b, c]. Thus, an article that had been commissioned by a journal regarded as the trumpet of American capitalism—respected, elegantly crafted, and a serious student of the business and financial Establishment—came to appear instead in the pages of a weekly magazine of liberal opinion.

The Nation also had a go against *Fortune*. In its May 20th issue, the former reported that MacNeal's article had been canceled by *Fortune* by order of Time, Inc. Publisher Henry Luce and Treasurer Charles Stillman, following pressure "brought on by an outstanding firm of accountants to have the article killed" ["In the Wind," 1939]. In a letter to *The Nation*, *Fortune's* Publisher and Managing Editor denied that pressure had been applied, and insisted that the magazine's decision not to run the MacNeal article had been based solely on editorial grounds ["Zounds!" 1939]. "The main controversy," they wrote, "was around Mr. MacNeal's propositions that accountants should become

appraisers and that a new set of conventions should govern the writing-up as well as the writing-down of assets" ["Zounds!" 1939]. As the McKesson & Robbins episode had exposed questionable auditing practices and did not turn on questions of accounting valuation and measurement, the editors of *Fortune* may have had reason to wince at a manuscript whose "punch line" dealt with valuation. Nonetheless, MacNeal had built the case that accountants' bookkeeping mentality, as he saw it, accounted for deficiencies in both auditing and accounting. The consequences of this mentality were, to MacNeal, inseparable.

MacNeal answered *Fortune* in the letters column of the same issue of *The Nation*. He contended that *Fortune*'s view that no pressure had been brought by an accounting firm or any other firm "is abundantly denied by facts known to me at first hand both from within and from without the *Fortune* offices" ["You Cur!" 1939, p. 158]. The name of Price, Waterhouse & Co. is mentioned in the MacNeal letter, and one supposes that this is the firm—an undoubted power in the affairs of the American accounting profession in the 1930s—which was suspected of bringing influence. In the letter, MacNeal asserts that the report carried in the May 20th issue of *The Nation* "agrees substantially with my understanding of what took place . . . " ["You Cur!" 1939, p. 158].

Less than a year after the MacNeal episode, *Fortune* published a recapitulation of the facts attending the McKesson & Robbins fraud, written by its editorial staff and devoid of any criticism of the principals ["McKesson & Robbins: Its Fall and Rise," 1940].

[25] A virtually identical passage appears in MacNeal [1939a, p. 18].

MacNeal's Contribution to What Went Before—A Brief Review

MacNeal was the first major accounting writer, at least in the English-language literature, to advocate a market-price system for financial statements. In 1918, Paton had argued for a thorough-going replacement-cost solution, including in income the unrealized changes in replacement cost. But he would not have abandoned the realization concept entirely, for the margin between selling price and the replacement cost of goods sold would not be accorded accounting recognition until the period of sale [Paton, 1918]. In subsequent years, Paton retreated from that position, and by the close of the 1930s, when he wrote the review of *Truth*, he was recommending that replacement costs not be allowed to obscure original-cost information in the financial statements (see Zeff [1979, pp. 111–117]).

Hatfield [1927, Chaps. X, XII, pp. 366–367] showed a marked tolerance for the recognition of unrealized appreciation in the accounts and ridicules the unthinking attachment by accountants to the realization concept. But Hatfield's is a "balanced" presentation, and he does not engage in advocacy.

Canning [1929], in a major work that was his doctoral dissertation at the University of Chicago, recommended the use of discounted present values for the valuation of balance-sheet assets.

Schmidt [1930; 1931] recommended the use of replacement costs, but he preserved a distinction between realized and unrealized profits, crediting the latter to capital.

Sweeney, while he is best known for his argument for general price-level accounting, also favored replacement-cost accounting, but he was even less inclined than the Paton of 1918 to ignore the realization concept. He did, however, include the current period's installment in unrealized profits and losses, labeled "unrealized," in the "final net income for the year" [Sweeney, 1936, Chap. III; 1932].

Other writers, such as Montgomery [1921, pp. 144–146], allowed inventories to be shown at replacement costs when in excess of original cost, and writers such as Castenholz [1931] welcomed fixed-asset appraisals. Rorem suggested that assets intended for sale should be valued at their selling prices, while assets intended for use be valued by reference to the present value of their future services [1928, pp. 286–287]. But until MacNeal [1939a], no one had presented an integrated proposal for the preparation of financial statements on a market-price basis. It was a daring argument to make even among accounting reformers.

Subsequent References to MacNeal's Work

What manner of mark did MacNeal leave in the accounting literature and on accounting practice? No definitive answer can be given to such a question, but it is possible to discern the degree of interest that his writings have attracted on the part of academics, professionals, and policy makers.

As suggested above, the reviewers of *Truth* gave MacNeal little encouragement. Moreover, Philips writes [1971, p. 634]:

> I can detect no sign that [MacNeal's] book had a major impact or even was taken seriously to any considerable extent [by practitioners] in the years following its publication.

Philips suggests that Editor Kohler's strong preference for original-cost accounting may explain why The Accounting Review did not even review the book.[26] He detects a lack of academic interest in other quarters as well, which is "perhaps the result of both the unpopularity of the views expressed and the narrow scope of the economic and accounting theory background presented" [1971, p. 634].[27] MacNeal was not an academic, and his propensity for direct prose and categorical pronouncements probably grated on academic sensibilities. More to the point, there probably were few academics in the 1940s and even in the 1950s who would have aligned themselves with a movement away from the original-cost convention in accounting. It was not a revolutionary era. For academics, the late 1930s and early 1940s were a period of codification and consolidation. Such works as Sanders, Hatfield and Moore [1938], Gilman [1939], and Paton and Littleton [1940] testified to the prevailing mood, and few path-breaking tracts appeared. The appearance of Edwards and Bell [1961], Chambers [1961], Moonitz [1961], and Sprouse and Moonitz [1962] marked an awakening of accounting academics to the deficiencies of original-cost accounting, and in the decade of the 1960s the early normative arguments of Paton, Canning, Sweeney, MacNeal, and Alexander were "discovered" time and again by academics. Doubtless the republication of *Truth* in 1970 by Scholars Book Co, and the reprinting of "What's Wrong with Accounting?" in Baxter [1950] and Baxter and Davidson [1962; 1977] did much to place MacNeal's argument before the academic audience.

On the professional side of the literature, it is of interest that Arthur Andersen & Co., in a tract which endorses current-value accounting, praises MacNeal's recommended treatment of liabilities and stockholders' equity as "unusually refreshing and clear" [1972, p. 47]. Like MacNeal, Arthur Andersen & Co. would not exhibit goodwill as an asset or apply current values to creditors' and stockholders' equities. To do otherwise would be "to introduce concepts identified with the valuation of a business as a whole" [Arthur Andersen & Co., 1972, p. 47].

Yet Chambers and Sterling are of a mind in lamenting MacNeal's lack of influence among his practicing brethren. Chambers places MacNeal in the same category as Paton, Hatfield, Canning, and Sweeney—all being critics who failed to make an impression on the practicing profession [1967, pp. 241–242; 1969, pp. 712–713]. Sterling [1970, p. 254] includes MacNeal with Canning as being among "the fringe group" of theorists, owing to "their lack of impact on the practice of accounting and the textbook literature."[28]

When assessing the impact of MacNeal and other critics of accounting practice in the U.S., one should recall that the Securities and Exchange Commission stood four-square behind original-cost

---

[26] William W. Cooper, in a letter to the writer dated April 13, 1981, relates that Eric Kohler regarded MacNeal's book as "superficial," which, adds Cooper, "would have been enough to motivate such a decision by Eric [i.e., not to have the book reviewed] even for a book that entirely agreed with his position on historical cost."

[27] I can find only three citations to MacNeal in the issues of THE ACCOUNTING REVIEW from 1940 to 1960. MacNeal is not mentioned in the chapters on "Income Determination" and "Plant Appraisals" in Paton's third edition of the *Accountants' Handbook* [1943]: nor is he cited in the fourth edition of the same work [Wixon, 1956]. MacNeal is nowhere mentioned in volume 1 of Newlove and Garner's *Advanced Accounting* [1951], which [unlike most textbooks] contains copious citations to the literature.

[28] While the works of MacNeal and other critics are frequently represented in the syllabi used for accounting theory seminars (see, e.g., Burns [1967–1981]), one seldom sees the influence of such writings in North American introductory or "intermediate" financial accounting courses. To be sure, the textbooks for such courses rarely engage the student in controversial debate of any kind, save for disputed methods of applying highly detailed official pronouncements.

accounting from its founding in 1934 to the early 1970s. The few attempts by the profession to depart from original-cost accounting were repulsed by the SEC [Zeff, 1972, pp. 155–157]; hence, one must appreciate that the obduracy of the SEC would have made professional debates over value-based accounting futile indeed.

Truth is quoted twice in the chapter on assets in the Financial Accounting Standards Board's Discussion Memorandum on the Conceptual Framework [1976, paras. 133, 136], although one suspects that MacNeal would have winced at the hilarious typographical error in the FASB's footnote to the second of the two quotations. It gives the title of MacNeal's book as "*Trust in Accounting*"! [1976, p. 78, ftn. 39].

In the writings of academics, including even those of non-North Americans, MacNeal's work is remembered. Hendriksen, in his three editions of *Accounting Theory* [1965; 1970; 1977], refers to MacNeal as a member of the school which employs the "Ethical Approach" to formulating accounting theory. Most, in his *Accounting Theory* [1977], discusses MacNeal's ideas at greater length than does Hendriksen, although one may be surprised by Most's suggestion that MacNeal may be associated with the future-oriented Fisher/Canning school [p. 10]. Most indicates how MacNeal's "true income" approach to theory development has largely been supplanted by other theory approaches in the 1960s and 1970s, most notably that of "decision usefulness" [p. 10]:

Since MacNeal wrote there have been innumerable restatements of his criticisms, but the rationale has changed subtly over the years. Although many critics still proceed from the assumption that accounting can be referred to a framework of economic theory, it has become unfashionable to call this the truth. Instead, critics direct attention to the need for information useful in making economic decisions. The desired values are not intrinsically good, but acquire their virtue from the decision models which call them forth.

In 1977, a committee of the American Accounting Association grouped MacNeal with Paton [1922], Canning [1929], Sweeney [1936], Alexander [1950], Edwards and Bell [1961], and Moonitz [1961] and Sprouse and Moonitz [1962] in the "true income" school of normative theorists, and the committee summarized MacNeal's argument in *Truth* in a brief appendix [AAA, 1977, Chap. 2].

Nelson [1973] includes MacNeal in his discussion of major "a priori" theorists, and McDonald [1972, p. 20] lists MacNeal among the major critics of accounting. Devine, after observing that accountants would refuse to recognize income even when a company, after having bought goods at a given cost, receives a "firm offer" of sale at twice that cost, is sympathetic to MacNeal's stand on realization [1962, II, p. 276]:

The conclusion is that accountants hold off recognition because of failure to meet the test of realization and not because the evidence is inadequate.... [T]he defense for omission of these gains is not always convincing and, as MacNeal and many others have pointed out, the practical consequences may be ghastly.

Solomons recalls MacNeal's "Fable of the Two Investment Trusts" and notes the "absurd result" yielded by applying the realization concept [1961, p. 378].

Davidson cites MacNeal's "Fable of the Two Investment Trusts" as the "classic accounting objection to the market transaction test for realization..." [1966, p. 104, ftn. 24]. Chatfield includes a discussion of MacNeal's argument in his chapter, "Changing Concepts of Asset Valuation," and contributes the unexpected characterization that "MacNeal was only trying to do on the conceptual level what Sweeney had done with the practical problem of asset valuation" [1977, p. 243]. Chatfield concludes that MacNeal's "criticisms were simplistic, but diagnostically correct, and of a type which would become familiar after World War II" [1977, p. 243].

Belkaoui writes that "The notion of current exit price was introduced by MacNeal and further developed by Sterling and Chambers" [1981, pp. 160–161].

Among non-North American academic writers, Lee [1975] refers to *Truth* in several places and credits MacNeal with being the first advocate of what is known today as "exit price" accounting [p. 88]. Scapens describes MacNeal as "an early supporter of selling prices" [1977, p. 54]. Barton remarks that two of MacNeal's fables "vividly portrayed" the deficiencies of the realization concept in accounting [1975, pp. 30–31]. Baxter [1975, p. 143, ftn. 4] quotes approvingly from MacNeal's "What's Wrong with Accounting?," and Gynther [1966, p. 164] cites the MacNeal article with favor.

Thus, it may be said that MacNeal is remembered among academics.[29] Yet the citations to his work are not nearly so frequent or substantive as are those to the writings of Paton, Hatfield, Canning, and Sweeney—most of whose major works have also been republished in recent years.

In most of the works cited above, MacNeal is mentioned once, briefly, and only in passing. Seldom is his argument treated at some length. Furthermore, MacNeal is not mentioned in quite a few places where one might have expected to see his name: Vatter [1947], Fitzgerald [1952], Edwards and Bell [1961], Mathews and Grant [1962], Sprouse and Moonitz [1962], Littleton and Zimmerman [1962], Roy [1963], Mattessich

[1964], Deinzer [1965], Goldberg [1965], Bedford [1965], Salmonson [1969], Thomas [1969], Skinner [1972], Rosen [1972], Backer [1973], Ijiri [1975], and Previts and Merino [1979]. These are all substantial works that evince a commendable awareness of the genre of writings of which MacNeal's are a part, but he is not cited.

CONCLUDING REMARKS

Kenneth MacNeal was a revolutionary in a non-revolutionary time. The late 1930s were hardly a propitious time for radical change in American accounting thought. The Securities and Exchange Commission, an ardent defender of original-cost accounting, had begun to assert its authority over accounting principles, and the normally defensive accounting profession was nervously contemplating

[29] In a recent article, Mumford [1980] criticizes MacNeal for having characterized Hatfield as a supporter of the "lower of cost or market" rule and as a defender of historical-cost valuation. Oddly, Mumford undertakes to refute MacNeal by citing passages from Hatfield [1927], a work that MacNeal never cites and shows no indication of having read: in fact, MacNeal cited Hatfield [1909 (1913 printing)]. In correspondence which I have seen, Hatfield complained to MacNeal about this misrepresentation, and MacNeal replied that, after all, on page 224 of his 1909 book, Hatfield used the term, "wise conservatism." MacNeal's riposte aside, I believe that Mumford's line of criticism in this regard is justified. In addition Mumford alleges [p. 153] that Hatfield had used two vivid examples (in Hatfield [1927]) that "bear rather too close a resemblance to MacNeal's [second and third fables]" for this to be entirely coincidental. . . . " I find this claim to be far-fetched, at best. In Hatfield's first example, the aim was to expose the "lower of cost or market" rule, whereas MacNeal, in his "Fable of the Two Flour Mills," was interested in exposing realization and "going value." The Hatfield example and the MacNeal fable are similar only in outline. In the second comparison, where both authors discuss the consequences of not booking unrealized appreciation on securities, Hatfield was concerned with misrepresentation, while MacNeal focused on *manipulation*. In the setting of Hatfield's example, the manipulation suggested by MacNeal could not have occurred. Finally, Hatfield's examples appeared in Hatfield [1927] and, from what I can tell, did not appear in any printings of Hatfield [1909]. As indicated above, MacNeal seemed to be aware only of Hatfield's 1909 book.

the repercussions of the McKesson & Robbins scandal [Carey, 1970, Chaps. 1, 2]. For academics, the late 1930s and early 1940s were evidently not a period of innovation.

While MacNeal would have preferred to abandon the realization concept *in toto*, he seemed at ease with this outcome only when discussing marketable securities and basic commodities. The markets for other assets were not acceptable to MacNeal, and he was obliged to retain the realization concept for the margin between selling price and replacement-cost Cost of Sales.

MacNeal was not alone in failing to attract an immediate following. Few, apparently, were lured by Canning.[30]

Sweeney's followers did not rise in large numbers until the 1960s. Paton had the benefit of turning out disciples at the University of Michigan, although his prolific writings have had a noticeable influence on others. MacNeal did not hold an academic post, and he discontinued his professional writing and speaking in 1941.

Although MacNeal and pioneers before him were seldom appreciated by their peers, they may have given later reformers the courage that comes from knowing that one is not alone.

[30] For a contemporary view of Canning's influence, see Whittington [1980, pp. 236–240].

REFERENCES

Alexander, Sidney S., "Income Measurement in a Dynamic Economy," in *Five Monographs on Business Income* (American Institute of Accountants, 1950), pp. 1–95.

American Accounting Association, Committee on Concepts and Standards for External Financial Reports, *Statement on Accounting Theory and Theory Acceptance* (AAA, 1977).

American Institute of Accountants, *Accounting Terminology*, A Preliminary Report of A Special Committee on Terminology (AIA, 1931).

American Institute of Certified Public Accountants, Committee on Investment Companies, *Audits of Investment Companies* (AICPA, 1973).

Arthur Andersen & Co., *Objectives of Financial Statements for Business Enterprises* (Arthur Andersen & Co., 1972).

Audits of Corporate Accounts (American Institute of Accountants, 1934).

Backer, Morton, *Current Value Accounting* (Financial Executives Research Foundation, 1973).

Barton, Allan, *An Analysis of Business Income Concepts*, ICRA Occasional Paper No. 7 (International Centre for Research in Accounting, University of Lancaster, England, 1975).

Baxter, W. T., *Studies in Accounting* (Sweet & Maxwell, 1950).

———, *Accounting Values and Inflation* (McGraw-Hill, 1975).

———, and Sidney Davidson, *Studies in Accounting Theory* (Sweet & Maxwell, 1962).

———, and Sidney Davidson, *Studies in Accounting* (The Institute of Chartered Accountants in England and Wales, 1977).

Beaver, William H., *Financial Reporting: An Accounting Revolution* (Prentice-Hall, 1981).

Bedford, Norton M., *Income Determination Theory: An Accounting Framework* (Addison-Wesley, 1965).

Belkaoui, Ahmed, *Accounting Theory* (Harcourt Brace Jovanovich, Inc., 1981).

Burns, Thomas J., editor, *Accounting Trends [I]-XV* (McGraw-Hill, 1967–1981).

Canning, John B., *The Economics of Accountancy* (Ronald Press, 1929).

———, review of *Truth in Accounting, Journal of the American Statistical Association* (December 1939), pp. 757–758.

Carey, John L., *The Rise of the Accounting Profession: To Responsibility and Authority, 1937–1969* (American Institute of Certified Public Accountants, 1970).

Castenholz, William B., *A Solution to the Appreciation Problem* (LaSalle Extension University, 1931).

Chambers, R. J., *Towards A General Theory of Accounting* (Australian Society of Accountants Research Lecture, The University of Adelaide, 1961).

——, *Accounting, Evaluation and Economic Behavior* (Prentice-Hall, 1966).

——, "Prospective Adventures in Accounting Ideas," THE ACCOUNTING REVIEW (April 1967), pp. 241–253.

——, "New Pathways in Accounting Thought and Action," *The Accountants' Journal* (July, 1968), reprinted in R. J. Chambers, *Accounting Finance and Management* (Arthur Andersen & Co., 1969), pp. 700–714.

Chatfield, Michael, *A History of Accounting Thought* (Krieger, 1977).

Daniels, M. B., *Financial Statements*, Monograph No. 2 (American Accounting Association, 1939).

Davidson, Sidney, "The Realization Concept," in Morton Backer, editor, *Modern Accounting Theory* (Prentice-Hall, 1966), pp. 99–116.

Deinzer, Harvey T., *Development of Accounting Thought* (Holt, Rinehart and Winston, Inc., 1965).

Devine, Carl Thomas, *Essays in Accounting Theory* (The Author, 1962).

Dickinson, Arthur Lowes, *Accounting Practice and Procedure* (Ronald Press, 1913).

Dicksee, Lawrence R., and Frank Tillyard, *Goodwill and Its Treatment in the Accounts* (Gee & Co., 1906).

Edwards, Edgar O., and Philip W. Bell, *The Theory and Measurement of Business Income* (University of California Press, 1961).

Esquerré, Paul-Joseph, *The Applied Theory of Accounts* (Ronald Press, 1914).

Financial Accounting Standards Board, *Conceptual Framework for Financial Accounting and Reporting: Elements of Financial Statements and Their Measurement*, Discussion Memorandum (FASB, December 2, 1976).

Fitzgerald, A. A., *Current Accounting Trends* (Butterworth & Co. (Australia) Ltd., 1952).

"Footnotes," Editorial, *The Journal of Accountancy* (August, 1939), p. 74.

Gilman, Stephen, *Accounting Concepts of Profit* (Ronald Press, 1939).

Goldberg, Louis, *An Inquiry into the Nature of Accounting* (American Accounting Association, 1965).

Green, Wilmer L., *History and Survey of Accountancy* (Standard Text Press, 1930).

Gynther, R. S., *Accounting for Price-Level Changes: Theory and Procedures* (Pergamon Press, 1966).

Hatfield, Henry Rand, *Modern Accounting: Its Principles and Some of Its Problems* (D. Appleton and Company, 1909).

——, *Accounting, Its Principles and Problems* (D. Appleton & Co., 1927).

——, review of *History and Survey of Accountancy*, *The Journal of Accountancy* (April, 1931), pp. 308–309.

——, review of *Truth in Accounting*, Review Supplement No. 10 [to *The Accountant*], The Accounting Research Association (January 1940), pp. 14–16.

Heckert, J. B., "Comments on the Definition of Earned Surplus," THE ACCOUNTING REVIEW (June 1930), pp. 168–174.

Hendriksen, Eldon S., *Accounting Theory* (Irwin, 1965).

——, *Accounting Theory* (Irwin, 1970).

——, *Accounting Theory* (Irwin, 1977).

Hunt, Pearson, review of *Accounting Concepts of Profit* and *Truth in Accounting*, *The Yale Law Journal* (November 1939), pp. 167–170.

Ijiri, Yuji, *Theory of Accounting Measurement*, Studies in Accounting Research No. 10 (American Accounting Association, 1975).

"In the Wind," *The Nation* (May 20, 1939), p. 588.

Jackson, J. Hugh, review of *Truth in Accounting*, *The American Economic Review* (December, 1939), pp. 853–855.

Lee, T. A., *Income and Value Measurement: Theory and Practice* (Thomas Nelson & Sons Ltd., 1975).

Lenhart, Norman J., review of *Truth in Accounting*, *The Journal of Accountancy* (June, 1939), pp. 395–396.

Littleton, A. C., and V. K. Zimmerman, *Accounting Theory: Continuity and Change* (Prentice-Hall, 1962).

MacNeal, Kenneth, *Truth in Accounting* (University of Pennsylvania Press, 1939a).

——, "What's Wrong with Accounting?", *The Nation* (October 7, 1939b), pp. 370–372.

——, "What's Wrong with Accounting?", *The Nation* (October 14, 1939c); pp. 409–412.

——, "Caveat Investor," *The Nation* (February 8, 1941a), pp. 151–153.

——, "Is Our System of Financial Reporting Sound?", *The Accounting Forum* (April 1941b), pp. 7–11, 56.

Mathews, Russell, and John McB. Grant, *Inflation and Company Finance* (The Law Book Co. of Australasia Pty Ltd., 1962).

Mattessich, Richard, *Accounting and Analytical Methods* (Irwin, 1964).

McDonald, Daniel L., *Comparative Accounting Theory* (Addison-Wesley, 1972).

"McKesson & Robbins: Its Fall and Rise," *Fortune* (March, 1940), pp. 72–75, 120, 123–126, 128, 130–131.

McLaren, N. Loyall, *Annual Reports to Stockholders: Their Preparation and Interpretation* (Ronald Press, 1947).

Montgomery, Robert H., *Auditing Theory and Practice* (Ronald Press, 1912).

———, *Auditing Theory and Practice*, Volume I (Ronald Press, 1921).

———, *Auditing Theory and Practice* (Ronald Press, 1934).

Moonitz, Maurice, *The Basic Postulates of Accounting*, Accounting Research Study No. 1 (American Institute of Certified Public Accountants, 1961).

Most, Kenneth S., *Accounting Theory* (Grid, 1977).

Mumford, M. J., "An Historical Defence of Henry Rand Hatfield," *Abacus* (December 1980), pp. 151–157.

Nelson, Carl L., "A Priori Research in Accounting," in Nicholas Dopuch and Lawrence Revsine, editors, *Accounting Research 1960–1970: A Critical Evaluation* (Center for International Research in Accounting, University of Illinois, 1973), pp. 3–19.

Newlove, George Hillis, and S. Paul Garner, *Advanced Accounting*, Volume I (D.C. Heath and Company, 1951).

Paton, W. A., "The Significance and Treatment of Appreciation in the Accounts," in G. H. Coons, editor, *Twentieth Annual Report* (Michigan Academy of Science, 1918), pp. 35–49.

———, *Accounting Theory—With Special Reference to the Corporate Enterprise* (Ronald Press, 1922).

———, review of *Truth in Accounting*, *Journal of Political Economy* (April, 1940), pp. 296–298.

———, and A. C. Littleton, *An Introduction to Corporate Accounting Standards*, Monograph No. 3 (American Accounting Association, 1940).

———, editor, *Accountants' Handbook* (Ronald Press, 1943).

Philips, G. Edward, review of republication of *Truth in Accounting*, THE ACCOUNTING REVIEW (July 1971), pp. 634–636.

Previts, Gary John, and Barbara Dubis Merino, *A History of Accounting in America: An Historical Interpretation of the Cultural Significance of Accounting* (John Wiley & Sons, 1979).

Rorem, C. Rufus, *Accounting Method* (The University of Chicago Press, 1928).

Rosen, L. S., *Current Value Accounting and Price-Level Restatements* (Canadian Institute of Chartered Accountants, 1972).

Roy, G. D., *A Survey of Accounting Ideas* (Calcutta: Alpha Publishing Concern, 1963).

Salmonson, R. F., *Basic Financial Accounting Theory* (Wadsworth, 1969).

Sanders, Thomas Henry, Henry Rand Hatfield and Underhill Moore, *A Statement of Accounting Principles* (American Institute of Accountants, 1938).

Scapens, Robert W., *Accounting in an Inflationary Environment* (Macmillan, 1977).

Schmidt, Fritz, "The Importance of Replacement Value," THE ACCOUNTING REVIEW (September 1930), pp. 235–242.

———, "Is Appreciation Profit?," THE ACCOUNTING REVIEW (December 1931), pp. 289–293.

Scholes, Myron S., "The Market for Securities: Substitution versus Price Pressure and the Effects of Information on Share Prices," *The Journal of Business* (April 1972), pp. 179–211.

Securities and Exchange Commission, "In the Matter of McKesson & Robbins, Inc.—Summary of Findings and Conclusions," *Accounting Series Release No. 19* (SEC, December 5, 1940a).

———, *In the Matter of McKesson & Robbins, Inc., Report on Investigation* (Government Printing Office, December, 1940b).

Shaplen, Robert, "Annals of Crime: The Metamorphosis of Philip Musica," *The New Yorker* I (October 22, 1955), pp. 49–81; II (October 29, 1955), pp. 39–79.

Skinner, R. M., *Accounting Principles: A Canadian Viewpoint* (Canadian Institute of Chartered Accountants, 1972).

Solomons, David, "Economic and Accounting Concepts of Income,'. THE ACCOUNTING REVIEW (July 1961), pp. 374–383.

Spacek, Leonard, "Treatment of Goodwill in the Corporate Balance Sheet," *The Journal of Accountancy* (February 1964), pp. 35–40.

Sprouse, Robert T., and Maurice Moonitz, *A Tentative Set of Broad Accounting Principles for Business Enterprises*, Accounting Research Study No. 3 (American Institute of Certified Public Accountants, 1962).

Sterling, Robert R., *Theory of the Measurement of Enterprise Income* (The University Press of Kansas, 1970).

Sweeney, Henry W., "Stabilized Appreciation," THE ACCOUNTING REVIEW (June 1932), pp. 115–121.

———, *Stabilized Accounting* (Harper & Brothers, 1936).

Thomas, Arthur L., *The Allocation Problem in Financial Accounting Theory*, Studies in Accounting Research No. 3 (American Accounting Association, 1969).

Vatter, William J., *The Fund Theory of Accounting and Its Implications for Financial Reports* (The University of Chicago Press, 1947).

Whittington, Geoffrey, "Pioneers of Income Measurement and Price-Level Accounting: A Review Article," *Accounting and Business Research* (Spring, 1980), pp. 232–240.

Wixon, Rufus, editor, *Accountants' Handbook* (Ronald Press, 1956).

"You Cur!", Letters to the Editors, *The Nation* (August 5, 1939), pp. 157–158.

Zeff, Stephen A., *Forging Accounting Principles in Five Countries: A History and an Analysis of Trends* (Stipes, 1972).

———, "Paton on the Effects of Changing Prices on Accounting: 1916–55," in Stephen A. Zeff. Joel Demski, and Nicholas Dopuch, editors, *Essays in Honor of William A. Paton: Pioneer Accounting Theorist* (Division of Research, Graduate School of Business Administration, The University of Michigan, 1979), pp. 91–137.

"Zounds!", Letters to the Editors, *The Nation* (August 5, 1939), p. 157.

THE ACCOUNTING REVIEW
Vol. LIX, No. 3
July 1984

Some Junctures in the Evolution of the Process of Establishing Accounting Principles in the U.S.A.: 1917–1972

Stephen A. Zeff

ABSTRACT: This paper reviews the circumstances attending five major turning points in the process by which accounting principles have been established in the United States. Particular attention is directed to the apparent reasons why the new approaches or reforms were undertaken. The review, which covers a 56-year period, concludes that generalizations about the factors that were influential in the shaping of the decision-making process, especially over so long a period, are difficult to make. Nonetheless, a motivating force seems to have been the accounting profession's fear of government involvement. The American Accounting Association is seen to have played a role at several of the junctures.

S EVERAL junctures in the evolution of the process of establishing accounting principles in the United States may be discerned. It is my purpose in this paper to identify the factors that seem to have been influential in shaping these events. The several junctures may be enumerated as follows:

1. Vote of the membership of the American Institute of Accountants (AIA), in 1918, to reject the capitalization of interest cost.
2. Vote of the AIA membership, in 1934, to adopt six "rules or principles" of accounting.
3. Decision by the Institute's Council, in 1938–39, to reorganize the Committee on Accounting Procedure, create a research department, and authorize the Committee to issue a series of bulletins on accounting without reference to Council.
4. Decision by the Institute's Council, in 1959, to supplant the Committee on Accounting Procedure by an

Accounting Principles Board, and also to replace the Institute's research department by an accounting research division.

5. Decision by the Institute's Council, in 1972, to adopt the recommendations of the Wheat Study, terminate the Accounting Principles Board and the accounting research division, and support the creation of a Financial Accounting Foundation, whose purpose would be to underwrite a Financial Accounting Standards Board.

Editor's Note: This paper served as the basis for a plenary address given at the 1983 Annual Meeting of the American Accounting Association. It was subsequently submitted and reviewed for publication.

Useful comments on an earlier draft were received from Richard Macve, Gary J. Previts, Andrew Barr, Paul Grady, and Reed K. Storey. The author is, of course, solely responsible for what remains.

Stephen A. Zeff is Herbert S. Autrey Professor of Accounting, Rice University.

Manuscript received November 1983. Accepted February 1984.

447

A theme that runs through the discussion of these events is that the actions of the Institute were precipitated by criticism voiced from inside or outside the profession, or by efforts of academics to influence the course of accounting principles. Especially in the 1930's, and even in the 1950's and 1970's, the American Accounting Association played a role.

Since accounting principles—which affect the behavior of independent auditors and their clients—have been set in the private sector, it is not surprising that, at each juncture, the American Institute of Accountants has been seen to seek support from authoritative bodies. At different times, these agencies have been in the government (e.g., the Federal Trade Commission, Federal Reserve Board, and Securities and Exchange Commission) or in the private sector (e.g., the New York Stock Exchange). In this context, the American Accounting Association has not been a support agency, but the Association has nonetheless been viewed by the Institute with concern and respect. Through its own initiatives, the Association could dilute the force of Institute pronouncements as well as suggest weaknesses (especially of the conceptual kind) in the Institute's program for establishing accounting principles.

"INTEREST AS A COST" IN 1917–18

In the early part of the second decade of the century, a number of articles began to appear in accounting journals which advocated the capitalization of interest. The controversy was precipitated, according to Wells [1978, p. 130], by the publication Arthur Lowes Dickinson's "The Fallacy of Including Interest and Rent as Part of Manufacturing Cost" [1911]. Dickinson was senior partner in the American firm of Price, Waterhouse & Co.

The FASB's Discussion Memorandum on "Accounting for Interest Costs" traces the background of the "interest as a cost" controversy:

> Towards the end of the nineteenth century, the issue of accounting for interest arose as part of a larger concern with developing realistic product costs to serve as a basis for establishing selling prices and measuring manufacturing efficiency. The increasing complexity of business, the increasing reliance on machinery, and the consequent need to invest large amounts of capital for long periods of time greatly increased the amount of overhead. The inclusion of overhead in product cost therefore became a major accounting issue [FASB, 1977, para. 174].

Along with the accounting treatment of depreciation, the manner of accounting for interest was born of the Industrial Revolution. The FASB adds,

> By the turn of the century, the general practice was to include in product costs virtually all costs of any nature, including interest. By 1910, however, most writers had concluded that manufacturing expenses should be distinguished from selling and administrative expenses, and that only manufacturing expenses should be included in product cost [FASB, 1977, para. 174].

Academics and practitioners were arrayed on both sides of the question of whether to include interest in production cost, and feelings were strong. Clark [1923, p. 255] was justified in observing that "The discussion of this question is a strange mixture of dogmatic assertion and arguments from expediency." The matter seemed to have been settled in 1917, when, acting at the request of the Federal Trade Commission (FTC), the newly formed American Institute of Accountants published a memorandum devoted mostly to auditing procedures, but which carried the following dictum regarding the composition of overhead cost:

That no selling expenses, interest charges, or administrative expenses are included in the factory overhead cost ["Uniform Accounts," 1917, p. 276].

But opposition to the Institute's position persisted. At the Institute's annual meeting in September 1917, Clinton H. Scovell, one of the leaders of the opposition, objected to the Institute's memorandum, published five months earlier, on the ground that it was unfavorable to the inclusion of interest in overhead. J. Lee Nicholson, another leader of the opposition, succeeded in persuading the Institute President to appoint a special committee "to gather statistics and facts and opinions on the treatment of interest and to report at the next meeting" ["Proceedings . . . ," 1917, p. 71]. The words of one observer testified to the hostile climate in which the action was taken:

A great many accountants felt that the appointment of such a committee was slaying the slain, but in order that both sides of the question should be heard the whole institute approved the passing of the resolution. For some years there has been a small but vociferous minority of the membership which has clung to the generally discarded idea that interest was properly an element of cost" [Richardson, 1918, p. 292].

At the Institute's next annual meeting, the committee's report was presented. Instead of fulfilling its charge to marshal "statistics and facts and opinions," the committee, in language hardly indicative of judicial balance, haughtily dismissed the arguments of the opposition, finding that "the inclusion in production cost of interest on investment is unsound in

theory and wrong, not to say absurd, in practice" ["Report . . . " 1918, p. 112].

It was a time when the leaders of the Institute were sensitive to the uses to which commercial bankers might put financial statements,[1] and the proposal to include interest in the cost of production probably was seen by most auditors as being inimical to a conservative and objective valuation of assets.[2]

At the Institute's 1918 annual meeting, the defenders of doctrine were so supremely confident of the rightness of their position that they sought and obtained the Institute membership's *approval*, not mere acceptance, of its report.[3] The following sentence, appearing in a footnote appended to the committee's report in the Institute's *1918 Year-Book*, clearly implies that Institute members were expected not to approve the inclusion of interest in production cost in financial statements:

Adoption of the report [by the Institute membership] did not debar any [Institute] member from including interest in cost of production when compiling . . . internal statistics—provided always that such statistics must not be

[1] Although the Institute's 1917 memorandum on balance-sheet audits had been solicited by the Federal Trade Commission, the document was published in the *Federal Reserve Bulletin* after having been approved by the Federal Reserve Board.

[2] Previts and Merino [1979, p. 184] view the dispute as a conflict between the entity and proprietary theories.

[3] In 1979, I brought the fact of the Institute membership's 1918 disapproval of interest capitalization to the attention of the Financial Accounting Standards Board, which was then considering a Statement on the subject. When Statement No. 34, "Capitalization of Interest Cost," was issued by the Board in October 1979, the following sentence was included in a footnote to paragraph 25:

Although the [1918] vote of the Institute's membership is of historical interest, it has not been incorporated into the body of authoritative pronouncements currently in force.

So much for the weight accorded the Institute membership's approval of accounting principles!

used to color financial statements ["Report . . . ," 1918, p. 112].

Why did the Institute's leaders act so categorically on the proper treatment of interest in the accounts? A likely reason was to establish credibility with the Federal Trade Commission and the Federal Reserve Board. Edward N. Hurley, FTC chairman, had become interested in promoting uniform accounting practices in certain industries, and he had horrified Institute leaders by suggesting that "consideration might be given to the possibility of developing a register of public accountants whose audit certificates would be acceptable to the Commission and the [Federal Reserve] Board" [Carey, 1969, p. 130]. For its part, the Federal Reserve Board was "keenly interested in the credit worthiness of organizations whose commercial paper was discounted by Federal Reserve banks. The Board, therefore, had an immediate and vital interest in the reliability of certified financial statements of such enterprises" [Carey, 1969, p. 132]. Evidently, the Institute sought to present a united front on the treatment of interest.

Scovell, Nicholson, and others of like mind on the interest question rightly concluded that the Institute hierarchy was unsympathetic to their cause (also see Carey [1969, p. 311]). In October 1919, they were among the leaders of the 37 men who met in Buffalo, New York to found the National Association of Cost Accountants, and in 1920 the new Association appointed a committee to study the question of including interest in production cost. At the Association's 1921 International Cost Conference, the committee's report was presented and the subject was discussed at length ["Interest as an Element of Cost," 1921]. No conclusion was reached, but at least a friendly forum for an exchange of views was provided.

While it is true, as Moonitz [1970] points out, that there were several concerted initiatives in the 1910's and early 1920's to influence accounting practice, the one involving the possible inclusion of interest in production cost is the best example from that period of an organized and persistent opposition to Institute doctrine. It was the first time that the membership of a national accounting body had taken a position on a matter of accounting principle. Had the Institute not then been under pressure from the FTC and Federal Reserve Board (FRB), it is very likely that no committee would have been formed by the Institute in 1917 to put an end to the controversy, and that no position would have been submitted to a vote of the Institute membership in 1918.

AIA Approval of Six "Rules or Principles"

The second juncture in the evolution of the process of establishing accounting principles covered the period 1926–34. William Z. Ripley, a Harvard economics professor, wrote an exposé of corporate financial reporting in the September 1926 issue of *The Atlantic Monthly*. Entitled "Stop, Look, Listen!", the article contained specific criticisms of reporting practices that Ripley regarded as deceptive. In the article, he referred to "enigmatic accounting" [p. 388] and directed much of his criticism to understated depreciation provisions and overstated asset valuations. His brief embraced both measurement and disclosure issues, including "the failure to disclose the method of the valuation [of assets], whether it be of property or of stock in trade" [p. 390]. Ripley concluded on an ominous note:

Let the word go forth that the Federal Trade Commission is henceforward to address itself vigorously to the matter of adequate and intelligent corporate publicity . . . [p. 399].

Ripley's article made an immediate impact. George O. May, senior partner in Price, Waterhouse & Co., commented critically on Ripley's article in a letter to *The New York Times* [1926a] and reacted more fully to Ripley's indictment in an address given a month after Ripley's article appeared [1926b].[4] May described the source of his concern as follows:

Unless some effective steps are taken to meet criticisms such as those voiced by Professor Ripley, the result will be some sort of bureaucratic control, and I am satisfied that through proper cooperation methods can be devised, without resort to government, which will be more effective and at the same time less burdensome and vexatious than control by a governmental body is likely to be [May, 1926c, p.42].

Not only did May dislike the prospect of government intervention, his words were well calculated to goad the profession into taking some concerted action to raise the standards of professional performance. In his address at the Institute's annual meeting in 1926, May proposed that the Institute sponsor a cooperative effort involving the leading stock exchanges, investment bankers, and commercial bankers so that

standards might be established for balance-sheets and income accounts which would be welcomed by many corporation executives and accountants who desire to be guided by the best practice, if they can be assured what that practice is [May, 1926b, p. 324].

The succeeding paragraphs in May's address make it clear that his recom-

mended standards would deal more with disclosure than with measurement. May was an Englishman, and he had received his accounting training in Exeter. In Britain (prior to 1981), the succession of Companies Acts largely confined their provisions on accounting to matters of disclosure, leaving the questions of how to value assets and determine net income to companies and their auditors. In his 1926 address, May favored the disclosure of the methods used to value capital assets and of any "extraordinary or extraneous profit" included in the profits of the year [pp. 324–325]. Of paramount importance would be the disclosure of any methods used "other than those commonly accepted" [p. 325].

May's philosophy, as set forth in the famous letter dated September 22, 1932 from the Institute's Committee on Cooperation with Stock Exchanges to the Committee on Stock List of the New York Stock Exchange, was that

[w]ithin quite wide limits, it is relatively unimportant to the investor what precise rules or conventions are adopted by a corporation in reporting its earnings if he knows what method is being followed and is assured that it is followed consistently from year to year [AIA, 1934, p. 9].

His committee proposed that corporations listed on the New York Stock Exchange (NYSE) formulate and approve a list of accounting methods used in the preparation of their financial statements; give assurances that the methods so adopted will be followed consistently from year to year, but that any material deviations should be disclosed; and

---

[4] May's talk was given at the annual meeting of the American Institute of Accountants. Carey [1969, Chap. 10] and May [Grady, 1962, Chap. 6] have discussed the series of initiatives by May and the Institute resulting from Ripley's critical writings on accounting and financial reporting.

furnish the list to the Exchange so that any stockholder might, upon payment of a fee, request a copy (1932 letter, in AIA [1934, p. 13]). In addition, May's committee recommended that the Exchange "make universal the acceptance by listed corporations of certain broad principles of accounting which have won fairly general acceptance, and within the limits of such broad principles to make no attempt to restrict the right of corporations to select detailed methods of accounting deemed by them to be best adapted to the requirements of their business"[5] (1932 letter, in AIA [1934, pp. 12–13]). May's "broad principles" encompassed the following:

1. Unrealized profit should not be credited to income, and expenses ordinarily chargeable against income should not be charged instead against unrealized profit.
2. Except for quasi-reorganizations, capital surplus (in today's jargon, additional paid-in capital) should not be charged with amounts that ordinarily would be charged to income.
3. "Earned surplus [today, retained earnings] of a subsidiary company created prior to acquisition does not form part of the consolidated earned surplus of the parent company and subsidiaries."
4. While "it is perhaps in some circumstances permissible" for treasury stock to be shown as an asset, the dividends declared on such stock may not be credited to the company's income.
5. "Notes or accounts receivable due from officers, employees, or affiliated companies must be shown separately and not included under a general heading such as Notes Receivable or Accounts Receivable"[6] (1932 letter, in AIA [1934, p. 14]).

Although the Institute's membership voted approval in 1934 of the committee's proposed principles, the Exchange did no more than agree to the list. Moreover, the Exchange never did impose a requirement on listed companies to compile a list of their accounting methods to be placed on public record. Yet much of what May's committee sought to achieve in this regard was implemented by the Securities and Exchange Commission (SEC) when it mandated the disclosure of certain accounting methods in the registration statements of listed companies [Blough, 1967, p. 3]. A further step was taken in 1972, when the Accounting Principles Board issued Opinion No. 22, requiring companies to disclose a summary of their "significant accounting policies" as an integral part of their annual financial statements.

Although the correspondence contained in *Audits of Corporate Accounts* [AIA, 1934] led to a successful collaboration between the Institute and the New York Stock Exchange, May's very substantial effort to ward off the intervention of the federal government in the establishment of accounting principles failed. Ripley's writings had spurred May and the Institute on, but the forces unleashed by the Great Depression were irreversible.

[5] The committee used the terms "principles," "practices," and "conventions" interchangeably, and at the 1934 Institute annual meeting, where the members were asked for their approval, the term "rules or principles" was employed. In a later article, May made clear that his committee did not use "principles" to suggest "fundamental principles," as in deductive logic. Instead, he preferred the following definition: "A general law or rule adopted or professed as a guide to action; a settled ground or basis of conduct or practice" [May, 1937, p. 423]. In 1939, when the Institute's Committee on Accounting Procedure reaffirmed the earlier "rules or principles," they were described as "rules formerly adopted." (Also see Grady [1962, pp. 73–74].)

[6] When these five "broad principles" were submitted for membership vote at the 1934 Institute annual meeting, a sixth was added, dealing with what is known as "treasury stock subterfuge." It was also approved by the membership.

AIA Decision to Empower the Committee on Accounting Procedure to Issue Pronouncements

Once the Securities and Exchange Commission came into existence in 1934, the leading edge of George O. May's effort to raise the standard of accounting practice seemed to lose its sharpness, as if the Institute leadership had been intimidated into silence by the new layer of federal bureaucracy and its broad statutory powers over accounting and auditing practice. At the same time, May was philosophically opposed to identifying "accepted principles of accounting" until an informed consensus was clearly discernible; this credo, coupled with his preference to allow corporations to adopt accounting methods that they believed to be "best adapted to the requirements of their business," did not portend an active, forceful program of raising the standard of accounting practice. May was not about to become the dictator of best practice.[7]

In 1933, May was named chairman of a new Institute committee, the Special Committee on Development of Accounting Principles, and in its first report, issued in October 1934, the committee bespoke a reluctance to forge ahead as confidently as had May's Special Committee on Cooperation with Stock Exchanges. A few excerpts from the committee's report exemplified the new mood:

> Since principles of accounting can not be arrived at by pure reasoning, but must find their justification in practical wisdom, the committee believes that the Institute should proceed with caution in selecting from the methods more or less commonly employed those which should be accorded the standing of principles or accepted rules of accounting. . . . The committee believes that the policy of the Institute should be to act with care and deliberation, and to endeavor whenever

possible to secure the concurrence of some body possessing high authority in the rules or principles which it lays down ["Report . . . ," AIA, 1935, p. 276].

This was the only report to emerge from the committee, and it was not reappointed in 1936, when its assignment was transferred to the new Committee on Accounting Procedure, of which May became chairman in 1937.

Eric L. Kohler, editor of The Accounting Review, journal of the American Association of University Instructors in Accounting (AAUIA), who wrote several biting editorials during the 1930's, professed a profound disappointment with the 1934 report of the Special Committee on Development of Accounting Principles:

> Little apparently may be hoped from the Committee. . . . Its recommendations are surface considerations and give no indication of any sound approach to the more general problem for which a solution is now so urgently necessary. In fact, it in substance confesses that it does not propose to exert any originality except that which will be required to restrain, shall we say, a securities and exchange commission that may get out of hand [Kohler, 1934b, pp. 335–336].

To be sure, the Institute committee was restating May's view that the profession required an authoritative ally in order to develop principles, as had been done with the FTC, FRB, and NYSE. But in 1934, the committee did not seem disposed to take the lead. In his editorials, Kohler began to adopt a cynical view toward the leaders of the Institute (see Kohler [1934a]), and he characterized himself as being among "the accounting radicals who advocate that accountants should not only think for themselves but also formulate their own rules without refer-

---

[7] For a discussion of May's philosophy, see Storey [1964, pp. 13–15] and May [1943].

ence to outside agencies" [Kohler, 1935, p. 372]. In December 1934, Kohler sternly criticized the Institute and issued a "call to arms" to his colleagues in the Association:

> For years [the Editor] has assailed the smugness of the profession and its inability to set standards for its own conduct and for the information of the public that relies upon its findings. . . . For years it has failed to see the problems before it: problems for the complexity of which it alone has been responsible. . . .
> To instructors of accounting, this condition of affairs should offer a challenge. Now, more than ever, the voice of enlightened opinion within the profession is needed. Shall we as accountants recognize that the responsibilities of the profession are large, particularly to third persons? Or shall we drift as we have done in the past, waiting, at first hopefully and now fearfully, for someone else to tell us what to do? Is it impossible for us to take any initial responsibility for defining our accountability to the business and financial world and to the investing public? [1934a].

It is hardly farfetched to believe that the Institute's apparent abdication as a leading force in the establishment of accounting principles was the principal catalyst for the reorganization of the AAUIA as the American Accounting Association in 1935–36. In the new Association's declaration of objectives, published early in 1936, its leaders rejected the view that "the only practicable means of improvement [in accounting practice] is the slow, evolutionary process involving persuasion and example through which the worst accounting practices may be gradually eliminated" [AAA, 1936, p. 2]. The new Association's program was defined as follows:

> Specifically, there should be a definitive, understandable explanation of what

a set of accounting statements purports to signify. . . . Such a body of principles would furnish an essential basis of judgment in constructing and appraising financial statements. . . . The essential of such a statement is that it constitute an integrated conception of the function of accounting as a means of giving financial expression to business facts [pp. 2–3].

One of the four official purposes of the new Association was

> To develop accounting principles and standards, and to seek their endorsement or adoption by business enterprises, public and private accountants, and governmental bodies [Zeff, 1966, p. 40].

This was a new objective that did not appear in the Constitution of the AAUIA. Thus was the impetus for the series of AAA statements on accounting principles, the first of which appeared in 1936.

There is ample reason to believe that the Institute leadership was not comfortable with the bold initiatives of the reborn Association. SEC Commissioner George C. Mathews was invited to attend the first meeting of the Association's 1936 executive committee, at which the Commissioner "asserted the need for an authoritative literature for use by governmental agencies" [Zeff, 1966, p. 43]. In June 1936, the Association's executive committee issued "A Tentative Statement of Accounting Principles Affecting Corporate Reports" and awaited the profession's reaction. Although numerous academics gave speeches and wrote articles that were critical of one or more sections of the principles statement, official comment from the Institute was nil. The Institute was evidently not pleased that the upstart organization of teachers was attempting to establish accounting principles that might, in the end, affect the performance standards expected of practitioners [Zeff, 1966, pp. 45–46]. Carman G. Blough, the SEC Chief Accountant, in a talk at the inaugural annual meeting of the Association, praised the body's principles statement as "a real contribution to the accounting profession" [1937, p. 30]. When, in early 1938, the Institute published a monograph entitled *A Statement of Accounting Principles*, written by three well-known academics [Sanders, Hatfield and Moore, 1938], a number of members of the Association believed that the Institute was trying to counter the recent achievement of the Association. The monograph had been commissioned in early 1935 by the Haskins & Sells Foundation, and the research was apparently completed before the Institute offered to publish it [Zeff, 1966, p. 47].

Annoyance at the growing role of the Association in the principles sphere was but one factor in impelling the Institute to regain the lead as a principles setter in 1938. The major factor was growing pressure being exerted by the SEC. Again, the specter of governmental intervention spurred the Institute's leadership.

During 1937–38, leaders of the Institute discussed whether, and if so, how, the Institute might reassert its leadership in the establishment of accounting principles. The SEC had been urging the Institute to take a more active role in promoting uniformity in accounting practice, and in April 1938, in one of Carman Blough's final acts as Chief Accountant, the Commission issued Accounting Series Release No. 4 which challenged the profession to provide "substantial authoritative support" for accepted accounting practices (see Zeff [1972, pp. 134–139]).

George O. May, for his part, proposed that his Committee on Accounting Pro-

cedure, rather than awaiting questions that might be raised by others (including the SEC), should act on its own initiative to give advice on matters meriting the Committee's attention. Previts and Merino report that May petitioned the Institute's executive committee in September 1937 to expand the Committee's membership, establish a research capability, and authorize it to initiate discussion on any problem area [1979, pp. 260–261] (also see Horne [1941, p. 47]).

The Institute's leadership moved cautiously in taking up May's suggestion. There was a concern that the Institute would suffer embarrassment if it were seen to issue pronouncements that failed to win the support of other authorities, or even of its own membership. May himself recognized the possible vulnerability of an Institute committee working alone in such sensitive waters. In a letter dated June 1, 1938 to Institute Secretary John L. Carey, May wrote:

> I feel it would be very unfortunate to have opinions put forward by the Institute which would be in direct conflict with those expressed by either the Securities and Exchange Commission or the New York Stock Exchange, or by an official body of accounting teachers, though I am quite prepared to express and maintain such dissent if it seems really necessary.

Other Institute leaders were impatient for signs of some progress. For example, on May 25, 1938, Will-A. Clader, a member of Council and a former Institute vice-president, wrote, in a letter to Frederick B. Andrews, also a member of Council and a former Institute President:

> For some reason the Institute's powers that be appear to be fearful of giving official approval to accounting principles. . . . I am getting old fast and fear that I may not see the day when the pro-

fession will have arrived to the point when it will have the final word in the accounting treatment of financial transactions.

Clader was concerned that Institute committees, including the Committee on Accounting Procedure when commenting on technical questions, were required to state that their views were given for information only "and that care must be taken so that there is no indication that they received the approval of the Institute or its governing body." Some, such as Clader, had suggested that the Institute's executive committee might allow statements drafted by technical committees to be issued under its imprimatur, but that idea was dismissed by Clem W. Collins, Institute President, in a letter to Clader dated June 2, 1938:

> The views of the members of the Executive Committee on such a controversial subject, would have no binding effect upon the profession or the members of the Institute if they did not represent the consensus of opinion and the prevailing best practice of the practitioners. It is quite conceivable that the views of the men constituting the Executive Committee might not represent that preponderance of opinion and practice; therefore until the profession has been given an opportunity to discuss proposed principles and procedures and to freely express opinions in regard thereto, I do not feel that any official group in the Institute should attempt to lay down the law.

Finally, acting on a proposal put forth in July 1938 by Patrick W. R. Glover, a partner in the major firm of Barrow, Wade, Guthrie & Co. and a member of the Institute's executive committee, the Institute leadership agreed to take a decisive step [Zeff, 1972, p. 135]. Glover's proposal contained the major points advanced by May in his recommendation

to the executive committee nine months earlier, and he added the proviso that the Committee should be authorized to issue bulletins without reference to the executive committee. In his Committee's report to Council in September 1938, May's proposal of September 1937 was reiterated. As approved by the Institute's Council, the plan provided for an enlargement of the Committee on Accounting Procedure from eight to 22 members, including the President as *ex officio* chairman, and authority to issue pronouncements in its own name. In 1939, also reflecting the proposals made by May and Glover, the Institute formed a research department to assist the Committee on Accounting Procedure in studying alternative solutions to accounting problems. These actions underscored the position that the Institute could not risk forfeiting its leadership in the establishment of accounting principles, especially in view of the restiveness of the SEC.

The essence of the compromise was that all interested parties and organizations whose support for pronouncements was required would be represented on the Committee. Three academics were named to the enlarged Committee: A. C. Littleton, William A. Paton, and Roy B. Kester, all of whom had led the reorganization of the AAA in 1935–36. Littleton and Paton were the Association's codirectors of research in 1938. (In all subsequent years, academics were included on the membership of the Committee.) The New York Stock Exchange was covered by the fact that George O. May, whose firm served as accounting adviser to the Exchange, was selected as vice-chairman of the Committee. (In actual fact, May chaired the Committee's meetings and led its work.) Since Carman G. Blough had concluded his service as SEC Chief Accountant on May 31, 1938 and had joined Arthur Andersen & Co. as a manager, he was an obvious candidate for Committee membership, and, indeed, his name appeared on the inaugural roll.[8] William W. Werntz, Blough's successor as SEC Chief Accountant, was invited to attend an early meeting of the Committee. Finally, a member was taken from each of the major public accounting firms, so that the likelihood of an important firm's disavowing the Committee's recommendations might be minimized. Another reason, of course, was to tap the substantial expertise in the larger firms, those whose clients were subject to the SEC's jurisdiction. The Committee membership in 1938–39 read like a "Who's Who" of the best-known technical experts in the U.S. accounting profession:

Clem W. Collins (Institute President), Chairman, Collins, Peabody and Young (Denver)

George O. May, Vice-Chairman, Price, Waterhouse & Co. (New York)

Frederick B. Andrews, F. B. Andrews & Company (Chicago)

George D. Bailey, Ernst & Ernst (Detroit)

Carman G. Blough, Arthur Andersen & Co. (Chicago)

Samuel J. Broad, Peat, Marwick, Mitchell & Co. (New York)

Arthur H. Carter, Haskins & Sells (New York)

Charles B. Couchman, Barrow, Wade, Guthrie & Co. (New York)

A. S. Fedde, Fedde & Company (New York)

Henry B. Fernald, Loomis, Suffern & Fernald (New York)

Stanley G. H. Fitch, Patterson, Teele & Dennis (Boston)

Henry A. Horne, Webster, Horne & Blanchard (New York)

Frederick H. Hurdman, Hurdman and Cranstoun (New York)

Lincoln G. Kelly, Lincoln G. Kelly & Company (Salt Lake City)

Roy B. Kester, Columbia University

Lewis Lilly, McLaren, Goode & Co. (San Francisco)

A. C. Littleton, University of Illinois

Warren W. Nissley, Arthur Young & Company (New York)

William A. Paton, University of Michigan

Charles F. Rittenhouse, Charles F. Rittenhouse & Company (Boston)

Walter A. Staub, Lybrand, Ross Bros. & Montgomery (New York)

Victor H. Stempf, Touche, Niven & Co. (New York)

Thus began the precedent of inviting one member to the Committee from each of the major national firms.[9] (This practice was continued with respect to the Big Eight firms on the Accounting Principles Board.) The Institute leadership was careful to provide representation on the Committee from both small and large firms, and from the Midwest, Rocky Mountains, and West Coast, as well as the East. Seven of the members were chairmen of other Institute committees. All angles were considered.

The Institute's first Director and Co-ordinator of Research was Thomas H. Sanders, an accounting professor at the Harvard Business School, who had served as a consultant to the SEC in 1934–35 and was the lead author of the Institute's 1938 publication, *A Statement of Accounting Principles*.

Hence, by 1939, the Institute's machinery was in place. Between 1934, when

[8] A measure of the importance of having the immediate past SEC Chief Accountant on the Committee is the fact that Blough was only a manager at Arthur Andersen & Co. He is probably the only representative of an accounting firm to serve on a standard-setting body prior to becoming a partner.

[9] With the merger of several firms in 1947 to form Touche, Niven, Bailey & Smart, and the merger in 1950 of Barrow, Wade, Guthrie & Co. into Peat, Marwick, Mitchell & Co., the eight largest firms came to be known as the Big Eight, a term whose popularity is traceable to Wise [1960].

the Institute membership had approved the six "rules or principles," and 1938–39, when the Institute reconstituted its Committee on Accounting Procedure and launched a research department, it had largely abandoned its leadership role in the establishment of accounting principles. The aggressiveness of the American Accounting Association in filling this void had been influential in inducing the Institute to find a way to recapture its leadership position. But the major influence had to be seen as the SEC. Yet notwithstanding the almost pathological fear by accounting practitioners of governmental intervention in their affairs, the Institute did not seize the initiative, following the passage of the securities acts, to develop and publicize its views on accounting principles. Kohler was probably right in believing that the leaders of the practicing profession, especially May, were exceedingly reluctant to "force" a consensus on accounting principles when a diversity of views prevailed among leading practitioners and other authorities. Throughout its life, the Committee on Accounting Procedure labored under this philosophical conflict—i.e., whether an authoritative professional body might insist upon the acceptability of only one accounting method when several enjoyed the support of leading CPA's and large corporations. The issue was not faced squarely until 1964, when the Institute, following 18 months of intensive study and debate, resolved to endow Opinions of the Accounting Principles Board with greater authority in the forging of "generally accepted accounting principles" (see Carey [1970, Chap. 5]). A burden was imposed on auditors to justify material departures from principles accepted in APB Opinions, and the APB was charged to "move toward the reduction of alternative practices in accounting" [*Report of the Special Committee on Opinions of the Accounting Principles Board*, 1965, p. 7].

AICPA DECISION TO SUPPLANT CAP WITH APB

Several factors seem to have driven the Institute's decision, made in 1959, to replace the Committee on Accounting Procedure (CAP) with the Accounting Principles Board (APB).

First, certain accounting problems had become increasingly difficult to resolve and had been causing serious divisions within the Committee on Accounting Procedure.

In several problem areas, the number of dissents and qualified assents (which often were tantamount, in their substance, to dissents) seemed to threaten further progress, and not a few of the dissenters and qualified assenters were representatives of the largest public accounting firms. Prominent instances were as follows:

"Accounting for the Use of Special War Reserves," Accounting Research Bulletin (ARB) No. 26 (October 1946)—three dissents (Haskins & Sells, Price Waterhouse, and Arthur Young).

"Emergency Facilities," ARB No. 27 (November 1946)—six dissents (including Price Waterhouse, Arthur Young, Touche Niven, and Barrow, Wade & Guthrie) and a qualified assent.

"Income and Earned Surplus," ARB No. 32 (December 1947)—three dissents (including Alexander Grant) and a qualified assent.

Letter dated October 14, 1948 from the Committee on Accounting Procedure reaffirming its ARB No. 33, "Depreciation and High Costs"—four dissents (including the chairman who was from Peat Marwick).

"Presentation of Income and Earned Surplus," ARB No. 35 (October 1948)—two dissents (Haskins & Sells and Ernst & Ernst) and four qualified assents.

"Depreciation and High Costs," Chapter 9(A) of ARB No. 43 (June 1953)—six dissents (including Peat Marwick and Price Waterhouse).

"Unamortized Discount, Issue Cost, and Redemption Premium on Bonds Refunded," Chapter 15 of ARB No. 43 (June 1953)—one dissent and four qualified assents (Peat Marwick, Haskins & Sells, Touche Niven, and Price Waterhouse).

"Accounting for the Costs of Pension Plans," ARB No. 47 (September 1956)—six qualified assents (including Price Waterhouse, Ernst & Ernst, Haskins & Sells, and Lybrand, Ross Bros. & Montgomery).

"Declining-Balance Depreciation," ARB No. 44 (Revised) (July 1958) —five qualified assents (including Arthur Andersen, Ernst & Ernst, Price Waterhouse, and Haskins & Sells).

Not only did these disagreements betray a difference in philosophy over the role of the Committee in narrowing the range of acceptable methods, but they also revealed fundamental disagreements over the proper methods of asset valuation and income determination. The latter discord suggested the need for more basic inquiries into the premises underlying broad accounting principles.

On at least four occasions during the Committee's history—1939, 1940, 1949, and 1956—it was proposed that the Committee develop a framework of fundamental principles that might serve to unite its members on the particulars of specific pronouncements, but no progress was ever reported (see Zeff [1972, pp.

141–143]). In his proposal for a reinvigorated accounting principles program in 1957, Institute President Alvin R. Jennings singled out research, especially fundamental research, as requiring a significant investment of resources [Jennings, 1958, pp. 31–33]. From this suggestion was born the accounting research division (of which Maurice Moonitz was the first director) to succeed the Institute's research department, which had been serving numerous other committees as well as the Committee on Accounting Procedure.[10]

Among the accounting research division's initial projects were, of course, the studies on postulates and basic principles by Moonitz and Robert T. Sprouse (see Zeff [1982]). Yet, upon the completion of this research phase, in 1962, the APB peremptorily dismissed the two studies as "too radically different from present generally accepted accounting principles for acceptance at this time" [APB, 1962]. The only fundamental research that reached fruition during the tenure of the APB were Accounting Research Study No. 7, *Inventory of Generally Accepted Accounting Principles for Business Enterprises* [Grady, 1965] and APB Statement No. 4, "Basic Concepts and Accounting Principles Underlying Financial Statements of Business

---

[10] Almost as soon as the Institute's research department was created in 1939, it was serving more than one demanding master. Although it had been established to assist the Committee on Accounting Procedure, by 1939–40 it was also conducting studies for the new Committee on Auditing Procedure. The number of Institute committees which it served continued to grow, and Carman G. Blough said that, in the 1950s, "As Director of Research, I complained because I had to spread my little staff of four CPA's over some 25 committees of the Institute, and we were not able to give enough time and attention to the Committee on Accounting Procedure" [Interview conducted by the author in January 1967]. Hence, the charge to the newly created accounting research division in 1959 was that its exclusive responsibility was to the Accounting Principles Board.

Enterprises" [APB, 1970]. Except for small portions of both studies (Chapters 2 and 9 in the former, and Chapter 4 in the latter), neither went beyond an exposition of accepted practice.

Second, representations had been made by the Controllers Institute of America (later to become the Financial Executives Institute) that company managements had not been given sufficient opportunity to comment on proposed bulletins prior to their issuance. (See Zeff [1972, pp. 145–148 and 168].) Since 1938, all of the members of the Committee on Accounting Procedure had been either accounting practitioners or academics, and the view had come to the fore that controllers and perhaps other interested parties should be integrated into the process of establishing accounting principles. In fact, the immediate past president of the Controllers Institute, Dudley E. Browne, was appointed in 1957 to the Institute's Special Committee on Research Program (which was formed in 1957 to study the implications of Jennings' presidential speech), evidently to underscore the newly acknowledged importance of the company controller in such matters. (From its founding, the APB always had between one and three financial executives as members. The Comptroller General of the United States was one of its charter members, and in the Board's final three years, 1971–73, one of its members was a financial analyst. Furthermore, the APB's exposure process and manner of consultation with interested parties eventually became considerably more elaborate than had been that of the Committee on Accounting Procedure.)

Third, the view had been gaining credence that the efforts of the American Accounting Association in the area of accounting principles reflected a more progressive spirit than did those of the Committee on Accounting Procedure. The AAA's Supplementary Statement No. 2, "Price Level Changes and Financial Statements" [1951], and the 1957 Revision of the Association's series of principles statements, "Accounting and Reporting Standards for Corporate Financial Statements," kept alive the interest, furthered more by academics than by practitioners, of general price-level accounting. The former had been cited by several members of the Committee on Accounting Procedure, when, in 1953–54, an effort was made to reverse the Committee's negative stand toward accounting recognition of changing prices (see AIA [1953, Chap. 9(A)]). (Later in the decade, the AAA studies by Jones [1955] and Mason [1956] attracted considerable interest among policy makers.) Also, in the debate over the "all-inclusive" vs. "current-operating-performance" conception of the income statement, the SEC made a point (at least as late as 1951) of citing the AAA's support of the former, which the SEC favored, while at the same time criticizing the Committee on Accounting Procedure's espousal of the latter (see Barr [1979, pp. 45, 49–51 and ftn. 3]; King [1948; 1951]; and SEC [1948, p. 112]).

Even George O. May, whose leadership of the Committee during its early years established the Committee's practice of addressing accounting principles on an issue-by-issue basis, conceded in 1958 that the AAA's approach might well be emulated by the Institute:

> The American Accounting Association from the time of its first pronouncement has sought to relate specific provisions to a broad concept. It would seem that the Institute must successfully undertake a similar task before it can claim with reason to be either the leading authority or one of the leading authorities upon the subject [Grady, 1962, p. 278].

The Association's series of principles statements, especially the eight supplementary statements issued on specific topics between 1950 and 1954, caused some to believe that the Institute's program could benefit from a firmer conceptual basis in its pronouncements, underscoring the need, mentioned above, for more fundamental research. It is noteworthy, therefore, that one of the individuals named to the Institute's Special Committee on Research Program in 1957 was R. K. Mautz, of the University of Illinois, who had been chairman of the AAA committee that had prepared the 1957 Revision of the Association's series of principles statements.

Fourth, the Institute's leaders were feeling the sting of Leonard Spacek's outspoken criticism of the profession's record in establishing accounting principles. In one speech, given in early 1957, he accused the Committee on Accounting Procedure of yielding to industry pressure on a proposed pronouncement. Institute Executive Director John L. Carey reported that "A wave of indignation greeted [Spacek's] speech" [1970, p. 77]. The Institute appointed a special committee to investigate Spacek's allegations, and it concluded that his assertions were unfounded [AIA, 1957]. In his presidential address the following October, in which he proposed a major research program to support the Institute's ongoing effort to establish accounting principles, Alvin R. Jennings went out of his way to defend the profession's record of independence [1958, p. 33]. Although Jennings did not identify the source of the challenge to the profession's independence, it can easily be inferred that he had Spacek in mind. Moreover, Spacek was among the ten individuals named by Jennings to the Special Committee on Research Program.

It is evident that Spacek's criticisms of the Institute's accounting principles program, as well as his proposal for an accounting court made in a widely reported speech in August 1957 [Spacek, 1958], were consequential in the Institute's high-level review in 1957–58 of its process of establishing accounting principles.

Fifth, the Committee on Accounting Procedure had crossed swords several times with the SEC's Chief Accountant, and the confrontations had evoked disquiet on both sides. The SEC was displeased with the Committee's preference for the "current-operating-performance" conception of the income statement, and several members of the Committee (as well as a number of widely known practitioners and academics—e.g., Grady, Spacek, and Paton) were upset at the SEC's unwillingness to allow the effects of changing prices to enter into the determination of companies' net incomes.[11] (This latter concern led some to believe that a vigorous attempt to lay a groundwork of fundamental accounting principles might be the only avenue to genuine progress.) Furthermore, the SEC had made it known that the Committee had not done enough to limit the alternatives available to management (see Storey [1964, pp. 48–51] and Zeff [1972, pp. 150–160]). The Institute was, as always, sensitive to the need to retain its credibility with the SEC. Among the individuals appointed to the Special Committee on Research Program were Andrew Barr, the SEC Chief Accountant,[12] and two of the three former SEC Chief Accountants,

[11] For the opinion of the then Chief Accountant of the SEC, see King [1952].

[12] It has been exceedingly rare for the SEC Chief Accountant to serve as a voting member on Institute policy committees. One supposes that the Commission regards such service, except in unusual circumstances, as having the potential to compromise, at least in appearance, the SEC's independence from those organizations that are subject to its regulation.

Carman G. Blough and William W. Werntz. Blough had been the Institute's respected Director of Research since 1944, and Werntz was the Chairman of the Committee on Accounting Procedure in 1957–59.

Other factors may have been at work, but I believe that the foregoing five factors were the most important. Some critics complained that a few of the larger accounting firms had begun to nominate less senior partners to the Committee on Accounting Procedure, and it was not unknown for members to call their home offices to ascertain the views of their more senior partners—who would not have heard the Committee's debate—prior to casting their vote. When the Institute's executive committee appointed the members of the inaugural Accounting Principles Board, it insisted that the accounting firms could be represented only by their firm-wide managing partners. Some firms balked at this restriction, but no exceptions were allowed (save for the chairman of the Board, Weldon Powell, who had also been chairman of the Special Committee on Research Program).

Criticism in the financial press was infrequent and thus seems to have been largely absent as a factor.

One can therefore say, after reviewing the factors enumerated and discussed above, that the Institute was reacting both to internal and external criticisms. In the main, it hoped that a much more heavily research-based approach to establishing accounting principles would facilitate a resolution of the growing number of seemingly intractable problems.

AICPA DECISION TO APPOINT A STUDY ON ESTABLISHMENT OF ACCOUNTING PRINCIPLES (THE WHEAT STUDY)

As has already been noted, the APB failed to fulfill its founders' hopes that fundamental research would reduce complex accounting problems to basic notions on which leading professionals could find agreement. Neither the Grady [1965] study nor the Board's Statement No. 4 [1970] was followed up by normative research that might have recommended a set of fundamental principles or accounting objectives. And except for its much more elaborate procedure for obtaining comments on its tentative positions (meetings with industry groups, symposia, public hearings, and a more extensive distribution of exposure drafts), the Board operated in a manner not greatly dissimilar from that of the Committee on Accounting Procedure.

Yet notwithstanding its new procedures and the fortified research commitment by the Institute, the APB compiled a record of dissents and qualified assents on matters involving asset valuation and income determination which exceeded that of the Committee on Accounting Procedure. Of the 12 substantive, single-issue Opinions issued by the Board through 1970 (see Exhibit 1), major disagreements among the Board members occurred on nine (i.e., excluding Opinions 5, 7, and 8).[13] These nine Opinions contained 35 dissents and 27 qualified assents, including in the former figure 13 dissents by Big Eight firm partners and eight dissents by academics. Indeed, of the 21 votes cast by the academics in the nine Opinions, 12 were either dissents or qualified assents. Three of the nine

[13] In fact, three Board members—two academics and a partner in a Big Eight firm—were prepared to file qualified assents to Opinion No. 7 owing to their belief that the Opinion proposed a kind of accounting for lessors that was inconsistent with the accounting for lessees specified in Opinion No. 5. At the eleventh hour, they were persuaded to withdraw their qualification in exchange for the insertion of paragraph 18, in which the Board acknowledged a possible inconsistency and said it "will continue to give consideration to this question." Yet the Board never addressed the alleged inconsistency in its later pronouncements.

Exhibit 1

Dissents and Qualified Assents in the 12 Substantive Single-Issue Opinions
of the Accounting Principles Board Through 1970

Opinion No. and Title	Total		Big Eight Firm Partners		Academics		No. of Academics on APB
	Dissents	Qualified Assents	Dissents	Qualified Assents	Dissents	Qualified Assents	
1 New Depreciation Guidelines and Rules	0	5	0	3	0	1	3
2 Accounting for the "Investment Credit"	6	1	4	1	0	0	3
4 Accounting for the "Investment Credit"	5	8	1	6	2	1	3
5 Reporting of Leases in Financial Statements of Lessee	1	2	1	0	0	1	3
7 Accounting for Leases in Financial Statements of Lessors	0	0	0	0	0	0	3
8 Accounting for the Cost of Pension Plans	0	0	0	0	0	0	2
9 Reporting the Results of Operations	0	5	0	3	0	1	2
11 Accounting for Income Taxes	6	1	2	1	1	0	2
14 Accounting for Convertible Debt and Debt Issued with Stock Purchase Warrants	4	2	2	1	1	0	2
15 Earnings per Share	3	5	2	2	0	1	2
16 Business Combinations	6	0	1	0	2	0	2
17 Intangible Assets	5	0	1	0	2	0	2
Totals	36	29	14	17	8	5	29
Totals for all but Opinions 5, 7 and 8	35	27	13	17	8	4	21

Note: Opinion No. 3, "The Statement of Source and Application of Funds," has been omitted as it did not affect the basic financial statements. Opinions 6, 10, and 12 dealt with a variety of matters, and Opinion 13 made a portion of Opinion 9 applicable to commercial banks.

Opinions (Nos. 2, 11, and 16) secured only the barest majority (i.e., two-thirds) required for passage. In Opinion No. 4, on the investment credit, the amount of space used to present the views of the five dissenters and eight qualified assenters well exceeded the space used to express the majority view.

The circumstances attending the approval of Opinions 16 and 17 appalled a number of APB members and close observers of the Board's operations (see Seligman [1982, pp. 416–430]). Pressure from both industry and government was especially intense and unrelenting, and, in one celebrated instance, a Board member astonished his colleagues by changing the vote he had cast at an earlier Board meeting at which a business combinations/goodwill Opinion was approved in principle by exactly a two-thirds majority. The previous meeting of the Board had been regarded as the climax of 18 difficult months of trying to fashion an Opinion that would secure at least a two-thirds majority, and it is not an exaggeration to say that the member's announcement of his change of mind provoked general consternation in the Board. In the end, the Board divided business combinations and goodwill into two Opinions, and the required majorities were somehow achieved.

Hard on the heels of the Institute's publication of Opinions 16 and 17 in August 1970, the senior partners of three

Big Eight firms wrote letters to the Institute President, Marshall S. Armstrong, in which they strongly criticized the Board's performance. In a letter dated November 11, 1970, Ralph E. Kent, managing partner of Arthur Young & Company, wrote that "A number of developments over the past several months have raised some doubts in my mind as to whether the present APB organization is the most appropriate ongoing mechanism for the establishment of accounting principles." Harvey E. Kapnick, chairman of Arthur Andersen & Co., in a letter dated November 16, 1970, wrote that "The Accounting Principles Board, in our view, has not successfully carried out its mission nor does it currently give promise of doing so." And Robert M. Trueblood (who had long been critical of the Board), chairman of the policy group of Touche Ross & Co., in a letter dated November 17, 1970, wrote that "we are presently reconsidering our entire participation in the affairs of the Board."

In the face of this barrage of criticism, Armstrong called an extraordinary conference of 35 prominent CPA's from 21 major accounting firms to discuss what should be done. The meeting was held in January 1971. Out of this conference came the recommendation that two study groups be appointed—one on the process of establishing accounting principles and the other on the objectives of financial statements (which came to be known as the Wheat and Trueblood Study Groups, respectively, after the names of their chairmen). In March 1972, the Wheat Study reported its unanimous recommendation that a Financial Accounting Standards Board, largely independent from the AICPA, be established [Study on Establishment of Accounting Principles, 1972], and within two months the Institute's Council adopted the Study's

recommendations. The Accounting Principles Board was terminated on June 30, 1973.

In the Institute leadership's deliberations in late 1970 and early 1971, it was noted that the American Accounting Association had, in August 1970, appointed a Committee on Establishment of an Accounting Commission, whose purpose was "to study the feasibility and desirability of a commission to inquire into the formulation of accounting principles" [AAA, 1971, p. 609]. The Association committee had been in touch with officers of the Institute and former members of the APB, so its existence was well known to the Institute hierarchy. Indeed, the Institute leadership was plainly nettled at the Association for trespassing on its turf. Both the Kent and Trueblood letters to Armstrong referred to the Association's initiative, and the AAA committee was mentioned during the high-level conference chaired by Armstrong in January 1971. The AAA committee recommended the establishment of a commission of inquiry, and in February 1971 the AAA's executive committee unanimously approved its report. But the Institute asked the Association to defer taking any action until after the report of its Wheat Study was received, and the Association acceded to this request. No further action was ever taken on the report of the Association's committee, but in its very creation and operation the committee had an impact on the actions taken by the Institute. In terms of practical effect, David Solomons, who had chaired the Association's committee, was named to the Wheat Study, and he became the principal draftsman of the Study's report. George H. Sorter, a member of the Association's committee, was appointed as research director for the Trueblood Study, and the 1968–69 and 1970–71 Association Presidents, Sidney Davidson and James Don Edwards, were made members of the nine-man Trueblood Study Group.

The report of the Association's committee [AAA, 1971] and the letters from Kent, Kapnick, and Trueblood, as well as other inquiries (e.g., see *AICPA Study . . .* [1972]), pointed to a number of deficiencies in the operation of the Board. An alleged lack of independence (a question raised in relation to the Committee on Accounting Procedure in the 1950's), possibly opening practitioner members to pressure from their firms' clients, was an issue. Others contended that the Board, e.g., in Opinion No. 15 on earnings per share, was producing rule books rather than statements of principles (see Paton [1971, p. 42]). Another concern felt strongly by a number of critics was the Board's failure (following on the failure of the Committee on Accounting Procedure) to establish fundamental principles, or objectives, to guide its work on specific topics. The Board's Statement No. 4, issued in early 1970, contained a strong dissent by one Board member (a Big Eight firm partner), and its status as a Statement rather than as an Opinion (which had been the original plan) was criticized by Maurice Moonitz, who had been a Board member in 1963–66, when the project was launched [1971]. As a Statement, the pronouncement could be ignored by practitioners.

One reason, seldom mentioned, why the APB foundered in its early years was the unexpected decision of the Institute's executive committee, in 1959, to insist that the accounting firms could be represented on the Board only by their firmwide managing partners. One surmises that the reason behind the executive committee's decision was that (as suggested above) some firms were seen as not taking the work of the Committee on Accounting Procedure seriously, by sending part-

ners of lesser stature to represent them. But the executive committee's policy was misconceived. Several of the managing partners had little interest in or aptitude for "theoretical" debates. Being the highest authority in their respective firms, they were disposed to pronounce their views rather than engage in a give-and-take discussion. Often they were not prepared for Board meetings, owing to the press of work in their firms. With strong-willed managing partners on the Board, a spirit of compromise was difficult to achieve. Especially when it was time for the Board to consider the Moonitz and Sprouse studies on accounting postulates and principles, the elder statesmen from the Big Eight firms were hardly of a mind to reexamine accounting from the ground up. Owing in part to this constitution of the Board's membership, relatively little genuine progress was made until 1964, when the Institute's executive committee, evidently having concluded that its membership policy was not working, began to replace most of the managing partners with their firms' senior technical partners.

After reviewing the history of the Committee on Accounting Procedure and the APB, Moonitz has concluded that "The evidence is clear that a professional accounting body, acting by itself, is incapable of obtaining agreement on a set of accounting standards" [1974, p. 67], as allies are needed to offset the power of management. While some have believed that outside pressures, such as those coming from government or industry, led to the downfall of the APB (e.g., see Zeff [1978]), George R. Catlett, a Board member from 1965 to 1971, disagreed:

> The Board's demise stemmed directly from the confusion and controversy stirred by efforts to halt alleged abuses and regulate accounting by means of arbitrary and uncoordinated rules based

on a chain of questionable compromises [1980].

Former APB members and close observers despaired of the "questionable compromises" that were required in order to obtain even fragile majorities in certain Opinions. This experience led some to recommend a Board of considerably smaller size.

To be sure, the APB had been held to a higher standard than the Committee on Accounting Procedure, as it was expected to deal in a definitive way—i.e., severely reduce or eliminate the range of accepted practices—in highly controversial areas, such as pensions, leases, price-level accounting, and income tax allocation. But because the APB *was* expected to make hard choices, outside pressures (exacerbated by constant media coverage) intensified. While the "questionable compromises" cited by Catlett served to debilitate the Board, it cannot be gainsaid that pressures from industry, the financial sector, and government played a significant role in the demise of the APB.

CONCLUSION

No common explanation may be found to describe the factors motivating the actions at all of the five junctures, especially as they cover a period of more than five decades. Perhaps the strongest force was the profession's fear of active involvement by government in the establishment of accounting principles. Criticism from within the Institute (in 1917, 1957 and 1970) also was a precipitating factor. Although Ripley's writings represented criticism from outside the profession, his call for government intervention endowed his words with special meaning for the Institute. The surge of the reborn American Accounting Association in 1936, coupled with Kohler's critical editorials, made a mark on Institute affairs in the 1930's, and the series of AAA principles statements, culminating in the 1957 Revision, together with the appointment in 1970 of the AAA's Committee on Establishment of an Accounting Commission, were contributing factors in later decades.

This is not to suggest that the Institute's leaders could be caricatured as reluctant plutocrats who could be moved only by fear of losing their control over events. Ripley's criticism gave George O. May the opportunity to fill a void in the Institute's leadership and launch a campaign to raise the standards of accounting and auditing practice. A call to ideals motivated the critics (e.g., Scovell, Kohler, Spacek and Trueblood) as it did those who engineered reforms (e.g., May, Glover and Powell). The tactics used by the several actors were different, but the cause was the same: to find a better way.

REFERENCES

Accounting Principles Board, "Statement by the Accounting Principles Board" (AICPA, 1962).
——— "Basic Concepts and Accounting Principles Underlying Financial Statements of Business Enterprises," *Statement No. 4* (AICPA, 1970).
AICPA Study on Establishment of Accounting Principles, Cases in Public Accounting Practice, Volume 11 (Arthur Andersen & Co., 1972).
American Accounting Association, "Statement of Objectives of the American Accounting Association," THE ACCOUNTING REVIEW (March 1936), pp. 1-4.
———, Committee on Concepts and Standards Underlying Corporate Financial Statements, "Price Level Changes and Financial Statements," *Supplementary Statement No. 2* (AAA, 1951).

——, Committee on Accounting Concepts and Standards, "Accounting and Reporting Standards for Corporate Financial Statements," *1957 Revision* (AAA, 1957).

——, Committee on Establishment of an Accounting Commission, "The Role of the American Accounting Association in the Development of Accounting Principles," THE ACCOUNTING REVIEW (July 1971), pp. 609-616.

American Institute of Accountants, *Audits of Corporate Accounts* (AIA, 1934).

——, Committee on Accounting Procedure, "Restatement and Revision of Accounting Research Bulletins," *Accounting Research Bulletin No. 43* (AIA, 1953).

——, Report of Special Committee Investigating Certain Phases of the Work of the Committee on Accounting Procedure and the Committee on Relations with the Interstate Commerce Commission (1957), reproduced in *A Search for Fairness in Financial Reporting to the Public, 1956-1969* (Arthur Andersen & Co., 1969), pp. 469-487.

Barr, Andrew, "Relations Between the Development of Accounting Principles and the Activities of the SEC," in William W. Cooper and Yuji Ijiri, Eds., *Eric Louis Kohler, Accounting's Man of Principles* (Reston Publishing Company, 1979), pp. 41-61.

Blough, Carman G., "The Need for Accounting Principles," THE ACCOUNTING REVIEW (March 1937), pp. 30-37.

——, "Development of Accounting Principles in the United States," in *Berkeley Symposium on the Foundations of Financial Accounting* (Schools of Business Administration, University of California, Berkeley, 1967), pp. 1-14.

Carey, John L., *The Rise of the Accounting Profession: From Technician to Professional, 1896-1936* (American Institute of Certified Public Accountants, 1969).

——, *The Rise of the Accounting Profession: To Responsibility and Authority, 1937-1969* (American Institute of Certified Public Accountants, 1970).

Catlett, George R., "Accounting: More Words, Less Reality," *The New York Times* (September 21, 1980).

Clark, J. Maurice, *Studies in the Economics of Overhead Costs* (The University of Chicago Press, 1923).

Dickinson, A. Lowes, "The Fallacy of Including Interest and Rent as Part of Manufacturing Cost," *The Journal of Accountancy* (December 1911), pp. 588-593.

Financial Accounting Standards Board (FASB), "Accounting for Interest Costs," Discussion Memorandum (FASB, 1977).

Grady, Paul (Editor), *Memoirs and Accounting Thought of George O. May* (The Ronald Press Company, 1962).

——, *Inventory of Generally Accepted Accounting Principles for Business Enterprises* (AICPA, 1965).

Horne, Henry A., "Accounting Procedure and Research," in *Experiences with Extensions of Auditing Procedure and Papers on Other Accounting Subjects*, Presented at the Fifty-third Annual Meeting of the American Institute of Accountants, 1940 (American Institute of Accountants, 1941), pp. 46-53.

"Interest as an Element of Cost," *Year Book 1921* (National Association of Cost Accountants, 1921), pp. 45-96.

Jennings, Alvin R., "Present-Day Challenges in Financial Reporting," *The Journal of Accountancy* (January 1958), pp. 28-34.

Jones, Ralph Coughenour, *Price Level Changes and Financial Statements, Case Studies of Four Companies* (American Accounting Association, 1955).

King, Earle C., "The Income Statement—Problem Child of Accountancy," *The New York Certified Public Accountant* (June 1948), pp. 413-418.

——, "What Are Accounting Principles?", *California Certified Public Accountant* (November 1951), pp. 12-27.

——, "Dissent," in Report of Study Group on Business Income, *Changing Concepts of Business Income* (The Macmillan Company, 1952), pp. 122-123.

Kohler, Eric L., "A Nervous Profession," THE ACCOUNTING REVIEW (December 1934a), p. 334.

——, "Standards Must Come," THE ACCOUNTING REVIEW (December 1934b), p. 334-336.

——, "Standards: A Dialogue," THE ACCOUNTING REVIEW (December 1935), pp. 370-379.

Mason, Perry, *Price Level Changes and Financial Statements, Basic Concepts and Methods* (American Accounting Association, 1956).

May, George O., "Publicity of Accounts" (1926a), in Bishop Carleton Hunt, Ed., *George Oliver May: Twenty-five Years of Accounting Responsibility, 1911-1936* (American Institute Publishing Co., Inc., 1936), pp. 49-52.

——, "Corporate Publicity and the Auditor," *The Journal of Accountancy* (November 1926b), pp. 321–326.

——, "A Proper Courage in the Assumption of Responsibility by the Accountant" (1926c), in Bishop Carleton Hunt, Ed., *George Oliver May: Twenty-five Years of Accounting Responsibility, 1911–1936* (American Institute Publishing Co., Inc., 1936), pp. 40–48.

——, "Principles of Accounting," *The Journal of Accountancy* (December 1937), pp. 423–425.

——, *Financial Accounting, A Distillation of Experience* (Macmillan Co., 1943).

Moonitz, Maurice, "Three Contributions to the Development of Accounting Principles Prior to 1930," *Journal of Accounting Research* (Spring 1970), pp. 145–155.

——, "The Accounting Principles Board Revisited," *The New York Certified Public Accountant* (May 1971), pp. 341–345.

——, *Obtaining Agreement on Standards in the Accounting Profession*, Studies in Accounting Research No. 8 (American Accounting Association, 1974).

Paton, W. A., "Earmarks of a Profession—and the APB," *The Journal of Accountancy* (January 1971), pp. 37–45.

Previts, Gary John, and Barbara D. Merino, *A History of Accounting in America* (Ronald Press-Wiley, 1979).

"Proceedings of the Annual Meeting Held at the New Willard Hotel, Washington, D. C., September 18 and 19, 1917," *1917 Year-Book of the American Institute of Accountants* (AIA, 1917), pp. 67–72.

"Report of Special Committee on Interest in Relation to Cost," *1918 Year-Book of the American Institute of Accountants* (AIA, 1918), pp. 110–112.

"Report of the Special Committee on Development of Accounting Principles," *1934 Year-Book of the American Institute of Accountants* (AIA, 1935), pp. 276–279.

Report of the Special Committee on Opinions of the Accounting Principles Board, Presented to Council of the American Institute of Certified Public Accountants (AICPA, Spring 1965).

Richardson, A. P., "Standardization of Accounting Procedure," *The Journal of Accountancy* (October 1918), pp. 292–295.

Ripley, William Z., "Stop, Look, Listen!", *The Atlantic Monthly* (September 1926), pp. 380–399.

Sanders, Thomas Henry, Henry Rand Hatfield and Underhill Moore, *A Statement of Accounting Principles* (American Institute of Accountants, 1938).

Securities and Exchange Commission, *14th Annual Report* (Government Printing Office, 1948).

Seligman, Joel, *The Transformation of Wall Street: A History of the Securities and Exchange Commission and Modern Corporate Finance* (Houghton Mifflin Company, 1982).

Spacek, Leonard, "Professional Accountants and Their Public Responsibility" (1957), in *A Search for Fairness in Financial Reporting to the Public, 1956–1969* (Arthur Andersen & Co., 1969), pp. 17–38.

——, "The Need for an Accounting Court," THE ACCOUNTING REVIEW (July 1958), pp. 368–379.

Storey, Reed K., *The Search for Accounting Principles* (American Institute of Certified Public Accountants, 1964).

Study on Establishment of Accounting Principles, *Establishing Financial Accounting Standards* (American Institute of Certified Public Accountants, 1972).

"Uniform Accounts," *Federal Reserve Bulletin* (April 1, 1917), pp. 270–284.

Wells, M. C., *Accounting for Common Costs* (Center for International Education and Research in Accounting, University of Illinois, 1978).

Wise, T. A., "The Auditors Have Arrived," *Fortune*, Part I (November 1960), pp. 151–157, 186, 191–192, 196, 198; Part II (December 1960), pp. 144–148, 239–240, 242, 244.

Zeff, Stephen A., *The American Accounting Association—Its First Fifty Years* (American Accounting Association, 1966).

——, *Forging Accounting Principles in Five Countries: A History and an Analysis of Trends* (Stipes, 1972).

——, "The Rise of 'Economic Consequences,'" *Journal of Accountancy* (December 1978), pp. 56–63.

——, *The Accounting Postulates and Principles Controversy of the 1960s* (Garland, 1982).

Resource note: Quotations are taken from correspondence that has been photocopied from the files of the American Institute of Certified Public Accountants and other sources, and these are in the possession of the author.

Big Eight Firms and the Accounting Literature: The Falloff in Advocacy Writing

STEPHEN A. ZEFF*

The author marshals evidence that partners in Big Eight firms, as well as the firms themselves, have engaged significantly less in advocacy writing in the accounting literature during the last decade compared with the output of articles and firm publications on controversial topics that appeared in the 1960s. He suggests several likely explanations for this trend in the literature, including the increasing competitiveness of public accounting and the transfer of standards-setting authority from a part-time board in which the Big Eight firms played a major role to the full-time Financial Accounting Standards Board. Other explanatory factors are the litigious climate and congressional oversight.

The vitality of a professional literature depends not only on the efforts of academic researchers but also on the intellectual leadership exerted by professionals. Some have commented on the recent trend in the academic accounting literature in which traditional normative research has largely been displaced by mathematical modeling and empirical studies with a high degree of rigor. (See, for example, [1,6].) While empirical research serves to identify and explain the phenomena with which accountants deal, it seldom will suggest directions toward which accounting policy making and practices might fruitfully proceed. In short, academic accountants in recent years have tended to retreat from the traditional normative literature and have had less to say about desirable improvements in policy making and practice.

Little has been written about recent trends in the literature produced by

*Stephen A. Zeff is the Herbert S. Autrey Professor of Accounting at Rice University.

Early drafts of this paper were delivered at the Eighth Annual Congress of the European Accounting Association in Brussels, on April 4, 1985; at the University of Cape Town on July 8, 1985; and at the 70th Annual Meeting of the American Accounting Association in Reno, on August 21, 1985. The author thanks the respondents and George Foster, Thomas R. Dyckman, Maurice Moonitz, Gary J. Previts, Lawrence D. Brown, William W Cooper, Murray Bryant, and Dennis R. Beresford for their helpful comments.

131

accounting professionals. My impression is that accounting professionals
have likewise retreated from normative discourse, and that the literature
produced by professionals in recent years has been characterized less by
normative argument than by neutral discussions and analyses of trends in
policy making and practice. Hector R. Anton, the editor-in-chief of the
Journal of Accounting, Auditing & Finance, has drawn attention to this
trend and has suggested some possible explanations [2]. If I am correct in
this belief, it may be argued that accounting professionals have become a
less fertile source of intellectual leadership in the affairs of the profession.
Specifically, it is my suspicion that the literature produced by partners in
U.S. Big Eight accounting firms has been marked less by advocacy about
accounting principles and the standards-setting process than it was in earlier
years. While it is useful and interesting to study actual trends in policy
making and practice, intellectual leadership requires a debating of contemporary issues with the aim of bringing about an improvement in policy
making and practice. The first is descriptive, while the second is normative.
Both are essential in a professional literature.

It is my purpose here to present some evidence on trends both in the
writings of Big Eight partners and in the publications issued by the Big
Eight firms. To acquire some insight into the reasons for these trends, I sent
a letter (the pertinent extract appears in the appendix) to twenty-six retired
partners of major accounting firms who were leaders of the profession when
they were active. The letter was also sent to a number of active audit partners
of major firms, and to several others. As will be evident from a reading of
the appendix, the letter-questionnaire is not a scientific instrument. It asks
several leading questions and was intended to be provocative. Hence, the
instrument contains some degree of bias, and the research presented in this
paper can only be said to suggest several hypotheses about trends that have
been occurring in the literature; it would be difficult to argue that findings
based on this kind of questionnaire actually confirm such trends. This paper
is intended, therefore, to be suggestive rather than definitive.

Results of the Questionnaire Study

Six of the twenty-six retired partners to whom I sent the letter-questionnaire did not reply; six of the replies were either very brief and general
or were otherwise not responsive to the inquiries in the questionnaire. Hence,
fourteen of the respondents provided useful replies. Their replies were in
the format of open-ended discussions of their views. They therefore are not
susceptible to a meaningful statistical analysis. There was generally strong
support for explanations 1 and 4 in my letter, namely, the influence of

heightened competition, and changes that have occurred in the standards-setting process. That managing partners no longer have the time or inclination to write about accounting principles (no. 7 in my letter) was a view that secured the greatest degree of agreement among the respondents. None of the other proffered explanations gained much support in the letters from the respondents.

The remainder of the paper is divided into three major sections. In the next two sections, I endeavor to examine the trends in the publishing behavior of the Big Eight firms as well as in the writing behavior of the partners of those firms. In the final section, drawing in part on the replies received to the questionnaire, I will suggest some possible explanations for the changes in publishing and writing behavior previously discussed.

Advocacy Papers Published by Big Eight Firms

Arthur Andersen & Co. was the first U.S. Big Eight firm to issue publications expressing the firm's views on accounting principles. Andersen used three basic formats: (1) white-covered booklets enclosing speeches by the firm's senior-level partners, and the firm's briefs filed before the APB, the FASB, and government bodies; (2) brown-covered books containing compendious summaries of current practice, authoritative positions, and the firm's views on about twenty-five to thirty controversial areas of accounting; and (3) brown- or blue-covered booklets or books consisting of explications of the firm's theoretical argument on broad issues of financial reporting.

The speeches and briefs were issued several times a year between 1956 and 1975.[1] The book-length compendium on assorted accounting practices was issued in five editions from 1960 to 1976 under the title, "Accounting and Reporting Problems of the Accounting Profession." The firm's conceptual statements included booklets on the basic postulate of accounting (1960), accounting for income taxes and pensions (1961–1962), and an argument for a court of accounting appeals (1965), among others. The book-length conceptual works were "Objectives of Financial Statements for Business Enterprises" (1972) and "Accounting Standards for Businesses throughout the World" (1974). The former was revised in 1984. Except for a 1984 revision of "Objectives," the firm's steady stream of advocacy papers terminated in 1975–1976. The firm has advised me that the 1984

---

[1] In addition, many of Chairman Harvey Kapnick's speeches during the 1970s were reproduced, in full or in part, in the firm's newsletter, *Executive News Briefs*. In 1985, Arthur Andersen issued its first speech booklet since the mid-1970s. It was an address by Duane R. Kullberg, the managing partner, given on January 17, 1985, which was provoked by the hearings scheduled by a congressional subcommittee on the performance of auditing firms and the SEC's oversight of the profession.

revision of "Objectives" is an occasional publication and does not necessarily signify a resumption of the earlier practice of publishing such works on a fairly systematic basis.

Few other U.S. Big Eight firms issued publications on accounting principles prior to the 1970s. In 1967, during the heat of the controversy over income tax allocation, Price Waterhouse broke its silence on accounting principles with a booklet carrying the provocative title, "Is Generally Accepted Accounting for Income Taxes Possibly Misleading Investors?" At the same time, Coopers & Lybrand declared its position on the issue [9]. Apart from Arthur Andersen's active publications program throughout the decade of the 1960s, these seem to have been the only publications issued by Big Eight firms giving prominence to their corporate views on accounting principles. All the while, of course, their partners on the APB were voting on Opinions.

In 1971–1973, apparently spurred by the inquiry of the AICPA's (the Institute) Trueblood Study Group into the objectives of financial statements, four other Big Eight firms—Price Waterhouse, Coopers & Lybrand, Arthur Young, and Peat, Marwick, Mitchell & Co.—inaugurated series of booklets drawing attention to their institutional positions on controversial areas of financial reporting: leases, materiality, business combinations, foreign currency translation, debt restructuring, changing prices, pensions, and the conceptual framework. These booklets consisted of the firms' written submissions to the Trueblood Study Group, the FASB, or the SEC, or of addresses given by leading partners. Curiously, all of these series terminated, as if on cue, in 1978–1979. Even Arthur Andersen's three-pronged series of advocacy publications ended in 1976 (except, as noted above, for the 1984 revision of the firm's "Objectives" study).

Between 1955 and 1974, Deloitte Haskins & Sells published annual volumes of "Selected Papers" containing speeches by partners on accounting principles and other subjects. No reason was given for its discontinuance after twenty years of publication. Until the latter 1970s, the firm gave summaries of its position on FASB and SEC initiatives in its weekly newsletter *The Week in Review*; extracts from the speeches of leading partners were occasionally reproduced in the newsletter. By the 1980s, however, the normative views of the firm and its senior partners had largely disappeared from the newsletter.

Two firms, Touche Ross & Co. and Ernst & Whinney, issued only a few advocacy papers during the period 1971–1978. In 1975, Touche Ross published a bold current-value proposal in a widely distributed pamphlet titled "Economic Reality in Financial Reporting," and the firm distributed a film to dramatize its argument. But the crusade was short-lived. The firm's

EXHIBIT 1
Newsletters Published for General Circulation
by the U.S. Big Eight Accounting Firms

Arthur Andersen & Co.:

Executive News Briefs (1973–1982)
Accounting News Briefs (1975–   )

Coopers & Lybrand:

Lybrand Newsletter (1958–1973)
Coopers & Lybrand Newsletter (1973–1982)
C&L Executive Alert Newsletter (1982–   )

Deloitte Haskins & Sells:

The Week in Review (1972–1984)
DH&S Review (1985–   )

Ernst & Whinney:

Financial Reporting Developments (1973–   )
Financial Reporting Briefs (1974–   )

Peat, Marwick, Mitchell & Co.:

Executive Newsletter (1975–   )

Price Waterhouse:

Accounting Events and Trends (1974–   )

Touche Ross & Co.:

In Perspective: Current Accounting Developments (1975–1981)
Open Line: A Letter to Accounting Educators (1977–   )

Arthur Young:

Arthur Young Views (1977–1981)

positions on pending FASB drafts were occasionally summarized in its newsletter *In Perspective*, but by the 1980s even this practice ceased, and the newsletter itself went out of existence in 1981. (See Exhibit 1.) Ernst & Whinney published an expansion of its views on the Trueblood inquiry in 1972, and in 1976 it issued a booklet in opposition to current value accounting.

By the end of the 1970s, with but few exceptions, all of the Big Eight firms had reoriented their publication programs primarily toward descriptive studies and client aids. Advocacy was no longer in fashion. Typical publications of the period contained overviews of recent FASB Statements and guides to their implementation, surveys of practice in light of recent pronouncements, objective analyses of the strengths and weaknesses of proposals under consideration by the FASB, and opinion surveys of the preparers and users of financial statements. In most instances that firms inserted normative comments in these publications, they were briefly stated and were typically accorded a low profile. In the 1980s, with but a few exceptions, this trend has continued.

In the period 1983–1985, three of the firms gave prominence to their views on income tax allocation and pension accounting. In March 1984, Deloitte Haskins & Sells issued a small booklet titled "Views on Accounting for Income Taxes," which expressed the firm's position. In 1983 and 1985, Coopers & Lybrand published critical analyses of successive FASB Exposure Drafts on pension accounting, the first appearing as a free-standing booklet and the second as a supplement to the June 1985 issue of the firm's *Executive Alert Newsletter.* Also in 1983, Ernst & Whinney issued a small booklet announcing its disagreement with the FASB's tentative views on pension accounting. A summary of Deloitte Haskins & Sells' transmission of views on pension accounting to the FASB was published in the July 22, 1985, issue of *DH&S Review,* the first number of the firm's new biweekly newsletter to discuss its views on financial reporting. One Big Eight firm has advised me that the disclosure of its views through the financial press is an effective means of according them the desired prominence.

Also in the 1970s and early 1980s, five of the Big Eight firms discontinued house organs that had been, to varying degrees, vehicles for technical articles on accounting. As indicated in Exhibit 2, Arthur Andersen, Coopers & Lybrand, Deloitte Haskins & Sells, Touche Ross, and Arthur Young ceased publication of their main-line house organs between 1973 and 1984. In the last years of those journals, as well as in the last several years' issues of the two main-line journals still being published by Peat Marwick and Price Waterhouse, technical discussions have given way to lighter articles of greater appeal to actual and prospective clients. Graphics and marketing tools have taken pride of place over the edification of professionals.

By the early and middle 1970s, all of the Big Eight firms had started newsletters designed to inform clients and others of recent and imminent developments in one or more of the following: financial reporting, auditing, taxation, and systems consulting. Some of the newsletters have been confined to an objective rendering of events and developments, while others occasionally contain capsule summaries of the firm's position on FASB Exposure Drafts. In one, the writer interposes normative judgments in a pungent style. (I refer here to the Price Waterhouse newsletter *Accounting Events and Trends.*) As indicated in Exhibit 1, three of the newsletters have been terminated. The Arthur Andersen newsletter that was dropped was more a vehicle for the firm's accounting philosophy than is the Andersen newsletter that continues in operation. Touche Ross is the only firm with a newsletter (*Open Line*) directed at accounting educators. When one com-

EXHIBIT 2
Journals Published for General Circulation by U.S. Big Eight Accounting Firms

	Of General Interest, Including Technical Articles on Accounting and Auditing	Oriented to Consulting and Business Developments	Oriented Chiefly to Profiling the Firm, Its Personnel, and Its Clients
Arthur Andersen & Co.	The Arthur Andersen Chronicle (1940–1981)		The People of Arthur Andersen (1973–)
Coopers & Lybrand	L.R.B & M. Journal (1920–1958) Lybrand Journal (1959–1972) Coopers & Lybrand Journal (1973)		
Deloitte Haskins & Sells	Haskins & Sells Bulletin (1918–1931) H&S Reports (1963–1978) DH&S Reports (1978–1982)		DH&S PLUS (1979–)
Ernst & Whinney		Ernst & Whinney Ideas (1981–)	E&E (1961–1976) E&E People (1978–1979) E&W People (1979–)
Peat, Marwick, Mitchell & Co.	World (1967–)	Management Controls (1954–1978) Management Focus (1979–)	
Price Waterhouse	The Price Waterhouse Review (1955–)	Today's Executive (1978–)	
Touche Ross & Co.	The Quarterly (1955–1967) TEMPO (1968–1983)		
Arthur Young	The Arthur Young Journal (1953–1978) The Quarterly (1980–1984)	Arthur Young Business View (1983–)	

pares *Open Line* with the firm's general circulation newsletter, *In Perspective*, it is evident that, since 1977–1978, Touche Ross has been more expansive about its position on FASB initiatives in its newsletter to educators than it was in the newsletter aimed more at clients.

Ernst & Whinney's series of Financial Reporting Developments (FRD) booklets is the most weighty of the firms' newsletters, and the firm regularly inserts its opinions in the mostly factual analyses of standards-setters' initiatives. In 1977, the FRD on the FASB's conceptual development was extensive and detailed, but in the last half-dozen years Ernst & Whinney's FRDs have appeared much less frequently than during most of the 1970s.

In sum, therefore, in the last six to ten years the Big Eight firms have almost wholly discontinued their systematic publication programs that gave prominence to their views on financial reporting. Their publications of this kind are now put out on an issue-by-issue basis and in varying formats. To an increasing degree, the firms' publishing resources have been dedicated to issuing booklets that alert clients to recent and pending accounting developments, including trends in the opinions and practices of other preparers, and that give advice on investment opportunities, financial planning, changing economic conditions, the ramifications of tax legislation, and other topics of operational interest to actual and prospective clients. The firms continue to submit their critical views to the FASB, but they are not as inclined to parade these views on a continuing basis before actual and prospective clients.

Advocacy Writing by Major-Firm Partners

In the first half of the twentieth century, it was commonplace for the partners of major U.S. accounting firms to engage in normative argument over accounting principles in professional journals and treatises. The following is a list of frequent authors during the period from 1910 to 1950:

Arthur E. Andersen	George O. May
George D. Bailey	Robert H. Montgomery
Samuel J. Broad	Warren W. Nissley
Charles B. Couchman	Maurice E. Peloubet
Arthur Lowes Dickinson	Clinton H. Scovell
Anson Herrick	Walter A. Staub
John B. Inglis	Edward B. Wilcox
Edward A. Kracke	John R. Wildman

During the 1950s and 1960s this tendency continued. Partners in major firms who were among the significant contributors to the normative dialogue on accounting principles were as follows:

Herman W. Bevis	Norman O. Olson
John C. Biegler	Weldon Powell
George C. Catlett	John W. Queenan
Philip L. Defliese	Leonard Spacek
Oscar S. Gellein	A. Carl Tietjen
Paul Grady	Robert M. Trueblood
Thomas G. Higgins	George C. Watt
Alvin R. Jennings	William W. Werntz
Harvey Kapnick	Frank T. Weston

The 1960s was a decade in which Big Eight firm partners wrote four Accounting Research Studies published by the Institute for use by the Accounting Principles Board. It was a time when Herman W. Bevis, the senior partner of Price Waterhouse, wrote a book on his philosophy of corporate financial reporting [3]. I believe that is the last book written by a Big Eight firm partner that charts a course for financial reporting.[2]

Also during the period from the 1930s to the mid–1970s, the five SEC Chief Accountants—Carman G. Blough, William W. Werntz, Earle C. King, Andrew Barr, and John C. Burton—frequently expressed their views on accounting issues, and Blough continued to write actively during his long tenure as the AICPA Director of Research (1944–1961). From 1967 to 1972, when he was the Institute's Executive Vice President, Leonard M. Savoie, formerly a partner in Price Waterhouse, was an active participant in the normative dialogue.

The pace of this normative writing activity declined precipitately in the mid–1970s and has not quickened in the 1980s.[3] The incidence of articles

---

[2]An interesting contrast may be drawn between the eighth edition of *Montgomery's Auditing*, published in 1957, and the ninth edition, published in 1975 The former, which was written by two partners of the deceased Montgomery, continued Montgomery's practice of pronouncing opinions on controversial accounting principles and procedures. In the 1975 edition, written by three partners of Coopers & Lybrand (including one who was a co-author of the 1957 edition), advocacy disappeared. In the preface to the 1975 edition, the authors wrote as follows:

> Tempting as it is, we have deliberately restrained ourselves from opining on the many and sundry issues that face the profession today, such as price-level and current value accounting and the new ways of auditing or reviewing interim financial statements That is not the purpose of this book. Our job is to catalog the status quo for reference and study; future editions will note the changes as they come [5:viii].

[3]Savoie was the Institute's principal full-time spokesman on professional and technical matters, and his output of published articles on financial reporting far exceeded that of his two immediate successors, Wallace E. Olson and Philip B. Chenok. The stark comparison between the volume of Savoie's writings on financial reporting, and that of Olson and Chenok, can be gauged by examining the lists of publications associated with Savoie in the 1967 through 1972 editions of the *Accountants' Index* and those of Olson and Chenok in the editions of the *Accountants' Index* beginning with 1972. That the Institute was no longer the parent of the principal standards-setting body in accounting from 1973 onward only partly explains this differential output. The Institute's Accounting Standards Executive

or books by the leading partners of major U.S. accounting firms, and especially the firms' managing partners, has dropped off sharply.

Actions by professional accounting bodies have been consistent with this trend. In the last few years, the *Journal of Accountancy* has actively sought "more practical articles," that is, those that might appeal to smaller practitioners. In the last fifteen years, three major state societies of CPAs have discontinued their journals (Illinois, Florida, and Texas), and the *California CPA Quarterly* has been changed to *Outlook*, the latter having a distinctly less technical flavor. The series of Seaview Symposia that the AICPA conducted every three years between 1968 and 1977 in concert with organizations representing preparers and users of financial statements are no longer held.[4] The first three Symposia were followed by the publication of proceedings volumes containing the papers and dialogue, but the fourth is represented only by an article in the journals of the four sponsoring bodies.

If one examines the record of articles published in the most important practitioner journal in the United States, the *Journal of Accountancy*, a revealing picture emerges. Between 1964 and 1984, the number of articles and "Statements in Quotes" that were written by Big Eight firm partners and that consist of reasoned advocacy on standards-setting and accounting principles is as follows:

1964 5	1970 3	1975 2	1980 0
1965 1	1971 2	1976 1	1981 0
1966 7	1972 2	1977 1	1982 3
1967 2	1973 0	1978 0	1983 1
1968 2	1974 0	1979 3	1984 0
1969 2			

In the first nine years, there were 26 such articles, while in the second twelve years there were but 11. Moreover, eight of the 11 articles appearing since 1974 were written by three authors: Joseph E. Connor, chairman of Price Waterhouse; Philip L. Defliese, managing partner of Coopers & Lybrand; and Arthur R. Wyatt, senior technical partner of Arthur Andersen & Co. A very few senior-level partners have done most of the advocacy writing, and two of those three (Defliese and Wyatt, both of whom retired) have left their firms. (I am not aware of current partners in Coopers & Lybrand and Arthur Andersen who are likely to carry forward the writing traditions of Defliese and Wyatt.) This is not to suggest that the *Journal of*

Committee has been an active standards-setter, and the Institute was the lead sponsor of the FASB (in its early years).

[4] One close observer of the Seaview Symposia has suggested to me that the sponsoring organizations believed that much of the exchange of views among preparers and users was taking place at meetings of the Financial Accounting Standards Advisory Council which is attached to the FASB and has its own staff.

Accountancy is the bellwether of the practitioner accounting literature; one must allow for the changing editorial policies of the *Journal*, and, as already noted, since 1982 the *Journal* has been on record as encouraging more "practical" articles. But this policy is, at least in part, a reflection of changes in the profession and in the role that the *Journal*'s publisher, the AICPA, envisions for itself.

The record of the *Financial Executive* suggests a somewhat different picture although, as in the case of the *Journal of Accountancy*, a few authors account for most of the recent articles. Since 1963, the year-by-year frequency of publication of advocacy-type articles written by Big Eight firm partners is as follows:

1963 1	1969 1	1975 1	1981 3
1964 0	1970 1	1976 1	1982 1
1965 1	1971 0	1977 2	1983 1
1966 3	1972 5	1978 2	1984 1
1967 2	1973 2	1979 1	
1968 1	1974 4	1980 2	

There was a flurry of articles in the early and mid–1970s, when several of the Big Eight firms began to give their views greater prominence in their own publications. Since 1977, nine of the 13 articles were written by the partners of three firms: Price Waterhouse, Arthur Andersen, and Ernst & Whinney. The Price Waterhouse partners were John C. Biegler and Joseph E. Connor, chairmen of the firm; Dennis R. Beresford was either the sole or lead author of the three Ernst & Whinney articles.

It is evident that Big Eight managing partners have tended in recent years to do less advocacy writing on standards setting and accounting principles. Only the Price Waterhouse chairman continues to give speeches on financial reporting (and other issues) that are widely distributed in reprint format. Even the incidence of such writing by the firms' senior technical partners seems to have diminished. In a few of the firms, only a handful of other partners have continued to contribute articles of an advocacy nature.

The writing behavior of Harvey Kapnick, chairman of Arthur Andersen from 1970 to 1979, reflects an interesting change of direction. His major speeches were published by the firm in two volumes. In the first volume, covering the period 1970–1974, 20 of his 23 reprinted speeches dealt with financial reporting or standards-setting issues, broadly defined. In the second volume, covering 1974–1979, 13 of the 18 speeches given through mid–1976 related to financial reporting or standards setting, while only five of the 18 speeches given between mid–1976 and 1979 were even remotely related to financial reporting or standards setting. Most of the speeches during the latter period dealt with broad economic and public policy issues.

When reviewing the recent literature written by Big Eight firm partners as well as that published by the Big Eight firms, a general conclusion is that the authors are reacting to pressures and standards setters' initiatives rather than leading the development and crystallization of accounting thought. While some articles are critical of existing accounting practices or of proposed accounting standards—and these have been written by a very small number of reformers—the majority of articles written by Big Eight firm partners in recent years deal with such matters as the burden of standards overload, self-regulation issues, current trends in international financial reporting, and the content of recent standards and the problems of their implementation. Rather than advance reasoned arguments that point toward directions of future improvement in financial reporting, most writers are disposed to engage in objective analysis of the pros and cons of proposals floated by the standards setters, leaving it to readers to draw their own conclusions. The Big Eight firms' recent publication activities reflect, in the main, a retreat from the earlier practice of systematically dispensing their reasoned views on major accounting issues of the day. The 1984 revision of the Arthur Andersen book on objectives is a departure from this trend, but it stands alone. To be sure, writings that structure arguments in a way that facilitates analysis by participants in the standards-setting process are a worthy contribution, but they do not sound the keynote for directions that the profession should take.

A final observation is that a significant number of papers in recent years have been written by standards setters and their staff. In the 1960s and early 1970s, many of the advocacy articles were written by Big Eight partners who were members of the APB. In recent years, members of the FASB and its staff have written quite a number of articles in which they analyze standards-setting initiatives and undertake to explain their implications. FASB Chairman Donald J. Kirk has, especially in the last several years, written extensively on the role of financial reporting in society. The normative articles written by the FASB members and staff have dealt with proposed standards as well as with the conceptual framework drafts. On the other hand, few of the normative articles written by Big Eight firm partners since the mid–1970s have discussed the conceptual framework; they have typically reacted to the FASB's initiatives on specific standards-setting projects.

Possible Explanations

An analysis of the reasons that firms and their partners have adopted a different role in the accounting literature might begin by offering some speculations on why they once viewed normative writing as an activity deserving of high priority. One explanation for this earlier attitude derives from the greater degree of flexibility of interpretation of ''generally accepted accounting principles'' in the 1960s and preceding decades. Prior to the 1970s, few U.S. accounting pronouncements were very detailed or definitive, especially when the subject was controversial among leading firms and practitioners. In that pioneering era, when the Securities and Exchange Commission was actively seeking to narrow the areas of accounting differences, there was more incentive for practitioners to create a literature that might, in the end, influence the course of accepted practice. In a profession that placed heavy emphasis on ''substantial authoritative support'' for practices that vied with others for the SEC's blessing, articles and books containing cogent and persuasive arguments for particular accounting practices might qualify as a benchmark or precedent in the eyes of the bureaucratic regulator.

Some firms (e.g., Arthur Andersen) expressed frustration in the 1950s after failing to persuade the SEC of the merits of general price level accounting, and they may have believed that major changes in accounting practice could be achieved only by rallying companies, firms, and academics to the support of such reforms. Since the 1930s, the contest over accounting principles has pitted the accounting standards-setting body against the federal regulator. When the practicing profession itself was divided, as it frequently was in the 1940s and 1950s [16:458–462], the creation of a supporting body of literature was probably seen as the best means for resolving controversy and influencing the SEC. One of the cornerstones of the Accounting Principles Board, erected in 1959, was that a reasoned discussion of the conceptual underpinnings of accounting would demonstrate the superiority of particular accounting principles and practices. In a climate in which written discourse was seen as a powerful arbiter of sound accounting practice, it followed that partners and firms might succeed in influencing the course of accounting practice by creating a persuasive literature. Yet in the 1950s and early 1960s, most firms were reluctant to take institutional positions lest they be accused of unprofessional advertising. By the end of the 1960s, however, this objection to publishing documents under firm names no longer was an issue. In 1966, a partner in the executive office of Price Waterhouse gave the following argument for actively contributing to the literature:

> As professional men, each of us has a duty to explain the firm's viewpoints to the business and financial community. This can be accomplished through discussions with businessmen, articles in publications which are read by people we want to reach, and speeches before ap-

propriate groups. Participation in this process by each member of our organization is called for. We want to reach all in the business and professional community—industrialists, lawyers, bankers, teachers— from those who have arrived in leadership positions to those who are just starting their careers [7:3].

Leonard Spacek, who was the architect of Arthur Andersen's postwar growth and development, gave the following reason for his firm's attitude toward writing and speaking out on accounting issues:

[T]he public accountant who wants to expand progressively and to obtain and hold the respect of his clients must also speak frankly about the shortcomings of his profession, and he must work vigorously to correct them. If he does this, he will find clients showing greater confidence in his judgment and increasing reliance on his services, because of his efforts to be forthright and truthful and to be helpful in bringing about improvement [13:146].

Firms were competing for a reputation as leaders of the profession, and the publication of influential books and articles was regarded as a means of establishing or enhancing a reputation. It was a time when corporations were only beginning to play an active role in influencing accounting principles.

Two important changes that have occurred since the late 1960s seem to have persuaded the firms and their partners to reassess their roles in the accounting literature. The market for accounting firms' traditional services became increasingly competitive, and the profit margins in auditing work began to narrow. Accounting firms therefore began to diversify their services and engage in a redoubled effort to retain their clients and expand their client base. At the same time, corporations were taking the offensive in their dealings with the accounting standards-setting body, coming to believe that some of the proposed accounting reforms might endanger their position in the marketplace.[5] When accounting firms declared themselves for or against proposed reforms, they would run the risk of offending important clients.

---

[5]Since the late 1960s, corporations have hardly been indifferent to the prospective impact of FASB actions. They have taken strong stands and have expressed their views forcefully to the FASB on such issues as accounting for business combinations, foreign currency fluctuations, restructuring of troubled debt, leasing, exploration costs in the oil and gas industry, and pensions. Indeed, a past Board Chairman of the Financial Executives Institute was moved to write recently: "I am particularly concerned about instances where advocates of a particular accounting concept feel so strongly about their views that they are willing to go to any extreme to defend their position, even if it might mean the demise of standard setting in the private sector" [15:39].

The second change relates to developments that have occurred in the standards-setting process. With the establishment of the FASB as a full-time body, the major accounting firms no longer dominated the setting of accounting standards. Rather than employ the literature to rally support for their favored positions, the firms dedicated their efforts to communicating with the FASB. The SEC had stated publicly that it would normally be guided by the FASB's advice; therefore, the writing of articles to establish "substantial authoritative support" would not influence the SEC's thinking as would a persuasive argument made orally or in writing to the FASB.

Competition

In the last twenty to twenty-five years, U.S. Big Eight firms have grown significantly in size, have expanded overseas, and have diversified their services. Their partners have become much more specialized, and, because a greater percentage of the firms' professionals come from educational and experiential backgrounds other than accounting, their identification with the organized accounting profession is more tenuous. All the while, the firms have become an increasing target of the plaintiff's bar and have endured more intensified scrutiny by federal agencies and the Congress.

In the 1970s, under persistent pressure from the Federal Trade Commission and the Justice Department, the AICPA amended its Code of Professional Ethics to permit competitive bidding, advertising, and uninvited solicitation [12:ch.6]. In the last several years, stories have circulated about companies' "shopping" among accounting firms for favorable opinions on the treatment of novel transactions, or of clients that have invited competitive bids for audit engagements which, in the end, were awarded to the incumbent audit firm at a fraction of the previous year's fee. The new reality of competitive bidding (including not only the results of actual bid taking but also the fear that certain clients might invite bids) has, in a climate of rising costs, led to a narrowing of profit margins in auditing. At the same time, firms have expanded the range and volume of their consulting services. Although the Big Eight firms are more secretive about their financial results than they were in the 1970s, one close observer of the U.S. profession reports that "though audit fees have continued to rise in absolute terms, it is now widely acknowledged that profit margins in this sector are rapidly eroding" [11:14]. This is not a climate in which professional idealism flourishes.[6]

---

[6]An AICPA committee has recently drawn attention to the impact of fundamental changes in the environment of auditing practice on the fabric of professionalism in accounting [10:esp.7-10]. In 1983,

As suggested, the very diversification of services deflects partners from an identification with the profession and, hence, a concern with financial reporting issues. One current partner in a Big Eight firm wrote:

> The major firms are on a growth treadmill that inevitably will stop, but each manager is determined to keep it moving ever faster during his regime. This has required diversification into many "information-based" services. The aggregate effect of these diversifications is to change the balance of the professional mindset—moving farther from an audit mentality and toward a consulting mentality. The diversified service draws the firms increasingly into competition with other disciplines that have few or no professional/competitive constraints, and our traditional professional standards of conduct are a competitive handicap.[7]

In such circumstances, it would be surprising if leading partners were to become parties to lofty debates over the role of corporate financial reporting in modern society. This is not to suggest that enlightened self-interest is a recent phenomenon in the profession. Where, in an earlier day, partners sought to build their firm's image among business leaders via addresses to important gatherings of accountants and articles published in the major accounting journals, today these channels may not be regarded as particularly productive. A current partner in a Big Eight firm wrote as follows in response to my letter of December 11, 1984:

> Written articles don't even do much any more to enhance a firm's professional reputation. The business community already perceives all of the large firms as highly competent in accounting and auditing. Even the most brilliant article will not add significantly to that perception. Firms now try to differentiate themselves in other ways, primarily by stressing their commitment to client service (We take business *personally*).

In the 1970s, when the founder and chairman of the Hayden, Stone Accounting Forums (which were held annually at New York University from 1962 to 1967) tried to reconstitute the forums under new sponsorship,

---

the AICPA appointed a special committee to "evaluate the relevancy of present ethical standards to professionalism, integrity and commitment to both quality service and the public interest, in the light of a changing economic, social, legal and regulatory climate" [4:111]. (See also [14,8].)

[7]This is one of several confidential communications received from respondents to my questionnaire survey. Only a minority of respondents have authorized me to reveal their identity. Since a revelation of the identities of some of the respondents may suggest clues to the identities, or firm affiliations, of the authors of other quotations, I have elected not to identify any of the respondents.

he had no difficulty in finding speakers, "but the [audience] interest in the sessions was just not there."

In the highly competitive accounting environment of the late 1970s and early 1980s, the cost of expensive publication programs apparently could not be justified in relation to the benefits likely to be conferred. One supposes that Big Eight firm partners saw little benefit in giving prominence to their firm's position on controversial accounting standards if many, or even some, actual or prospective clients were to be irritated by these views. One close observer of the profession wrote: "Given the environment presently prevailing among the major firms in the accounting profession, taking a position in a house organ, professional journal, or speech that might be objectionable to a current or potential client would be considered by one's partners to be unacceptable behavior." The firms continue to submit their views to the FASB, but they make less of an issue of their position, unless, perhaps, it might secure client approval.

That the incidence of normative writing by managing partners has dropped precipitately is not surprising in light of the aforementioned changes that have been occurring in the major accounting firms. The firms have become conglomerate enterprises; their organization is more complex, and they are either multinational in scope or are linked to an international network of firms. The managing partner's responsibilities are predominantly managerial and leave little time for technical sorties. The fall-off in normative writing by most of the senior technical partners may perhaps be explained by the other factors discussed in this section.

Finally, in light of trends in the incidence of litigation and the periodic inquiries by congressional committees, firms are not eager to engage in the kind of public dialogue that would raise questions about the propriety of accounting standards and practices. The Moss and Metcalf investigations of 1976–1978 not only affected the operating behavior of the AICPA and the FASB, but also may have had a chilling effect on the outspokenness by leading partners and accounting firms. A current Big Eight partner wrote: "The dual concerns of Congressional oversight and the litigious environment have made CPA's nervous about criticizing the status quo. Some even consider it dangerous. So, controversial articles on accounting/professional matters are not in style."

Standards Setting

Another major source of explanation centers on trends in accounting standards and in the standards-setting process. One current partner in a Big Eight firm wrote:

As standard setting has moved farther from broad, basic fundamentals and more into the detailed, nitty-gritty rules, the big picture people have lost interest in accounting principles, and leave them to the technical boffins. I remember vaguely [Robert] Trueblood saying or writing that he began to give up in disgust when the APB came up with Opinion 15 on Earnings per Share.

The heady days of pioneering in accounting principles have given way to an era in which carefully chiseled accounting rules are formulated to cope with a complex transaction that was structured solely to escape the ill accounting effects of other forms of the same transaction. An academic who is a close student of the profession wrote:

Accounting reporting keeps coming closer to tax reporting in the sense of principles, interpretations and precedents. Loop-hole plugging, a long-time indoor sport of the Congress and the Internal Revenue Service, is now a key occupation of the FASB. This activity consumes a very large amount of the energies of the FASB, and, like the Congress and the IRS, they never catch up with the loop-hole maker.

At the same time, Big Eight partners have narrowed their focus to become industry specialists, and, as a former member of the Institute's Accounting Standards Executive Committee wrote, "my experience has been that as one becomes more of an industry specialist he tends to become somewhat of an apologist for the industry." As accounting standards become more rule-oriented and as partners become experts at applying the rules to the industries that command their attention, the likelihood diminishes that the firms or partners will address "big picture" issues. Again, Arthur Andersen's 1984 revision of its "Objectives" study is an exception.

A related matter concerns the full-time nature of the FASB. As one retired partner wrote:

The advent of a truly capable, truly independent, full-time free-standing body of accounting standard-setters [is a major factor]. The demise of the APB at midnight, June 30, 1973 was the end of roughly 40 years of AI(CP)A responsibility—and, hence, individual responsibility of leading practitioners—for developing, promulgating, and enforcing consensus solutions to cutting-edge problems of accounting and reporting. And with it died, understandably, the widespread effort of such practitioners to shape and mold consensus, to persuade others to embrace a particular view by printing that view in the accounting journals.

With the establishment of the FASB, the Big Eight firms may have come to sense a remoteness from the standards-setting process. No longer would each Big Eight firm be represented by a senior partner on the standards-setting body, and the research apparatus that had been erected in each firm to support its partner on the board would, if it were to be retained at all, be redirected toward commenting on FASB initiatives. With the transition from a part-time to a full-time board, Big Eight firms suddenly found themselves on the "outside" of the standards-setting activity, together with their clients.

Of importance, therefore, would have been the firms' perception of how they might best achieve an impact on the FASB's deliberations. Eventually, it may have been discovered that the publication of articles, which may have been influential in the days of the APB, did not weigh as heavily with the FASB. A retired Big Eight partner wrote:

> The new system [i.e., the FASB] shifted materially the burden of using sound accounting in financial reporting from practitioners and their clients to the central rule makers. The practitioner's problem became largely one of finding the applicable rule (or the central board's reasoning) and following it.
>
> Suppose the practitioner who once published widely now wants to influence an accounting treatment or change one already centrally established. To do this he has to be persuasive to a majority of the current FASB members. Chances are that articles in general publications are an insufficient—probably ineffective—way to do this. A more promising approach would be to use in-house full-time accounting researchers to communicate a firm's views to FASB members and (of great importance) their staffs.

Whether articles in professional journals that are based on the contents of comment letters submitted to the FASB could succeed in enhancing the persuasiveness of the arguments and evidence already contained in the comment letters is open to debate. As one current Big Eight partner wrote:

> Today, GAAP largely takes the form of authoritative pronouncements issued by small, easily identifiable groups. Moreover, these groups follow prescribed standard-setting procedures that include designated opportunities for public input. It no longer makes sense, therefore, to spend the considerable time necessary to prepare an article for the entire readership of the *Journal of Accountancy* when all you have to do to change GAAP is persuade the seven members of the FASB. Most large firms accordingly invest a lot of time preparing their communications with the FASB—time that twenty years ago might have been spent writing articles.

These arguments concerning the full-time nature of the standards-setting body might not apply in all cultural settings, but policymakers in other countries who are thinking of moving toward full-time standards setting might reflect on the American experience.

If in-depth studies were conducted for each of the Big Eight firms, it is likely that firm-specific explanations could be adduced as well. Nonetheless, there appear to be several pervasive explanations. The increasingly competitive climate in which public accounting is practiced, together with the transformation of accounting standards setting into a full-time activity with a highly structured process for entertaining comments, seems to be the most important changes in the environment that have led to the shifts in publication and writing behavior. The twin specters of litigation and congressional oversight can hardly be dismissed as contributing factors.

In addition, some of the respondents to my December 11, 1984, letter criticize the AICPA for not playing a leadership role in the setting of accounting standards following the establishment of the FASB. One retired Big Eight partner wrote:

> Unfortunately, the AICPA has not adopted policies that further the role of financial reporting. It escapes me why the AICPA is not guided by the notion that an important role for financial reporting in society makes auditing important. A more important role for financial reporting elevates the importance of auditing. . . . Apparently the *Journal of Accountancy* believed it could change the perception of the usefulness of the AICPA to smaller firms if it emphasized so-called practical matters instead of theoretical issues. The annual meeting of the AICPA manifests the same emphasis. It is indeed unfortunate that the AICPA has not, at the same time, emphasized the importance of financial reporting in society's affairs. It amounts to almost an abrogation. Surely, auditing will not be very important if what is audited serves a relatively minor role in the affairs of society.

Another retired partner criticizes the Institute for adopting a policy of not printing anything controversial or critical about financial reporting once the FASB replaced the Institute's APB. He added: "As a result, the *Journal of Accountancy* stayed away from controversial subjects and thus couldn't print anything that was interesting. Whether they admit it or not, that policy still exists and it has been a mistake." The foregoing analysis of normative articles written by Big Eight partners tends to be consistent with this perception.

Concluding Remarks

Publishing and writing have been assigned a lower priority within the Big Eight firms in recent years, principally owing to changes in the competitive environment, the reorganization of the standards-setting function, and increasing levels of litigation and congressional oversight. Most firms evidently do not see the benefit, either in terms of enhancing their image or, when dealing with clients, from using their publications or partner writing time to advance the professional dialogue over the aims of financial reporting or the comparative merits of particular accounting standards. In the current competitive environment, the imperative of serving one's clients has become paramount.

Most firms and partners have largely withdrawn from active publishing and writing in the normative vein, preferring instead to publish booklets or write articles that guide clients in understanding and implementing recent pronouncements and that assist clients in responding more effectively to the FASB on pending proposals. A recent booklet on pension accounting published by a Big Eight firm exemplifies this latter mission. The booklet was issued "to suggest ways to maximize the effect of your [company's] response to the FASB." It goes on:

> [Our firm] is in a position to assist you in preparing an effective and persuasive response. Our experience in dealing with the FASB allows us to identify the critical issues on which they seek response. We would assist your company in evaluating the effects, developing empirical evidence, and identifying the economic consequences of the positions your company supports and rejects.

This form of client service is probably not unrepresentative of the role that at least some firms adopt in today's competitive environment.

The removal of the Big Eight firms from the center stage of standards setting has led to a redirection of their publication and writing efforts toward forums within the FASB. Both the firms and their clients are now on the outside of the standards-setting process, and the firms' writing efforts now take the form, more likely than not, of comments submitted on Discussion Memorandums and Exposure Drafts. While the Financial Accounting Standards Advisory Council and the Emerging Issues Task Force can have an impact on the FASB's agenda, the Big Eight firms do not have as much influence over the standards setter's agenda as they did during the tenure of the APB. The FASB has, as it was charged to do, seized the initiative, and the firms react rather than lead. To the extent that an active written dialogue exists on the broad subject of financial reporting and on specific accounting standards, it is found more in the public files of the FASB than in the professional journals or in firms' publications.

Nothing in this paper is intended to imply that the firms' partners are speaking less than in previous years. The evidence adduced in this paper deals with institutional publications and the writing behavior of partners. One respondent to my letter suggested that there are even more forums for delivering speeches than in the past, and he allowed the inference that even more speeches are being given than before. Whether the speeches are normative or descriptive is not known.

The notion implicit in the conduct of this study is my belief that intellectual leadership is essential to the progress of accounting as a profession. One may justifiably express concern if the largest and most influential practice units in a profession remove themselves from active leadership in advancing the quality of its technical literature as well as in forging a consensus over the proper directions that its service to society should take. In the context of accounting, a literature should reflect both a normative and descriptive vitality, and it is with respect to a decline in the former that the profession should be concerned.

APPENDIX

Extract from letter dated December 11, 1984

Today, one notices *very* few firm partners who speak out on the controversial issues of the day. It can hardly be maintained that a dialogue even exists. As if to confirm this trend, the firms' house organs seldom contain articles any more which advocate desirable directions for financial reporting. In fact, several of the firms have discontinued the publication of house organs, and only one firm in recent years has distributed printed copies of its partners' speeches. I find it difficult to name most of the firms' national managing partners or even their national technical or research partners. They are not leading contributors to an active dialogue over financial reporting issues.

I am doing some research on why today's accounting literature fails to reflect the continuing dialogue on accounting principles and standards which was so commonplace in the 1960s. Perhaps there are fewer forums at which such views might be expressed, and when they are expressed there may be less of an inclination to disseminate those views in written form. Several reasons seem plausible:

1. The accounting firms have become much more intensely competitive,

and partners do not see it in their firm's interest to take public positions on controversial financial reporting matters which might annoy clients or prospective clients.

2. Also for competitive reasons, a much greater percentage of a partner's time is devoted to attracting and retaining clients, leaving much less time for preparing and delivering speeches at professional meetings.

3. The increasing degree to which partners have become industry specialists has diluted their interest in the broad questions of corporate financial reporting. As one commentator has suggested, "there are no 'big picture' people any more."

4. Owing to the fact that the FASB has replaced the APB, and that none of the firms any longer have partners who serve on the principal standard-setting body (i.e., the FASB), there is less of an active interest within the firms in mounting a debate over issues under active consideration. When the APB was in existence, each firm knew that its member-partner was preparing to cast a vote, and the competition among firms for the minds of those who might be undecided was keener than now.

5. Accounting firms no longer attract or promote individuals who maintain an active interest in the "philosophical" or "theoretical" issues in financial accounting.

6. Along with many American institutions, accounting firms operate along more pluralistic, democratic lines than in an earlier day. Partners are more independent-minded and are less inclined to defer to senior partners on the grounds of their stature in the firm or eminence in the profession. An accounting philosophy may not be as clearly defined or as widely shared within a firm as in the 1950s and 1960s, and firm partners may be more uncomfortable with views that are publicly expressed by other partners which are not consistent with their own.

7. Firms are much larger and more complicated organizations than they were in the 1960s, and most national managing partners do not have the time to devote to professional dialogues over accounting principles.

I do not mean to suggest that these are the only plausible explanations, and none of these may, in your opinion, satisfactorily describe the significant dropoff in the professional dialogue on financial reporting issues.

REFERENCES

1. Hector R Anton, "From the Editor," *Journal of Accounting, Auditing & Finance* (Fall 1984), pp. 3–4.

2. Hector R. Anton, "From the Editor," *Journal of Accounting, Auditing & Finance* (Winter 1985), pp. 83–85.
3. Herman W. Bevis, *Corporate Financial Reporting in a Competitive Economy* (New York: Macmillan, 1965).
4. *Committee Handbook 1984/85* (New York: AICPA, 1984).
5. Philip L. Defliese, Kenneth P. Johnson, and Roderick K. Macleod, *Montgomery's Auditing*, 9th ed. (New York: The Ronald Press Company, 1975).
6. Thomas R. Dyckman and Stephen A. Zeff, "Two Decades of the *Journal of Accounting Research*," *Journal of Accounting Research* (Spring 1984), pp. 225–297.
7. Thomas A. Ganner, "Speak Up . . . It's Your Profession," *The Price Waterhouse Review* (Summer 1966), pp. 2–3.
8. Harold Q. Langenderfer, "President's Message," *Accounting Education News* (June 1984), pp. 1, 3.
9. Lybrand, Ross Bros. & Montgomery, "Why Retrogress to a Cash Basis of Accounting for Income Tax Expense?" *Financial Executive* (September 1967), pp. 75, 78–79.
10. *Major Issues for the CPA Profession and the AICPA*, A Report by the AICPA Future Issues Committee (New York: AICPA, 1984).
11. Peter Mantle, "More Offices, More Staff, More Fees but Audit Continues Relative Decline," *International Accounting Bulletin* (November 1984), pp. 14–16.
12. Wallace E. Olson, *The Accounting Profession: Years of Trial: 1969–1980* (New York: AICPA, 1982).
13. Leonard Spacek, "Development and Expansion of an Accounting Practice," address delivered on June 7, 1960, and reproduced in *A Search for Fairness in Financial Reporting to the Public* (Chicago: Arthur Andersen & Co., 1969), pp. 143–147.
14. Edward Stamp, "Is Professionalism Dead?" *International Accounting Bulletin* (October 1984), pp. 22–23.
15. Robert C. Thompson, "How Do You View the FASB?" *Financial Executive* (May 1984), pp. 38–42.
16. Stephen A. Zeff, "Some Junctures in the Evolution of the Process of Establishing Accounting Principles in the U.S.A.: 1917–1972," *The Accounting Review* (July 1984), pp. 447–468.

Arthur Andersen & Co. and the two-part opinion in the auditor's report: 1946–1962*

STEPHEN A. ZEFF *Rice University*

Abstract. This paper constitutes a historical study of the roots of the decision by Arthur Andersen & Co. in 1946 to adopt a two-part auditor's opinion for all of its engagements, and of its eventual decision in 1962 to return to the standard form of the auditor's report. The essence of the two-part opinion was to decouple the auditor's opinion on fairness of presentation from the opinion on conformity with generally accepted accounting principles. The paper also treats the factors that prompted the Canadian Institute of Chartered Accountants to adopt a two-part opinion, and the reasons why it opted to return to the single-opinion format in 1976.

Résumé. L'auteur retrace l'historique de la décision prise en 1946 par Arthur Andersen & Cie de présenter l'opinion du vérificateur en deux volets dans toutes ses missions, et de sa décision ultérieure, en 1962, de ramener le rapport du vérificateur à sa forme standard. Le choix de l'opinion en deux volets reposait sur l'intention de distinguer l'opinion du vérificateur quant à la fidélité avec laquelle est présentée l'information de l'opinion du vérificateur relative au respect des principes comptables généralement reconnus. L'auteur traite également des facteurs qui ont amené l'Institut Canadien des Comptables Agréés à adopter l'opinion en deux volets, et des raisons pour lesquelles il a choisi de rétablir l'opinion unique en 1976.

Introduction

Since 1939 in the United States, the standard form of the auditor's report has contained the phrasing, "present fairly... in conformity with generally accepted accounting principles...." In the last 25 years, the role of "present fairly" in relation to "in conformity with generally accepted accounting principles" in the auditor's report has been a controversial topic in North America (see Carmichael, 1974; Rosenfield and Lorensen, 1974; and Johnston, 1979). The Auditing Stan-

---

* The author appreciates the cooperation of Arthur Andersen & Co. in the preparation of this paper. The author gratefully acknowledges the helpful comments on earlier drafts by Timothy T. Griffy, Haim Falk, Douglas R. Carmichael, Frederick L. Neumann, Jack C. Robertson, Philip W. Bell, Ken Trotman, Stephen Taylor, Barbara D. Merino, Gary J. Previts, George R. Catlett, Leonard Spacek, Leonard G. Eckel, and Lee D. Parker, as well as by the anonymous reviewers. He also appreciates the historical insights into the Canadian experience provided by Ross Skinner, Doug Thomas, Rod Anderson, Stephen Elliott, David Selley, Kenneth Gunning, G. Kenneth Carr, and Gertrude Mulcahy. He is solely responsible for what remains.

dards Board of the American Institute of Certified Public Accountants (AICPA), seeking to implement a recommendation made by the Commission on Auditors' Responsibilities (1978, p. 14), proposed in 1980 that "fairly" be deleted altogether from the auditor's standard report because "the word is subjective and is interpreted differently by different users of the auditor's report" (AICPA, 1980, p. 6). The board's proposal provoked considerable debate and disagreement because it was not clear whether the deletion of "fairly" would contribute to, or lessen, the alleged confusion over the meaning of the auditor's report (see Carmichael and Winters, 1982, p. 18). In the end, the board's proposal was withdrawn.

In Canada, for a period in the 1960s and 1970s, the accounting profession supported a two-part opinion, in which separate opinions were to be given on "present fairly" and on "conformity with generally accepted accounting principles."

In addition, although it was not widely known, the accounting firm of Arthur Andersen & Co. used a two-part opinion in all of its engagements between 1946 and 1962.

It is the purpose of this article to suggest the reasons behind the firm's decision to adopt a dual-opinion format and, in the end, to return to the single-opinion format endorsed by the AICPA. In the first part of the paper, the Canadian experience with the two-part opinion will be reviewed because it may be instructive to compare the experience of a national accounting profession with that of a major accounting firm at odds with the leadership of its national accountancy body.

Canadian experience with the two-part opinion

In Canada, the auditing pronouncements of the Canadian Institute of Chartered Accountants (CICA) called for a two-part opinion between 1968 and 1976 (some would say from 1959 to 1976). The auditor was expected to express two opinions, one on whether the financial statements present fairly, the other on whether they were prepared in accordance with generally accepted accounting principles (GAAP) (see Eckel, 1973; and Johnston, 1979).

The CICA's Accounting and Auditing Research Committee, evidently more through inadvertence than design, created the impression in *Bulletin No. 25* (CICA, 1967) that it was recommending a two-part opinion. In fact, it appears that the committee had no such intention.[1] The purpose of *Bulletin No. 25* was to

---

1   Eckel (1973, p. 41), a close student of these developments, finds language in *Bulletin No. 25* that supports the concept of a two-part opinion, although the language used by the committee was less than explicit. Moreover, in a communication with the author, Gertrude Mulcahy, who was CICA research associate, then associate research director, and (from 1969 onward) research director during the 1970s, maintains that the two-part opinion was first introduced in *Bulletin No. 17*, issued in 1959, and was reiterated and clarified in *Bulletin No. 25*. Yet, in other communications with the author, R.M. Skinner, a member of the committee that drafted *Bulletin No. 17*, and G.K. Carr, the deputy chairman of the committee that drafted *Bulletin No. 25*, both affirm that there was no intention by their respective committees to call for a two-part opinion. (Letter, 1990, from Gertrude Mulcahy; letter, 1988, and telephone conversation (1990) with R.M. Skinner; letter 1990, from G.K. Carr.)

add a reference to the funds statement in the auditor's report. It also restated the auditor's obligations set forth in *Bulletin No. 17* (CICA, 1959). The principal object of the latter was to recommend the inclusion in the auditor's report of a reference to conformity with GAAP and consistency in their application. Another aim of *Bulletin No. 17* was to recommend the use of "present fairly" in the opinion paragraph of the auditor's report unless a different wording was required by statute. Prior thereto, the opinion to be given in the auditor's report was confined to whether (1) the financial statements "present fairly" the financial position and results of operations (for Ontario corporations) or (2) the financial statements "exhibit a true and correct view" (for corporations subject to the companies legislation of other jurisdictions). The purport of *Bulletin No. 17* was to favor the American-style opinion paragraph in the auditor's report.

Since *Bulletin No. 17* had introduced the auditor's obligation to comment on conformity with GAAP and consistency in addition to the previous obligation that the auditor give an opinion on "true and correct view" or "present fairly," the committee found it necessary to discuss how the *two* obligations were related to one another. Some drew the inference from the committee's discussion that two *opinions* were required. A similar discussion appeared in *Bulletin No. 25*. In 1967–1968, when the Accounting and Auditing Research Committee codified the previous bulletins and compiled the new *CICA Handbook*, the committee used language that was construed as constituting an *explicit requirement* for a two-part opinion (Sec. 2500.06) (see, e.g., Eckel, 1973, p. 41), even though the committee may not have had that intention.[2]

Since the CICA had switched to the American-style opinion paragraph, there was keen interest in Canada in the decision rendered in the Continental Vending case in 1969 by the U.S. Second Court of Appeals in which the court said that the "critical test" for determining the adequacy of financial statements was fair presentation. Compliance with GAAP, the court said, was persuasive but not necessarily conclusive. The case attracted comment in the Canadian accounting literature (see, e.g., Eckel 1973, p. 43; and Anderson, 1977, p. 484), and the Second Circuit's establishment of the primacy of fairness may have emboldened the CICA's leaders to support a two-part opinion in the auditor's report.

Indeed, in May 1972, the CICA research director wrote a letter on behalf

2   G.K. Carr, who served as 1967–1968 chairman of the Accounting and Auditing Research Committee, advises the author that the issue of a two-part opinion "did not come to the fore" in the committee's discussions. (Telephone conversation, 1991.) When the *CICA Handbook* was unveiled in December 1968, the research director reported that the committee had "made a number of wording changes in recommendations to eliminate ambiguities" (Mulcahy, 1968, p. 433), but the changes were not identified.

Eckel (1973, p. 42) has pointed out that the CICA's Accounting and Auditing Research Committee never actually added an "and" between "present fairly" and "in accordance with generally accepted accounting principles" to signify, unequivocally, the intention to call for two separate opinions. As will be seen below, when Arthur Andersen & Co. decided in the 1940s to express two opinions instead of one, the firm believed it was necessary to insert "and were prepared" between "present fairly" and "in conformity with generally accepted accounting principles."

of the Accounting and Auditing Research Committee to all CICA members to remind them of the dual obligation imposed by the requirement of a two-part opinion (see Eckel, 1973, p. 43). The CICA's letter of clarification had been provoked by concern over the 1971 annual report of Trizec Corporation, a Montreal-based real estate development company, in which the company boosted its reported net income by 60 percent by means of a decision to account for deferred income taxes on a discounted basis. The company's auditor, one of Canada's best-known firms, did not qualify its opinion on conformity with GAAP even though there was little, if any, support for this discounting practice in Canada. After some discussion, the Ontario Securities Commission eventually accepted a filing of the company's prospectus that incorporated the financial statements reflecting the disputed practice. Eventually, in connection with the issuance of Trizec's 1972 financial statements, the 1971 statements were restated to eliminate the discounting of deferred taxes, and two partners of the audit firm were censured by their professional institute (see Elliott, 1974).

One consequence of the Trizec affair was that questions began to be raised about the criteria that auditors should be expected to use when deciding whether a client's practices are in conformity with GAAP. Companies and securities legislation were silent on the point. Although CICA members were required to base their judgments on the *CICA Handbook*, the Trizec affair drew attention to the auditor's responsibility to determine the content of GAAP when there was a departure from the *Handbook* or, as in the case of Trizec, where the *Handbook* was silent.

In December 1972, the Canadian Provincial Securities Administrators declared in a national policy statement that GAAP, for purposes of yearly and half-yearly financial statements filed with them, would be defined by reference to the recommendations in the *CICA Handbook*. This action was, without doubt, precipitated by the embarrassment surrounding the questionable judgment used by the Trizec auditors in deciding what practices qualified as GAAP. The securities administrators preferred an objective source of authority rather than reliance on the judgments of individual auditors that could be based on largely undefined criteria. A similar provision was included in the 1975 Canada Business Corporations Act Regulations. Hence, the legal status accorded to the CICA's accounting recommendations as the arbiter of GAAP suggested to the CICA's Auditing Standards Committee that they should constitute the sole framework for judging fair presentation. The decision taken in 1976 by the CICA's committee to revert to a one-part opinion was, therefore, taken mainly to establish a generally understood framework for use by auditors when making this judgment (see Thomas, 1976, pp. 57–58).

Another more subtle factor may also have been influential in the committee's 1976 decision. In the 1950s and early 1960s, when accounting pronouncements were issued relatively infrequently and were concerned, in the main, with broader and less contentious questions, auditors may have found themselves in easier agreement with one another, and with their client companies, on matters of judgment in the application of accounting principles. As the standard setters began to pronounce upon specific and controversial questions in the late 1960s and early 1970s, auditors were increasingly likely to find themselves disagreeing with their peers, and with their client companies, on such judgments. Companies wishing to avoid the adverse effects of disagreeable pronouncements on touchy subjects were likely to be questioning the wisdom of their auditors' judgment. The level of tension in such relationships must have been rising. By the mid-1970s, therefore, auditors themselves may have preferred to substitute the *CICA Handbook* for the broader exercise of professional judgment.

It is interesting to note that the CICA's Auditing Standards Committee, as part of its decision in 1976 to revert to the one-part opinion, included the suggestion that "the auditor must exercise his professional judgment as to the appropriateness of the selection and application of principles to the particular circumstances of an enterprise and as to the overall effect on the financial statements of separate decisions made in their preparation." This passage prompted one commentator to remark, "In effect, we still have a two-part opinion!" (Johnston, 1979, p. 53). Johnston's dictum may have been premature since the committee's suggestion was made as background discussion, but not as part of the formal recommendation. Eight years later, in 1984, the CICA's Auditing Standards Committee converted the "appropriateness test" from a suggestion to a formal recommendation (*CICA Handbook* para. 5400.13), to increase the emphasis on professional judgment in the audit function (see Jeffreys, 1984; and Gibbins, 1983).

Hence, although the dual (or two-part) opinion was mandatory in Canada for almost a decade, the auditor's standard report in the United States has, since the 1930s, joined fair presentation and conformity with GAAP in a single opinion.

Arthur Andersen & Co.: Rationale behind the decision in 1946

In 1934 in the United States there was "almost instant and widespread acceptance" (Staub, 1942, p. 76) of the standard form of the auditor's report (or certificate, as it was then called) recommended by the American Institute's Special Committee on Co-operation with Stock Exchanges and endorsed by the Committee on Stock List of the New York Stock Exchange and by the Committee on Stock Exchange Relations of the Controllers Institute of America. The opinion paragraph was as follows:

In our opinion, based upon such examination, the accompanying balance-sheet and related statement of income and surplus fairly present, in accordance with accepted principles of accounting consistently maintained by the Company during the year under review, its position at December 31, 1933, and the results of its operations for the year (American Institute of Accountants, 1934, p. 47).

It was originally envisaged that "accepted principles of accounting" would be expressions of broad principles and would be few in number. The Special Committee suggested that a statement of such principles might be developed in consultation with "a small group of qualified persons, including corporate officials, lawyers and accountants" (AIA, 1934, pp. 13–14). Within the limits of these broad principles, corporations were to be free to choose accounting and reporting methods, and were expected to file a public statement of these methods with the New York Stock Exchange. In its report, the Special Committee proposed five broad principles, which were, together with a sixth, approved by the membership of the American Institute of Accountants (as the AICPA was then known). Yet neither the New York Stock Exchange nor the Securities and Exchange Commission (SEC) acted to require corporations to provide a publicly available list of the accounting and reporting methods they used. Storey writes: "The failure to adopt the limitations recommended by the special committee to accompany the freedom given management in the choice of accounting methods sowed the seeds of the subsequent proliferation of accepted methods" (Storey, 1964, p. 27). In 1939, the Institute's Committee on Auditing Procedure modified the opinion paragraph by transposing "present" and "fairly," replacing "in accordance" with "in conformity," and inserting "generally accepted accounting principles" in place of "accepted principles of accounting": "... present fairly ..., in conformity with generally accepted accounting principles ..." (AIA, 1939, p. 12). The term *generally accepted accounting principles* came to refer not only to broad principles but also to accounting methods. In 1939, the Institute's Committee on Accounting Procedure began issuing bulletins to provide the SEC with "substantial authoritative support" for the principles and methods comprehended by GAAP. In instances where alternative methods or practices commanded strong support within the Committee, the resulting bulletins allowed optional treatments, contributing to the proliferation cited by Storey.

As a firm, Arthur Andersen & Co. was concerned that questionable methods and practices had become justified under the imprimatur of GAAP, and the firm believed that the formal link between fair presentation and conformity with GAAP might preclude auditors from taking exception to the application of accounting principles (i.e., methods) of which they disapproved but which were nonetheless believed to be generally accepted. In an internal memorandum dated November 21, 1941, the firm indicated its uneasiness with the link between fairness and GAAP:

The reputation and standing of the firm have been built upon a foursquare policy of honesty and forthrightness. If, after the most thorough investigation and careful consideration, we are convinced that a certain accounting policy is fundamentally unsound and that its application will result in financial statements that are materially misleading, we must take exception to the policy in our certificate; we will not avail ourselves of the technicality that the principles to which we object may be quite generally accepted.

This policy reflected the view of Arthur Andersen himself that the partners in the firm, no less than other members of the profession, should use their independent judgment when assessing the propriety of accounting principles, and should not unquestioningly subordinate their professional opinions to the rules and procedures approved by a committee of the Institute.

In 1944, the Institute's Committee on Accounting Procedure approved *Accounting Research Bulletin No. 23*, "Accounting for Income Taxes." The committee accepted interperiod tax allocation except "in the case of differences between the tax return and the income statement where there is a presumption that they will recur regularly over a comparatively long period of time" (AIA, 1944, p. 190). Arthur Andersen & Co., however, favored interperiod tax allocation for oil and gas companies that capitalized the drilling costs of productive wells for financial accounting purposes while deducting them immediately for tax purposes—a difference that could well persist for a considerable number of periods.

Finally, in 1946, the firm concluded that the auditor's standard report, with a single opinion, placed it in an indefensible position. The decision was made to decouple the opinion on fair presentation from that on conformity with GAAP.

In an internal memorandum dated July 2, 1946, the firm "reemphasized the established policy of the firm to take exception in our certificate to accounting principles or procedures of which we cannot approve, regardless of the fact that there may be a substantial weight of accounting authority or usage in support thereof." The 1946 memorandum continued:

A corollary of this policy is the proposition that the certifying paragraph expresses three separate and distinct opinions: (1) that the financial statements present fairly the financial position and results of operations, (2) that the statements have been prepared in conformity with generally accepted accounting principles and (3) that these principles have been consistently applied.

The fact that the certifying paragraph in its standard form is an expression of more than a single opinion may not have been uniformly understood in the past. Some of the misunderstanding, if any, may have resulted from a lack of clarity in the wording of the paragraph, and it is the purpose of this release to revise this wording so that it will hereafter more clearly convey the appropriate meaning of the paragraph. Insertion of the words "and are" just preceding the present reference to conformity with generally accepted accounting principles will accomplish this purpose. Therefore, in the future the standard certifying paragraph in our certificate will read as follows:

"In our opinion, the accompanying balance sheet and related statements of income and surplus present fairly the position of the XYZ Company at _____ and the results of its operations for the year ended that date and are in conformity with generally accepted accounting principles applied on a basis consistent with that of the preceding year."

Somewhat more than a year later, the firm replaced "are" with "were prepared," as an investment banker had suggested that this revised wording would improve the clarity. One supposes that the phraseology in *Accounting Series Release No. 4*, the SEC's basic statement of its administrative policy on accounting principles, commended the word "prepared" in the firm's opinion paragraph. *ASR No. 4* (1938) begins as follows:

In cases where financial statements filed with this Commission ... are *prepared* in accordance with accounting principles for which there is no substantial authoritative support, such financial statements will be presumed to be misleading or inaccurate despite disclosures contained in the certificate of the accountant or in footnotes to the statements provided the matters involved are material (emphasis supplied).

Another motivation behind the firm's decision was to differentiate its services from those of other firms: to create the image that principle, not expediency, governed its actions and that the firm had the courage to break with tradition. Leonard Spacek, who was the firm's partner in charge of the Chicago office when the decision was made, subsequently said, "Of course a lot of our attraction to clients was the fact that we would do things if we thought they were right" (Spacek, 1985, p. 238). Moreover, in a conformist profession the firm was willing, even eager, to break ikons. Spacek recalls that Arthur Andersen himself "liked the idea of bucking a trend" (p. 231). In 1970, *Fortune* magazine wrote that "Arthur Andersen [& Co.] ... has long been regarded as the maverick of the profession, a role the firm obviously relishes" (Louis, 1970, p. 96). The decision to opt for a two-part opinion in the auditor's report was tailor-made to demonstrate these virtues.

In the mid-1940s, Arthur Andersen & Co. was known as "a small [public] utility firm" (Spacek, 1985, p. 8) and was based in the Middle West, when all of the country's major accounting firms had their headquarters in New York City. Shortly after Spacek became the firm's managing partner in 1947, following Andersen's death, he gave several speeches that ruffled the feathers of the profession's elders. Spacek was asked to meet with the heads of other firms at a prominent New York City club. All of the large firms were represented, as were a number of middle-sized firms. The session was chaired by George O. May, the retired senior partner of Price Waterhouse & Co. and the *éminence grise* of the profession. Spacek (1985, p. 55) recalls the encounter as follows:

I remember George O. May telling us, but looking me straight in the eye, and said that the leadership of the accounting profession must rest in the hands of the larger, successful firms and that the smaller firms can enjoy the success but must acknowledge that the leadership of the profession is in the hands of the larger firms. It had a terrific impression on me because I was just trying to work out our own leadership in the profession. But I said to myself, at that time, if it is bigness that it takes to have any say in the accounting profession, why then we will concentrate on first things first. We'll get big. That's when I really went out for promotion. I really–everything I did in one way or the other was to see that it eventually resulted in promotion.

One could easily imagine that this encounter with the Eastern establishment served only to redouble Spacek's determination to differentiate his firm from the others.[3]

---

3   Spacek's fiery personality and the dominant role that he played as unquestioned leader of Arthur Andersen & Co. from 1947 to 1963 combine to make this as much a study of Leonard Spacek as of his firm. Indeed, in his oral history, he takes credit for having made the decision in 1946 to shift to the two-part opinion (Spacek, 1985, p. 238). For a further discussion of Spacek and his role in the firm, see *A Vision of Grandeur* (1988, esp. pp. 107–112 and 118–122).

Amplification of the firm's rationale

On May 7, 1957, almost ten years after Arthur Andersen & Co. abandoned the single-opinion format of the auditor's report, Carman G. Blough, the Institute's full-time Director of Research and former SEC chief accountant, questioned the firm's practice in a letter to Richard S. Claire, an Andersen home-office partner. Blough, as it happened, had become a manager in the firm in 1938, following his departure from the SEC; he was admitted to the partnership in 1940 and left to join a federal government agency in 1942. (He had represented Arthur Andersen & Co. on the Institute's Committee on Accounting Procedure between 1938 and 1942.) Blough and Claire had discussed the firm's preferred format of the auditor's report during the April 1957 meeting of the Institute's Council. Claire replied to Blough in a lengthy letter dated May 15, 1957. In his letter, Claire (1957, p. 2) said that

we view the distribution of significance to each of the three parts of the opinion paragraph in the standard certificate to be roughly 85% to the fair presentation of financial position and results of operations, 10% to generally accepted accounting principles, and 5% to consistency. Any exaggeration that there may be in the foregoing distribution of values is done just to make clearer what we consider to be a most important point. The reference to generally accepted accounting principles we regard as a statement of the objective standards by which the fairness of presentation is judged. We recognize also that the term "generally accepted accounting principles" as used in certificates today is applied both to principles and to practices. Improvements in accounting practices are continually in process. A practice generally accepted today may a few years from now not be generally accepted. During the interim period there may be two practices covering the same accounting matter, both of which may be said to be generally accepted. One, however, may clearly result in a better statement of net income.

Claire illustrated his argument with two cases. In the first, he compared the income statements of a small oil company on two different bases: successful-efforts costing and full costing. The latter practice, he said, was in accordance with GAAP, while the former had the support of "substantial precedent and authority." By adhering to the Institute's standard form of auditor's report, an accounting firm could, Claire argued, give an unqualified opinion for either practice. With respect to the financial statements prepared in accordance with the successful-efforts practice (of which the firm disapproved), Arthur Andersen & Co. would insert a middle paragraph in its auditor's report that would include the following sentence:

While the practice of expensing such costs for financial reporting purposes was generally followed in the petroleum industry some years ago, the practice of capitalizing such costs and amortizing them over the productive lives of the properties is now more generally followed and, in our opinion, is preferable ... (Claire, 1957, p. 3).

Since, in Claire's factual case, the full-costing net income for the year was 10 times the successful-efforts costing net income, he said (1957, p. 3) that his firm would conclude with the following opinion paragraph:

Because of the significance of the matter referred to in the preceding paragraph, we are of the opinion that the accompanying balance sheet and statements of income and earned surplus do not fairly present the financial position of X Company as of ____, 195__, nor the results of its operations for the __ months then ended.

In his second illustrative case, Claire referred to the prevailing practice of auditors with respect to railroad clients. Since interperiod tax allocation was not required for railroads by the Interstate Commerce Commission, most auditors followed a practice of giving an opinion on railroads' financial statements "in accordance with accounting principles and practices prescribed or authorized by the Interstate Commerce Commission," rather than in accordance with GAAP. Arthur Andersen & Co.'s practice, wrote Claire, was to draw attention to, and quantify the effect of, the railroad's departure from GAAP, and to state the firm's opinion on what was the *proper* practice (which, in this instance, conformed to GAAP). The firm's opinion on fair presentation would be qualified in the light of the railroad's departure from proper practice (or, one assumes, an adverse opinion would be given if the effect of the departure were very significant).

In closing his letter, Claire contended that his firm believed that its form of the auditor's report "conforms more closely to Rule 202 [of SEC's Regulation S-X] that the accountant's certificate shall state clearly 'the opinion of the accountant in respect of the financial statements covered by the certificate and the accounting principles and practices reflected therein'" (Claire, 1957, pp. 4–5). Claire reported to Blough that "we have never discussed [our form of the auditor's report] with the Securities and Exchange Commission ..." (Claire, 1957, p. 4). One therefore infers that the SEC's accounting staff had never registered a formal objection to the use of Arthur Andersen & Co.'s dual-opinion format in the filings by its clients.

On May 8, 1958, two senior partners of Arthur Andersen & Co. met in Washington with Andrew Barr, the SEC's chief accountant, and three of his aides. The meeting had been requested the previous fall by the firm, owing apparently to Claire's letter to Blough. The firm sought to ascertain the accounting staff's reaction to the form of its audit opinion. According to the firm's report of the meeting, Barr said it was "unfortunate that [the firm] adopted this wording because it created dissension in the profession" (Arthur Andersen & Co., 1958, p. 1). Asked whether, in his view, the firm should not have adopted the two-part opinion, Barr avoided a direct reply and repeated his expression of disquiet about dissension in the profession (p. 1). Barr allowed the inference that the two-part opinion, while unfortunate and perhaps ill-advised, was not objectionable. This seems to have been the only recorded reaction of the SEC to the firm's practice of using a two-part opinion. There is no indication that the SEC ever declined to accept financial statements with the firm's two-part opinion attached.

Partners vote on returning to single opinion

By 1957, leading partners in the firm were troubled by the apparent conflict between the firm's espousal of price-level-adjusted depreciation and its practice of not expressing an exception in its auditor's report when clients did not follow this practice.

In 1954, Arthur Andersen & Co. had petitioned the SEC "to formally require disclosure of the effect on income of depreciation adjustments related to price level changes in financial statements filed for purposes of public record" (Spacek, 1956, p. 5), but the petition was denied. Also in 1954, Garrett T. Burns, an Arthur Andersen & Co. partner, made a determined effort to persuade the Institute's Committee on Accounting Procedure, of which he was a member, to reverse its long-standing opposition to the recognition of price-level-adjusted depreciation in companies' financial statements. In Chapter 9A of *Accounting Research Bulletin No. 43*, issued in 1953, the Committee had once again reaffirmed its earlier position, but only by the narrowest majority. Burns' effort within the Committee failed, if only because of the SEC's known antipathy to departures from traditional historical cost.

Since 1954, Leonard Spacek, the firm's managing partner and an uncompromising advocate of the principles and standards in which he believed, had been promoting the cause of price-level depreciation in speeches before academics and professionals. Spacek's campaign for price-level depreciation further served to differentiate Arthur Andersen & Co. from other firms. Not only did price-level depreciation raise a central question about the meaningfulness of corporate financial statements, it would also have struck a responsive chord among companies who believed that the federal income tax was a levy upon capital, and among public utilities who questioned the fairness of a rate-base determination without considering the effect of changing prices (see, e.g., Chandler, 1953).

There was, some noticed, a discordance between Spacek's aggressive espousal of price-level depreciation and his firm's failure to take exception in the "present fairly" portion of its two-part opinion when clients did not accept the practice. In a widely reported speech in February 1957, Spacek gave his own answer to this apparent conflict (p. 21):

Our clients have the right to prepare their financial statements on the same basis as the financial statements of the corporations with which they are competing. We cannot interfere with this right. We, as auditors, cannot impose upon our clients new principles of financial accountability when those principles are not accepted by the accounting profession and business generally, even though we are strongly convinced of their merit .... We will give each of our clients and their shareholders all the benefits accruing to them under "generally accepted accounting principles," except in those cases where we believe that such "principles" are at variance with the concepts for which there is, or has been, substantial acceptance.

In an internal memorandum dated February 19, 1957, the firm's partners were asked whether the policy of giving a two-part opinion should be continued. The alternatives were laid before the partners. The firm could

1. Revert to the single-opinion format, continue to take exception to practices that do not "fairly present," but omit any exception in cases, like price-level depreciation, where the practice had not secured substantial acceptance.
2. Revert to a single-opinion format but omit an exception "in all cases in which the practice of a client, with which we disagree, has the support of the American Institute of Accountants or is supported by substantial precedent in actual practice."
3. "Retain our present form of certificate and continue to explain frankly (outside the certificate) why we do not believe we have a right to take exception to a failure to recognize price level depreciation or other practice [which we believe is sound and] for which there is no authoritative support or precedent in practice" (Arthur Andersen & Co., 1957, p. 5).

In the six-page memorandum, arguments were presented on both sides of the question of whether to retain the two-part opinion, but by far the longest and more impassioned argument was given in defense of continuing to give the two-part opinion. Spacek's views in his February 1957 speech (quoted above) were reflected in the latter argument. Among the points made in favor of retaining the two-part opinion were the following:

To revert back to the other form at this time would mean an abandonment of a long-established policy which is just as sound today as it was twenty years ago. It would represent a departure from a policy based upon principles and the adoption of one justified only by considerations of expediency .....
Rule 202 of the Securities and Exchange Commission states: "The accountants' certificate shall state clearly (i) the opinion of the accountant in respect of the financial statements covered by the certificate and the accounting principles and practices reflected therein." We *should* be advocating the universal adoption of a certificate that does that, but the adoption of the proposed revision would forever bar us from recommending such a change (pp. 3, 4).

Also in support of the argument for retaining the two-part opinion, it was stated that legal counsel had given the firm an opinion that a change to the single-opinion format would not lessen any liability of the firm, "but on the contrary might *jeopardize* our position because the change might be construed as a course of action designed to conceal rather than to disclose." (Arthur Andersen & Co., 1957, p. 4).

The principal argument in favor of making the change was given in the 1957 Arthur Andersen memo as follows:

Admittedly this is a compromise, but since there is no satisfactory way out of our present dilemma, it represents a better policy than the one we now follow. Anyone who reads our present certificate could assume that we judge independently of generally accepted accounting principles as well as in conformity with them. This is not true at the present time in those cases involving price level depreciation (p. 2).

As these excerpts suggest, one side could claim principle, while the other was supported only by expediency.

At the partners' meeting in May 1957, the matter was discussed at length, and their decision was to retain the two-part opinion. No transcript was preserved, and the reasons that were considered the most persuasive were not recorded.

Public criticism by Carman G. Blough

Following the exchange of correspondence between Carman G. Blough and Richard S. Claire in May 1957, there was no indication that Blough intended to carry the matter further. It came as a surprise, therefore, when Blough devoted a portion of his "Accounting and Auditing Problems" department in the March 1958 issue of *The Journal of Accountancy* to a criticism of the dual-opinion format of the auditor's report. Without naming Arthur Andersen & Co., Blough wrote that "At least one accounting firm has, for some time, been using a variation of the standard form of auditor's report which apparently uses some other basis, which is not disclosed, for the judgment as to 'fairness'" (Blough, 1958a, p. 76). After stating "we feel that this is a most unfortunate practice," he added:

If every accountant were to decide for himself what a "fair presentation" is, there would be no standards to go by. One person might consider that a certain presentation was fair while someone else might feel that it was unfair and that something very different was fair. Both might be very honest in their convictions yet be miles apart in their presentations. It is only if their judgments are reached within the framework of generally accepted principles of accounting, i.e., the recognized and widely accepted conventions and procedures, that there can be any test of the reasonableness, or even the honesty, of a particular representation.

. . . it seems to us the accountant puts himself in a dangerous position when he departs from established ground rules in determining the fairness of a financial presentation (Blough, 1958a, p. 76).

A reply to Blough's position appeared in the May 1958 issue of the *Journal*. It was written not by a partner of Arthur Andersen & Co. but by Maurice E. Peloubet, to whom Blough referred as "a well-known and highly regarded member of our profession, for whose views we have the highest respect" (Blough, 1958b, p. 73). Peloubet, in fact, had been one of the original members (1939–1941) of the Institute's Committee on Auditing Procedure and had been a long-time member (1941–1953) of the Committee of Accounting Procedure. He was a partner in a small firm, Pogson, Peloubet & Co., which merged into Price Waterhouse & Co. in 1963. In his reply, Peloubet criticized Blough for suggesting that "present fairly" means no more than "in conformity with GAAP." He argued (1958, p. 73) that

Wherever choices are presented or where the exercise of judgment is required, either on the part of the management or the accountant, I do not think the full responsibility has been discharged by merely stating that the accounts have been prepared on the basis of generally accepted accounting principles.

If this is sufficient, why bother about "present fairly"? It seems to me that the phrase "present fairly in conformity with generally accepted accounting principles" means that the accounts are prepared in accordance with appropriate and applicable generally accepted accounting principles, and that where there are choices, and where alternative methods are permitted, the methods under which the accounts have been prepared are either the most appropriate under the circumstances, or are one of possibly several alternative methods, any of which, in the judgment of the accountant, are applicable.

Although Peloubet seems to dilute his argument by suggesting, at the close of the foregoing quotation, that applicability can be substituted for appropriateness, he added (1958, p. 74) that "in the vast majority of cases some one of the accepted principles or methods will be applicable, but the accountant will still be forced to decide on the propriety of the method used." Blough did not agree. He wrote (1958b, p. 75):

If there are two or more such alternatives, we agree that the auditor may use his influence to have management adopt his choice, but if the management chooses an accepted alternative that he agrees is appropriate, though not what he considers the best, we question whether he can properly deny its fairness in accordance with generally accepted accounting principles.

Blough contended that, until the accounting profession could get together and agree upon criteria for assessing appropriateness, the determination of "fairness" should be guided by generally accepted accounting principles that are applicable in the circumstances.

Yet the premise underlying Arthur Andersen & Co.'s decision in 1946 to adopt the two-part opinion was that the auditor has a professional responsibility to determine appropriateness when deciding whether the financial statements "present fairly." The issue of appropriateness was, in one sense, more serious in the 1940s and even in the 1950s than it is today. In the years prior to the establishment in 1959 of the Accounting Principles Board, the number of pronouncements was relatively few and there was resistance within the profession to narrowing the range of acceptable methods (see Zeff, 1984, pp. 458–459). In such controversial areas as inventory valuation, depreciation, tax allocation, goodwill amortization, pensions, leases, business combinations, and the treatment of unamortized discount, issue cost, and redemption premium on refunded bonds, the Institute's pronouncements either were silent or admitted of alternatives, usually with scant regard for differing circumstances.[4]

4   A profound difference in accounting ideology existed between Arthur Andersen & Co., a firm whose early development had been primarily in the regulated public utility field, and Price Waterhouse & Co. and Haskins & Sells, which had developed client bases composed heavily of major industrial corporations whose presidents were among the early captains of American industry. Companies in regulated industries were accustomed to uniform accounting systems imposed by governmental fiat, while unregulated businesses were disposed toward freedom of enterprise. Not surprisingly, Arthur Andersen & Co. urged a greater degree of company-to-company uniformity in financial reckonings (see, e.g., Spacek, 1961), while PW and H&S were defenders of flexibility (see, e.g., Grady, 1965, pp. 32–35; and Powell, 1965). Prior to

Leonard Spacek believed that, in such a permissive climate, it was incumbent on the auditor to make a judgment on the appropriateness of alternative methods. In an August 1957, speech, he reiterated that view and said that the profession would "at least put the teeth of responsibility into the present form of audit certificate" if it were to modify the opinion paragraph as follows:

In our opinion (the statements) present fairly the financial position and results of operation in conformity with *those* generally accepted accounting principles *considered appropriate in the circumstances* and applied on a basis consistent with that of the preceding year (Spacek, 1958, p. 374, italics added).

In the same speech, Spacek proposed that the Institute establish "a court or professional tribunal of accounting principles" and charged the Institute with responsibility for "defining the criteria of accounting principles" (1958, p. 377).

According to Blough, the auditor's determination of appropriateness had to await the day when the profession could agree upon suitable criteria, and until then the auditor should not be basing judgments on his own personal opinion (1958b, p. 74). Spacek, ever the activist, was pressing the profession to develop criteria for evaluating appropriateness and, in the end, to eliminate alternative accounting principles.

The controversy over appropriateness flared anew in the 1970s, when the SEC proposed to charge auditors with the responsibility for determining whether a client company's switch from one accounting principle to another "is preferable under the circumstances." The SEC eventually lightened the burden by permitting the auditor to rely on the client's business judgment. Nonetheless, issues were raised about how an auditor might determine preferability in the absence of agreed-upon objectives and established criteria (see Revsine, 1977, and footnote 8, *infra*). It will be recalled that an appropriateness test currently exists as a formal recommendation in Canada, yet criteria for making such judgments seem to be lacking there as in the United States (see Gibbins and Mason, 1988, chap. 6).

Two-part opinions on price-level depreciation

As demonstrated by the firm's internal debate during 1957, its advocacy of price-level depreciation was testing the partners' depth of support for the two-part opinion. Evidently, it was not contemplated by the firm in the 1940s that it might one day espouse an accounting principle, such as price-level depreciation, for which there was no general acceptance, thus placing the firm in the unacceptable position of imposing on its clients "new principles of financial accountability," as Spacek termed it in his February 1957 speech.

In audit reports given to three of its clients who adopted price-level depre-

the showdown in AICPA Council in 1964 (Zeff, 1972, pp. 180–183), the flexibility school was the dominant force in the AICPA committees that pronounced upon accounting principles. In this arena as well, Arthur Andersen & Co. was "bucking the trend."

ciation during the 1950s, Arthur Andersen & Co. used its two-part opinion to lend support to this departure from GAAP.[5]

Ayrshire Collieries Corporation, an Indianapolis client, reflected price-level depreciation in the Comparative Statement of Earnings included in its 1958 annual report as follows:

	Year Ended June 30, 1958	Year Ended June 30, 1957
Net income for the year	$2,884,256	$2,904,730
Provision for price-level depreciation (See note)	195,429	143,587
Balance of Net Income	$2,688,827	$2,761,143

After giving its usual two-part opinion on the company's financial statements, Arthur Andersen & Co. added the following paragraph as part of its auditor's report:

In our opinion, however, the net income for the year is more fairly presented after deducting the provision for price-level depreciation, since current price levels have been recognized in determining the current cost of property consumed in operations. Generally accepted principles of accounting for cost of property consumed in operations are based on historical costs and do not reflect the effect of price-level changes since dates of acquisition or construction of the companies' depreciable property.

In the 1957 annual report of Sacramento Municipal Utility District (SMUD), the Operating Expenses section of the Income Statement included the following breakdown:

Provision for depreciation—Computed on historical cost	$1,506,624
Additional provision to reflect increase in price level (Note 1)	665,000

In the auditor's report, the following two paragraphs were given after the scope paragraph:

As set forth in Note 1 to the accompanying financial statements, the statement of net revenue reflects an additional charge for depreciation of $665,000; this charge is equivalent to the amount by which depreciation computed on the cost of depreciable property adjusted to reflect current price levels exceeds depreciation computed on cost. Although this practice is not yet recognized as a generally accepted principle of accounting, it is our opinion that, for the District, it results in a fair statement of net revenue for the year, and we have approved its adoption. In other respects, the financial statements, in our opinion, were prepared in accordance with generally accepted accounting principles applied on a basis consistent with that of the preceding year.

---

5   Expanded treatment of these company disclosures and the resulting auditors' reports may be found in a news feature in *The Journal of Accountancy* ("Price-level Depreciation ... ," 1959) and in Appendix D in *Accounting Research Study No. 6* (Staff of the Accounting Research Division, 1963, pp. 211–217).

In our opinion, the accompanying balance sheet and statement of net revenue present fairly the financial position of Sacramento Municipal Utility District as of December 31, 1957, and the results of its operations for the year then ended.

Iowa-Illinois Gas and Electric Company, which had been authorized by the Iowa Supreme Court to recover, through rates charged to customers, the fair value of the property used to provide customer service, also recognized fair value depreciation in its financial statements. In its 1958 annual report, the company included fair value depreciation in the operating expenses in its Statement of Income. Included in the middle paragraph of the auditor's report were the following two sentences:

We approve the practice adopted by the Company, since it results, in our opinion, in a fairer statement of income for the year than that resulting from the application of generally accepted accounting principles. In all other respects, the financial statements were prepared in conformity with generally accepted accounting principles applied on a basis consistent with that of the preceding year.

Arthur Andersen & Co. concluded its auditor's report with an opinion on fair presentation similar to the final paragraph in its auditor's report given to SMUD.

Both Ayrshire and Iowa-Illinois were subject to SEC jurisdiction, and the Commission's accounting staff took exception to the treatment of price-level depreciation as an expense. As a result of the SEC's objection, the companies amended their presentation to show price-level depreciation as an appropriation of earned surplus (i.e., retained earnings).

The auditors' report in these three instances illustrate Arthur Andersen & Co.'s use of its two-part opinion to express approval of companies' use of price-level depreciation. The dilemma that faced the firm, however, was the inconsistency between these opinions and those given to companies whose financial statements reflected traditional historical cost depreciation.

The firm reverts to the single-opinion format

Spacek's despair in 1957 was that the Institute's Committee on Accounting Procedure was making no progress toward reducing the number of alternative accounting principles, and that no one in the Institute's hierarchy seemed interested in actively developing criteria for judging appropriateness when alternatives were available. In that climate, his firm had decided to continue its policy of giving two-part opinions.

During 1957, the stridency of Spacek's public criticisms of the accounting profession's record in improving financial reporting accelerated, and the Institute appointed a special committee to investigate Spacek's charge that an Institute committee had yielded to industry pressure. The committee, composed of Institute leaders, found his claims to be unsupported by the facts (see Zeff, 1984, p. 461). The firm's strong view that it should base its auditor's opinion on only those accounting principles that it believed were proper led to the loss of some of its railroad clients (Spacek, 1985, pp. 248–249).

In October 1957, changes began to occur that, for the first time, gave Spacek and his firm some basis for believing that progress might soon be made on both fronts. Institute President Alvin R. Jennings, a senior partner in Lybrand, Ross Bros. & Montgomery (as the U.S. firm of Coopers & Lybrand was then known), delivered a major address in which he responded to criticisms (including Spacek's) of the performance of the Committee on Accounting Procedure. Jennings (1958) proposed the creation of an independent research organization that would be more attuned to the changing economic and financial times.

In December 1957, Jennings appointed a blue-ribbon Special Committee on Research Program "to consider a new approach to the means whereby accounting research should be undertaken, accounting principles should be promulgated, and adherence to them should be secured" (Report to Council of the Special Committee on Research Program, 1958, p. 62). The committee's charge was broad and dealt with fundamental issues. Spacek was among those invited to serve, and he accepted. Other members of the special committee included Carman Blough, Paul Grady, William W. Werntz, Andrew Barr, and Weldon Powell— all leaders of the profession. Werntz was chairman of the Institute's Committee on Accounting Procedure, and Barr was the SEC's chief accountant. Blough and Werntz were former chief accountants.

In its historic report issued in September 1958, the special committee unanimously recommended a major reform in the Institute's accounting principles program, which included the following points:

- the Committee on Accounting Procedure be replaced by an Accounting Principles Board (APB),
- an accounting research division be created within the Institute to serve the Board,
- two initial research projects be directed at identifying the basic accounting postulates and broad accounting principles, and
- the Board use these and subsequent research studies as a basis for its accounting pronouncements.

As Spacek saw it, the high priority given to the two research projects on postulates and broad principles inspired hope that the Institute would finally develop criteria for assessing appropriateness and that, as a consequence, the Board's pronouncements would lead to a reduction in the number of alternative accounting principles. This was Spacek's first service on an Institute committee, and one may infer from his unqualified assent to the special committee's report that he believed that the profession's leaders were of a mind to make real progress toward solving the problems of which he had been complaining. The Institute swiftly approved the special committee's recommendations and established the

APB and its accounting research division in 1959. One year later, after resolving some initial concerns, Spacek accepted an appointment to the Board.[6]

In his address to the Institute's 1960 Annual Meeting, Spacek voiced support for the goals implicit in the special committee's report. He referred to two publications recently issued by his firm that supplied agenda material for the newly formed Accounting Principles Board. One, a 127-page booklet, *Accounting and Reporting Problems of the Accounting Profession* (Arthur Andersen & Co., 1960a), was a critical analysis of alternative accounting principles in 20 major problem areas. The second of the two publications, a 43-page booklet on "the basic postulate of accounting," discussed his firm's views on the Board's research project on basic accounting postulates (Arthur Andersen & Co., 1960b).

Spacek's avowed endorsement of the aims of the APB, coupled with his firm's emerging policy of publishing technical booklets dealing with matters coming before the Board, created a climate in which the firm could consider abandoning its departure from the Institute's standard form of the auditor's report and instead channel its efforts at achieving accounting reform through the Institute's new accounting principles program.

In an internal memorandum dated October 2, 1962, a proposed revision of the firm's dual-opinion auditor's report was again placed before the partners for a vote. Only the argument in favor of reverting to the single-opinion format was presented, and it was stated that Spacek, the firm's managing partner, concurred with that argument. The memorandum drew attention to the booklets in which the firm took issue with settled practice in a number of problem areas. The memorandum (Arthur Andersen & Co., 1962, p. 2) added:

In some of these areas where the effect is very substantial, we have qualified and would currently qualify our opinions on financial statements, and in some of the other areas we have not qualified and ordinarily would not qualify our opinions.

In articles, speeches and other communications, as well as in our booklets, we have emphasized to businessmen and accountants that "fairness" in financial reporting is not being achieved through some of the present accounting practices. The continued use of our present form of opinion, in the light of the position we have taken publicly on many of these practices and the general recognition by the profession that these problems do exist, could easily create the impression that we are being hypocritical or intellectually dishonest.

---

6   The Institute's executive committee had insisted that, apart from Weldon Powell (who was to be the chairman), all representatives on the APB from the Big Eight firms must be their firm-wide managing partners. Spacek balked at this requirement, believing that his firm's senior technical partner should represent the firm. William M. Black, the managing partner of Peat, Marwick, Mitchell & Co., held the same view. Consequently, only six of the Big Eight firms were represented on the APB during 1959–1960, its inaugural year. J.S. Seidman, the Institute's 1959–1960 President, believed it was essential to the success of the APB for all of the Big Eight firms to be represented. A close professional acquaintance of Spacek's, Seidman succeeded in persuading Spacek and Black to join the APB in 1960, when its size was increased from 18 to 21 to accommodate the new members. Seidman was also instrumental in arranging for Spacek, whose aggressive manner and outspoken criticism had irritated many members of the profession's establishment, to deliver a major address at the Institute's 1960 Annual Meeting.

By the early 1960s, price-level depreciation was not the only subject on which the firm was recommending a practice that was not generally accepted. In October 1962, when the memorandum was issued, the Accounting Principles Board was embroiled in a controversy over accounting for the investment credit, and Arthur Andersen & Co. had announced its position in favor of deferral.[7] Since the investment credit was without precedent, neither the flow-through nor the deferral approach to accounting for the credit could be said to enjoy general acceptance. Perhaps the firm sensed that, in the event that the Board were to support only the flow-through approach, it would find itself (as with price-level depreciation) in opposition to the only practice that was generally accepted. It may not have been entirely an accident in timing that the memorandum was issued in the thick of the controversy over accounting for the investment credit. Furthermore, if the firm's managing partner was serving on a board that would have a large hand in determining GAAP, it might have seemed incongruous if the firm were to continue giving opinions on fairness of presentation not predicated on GAAP.

The vote of the partners was not recorded, but on October 25, 1962, the firm issued an internal accounting release in which the single-opinion auditor's report was presented as firm policy.

The reversion decision: Some major influences

What had happened since 1957? For one thing, the firm had adopted a strategy of publicly venting its views on a wide range of financial reporting issues. The number of problem areas in which the firm took issue with generally accepted accounting principles was considerable. Prior to 1957, by contrast, the firm had focused its public criticism on the unwillingness of the profession and the SEC to approve price-level depreciation as an accepted principle. The inconsistency between the firm's public advocacy of price-level depreciation and its policy of giving clean "fairness" opinions to companies not adopting price-level depreciation had troubled many of the partners at the time of the reconsideration of the two-part opinion in 1957. Owing to the firm's outspokenness on the entire agenda of issues coming before the APB, the number and variety of potential inconsistencies between what it said and what it did multiplied between 1957 and 1962. The firm's internal memorandum of October 2, 1962, stated the dilemma as follows:

If we retain our present form of opinion, we would be continuing to state that, in our opinion, the financial statements "present fairly," while at the same time we are saying publicly in booklets, articles, addresses, etc. (in order to obtain corrective action by the accounting profession), that some of the practices on the basis of which we give unqualified opinions do not result in financial reporting that meets the test of "fairness."

---

7   For a discussion of the controversy over the investment credit in 1962, see Moonitz (1966).

It was awkward, to say the least, for the firm to be giving an unqualified opinion on the "fairness" of financial statements that reflected the use of accounting principles that the firm publicly criticized.

Second, the firm's practice of championing price-level depreciation in some of its auditors' reports, as illustrated in the previous section, had drawn even further attention to the inconsistency dilemma. In 1957, a problem that concerned the firm was the juxtaposition of Spacek's public utterances on price-level depreciation as against the firm's policy of giving clean "fairness" opinions to companies not adopting the practice. In 1958, as reported above, the firm began to carry its advocacy of price-level depreciation into its reports on the financial statements of companies that had adopted the practice. Yet the firm continued, as it knew it must, to give clean opinions to nonadopters.[8]

Third, the Institute in the 1960s seemed to be committed to abandoning its earlier tolerance of alternative accounting principles, and the firm, as suggested above, believed that its advocacy in the form of publications, speeches, and articles might gain support within the APB for a reduction in the number of alternatives. To Spacek's disappointment (1962a), the Board's research studies on postulates and principles did not become the building blocks for later pronouncements, and the Board itself disavowed the two studies in June 1962. By mid-1962, the APB still had not been tested on a major accounting pronouncement, yet Spacek continued to believe in the Board. In July 1962, he said, "I do believe that our Accounting Principles Board will eventually succeed in coming to the right answer" (1962b, p. 205).

Fourth, the firm's policy of tackling controversies in its auditors' report was not working. The policy was having no perceptible impact on practice or on the literature. No other firms had followed suit even though the SEC's accounting staff did not object to the practice, and no evidence has come to light that it influenced companies in their choice of accounting principles. Apart from Blough's 1958 column in *The Journal of Accountancy*, and some discussion in one of the firm's publications (Arthur Andersen & Co., 1960a, pp. 4–5), nary a reference to Arthur Andersen & Co.'s two-part opinion can be found in the academic or professional accounting literature, or even in the minutes of the

8   A somewhat similar problem involving the preferability dilemma (see discussion on p. 457, *supra*) arose in the mid-1970s, when Arthur Andersen & Co. challenged the SEC's *Accounting Series Release No. 177* (1975). The SEC required that, when a registrant company seeks to change an accounting principle, "a letter from the registrant's independent accountants shall be filed as an exhibit indicating whether or not the change is to an accounting principle which in his judgment is preferable under the circumstances ... ." In response, the firm wrote: "A letter from our firm stating that a particular principle is preferable for one client could adversely affect many other clients not participating in such a decision and could adversely affect the reputation and credibility not only of such clients but also of our firm in giving reports on the financial statements of those other clients, whether or not they ever make accounting changes, and thus open our clients and our firm to potential costly litigation" (Arthur Andersen & Co., 1976, p. 8). The threat of litigation, while considered in the firm's 1957 internal debate and perhaps also in the decision to abandon the two-part opinion in 1962, had become a significantly more serious issue in the 1970s.

Institute's Committee on Auditing Procedure. The firm's practice had attracted virtually no notice.

Fifth—and perhaps the pivotal factor—was Spacek's interest in taking over a long-time client from Price Waterhouse & Co. Superior Oil Co. had been a Price Waterhouse client since 1933, and the company's management wished to change auditors. If only because of George O. May's condescending manner in the meeting with Spacek in the late 1940s, the prospect of acquiring a Price Waterhouse client must have been irresistible. Moreover, Superior Oil was thinking of moving its headquarters from Los Angeles to Houston, where Arthur Andersen & Co.'s major oil and gas audit work was based. But there was a problem. Superior Oil, with conservative management, followed the minority but accepted practice of expensing not only the cost of unsuccessful wells but also the cost of successful wells. Arthur Andersen & Co. had been very critical of this practice and did not have any clients following it. The firm was an avowed advocate of capitalizing the costs of both successful and unsuccessful wells. Before accepting the engagement, Spacek asked SEC Chief Accountant Andrew Barr, "If we took over an oil company who was charging all their drilling cost to expenses, including the good wells, I mean the successful wells as well as the dry holes, and we qualified it, would [you] stand behind us and require the capitalization of the successful wells?" (Spacek, 1985, p. 239). Barr responded that, in his view, the company's practice was "generally accepted." It therefore became necessary for the firm to endorse what was "generally accepted" in this regard if it wanted to obtain the new client. As Spacek later said, "That triggered [the firm's decision to revert to the one-part opinion] because the accounting profession always said 'You preach all these things but you don't follow them.' I just said okay, [from] now on we will follow generally accepted accounting principles [in our auditor's report] but nobody will stand in our way in our efforts to improve them" (Spacek, 1985, p. 239). Arthur Andersen & Co. acquired the audit of Superior Oil in 1962, and the firm's report issued in 1963 in the one-part format was not qualified.[9]

The Superior Oil incident was the last straw. In a permissive climate, when other major firms were willing to give unqualified opinions on a wide range of alternative accounting principles, Arthur Andersen & Co. ran the risk of offending newly acquired clients that were accustomed to the flexibility of their previous auditors. The advocacy of the firm's views through the medium of its auditor's report had become too costly. It was thought wiser to promote the firm's views on accounting principles through its publications and the speaking and writing activities of its partners.

References

A Vision of Grandeur (75th Anniversary publication of Arthur Andersen & Co.) (1988).

9   The author is grateful to George R. Catlett for advice in characterizing this episode.

American Institute of Accountants, Special Committee on Co-operation with Stock Exchanges, *Audits of Corporate Accounts 1932–1934* (New York: AIA, 1934).
————, Committee on Auditing Procedure, "Extensions of Auditing Procedure," *Statement on Auditing Procedure No. 1* (New York, AIA, October 1939).
————, Committee on Accounting Procedure, "Accounting for Income Taxes," *Accounting Research Bulletin No. 23* (New York: AIA, December 1944) pp. 183–194.
————, Committee on Accounting Procedure, "Restatement and Revision of Accounting Research Bulletins," *Accounting Research Bulletin No. 43* (New York: AIA, 1953).
American Institute of Certified Public Accountants, Auditing Standards Board, "The Auditor's Standard Report," proposed statement on auditing standards (New York: AICPA, September 10, 1980).
Anderson, Rodney J., *The External Audit 1: Concepts and Techniques* (Toronto: Pitman Publishing, 1977).
Arthur Andersen & Co., *P & M Series Release No. 16* (November 21, 1941).
————, *Firm Accounting Release No. 27, Re: Certifying Paragraph of Auditors' Certificate* (July 2, 1946).
————, Memorandum to All Partners, Subject: Suggested Change in our Present Certificate (February 19, 1957).
————, "Meeting with SEC Accounting Staff, May 8, 1958, to Discuss the Form of Our Certificate (FAR 15) and Various Other Matters."
————, *The Postulate of Accounting—What It Is, How It Is Determined, How It Should be Used* (Chicago: Arthur Andersen & Co., 1960b).
————, *Accounting and Reporting Problems of the Accounting Profession* (Chicago: Arthur Andersen & Co., 1960a).
————, Memorandum to Each Partner and Principal, Subject: Proposed Revision of the Form of Auditors' Opinion (October 2, 1962).
————, "Request for Action by Commission with Respect to Certain Rules and Pronouncements Relating to Accounting Principles," *Before the Securities and Exchange Commission* (Chicago: Arthur Andersen & Co., June 15, 1976).
Blough, C.G., "Implications of 'Present Fairly' in the Auditor's Report," Accounting and Auditing Problems, *The Journal of Accountancy* (March 1958a) pp. 76–77.
————, "More About 'Present Fairly' in the Auditor's Report," Accounting and Auditing Problems, *The Journal of Accountancy* (May 1958b) pp. 73–75.
Canadian Institute of Chartered Accountants, The Committee on Accounting and Auditing Research, "The Auditor's Report," *Bulletin No. 17* (October 1959).
————, The Accounting and Auditing Research Committee, "The Auditor's Report," *Bulletin No. 25* (September 1967).
Carmichael, D.R., "What Does the Independent Auditor's Opinion Really Mean?" *Journal of Accountancy* (November 1974) pp. 83–87.
————, and A.J. Winters, "The Evolution of Audit Reporting," in D.R. Nichols and H.F. Stettler (eds.), *Auditing Symposium VI* (Lawrence: School of Business, University of Kansas, 1982) pp. 1–20.
Carr, G.K., letter to the author (October 12, 1990), telephone conversation with the author (April 1, 1991).
Chandler, G., "The Impact of Inflation upon Depreciation Requirements," *The Arthur Andersen Chronicle* (April 1953) pp. 112–124.
CICA Handbook (Toronto: Canadian Institute of Chartered Accountants, revised with periodic supplements).
Claire, R.S., letter to C.G. Blough (May 15, 1957).
Commission on Auditors' Responsibilities, *Report, Conclusions, and Recommendations* (New York: Commission on Auditors' Responsibilities, 1978).

Eckel, L.G., "The Two-Part Audit Opinion," *CAmagazine* (June 1973) pp. 40–43.

Elliott, S., "Accounting and Canada," *The Arthur Andersen Chronicle* (July 1974) pp. 78–82.

Gibbins, M., "Easing the Tension Between Professional Judgment and Standards," *CAmagazine* (May 1983) pp. 38–43.

———, and A.K. Mason, *Professional Judgment in Financial Reporting* (Toronto: Canadian Institute of Chartered Accountants, 1988).

Grady, P., *Inventory of Generally Accepted Accounting Principles for Business Enterprises*, Accounting Research Study No. 7 (New York: American Institute of Certified Public Accountants, 1965).

Jeffreys, D.E., "'The Auditor's Standard Report' Revisited," *CAmagazine* (October 1984) pp. 107–109.

Jennings, A.R., "Present-Day Challenges in Financial Reporting," *The Journal of Accountancy* (January 1958) pp. 28–34.

Johnston, D.J., "Fairness and the One-Part Opinion," *CAmagazine* (February 1979) pp. 46–54.

Louis, A.M., "A Fat Maverick Stirs Up the Accounting Profession," *Fortune* (December 1970) pp. 96–99, 122–125.

Moonitz, M., "Some Reflections on the Investment Credit Experience," *Journal of Accounting Research* (Spring 1966) pp. 47–61.

Mulcahy, G., "The CICA Handbook—Research Recommendations," *Canadian Chartered Accountant* (December 1968) pp. 432–433.

———, letter to the author (October 12, 1990).

Peloubet, M.E., letter to Carman G. Blough, in Blough (ed.), "More About 'Present Fairly' in the Auditor's Report," in Accounting and Auditing Problems, *The Journal of Accountancy* (May 1958) pp. 73–74.

Powell, W., "Putting Uniformity in Financial Accounting into Perspective," *Law and Contemporary Problems* (Autumn 1965) pp. 674–689.

"Price-level Depreciation in Annual Statements," *The Journal of Accountancy* (September 1959) pp. 16, 18.

"Report to Council of the Special Committee on Research Program," *The Journal of Accountancy* (December 1958) pp. 62–68.

Revsine, L., "The Preferability Dilemma," *Journal of Accountancy* (September 1977) pp. 80–89.

Rosenfield, P., and L. Lorensen, "Auditors' Responsibilities and the Audit Report," *Journal of Accountancy* (September 1974) pp. 73–83.

Securities and Exchange Commission, "Administrative Policy on Financial Statements," *Accounting Series Release No. 4* (April 25, 1938).

———, "Notice of Adoption of Amendments to Form 10-Q and Regulation S-X Regarding Interim Financial Reporting," *Accounting Series Release No. 177* (September 10, 1975).

Skinner, R.M., letter to the author (July 11, 1988) and telephone conversation with the author (October 28, 1990).

Spacek, L., "Accounting Has Failed to Prevent Major Misrepresentations" (April 19, 1956), in *A Search for Fairness in Financial Reporting to the Public* (Chicago: Arthur Andersen & Co., 1969) pp. 1–7.

———, "Professional Accountants and Their Public Responsibility" (February 12, 1957), in *A Search for Fairness in Financial Reporting to the Public* (Chicago: Arthur Andersen & Co., 1969) pp. 17–26.

———, "The Need for an Accounting Court," *The Accounting Review* (July 1958) pp. 368–379.

————, "Are Accounting Principles Generally Accepted?" *The Journal of Accountancy* (April 1961) pp. 41–46.

————, "Comments of Leonard Spacek," in R.T. Sprouse and M. Moonitz, *A Tentative Set of Broad Accounting Principles for Business Enterprises*, Accounting Research Study No. 3 (New York: American Institute of Certified Public Accountants, 1962a) pp. 77–79.

————, "Presentation on Accounting Principles" (July 6, 1962b), in *A Search for Fairness in Financial Reporting to the Public* (Chicago: Arthur Andersen & Co., 1969) pp. 197–208.

————, *The Growth of Arthur Andersen & Co., 1928–1973: An Oral History by Leonard Spacek* (Chicago: Arthur Andersen & Co., 1985).

Staff of the Accounting Research Division, *Reporting the Financial Effects of Price-level Changes* (New York: American Institute of Certified Public Accountants, 1963).

Staub, W.A., *Auditing Developments during the Present Century* (Cambridge, MA.: Harvard University Press, 1942).

Storey, R.K., *The Search for Accounting Principles: Today's Problems in Perspective* (New York: American Institute of Certified Public Accountants, 1964).

Thomas, R.D., "Research," *CAmagazine* (December 1976) pp. 54–58.

Zeff, S.A., *Forging Accounting Principles in Five Countries: A History and an Analysis of Trends* (Champaign, IL: Stipes Publishing Company, 1972).

————, "Some Junctures in the Evolution of the Process of Establishing Accounting Principles in the U.S.A.: 1917–1972," *The Accounting Review* (July 1984) pp. 447–468.

Case cited

United States v. Simon, 425 F.2d 796 (2d Cir. 1969), cert. denied 397 U.S. 1006 (1970). (Continental Vending case)

British Accounting Review (1997), **29** (Special Issue), 3–39

THE EARLY YEARS OF THE ASSOCIATION OF UNIVERSITY TEACHERS OF ACCOUNTING: 1947–1959

STEPHEN A. ZEFF

Rice University

The first organization of accounting academics in the UK, the Association of University Teachers of Accounting, was launched in 1947. Today it is known as the British Accounting Association. The Association was initially an enterprise of teachers in English and Welsh universities. It was founded at a time when impetus was being given to the study of accounting in their universities, and the first full-time accounting chairs were established in Britain. It was also a period in which serious efforts were made to stimulate accounting research.

The paper will begin with a discussion of the changing climate in accounting education and research, and is followed by a history of the Association's first 12 years.

© 1997 Academic Press Limited

EVOLUTION OF UK ACADEMIC ACCOUNTING TO 1947

Early Accounting Chairs

Prior to 1947, academic accounting in the UK was dominated by practical men with an interest in accounting education, who took part-time positions in the universities. All of the chair holders in England and Scotland during this period served on a part-time basis. Some, such as L. R. Dicksee, S. S. Dawson and F. R. M. de Paula, were progressive thinkers and made important contributions to the literature (see Brief, 1980; Kitchen & Parker,

The author owes a large debt of gratitude to the late David Solomons, who graciously contributed his files relating to his involvement in the Association of University Teachers of Accounting (AUTA) during the period 1947–1959. Without these files, the history of the AUTA prior to 1960 could not have been written. The author is also grateful to Lou Goldberg for furnishing a copy of Issue No. 2 of the AUTA Newsletter and for comments on an earlier draft, to Keith Maunders for providing a large file of AUTA correspondence, to Richard Macve for his diligent searches in the LSE library, and to Will Baxter, Harold Edey, Vyvyan Cornwell, Steve Walker, Tom Lee, Michael Mumford, Bob Parker, Christopher Napier, Michael Bromwich, David Flint and Dick Edwards, as well as the participants in the 8th Annual ABFH Conference, held at the Cardiff Business School on 18–19 September 1996, for their comments on earlier drafts. This paper is dedicated to the memory of David Solomons (1912–1995).

Correspondence should be addressed to: Professor S. A. Zeff, Jesse H. Jones Graduate School of Administration – MS 531, Rice University, Houston, TX 77005–1892, USA.

0890–8389/97/0S0003 + 37 $25.00/0   ba970027

1980; Parker & Zeff, 1996). A full-time chair, initially combining accountancy with commerce, was installed at University College Galway in 1914 and, with the addition of economics, continued in existence for 55 years.

On 1 October 1902, Lawrence R. Dicksee took up a post as Professor of Accounting, part-time, in the University of Birmingham, the first such appointment in a UK university.[1] Dicksee was already well known for his pioneering work, *Auditing: A Practical Manual for Auditors*, first published in 1892, as well as for other books and articles that flowed from his prolific pen. He was the senior partner in the London firm of Sellars, Dicksee & Co. Also, in 1902, he began lecturing at the London School of Economics (thus becoming the first accounting lecturer at LSE), and, in 1906, he resigned the Birmingham Chair 'to spend more time on a post concerned with business training of Army officers, at the LSE' (Craner & Jones, 1995).[2] He continued to lecture at LSE for the next 25 years, always in a part-time capacity.

In 1907, Sidney S. Dawson, a Liverpool practitioner, succeeded to the Birmingham Chair. Dawson, also a frequent contributor to the literature, was best known as compiler of *The Accountant's Compendium*, published in 1898. After 3 years, he resigned the chair 'owing to the pressure of professional engagements' (Craner & Jones, 1995; 1996, p. 8). At the time of their respective appointments, both Dicksee and Dawson were fellows of The Institute of Chartered Accountants in England and Wales (ICAEW).

Following two incumbencies of such short duration, held by professionals practising in other cities, the University turned to a scion of one of Birmingham's prominent families, Charles E. Martineau, an export merchant. He occupied the Chair as a part-timer from 1910 until his retirement in 1931. A graduate of Cambridge and a member of ICAEW,[3] Martineau was the most obscure of the chair holders in England prior to 1947. He is not credited with any publications in the *Accountants' Index*. Upon Martineau's retirement, the Birmingham Chair was converted to a full-time Readership in Accounting and Administration, to which Donald Cousins was appointed. Cousins continued in the readership until 1947, when it was reinstated as a chair. From 1906 onward, it had been expected that the Chair holder would emphasize the user's perspective, as it was not anticipated that Bachelor of Commerce students would, in the normal course, intend to become professional accountants. This expectation was extended to the readership as well. During his tenure, Cousins wrote introductory texts on bookkeeping, costing and general business finance, which apparently also found favour with a wider commercial audience (Craner & Jones, 1995; 1996).

In the University of London, Dicksee became Reader in Accountancy in 1913, and, somewhat more than a year later, was appointed to the personal chair of Professor of Accounting and Business Organisation, the first accounting chair in the university.[4] Both appointments were on a part-time basis. In 1920, he was appointed the inaugural Sir Ernest Cassel Professor of Accountancy and Business Methods, part-time, tenable at LSE.[5] He became *emeritus* in 1926, although he continued to lecture from time to time. Dicksee was immediately succeeded in the part-time chair by F. R. M. de Paula, a fellow of the ICAEW and a partner in a London practice. Prior to accepting the chair, de Paula had been a part-time lecturer for some years at LSE and then became Reader in Accounting and Business Organization, part-time, when the readership was instituted in 1924 (Kitchen & Parker, 1980, pp. 60–61, pp. 85–86).[6] De Paula resigned both the Chair and his partnership at the end of 1929 to become chief accountant, and later controller, of Dunlop Rubber Company. Following de Paula's departure, LSE went without a chair in accounting until after the war. As de Paula himself wrote in 1933, 'when I retired at the end of 1929 this chair was utilized for another purpose and therefore there is no such chair of accountancy'.[7]

In Scotland, part-time professors of accounting were first appointed in the University of Edinburgh in 1919, and in the University of Glasgow in 1926. The Council of The Society of Accountants in Edinburgh (Edinburgh Society), led by Richard Brown, the Society's secretary (who died in 1918), promoted the Edinburgh Chair and did much to secure its financing (Lee, 1996, pp. 192–194). T. P. Laird, an accountancy practitioner and a frequent contributor to *The Accountants' Magazine*, became the inaugural Professor of Accounting and Business Method in the University of Edinburgh. An acknowledged expert on trust accounting, he served until his death in 1927, at which time he was president-elect of the Edinburgh Society (Lee, 1983). Laird was succeeded in the same year by William Annan, who held the Chair until 1943, a year following normal retirement age. Annan, also a practitioner, often contributed to *The Accountants' Magazine* and was President of the Edinburgh Society from 1939 to 1942, thus becoming the first occupant of a university chair in Britain to serve as president of an accountancy body.[8] A. G. Murray filled the Edinburgh Chair from 1945 until his death in 1957. A practitioner, Murray is best known for being joint editor of *The Accountants' Magazine* from 1923 to 1930, and Editor from 1930 to 1952 (Lee, 1983; Walker, 1994, pp. 89–90).

In 1926, John Loudon, a partner in a Glasgow firm, became the first Johnstone Smith Professor of Accountancy in the University of Glasgow, the Chair having been endowed the previous year with a gift of £20,000 by David Johnstone Smith, the immediate past President of The Institute of Accountants and Actuaries in Glasgow (Flint, 1978).[9] Loudon served until 1938, when he was succeeded in the Chair by Ian W. Macdonald, a practitioner who became a leading banker following the war. Macdonald remained in the Chair until 1950 (*A History of The Chartered Accountants of Scotland*, 1954, p. 171). While both Loudon and Macdonald published several articles during their respective tenures, neither was an author of note.

At University College Galway, Bernard Francis Shields, M.A., who had previously been in business and engaged in commercial instruction, was appointed, at the age of 30, the first Professor of Commerce and Accountancy in October 1914.[10] This was the earliest full-time chair in a UK university with Accountancy or Accounting in its title. In 1916, the title of the Chair was broadened to Economics, Commerce and Accountancy, which continued in effect until 1969, when the Chair was abolished. In 1918, Shields resigned to become Professor of Commerce at University College Dublin, where he remained until his retirement in 1951. Francis McBryan, B.A., H.Dip. in Ed., who had been a commercial teacher in secondary schools, thereupon succeeded to the Galway Chair, and remained in post until his retirement in 1952. Neither Shields nor McBryan was a qualified accountant, and neither published any works on accountancy.[11]

In 1926, *The Financial Times* surveyed accountancy appointments in UK and overseas universities. After noting the existence of chairs or lectureships in Birmingham, London, Edinburgh, Glasgow, Liverpool, Manchester, Durham and Aberdeen Universities (and pointing out that accountancy was coupled with business methods in the chair appointments at London and Edinburgh), the newspaper raised a question about the other universities:

'This [enumeration] leaves a considerable proportion of our Universities— about ten—that make no special teaching provision in [accountancy]—so very important to modern commerce and industrialism. One is hardly surprised at Oxford and Cambridge, but that Bristol, Leeds, Sheffield, Nottingham and Reading should all be in the same boat is rather astonishing.'[12]

Reviewing the positions in Canada, Australia, New Zealand, South Africa and Hong Kong, *The Financial Times* concluded: 'In comparison with Great Britain, the Universities of the newer world of the Colonies exhibit a much keener appreciation of the value of accountancy in the educated business life of today.'[13]

Early Institutional Efforts to Foster Research

In 1935, The Society of Incorporated Accountants and Auditors established a research committee whose work 'should include, in the first instance, arrangement for the publication of monographs on professional subjects, for the formation of Research Groups, and special educational work as regards the technique of the profession'.[14] It was not one of the formal committees of the Society's Council, suggesting that its very creation was thought by some to be a radical step. A. A. Garrett, the Society's long-time secretary and its historian, claimed that 'in the United Kingdom and Ireland—and probably in the British dominions—it was the first Research Committee in the accountancy profession' (1961, p. 197). Although Garrett acknowledged that the American Institute of Accountants had previously undertaken research work, the Society may well have been the first professional accountancy body in the English-speaking world to include 'research' in a committee title. At the time, the ICAEW's Council, dominated by conservative practitioners, would not have countenanced a committee with such a title and charge. It was not until 1949 that the ICAEW finally allowed 'research' to appear in a committee title, and even then, not without some trepidation (Zeff, 1972, pp. 13–14).

The output of the Society's research committee was modest in the 1930s, but its pace accelerated in the 1940s and 1950s, consisting primarily of books written by F. Sewell Bray and the sponsorship of an academic journal, *Accounting Research*, which was jointly edited by Bray and Leo T. Little from 1948 to 1958 (see Solomons & Zeff, 1996).[15] In 1952, the Society created the Stamp–Martin Chair of Accounting, tenable, not in a university, but at Incorporated Accountants' Hall, the Society's head office.[16] Bray, a London practitioner who was a research fellow in the department of applied economics at Cambridge University, was the sole occupant of the Chair until its discontinuance in 1957, upon the integration of the Society into the three chartered institutes in the British Isles.

In 1936, the Accounting Research Association (ARA) was formed, mainly through the efforts of Ronald S. (later Sir Ronald) Edwards, a lecturer at LSE, and Cosmo Gordon, the librarian of the ICAEW.[17] Eric Hay Davison (an ICAEW member in industry), several practitioners, and the editor of *The Accountant* were also active in the ARA.[20] Davison did much to encourage accountants to join the group. Its objects were:

'(1) To promote research into the history and development of accounting.
(2) To discover, in particular, how economic, social and legal changes have affected the development of methods of accounting.
(3) To examine the present position of accounting theory and practice with the object of formulating basic principles' (Bircher, 1991, p. 158, p. 160).

The speaker at the ARA's inaugural meeting on 14 December 1936, at which over 100 people were present, was Sir Josiah (later Lord) Stamp, GCB, GBE, DSc(Econ.). In a celebrated speech in 1921 to the Society, Sir Josiah had challenged accountants to become researchers and thus join in 'the quest for truth and the advance of knowledge' (Stamp, 1921, p. 507; Garrett, 1961, pp. 125–128). In his talk to the ARA, he reiterated some of the arguments he had made 15 years before, and suggested some fruitful lines of research.[19]

The ARA was launched with optimism that a vehicle had finally been found for the encouragement and dissemination of scholarly research into the history, development and present state of accounting, unconstrained by the rigid boundaries of established practice. The ICAEW officially ignored the ARA, but the young organization succeeded in publishing a series of papers, reprints and book reviews, which were issued as supplements to

The Accountant or were put out separately by Gee and Co., then the leading UK publisher of books on accountancy and kindred subjects, as well as proprietor of *The Accountant*. Edwards recalled that 'Our reviews were critical and analytical and regarded, therefore, as rather shocking'.[20]

The ARA's membership reached a high of 239, yet the organization ceased functioning by 1941. The war took its toll. Once peace was restored, it was evident that most of the idealistic founders had either lost their ardour or had gone off into other pursuits. Ronald Edwards, the driving force during ARA's short life, had become interested in the interplay between engineering and economics (Zeff, 1972, pp. 2–3; Bircher, 1991, pp. 156–183).[21]

LSE from the 1930s to 1947

Harold Edey (1974, pp. 1–2) has remarked that the course syllabuses prior to the 1930s at LSE contained 'a greater dose of the "impedimenta of subordinate detail" than would now be thought desirable' and that the published work of Dicksee and de Paula 'leaned, as one would expect in a young subject, more towards clear exposition of practice than critical analysis'. (Dicksee and de Paula were, however, leading figures in the improvement of practice.) 'The period from the thirties to the present day', he added, 'saw the study of the subject in the School more firmly anchored to the bedrock of economic theory'.[22]

In the 1930s, Ronald Edwards, Ronald Coase and Ronald Fowler—the 'three Ronalds', as they have been called—had the good fortune to come under the spell of an inspiring teacher, Professor Arnold Plant. In turn, Plant was fortunate to have three such talented disciples. He recruited them to his staff at LSE, and the three assistant lecturers wrote a number of scholarly articles on accounting history, accounting theory and costing in the latter 1930s. Edwards and Coase published much of their work in *The Accountant*, not a learned journal, but a weekly practitioner magazine whose editor, Miss V. M. Snelling, was courageous not only in supporting the ARA but also in publishing lengthy, theoretical articles (Baxter, 1991, p. 139).

The most memorable of Edwards' papers on accounting was a 13-part article in 1938 on 'The Nature and Measurement of Income'. In the article, he drew extensively on the work of economists and accounting theorists, and seemed to be especially influenced by the major treatises of Professors John B. Canning (1929) and James C. Bonbright (1937). He propounded a future-oriented, increased-net-worth concept of income that provoked expressions of outrage from Stanley W. Rowland, a practitioner and a part-time lecturer in Edwards' own department (Bircher, 1991, pp.178–180; Parker & Zeff, 1996).[23] Edwards' 1938 article nonetheless had a large impact on W. T. Baxter, who was then a full-time Professor of Accounting in the University of Cape Town (Baxter, 1978, pp. 16–17 of Preface), and eventually also on David Solomons, who joined the department as a part-time lecturer in 1946 (converted to full-time in 1947), having been a student of Plant's during his undergraduate days at LSE (Solomons, 1984, vol. 1, p. xv). When Solomons joined the LSE faculty, he found a mentor in Edwards, and Solomons' writings on asset valuation in the 1960s may be traced directly to Edwards' influence (Zeff, 1995).

In several of their published papers during that period, Edwards and Coase applied economic reasoning to cost analysis, thus defining the LSE's approach to the subject and setting the stage for a series of later LSE contributions in the area (Gould, 1974; Arnold & Scapens, 1981; Coase, 1982; Coase 1990; Baxter, 1991).

On 1 May 1947, LSE appointed Baxter as its first full-time Professor of Accounting, which was also the first full-time accounting chair in Britain. Apparently by coincidence, on 1 October 1947, the University of Birmingham also instituted a full-time chair in Accounting and Administration, and elevated Donald Cousins, the University's full-time Reader in Accounting and Administration since 1931, to the post (Craner & Jones, 1995).[24]

In his inaugural lecture, Baxter surveyed the accounting scene in Britain:

'While accounting managed to win its way into some British universities several decades since, its place has so far been small and uncertain. Mine is, I think, the first full-time chair to be created in Britain; and many universities are only this year appointing their first full-time—or even part-time—instructors ...' (Baxter, 1948, p. 181).

'... the most remarkable thing about accounting as a field of study is that it is not so much a subject by itself as a synthesis of other subjects' (p. 181).

'The lack of any liaison between accounting and economic theory is so marked and so astonishing as to call for a whole lecture to itself. Each subject has grown up in serene indifference to the other, although both try to solve much the same problems, and in certain places the degrees of overlapping is remarkable.' (p. 182)

Baxter cited the works of two economists (Canning and Bonbright) and no accounting academics.

The Universities and the Accountancy Profession

In September 1944, the McNair Committee, known formally as the Joint Committee Representing the Universities and the Accountancy Profession, rendered a momentous report.[25] Composed of representatives of the Universities and University Colleges, the ICAEW, the Society and The Association of Certified and Corporate Accountants, the committee (which was chaired by Sir Arnold McNair, Vice-Chancellor of the University of Liverpool) recommended a 'Universities scheme', under which co-operating universities in England and Wales would introduce new options in accountancy, law, a modern foreign language and government in the curriculum for their degrees offered in economics and commerce. In return, the professional bodies would undertake to exempt 'scheme' graduates from their Intermediate examinations (see Solomons & Berridge, 1974, pp. 37–40). The committee continued in existence as the Joint Standing Committee of the Universities and the Accountancy Profession, and conferences to discuss the evolution of its work were held at Easter during odd-numbered years, beginning in April 1947.[26] In this setting, accounting academics were brought into closer contact with leading members of the accountancy bodies who were sympathetic with the role that universities might play in preparation for entry into the profession.[27]

One of the members of the Joint Committee, Sir Alexander Carr-Saunders, who was Director of LSE and co-author of an important book on the professions (1933), was invited by the Minister of Education in 1946 to chair a special committee 'To consider the provision which should be made for education for commerce and for the professions relating to it, and the respective contributions to be made thereto by universities and by colleges and departments of commerce in England and Wales'.[28] The committee's report, submitted in 1949, contained, *inter alia*, the suggestion that 'part-time day courses, possibly on the "sandwich" principle, giving preparation for the intermediate and final examinations of the three main bodies of accountants, should be organised by the colleges of commerce and the major technical colleges on a regional basis and in conjunction with the accountancy bodies'.[29] *The Accountant* greeted the report with 'astonishment',[30] and the Council of the ICAEW, in a 50-page rejoinder, declared that 'the recommendations of the Carr-Saunders Committee are wholly inappropriate for persons wishing to become members of the Institute ... [and] would undermine the Institute's whole system of training under articles' (Solomons & Berridge, 1974, p. 24).[31]

The situation in Scotland was much different than in England and Wales. A 'distinctive feature of the Scottish profession from the outset was its close links with the universities. Part-time attendance at university classes in law was compulsory from the outset for non-graduate apprentices, and attendance at classes in economics and accountancy on a part-time basis was required for many years ...' (Solomons & Berridge, 1974, p. 17).[32] Moreover, the accountancy bodies in Edinburgh and Glasgow evinced an almost paternal interest in the accounting chairs founded in 1919 and 1926 in the two universities, and they played a role in identifying candidates when vacancies arose. The chairs in the two Scottish universities were not allowed to lapse. In England and Wales, by contrast, there was no protest from the accountancy bodies when, during the period from 1931 to 1947, there were no professors of accounting in Birmingham and London.[33]

ACADEMIC ACCOUNTING BODIES IN OTHER COUNTRIES

Formation of the Association of University Teachers of Accounting was preceded by associations of accounting academics in two other countries: the United States and Japan. The oldest organization of accounting academics is the American Accounting Association (AAA), which was founded in 1916 as the American Association of University Instructors in Accounting. The AAA adopted its present name in 1935, its intention being to broaden the scope of the Association to include the encouragement and sponsorship of research and the development of accounting principles and standards.[34]

The growth of business schools in US universities during the first three decades of the century created a demand for accounting educators, and the number of accounting academics burgeoned. Accounting textbooks proliferated, and articles written by academics filled the practitioner journals and *The Accounting Review*, the AAA's quarterly journal launched in 1926. In 1936, the AAA's executive committee published its views on the accounting principles underlying corporate financial reports, in order to provide the recently established Securities and Exchange Commission (SEC) with guidance on proper practice, an initiative not altogether welcomed by the practitioner community (see Zeff, 1966, pp. 45–49). In 1940, the AAA collaborated with the American Institute of Accountants, the practitioners' organization, in the distribution to members of the influential monograph, *An Introduction to Corporate Accounting Standards*, by W. A. Paton and A. C. Littleton. In the monograph, the authors presented an elegant defence of historical cost accounting, which, with the SEC's strong support for historical cost accounting, effectively precluded any serious consideration of other valuation bases in corporate financial reporting until the inflationary decade of the 1970s. The AAA has also been active on a wide range of matters relating to accounting education.

In 1937, the Japan Accounting Association (JAA) was founded 'as a purely academic association' along lines similar to the AAA ('The Japan Accounting Association', 1993). British accounting academics were, however, unlikely to have known of the JAA.

Hence, there were two precedents when, in 1947, British accounting academics undertook to form an organization.

INAUGURAL MEETING OF THE ASSOCIATION

The Association of University Teachers of Accounting held its inaugural meeting at the London School of Economics on 22/23 December 1947.[35] In attendance were 13 teachers representing the following universities:

Birmingham: Prof. Donald Cousins, BCom, ACA
                Mr E. J. Newman, BA, ACA

Bristol:	Mr Brian Magee, BCom, ACA
Cardiff:	Mr Charles Magee, BCom, ACA
Durham:	Mr Albert Bell, FCA
Hull:	Dr L. M. Lachmann, Dr rer. pol., MSc(Econ.)
Leeds:	Mr A. McCarmick, ACA
Liverpool:	Mrs Bramwell McCombe, MA, BCom
London:	Prof. W. T. Baxter, BCom, CA
	Mr D. Solomons, BCom, ACA
Manchester:	Mr G. W. Murphy, BA(Com.), FCA
Sheffield:	Mr Frank Downing, FCA
	Mr C. A. Smith, LLM, FCA

Cousins proposed, and it was unanimously accepted, that Baxter occupy the chair during the meeting.

It was reported in the Minutes that Cousins and Baxter

'had decided to convene the conference as a result of discussions which they had had following on the conference, which was held at Oxford in April 1947, between representatives of the universities and the accountancy profession. They had in mind the formation of an association which would act as a link between the teachers of accounting within the universities and the professional accountancy bodies. The Association should have a simple constitution and could perform a number of very useful functions, including the holding of an annual conference, the circulation of a periodical bulletin for the exchange of information between members, promotion of research work in accounting, and possibly cooperation in the work of the professional journals.'[36]

It was resolved to adopt the name of The Association of University Teachers of Accounting (patterned after the Association of University Teachers of Economics, AUTE) and that the officers shall consist of a president, a chairman and a secretary, and 'that there shall in addition be a committee of three members'.[37] The object of the Association, it was agreed, 'shall be the promotion of the study and teaching of accounting, especially within the universities'. The membership was to be restricted to 'teachers of accounting and allied subjects in universities or university colleges in the British Isles, and to such other persons as may be elected by the Association to be honorary members thereof'. The annual subscription was set at 10s 6d, and the following executive officers were chosen:

Chairman:	Prof. Donald Cousins
Secretary:	Mr David Solomons
Committee:	Prof. W. T. Baxter
	Mrs Bramwell McCombe
	Mr Brian Magee

It was resolved that Lord Eustace Percy, Vice-chancellor of the University of Durham and Chairman of the Joint Standing Committee of the Universities and the Accountancy Profession, should be invited to become President of the Association, and he subsequently accepted (although he never attended an Association conference).

Baxter agreed to serve as Editor of a periodic newsletter.

In order to avoid a 'clash' with the annual conferences of the AUTE, which were held during January, it was decided to hold the next conference during the Easter vacation in 1949, and Cousins' invitation that the conference be held in Birmingham was accepted.

It was mentioned in the minutes that invitations to the inaugural meeting 'had been sent only to those universities and university colleges in England and Wales which were at present participating in the joint scheme with the professional accountancy bodies'. The Committee:

> 'was instructed to investigate the position of the teaching of accounting in the universities of Scotland, Northern Ireland and Eire, with a view to inviting the university teachers of accounting in those countries to join the Association, if it should be found that there was sufficient similarity between the work done in the universities of England and Wales and in those of the other parts of the British Isles to make such a step desirable.'[38]

A table was presented which gave the number of students receiving tuition in accounting at the 10 universities represented in the meeting. There were 203 specialist students (i.e. 'those students taking special courses in accounting designed to give exemption from the intermediate examinations of the professional bodies') and 502 non-specialist students, the largest number of the latter being at London and Manchester. In a report of the meeting in *The Accountant*, Solomons wrote, 'Compared with similar figures for the United States, these numbers are minute. But they represent a solid achievement of the last 3 years, and real progress is now being made'.[39] Some regret was expressed at the meeting that 'the absence of honours degrees in accounting (which apparently extends to all universities except London and Birmingham)—sometimes tended to discourage outstanding students from taking up the subject'.

The tension between the universities and conservative members of the profession led to a comment that some of the latter 'had shown some reluctance to accept articled clerks who intended to spend the first 3 years of their articles at the university'.

On the subject of teaching materials, it was noted that:

> 'A great deal of dissatisfaction was expressed with the text books at present available. Most of the English standard works were regarded as too "tabloid" to be suitable for university students, that they were unduly dogmatic, and did not encourage independent thought. They also tended to divorce study of accounting from the student's other studies, especially by ignoring the work of economists.'[40]

Discussion was also devoted to the content of examinations and to contacts between the universities and industry, commerce and the professions.

On the subject of research and book reviews, it was observed that the Accounting Research Association, 'which had done valuable work before the war', was 'in a state of suspended animation' and there was 'no prospect of the former officers of the ARA taking the initiative in reviving its work, and such initiative might therefore well come from the new Association'. Solomons reported that Sewell Bray 'had informed him of the steps already taken to produce a new journal to be known as "Accounting Research". This was being financed by the Society of Incorporated Accountants and Auditors, but would not otherwise be a specifically Society publication'. It was decided that 'the officers of the Association should get in contact with Mr. Bray, and with the [former] officers of the A.R.A. with a view to exploring the possibilities of co-operation between the three bodies'.[41]

Following the meeting, an inaugural dinner was given by LSE for the university representatives, at which the following were also in attendance: Sir Harold Barton, Governor of LSE; Donald V. House, of the ICAEW; Sewell Bray, representing the Society of Incorporated Accountants and Auditors; F. G. Wiseman, of the Association of Certified and Corporate Accountants (ACCA); Derek du Pré, Editor of *The Accountant*; and Ronald S. Edwards, of LSE.[42]

COUSINS AND SOLOMONS COMMENT ON THE IMPORTANCE OF RESEARCH

At the meeting of the Committee on 14 July 1948, the question of teaching *vs* research arose. Mrs. McCombe had submitted an agenda paper on 'the possibilities of co-operation in accounting research between the Association and the professional accounting bodies'. Cousins, who was not himself a researcher, interposed that:

> 'the time was not ripe for this work as university departments of accounting had not yet developed any settled policy in connection with the content of undergraduate courses and examinations and that the pressure of work on teachers left little time for outside activity of the kind proposed. There was no magic in the word "research" and co-operation between the universities and the accounting bodies might be allowed to grow naturally out of the published research work done as part of the universities' [normal activities]'.

Solomons, however, 'drew attention to the fact that virtually no accounting research of any kind had yet been done by the universities and that the first duty of members of the Association was to produce results themselves rather than to discuss the organisation of research work by other people'.[43] Baxter was reported in the Minutes as concurring in this view.

To what degree did the members of university accounting departments actually publish research from 1948 to the end of the 1950s? In the nine volumes of *Accounting Research* between 1948 and 1958, only 10 of the approximately 180 articles were authored or co-authored by accounting academics in UK universities, all but one of whom were at LSE: Baxter, Harold Edey, Solomons and Jack Kitchen. No article by an accounting academic at a UK university appeared in *The Accounting Review* from 1948 to 1959.[44] To the degree that such research was published, it most likely appeared in the professional accountancy journals or in journals in neighbouring fields.

THE NEWSLETTER APPEARS

The first number of the Association's Newsletter, edited by Baxter, was issued in July 1948. It ran seven single-spaced, typescript pages, of which two pages consisted of news from university departments of accounting and a further two pages were given over to a list of suggested works for inclusion in a university library of accounting. The Secretary reported that membership invitations had been sent to the three Scottish universities, and that 'Edinburgh, led by Professor Murray, is joining in strength . . .'. Owing to expressions of interest in the Association received from Canada, South Africa, New Zealand, India and Israel, the Committee decided to set up a special class of membership, whose holders would be known as corresponding members. Solomons also reported that honorary membership had been conferred on F. R. M. de Paula, OBE, FCA, 'in recognition of his past and present services to the teaching of accounting', and on F. Sewell Bray, FCA, FSAA, 'by virtue of his position as Nuffield Research Fellow in the Department of Applied Economics at Cambridge'.

At the conclusion of his Secretary's report, Solomons wrote, 'At this early stage in the Association's history, it is relatively easy to expand membership—we are ploughing virgin soil. The next twelve months will provide the answer to a more important question—is the Association well adapted to do a really important job of work?' At the first annual conference, by then scheduled for Birmingham during the weekend of 23–25 September 1949 (instead of at Easter, evidently to avoid a conflict with the second conference of the Joint Standing Committee of the Universities and the Accountancy Profession), he said, 'members will have an opportunity to pronounce their own verdict on this question . . .'

BAXTER PROPOSES PUBLICATION OF TEACHING MATERIALS

At the meeting of the Committee on 9 December 1948, Baxter:

'put forward a proposal that the Association should make itself responsible
for two or three volumes which would bring together, for the benefit of
students, material of a high quality already published in periodicals and
in other forms which prevented them from being readily available to
students. He envisaged that the first volume might cover general accounting, and the second volume cost accounting. The National Joint
Committee had considered the proposal earlier that day but had decided
that it was not itself the appropriate body to handle this matter. After
discussion it was agreed that the Association should sponsor these publications and that consideration should be given to the addition of a third
volume on trust accounting. Professor Baxter and the Secretary undertook
to circularise members asking for suggestions as to the contents of the
volumes.'[45]

This action led to the publication in 1950 of Baxter's pioneering reader,
Studies in Accounting, which was 'Edited on behalf of the Association of
University Teachers of Accounting'. The publisher, Sweet & Maxwell,
presented a copy to each member of the Association. Two years later, Sweet
& Maxwell published Solomons' equally celebrated reader, *Studies in Costing*,
which was likewise edited on behalf of the Association. In view of the higher
price of this second volume (35s for Solomons vs 23s 6d for Baxter), as
well as the increase in the number of members, the publisher was prepared
to offer each member a concessional price of 22s. The Committee, however,
decided that the funds of the Association made it possible to cover the cost
of providing a copy of Solomons' book to 'all members who pay their 1953
subscription (10s. 6d)',[46] which had been unchanged since the founding of
the Association.

THE SECOND NEWSLETTER

Issue No. 2 of the Association's Newsletter was distributed in July 1949,
and ran to 10 pages. It began with the Chairman's Foreword, by Donald
Cousins, and the Secretary's report, in which Solomons disclosed that the
Association's membership had risen over the year from 17 to 26 full
members, including six in Scotland.

A report published in June gave testimony to the small number of
accountancy teachers in England and Wales who might be tapped for
membership: 29 (apart from special lecturers), of whom only seven were
full-time.[47] The distribution by university was as follows:

	Full-time	Part-time
Birmingham	1	1
Bristol	0	2
Durham (Newcastle)	1	0
Hull	0	1
Leeds	0	3
Liverpool	1	0
London	2	8
Manchester	1	2
Nottingham	0	1
Sheffield	1	1
Southampton	0	2
Wales	0	1

The dominance of the University of London is evident, representing more than one-third of the total.

In the Newsletter, three signed book reviews were followed by reports from Australia and New Zealand, submitted by Louis Goldberg and W. G. (later Sir William) Rodger, respectively.

The Newsletter closed with a belated note on the death in December 1945 of Henry Rand Hatfield. The Editor wrote that 'Professor Hatfield is probably better known in this country than any other American writer on accounting. His works are characterised not only by a rare simplicity and penetration, but also by frequent glimpses of humour', and then proceeded to give an example of the latter. It was a footnote in Hatfield's *Accounting—Its Principles and Problems* (1927, p. 460) in the section on the Statement of Sources and Disposition of Funds, in which he commented on the clumsiness of this title:

> 'Professor [William Morse] Cole in the first edition of his *Accounts* uses the title "Where–Got–Gone" Statement, but this has apparently been abandoned even by its author. It is a source of regret that a colorful term introduced into the drab literature of accounting should have fallen into disuse. But it hardly seems the function of this treatise to serve as an asylum for a foundling abandoned by its progenitor.'

THE 1949 CONFERENCE

On the weekend of 23–26 September 1949, 21 months after the founding of the Association, its second conference was held at University House, Edgbaston, Birmingham. Members attended from nine English universities. The proceedings began on Friday evening with the Chairman's address, followed by an informal discussion on teaching methods, curricula and textbooks. On Saturday, the morning was given over to a symposium on 'The Content and Aims of a University Course in Accounting', with four short papers by a professional accountant (W. H. Newton, senior partner in the firm of Newton & Co., Chartered Accountants, as well as Treasurer of Birmingham University), an industrial accountant (W. W. Fea, Chief Accountant of Guest, Keen & Nettlefolds Ltd), a business man (Eric W. Vincent, Director of Harry Vincent Ltd) and an academic economist (J. Glyn Picton, Lecturer in industrial economics at Birmingham University). In the report of the conference published in *The Accountant*, which was almost certainly written by David Solomons, the Association's Secretary, the following observation in support of university study in accounting was noted:

> 'Perhaps the most important point which emerged from the ensuing discussion was the unanimity among university teachers of accounting that professional firms who took newly-articled clerks immediately on the completion of their university studies in accounting might be disappointed if they expected these clerks to compete at once on level terms with clerks who had completed two years of the normal five-year period of articles. The graduate articled clerk would, of course, lack the practical experience that the five-year man would have begun to gain, and it was only at the end of their respective articles that a comparison of the two types of articled clerk ought to be made. In such a comparison, the graduate articled clerk would have nothing to fear.'[48]

The afternoon was free, and the evening session on the theme of 'Weaknesses in Orthodox Accounting Theory' began with a short paper by Harry Norris, an industrial accountant who was the author of *Accounting Theory: An Outline of Its Structure* (1946). On Sunday morning, Solomons opened the discussion of 'Accounting Research—Illusion or Reality?' Following a free afternoon, an informal dinner was held, following which the Association's members entertained the Vice-chancellor of Birmingham University, a Member of the Council of the ICAEW (W. L. Barrows, a Birmingham practitioner), and the Presidents of the Birmingham and District Society of Chartered Accountants, and of the Birmingham District Society of Incorporated Accountants and Auditors. On Monday morning, members visited the Shaftmoor Lane works of Joseph Lucas Ltd, 'which included not only a brief inspection of the factory, but also an extremely instructive review of the company's costing methods'.[49]

At the general meeting of the Association held on Sunday morning, it was announced that G. W. Murphy, of the University of Manchester, would succeed to the Editorship of the Newsletter, as Baxter had asked to be relieved of his post. Cousins and Solomons were to continue in their respective capacities as Chairman and Secretary. The frequency of the Association's conferences was discussed. Since the joint meeting, held in

Oxford, between representatives of the Universities and the Accountancy Profession was held biennially (in odd-numbered years), it was thought by some that the Association's conferences might also be held biennially in the years between the Oxford meetings. Reactions to this suggestion must have varied, since it was decided to hold the next conference in September 1950 and to defer until then a discussion of the timing of future conferences.

THE 1950 CONFERENCE

Another weekend conference, this time labelled 'Annual' and a day shorter than its predecessor, was held from Friday evening to Sunday afternoon, 22–24 September 1950 at St. Anselm Hall, Victoria Park, Manchester. Friday evening was organized along the same lines as at the 1949 conference. G. W. Murphy, of the University of Manchester, was in charge of the arrangements. On Saturday morning, according to the conference announcement (no report of the conference appeared in *The Accountant*), W. Arthur Lewis, Stanley Jevons Professor of Political Economy in the University of Manchester, was to open a discussion on 'Accounting for Monopoly Control'. In the afternoon, members were to have a tour of the offices of Messrs Hartley Turner & Son, Chartered Accountants, 'where the partners will present and explain a system of control of professional work and charges'. In the evening there was to be a dinner at which 'a number of distinguished local accountants and university representatives' were to be guests. On Sunday morning, Ely Devons, Robert Ottley Professor of Applied Economics in the University of Manchester, was to open a discussion on 'Some Problems Arising from an Analysis of Costs and Prices in the Cotton Industry'. A short business session was to close the conference.

W. T. Baxter was elected as Chairman to succeed Cousins, and David Solomons, who was prevented from attending the conference owing to an attack of the flu, submitted his resignation as Secretary 'owing to other claims on my time' (Newsletter No. 3, p. 3).[50] C. A. Smith, of the University of Sheffield, was elected to succeed him. H. C. Edey, of LSE, and S. V. P. Cornwell, a practitioner in Bristol and part-time lecturer at the University, were elected to the Committee.

The members of the Association may have been hopeful that the ICAEW might become interested in supporting accounting research when the Institute announced in early 1950 that a London practitioner and well-known author, the late P. D. Leake, had bequeathed the residue of his estate, estimated to be £80,000, to the Institute. The bequest was to be held as the 'P. D. Leake Trust Fund' 'for such purposes falling within the legal definition of charity as are likely to benefit and advance the science of accounting and political economy including the subject of public finance and taxation'.[51] The Institute's Council must have been in a quandary over how to use the fund, since the conduct and support of studies in 'the science of accounting and political economy' had never been one of the Councillors' interests. Finally, in 1954, the Council decided to establish the P. D. Leake Professorship of Finance and Accounting in the University of Cambridge, to be financed by an annual grant of £3,000. The professorship was awarded the following year to Richard N. (later Sir Richard) Stone, an economic statistician who was developing a system of national accounts (for which he received the Nobel Prize in economic sciences in 1984).[52] Howitt (1966, p. 113) has written that 'Grants have since been made for the establishment of a P. D. Leake Research Fellowship at Balliol College, Oxford, and for other Fellowships tenable at Oxford, London and Birmingham Universities'.

THE THIRD NEWSLETTER—17 MONTHS AFTER NO. 2

G. W. Murphy, the new Editor, apologised profusely in Issue No. 3 of the Newsletter, dated December 1950, for the long delay in its publication. In his final Chairman's Foreword, Cousins wrote,

> 'The name and purpose of the Association have been most felicitously put on the map by the recent appearance of the volume "Studies in Accounting", edited by our new Chairman, William Baxter. He deserves a whole bunch of good marks for bringing together the twenty-six contributions which fill its pages, and I think the best tribute we can pay him in the first place to the very considerable amount of work that has gone into its compilation is to do our utmost to make its existence widely known.'

In the Secretary's report that had been submitted to the conference, Solomons wrote that, in somewhat less than 3 years since the Association's founding, its membership had increased from 13 persons representing 10 English and Welsh universities who attended the inaugural meeting, to 48 members from 23 universities, including six from Scotland and 11 from overseas, representing, Australia (A. A. Fitzgerald and Louis Goldberg, both of the University of Melbourne), Canada (Professor Kenneth F. Byrd, McGill University), Israel (David Rosolio, a practitioner in Tel Aviv and part-time lecturer at Hebrew University of Jerusalem), India (G. Basu, a practitioner in Calcutta), New Zealand (W. G. Rodger, of Victoria University College, and T. R. Johnston and Professor L. W. Holt, both of Auckland University College), South Africa (Thomas Cairns and Professor B. J. S. Wimble, both of the University of the Witwatersrand) and Thailand (Phya Jaiyos Sompati, University of Chulalongkorn, Bangkok). B. S. Yamey, by then at the London School of Economics, had joined whilst he was at the University of Cape Town. Of the 48, 16 were full-time teachers, 25 were part-time teachers, five were former teachers (a new category authorized at the 1949 conference), and two (Bray and de Paula) were honorary members.

The Newsletter again contained reports from the antipodes, written, as before, by Goldberg and Rodger.[53] There were three signed book reviews, two by Baxter, and a long list of 'books on accounting or relevant to accounting', evidently compiled by Baxter. The Newsletter concluded with the first published list of members.

NEWSLETTER NO. 4—THE LAST TO APPEAR

After a year's lapse, Issue No. 4, the last in the series of Newsletters, came out in December 1951. In his Chairman's Foreword, Baxter reflected on a recent book published by an economic historian who had made heavy use of old accounts and business documents, and he challenged his colleagues in the Association either to rise to new heights in their research or to accept a supporting role in the research conducted in established disciplines. Baxter's message caught the attention of the Editor of *The Accountant*, who reproduced the following extract:

> 'From every point of view, it is extremely desirable that the discussion of accounting theory should flourish. Ultimately, such speculations will be useful to professional life, besides enriching our academic studies. But somehow our work is not yet very impressive. Indeed, much of it seems hardly to merit the name "research". That word suggests—to my mind at least—something of rare quality and originality . . .

> 'The fundamental issues of accounting (e.g. theories of capital and revenue) have still to be explored, but only the most brilliant and ambitious student has any chance of doing useful work here.

> 'Does this mean that we should discourage the would-be researcher? To some extent, yes; a continuation of the present flow of third-rate output can lead only to the discredit of accounting research. Where an inquiring mind refuses to be discouraged, perhaps the best route for it to follow is one in which accounting knowledge can throw light on another subject. There is much to be said for winning one's spurs in a field whose standards have long been regarded as rigorous . . .

> 'Research in economic history offers great scope for accounting methods. Some aspects of national statistics may well do likewise. Detailed studies of the law's inter-relations with accounting should also be fruitful. In short, our best plan may for the nonce be to treat accounting as a tool rather than an end.'[54]

It was reported in the Newsletter that an Association sub-committee was preparing a memorandum to be submitted on behalf of the Association to the Royal Commission on Taxation of Profits and Income. The sub-committee was composed of Baxter, Solomons and H. C. Edey (Association members at LSE) and two economists, R. C. Tress and A. T. (now Sir Alan) Peacock.

The Newsletter contained some correspondence from Australia and South Africa, a report from New Zealand, three signed book reviews (including one each by Solomons and Baxter), a list of members, and the memorandum shortly to be submitted to the Royal Commission.

THE 1952 CONFERENCE

The Association's fourth conference was held on the weekend of 28–30 March 1952 at Burwalls, a hall of residence in the University of Bristol.[55] A meeting in the spring was believed to be more convenient for members than in September. S. V. P. Cornwell was primarily responsible for the administrative arrangements. On Saturday morning, papers were read by two visitors, R. C. Tress, Professor of Political Economy in the University of Bristol, on 'The Use of Accounting Terms and Concepts by Economists',[56] and I. F. Pearce, Lecturer in industrial administration in the University of Nottingham, on 'Cost Accounting and Economic Theory'. On Saturday afternoon, a discussion was held between those members interested in teaching in taxation.

A business meeting was held on Sunday morning, following which F. J. Weeks, who was a member of the management accounting team of the Anglo–American Council on Productivity, spoke on 'Some Impressions of American Industrial Accountancy'.

At the business meeting, Brian Magee, of the University of Bristol,[57] was elected to succeed Baxter as Chairman on 1 August 1952. C. C. Magee (Brian Magee's brother), of the University of Wales, was elected Secretary and Treasurer, and H. C. Edey and J. Kitchen, both of LSE, were elected as Joint Editors of the Newsletter. The Committee was to be composed of Donald Cousins, C. A. Smith, and, upon his retirement as Chairman, Baxter.[58]

During the week following the Sixth International Congress on Ac-' counting, held in June 1952 in London, the Association scheduled a meeting at LSE 'at which members of similar bodies from oversea will have a chance to meet one another and discuss matters of common interest'.[59]

THE 1955 CONFERENCE

No further activity was reported until 1955, when the Association held its fifth conference on the weekend of 25–27 March at Hugh Stewart Hall, University of Nottingham.[60] Following tea and dinner on Friday, David Solomons gave an address entitled 'The Teaching of Accounting in American Universities'. Solomons had spent a term in 1954 as a visiting professor at the University of California. On Saturday morning, Donal O'Donovan, of the Organisation and Methods Division of HM Treasury, spoke on the work of his department. Three films were shown in the afternoon: 'Accounting—the Language of Business', borrowed from *The Accountant*, and 'Enterprise' and 'Balance 1950', obtained from the Imperial Chemical Industries Film Library. A dinner was held in the evening. A short business meeting took place on Sunday morning, following which Brian Tew, Professor of Economics at Nottingham, addressed the conference on 'Company Accounts as a Source of Economic Statistics'.

At the business meeting, Solomons was elected Chairman, and S. V. P. Cornwell was elected Secretary. Members attended from Birmingham, Bristol, Cardiff, London, Manchester, Nottingham, Sheffield and Southampton, as well as from Melbourne.[61]

ACTIVITIES DURING 1957

A meeting of the Committee was held on 30 March 1957 in conjunction with the fifth conference of the Joint Standing Committee of the Universities and the Accountancy Profession, which took place at the University of Liverpool on the weekend of 29–31 March.[62] Solomons, who was in the chair, proposed that:

'the Association should undertake a specific piece of work partly because the work was necessary and partly to enliven the Association's activities. His proposal was that the Association should sponsor a study group on accounting education'.[63]

The other members of the Committee—Edey, Baxter (who had just been co-opted), Brian Magee, C. A. Whittington-Smith (formerly C. A. Smith) and Cornwell—agreed the proposal and authorized the Chairman to 'put out feelers' to the individuals tentatively suggested for membership on the study group. The Committee decided, however, 'To do nothing overt until the dust of the integration arrangements [between the Society of Incorporated Accountants and the three chartered institutes in the British Isles] had settled, except to get the group organised'.[64]

Among the individuals suggested for the education study group were Solomons and Baxter; Sir Harold Barton, a past President and long-time member of the Council (1928–1957) of the ICAEW; Eric Hay Davison, an industrial accountant who was known for his reformist views; Leo T. Little, an economist who was the Editor of *Accountancy* and Joint Editor of *Accounting Research*; and W. E. Parker, a senior partner in Price Waterhouse & Co. and a member of the Council of the ICAEW.

Solomons' views on accounting education were diametrically opposed to those held by most leaders of the ICAEW. On 10 November 1955, Solomons (and Whittington-Smith) had attended the annual dinner of the Bristol and West of England Society of Chartered Accountants, at which W. S. (later Sir William) Carrington, the President of the ICAEW and a senior partner in one of the oldest English accountancy firms, set out his views on accounting education with pungent directnesss:

'Whilst I think that the special degree courses now being provided at certain of the universities have a place in our system of professional education, I can foresee grave dangers unless university lecturers and professors are careful to avoid feeding their students with arguments and propositions which they are not mature enough fully to appreciate or even digest properly ... In saying this, I am not seeking to detract at all from the value of university chairs of accounting, but I do think that their main value will be in the field of research and post-graduate study and I don't want them to feed the young on champagne and caviare before they are properly weaned.'[65]

Four weeks later, Solomons delivered his inaugural lecture as Professor of Accounting at Bristol under the title, 'Accounting Education for New Responsibilities', in which he derided the Institute's total reliance on articles of apprenticeship and correspondence tuition in the preparation of future chartered accountants. He said, 'much of the educational value of practical experience will be lost if the ground has not adequately been prepared in advance' and 'I find it utterly incomprehensible that any profession should think [correspondence tuition is] other than a third-rate substitute for real education' (Solomons, 1956, p. 117). He proposed instead that candidates for membership in the Institute be required to complete 3 years of university study in economics, accounting and law, to be followed by 3 years of office work, interspersed with periods of full-time practical training. At the conclusion of his address, Solomons quoted from Carrington's speech and asked why the Institute should fear that students be exposed to 'the critical discussion of accepted ideas' (Solomons, 1956, p. 120). Solomons was vexed by views such as Carrington's, and he was looking for ways to engage the Institute leadership in a dialogue. Also, as noted above, Solomons was keen to 'enliven' the Association's activities. On 6 November 1957, Solomons wrote to Sidebotham that the Association:

'has shown only the barest signs of life since it held its last conference in Nottingham at Easter 1955. There would have been a conference last Easter but for the fact that many members attended the conference on the "Universities and the Accountancy Profession" at Liverpool ... I do not think we can go much longer without calling the members together and my idea is that we should organize a conference for Easter 1958.'

At the meeting of 30 March, it became known that Cornwell wished to be relieved of his duties as Secretary and Treasurer, owing to the pressure of professional and other commitments. (Sometime between 1955 and 1957 the title of the position was altered to include 'and Treasurer'.) It was unanimously agreed that Solomons should approach Roy Sidebotham, of the University of Manchester, about taking on the job. In April, Sidebotham, who had never attended an Association conference, accepted the position 'for a while, anyway', since, as he wrote to Solomons on 25 October 1957, 'As you will appreciate, I feel my position in AUTA to be rather curious. I am, in effect, the executive officer of an organisation only two of whose members (Mr. Murphy and Professor Baxter) have I ever met'.

Also at the meeting there was concern expressed over the future of *Accounting Research* in the light of the proposed integration of the Society of Incorporated Accountants into the three chartered institutes in the British Isles, which had been announced the previous December.[66] Edey was asked 'to make an entirely informal approach, in a guarded manner, to Mr. Leo T. Little, one of the joint editors'.[67] The Committee also resolved to ask Sweet & Maxwell, Ltd, the UK publishers of *Studies in the History of Accounting*, edited by A. C. Littleton and B. S. Yamey, if copies could be made available to Association members on trade terms comparable to what had been done for the first two collections in the series, edited by Baxter and Solomons. (In the event, Sweet & Maxwell granted Association members a discount of 25%, at a price of £1 17s 6d. Fifteen members ordered the book.) The Littleton and Yamey collection had been 'Edited on behalf of The Association of the University Teachers of Accounting and the American Accounting Association', and was published in 1956 simultaneously by Richard D. Irwin, Inc. in the United States and Sweet & Maxwell in the UK. It was Baxter's suggestion that Yamey do a book on history for the series, and he also proposed that it be done in concert with the AAA.[68] Baxter exchanged correspondence with Professor Frank P. Smith, the AAA President in 1954, on the publication arrangements.[69] Unlike the Baxter and Solomons volumes, which were collections of previously published writings, almost every article was commissioned specifically for the volume by Littleton and Yamey.

The Association continued to be small. In September 1957, its list of members showed 66 individuals, of whom 23 were resident outside the British Isles. As no subscription reminders had been sent out since 1953, much of the list might have been out of date. At the bottom of a copy of the list seen by the author, the following note was written by hand: 'Some of these members we have not heard of or from for a long time'.

At a meeting of the Committee on 17 December 1957, held at LSE, with Solomons in the chair, and Edey, Magee and Sidebotham in attendance, it was decided that the 1958 conference should be on accounting education, and that the proposal for a study group on education be deferred for further consideration after the conference. Sidebotham reported that the Association had a balance of cash on hand of £89 5s 8d.[70]

THE EDUCATION CONFERENCE IN 1958

It was announced in *The Accountant* of 8 March 1958 that the Association would be holding a conference on accounting education on 28/29 March at LSE.[71] Solomons, who was principal organizer of the conference and the editor of its proceedings, believed that 'there had never been an opportunity in this country for members of all the principal bodies in the accountancy profession to meet together and discuss the problems of professional education and training which are of concern to them all' (*Accounting Education*, 1958, p. i).[72] Thus, Solomons set the stage for the dialogue between academics and practitioners that he had envisaged in his inaugural lecture given in December 1955.

The conference consisted of three panel sessions: The Professional Bodies and Accounting Education, chaired by Solomons; Educational Arrangements of Solicitors, Architects and Scottish Chartered Accountants, chaired by Baxter; and General Discussion, chaired by Brian Magee. There were 21 principal participants, of whom four were panellists in the first session and another four were panellists in the second session. The longest presentation was made by Edey, who opened the final session. In advance of the conference, Solomons had sent each of the panel members a list of possible questions, and solicited their comments. During each of the first two sessions, the chairman addressed questions to the panellists, and an active discussion ensued.

A General Meeting of the Association was held immediately following the third session. Edey was elected Chairman,[73] and Sidebotham was re-elected as Secretary and Treasurer. The following were elected to the Committee: Cousins, Baxter, Solomons, Brian Magee and C. A. Whittington-Smith. In discussion, it was suggested that future conferences might be held in 2 out of every 3 years.[74] Concern was expressed about the future of *Accounting Research*, and it was resolved unanimously:

'That in the opinion of this Association, the discontinuance of the publication of "Accounting Research" would be regrettable. In the event of this becoming reality, the committee are empowered to take such action as they deem desirable.'

Accounting Research ceased publication following its issue for October 1958, a year following the transfer of the journal from the Society of Incorporated Accountants to the ICAEW.[75]

The education conference was supported with some funds from the Society of Incorporated Accountants. Leo T. Little, the Editor of *Accountancy* (the Society's journal until November 1957, when it was transferred to the ICAEW), provided recording facilities for the conference, and Solomons undertook to edit a volume of proceedings. Since an approach for funds to the P. D. Leake Committee of the ICAEW had been unavailing, and in view of the fact that the transcript consisted of dialogue involving as many as 21 participants, Solomons had concluded that it would be infeasible, if only on grounds of cost, to verify the text with each speaker. However, in November, after 500 copies of the proceedings volume had been printed and copies were distributed to participants, one of the panellists, H. O. H.

Coulson, a partner in the London firm of Barton, Mayhew & Co. and a fellow of the ICAEW, complained of several misquotations and that an important part of his remarks had been omitted from the proceedings.[76] In fact, part of Coulson's remarks, as well as some of Solomons' own remarks, had been lost, owing to the fact that a reel of recording tape had been burnt in *Accountancy*'s office. Solomons offered 'to insert an erratum slip correcting any instances of material misreporting before distribution is resumed',[77] but Coulson contended that the errors of commission and omission in the conference report were too pervasive and extensive to be handled in such a manner.[78] He was irate that he had not been given the courtesy of reviewing the transcript prior to publication. A further obstacle to resuming distribution was the decision announced by the ICAEW's Investigation Committee that it was impermissible to show its members' designatory initials and firm names in the 'List of Principal Participants' in a generalist publication such as the proceedings volume, as these would allow improper inferences of authority and, one supposes, an appearance of self-promotion. In the end, following a tense exchange of letters, Coulson vaguely threatened legal action if distribution of the conference report were resumed. Solomons, who had done yeoman's work in directing the conference and editing the proceedings, must have been bitterly disappointed. All of the undistributed copies of the volume of proceedings, which ran to 54 pages of single-spaced typescript, had to be destroyed, and the copies sent to journals for review were withdrawn.[80]

SUBMISSIONS AND ORAL TESTIMONY TO THE PARKER COMMITTEE

In August 1958, the ICAEW's Council appointed a Committee on Education and Training, chaired by W. E. Parker, of Price Waterhouse & Co., with the following terms of reference:

> 'To consider the education and training appropriate for entrants to the profession, the existing arrangements and facilities therefor, and the changes, if any, which should be made so as to ensure the provision of an adequate supply of trained candidates suitable in all respects for admission to membership of the Institute; and to make recommendations.'[80]

Parker had given an address at the ICAEW's summer course in July 1957 on 'Training for the Profession', in which, amongst other things, he was sceptical of any role that full-time or even part-time academic study might play in preparing candidates for entry into the profession (1957). In any event, the 11-member Parker Committee was safely in the hands of the conservative Establishment: six of its members were past Presidents or would soon become Presidents of the Institute, including Parker himself.

In response to the Parker Committee's request for written comments, the Association submitted a memorandum on 15 January 1959 that had been drafted by Solomons (with advice from Edey and Baxter) and reviewed by members of its Committee.[81] Submitted under the name of the Association's office-bearers, Edey and Sidebotham, the memorandum struck a chord that would have resonated with many of the Association's members:

> 'It is probably not too much to say that on no profession of comparable importance in England and Wales have the universities made so little impact as on the accountancy profession' (para. 35).

The memorandum adopted as self-evident the importance of theoretical study in the preparation of Chartered Accountants, and it proposed that non-graduate clerks should spend an aggregate of 30% of their 5-year articles in block-release courses at a technical college.

In July 1959, David Solomons left the UK for a professorship at the Wharton School of the University of Pennsylvania. The long-standing antipathy of some, though not all, of the leading members of the ICAEW toward a place for universities in the education and training of articled clerks, compounded by the distressing correspondence with Coulson during the winter of 1958–1959, were important reasons why Solomons, who had been the catalyst in the Association, resigned his professorship at Bristol and left for the United States.

Also in July, the Parker Committee invited the Association to send a delegation to give oral evidence to the Committee. At Parker's request, the Association set about preparing a supplementary written submission. After extensive correspondence among members of the Committee, including suggestions by mail from Solomons, the Association provided 'twenty copies of draft syllabuses in economics, statistics and financial mathematics and some examples, with feasible solutions, of the type of question [the] Association would like to see set in the Institute's examinations'.[82] In the Association's submission of 15 January, these subjects were recommended to broaden the Institute's syllabus. In a passage surely written by Solomons, the Assocation had said: '[These subjects] are surely of greater importance than the minutiae of bankruptcy law or executorship' (para. 24).

Edey, Sidebotham, Baxter and Cousins met with the Parker Committee on 17 December 1959 to discuss the Association's submissions. They were accompanied, at Parker's request, by Professor F. A. Wells, of the University of Nottingham's Department of Industrial Economics, who had made a separate submission to the Committee.

In its report issued in 1961, the Parker Committee rejected the Association's proposals and gave scant encouragement to those who favoured a role for the universities in the preparation of Chartered Accountants (*Report of the Committee on Education and Training*, 1961).[83]

STATE OF THE ASSOCIATION IN 1959

At a meeting of the Committee on 5 January 1959, the Secretary was instructed to levy a subscription of 10s on each member. Although the membership list drawn up in September 1957 had shown 66 names, in May 1959 the Secretary reported that only 32 members had paid the subscription levy, including 10 who were outside the UK. Of the 22 members residing in the UK, 19 were academics, of whom 13 were said to be full-time.[84] The Secretary said that the balance in the Association's account was £80. Interest in the Association's affairs clearly was on the wane.

REVIEW OF THE PERIOD 1947–1959

The influence of Baxter, Solomons and Edey in the early stages of the Association's development was palpable. When one or two of this trio were active in the Association's leadership, conferences were held with regularity, a Newsletter was put out in a timely manner, publications were issued in the Association's name, gauntlets were thrown down to stimulate a higher quality of accounting research, and submissions were made to policy-making bodies.

Conferences were held in 1947, 1949, 1950, 1952, 1955 and 1958, and one or both of Baxter and Solomons were leading figures in each of the six. Baxter was Chairman from 1950 to 1952 and Solomons was Secretary from 1947 to 1950 and Chairman from 1955 to 1958, and one or both served on the Committee during most of its existence. Baxter was Editor of the first two issues of the Newsletter, and much of the content of Nos 3 and 4 was the work of Baxter and Solomons. It was Baxter and Solomons who compiled the first two anthologies of articles that were published in the name of the Association. Baxter, Solomons and Edey were the three Association members who, together with two economists, wrote the Association's memorandum to a Royal Commission, and Solomons drafted the Association's submission to the Parker Committee. Solomons, with help from Baxter and Edey (and Sidebotham), directed the accounting education conference held at LSE in 1958, which, but for the accidental loss of some of the transcript, would have led to another publication in the Association's name.

S. V. P. Cornwell, the former Association Secretary and Solomons' colleague at Bristol, writes: 'From 1954 to 1960 the motivating force in AUTA was (almost exclusively) David Solomons'.[85] Following Solomons' departure for America in 1959 and the preparation a few months later of the Committee's testimony to the Parker Committee (to which Solomons contributed from overseas), the Association became dormant.

AFTERWORD

The 1960s were a decade in which no activities of the Association were reported in *The Accountant*. Following the 1958 education conference, the next notice to appear in *The Accountant* was in 1971, when it was announced that B. V. Carsberg, of the University of Manchester, had succeeded P. A. Bird, of the University of Kent, as Chairman. Other newly elected office-bearers were J. F. Flower, of the University of Bristol, as Vice-Chairman; E. A. Lowe, of the Manchester Business School, as Secretary/Treasurer; and K. Wallis, of the University of Manchester, as *News Review* Editor. It was reported that a new constitution had been adopted at general meetings the Association held on 30 March at Darwin College, University of Kent.[86]

That the Association's institutional memory may have become a blank after a long period of apparent inactivity is borne out by the following report in *The Accountant* in 1973:

'It came as something of a surprise to both members and committee members attending the annual conference of the Association of University Teachers of Accounting in Edinburgh last week, when Professor David Solomons announced during his talk that he "could claim credit for being a founder member of the Association" and that 1973 appeared to be its 25th year of life.'[87]

In 1965, it was reported in *The Accountant* that an Association of Lecturers in Accountancy had been formed,[88] evidently to serve the interests of lecturers in the colleges, but none of those who had been active in the AUTA were mentioned in successive reports, which continued into the 1970s.

NOTES

1. In the United States, where academic accounting developed earlier than anywhere else among English-speaking countries, the first full professors of accounting, all serving part-time, were appointed in 1900 by New York University (Lockwood, 1938, pp. 141–144). In 1904, Henry Rand Hatfield became the first full-time academic with a professorial title in accounting at a US university (Associate Professor of Accounting, University of California). He became Professor of Accounting in 1909.
2. In 1903, Dicksee was named to LSE's newly created Professorial Council, which dealt with matters of academic policy. In its annual calendar, LSE referred to Dicksee as Professor, in deference to his appointment at Birmingham.
3. Craner & Jones (1996, 11) report that Martineau 'went to Emmanuel College, Cambridge where he won Exhibitions in his first and second years and graduated "Senior Optime" in 1884 in the Mathematics Tripos'. He was admitted to the ICAEW in 1888, 'having passed the Final with "Distinction" and gained the Institute prize'. He practised for 3 years, up to 1891, and then entered the export trade, from which he retired in 1932.
4. In 1912, degrees containing an accounting element were offered at only the following British universities: Birmingham, Manchester, Leeds, Liverpool and LSE (only as an optional subject) (Edwards, 1989, p. 284).

5. The Senate conferred the lectureship on Dicksee in November 1913 and the personal professorship in January 1915. He was appointed to the Cassel Chair in July 1920. This information was supplied by Miss Ann Hewison, Academic Office, Senate House, University of London, by letter dated 22 October 1996.

6. In a letter to Sir William (later Lord) Beveridge, director of LSE, dated 2 December 1929, de Paula expressed confusion over the use of different titles: 'The title of the Chair is—Accountancy and Business Methods', and the title of the Reader's appointment is—'Accounting and Business Organisation'. I do not understand quite why there is this difference in the two titles, nor do I fully appreciate what is meant by "Business Methods"'.

7. *The Accountant*, 7 January 1933, p. 11. In a letter written by Mrs. J. Mair, secretary of LSE, dated 2 December 1929, Professor Harold Laski is reported to have said 'that the chair should be converted into something else because there wasn't an individual in the School who thought accountancy a subject for a chair' (anecdote supplied by LSE). It thereupon became a chair of commerce. De Paula's successor in the Chair was Arnold Plant as Cassel Professor of Commerce, who, as it happens, created an intellectual climate that did much to stimulate accounting research at LSE in the 1930s (Baxter, 1991, p. 139) and served on the Committee of the Accounting Research Association (ARA) (see below) (Napier, 1996a, p. 442). For references to Plant's role in the ARA, see *The Accountant*, 28 November 1936, p. 730, and 19 December 1936, p. 841.

8. Some indication of the pressures with which part-time professors had to cope is suggested by W. T. Baxter's recollection of a constraint under which Annan said he laboured: 'he was a partner in a busy firm, and his university work was limited to three lectures a week; lack of time thus made it impossible for him to do as good a job as he wanted' (Baxter, 1978, p. 4 of Preface). Between 1934 and 1936, Baxter, who had previously been employed in Annan's firm, was a lecturer at the University of Edinburgh. He has written, 'Though my job was described as part-time, in fact I made it full-time'. Letter to the author from Baxter, dated 18 November 1995.

9. The University ordinance setting up the Chair prescribed a limited tenure of 12 years. Letter to the author from David Flint, dated 8 December 1995.

10. Letter to the author from Nóirín Moynihan, of The National University of Ireland, dated 30 August 1996.

11. The author is grateful to David Flint for apprising him of the Chair and to Professor S. Collins, of the University College Galway, for furnishing particulars. Useful information was also supplied by Peter Clarke and Niamh Brennan, both of University College Dublin. The biographical information about Shields was obtained from his listing in *Who's Who*, and that about McBryan was found in Fanning (1984, p. 142). Prior to 1922, when the Irish Free State came into existence, Ireland was part of the UK.

12. An extract from *The Financial Times* article was reproduced in *The Accountant*, 16 October 1926, pp. 515–516; the quotation is from p. 515. A week later, *The Accountant* reported that Nottingham and Leicester indeed had accountancy lectureships, and observed: 'It is apparent that accountancy is becoming more and more a part of the regular curriculum of modern universities' (23 October 1926, p. 552). 'It has been suggested that one reason why accounting has struggled to achieve academic status in Britain is because universities saw themselves as institutions capable of producing "well-rounded gentlemen" rather than an individual trained to enter the market' (Edwards, 1989, p. 284).

13. *Accountant*, 16 October 1926, p. 515. The condition in India, including Ceylon, was found to be 'lamentable' (at p. 516).

14. *The Incorporated Accountants' Journal*, February 1935, p. 161.

15. *Accounting Research* thus became only the second English-language journal in the world devoted to accounting theory and research. The first was *The Accounting Review*, begun in 1926.

16. See *Accounting Research*, January 1953, pp. 103–104.

17. For a report of the organizational meeting, see *The Accountant*, 28 November 1936, pp. 730–731. Gordon writes: 'The project [to form the ARA] was due to our realization of the fact that up to that time hardly any work which could rank as *research* had been done in England, least of all by the professional bodies'. Letter to the author from Cosmo Gordon, dated 9 December 1964.

18. *The Accountant* ran a leader in which the Editor welcomed the ARA and ventured the view that accounting should be a learned profession as well as a practical profession. *The Accountant*, 5 December 1936, p. 759. A recollection by Davison concerning the founding of the ARA is reported in Mumford (1991, p. 136).

19. Sir Josiah's speech was reproduced in *The Accountant*, 2 January 1937, pp. 15–19.

20. Letter to the author from Sir Ronald Edwards, dated 30 November 1964.

21. Edwards writes: 'The Accounting Research Association really came to an end during the war years. Those of us who started it were unable to do anything to keep it going for about seven years, and afterwards some thought that it was unnecessary to revive it. Personally, I have some doubt about that, but I had to some extent by then shifted my interest. I tend to alter my career about once every ten years'. Letter to the author from Sir Ronald Edwards, dated 30 November 1964.

22. The efforts at LSE to integrate economics and accounting are treated by Napier (1996a). A useful source on the stages of evolution of accounting at LSE is Dev (1980).

23. Kitchen reports that 'Rowland in fact followed de Paula at LSE in taking charge of the work there in accounting until 1946 (the year of his death), though he was not granted the status of professor' (1978, 29). Edey observes that Rowland's published work carried forward the practice-orientated tradition of Dicksee and de Paula (1974, pp. 1–2).

   In January 1939, Rowland gave an address at the inaugural meeting of The Accountants' Group, which appears to have been more of an activist discussion group than a research forum (as was the ARA). In his address, Rowland insisted that 'Accounting must remain in its essence a record of past events . . .' (1939a, p. 131). In an address the following month to the annual general meeting of the ARA, Rowland inveighed against researchers who, not bred of experience in the practice of accountancy, would instruct the profession (1939b, p. 444). The reference to Edwards and other like-minded researchers (such as Coase, whose article he cited) was evident.

24. Baxter's appointment took effect on 1 May instead of on the usual 1 October owing to an agreement reached between LSE and the University of Cape Town (UCT) at Baxter's request. In March 1947, when Baxter's LSE appointment was approved, he was residing in Edinburgh on leave from UCT. His leave expired on 30 June, and, as a convenience to Baxter, LSE and UCT agreed the date of 1 May for both his resignation from UCT and appointment at LSE so as to make it unnecessary for him to return to UCT for the months of July and August following the expiry of his leave. (This information was found in Baxter's personnel file at LSE.)

25. The report was published in *The Accountant*, 28 April 1945, pp. 202–204, together with an introductory article on pp. 198–199. Commenting on the report, *The Economist* wrote, 'Accountancy has hitherto tended to be one of those professions—banking, insurance and the solicitor's branch of the law are other examples—which have, by the force of circumstances and their own professional requirements, held themselves somewhat aloof from the main stream of the nation's intellectual life' (5 May 1945, p. 576).

26. A report of the first conference appears in *The Accountant*, 3 May 1947, p. 248.

27. Although he judged the progress of the 'Universities scheme' to be 'satisfactory' following the first 5 years after it went into effect in 1946, Nicholas Stacey nonetheless concluded that its impact on the overall intake of new accounting professionals was insignificant. By 1950–1951, he reported, the number of university students enrolled in the 'scheme' was 350, compared with 'the number of students of the recognized accountancy societies, which in 1951 numbered over 30,000' (1954, p. 254). Solomons (1951, p. 40) attributed the slow start to the immediate post-war need to reserve a large number of university places for ex-service men, who were usually well above the normal age of university

students and 'were not attracted to a scheme which demanded of them a minimum of five years between entering the university and finally obtaining membership of a professional body, as compared with a minimum of three years for non-graduate ex-service candidates'. With the return to normal conditions, Solomons reported a 'distinct increase' in applications for admission to accounting courses.

28. *The Accountant*, 14 January 1950, p. 29.
29. *Ibid.*, p. 30.
30. *Ibid.*, p. 29.
31. One of the members of Carr-Saunders' Committee on Education for Commerce was F. R. M. de Paula, an industrial accountant who was on the Council of the ICAEW. De Paula resigned from the Council at the end of 1949 'on grounds of health and other commitments', a few weeks after publication of the committee report (Kitchen & Parker, 1980, p. 120). De Paula clearly would have supported the committee's recommendations, and might even have believed that they did not go far enough. As long ago as 1928 he had written, 'In my opinion our professional education requires to be raised to a University level . . .' (*The Accountant*, 1 December 1928, p. 711). Whether his resignation was prompted by the abhorrence expressed in the ICAEW Council toward the report is not known.
32. The decision by The Society of Accountants in Edinburgh to initiate compulsory attendance in law classes at the University of Edinburgh was taken in 1866 (Walker, 1988, p. 151). Part-time attendance at university classes in economics and accountancy began to be required in 1926 (Shackleton, 1992, p. 420).
33. Early in 1933, de Paula wrote to *The Accountant*, 'I would . . . suggest that the [English] Institute should take a direct interest in the teaching of accountancy at the modern universities. So far as I am aware, up to date it has not done so'. *The Accountant*, 7 January 1933, p. 11. Eight months later, in another letter to *The Accountant*, de Paula wrote that, 'so far as I can judge, [the discontinuance of the chair of accountancy at LSE] has passed unnoticed by the profession' (9 September 1933, pp. 419–420). Also see his letter in *The Accountant*, 1 January 1927, p. 31.
34. For a history of the first 50 years of the AAA, see Zeff (1966).
35. Minutes of the Inaugural Meeting of the Association of University Teachers of Accounting, held at the London School of Economics, on 22/23 December 1947.
36. *Ibid.*, p. 1.
37. Edey writes that the 'mechanics and name [of the Association] were stimulated by the existence of the AUTE'. Letter to R. H. Parker from H. C. Edey, dated 5 September 1996. That the American Accounting Association was not a likely organizational model is suggested by the fact that Cousins, Baxter, Solomons and Edey were not members of the AAA in the 1940s. Of the four, Solomons was the first to join the AAA, in 1954 (information supplied by the AAA). Moreover, the AAA is not mentioned in Baxter's introduction to his *Studies in Accounting* (1950), although it is cited by Solomons in the Preface to his *Studies in Costing* (1952, p. vi).
38. Minutes, *op. cit.*, p. 2.
39. *The Accountant*, 31 January 1948, p. 94.
40. Minutes, *op. cit.*, p. 4.
41. *Ibid.*, p. 5. On 16 January 1948, Sewell Bray wrote to Baxter concerning the plans for his new journal. In the attached prospectus, it was rather grandly stated that the journal 'will provide for accountancy a periodical of the standing of "The Economic Journal" in economics, or "The Journal of the Royal Statistical Society" in statistics', and 'the intention is to provide a scholarly medium for making known advanced work undertaken by accountants whether they are engaged in professional practice, in industry or in University or other teaching'. On 21 January, Baxter replied that 'There is certainly a great need for such an undertaking and I think that the profession owes you and Mr. [Leo T.] Little a debt for shouldering the burden. I hope that the venture is a great

success, and I should like to be one of the subscribers'. He foresaw no conflict between Bray's journal and the activities of the Association. Also see Bray (1949).

42. Sir Harold had served as President of the ICAEW in 1944–1945, and House was to become ICAEW President in 1954–1955. In December 1947, at the time of the dinner, both were members of the Council of the ICAEW. House and Wiseman had represented the Institute and the ACCA, respectively, on the McNair Committee and were serving on the Joint Standing Committee of the Universities and the Accountancy Profession. See *Accountancy*, May 1945, p. 143, and April 1948, p. 81.

43. Minutes of Meeting of the Committee of the Association of University Teachers of Accounting, held at London School of Economics, Houghton Street, Aldwych, London, WC2, on 14 July 1948, p. 3.

44. Basil Yamey, who, though an academic economist, was a member of the Association, published three articles in the last four issues of *Accounting Research* and had an article in the 1959 volume of *The Accounting Review*. Sewell Bray, a practitioner who held academic posts (but not in a university accounting department), published many articles in *Accounting Research* and one in *The Accounting Review* during the 12-year period. In 1956–1957, Gerald H. Lawson, then an economic research student at the University of Durham, published two comments on a joint costing article in the *Review*. Lawson later became a finance professor at Manchester Business School and has written extensively in the accounting literature.

45. Minutes of Meeting of the Committee of the Association of University Teachers of Accounting, held at the London School of Economics, Houghton Street, Aldwych, London WC2 on 9 December 1948, p. 2.

46. Letter to Association members from C. C. Magee, Hon. Secretary, dated March 1953.

47. 'The Universities and the Accountancy Profession: Report of the Conference', *The Accountant*, 18 June 1949, p. 522.

48. *The Accountant*, 22 October 1949, p. 448. Some of the information in this section is based on the provisional programme for the conference, which was distributed by the Secretary.

49. *Ibid.*

50. A year earlier, Solomons had been promoted to a readership (the first full-time accounting readership at LSE), and the demands imposed by this appointment may have played a role in his resignation.

51. *Report and Accounts 1949*, The Institute of Chartered Accountants in England and Wales, p. 37.

52. Napier (1996b, p. 469) reports that the Institute initially offered the funding for accounting education at Oxford University, which turned it down, and then made its approach to Cambridge, which used the funding to endow a chair for Stone. Stone held the Leake Professorship until his retirement in 1980, following which the funding was not renewed.

53. In the 1950s, Goldberg was active in discussions that led, in 1958, to the founding of what eventually became the Australasian Association of University Teachers of Accounting, which, in 1972, changed its name to the Accounting Association of Australia and New Zealand (Goldberg, 1987, chaps. 1–2).

54. *The Accountant*, 1 March 1952, p. 234.

55. At the time of the conference, accountancy was a field in England and Wales in which all but three university appointments were at a junior level. In a letter dated 8th January 1952 to the editor of *Der Wirtschaftsprüfer*, Solomons wrote that, apart from the two professors (Baxter and Cousins) and himself as reader, 'There are no other persons in this country teaching accounting at universities who hold positions above that of lecturer' (in the Solomons files).

56. In 1951, a committee composed of distinguished accountants and economists, formed under the auspices of the ICAEW and the National Institute of Economic and Social Research, issued a booklet entitled *Some Accounting Terms and Concepts* (1951), which

reported the results of 'an examination of the major accounting concepts and of the more important terms commonly used by both accountants and economists' (Foreword). In his paper, which was published in *Accounting Research* (1952), Tress did not mention the Committee's report.

Tress was 'a convinced supporter of the importance of Accountancy as a subject in the [Bristol] Economics Department, and he was the motivating force in the establishment of a separate Chair of Accountancy, and its acceptance in 1954 by David Solomons'. Communication to the author from S. V. P. Cornwell, dated 14 September 1995. The Bristol Chair was the third in Britain to be established on a full-time basis, but was only the second to be devoted solely to accounting.

57. Magee, then a lecturer at Bristol, was a graduate of LSE (BCom, 1926) and from 1931 to 1935 he had been Assistant in Commerce (with special reference to Accounting) under Plant at LSE.

58. *The Accountant*, 3 May 1952, p. 476.

59. *The Accountant*, 14 June 1952, p. 635.

60. It is not known who was in charge of arrangements, but it seems likely to have been Arthur Lionel Morell, a practitioner who was a part-time lecturer at the University. He was then the only Association member from Nottingham.

61. *The Accountant*, 16 April 1955, p. 443.

62. *The Accountant*, 6 April 1957, p. 410.

63. Minutes of a Meeting of the Committee of AUTA held at Derby Hall, Liverpool on 30 March 1957.

64. *Ibid.*

65. *The Accountant*, 19 November 1955, pp. 589–590.

66. *The Accountant*, 22 December 1956, pp. 637–639 and 660–664.

67. Minutes of a Meeting of the Committee of AUTA held at Derby Hall, Liverpool on 30 March 1957.

68. Letter to the author from B. S. Yamey, dated 12 October 1995.

69. Minutes of the AAA executive committee meeting, held in Urbana, Illinois, 30/31 August 1954, p. 3, and Minutes of the AAA executive committee meeting, held in Austin, Texas, 4/5 December 1954, p. 4 (supplied by the AAA office in Sarasota, Florida).

70. Minutes of a committee meeting held at the London School of Economics on 17 December 1957.

71. At p. 299. This was the first reference in *The Accountant* to the affairs of the Association since 1955. The next such reference did not appear until 1971.

72. *Accounting Education* was the proceedings booklet from the 1958 conference which was printed but never officially distributed, for the reason given below.

73. Edey, who had joined LSE as a lecturer in 1949, was made a reader in 1955 upon Solomons' departure for the new chair at Bristol. In 1962, LSE awarded Edey a personal chair.

74. Minutes of a General Meeting of the Association held in the London School of Economics on 29 March 1958.

75. See the announcement that *Accounting Research* will henceforth 'be incorporated with *Accountancy*, the monthly journal of The Institute' (*The Accountant*, 15 November 1958, p. 607), and the letter from Louis Goldberg in which he 'deplore[d] the circumstances, whatever they may have been, that made such a decision necessary' (*The Accountant*, 13 December 1958, p. 737).

76. After Solomons' successive invitations to two members of the ICAEW's Council were declined by each man owing to a concern that any views he would express might be taken as authoritative opinions of the Council and therefore of the Institute, Solomons approached the Vice-President of the Institute for the name of a leading English Chartered Accountant who might be willing to participate. Coulson, who was not a member of the Council, was recommended, and he accepted.

77. Letter from Solomons to Coulson, dated 1 December 1958 (in the Solomons files).
78. On 23 December 1958, Coulson sent Solomons a six-page memorandum, with a copy to the Institute, in which he set out his criticisms of the proceedings report. Coulson's feelings toward Solomons were summed up by the following passage: 'In particular, the report, certainly in the first session [which Solomons chaired], fails to reflect adequately the provocative and partial tone of much of the comment of the Chairman, as a result of which the level of discussion was not improved and many of the recorded utterances of the speakers were phrased in terms which would better not have been reported' (in the Solomons files). Coulson also alleged that Solomons had been partial in the editing of the proceedings. Solomons conceded none of these points, but largely confined his replies to the matters of detail that could be handled in an addendum.
79. Most of the transcript from the second of the three panel sessions, although reflecting a number of differences from the text in *Accounting Education* (1958), was printed in the April and May 1958 issues of *Accountancy*, at pp. 175–178 and 229–232, respectively.
80. *The Accountant*, 16 August 1958, p. 205.
81. A summary of most of the important points in the report was published in Lorig (1960, pp. 459–461).
82. Letter from Roy Sidebotham, Hon. Secretary, to W. E. Parker Esq., dated 2 December 1959.
83. Writing from the United States, Solomons published a scathing critique of the Parker Committee Report (Solomons, 1961).
84. In Table 1 of his paper in this special issue, Parker (1997) reports the names of 21 full-time accounting academics in UK universities in 1960.
85. Letter to the author from Cornwell, dated 14 September 1995.
86. *The Accountant*, 8 April 1971, p. 468.
87. *The Accountant*, 12 April 1973, p. 519. In fact, it was the 26th year.
88. *The Accountant*, 18 December 1965, p. 824, and 22 January 1966, p. 120.

REFERENCES

Accounting Education, A Report of a Conference of the Association of University Teachers of Accounting held in London, March (1958). London, Sweet & Maxwell for the Association.

Arnold, J. & Scapens, R. (1981). 'The British contribution to opportunity cost theory'. In M. Bromwich & A. Hopwood (eds), *Essays in British Accounting Research*, pp. 155–173, London, Pitman.

Baxter, W.T. (1948). 'Accounting as an academic study', *The Accountant*, 6 March, pp. 181–185.

Baxter, W.T. (1950). *Studies in Accounting*, London, Sweet & Maxwell.

Baxter, W.T. (1978). *Collected Papers on Accounting*, New York, Arno Press.

Baxter, W.T. (1991). 'Early critics of costing: LSE in the 1930s'. In O.F. Graves (ed), *The Costing Heritage: Studies in Honor of S. Paul Garner*, pp. 138–149, Harrisonburg, Virginia, The Academy of Accounting Historians.

Bircher, P. (1991). *From the Companies Act of 1929 to the Companies Act of 1948: A Study of Change in the Law and Practice of Accounting*, New York, Garland.

Bonbright, J.C. (1937). *The Valuation of Property: A Treatise on the Appraisal of Property for Different Legal Purposes*, New York, McGraw-Hill Book Company.

Bray, F.S. (1949). 'The English universities and the accounting profession', *The Accounting Review*, July, pp. 273–276.

Brief, R.P. (ed.) (1980). *Dicksee's Contribution to Accounting Theory and Practice*, New York, Arno Press.

Canning, J.B. (1929). *The Economics of Accountancy: A Critical Analysis of Accounting Theory*, New York, The Ronald Press Company.

Carr-Saunders, A.M. & Wilson, P.A. (1933). *The Professions*, Oxford, The Clarendon Press.

Coase, R.H. (1982). 'Economics at LSE in the 1930's: A personal view', *Atlantic Economic Journal*, March, pp. 31–34.

Coase, R.H. (1990). 'Accounting and the theory of the firm', *Journal of Accounting and Economics*, January, pp. 3–13.

Craner, J. & Jones, R. (1995). *The First Fifty Years of the Professors of Accounting at The University of Birmingham*, Birmingham, Birmingham Business School.

Craner, J. & Jones, R. (1996). 'The First Four Professors of Accounting at The University of Birmingham', Working Paper, University of Birmingham.

Dawson, S.S. (1898). *The Accountant's Compendium*, London, Gee and Co.

De Paula, F.R.M. (1943). 'The future of the accountancy profession', *The Accountant*, 8 May, pp. 239–242.

Dev, S. (1980). *Accounting and the L.S.E. Tradition*, London, The London School of Economics and Political Science.

Dicksee, L.R. (1892). *Auditing: A Practical Manual for Auditors*, London, Gee and Co.

Edey, H.C. (1974). 'The Department of Accounting', *LSE*, June, pp. 1–3.

Edwards, J.R. (1989). *A History of Financial Accounting*, London, Routledge.

Edwards, R.S. (1938). 'The nature and measurement of income', *The Accountant*, 2 July-24 September (reprinted in Parker & Zeff).

Fanning, R. (1984). 'Economists and Governments: Ireland 1922–52'. In: A.E. Murphy (ed.), *Economists and the Irish Economy from the Eighteenth Century to the Present Day*, pp. 138–156, Dublin, Irish Academic Press.

Flint, D. (1978). 'Fifty years of accountancy in the University of Glasgow 1926–1976', *Financial Reporting and Accounting Standards*, University of Glasgow Press, pp. 1–5.

Garrett, A.A. (1961). *History of The Society of Incorporated Accountants 1885–1957*, London, Oxford.

Goldberg, L. (1987). *Dynamics of an Entity: The History of the Accounting Association of Australia and New Zealand*, Accounting Association of Australia and New Zealand.

Gould, J.R. (1974). 'Opportunity cost: the London tradition'. In H. Edey & B.S. Yamey (eds), *Debits, Credits, Finance and Profits*, pp. 91–107, London, Sweet & Maxwell.

Hatfield, H.R. (1927). *Accounting—Its Principles and Problems*, New York, D. Appleton and Company.

Howitt, Sir Harold (1966). *The History of The Institute of Chartered Accountants in England and Wales 1880–1965 and of Its Founder Accountancy Bodies 1870–1880*, London, The Institute of Chartered Accountants in England and Wales.

A History of The Chartered Accountants of Scotland From the Earliest Times to 1954 (1954), Edinburgh, The Institute of Chartered Accountants of Scotland.

'The Japan Accounting Association' (1993). *Japanese Accounting Forum* (annual publication of the Japan Accounting Association), pp. 3–9.

Kitchen, J. (1978). *Accounting: A Century of Development*, University of Hull.

Kitchen, J. & Parker, R.H. (1980). *Accounting Thought and Education: Six English Pioneers*, London, The Institute of Chartered Accountants in England and Wales.

Lee, T.A. (1983). *Professors of Accounting at the University of Edinburgh—A Selection of Writings 1919–1983*, Department of Accounting and Business Method, University of Edinburgh.

Lee, T.A. (1996). 'Richard Brown, Chartered Accountant and Christian Gentleman'. In T.A. Lee (ed.), *Shaping the Accountancy Profession: The Story of Three Scottish Pioneers*, pp. 153–221, New York, Garland.

Littleton, A.C. & Yamey, B.S. (1956). *Studies in the History of Accounting*, London, Sweet & Maxwell, and Homewood, Illinois, Richard D. Irwin.

Lockwood, J. (1938). 'Early university education in accountancy', *The Accounting Review*, June, pp. 131–144.

Lorig, A.N. (1960). 'Training accountants in Great Britain', *The Accounting Review*, July, pp. 455–463.

Mumford, M.J. (1991). 'Chartered accountants as business managers: an oral history perspective', *Accounting, Business & Financial History*, March, pp. 123–140.

Napier, C.J. (1996a). 'Academic disdain? Economists and accounting in Britain, 1850–1950'. *Accounting, Business & Financial History*, 6, pp. 427–450.

Napier, C.J. (1996b). 'Accounting and the absence of a business economics tradition in the United Kingdom', *The European Accounting Review*, 5, pp. 449–481.

Norris, H. (1946). *Accounting Theory: An Outline of Its Structure*, London, Sir Isaac Pitman & Sons.

Parker, R.H. (1997). 'Flickering at the margin of existence: the Association of University Teachers of Accounting, 1960–1971', *The British Accounting Review*, March, pp. 41–61.

Parker, R.H. & Zeff, S.A. (1996). *Milestones in the British Accounting Literature*, New York, Garland.

Parker, W.E. (1957). 'Training for the profession—II', *The Accountant*, 3 August, pp. 122–127.

Paton, W.A. & Littleton, A.C. (1940) *An Introduction to Corporate Accounting Standards*, American Accounting Association.

Report of the Committee on Education and Training ('The Parker Committee Report') (1961). London, The Institute of Chartered Accountants in England and Wales.

Rowland, S.W. (1939a). 'New movements in accountancy', *The Accountant*, 28 January, pp. 131–132.

Rowland, S.W. (1939b). 'Experience, research and speculation in accounting', *The Accountant*, 1 April, pp. 442–444.

Shackleton, K. (1992). 'The evolution of education policy within the Institute of Chartered Accountants of Scotland'. In K. Anyane-Ntow (ed.), *International Handbook of Accounting Education and Certification*, pp. 417–444, Oxford, Pergamon Press.

Solomons, D. (1951). 'The universities and the accountancy profession', *The Accountants Journal*, February, pp. 40–43.

Solomons, D. (1952). *Studies in Costing*, London, Sweet & Maxwell.

Solomons, D. (1956). 'Accounting education for new responsibilities', *The Accountant*, 28 January, pp. 83–86; 4 February, pp. 114–120.

Solomons, D. (1961). 'The report on education and training: failure of a mission', *Accountancy*, July, pp. 407–412 (reprinted in Parker & Zeff).

Solomons, D. (1984). *Collected Papers on Accounting and Accounting Education*, New York, Garland (2 vols).

Solomons, D. & Zeff, S.A. (1996). *Accounting Research, 1948–1958*, New York, Garland (2 vols).

Solomons, D. & Berridge, T.M. (1974). *Prospectus for a Profession*, London, Advisory Board of Accountancy Education.

Some Accounting Terms and Concepts, A Report of a Joint Exploratory Committee appointed by The Institute of Chartered Accountants in England and Wales and by the National Institute of Economic and Social Research (1951). Cambridge, The University Press.

Stacey, N.A.H. (1954). *English Accountancy: A Study in Social and Economic History 1800–1954*, London, Gee and Company.

Stamp, Sir J. (1921). 'The relation of accountancy to economics', *The Accountant*, 15 October, pp. 501–507 (reprinted in Parker & Zeff).

Tress, R.C. (1952). 'The use of accountancy terms and concepts by economists', *Accounting Research*, October, pp. 317–331.

Walker, S.P. (1988). *The Society of Accountants in Edinburgh 1854–1914: A Study of Recruitment to a New Profession*, New York, Garland.

Walker, S.P. (1994). *Accountancy at the University of Edinburgh 1919-1994: The Emergence of a 'Viable Academic Department'*, Edinburgh, The Institute of Chartered Accountants of Scotland.

Zeff, S.A. (1966). *The American Accounting Association—Its First 50 Years*, American Accounting Association (reprinted in 1991 by the AAA).

Zeff, S.A. (1972). *Forging Accounting Principles in Five Countries: A History and an Analysis of Trends*, Champaign, Illinois, Stipes.

Zeff, S.A. (1995). 'David Solomons (1912–1995)—An Appreciation', *Accounting and Business Research*, Autumn, pp. 315–319.

Accounting Historians Journal
Vol. 26, No. 2
December 1999

Stephen A. Zeff
RICE UNIVERSITY

THE EVOLUTION OF THE CONCEPTUAL FRAMEWORK FOR BUSINESS ENTERPRISES IN THE UNITED STATES

Abstract: Institutional efforts in the U.S. to develop a conceptual framework for business enterprises can be traced to the Paton and Littleton monograph in 1940 and later to the two Accounting Research Studies by Moonitz and Sprouse in 1962-1963. A committee of the American Accounting Association issued an influential report in which it advocated a "decision usefulness" approach in 1966, which was carried forward in 1973 by the report of the American Institute of CPAs' Trueblood Committee. All of this laid the groundwork for the conceptual framework project of the Financial Accounting Standards Board (FASB), which published six concepts statements between 1978 and 1985. A seventh concepts statement is likely to be published in 2000. It is still not clear how the FASB's conceptual framework has influenced the setting of accounting standards, and some academic commentators are skeptical of the usefulness of all normative conceptual framework projects.

THE BEGINNINGS[1]

The earliest attempts to develop a "conceptual framework" in the U.S. accounting literature were by William A. Paton and John B. Canning. In his *Accounting Theory* [1922], Paton presented "a restatement of the theory of accounting consistent with the conditions and needs of the business enterprise *par excellence*, the large corporation" [pp. iii-iv], and in the final

---

Acknowledgments: The writer is grateful to Allister Wilson, Tom Dyckman, Larry Revsine, Chuck Horngren, Denny Beresford, and Jim Leisenring for comments on an earlier draft. The responsibility for what remains is solely the writer's. A similar version of the article was originally published in Spanish in Vol. 28, No. 100 (1999) of the *Revista Española de Financiación y Contabilidad*. The editor is grateful to Professor Zeff for allowing *AHJ* to publish the article in English.

[1]For a review of the early efforts by the American Accounting Association and the American Institute of (Certified Public) Accountants, see Storey [1964] and Zeff [1972, pp. 129-178; 1984].

chapter he discussed a series of basic assumptions, or "postulates," that underpin the structure of modern accounting. In *The Economics of Accountancy* [1929], Canning was the first to develop and present a conceptual framework for asset valuation and measurement founded explicitly on future expectations. Paton's book was an expansion of his doctoral dissertation done at the University of Michigan, and Canning's was his doctoral dissertation accepted by the University of Chicago. Through these works, Paton and Canning influenced many other writers over the years [for Canning, see Zeff, 2000].

Probably the first institutional attempt to lay the foundations of a conceptual framework was the "Tentative Statement of Accounting Principles Affecting Corporate Reports," issued in 1936 by the executive committee of the American Accounting Association (AAA) and published in *The Accounting Review*.[2] The main reason for preparing the "Tentative Statement," a paean to historical cost accounting, was to provide authoritative guidance to the recently established Securities and Exchange Commission (SEC). In fact, the SEC's accounting staff frequently cited the "Tentative Statement" with favor, as well as the revisions thereof issued in 1941 and 1948 and the eight supplementary statements issued between 1950 and 1954. The final revision of the Statement, issued in 1957, proved to be too venturesome beyond established practice for easy acceptance by the SEC.

An outgrowth of the AAA's 1936 "Tentative Statement" was perhaps the most influential monograph in the U.S. accounting literature, *An Introduction to Corporate Accounting Standards*, written by Paton and A. C. Littleton, two of the foremost accounting academics of their day, and published in 1940 by the AAA. Above all, it was an elegant explication and rationalization of the historical cost accounting model that was already widely accepted in the U.S. It met with general acclaim and was used for many years in accounting courses throughout the country. The Paton and Littleton monograph, as it came to be known, probably did as much as any single publication to perpetuate

---

[2]The most comprehensive review and analysis of the evolution of the efforts to formulate a conceptual framework in the U.S. is Storey and Storey's *The Framework of Financial Accounting Concepts and Standards* [1998], which should be consulted by any serious student of the subject. Reed K. Storey, the senior author of this study, was a long-time member of the FASB's research staff and was a major contributor to the board's conceptual framework project. For a skeptic's view of conceptual framework projects, see Macve [1997].

the use of historical cost accounting in the U.S. Their monograph also popularized the use of "matching" costs and revenues, widely known as the matching convention. Reed K. Storey [1981, p. 90], who devoted most of his professional career to guiding the research for the Accounting Principles Board and the Financial Accounting Standards Board, wrote:

> The [Paton and Littleton] monograph was a startling exception to the general proposition that academic writing has had little effect on accounting practice. . . . Generations of accountants learned to use it as scripture. . . .

> During the 40 years since the Paton and Littleton monograph, accounting practice has developed substantially along the lines specified in the monograph, and rationalization and theory consistent with the monograph have been widely used and have been common in authoritative pronouncements.

Two years before the Paton and Littleton monograph appeared, the American Institute of Accountants (AIA) published *A Statement of Accounting Principles*, by Thomas H. Sanders, Henry Rand Hatfield, and Underhill Moore — two accounting academics and a law academic — which was, in large measure, a defense of accepted practice. The monograph had been commissioned in 1935 by the Haskins & Sells Foundation in order that the fledgling SEC, which had declared an interest in prescribing the form and content of financial statements in registration statements, might be provided with some authoritative guidance on best accounting practice. In 1938-1939, the AIA became even more active in providing guidance to the SEC when it authorized its Committee on Accounting Procedure (CAP) to issue Accounting Research Bulletins. In one of its first decisions, the committee rejected the option of developing a comprehensive statement of accounting principles — a kind of "conceptual framework" — because the project would take perhaps five years to complete, during which time the SEC might lose patience with the committee and instead begin to make its own accounting rules [Zeff, 1972, p. 137]. Several times in the 1940s and 1950s during the tenure of the CAP, proposals to develop a set of basic accounting concepts were expressed, and in the 1940s the Institute's research department actually issued an eight-page review of basic accounting principles [AIA, 1945]. However, none of these initiatives was taken up by the committee as part of its program of work [Zeff, 1972, pp. 141-143].

Also during the 1940s and 1950s, both within the Institute's committee and between the committee and the SEC's accounting staff, an accumulated frustration arose from disagreements on a number of controversial accounting issues, including deferred tax accounting, historical cost v. current value, the propriety of general price-level adjustments, and the treatment of unusual items in the profit and loss statement. Representatives on the committee from the major public accounting firms differed philosophically on the pervasive issue of whether to impose a greater degree of uniformity or to permit flexibility in the choice of accounting methods [see Zeff, 1984, pp. 458-459]. This continuing discord reflected unfavorably on the work of the committee. Believing that a stronger research component was needed to support the committee's deliberations, the Institute's incoming president, Alvin R. Jennings [1958, p. 32], proposed establishment of a research foundation that would "carry on continuous examination and re-examination of basic accounting assumptions and to develop authoritative statements for the guidance of both industry and our profession." At the same time, Leonard Spacek [1957, p. 21], the pugnacious managing partner of Arthur Andersen & Co., was publicly criticizing the accounting profession for not establishing the premises and principles of accounting. Pressure began to build for a better approach to establishing "generally accepted accounting principles" (GAAP) than was being done on a case-by-case basis by the CAP. It was hoped that a program of fundamental research could enable the committee to resolve some of its deep disagreements and also to persuade the SEC of the merit of new approaches. Jennings thereupon set up a Special Committee on Research Program to study and make recommendations on the Institute's role in establishing accounting principles, including especially the research component.

ERA OF THE ACCOUNTING PRINCIPLES BOARD

The Institute's Special Committee on Research Program was composed of leading figures from the ranks of auditors, preparers, and academics, and also included the SEC chief accountant. In its path-breaking report published in 1958, the committee proposed the establishment of both an Accounting Principles Board (APB) to replace the CAP and an accounting research division to support the APB. The committee identified four broad levels at which financial accounting should be addressed: postulates, principles, rules or other guides for the application of principles to specific situations, and research [Report to Council of the Special Committee on Research Program, 1958, p. 63]. The term "postulates" had been little used in the accounting literature. The committee asserted that postulates "are few in number and are the basic assumptions on which principles rest. They necessarily are derived from the economic and political environment and from the modes of thought and customs of all segments of the business community" [p. 63]. It added that "a fairly broad set of co-ordinated accounting principles should be formulated on the basis of the postulates" [p. 63]. The first priority of the research division was to commission studies on the accounting postulates and broad accounting principles. The committee said that "the results of these [studies], as adopted by the [Accounting Principles] Board, should serve as the foundation for the entire body of future pronouncements by the Institute on accounting matters, to which each new release should be related" [p. 67]. Thus was born the first institutional program to establish a conceptual framework — with principles predicated on postulates — although the term "conceptual framework" itself did not come into vogue until the 1970s.

The Institute accepted the committee's recommendations, and in 1959 the APB succeeded the CAP. An accounting professor at the University of California at Berkeley, Maurice Moonitz, was appointed the full-time director of accounting research, and he proceeded to commission the research studies on postulates and broad principles. Moonitz assigned to himself the project on postulates, and he collaborated with his Berkeley colleague, Robert T. Sprouse, on the research study dealing with broad principles.

Moonitz's *The Basic Postulates of Accounting*, Accounting Research Study No. 1, was published in 1961, and it consisted of an exposition and explanation of three tiers of accounting postulates, treating the environment, the field of accounting, and the imperatives (such as going concern, objectivity, consistency, the monetary unit, materiality and conservatism, and disclosure). It was not clear from Moonitz's study whether he favored historical cost accounting or a version of current value accounting; thus, many readers found his study to be too abstract and general to engage their interest and critical thought. The follow-up study by Sprouse and Moonitz, *A Tentative Set of Broad Accounting Principles for Business Enterprises*, Accounting Research Study No. 3, which was published in 1962, evinced no such neutrality. Drawing on Moonitz's postulates, the authors argued that less reliance should be placed on the realization concept "as an essential feature of accounting" [p. 15] and that the use of current values should be expanded, which, in view of the SEC's long-standing antipathy to departures from historical cost accounting, immediately became controversial if not objectionable. Sprouse and Moonitz advocated the use of current replacement costs for merchandise inventories and for plant and equipment, as well as the use of discounted present values for receivables and payables to be settled in cash. In the early 1960s, the use of present values of expected future cash receipts was virtually unknown in U.S. financial reporting, and current values (except in "lower of cost or market") were hardly to be found. Sprouse and Moonitz also recommended that the holding gain or loss from revaluing inventories should be taken to profit [p. 30]. Nine of the 12 members of the project advisory committees for the postulates and principles studies commented on Sprouse and Moonitz's recommendations in a section appended to their study, and the reactions of eight of the nine ranged from tepid to dismissive. Three of the sternest critics were the SEC chief accountant and two previous SEC chief accountants. The APB itself, which was charged with deciding whether to adopt the two research studies or not, issued a famous statement in which it discarded the two studies as "too radically different from present generally accepted accounting principles for acceptance at this time" [APB, 1962].

Moonitz and Sprouse had thought their assignment was to develop a rational argument for a sound approach to financial reporting. Most members of the APB and other leaders of the accounting profession, by contrast, looked upon basic research as an instrument for rationalizing the *status quo* (in the tradition of the Paton and Littleton monograph), rather than as a normative argument for fundamental change in accounting. Above all, the SEC was at that time a conservative regulator, which regarded departures from the "objectivity" of historical cost accounting as possessing the potential to deceive the readers of financial statements. In the 1960s, the SEC saw its mission chiefly as one of guarding against misleading financial statements rather than of improving the information content of the statements. As a result of the APB's rejection of the postulates and principles studies, the cause of basic accounting research as a foundation stone for pronouncements on specific subjects suffered a severe setback, and the board instead began to deal with specific issues, much as had the CAP before it, without a body of underlying concepts on which to draw.

One of the project advisory committee members, Paul Grady, a retired partner of Price Waterhouse & Co. who was a protégé of the former *doyen* of the accounting profession, George O. May, argued that a summary of GAAP would be timely. He believed, much as did his academic mentor, A. C. Littleton, that theoretical explanations should be derived inductively from practice. The APB commissioned Grady to undertake such a study, and in 1965 the Institute published his *Inventory of Generally Accepted Accounting Principles for Business Enterprises* (Accounting Research Study No. 5), which, he hoped, would be kept up to date by periodic supplements. The study was in great demand overseas, for it was seen as an authoritative compilation of accepted U.S. practice. Although Grady's study undertook to identify basic concepts, objectives, and principles implicit in current pronouncements, it offered little to portend an improvement in practice. At the least, his study purported to show that accounting rested on basic concepts, objectives, and principles, contrary to the view held by skeptics.

In the mid-1960s, the APB responded to the recommendation of a special committee that the board "enumerate and describe the basic concepts to which accounting principles *should be* oriented" and "state the accounting principles to which practices and procedures *should* conform" [emphasis supplied; Zeff, 1972, p. 196]. This was, at last, a charge that the board should adopt a normative stance toward the development of basic concepts, and not just synthesize accepted practice. It was intended that the final product would be an Opinion of the board, carrying status as a mandatory pronouncement. The board and one of its committees labored for five years, during which its members had great difficulty reaching agreement on the normative propositions. In the end, it was easiest to achieve agreement on a mostly descriptive statement, which was published as Statement No. 4 in 1970 under the title, *Basic Concepts and Accounting Principles Underlying Financial Statements of Business Enterprises.* As a Statement, instead of an Opinion, the document was not mandatory and its contents could be ignored. The issuance of a mostly descriptive statement greatly disappointed those who had hoped that the board finally would provide a blueprint for principled improvement in financial reporting. A member of the APB, George R. Catlett of Arthur Andersen & Co., dissented to the Statement "because in his view it fails to provide what purports to be 'a basis for guiding the future development of financial accounting'" [APB, 1970, p. 105]. Nonetheless, even as a descriptive statement, the document was comprehensive, perceptive, and deeply analytical, and its contents have frequently been cited when insights into existing practice were being discussed.

AAA'S *A STATEMENT OF BASIC ACCOUNTING THEORY*

While the CAP and the APB, which were composed mostly of accounting practitioners, were unable or unwilling to develop a normative set of underlying concepts and basic principles, committees of accounting academics had no such reluctance. In 1966, a committee of the American Accounting Association published a pioneering monograph, entitled *A Statement of Basic Accounting Theory* (*ASOBAT*), which redirected attention away from the inherent virtues of asset valuation models and toward the "decision usefulness" of financial statements.[3] It defined accounting as "the process of identifying, measuring, and communicating economic information to permit informed judgments and decisions by users of the information" [AAA, 1966, p. 1]. While that definition would hardly be exceptional today, in the 1960s, when theorists were actively debating the superiority of alternative asset valuation models [see, for example, Nelson, 1973; Henderson and Peirson, 1983, chs. 8 and 9; Lee, 1996], an explicit orientation toward the users of information was a breath of fresh air. The committee [AAA, 1966, pp. 23-24] also placed emphasis on futurity:

> The committee suggests that accounting information for external users should reflect their needs by reporting measurements and formulations thought to be relevant in the making of forecasts without implying that the information supplied is wholly adequate for such prediction.
>
> Almost all external users of financial information reported by a profit-oriented firm are involved in efforts to predict the earnings of the firm for some future period. Such predictions are most crucial in the case of present and prospective equity investors and their representatives — considered by many to be the most important of the user groups. . . . The past earnings of the

---

[3]For a discussion of the "decision usefulness" approach, see the AAA's *Statement on Accounting Theory and Theory Acceptance* [AAA, 1977, pp. 10-21]; much fuller coverage appears in Staubus [forthcoming].

firm are considered to be the most important single item of information relevant to the prediction of future earnings. It follows from this that past earnings should be measured and disclosed in such a manner as to give a user as much aid as practicable in efforts to make this prediction with a minimum of uncertainty [pp. 23-24].[4]

The committee identified and elaborated upon "four basic standards for accounting information ... that provide criteria to be used in evaluating potential accounting information": relevance, verifiability, freedom from bias, and quantifiability [p. 8]. It then judged a number of accounting problem areas against those standards [pp. 27-36]. In one of its more important judgments, on historical cost v. current value, the committee [pp. 30-31] concluded, after weighing verifiability against relevance, that financial reporting should display information drawn from both models (which was a radical recommendation at the time):

> The presentation of historical [transaction-based] information alone excludes the full impact of the environment on the firm; presentation of current cost information alone obscures the record of consummated market transactions. The committee recommends that both kinds of information be presented in a multi-valued report, in which the two kinds of information appear in adjacent columns.

In a little-noticed section of the report, the committee [p. 29] suggested that "accountants usually have required too narrow a view of compliance with the standard of quantifiability" and that, in the light of the uncertainty surrounding accounting measurements, "there is no compelling reason why the accountant should not report in terms of interval estimates or probability distributions."

Robert R. Sterling [1967a, pp. 99-100], an important accounting theorist of the day, assessed *ASOBAT* as follows:

> The committee has invited us to view accounting as a measurement-information system. This new view precludes some questions but poses others. In their refer-

---

[4]In 1969, another AAA committee issued a major report on the extent to which current financial reporting practices satisfy the needs of investors and creditors in the light of *ASOBAT*'s suggested standards for accounting information [AAA, 1969].

ence frame, it is no longer appropriate to argue about which convention or assumption comes closest to the 'actual' cost or income; it is not appropriate to assume that if we carefully describe (fully disclose) the methods used, then the figures will be meaningful, or that only invested costs or transaction data are the subject matter of accounting or that by its very name accounting reflects costs. Under the new view, measurements in accounting are a function of some end.

This is a change in 'world-view' and is the stuff that revolutions are made of [footnote omitted].

A BIG EIGHT FIRM ANNOUNCES ITS OWN STATEMENT OF OBJECTIVES

In 1972, the Big Eight firm of Arthur Andersen & Co. (AA) issued a 130-page booklet entitled *Objectives of Financial Statements for Business Enterprises*. The development of this unique publication grew out of the firm's frustration with the failure of the APB to agree on a normative statement of concepts and principles in its Statement No. 4 in 1970 [Wyatt, 1999, p. 161]. The firm focused on "objectives" because the Institute's Trueblood Committee was then engaged in a major study of the objectives of financial statements (see the next section). AA's booklet was critical of existing accounting practice, especially its emphasis on conservatism and historical cost as a goal instead of as a method toward a goal [pp. 34-38]. It emphasized instead that "financial statements must be fair to all users and should provide the basis for resolving [their] conflicting interests..." [p. 8], a view that the firm's former managing partner and chairman, Leonard Spacek, had been advocating in speeches since the 1950s [see *A Search for Fairness...*, 1969]. The firm [p. 116] concluded that the overall purpose of financial statements:

> ... is to communicate information concerning the nature and value of the economic resources of a business enterprise, the interests of creditors and the equity of owners in the economic resources, and the changes in the nature and value of those resources from period to period.

One implication of this objective was that assets should be measured at current value, and the firm recommended that unrealized holding gains and losses be disclosed in the income statement [chs. 7 and 8].

AA's proposal was a bold one, and it was the only accounting firm to issue such an elaborate statement of its views.

THE TRUEBLOOD REPORT:
OBJECTIVES OF FINANCIAL STATEMENTS

The decision usefulness approach that found acceptance in *ASOBAT* was carried forward into a major report issued in 1973 by a special committee of the American Institute of Certified Public Accountants (AICPA)[5] on the objectives of financial statements. The committee was formed in 1971, after three of the Big Eight firms (including AA) had made known their concerns over the ineffectiveness of the APB, including its inability to resist pressures from special interests, especially preparers [see Zeff, 1984, pp. 463-464]. The AICPA formed two special committees in this crisis setting. The first, known as the Study Group on the Establishment of Accounting Principles, or the Wheat Committee, met to recommend improvements in the process of establishing those principles. In its report [*Establishing Financial Accounting Standards*, 1972], the committee proposed a full-time, independent body known as the Financial Accounting Standards Board (FASB) under the wing of a new Financial Accounting Foundation. The AICPA promptly approved the Wheat Committee's report and created the FASB to succeed the APB in July 1973. The second special committee, the Study Group on the Objectives of Financial Statements, or the Trueblood Committee, was composed of leading practitioners, academics, and users of accounting information, and was charged with proposing the fundamental objectives of financial statements to guide the improvement of financial reporting. It was to produce a normative statement, not an inference drawn from practice. Importantly, the research director of the Trueblood Committee, George H. Sorter, an accounting professor at the University of Chicago, had been one of the most influential members of the AAA committee that had developed *ASOBAT*.[6] Sorter also played a major role in the drafting of the Trueblood Committee's report.[7]

---

[5]In 1957, the American Institute of Accountants changed its name to the American Institute of Certified Public Accountants.

[6]Telephone interview with Charles T. Zlatkovich, chairman of the *ASOBAT* Committee, April 3, 1999.

[7]Telephone interview with Oscar S. Gellein, a member of the Trueblood Committee, March 19, 1999. See Sorter [1973] for a discussion of the main points in the Trueblood report and of the approach used by the committee.

The Trueblood Committee's report, *Objectives of Financial Statements,* which was issued in October 1973, embraced *ASOBAT*'s decision usefulness approach and focused even more specifically on future cash flows [p. 20]:

> An objective of financial statements is to provide information useful to investors and creditors for predicting, comparing, and evaluating potential cash flows to them in terms of amount, timing, and related uncertainty.

The committee said that financial statements should "serve primarily those users who have limited authority, ability, or resources to obtain information and who rely on financial statements as their principal source of information about an enterprise's economic activities" [p. 17]. While the committee devoted primary attention to investors and creditors, it also regarded managers and employees as coming within the set of financial statement users, and it concluded, "While users may differ, their economic decisions are similar. Each user measures sacrifices and benefits in terms of the actual or prospective disbursement or receipt of cash" [p. 18].

Following in the steps of *ASOBAT,* the committee thought it desirable to enumerate several "qualitative characteristics of reporting": relevance and materiality, form and substance, reliability, freedom from bias, comparability, consistency, and understandability [ch. 10]. The committee concluded, much as had the AAA committee that had prepared *ASOBAT,* that "the objectives of financial statements cannot be best served by the exclusive use of a single valuation basis" [p. 41]. The Trueblood Committee considered an even broader array of valuation bases than did the AAA committee: historical cost, exit values, current replacement cost, and discounted cash flows, and it counseled that "the specific combination of valuation bases to be used is an implementation issue" [p. 42]. The committee helpfully suggested how each of the valuation bases could be fitted to the information requirements they most likely would fulfill.

In two sections of the Trueblood report that are often overlooked, the committee commented on the fallibility of single numbers in financial statements as well as on the use of financial statements to help achieve social goals. As to the former, the committee followed *ASOBAT* by observing that "measurements in terms of single numbers that do not indicate possible ranges and dispersions pose problems in describing events subject to uncertainty" [p. 39]. This is a point that has seldom been raised explicitly in policy-making circles. The committee concluded by suggesting [p. 40]:

> To satisfy the individual preferences of users for predicting and controlling the impact of current events on enterprise earning power, some apparently simple quantifications should be supplemented to represent their actual complexities by disclosing ranges of precision, reliability, and uncertainty.

In a broader societal context, the Trueblood Committee stated that the social goals of enterprise are no less important than the economic goals. Citing pollution as an example, the committee drew attention to "those enterprise activities which require sacrifices from those who do not benefit" [p. 54]. It concluded that [p. 55]:

> An objective of financial statements is to report on those activities of the enterprise affecting society which can be determined and described or measured and which are important to the role of the enterprise in its social environment.

The Trueblood report was remarkable for the freshness of its approach. It did much to refocus discussions in the accounting policy arena from stewardship reporting to providing information useful for decision makers. The report became a kind of blueprint for the conceptual framework project that the newly established FASB was just beginning.[8]

ERA OF THE FASB: EARLY DEVELOPMENTS

The Wheat Committee, in its report which recommended the establishment of the FASB, did not envision that the board would undertake to develop a conceptual framework. In its report, the committee [1972, pp. 19, 78] wrote as follows:

> The need for a fundamental conceptual foundation has been much debated in accounting circles for many years. We believe this debate may have produced more heat than light. Financial accounting and reporting are

---

[8]The transcript of proceedings from the Trueblood Committee's public hearing held in May 1972 was published in a two-volume typescript. In addition, significant research, reference, and resource materials that were considered by the Trueblood Committee during the development of its report were reproduced in *Objectives of Financial Statements: Selected Papers* [1974]. For a discussion of the Trueblood report, see "Studies on Financial Accounting Objectives: 1974" [1974].

not grounded in natural laws as are the physical sciences, but must rest on a set of conventions or standards designed to achieve what are perceived to be the desired objectives of financial accounting and reporting. We understand the primary work of the [Trueblood Committee] to be the development of such objectives and some guidelines for their achievement.

The work of the ongoing standard-setting body should be to develop standards for preparing financial accounting information that will be consistent with these objectives.

and

We do not believe that the [FASB's] staff should be expected to conduct a broad, fundamental research program dealing with basic concepts on an ongoing basis, since we believe that this type of research is best left to those in the academic field.

Nonetheless, in November 1973, five months into its first year of operation as successor to the APB, the FASB ["Board Meets with Trueblood Study Group," 1973] reported that it would be tackling "the entire hierarchy of financial accounting theory," beginning with the Trueblood report:

Once objectives are agreed upon, the Board intends to address itself to the entire hierarchy of financial accounting theory, including qualitative characteristics, the types of information needed by users of financial statements, and basic accounting concepts.

A month later, in December 1973, the board announced that its project on "Broad Qualitative Standards for Financial Reporting," which had been set the previous April, was being enlarged under a new and more impressive title, "Conceptual Framework for Accounting and Reporting: Objectives, Qualitative Characteristics and Information" ["Task Force Appointed," 1973, p. 1]. There was thus no doubt that the board intended to develop a full-fledged conceptual framework, and the board's term, "conceptual framework," came to be widely used for such an undertaking.[9]

---

[9]Gore [1992] has provided a critical analysis of the development of the board's conceptual framework project. See Agrawal [1987] for an analysis of the logical structure of the conceptual framework. For insights into the dynamic within the board and the politics affecting its decisions on the conceptual framework, see Miller et al. [1998, ch. 4].

Robert T. Sprouse, an original member of the board who served as its vice chairman from 1975 to 1985, has said that two factors drove the board to embark on a conceptual framework. First, the board felt obliged to carry on the work of the Trueblood Committee [Sprouse, 1988, p. 124]. Second, the board required a framework of concepts to help it address the six technical projects on its initial agenda: research and development, contingencies, leases, foreign currency translation, business segments, and materiality. Sprouse [1984/85, p. 25][10] has written:

> Almost immediately the board recognized the need to develop certain fundamental concepts that it could look to for rational and consistent guidance in analyzing and resolving issues. The absence of an established concept of something as basic as an asset was a handicap in addressing accounting for research and development costs; the absence of an established concept of something equally as basic as a liability made resolving the issues in accounting for contingencies more difficult. Those first experiences strengthened the new board's recognition of the importance of establishing a conceptual framework for analyzing issues and relating its decisions to that framework.

The following year, in June 1974, the board issued its first discussion memorandum in the "Conceptual Framework for Accounting and Reporting" project, dealing with the objectives and qualitative characteristics recommended by the Trueblood Committee [FASB, 1974]. Discussion memoranda are objective analyses of issues facing the board, without any indication of the board's views or preferences. The board held a public hearing on the discussion memorandum in September 1974.

In December 1976, the board issued two important documents relating to the conceptual framework project. One was *Tentative Conclusions on Objectives of Financial Statements of Business Enterprises* [FASB, 1976], based on an analysis of the written comments received and oral testimony at the public hearing held on the June 1974 discussion memorandum. The other document was a 360-page discussion memorandum subtitled *Elements of Financial Statements and Their Measurement*. The discussion memorandum on elements also included an extensive treatment of both the qualitative characteristics of

---

[10]See also Kirk [1989, pp. 89-90].

financial information and the measurement of the elements. Both the board's tentative conclusions on objectives and the contents of its lengthy discussion memorandum on the rest of the conceptual framework were the subject of a public hearing set for June 1977.

The board's tentative conclusions on objectives were noteworthy for the inclusion of an appendix on modern capital market theory, which represented the first acknowledgment by a U.S. standard setter of this important stream of research in the finance literature. The December 1976 discussion memorandum devoted an important section to the choice to be made between the "asset and liability view" and the more traditional "revenue and expense view" (associated with the Paton and Littleton monograph) for defining earnings [paras. 32-70 and ch. 5]. Under the "asset and liability view," which the board eventually came to favor, the definition of earnings depends on the definitions of assets and liabilities, so that a balance sheet test must be invoked to validate the existence of earnings, revenues, and expenses.[11] The discussion memorandum also contained a chapter on the important distinction between "financial capital maintenance" and "physical capital maintenance" [ch. 6], which had not received much explicit attention in the U.S. accounting literature. It also presented an extensive discussion of the "attributes of assets": historical cost, current cost, exit value, and present value [ch. 8].

Between 1974 and 1985, the FASB issued 30 publications (eight discussion memoranda, seven research reports, eight exposure drafts, one invitation to comment, and six concepts statements) in its massive conceptual framework project, totaling over 3,000 pages.[12] In addition, the board received more

---

[11]Storey and Storey [1998] have written that the board's adoption of the primacy of the asset and liability view "still is undoubtedly the most controversial, and the most misunderstood and misrepresented, concept in the entire conceptual framework" [p. 76], chiefly because the asset and liability view was seen by many as a device to "impose some kind of current value accounting on an unwilling world" [p. 83]. They discussed the controversy at some length [pp. 47-66, 76-85].

Robert T. Sprouse believed that the asset and liability view would rid balance sheets of "what-you-may-call-its," which were the unintelligible residues produced by the matching convention [Sprouse, 1966]. Also see Sprouse [1977, pp. 12-13; 1988, pp. 126-127].

[12]For a complete list of the publications, see Gore [1992, Appendix 2]. One discussion memorandum, two research reports, two exposure drafts, and two concepts statements (4 and 6) constituted the adaptation of the conceptual framework to nonbusiness entities, which is not discussed in this paper. Two

than 1,000 letters of comment in response to its discussion memoranda and exposure drafts, and it held eight public hearings covering 20 days of oral testimony, which was transcribed and placed on the public record. The written record and the amount of board member and staff time dedicated to the project were immense. It was estimated that, in the early 1980s, the conceptual framework project accounted for as much as 40 percent of the board's technical staff time [Van Riper, 1994, p. 81].

ERA OF THE FASB: THE CONCEPTS STATEMENTS[13]

The FASB issued six Statements of Financial Accounting Concepts, known as concepts statements, of which two (Nos. 4 and 6) represented adaptations to nonbusiness entities. The FASB [Concepts Statement 2, pp. i-ii] stated the purpose of the concepts statements as follows:

> Statements in the series are intended to set forth objectives and fundamentals that will be the basis for development of financial accounting and reporting standards. . . .
>
> The conceptual framework is a coherent system of interrelated objectives and fundamentals that is expected to lead to consistent standards and that prescribes the nature, function, and limits of financial accounting and reporting. It is expected to serve the public interest by providing structure and direction to financial accounting and reporting to facilitate the provision of evenhanded financial and related information that is useful in assisting capital and other markets to function efficiently in allocating scarce resources in the economy. . . .

---

discussion memoranda and the invitation to comment, which dealt with matters of the display of accounting information, treated subjects that were included in the exposure draft entitled *Reporting Income, Cash Flows, and Financial Position of Business Enterprises* [FASB, 1981] but which did not eventually mature into a concepts statement. Included in the above enumeration of FASB documents is the discussion memorandum on *Criteria for Determining Materiality*, issued on March 21, 1975, which was not formally part of the conceptual framework project. Nonetheless, the conceptual aspects of the materiality project were incorporated into the qualitative characteristics project in 1978.

[13]For more extensive discussion of the board's concepts statements, see Davies et al. [1997, pp. 46-63], Pacter [1983], Solomons [1986], Wolk et al. [1992, ch. 6], and Miller et al. [1998, pp. 105-115].

Statements of Financial Accounting Concepts do not establish standards prescribing accounting procedures or disclosure practices for particular items or events, which are issued by the Board as Statements of Financial Accounting Standards. Rather, Statements in this series describe concepts and relations that will underlie future financial accounting standards and practices and in due course serve as a basis for evaluating existing standards and practices.

Objectives: The comments received on the discussion memorandum on objectives proved to be an education for board members. In 1975, the board conducted a survey of opinion on the Trueblood recommendations. Marshall S. Armstrong [1977, p. 77], the board chairman, reported one finding that disturbed him:

In our first discussion memorandum on the conceptual framework of accounting, the most important project on our agenda, we sought an expression of opinion from respondents on the following as a basic objective of financial statements; it is taken directly from the Trueblood report:

'The basic objective of financial statements is to provide information useful for making economic decisions.'

Could there be disagreement with a statement such as this? I am sure you will be astounded to learn that only 37 percent of our respondents were able to recommend the adoption of this objective. Twenty-two percent recommended that it be rejected out of hand; and 10 percent insisted that it needed further study. It is difficult to believe that only 37 percent can agree that the basic objective of financial statements is to provide information useful for making economic decisions. I think this suggests the problem quite clearly.

Those who disagreed took the position that the basic function of financial statements was to report on management's stewardship of corporate assets and that the informational needs of readers was of secondary importance. It follows from this line of thinking that management can best determine the principles to be employed in reporting on their firms, and that standards — standards almost of any sort — can only impede management in its effort to fulfill this responsibility.

Two accounting academics observed that the respondents to the FASB survey probably thought of furthering their own personal interests rather than promoting the interests of readers generally. Reflecting on Armstrong's expression of concern, Dopuch and Sunder [1980, p. 13][14] wrote:

> Why should we believe all groups of interested parties would adopt the provision of information useful for making economic decisions as their motivation for being involved in the financial reporting process? For example, we should not be surprised if auditors, like everyone else, seek to maximize their own wealth through participation in the accounting process. If the provision of economically useful information implies greater exposure to the risk of being sued without corresponding benefits of higher compensation, they will not see the provision of economically useful information (however defined) as *their* objective of the financial accounting process.

One might have added that most auditors had probably been educated to believe that accounting serves primarily a stewardship function, and that they would find it somewhat threatening to contemplate that accounting should have a more activist function in economic society. Such preconceptions and predispositions made it difficult for the board to impose a decision usefulness objective on a profession that had been accustomed to view accounting as basically a passive record-keeping activity.

Concepts Statement 1, *Objectives of Financial Reporting by Business Enterprises*, issued in November 1978, closely followed Trueblood's emphasis on futurity, as indicated by the following key passage [para. 37]:

> Financial reporting should provide information to help present and potential investors and creditors and other users in assessing the amounts, timing, and uncertainty of prospective cash receipts from dividends or interest and the proceeds from the sale, redemption, or maturity of securities or loans.

In Statement 1, the board preferred the broader term, financial reporting, over the narrower term, financial statements,

---

[14]For further discussion of the "politics" of developing a conceptual framework, see Rappaport [1977], Horngren [1981], Miller [1990], and Van Riper [1994, pp. 20-22, 75-82].

used in the Trueblood report. Donald J. Kirk [1988, p. 13], the FASB chairman when all of the concepts statements were approved, later explained how this decision "blunted" some of the opposition to the evolving conceptual framework, which seemed to many to raise the specter of current value accounting:

> It was thought by this broadening that, as under the securities laws, the needs of users could be satisfied through disclosures, possibly even separate from the financial statements, and, therefore, not require the type of income measurement changes that opponents feared [that is, current value accounting].

David Solomons, an accounting professor at the University of Pennsylvania and the principal draftsman of the Wheat report, wrote a critique of the board's Concepts Statements 1-4 in which he gave the statement on objectives a grade of C, because, he said, "the purposes that the board has defined for financial reporting are excessively narrow" [Solomons, 1986, p. 118]. He wrote [p. 118]:

> ...while the Trueblood report recognized, however briefly, that business enterprises had a responsibility to society and not just to their stockholders, the board's statement on objectives substantially confines its attention to the needs of investors and creditors, barely recognizes the needs of managers, and ignores altogether the interests of other groups with an interest in enterprise productivity, such as labor and the tax authorities.

To this writer, Solomons' overall evaluation of the statement seems to be more critical than necessary.

Qualitative Characteristics: Concepts Statement 2, *Qualitative Characteristics of Accounting Information,* was issued in May 1980.[15] Donald Kirk [1988, p.13] has written that "defining the characteristics of useful financial information was the least controversial of the conceptual framework projects, in part because readers did not see implications that portended current value accounting."

Statement 2 followed in the tradition of *ASOBAT* and the Trueblood report and, in the decision usefulness mode,

---

[15]For an analysis of Statement 2, see Storey and Storey [1998, pp. 98-119].

enumerated and explained a hierarchy of qualities of accounting information. David Solomons, who drafted the statement at the invitation of the board, rectified the overemphasis on investors and creditors in Statement 1 [see para. 26 of Statement 2], which he was later to criticize. "Relevance" and "reliability" were the two pillars, and at several places the inevitable tradeoffs between the two were discussed. "Reliability" was supported by "representational faithfulness" (a term coined by Solomons) and "verifiability." Representational faithfulness, which was defined as "correspondence or agreement between a measure or description and the phenomenon it purports to represent" [para. 63], was a more elegant and comprehensive concept than "freedom from bias" in *ASOBAT* and the Trueblood report. In the discussion of verifiability, the term "objectivity" was nowhere to be found, probably to allow for the admissibility of departures from historical cost accounting. "Objectivity" was similarly absent in *ASOBAT* and the Trueblood report. "Verifiability," it was stated, "implies consensus. Verifiability can be measured by looking at the dispersion of a number of independent measurements of some particular phenomenon" [para. 84].

In contrast to *ASOBAT* and the Trueblood report, the board envisioned a role for "conservatism," albeit constrained: "There is a place for a convention such as conservatism — meaning prudence — in financial accounting and reporting, because business and economic activities are surrounded by uncertainty, but it needs to be applied with care" [para. 92]. But the board made clear that "conservatism in financial reporting should no longer connote deliberate, consistent understatement of net assets and profits" [para. 93].[16] The board carefully limited the use of conservatism as follows [para. 95]:

> Conservatism is a prudent reaction to uncertainty to try to ensure that uncertainties and risks inherent in business situations are adequately considered. Thus, if two estimates of amounts to be received or paid in the future are about equally likely, conservatism dictates using the less optimistic estimate; however, if two amounts are not equally likely, conservatism does not necessarily dictate using the more pessimistic amount rather than the more likely one.

---

[16]Sterling [1967b] has reported finding considerable support for the hypothesis that conservatism is the fundamental principle of valuation in traditional accounting.

The board's discussion of "neutrality" very much followed from Solomons [1978] and alerted readers to the proper posture of the standard setter in a politicized world [see Kirk, 1988, pp. 13-14]. The essential position set forth in the statement was [para. 106]:

> While rejecting the view that financial accounting standards should be slanted for political reasons or to favor one economic interest or another, the Board recognizes that a standard-setting authority must be alert to the economic impact of the standards that it promulgates.

Finally, "comparability" was introduced as a *desideratum* [paras. 111-122], and it was stated that accounting decisions must satisfy a materiality screen or threshold [paras. 123-132]. Invoking a variant on a passage that has been used since the 1960s to characterize "comparability," the board asserted that greater comparability "is not to be attained by making unlike things look alike any more than by making like things look different" [para. 119].

Statement 2 is perhaps the most admired and most emulated of the board's concepts statements. The analysis is logically and sensibly ordered, it is well explained (reflecting Solomons' penchant for metaphors), and the terms are carefully defined. Miller et al. [1998, p. 110] have written that Statement 2 "provides a set of definitions that the Board and its constituents can and do use to communicate with each other. The definitions bring more rigor to the due process, and possibly to the thought processes of the participants." Former chairman Kirk [1988, p. 13] has written that Statement 2 "has contributed greatly to the understanding of the need for and purpose of standards." Davies et al. [1997, p. 63], three partners in the U.K. firm of Ernst & Young who have studied the FASB's conceptual framework in depth, praised Statement 2 as "outstanding work."

An empirical study of the views of 26 former members of the APB and of the FASB, however, yielded an opposite finding. The subjects were tested for their views on whether the 11 qualitative characteristics were operational, comprehensive, and parsimonious (i.e., free of significant redundancies in meaning). The researchers [Joyce et al., 1982, p. 670] concluded as follows:

> Many of the results reported here are not favorable to the *Statement*. Nine of the 11 qualitative characteris-

tics clearly fail the tests of operationality. Not only is there considerable disagreement among experienced policy makers on what the qualitative characteristics mean in the context of particular accounting policy issues, there is also considerable disagreement on their relative importance. While the qualitative characteristics appear to comprise a comprehensive set for choosing among accounting alternatives, the set is not a parsimonious one. Thus the *Statement* fails to meet two out of its three desired criteria.

This casts doubt on the ability of the qualitative characteristics defined in the *Statement* to facilitate accounting policy making.

Elements: Concepts Statement 3, *Elements of Financial Statements for Business Enterprises*, was issued in December 1980, seven months after Statement 2. It sets forth the definitions of assets, liabilities, equity, investments by and distributions to owners, and comprehensive income and its components (revenues, expenses, gains, and losses) that are collectively the "elements" of financial statements. As motivation, former board chairman Kirk [1988, p. 15] wrote that the need for workable definitions of assets and liabilities on such projects as research and development costs and accounting for contingencies, both of which were on the board's initial agenda, "served as a catalyst" for the elements project.

This is the statement in which the board made known its preference for the "asset and liability view" over the "revenue and expense view" for defining earnings. While the board did not actually discuss the two views in the statement, one notices that revenues, expenses, and gains and losses were defined in terms of assets and liabilities. Hence, revenues were defined as "inflows or other enhancements of *assets* of an entity or settlements of its *liabilities* (or a combination of both) during a period from delivering or producing goods, rendering services, or other activities that constitute the entity's ongoing major or central operations" [emphasis supplied, footnote omitted; para. 63]. By contrast, the definition of revenues propounded 25 years earlier in the Institute's Accounting Terminology Bulletin No. 2 reflected the traditional "revenue and expense view," without a reference to assets or liabilities. It was: "*Revenue* results from the sale of goods and the rendering of services and is measured by the charge made to customers, clients, or tenants for goods and services furnished to them" [*Proceeds,*

Revenue, Income, Profit, and Earnings, 1955, p. 34].

It was in this statement (presaged in the exposure draft of December 28, 1979) that the board unveiled its new terminology, "comprehensive income," to describe "the change in equity (net assets) of an entity during a period from transactions and other events and circumstances from nonowner sources" [para. 56]. In the context of the choice between financial capital maintenance and physical capital maintenance, on which the board deferred a decision until a later statement, comprehensive income was viewed as "a return *on* financial capital" [para. 58].[17] Comprehensive income would thus include unrealized holding gains and losses, if they were adjudged to be recognizable accruals.

Two facets of Statement 3 caused trepidation, especially among practitioners and financial executives — that the board's adoption of the "asset and liability view," together with its comprehensive income proposal, would inevitably lead to some form of current value accounting [see, e.g., Way, 1977, pp. 40-41; Schuetze, 1983, p. 260; Beresford, 1983, p. 67; Pacter, 1983, p. 84; Gore, 1992, pp. 94-95; Van Riper, 1994, p. 75].[18] Expressions emanating from the board and elsewhere that this implication was unfounded may not have allayed many fears. And a forthright statement by Reed K. Storey [1981, pp. 94-96], a senior member of the FASB's research staff, may have added to the anxiety:

> I think the handwriting is already on the wall for the present model (which is often mislabeled 'historical cost accounting') because, among other things, it can't cope with everyday complications, such as changing prices and fluctuating foreign exchange rates. . . .
>
> Those who feel threatened by the conceptual framework or hope that it will maintain the status quo will be disappointed. Change is coming, even if the concep-

---

[17]For an extensive treatment of financial v. physical capital maintenance, see Sterling and Lemke [1982].

[18]In fact, as early as 1977, one of the Big Eight accounting firms, Ernst & Ernst, was alarmed that the "asset and liability view" would lead inevitably to current value accounting, which it opposed. Its concern that the board had not clearly explained the implications of its thinking led the firm "to mount a campaign to educate financial executives about the conceptual framework and the potential dangers it presented" [Beresford, 1983, p. 66]. By July of that year, the firm had presented more than 50 conceptual framework seminars around the country to over 5,000 people [Ernst & Ernst, 1977, p. 1].

tual framework is never adopted, because of weaknesses in the existing accounting model.

Solomons, in his critique of the concepts statements, gave Statement 3 a B-. Although he regarded the board's definitions as "a distinct improvement on the earlier definitions in APB Statement no. 4" [1986, p. 120], he nonetheless believed that the definitions were not sufficiently robust to deal with the most difficult accounting problems. He illustrated this point by attempting to apply the definition of liabilities to pensions, and he found it wanting. Yet Solomons, who was an advocate of the "asset and liability view," noted with satisfaction that "the definitions have been formulated in such a way as to leave no room for reasonable doubt about the primacy of assets and liabilities and the dependency of the other elements on these two" [pp. 120-121].

It is of interest that Dennis R. Beresford, who would become FASB chairman in 1987, wrote in 1981, while he was still a partner in Ernst & Whinney (and chairman of the Institute's Accounting Standards Executive Committee), that he found Statements 1, 2, and 3 (and 4) to be "broad, abstract statements or proposals which in my opinion have provided little, if any, help in deciding the accounting issues of the day" [Beresford, 1981, p. 66]. He described himself as a pragmatist, and he was, from the start, a skeptic of the conceptual framework project [see Beresford, 1983].

Recognition and Measurement: In December 1984, a full four years after the issuance of the statement on elements,[19] the board issued Concepts Statement 5 on *Recognition and Measurement in Financial Statements of Business Enterprises.*[20] This was the long-awaited statement that would announce the board's position on the most controversial issues in the conceptual framework project, including its view on which measurement attribute(s) were to be central to the framework. On this statement, the board equivocated badly, which led Solomons [1986, p. 124] to give it a grade of F and "require the board to take the course over again — that is, to scrap the statement and start afresh." It was also the first concepts statement in which a board member dissented.

---

[19]Miller [1990] and Gore [1992, pp. 105-109] have explained the delay: the board was divided both on how to proceed and on what to conclude.

[20]For an analysis of Statement 5, see Storey and Storey [1988, pp. 145-160].

Early in the statement, the board gave notice that it would not be advancing the literature in a way so as to alter practice [para. 2]:

> The recognition criteria and guidance in this Statement are generally consistent with current practice and do not imply radical change. Nor do they foreclose the possibility of future changes in practice. The Board intends future change to occur in the gradual, evolutionary way that has characterized past change.

The major disappointment to many readers was the board's disinclination in Statement 5 to make a decision on the preferred measurement attribute. The board enumerated the attributes that are "used in present practice": historical cost, current cost, current market value, net realizable value, and present value of future cash flows [para. 67], but could only conclude the following [para 70]:

> Rather than attempt to select a single attribute and force changes in practice so that all classes of assets and liabilities use that attribute, this concepts Statement suggests that use of different attributes will continue, and discusses how the Board may select the appropriate attribute in particular cases [footnote omitted].

The Trueblood report at least undertook to suggest how different measurement attributes might be more or less helpful in fulfilling certain information requirements [*Objectives of Financial Statements*, 1973, ch. 6]. But the board, after ten years of unrelenting work on the conceptual framework project, could not achieve as much on measurement attributes as the part-time Trueblood Committee had done in 30 months.

On recognition, the board was clearly reluctant to innovate. It did not, for example, undertake to discuss whether to accord recognition to the "firm" commitments under wholly executory contracts, that is, those on which no party has yet performed any of its promises [para. 107]. Yuji Ijiri [1980] argued the case eloquently in a research report written at the invitation of the board, and the subject was again treated in another research report by L. Todd Johnson and Reed K. Storey [1982, ch. 11].

In the section on recognition, Statement 5 did contain a carefully worded proposition that "information based on current prices should be recognized if it is sufficiently relevant and reliable to justify the costs involved and more relevant than alternative information" [para. 90], which Storey and Storey

[1998, p. 159] criticized as "extremely weak guidance." Miller et al. [1998, p. 115] complained that the criteria of "relevant" and "reliable" in this proposition "are too broad to provide helpful guidance either to standards setters or to individual account-ants who are attempting to resolve a new issue." David Mosso [1998, p. 7], a member of the board from 1978 to 1987 who continued as a member of the board's senior staff until 1996, has said that this proposition "may sound like a weak endorse-ment but at the time it was extremely contentious and a major concession to the Board members who favored more market value accounting." He added that "it is the concept that under-lies the progress that has been made in marking financial instruments to market." As Kirk has pointed out, the board's assent even to this proposition, hedged as it was, was contin-gent on how the unrealized holding gains and losses were to be reported. Preparers felt strongly that any unrealized holding gains and losses should not affect earnings. In the end, the board settled on a compromise presentation by which both con-ventional net income (retitled "earnings" in Statement 5) and comprehensive income, which would essentially consist of earnings plus or minus unrealized holding gains and losses, should be reported. As the choice of measurement attribute could not be disengaged from the income-reporting implica-tions of unrealized holding gains and losses, this compromise was necessary for Statement 5 to survive [Kirk, 1989, pp. 100-103].

As will be seen, one advance that did have future ramifica-tions was the board's focus on comprehensive income. In State-ment 5, the board proposed the preparation of both a statement of earnings and a statement of comprehensive income, and it said that the "full set of articulated financial statements dis-cussed in this Statement is based on the concept of financial capital maintenance" [para. 45]. In this somewhat indirect way, it signified that financial capital maintenance had won its favor.[21] The dissenter to Statement 5, John W. March, who was a former partner of Arthur Andersen, objected to comprehen-sive income "as a concept of income because it includes all recognized changes (including price changes) in assets and liabilities . . . " [p. 32]. March was a partisan of the physical capital maintenance concept [pp. 32-33].

---

[21]Robert T. Sprouse [1988, p. 126], the board's vice chairman, later wrote that Concepts Statement 5 "comes down solidly on the side of financial capital maintenance."

Although the board was not prepared in the 1980s to issue a standard requiring that comprehensive income should be reported in the basic financial statements, it returned to the issue vigorously in the mid-1990s. It was then that the board built on the definition of comprehensive income in Statement 3 and on paragraphs 13 and 39-44 of Statement 5 to issue an exposure draft proposing a requirement that net income and comprehensive income be accorded equal prominence in either one or two statements of financial performance [FASB, 1996]. But strong resistance from preparers forced the board to accept a compromise, permitting a third option — to display comprehensive income in the statement of changes in equity [FASB, 1997]. Thus, the board enabled preparers to exclude such items as unrealized gains and losses from a statement of financial performance.[22]

At several places in Statement 5, including two quoted above, the board left change to a process of evolution [also see para. 35]. Solomons [1986, p. 122], in his critique, skewered this approach:

> These appeals to evolution should be seen as what they are — a cop-out. If all that is needed to improve our accounting model is reliance on evolution and the natural selection that results from the development of standards, why was an expensive and protracted conceptual framework project necessary in the first place? It goes without saying that concepts and practices should evolve as conditions change. But if the conceptual framework can do no more than point that out, who needs it? And, for that matter, if progress is simply a matter of waiting for evolution, who needs the FASB?

Solomons [p. 193] complained that the board's non-committal listing of measurement attributes in Statement 5 showed that it had not progressed beyond its December 2, 1976 discussion memorandum, which had done the same.

Oscar S. Gellein [1986, p. 14], who had served on the board from 1975 to 1978, also was critical of the board's failure to provide conceptual guidance, without which, he said, "there is the risk of reversion to ad hoc rules in determining accounting methods." Wolk et al. [1992, p. 177] wrote that Statement 5

---

[22]For further discussion of comprehensive income, see Johnson and Reither [1995].

"must be considered a distinct letdown, if not an outright failure."

Storey and Storey [1998, p. 159], who have been staunch supporters of the conceptual framework approach, criticized the board for abdicating its responsibility in Statement 5:

> Whereas a neutral exposition of alternatives was appropriate for a Discussion Memorandum, a litany of present measurement practices with neither conceptual analysis or evaluation nor guidance for making choices was not proper for a Concepts Statement.

In merely describing current practice, Concepts Statement 5 is a throwback to statements of accounting principles produced by the 'distillation of experience' school of thought [e.g., Paul Grady's approach in the APB's Accounting Research Study No. 5] — an essentially practical, not a conceptual, effort. Its prescriptions for improving practice are reminiscent of those of the Committee on Accounting Procedure or the Accounting Principles Board; measurement problems will be resolved on a case-by-case basis. Unfortunately, that approach worked only marginally well for those now-defunct bodies.

One close observer of the board has written that the board's decision not to disturb the *status quo* on recognition and measurement "was led by representatives of the preparer constituency, particularly members of the Financial Executives Institute, and was supported by three Board members [including March]" [Miller, 1990, p. 28].

Role of Statement 33: No reference has previously been made to the board's Statement of Financial Accounting Standards 33, *Financial Reporting and Changing Prices*, issued in September 1979, which required more than 1,300 large corporations to disclose in an unaudited supplementary note certain general price-level information and current cost accounting information.[23] Yet it is impossible to discuss the board's recognition

---

[23]The current cost accounting portion of Statement 33 reflected the influence of the report of the Sandilands Committee [1975, ch. 12] in the U.K., which gave prominence to the "value to the business" (or "deprival value") approach to current value accounting. For a review of this and other intellectual influences on the board's thinking, including the interaction between Statement 33 and the board's conceptual framework project, see Tweedie and Whittington [1984, ch. 7 and entries in their subject index under *FAS33*].

and measurement project without taking into account the impact on the board of preparers' and users' reactions to Statement 33. As former board chairman Kirk [1988, p. 16], who previously was an audit partner in Price Waterhouse, has written:

> While not formally a part of the conceptual framework project on recognition and measurement, Statement 33 was the laboratory for the conceptual project. It was the testing ground for the application of the current cost system to the most difficult of valuation problems — fixed assets — and the testing ground for the validity and utility of the concept of physical, rather than financial, capital.
>
> ... the experience with Statement 33 by the time we were debating Concepts Statement No. 5 told me that use of the current cost information was very limited, and that there were serious questions about its reliability. I could find little reason to endorse on a conceptual level a current value or current cost measurement system for future standards when it appeared that the utility of such a system in Statement 33 was going to be seriously challenged.

In August 1984, just as the board was completing work on Statement 5, it was disclosed in the board's *Status Report* that:

> ... research studies and responses to the Invitation to Comment [entitled *Supplementary Disclosures about the Effects of Changing Prices* (FASB, 1983)] indicate that Statement 33 information has not been widely used. Both the number of users and extent of use have been limited. A large number of responses to the Invitation to Comment indicate that the costs of preparing the disclosures have outweighed the benefits to date ["Financial Reporting and Changing Prices," 1984].

In November 1984, the board issued Statement of Financial Accounting Standards No. 82, in which it eliminated the requirement for supplementary disclosure of the inflation accounting information, and two years later, in December 1986, it issued Statement of Financial Accounting Standards No. 89, in which it eliminated altogether the requirement for the supplementary disclosure on changing prices.

Present Value: In the late 1980s, the board, aware of the increasing importance of present value as a decision-making tool and sensitive to the widely differing approaches adopted over the years by the FASB and other U.S. standard setters for implementing present value-based measurements, began to develop a common framework for using present value and estimates of future cash flows in accounting measurement.[24] It issued a discussion memorandum in 1990 [*Present Value-Based Measurements in Accounting*], held a public hearing in 1991, published a special report [Upton, 1996], and issued an exposure draft for a proposed standards statement [1997]. In the end, the board concluded that the subject should form part of the conceptual framework project, and it proceeded to issue an exposure draft of a proposed concepts statement [1999]. The proposed statement will not deal with the larger question of recognition but will instead provide "a framework for using future cash flows as the basis for an accounting measurement" [FASB exposure draft, 1999, para. 10]. Publication of the concepts statement is planned for early in the year 2000.

An Assessment: The many disappointments expressed about the concepts statement on recognition and measurement meant that the board's conceptual framework project ended on a "down" note. The hope, perhaps naïve, that the framework might point a clear path toward improvement in financial reporting was not fulfilled.

Richard Macve, a British accounting academic who has been a close student of the FASB's conceptual framework, has been skeptical of such claims. Macve [1997, p. xxii] wrote:

> Given the inherent conceptual limitations of 'income' and 'value' measurement, it remains unrealistic to expect official attempts to develop 'conceptual frameworks' for financial accounting and reporting to be able to provide a coherent basis for the resolution of accounting problems. . . . Moreover, standard setters' major problems are more often political. A framework, however technically correct, cannot solve the political problems of different interests and needs at the level of individual standards [footnote omitted].

Commentators have generally rendered a negative assessment of the board's conceptual framework. Solomons [1986, p. 122], who was a fervent supporter of the board's project, regret-

---

[24]Miller and Bahnson [1996, pp. 94, 96, 98] have cited defects in the application of present value in seven previous pronouncements.

fully concluded that "my judgment of the project as a whole must be that it has failed." In particular, he regarded Statement 5 as a "dismal failure" [p. 118]. Miller et al. [1998, p. 105], however, saw a silver lining in the dark clouds:

> Although it is probably an overstatement to call the project a complete failure, it is certainly a disappointment. On the other hand, it makes a significant contribution to the accounting literature by establishing that service to user needs is the primary objective of financial accounting. It has also contributed to the efficiency of the due process procedures by defining a number of key terms that are indeed used by the Board and its constituents. These accomplishments may bring more rigor and efficiency to the Board's deliberations, but that conclusion can be safely reached only in the long run.

In regard to user needs, one could argue that the literature had already been enriched by the Trueblood report.

Kenneth Most [1993, pp. 107, 109] saw the project as "seriously flawed," and he registered his "great surprise . . . that the FASB's conceptual framework has been imitated in other countries." Davies et al. [1997, p. 63] opined that the weakness of the board's conceptual framework project was probably most attributable to the "Board's failure to deal with the fundamental issues of recognition and measurement." Archer [1993, p. 113] has written that "the FASB's attempt involved massive effort; but, in terms of conveying an increased degree of either intellectual or institutional authority upon the standard-setting process, the mountains evidently brought forth a mouse."

A favorable review was given by Kevin Stevenson [1987, p. 49], director of the Australian Accounting Research Foundation, who said, "I must say I regard the work of the FASB on their conceptual framework as extremely valuable." His disappointment with Statement 5 was that "it did not provide a full analysis of the issues" [p. 51].

In late 1984, Arthur Andersen, once it had seen the board's exposure draft [1983] on recognition and measurement, issued a second edition of its *Objectives of Financial Statements for Business Enterprises,* in which it restated the importance it attributed to value. The firm pointedly differentiated the reference to "economic resources" in its overall objective (see above) from the board's, arguing that there is a "vast difference . . . since we specifically call for the 'nature and value' of economic resources, while the FASB merely asks for information about them" [1984, p. 8n]. The firm reiterated its support for financial capital maintenance, and it expanded its recommended coverage of current value accounting to include liabilities. As a contribution to the dialogue, the firm's revised booklet constituted an implied criticism of the board's noncommittal position on measurement.

Reaction to the board's conceptual framework necessarily depended on one's expectations. At one extreme, Sterling [1982, p. 106] argued as follows:

> In my view the next essential step [after Concepts Statements 1-3] is to display replicable logical connections between the concepts and the conclusions about specific practices. Provision of such connections is likely to require honing the concepts to make them logically fertile. ... if the concepts aren't honed to the point where the logical connections are at least plausible, preferably replicable, the framework is likely to be at best useless and at worst used to rationalize preconceived positions that are likely to be contradictory.

At the other extreme, Peasnell [1982, p. 255] suggested that the conceptual framework:

> ... could be intended to do no more than provide very broad general objectives for financial reporting to which no one could take serious objection; the aim would be to 'raise the moral tone' of the profession.

Perhaps closure on specific accounting standards was too much to expect from a conceptual framework.

In 1977, an AAA committee composed of nine academics pessimistically concluded, after three years of study, that "theory closure cannot be dictated" and that "all theory approaches are flawed when viewed from the perspective of some alternative approach" [AAA, 1977, pp. 49, 50]. Each conceptual framework, it added, "implicitly incorporates individual beliefs and premises that cannot be proved or disproved in a logical sense" [p. 48]; hence, the committee concluded that it cannot be demonstrated that one framework is superior to all others.[25]

Dopuch and Sunder [1980] were similarly pessimistic of any attempt to impose a normative conceptual framework on

---

[25]Lawrence Revsine was chairman of the committee. For his views on the implication of the report for the development of a conceptual framework, see Revsine [1977, pp. 35-39].

society, for the groups and individuals who are concerned with financial reporting possess their own private motives and objectives. In the end, they argued, standards will inevitably be compromises to appease these conflicting interests.

Storey and Storey [1998, p. 161], on the final page of their comprehensive study, preferred to accentuate the achievements of the board's conceptual framework:

> The FASB has used the completed parts of the framework with considerable success. The Board's constituents also have learned to use the framework, partly at least because they have discovered that they are more likely to influence the Board if they do. Both the Board and the constituents have also found that at times the concepts appear to work better than at other times, and undoubtedly they sometimes could have been more soundly applied. . . . some parts of the conceptual framework are still controversial, partly at least because long-held views die hard. The framework remains unfinished, although the Board gives no sign of completing it in the near future.

> Despite the fact that the Board has left it incomplete, the FASB's conceptual framework

> - Is the first reasonably successful effort by a standards-setting body to formulate and use an integrated set of financial accounting concepts
> - Has fundamentally changed the way financial accounting standards are set in the United States
> - Has provided a model for the International Accounting Standards Committee and several national standards-setting bodies in other English-speaking countries, which not only have set out their own concepts but also clearly have been influenced by the FASB's Concepts Statements, sometimes to the point of adopting the same or virtually the same set of concepts.

This writer would interpose three reactions to the views expressed by Storey and Storey. (1) Without question, the board has shown that it can bring an immense project of this kind to completion, but whether the effort has been "reasonably successful" is still an open question. (2) One doubts that the board's approach to setting standards has been "fundamentally changed" by the conceptual framework — changed, yes, but not fundamentally. (3) It is true that the board's conceptual framework has been imitated in other countries and by the International Accounting Standards Committee (IASC). But the IASC's framework is no more helpful on measurement than is the FASB's Statement 5. The U.K. Accounting Standards Board (ASB), in the 1999 redraft of its Statement of Principles, also declined to choose between historical cost and current value as the measurement basis [para. 6.4]. And the ASB, unlike the FASB, is not constrained by a conservative securities commission or by an entrenched tradition of historical cost accounting. The Australian Accounting Research Foundation, which began the research for its conceptual framework in the 1970s, has yet to issue even an exposure draft for a concepts statement on recognition and measurement. So, the exportation of the board's conceptual framework has not led to marked success overseas.

When judging the overall product of the FASB's conceptual framework, one can justifiably fault the board for not having chosen, as a matter of principle, the relevant measurement attribute or attributes that should govern the preparation of financial statements. That was, after all, the *raison d'être* for the entire exercise — everything pointed toward that end. What reasons serve to explain the board's indecisiveness? Resistance to change — from preparers, practitioners, and the SEC, as well as within the board — coupled with an indifference, at best, by users constituted a high barrier for the board to surmount. The SEC's well-known antipathy toward departures from historical cost accounting in the financial statements might have been seen by some members of the board as an obstacle to a principled choice. Memories were still fresh of the condemnation by the APB (and by the SEC's chief accountant) of Sprouse and Moonitz's advocacy of current value accounting in their accounting research study published in 1962, resulting in the APB's decision to consign both the postulates and principles studies to oblivion. Some FASB members may not have wanted to risk having the board's conceptual framework similarly marginalized as "too radically different." Furthermore, departures from historical cost accounting represented a potential threat not only to the preparer community but also to accounting practitioners [see Revsine, 1991]. To preparers, the use of current value raised the specter of including potentially volatile unrealized holding gains and losses in the income statement. As regards practitioners, few would have possessed any knowledge of measurement attributes other than modified historical cost accounting because of the monopoly that the latter had so long enjoyed in the U.S. Practitioners may have feared that their expertise would become obsolete by the imposition of an unfamiliar system of accounting. Macve [1997, p. xxii] has characterized these sources of resistance as "the political problems of different interests and needs." Even within the board, the members differed intellectually and emotionally on the choice of measurement attribute — reflecting what Horngren [1981, p. 90] has called their "individual conceptual frameworks." This built-in resistance to change on so many sides must have been a brooding omnipresence in the board's deliberations.

What has been the practical effect of the board's conceptual framework? Unless one is on the inside and listens to the board deliberations — or, as a researcher, interviews the principals and examines the board's minutes and files — it is difficult to know whether the evolving conceptual framework actually changed minds or was cited in subsequent standards statements to buttress a preconceived view. To be sure, Arthur R. Wyatt [1987, p. 46], who joined the board just after the issuance of Statement 5, has said that "the current FASB members and staff refer to the framework constantly," especially the qualitative characteristics and the definitions of elements. Further, he said that "constituents particularly refer to the conceptual framework when they do not agree with a tentative conclusion that we have reached on a practical issue and argue that it is inappropriate because it does not follow logically from the conceptual framework." But it would be useful to have the findings from an empirical research study.

Former board member Mosso [1998, p. 7] has said that "Concepts Statement 5 laid the groundwork" for the board's decision in 1987 (Statement 95) to replace the funds statement with the statement of cash flows "by further developing Concept Statement 1's emphasis on cash flows as a tool of investment decision making."

To demonstrate impact, Miller [1990, p. 27] has claimed that three subsequent standards statements incorporate the board's preference for the "asset and liability view": Statement 76, on in-substance defeasance [1983]; Statement 87, on pensions [1985]; and Statement 96, on deferred tax [1987]. He noted as well that three of the board's early standards statements, issued between 1974 and 1976, also embraced the "asset and liability view" [Miller, 1990, p. 27]. Evidently, the board did not require a concepts statement in order to adopt this premise in its standards.

As part of his major study of the conceptual framework

project, Gore sought to discern the impact of the completed conceptual framework on three standards statements: Statement 87, on pensions [1985]; Statement 95, on cash flow statements [1987]; and Statement 96, on deferred tax [1987]. Gore [1992, p. 124] concluded that the board's conceptual framework "can claim little effect on the various outcomes."

Yet Daley and Tranter [1990, p. 15] have contended that it is pointless to attempt to judge specific accounting standards in terms of a conceptual framework that includes neutrality as a desired characteristic of reliability. They argued that "the significant role that economic and political pressures play in the development of accounting standards" must be factored in to the conceptual framework and therefore into any such analysis of the conformity of standards to a framework.

To what extent have members who joined the board after the conceptual framework was completed in 1985 "signed on" to the conceptual framework? At the end of 1986, only 12 months after Statement 6 was issued, Chairman Kirk [1986, p. 8] wrote, "I have already noticed that board members who were not involved in the lengthy debates preceding [the six] Concepts Statements, especially No. 5 on recognition and measurement, have less attachment or proprietary interest in them." By 1993, all of the members who voted on Statement 5 had left the board. In a standard-setting body with rotating membership, how long will an approved conceptual framework retain its authoritativeness within the body? To its credit, the board has taken steps to keep the conceptual framework on the table. At some of the board's professional development sessions that are held for the benefit of members and the research staff, issues relating to the conceptual framework are periodically scheduled for discussion. Also, a number of recent agenda projects, especially the current one on present value, has led the board to revisit the earlier concepts statements. Finally, the annual performance review of board members can point up a lack of knowledge of the concepts statements. But the question remains, to what extent do the current board members subscribe to the conceptual framework?

These are interesting questions on which, it is hoped, empirical research will be conducted. Until then, we live with opinions.

REFERENCES

A Search for Fairness in Financial Reporting to the Public (1969), selected addresses by Leonard Spacek (Chicago, IL: Arthur Andersen & Co.).

Accounting Principles Board (1962), *Statement by the Accounting Principles Board* (New York: American Institute of Certified Public Accountants), April.

Accounting Principles Board (1970), *Basic Concepts and Accounting Principles Underlying Financial Statements of Business Enterprises*, Statement No. 4 (New York: American Institute of Certified Public Accountants), October.

Accounting Standards Board (1999), *Statement of Principles for Financial Reporting*, Revised Exposure Draft (London: ASB).

Agrawal, Surendra P. (1987), "On the Conceptual Framework of Accounting," *Journal of Accounting Literature*, Vol. 6: 165-178.

American Accounting Association (1936), "Tentative Statement of Accounting Principles Affecting Corporate Reports," *Accounting Review*, Vol. 11, No. 2: 187-191.

American Accounting Association (1966), *A Statement of Basic Accounting Theory* (Evanston, IL: AAA).

American Accounting Association (1969), "An Evaluation of External Reporting Practices: A Report of the 1966-68 Committee on External Reporting," *Accounting Review*, Vol. 44 (Supplement): 78-123.

American Accounting Association (1977), *Statement on Accounting Theory and Theory Acceptance* ([no place]: AAA).

American Institute of Accountants (1945), "Corporate Accounting Principles: A Statement by the Research Department," *Journal of Accountancy*, Vol. 80, No. 4: 259-266.

Arthur Andersen & Co. (1972), *Objectives of Financial Statements for Business Enterprises* ([no place]: Arthur Andersen & Co.).

Arthur Andersen & Co. (1984), *Objectives of Financial Statements for Business Enterprises* (Chicago: Arthur Andersen & Co.).

Archer, Simon (1993), "On the Methodology of Constructing a Conceptual Framework for Financial Accounting," in Mumford, M. J. and Peasnell, K. V. (eds.), *Philosophical Perspectives on Accounting: Essays in Honour of Edward Stamp* (London: Routledge): 62-122.

Armstrong, Marshall S. (1977), "The Politics of Establishing Accounting Standards," *Journal of Accountancy*, Vol. 143, No. 2: 76-79.

Beresford, Dennis R. (1981), "A Practitioner's View of the FASB Conceptual Framework," *Ohio CPA Journal*, Vol. 40: 65-67.

Beresford, Dennis R. (1983), "Observations on the FASB's Conceptual Framework," in Elam, Rick (ed.), *DR Scott Memorial Lectures in Accountancy*, Vol. 12 (Columbia, MO: University of Missouri-Columbia): 53-69.

"Board Meets With Trueblood Study Group" (1973), *Status Report* of the Financial Accounting Standards Board, No. 6, November 28: 2.

Canning, John B. (1929), *The Economics of Accountancy* (New York: The Ronald Press Company).

Daley, Lane A. and Tranter, Terry (1990), "Limitations on the Value of the Conceptual Framework in Evaluating Extant Accounting Standards," *Accounting Horizons*, Vol. 4, No. 1: 15-24.

Davies, Mike, Paterson, Ron, and Wilson, Allister (1997), *UK GAAP: Generally Accepted Accounting Practice in the United Kingdom* (London: Macmillan/Ernst & Young).

Dopuch, Nicholas and Sunder, Shyam (1980), "FASB's Statements on Objectives and Elements of Financial Accounting: A Review," *Accounting Review*, Vol. 55, No. 1: 1-21.

Ernst & Ernst (1977), "Information Release," national office, retrieval no. 38628, July 27.

Establishing Financial Accounting Standards (Wheat report) (1972) (New York: American Institute of Certified Public Accountants).

Financial Accounting Standards Board: Discussion Memoranda on the Conceptual Framework for Accounting and Reporting

Consideration of the Report of the Study Group on the Objectives of Financial Statements (1974) (Stamford, CT: FASB), June 6.

Elements of Financial Statements and Their Measurement (1976) (Stamford, CT: FASB), December 2.

Financial Accounting Standards Board: Exposure Drafts

Elements of Financial Statements for Business Enterprises (1979) (Stamford, CT: FASB), December 28.

Reporting Income, Cash Flows, and Financial Position of Business Enterprises (1981) (Stamford, CT: FASB), November 16.

Recognition and Measurement in Financial Statements of Business Enterprises (1983) (Stamford, CT: FASB), December 30.

Present Value-Based Measurements in Accounting (1990) (Norwalk, CT: FASB), December 7.

Reporting Comprehensive Income (1996) (Norwalk, CT: FASB), June 20.

Using Cash Flow Information in Accounting Measurements (1997) (Norwalk, CT: FASB), June 11.

Using Cash Flow Information and Present Value in Accounting Measurements (1999) (Norwalk, CT: FASB), March 31.

Financial Accounting Standards Board: Statements of Financial Accounting Concepts

Objectives of Financial Reporting by Business Enterprises (1978), No. 1 (Stamford, CT: FASB), November.

Qualitative Characteristics of Accounting Information (1980), No. 2 (Stamford, CT: FASB), May.

Elements of Financial Statements of Business Enterprises (1980), No. 3 (Stamford, CT: FASB), December.

Objectives of Financial Reporting by Nonbusiness Organizations (1980), No. 4 (Stamford, CT: FASB), December.

Recognition and Measurement in Financial Statements of Business Enterprises (1984), No. 5 (Stamford, CT: FASB), December.

Elements of Financial Statements (1985), No. 6 (Stamford, CT: FASB), December.

Financial Accounting Standards Board: Statements of Financial Accounting Standards

Financial Reporting and Changing Prices (1979), No. 33 (Stamford, CT: FASB), September.

Extinguishment of Debt (1983), No. 76 (Stamford, CT: FASB), November.

Financial Reporting and Changing Prices: Elimination of Certain Disclosures (1984), No. 82 (Stamford, CT: FASB), November.

Employers' Accounting for Pensions (1985), No. 87 (Stamford, CT: FASB), December.

Financial Reporting and Changing Prices (1986), No. 89 (Stamford, CT: FASB), December.

Statement of Cash Flows (1987), No. 95 (Stamford, CT: FASB), November.
Accounting for Income Taxes (1987), No. 96 (Stamford, CT: FASB), December.
Reporting Comprehensive Income (1997), No. 130 (Norwalk, CT: FASB), June.

Financial Accounting Standards Board: Sundry

Criteria for Determining Materiality (1975), Discussion Memorandum (Stamford, CT: FASB), March 21.
Tentative Conclusions on Objectives of Financial Statements for Business Enterprises (1976) (Stamford, CT: FASB), December 2.
Supplementary Disclosures about the Effects of Changing Prices (1983), Invitation to Comment (Stamford, CT: FASB), December.

"Financial Reporting and Changing Prices" (1984), *Status Report* of the Financial Accounting Standards Board, No. 159, August 20: 1.
Gellein, Oscar S. (1986), "Financial Reporting: The State of Standard Setting," *Advances in Accounting*, Vol. 3: 3-23.
Gore, Pelham (1992), *The FASB Conceptual Framework Project 1973-1985: An Analysis* (Manchester: University of Manchester Press).
Grady, Paul (1965), *Inventory of Generally Accepted Accounting Principles for Business Enterprises* (New York: American Institute of Certified Public Accountants).
Henderson, Scott and Peirson, Graham (1983), *Financial Accounting Theory: Its Nature and Development* (Melbourne, Australia: Longman Cheshire Pty Limited).
Horngren, Charles T. (1981), "Uses and Limitations of a Conceptual Framework," *Journal of Accountancy*, Vol. 151, No. 4: 86, 88, 90, 92, 94-95.
Ijiri, Yuji (1980), *Recognition of Contractual Rights and Obligations: An Exploratory Study of Conceptual Issues* (Stamford, CT: FASB).
Jennings, Alvin R. (1958), "Present-Day Challenges in Financial Reporting," *Journal of Accountancy*, Vol. 105, No. 1: 28-34.
Johnson, L. Todd and Reither, Cheri L. (1995), "Reporting Comprehensive Income," *Status Report* of the Financial Accounting Standards Board, No. 270, November 28: 7-11.
Johnson, L. Todd and Storey, Reed K. (1982), *Recognition in Financial Statements: Underlying Concepts and Practical Conventions* (Stamford, CT: FASB).
Joyce, Edward J., Libby, Robert, and Sunder, Shyam (1982), "Using the FASB's Qualitative Characteristics in Accounting Policy Choices," *Journal of Accounting Research*, Vol. 20, No. 2, Pt. II: 654-675.
Kirk, Donald, J. (1986), "The Increasing Quest for Certainty in an Increasingly Uncertain World," *FASB Viewpoints*, December 23: 5-8.
Kirk, Donald J. (1988), "'Looking Back on Fourteen Years at the FASB: The Education of A Standard Setter,'" *Accounting Horizons*, Vol. 2, No. 1: 8-17.
Kirk, Donald J. (1989), "Reflections on a 'Reconceptualization of Accounting': A Commentary on Parts I-IV of Homer Kripke's Paper, 'Reflections on the FASB's Conceptual Framework for Accounting and on Auditing,'" *Journal of Accounting, Auditing & Finance*, Vol. 4, No. 1 (New Series): 83-105.
Lee, Tom (1996), *Income and Value Measurement* (London: International Thomson Business Press).
Macve, Richard (1997), *A Conceptual Framework for Financial Accounting and Reporting: Vision, Tool, or Threat?* (New York: Garland Publishing).

Miller, Paul B. W. (1990), "The Conceptual Framework as Reformation and Counterreformation," *Accounting Horizons*, Vol. 4, No. 2: 23-32.

Miller, Paul B. W. and Bahnson, Paul R. (1996), "Four Steps to Useful Present Values," *Journal of Accountancy*, Vol. 181, No. 5: 91-94. 96, 98.

Miller, Paul B. W., Redding, Rodney J., and Bahnson, Paul R. (1998), *The FASB: The People, the Process, and the Politics* (Burr Ridge, IL: Irwin/McGraw-Hill).

Moonitz, Maurice (1961), *The Basic Postulates of Accounting* (New York: American Institute of Certified Public Accountants).

Mosso, David (1998), "Developing and Adhering to a Conceptual Framework," *Status Report* of the Financial Accounting Standards Board, No. 305, September 30: 5-7.

Most, Kenneth S. (1993), *The Future of the Accounting Profession: A Global Perspective* (Westport, CT: Quorum Books).

Nelson, Carl L. (1973), "A Priori Research in Accounting," in Dopuch, Nicholas and Revsine, Lawrence (eds.), *Accounting Research 1960-1970: A Critical Evaluation* ([no place]: Center for International Education and Research in Accounting, University of Illinois): 3-19.

Objectives of Financial Statements (Trueblood report) (1973) (New York: American Institute of Certified Public Accountants).

Objectives of Financial Statements: Selected Papers (1974) (New York: American Institute of Certified Public Accountants).

Pacter, Paul A. (1983), "The Conceptual Framework: Make No Mystique about It," *Journal of Accountancy*, Vol. 156, No. 1: 76-78, 86-88.

Paton, William Andrew (1922), *Accounting Theory—With Special Reference to Corporate Enterprise* (New York: The Ronald Press Company).

Paton, W. A. and Littleton, A. C. (1940), *An Introduction to Corporate Accounting Standards* ([no place]: American Accounting Association).

Peasnell, K. V. (1982), "The Function of a Conceptual Framework for Corporate Financial Reporting," *Accounting and Business Research*, Vol. 12, No. 48: 243-256.

Proceeds, Revenue, Income, Profit, and Earnings (1955), Accounting Terminology Bulletin No. 2, in *Accounting Research and Terminology Bulletins, Final Edition* (New York: American Institute of Certified Public Accountants, 1961): 33-36.

Rappaport, Alfred (1977), "Economic Impact of Accounting Standards — Implications for the FASB," *Journal of Accountancy*, Vol. 143, No. 5: 89-90, 92, 94, 96-98.

Report to Council of the Special Committee on Research Program (1958), *Journal of Accountancy*, Vol. 106, No. 6: 62-68.

Revsine, Lawrence (1977), in *The Conceptual Framework of Accounting*, proceedings of a conference held on May 4, 1977 at the Wharton School, University of Pennsylvania ([place and publisher not given]).

Revsine, Lawrence (1991), "The Selective Financial Misrepresentation Hypothesis," *Accounting Horizons*, Vol. 5, No. 4: 16-27.

Sanders, Thomas H., Hatfield, Henry Rand, and Moore, Underhill (1938), *A Statement of Accounting Principles* (New York: American Institute of Accountants).

Sandilands Committee (1975), *Inflation Accounting: Report of the Inflation Accounting Committee*, F. E. P. Sandilands Esq., CBE, Chairman (London: Her Majesty's Stationery Office, Cmnd 6225).

Schuetze, Walter P. (1983), "The Significance and Development of the Conceptual Framework," *Journal of Accounting, Auditing & Finance*, Vol. 6, No. 3: 254-262.

Solomons, David (1978), "The Politicization of Accounting," *Journal of Accountancy*, Vol. 146, No. 5: 65-72.

Solomons, David (1986), "The FASB's Conceptual Framework: An Evaluation," *Journal of Accountancy*, Vol. 161, No. 6: 114-116, 118, 120-122, 124.

Sorter, George H. (1973), "Objectives of Financial Statements: An Inside View," *CAmagazine* (Canada), Vol. 103, No. 5: 30-33.

Spacek, Leonard (1957), "Professional Accountants and Their Public Responsibility," in *A Search for Fairness in Financial Reporting to the Public* (Chicago: Arthur Andersen & Co., 1969): 17-26.

Sprouse, Robert T. (1966), "Accounting for What-You-May-Call-Its," *Journal of Accountancy*, Vol. 122, No. 4: 45-53.

Sprouse, Robert T. (1977), in *The Conceptual Framework of Accounting*, proceedings of a conference held on May 4, 1977 at the Wharton School, University of Pennsylvania ([place and publisher not given]).

Sprouse, Robert T. (1984/85), "The Dynamics of Financial Accounting Standard Setting," *Jones Journal* (of the Jesse H. Jones Graduate School of Administration, Rice University), Fall/Winter: 21-29.

Sprouse, Robert T. (1988), "Financial Reporting," *Accounting Horizons*, Vol. 2, No. 4: 121-127.

Sprouse, Robert T. and Moonitz, Maurice (1962), *A Tentative Set of Broad Accounting Principles for Business Enterprises* (New York: American Institute of Certified Public Accountants).

Staubus, George J. (forthcoming), *Development of the Decision-Usefulness Theory of Accounting* (Hamden, CT: Garland Publishing).

Sterling, Robert R. (1967a), "A Statement of Basic Accounting Theory: A Review Article," *Journal of Accounting Research*, Vol. 5, No. 1: 95-112.

Sterling, Robert R. (1967b), "Conservatism: The Fundamental Principle of Valuation in Traditional Accounting," *Abacus*, Vol. 3, No. 2: 109-132.

Sterling, Robert R. (1982), "The Conceptual Framework: An Assessment," *Journal of Accountancy*, Vol. 154, No. 5: 103-106, 108.

Sterling, Robert R. and Lemke, Kenneth W. (eds.) (1982), *Maintenance of Capital: Financial Versus Physical* (Houston, TX: Scholars Book Co.).

Stevenson, Kevin M. (1987), "The Role of A Conceptual Framework," in *Standard Setting for Financial Reporting*, an international conference sponsored by the American Accounting Association with Klynveld Main Goerdeler ([no place]: Peat Marwick Main & Co.): 49-56.

Storey, Reed K. (1964), *The Search for Accounting Principles: Today's Problems in Perspective* (New York: American Institute of Certified Public Accountants).

Storey, Reed K. (1981), "Conditions Necessary for Developing a Conceptual Framework," *Journal of Accountancy*, Vol. 151, No. 6: 84, 86, 88, 90, 92, 94-96.

Storey, Reed K. and Storey, Sylvia (1998), *The Framework of Financial Accounting Concepts and Standards* (Norwalk, CT: FASB).

"Studies on Financial Accounting Objectives: 1974" (1974), *Journal of Accounting Research*, Vol. 12 (Supplement).

"Task Force Appointed to Study Conceptual Framework for Accounting and Reporting; Will Meet With Members of Trueblood Study Group" (1973), *Status Report* of the Financial Accounting Standards Board, No. 8, December 27: 1-2.

Tweedie, David and Whittington, Geoffrey (1984), *The Debate on Inflation Accounting* (Cambridge: Cambridge University Press).

Upton, Wayne S., Jr. (1996), *The FASB Project on Present Value Based Measurements, an Analysis of Deliberations and Techniques* (Norwalk, CT: FASB), February.

Van Riper, Robert (1994), *Setting Standards for Financial Reporting: FASB and the Struggle for Control of a Critical Process* (Westport, CT: Quorum Books).

Way, Alva O. (1977), in *The Conceptual Framework of Accounting*, proceedings of a conference held on May 4, 1977 at the Wharton School, University of Pennsylvania ([place and publisher not given]).

Wolk, Harry I., Francis, Jere R., and Tearney, Michael G. (1992), *Accounting Theory: A Conceptual and Institutional Approach* (Cincinnati, OH: South-Western Publishing Co.).

Wyatt, Arthur R. (1987), "The Role of A Conceptual Framework," in *Standard Setting for Financial Reporting*, an international conference sponsored by the American Accounting Association with Klynveld Main Goerdeler ([no place]: Peat Marwick Main & Co.): 44-48.

Wyatt, Arthur R. (1999), "Accounting Hall of Fame 1998 Induction: Response," *Accounting Historians Journal*, Vol. 26, No. 1: 158-163.

Zeff, Stephen A. (1972), *Forging Accounting Principles in Five Countries: A History and an Analysis of Trends* (Champaign, IL: Stipes Publishing Co.).

Zeff, Stephen A. (1984), "Some Junctures in the Evolution of the Process of Establishing Accounting Principles in the U.S.A.: 1917-1972," *Accounting Review*, Vol. 59, No. 3: 447-468.

Zeff, Stephen A. (2000), "John B. Canning: A View of His Academic Career," *Abacus*, Vol. 36, No. 1, forthcoming.

ABACUS, Vol. 36, No. 1, 2000

STEPHEN A. ZEFF

John B. Canning: A View of His Academic Career

Although his major published work on accounting spanned only four years, from 1929 to 1933, of his career as an economist, John B. Canning was author of a major treatise on accounting theory, *The Economics of Accountancy*. Yet little is known about his academic career, including when and why he became interested in accounting, and when and why his interest shifted to other subjects. The aim of this article is to endeavour to trace the impact of his book on later contributors to the accounting literature and to review his academic career, especially in relation to his work in accounting, drawing on interviews with former colleagues and students.

Key words: Accounting education; Accounting theory; History of thought.

John Bennet Canning[1] was a son of the U.S. Middle West, grew up in Michigan and Oklahoma, took bachelor's and doctor's degrees at the University of Chicago, was on the Stanford University economics faculty for twenty-seven years, and served as an economics expert to the U.S. government on food and agricultural problems.

Professional and social problems intrigued Canning. In the 1920s, he assiduously developed an elaborate accounting curriculum within the Stanford economics department with a view toward upgrading the public accounting profession. To Canning, mathematics, law and economics formed the base of a proper accounting education. In the 1930s and 1940s, he turned his attention to problems at the macro level: the government's fiscal policy, its programs of unemployment insurance, social security and health insurance, and eventually its agricultural policy.

Canning was not a prolific writer. He wrote one book and a dozen journal articles, of which five pertained to accounting.[2] His *magnum opus, The Economics of Accountancy: A Critical Analysis of Accounting Theory* (1929b), was primarily

---

[1] Canning's middle name was correctly spelled with one 't', although a few authors have written it as Bennett (e.g., Smith, 1974).

[2] A complete list of Canning's published work is appended to this article.

STEPHEN A. ZEFF is the Herbert S. Autrey Professor of Accounting, Rice University, Houston, Texas. I am grateful to Philip W. Bell, Maurice Moonitz, Ilia Dichev, Geoffrey Whittington, Dale L. Flesher, J. R. Edwards, Sidney Davidson, W. T. Baxter, Charles T. Horngren, Reed K. Storey, George J. Staubus, Ray Ball, and the editor and anonymous referees for comments and suggestions on earlier drafts, to William R. Smith for his file of correspondence and his unpublished paper on Canning, and to those who graciously acceded to interviews or responded to my letters and telephone calls. I am also grateful to the staff members of the Department of Special Collections, Stanford University Libraries, and of the Department of Special Collections, Regenstein Library, the University of Chicago. I am alone responsible for what remains.

4

intended to provide accountants with an understanding of economics that is relevant, indeed essential, to the theory and practice of accounting. Canning's book is regarded by many as one of the major works on accounting theory, and it was republished by Arno Press in 1978.

Most of the particulars contained herein have not previously been reported in the literature.[3] This research project began in 1964, when the author conducted interviews with Canning's widow and former colleagues in the Stanford University economics department, and corresponded with former students. In recent years, the author conducted further interviews and inquiries, and William R. Smith, who had communicated with some of Canning's former colleagues and students in the early 1970s, generously provided the author with his file of correspondence.

This article proposes to address the following questions: What was Canning's background and why did he become interested in accounting? What was his impact on the accounting literature, and how was he regarded by his students? Why did he largely withdraw from the accounting literature in the 1930s?

The article will begin by examining the impact of *The Economics of Accountancy* on subsequent theorists and other writers, and will proceed to review Canning's childhood and his undergraduate and graduate years at the University of Chicago, his single-handed effort to develop a fully-fledged accounting curriculum in the economics department at Stanford University (which was dismembered as soon as he retired), his manner as a teacher, the preparation and completion of his doctoral dissertation in mid-career, and the implications of his expanding interests in the 1930s and 1940s.

OVERVIEW OF CANNING'S IMPACT

Canning's impact on accounting thought is traceable almost entirely to *The Economics of Accountancy* rather than to his articles or to the work of his disciple, Edward G. Nelson.[4] In his book, Canning was, together with Paton (1922), the first to attempt development of a comprehensive accounting theory. Moreover, Canning was the first to develop and present a conceptual framework for asset valuation and measurement founded explicitly on future expectations. An emphasis on futurity has since come to be embraced by the American Institute of Certified Public Accountants' Study Group on the Objectives of Financial Statements (Study Group, 1973) and by leading national standard setters.[5] His emphasis on asset valuation, and thus on the balance sheet, has also become the dominant focus of

---

[3] Biographical data in a previous article on Canning (Gibson, 1993) are based on published materials. A brief profile of Canning (Smith, 1974) reflects the latter's correspondence with some of Canning's former colleagues and students.

[4] For three related examples of Nelson's influence, however, see Moonitz and Staehling (1950, p. 212), Storey (1960) and Sprouse and Moonitz (1962, p. 15). For more about Nelson, see note 26, *infra*.

[5] See, e.g., SFAC 1 of the Financial Accounting Standards Board (1978); Statement of Accounting Concepts (SAC) 2 of the Public Sector Accounting Standards Board and the Accounting Standards Review Board (1990), in Australia; and the U.K. Accounting Standards Board's revised exposure draft, *Statement of Principles for Financial Reporting* (1999).

5

the same leading standard setters, as well as of a number of important modern theorists, including R. J. Chambers (1966), W. T. Baxter (1971) and David Solomons (1995). At the very least, one can say that Canning was ahead of his time.

One-third of Canning's book consists of a critical analysis of accounting practice. As an outsider looking in, he was an insightful observer of the product of accountants, and he tried to make sense of what they did. (See also Canning, 1929a.) He was frustrated by their confusing terminology (1929b, pp. 92–4), their misguided use of 'conservatism' (pp. 194–5) and their 'astonishing lack of discussion of the nature of income' (p. 93). He ruefully concluded that 'what is set out as a measure of net income can never be supposed to be a fact in any sense at all except that it is the figure that results when the accountant has finished applying the procedure which he adopts' (pp. 98–9). He added that 'accountants have no complete philosophical system of thought about income; nor is there evidence that they have ever greatly felt the need for one' (p. 160).[6]

Yet Canning admired much of what accountants had achieved and was fully aware of the difficulty and importance of the task facing them (e.g., chaps VII, XII and XV). George O. May, a leading American accounting practitioner who was critical of Canning's characterization of accounting as essentially a process of valuation, nonetheless conceded that 'Professor Canning displays a sympathy with accountants and a knowledge and an appreciation of their work that is not common in other than purely professional writers' (Hunt, 1936, Vol. 2, p. 406; also p. 309).

Canning was the first to point out that the accountant's implied definition of assets omits 'those services arising from contracts the two sides of which are proportionately unperformed' (p. 22), an observation that has been cited by a number of authors, especially when the capitalization of long-term, non-cancelable leases began to be an important accounting issue in the 1960s.[7]

On the most ephemeral of balance-sheet items, goodwill, Canning wrote:

> Goodwill, when it appears in the balance sheet at all, is but a master valuation account—a catch-all into which is thrown both an unenumerated series of items that have the *economic*, though not necessarily the *legal*, properties of assets, and an undistributed list of undervaluations of those items listed as assets. It is the valuation account *par excellence*. (pp. 42–3)

Goodwill, he said, 'cannot under any circumstances be called an "asset"'. Instead, it properly belongs to the class of 'valuation accounts that are set out as adjuncts' to true asset accounts (p. 43). Canning's characterization of goodwill as 'a master valuation account' has also been frequently cited in the literature.[8]

---

[6] Both of these passages have been cited by later writers: for the first, see, e.g., Norris (1946, pp. 3, 115), Chambers (1955, p. 17; 1979, p. 767) and Solomons and Zeff (1996, p. xiii), which was drafted by Solomons; for the second, see, e.g., Vatter (1947, p. 76), Bedford (1965, pp. 71–2), Ball and Brown (1968, p. 160), Henderson and Peirson (1983, pp. 93–4) and Devine (1985, Vol. II, pp. 57, 135).

[7] See, e.g., Myers (1962, p. 5), Wojdak (1969, p. 563), Most (1977, p. 217) and Miller and Islam (1988, p. 17).

[8] See, e.g., Morrison (1956, chap. 19, p. 2), Hendriksen (1965, p. 348), Gynther (1969, p. 249), Most (1977, p. 241), Devine (1985, Vol. II, p. 92) and Miller and Islam (1988, p. 91).

6

Two-thirds of Canning's book is an argument for an improved measurement system for accounting, predicated on Irving Fisher's classic treatise, *The Nature of Capital and Income* (1906).[9] Chambers (1979) and Whittington (1980) have ably analysed and assessed Canning's theory, and no attempt will be made here to duplicate what they have done. According to Whittington, Canning's 'fundamental contribution to accounting thought' was his emphasis on the forward-looking valuation of assets (1980, p. 238). In today's jargon, he treated two aspects: definition and measurement. In regard to definition, he wrote: 'An asset is any future service in money or any future service convertible into money (except those services arising from contracts the two sides of which are proportionately unperformed) the beneficial interest in which is legally or equitably secured to some person or set of persons' (1929b, p. 22).

Measurement occupied much of Canning's attention (see Chambers, 1979). As an ideal, he favoured the 'direct valuation' of assets, that is, the discounted present value of what Fisher called 'realized [money] income'. He believed that this ideal could be applied to such assets as cash, receivables and finished goods inventory, for which 'a realized money income exists and is statistically determinable' (1929b, p. 207). In this respect, he departed from the emphasis placed on contemporary replacement costs or market values by Paton (1918, 1922) and Schmidt (1921) and soon to be advocated by Sweeney (1932) and MacNeal (1939).

With respect to other assets, Canning recommended 'indirect valuation': '(1) the present worth of future outlays necessary to obtain like services in like amounts by the *best available alternative means*, less (2) the present worth of future outlays necessary to obtain the agent's future service in the *most economical manner*' (p. 188). Whittington wrote that Canning's 'main contribution to valuation is the advocacy of the "opportunity difference" principle for indirect valuation, i.e. valuing the asset in terms of the minimum cost of replacing its services, on the assumption that the services are essential to business operations and that it is economically worthwhile to continue operating' (1980, p. 238).

These two important contributions, the explicit emphasis on futurity and the use of opportunity differences as a proxy for direct valuation, arguably influenced subsequent theorists. In their important 1940 monograph, *An Introduction to Corporation Accounting Standards*, Paton and Littleton also emphasized futurity. They argued that '"Service" is the significant element behind the accounts, that is, service-potentialities, which, when exchanged, bring still other service-potentialities into the enterprise' (p. 13). While Paton and Littleton did not cite previous authorities, Paton (as will be shown below) knew and admired Canning's book. But no more than a weak case can be made for actual influence.

Next in the chronological line were William J. Vatter, the originator of the 'fund theory of accounting' (1947), and George J. Staubus, a Vatter disciple. After citing Canning's 'future service' definition of an asset (Canning, 1929b, p. 22; quoted above) and Paton and Littleton's reference to 'service potentialities' (Paton and Littleton, 1940, p. 13), Staubus noted that 'It was William J. Vatter, however, who

---

[9] Chambers (1971) has written a retrospective review of Fisher's book.

7

set the pattern for modern definitions (1947, p. 17): "Assets are service potentials, not physical things, legal rights, or money claims". Service potential is now commonly accepted as the central characteristic of assets' (Staubus, 1977, p. 123).[10] In his influential doctoral thesis, completed in 1947, Vatter was much aware of Canning, and he evidently transmitted this appreciation to his own doctoral students. Two of his disciples, George H. Sorter and Charles T. Horngren (1962, p. 394, n. 9), quoted Canning's proposal for indirect valuation with favour. Another Vatter disciple, David Green, Jr. (1960), quoted Canning's definition of an asset and drew heavily on his indirect valuation when fashioning his own notion of 'cost obviation'. Staubus, an advocate of futurity, wrote in the published version of his doctoral dissertation, which was the first major articulation of the 'decision-usefulness theory of accounting', that 'this essay would never have been started if Paton, Canning, and Vatter (in chronological order) had not made their stimulating contributions to accounting theory' (1961, p. ix). Subsequently, Staubus drafted the policy recommendations in the first Australian study of objectives and concepts of financial statements (Kenley and Staubus, 1972) and served as the Financial Accounting Standards Board's director of research and technical activities in 1976–8, during the early development of the board's conceptual framework (see Gore, 1992, p. 112).[11]

For his part, Sorter served as an influential member of the American Accounting Association's committee[12] that prepared the path-breaking monograph, *A Statement of Basic Accounting Theory* (known as *ASOBAT*: AAA, 1966) and as research director of the AICPA's Study Group on the Objectives of Financial Statements. He played a major role in drafting the Study Group's report, *Objectives of Financial Statements* (1973), known as the Trueblood Report, which advocated the forward-looking orientation of financial statements, with a strong emphasis on estimating future cash flows.[13] The Trueblood Report, in turn, became the template for the FASB's SFAC 1, *Objectives of Financial Reporting by Business Enterprises* (1978). All three of these statements embodied the decision-usefulness approach. Sorter, who had earlier reviewed Staubus (1961), and characterized it as 'a stimulating work which presents a new approach to the purpose and structure of accounting theory' (1963, p. 223), played a role in advancing the cause of decision-usefulness in both *ASOBAT* and the Trueblood Report.

R. J. Chambers, whom Barton has described as 'one of the few giants of contemporary accounting thought' (1982, p. 128), has written that Canning's *Economics of*

---

[10] Horngren has written that Vatter's 'adoption of "service potential" as the key characteristic of an asset has been particularly influential' in the financial accounting literature (Horngren, 1991, p. 234).

[11] A more extensive treatment of Staubus' role in the evolution of the decision-usefulness theory literature may be found in his forthcoming book, *Development of the Decision-Usefulness Theory of Accounting*. For a further treatment of the evolution of the decision-usefulness approach, see AAA (1977, pp. 10–21).

[12] Telephone interview with Charles T. Zlatkovich, chairman of the committee, 3 April 1999.

[13] Telephone interview with Oscar S. Gellein, 19 March 1999. Gellein was a member of the Study Group.

8

Accountancy was an early influence in his own thinking (Chambers, 1979, pp. 764–5), and Whittington has observed that 'in some respects [Chambers is] an intellectual successor to Canning' (1980, p. 238).[14] Chambers' influence in Australia and overseas has been immense. In Australia, his exit price system was one of the alternative valuation approaches considered in the mid-1970s by the Australian Accounting Research Foundation (1975), and in 1978 Chambers chaired the Accounting Standards Review Committee which rendered a report on company accounting standards to the New South Wales government. Chambers' continuously contemporary accounting (CoCoA, as his system came to be known) was one of the three accounting methods studied in New Zealand's government- and private-sector-sponsored Inflation Accounting Research Project in the 1970s and was expressly considered in two government-sponsored inquiries: New Zealand's Richardson Report (*Report of the Committee of Inquiry into Inflation Accounting*, 1976) and the United Kingdom's Sandilands Report (Inflation Accounting Committee, 1975), as well as in the discussion paper, *Current Value Accounting*, published in 1976 by the Accounting Research Committee of the Canadian Institute of Chartered Accountants.

Maurice Moonitz and Robert T. Sprouse, two major figures in the U.S. literature and in U.S. standard setting, have also been touched by Canning. Through Charles C. Staehling, Canning had a considerable influence on Moonitz, Staehling's younger colleague at Berkeley[15] (Moonitz, 1984, pp. 2–3). This appreciation of Canning was shortly transmitted to Sprouse. In 1955, Sprouse joined the Berkeley faculty where, he later wrote, Moonitz 'was in fact my mentor' (1994, p. 156). For a textbook in his intermediate accounting classes, Sprouse used Moonitz and Staehling (1950), with its 'valuation experiment' derived explicitly from Canning's direct valuation model. Intrigued by this section of the book, he proceeded to study and become impressed with Canning's argument.[16] Canning's influence is well exemplified in Sprouse (1966, pp. 111–12). Of course, Moonitz and Sprouse have had an impact on others. In particular, Moonitz was the AICPA's director of accounting research in 1960–3 and served as a member of the Accounting Principles Board (APB) from 1963 to 1966, Moonitz and Sprouse wrote the monographs on accounting postulates and principles which the APB commissioned in 1960 (Moonitz, 1961; Sprouse and Moonitz, 1962), and Sprouse served on the FASB from 1973 to 1985 and played a major role in the development of the board's entire conceptual framework (see Gore, 1992, p. 113).

Oscar S. Gellein, a former accounting academic and research partner of Haskins & Sells (today part of Deloitte & Touche), has written of his high regard for Canning's book: 'Canning proceeded with great skill, and with considerable foresight of a growing need, to deduce the fundamentals underlying the accounting practices

---

[14] In Chambers' monumental *An Accounting Thesaurus: 500 Years of Accounting* (1995), no work is quoted more times than Canning's *Economics of Accountancy*.

[15] Interview with Maurice Moonitz, 19 April 1995. For evidence of this impact, see Moonitz and Staehling (1950, chaps 2 and 5–7) and Sprouse and Moonitz (1962, p. 15).

[16] Telephone interview with Sprouse, 1 October 1997.

9

of his day' (1981, p. 2–27). Gellein also had occasion to become familiar with Staubus' work on decision-usefulness accounting, for he served as discussant on Staubus' paper on 'The Relevance of Evidence of Cash Flows' at a research conference held in 1970 (Staubus, 1971). Gellein was an influential member of the Trueblood Study Group and served as well as on the FASB from 1975 to 1978, where he played an important role in shaping the board's conceptual framework (see Gore, 1992, p. 113).

In its treatment of 'opportunity differences', Canning's *Economics of Accountancy* influenced James C. Bonbright and F. K. Wright directly and others (e.g., W. T. Baxter and David Solomons) indirectly in the formulation of 'value to the owner', or 'deprival value', which has become one of the leading concepts underpinning the current valuation of assets (Whittington, 1980, pp. 237–39; Whittington, 1994, pp. 254, 259; Bonbright, 1937, esp. p. 227n.; Henderson and Peirson, 1983, p. 133; Wright, 1964, p. 82n.).[17] Solomons and Baxter have been the 'two main supporters' of deprival value (Ashton, 1987, p. 1).

Yet Carl T. Devine, one of the foremost accounting scholars, was moved to write: 'It still amazes me that Canning's major contribution to the accounting profession continues to be under-estimated generation after generation' (1985, Vol. V, p. 88n.). He said that Canning's 'rule for handling indirect valuations is certainly one of the best available' (1985, Vol. V, p. 88).

Canning's book was not mentioned by a number of important subsequent authors who have fashioned accounting theories or conceptual frameworks. He was not cited by Sweeney (1936), MacNeal (1939) or Alexander (1950), another economist who propounded a future-oriented valuation framework, nor by Edwards and Bell (1961). Solomons, who was actively involved in developing the statement on qualitative characteristics for the FASB's conceptual framework as well as with the evolving conceptual framework in the U.K., was much more impressed by Alexander than Canning (see, e.g., Solomons 1961).[18] Reed K. Storey, who had much to do with the research studies of the APB as well as with the FASB's conceptual framework (see Gore, 1992, p. 113), did not mention Canning in his two most important works on the subject (Storey, 1964; Storey and Storey, 1998). Yet, in his doctoral dissertation completed in 1958 (published in 1978), Storey, a Moonitz disciple, drew on Canning (1929b), Canning's disciple Nelson (1942), and Moonitz and Staehling (1950).

While virtually all citations to Canning's book have been non-negative, several major authors have taken issue with his analysis.[19] In particular, Ball and Brown

---

[17] In the 1930s, Canning's and Bonbright's books influenced Ronald S. Edwards, at the London School of Economics, who transmitted this influence in the 1940s to David Solomons, who was then a junior faculty member at LSE. Also in the 1930s, Bonbright's book influenced W. T. Baxter, who later coined the term 'deprival value'. (Letter to the author from Baxter, dated 23 October 1997.) See Baxter, 1967, pp. 212–13; 1971, chap. 4; and 1978, pp. 15–16 of the Preface. Also see the biographical essays on Baxter, Edwards and Solomons, as well as the editors' introductory notes, in Parker and Zeff (1996).

[18] Confirmed in conversations with Solomons.

[19] See Preinreich (1937), Bedford (1965, pp. 71–72), Ijiri (1967, p. 64n) and Chambers (1979).

10

(1968) reacted to Canning's conclusion that accounting income is meaningless, a mere consequence of an illogical set of procedures used in its calculation. Their well-known empirical work was designed to demonstrate that one important category of users—shareholders—do not find accounting income to be meaningless at all. Ball and Brown rejected the argument by Canning and others that the only meaningful accounting information could be current market values. They found that accounting income (and thus change in book value of equity) is correlated with change in the current market value of equity, as observed in the share market. Hence, they concluded, accounting income already impounds information about economic income.

Canning's influence cannot be detected in most of the tradition-encrusted textbook literature in accounting or in accounting practice, especially in the U.S.A.,[20] where the Securities and Exchange Commission (SEC) declared its unwavering support of historical cost accounting in the 1930s, a policy it did not seriously reconsider until the inflationary decade of the 1970s (see Walker, 1992). In the U.S.A., textbooks march to the tune of the Uniform Certified Public Accountants Examination, and the examination in turn is attuned to 'generally accepted accounting principles' as enforced by the SEC. Canning was, however, amply noticed by other reformers, by students of accounting theory and also by the early leaders of agency theory research (Watts and Zimmerman, 1979, p. 298). His book has been discussed, sometimes at length, in most treatises on accounting theory, and it was included amongst the thirteen most important writings in the classical genre of theory development by an American Accounting Association committee that comprehensively reviewed the literature in the mid-1970s (1977, Chap. 2).

Views on Canning's Contribution
Chambers (1979) was impressed by Canning's criticisms of accounting theory and practice and by the rigour he brought to his analysis. Whittington (1980, p. 237) said that Canning's book 'represented an important step forward in accounting thought and can still be read with benefit by those concerned with current developments in the subject'. Moonitz and Littleton (1965, p. 84) have written that Canning 'was primarily a statistician and economist who found accounting of interest because of the wealth of data it provides for analysis and evaluation. He is one of the first to observe that what accountants do is better than what they say about what they do—their actions are better than their explanations.'[21] Schumpeter regarded Canning's *Economics of Accountancy* as an 'important . . . response' to Irving Fisher's 'first step toward co-ordinating the economist's and the accountant's work' (1954, p. 945). Fisher himself wrote that 'It would not seem an exaggeration to say

---

[20] Indeed, Sterling (1970, p. 254) placed Canning in a 'fringe group' of theorists for 'their lack of impact on the practice of accounting and the textbook literature'.

[21] That Canning viewed accounting through the eyes of an economic statistician is often overlooked. Vatter (1961, pp. 589–90) has written, 'Canning's attempt to explain and systematize the philosophical basis of accounting in an economic world stressed the nature of accounting measurements as essentially statistical, even as related to valuation and the measurement of income'. Also see Mattessich (1964, pp. 248, 250).

11

that [Canning's book] marks an epoch in the two branches of knowledge to which it relates—economics and accountancy—and none the less because it is a border-line study rather than strictly within the domain of either branch' (1930b, p. 603). Preinreich wrote that Canning 'has done valuable work in defining direct and indirect valuation', but added that 'his thoughts are not always carried to their logical conclusion' (1937, p. 211).

Tweedie and Whittington viewed *The Economics of Accountancy* as 'a thorough critique of contemporary accounting practice [that] offered alternatives which were designed to bring the accountant's practices more in line with the economist's forward-looking methods of valuation' (1984, p. 25). Wheeler, in his essay, 'Economics and Accounting', regarded Canning's book as the 'outstanding attempt' to bridge the two fields (1955, p. 45).

This review provides considerable evidence that a number of the important theoretical developments during the latter half of the century owe much to Canning's direct and indirect influence. An impact on accounting practice, however, is much less discernible.

CANNING'S EARLY YEARS

Canning was born in Huron County, Michigan, near the border with Canada, on 25 November 1884, the first son of John and Cora Julia (Ford) Canning. His father, a Canadian, had come to the U.S.A. in 1881 and was a farmer.[22] In 1901, the Canning family moved to Oklahoma where, as the eldest of six children, John was expected to help his father on the family dairy farm, although it has been reported that he hated farming. At age eighteen, he took active charge of the farm. He received some academic instruction at home, but it was not until age twenty-one that he enrolled in Oklahoma City High School. During his spare time and summers, he continued to work on the family farm. He later reported that, in his six years' management, he increased the value of the farm threefold. The school offered a rigorous curriculum, which included four years of Latin. In his senior year, Canning was editor-in-chief of *The Student*, the monthly, student-run publication, and he played left tackle and fullback on the school's football team. He received his graduation diploma in May 1909.[23]

AT THE UNIVERSITY OF CHICAGO

In the fall of 1909, at the age of twenty-four, Canning matriculated at the University of Chicago. As he had developed a strong interest in football, the presence at

[22] Details about Canning's early life have been culled from a biographical entry ('Canning, John Bennet', 1968), from interviews with Dorothy P. (Mrs John B.) Canning, 5 December 1964, and with Thomas N. Canning (John B. Canning's youngest son), 16 October 1994, and from articles in *The Daily Palo Alto*, predecessor of *The Stanford Daily* ('John Bennett [sic] Canning Has Varied Interests', 1921; and 'Professor Canning Managed Family Dairy In Oklahoma Before Entering High School', 1923).

[23] 'Seventy Enter Higher School' (1909).

12

Chicago of Amos Alonzo Stagg, the most famous football coach in the country, may have drawn him there. At Chicago, he majored in political economy and took considerable work in French and German.[24] His further studies embraced mathematics, English language and literature, political science, sociology, anthropology, physiology and geography. He apparently considered studying law, but changed his mind.[25] He was supported financially by scholarships throughout his four undergraduate years, during which he played fullback on the freshman football team in 1909 and was a right guard on Stagg's varsity football teams of 1911 and 1912. In the spring of his senior year, Canning went out for the track and field team, also coached by Stagg, and succeeded in making the squad in the hammer throw.

During the spring quarter of his sophomore year, Canning took a course in accounting from Nathan C. Plimpton, who was then the university's chief accountant (and eventually became its comptroller). Edward G. Nelson, who studied under Canning in the late 1920s and became his close colleague and friend, recalls that Canning said it was Plimpton who got him to see that 'accounting was more than just bookkeeping'.[26] But there was also a practical reason for Canning's interest in accounting: he needed to earn his expenses, and Plimpton found him a job in which he was to help settle a large estate whose financial affairs were in disarray. That experience may have heightened his interest in accounting and valuation issues.

Two of Canning's best grades were in a pair of courses on distribution of wealth, taught by A. C. Whitaker, a visiting professor from Stanford University. Whitaker was impressed with Canning's intellect, and he was later to recommend that he be brought to Stanford.[27]

Following receipt in June 1913 of his Bachelor of Philosophy degree in arts and literature, with honours in political economy, Canning was awarded a scholarship for graduate study, and he entered Chicago's doctoral program in political economy. During the next four years, he took graduate courses in 'special research in insurance (both law and economics), accounting, statistics, industrial management, money and banking, value, distribution, history of economic thought, population, corporation finance, investments, and with some work in cognate fields such as commercial law, political science, sociology and mathematics'.[28] Of his four courses in accounting,

---

[24] Information on Canning's academic work was obtained from the Registrar, The University of Chicago, and was reported in a letter from Canning to Jacob Viner, dated 20 October 1928.

[25] Canning's forensic ability was recognized by his peers. In *The Cap and Gown* for 1913, the student yearbook, it was said of Canning: 'If you want some one to do your arguing for you, you could not get a more efficient artist' (p. 437).

[26] Interview with Edward G. Nelson, 8 June 1965. Nelson (1904–72) completed his doctorate under Canning in 1932 and served on the Stanford economics faculty from 1929 to 1932 (as assistant in instruction) and from 1932 to 1941 (as assistant professor), mainly teaching the introductory accounting courses. From 1945 onward, he was at the University of Kansas. Nelson was Canning's best-known disciple (see, e.g., Nelson's articles published in 1935 and 1942), and the two men and their wives remained friends until Canning's death.

[27] Interviews with A. C. Whitaker (1877–1965), 12 January 1965, and with Dorothy P. (Mrs John B.) Canning, 5 December 1964.

[28] Letter from Canning to Jacob Viner, dated 20 October 1928.

13

one was given by a visiting faculty member from the University of Illinois, John Christie Duncan; two courses, in intermediate and advanced accounting,[29] were from Jay Dunne (AB, University of Michigan); and the fourth was an accounting principles course taught by George E. Frazer, a practitioner. The courses taken from Duncan and Frazer were as a visiting student, without a grade.

Among Canning's political economy instructors were Robert F. Hoxie in economic history, J. Laurence Laughlin (the department's founder and head professor) in money and distribution of wealth, Chester W. Wright in trusts and corporation finance, and Lewis H. Haney in the theory of value. John Maurice Clark joined the Chicago faculty from Amherst College in 1915, Jacob Viner came as an instructor in 1916, and Frank H. Knight was an instructor at Chicago in 1916–17, and Canning came to know all three. By the time of Laughlin's retirement in 1916, 'Chicago had become widely recognized as one of the nation's leading centers of academic economics' (Coats, 1963, p. 491).

On 23 December 1915, Canning married Dorothy Helen Plumb (1894–1979), a University of Chicago classmate, in a wedding held in Oklahoma City. They had three sons: John Howard (1917–83), James Gilmore (1920–44), and Thomas Norman (1921–).

During his four years of graduate study, Canning was an assistant in the department in 1914–15 and was an instructor in the College of Commerce and Administration[30] in 1915–17, teaching courses in elementary economics, statistics, insurance, and corporation finance. (Canning's interest in sports did not disappear: during his first two graduate years 1913–14 and 1914–15, he was the assistant football coach under Stagg.) In 1917, evidently with some coursework yet to be taken, let alone the writing of a doctoral dissertation, he accepted Stanford's offer to become assistant professor of economics. Before he could take up the appointment, however, war intervened. He served in the U.S. Army for two years, becoming a major and spending several months in France. Following his discharge in September 1919, at age thirty-four, he joined the Stanford economics faculty.

FIRST DECADE AT STANFORD UNIVERSITY: 1919–29

Involvement in Varsity Athletics
Perhaps it was just as well that Canning's arrival at Stanford was delayed until 1919, for it was in that year that Stanford revived its varsity sport of American football after having abandoned it in 1906 (as had the University of California) for rugby football, which was regarded as the less dangerous of the two football games. From 1919 to 1921, Stanford employed only a few salaried coaches and experimented

[29] In U.S. universities during most of the century, the sequence of financial accounting courses in a curriculum has typically been labelled as elementary (introductory), intermediate and advanced, followed by 'theory'. These terms were coined in the 1910s and are mere place-holders. Intermediate and advanced accounting signify the second and third tiers, respectively, in a course of study. As will be shown below, Canning preferred a stricter meaning of 'advanced' in matters of curriculum and textbook titles.

[30] In 1916, the college became a school.

14

with a different head coach in each year, and Canning, the one-time right guard and assistant coach under the revered Amos Alonzo Stagg, gladly filled in as the varsity line coach during the three seasons. On 2 November 1921, he gave a talk on 'Straight Football, Line Plays' as part of a university lecture series on 'The Technique of American Football', which was reported in the student newspaper to have been '[t]he best lecture Professor Canning has ever given'.[31] It was said, however, that Murray Shipley Wildman (1868–1930), the chairman of the economics department, did not look favourably on Canning's use of his afternoons on the football field, which may have hurt his case for promotion.[32] For many years, Canning also served as an official at Stanford track meets, as a timer for the races and as a judge for the high jump.[33]

Development of an Accounting Curriculum
In the Stanford economics department of that day, a faculty member had great freedom to choose the courses he wished to offer.[34] In 1919–20, the department had only seven faculty members: Wildman (money and banking), Walter Greenwood Beach (sociology and labour economics), and A. C. Whitaker (corporation finance and foreign exchange), the full professors; Eliot Jones (railway and water transportation), the associate professor; Canning, the assistant professor; and two instructors. The departmental offerings were heavily focused on applied issues. Indeed, beginning in the *Register for 1920–21*, it was stated that, 'The courses offered in this department are not confined to the subject of Economics as properly defined, but include a number of topics often given in departments of sociology and schools of commerce' (p. 138). It was not until 1925 that Stanford launched its Graduate School of Business. The economics department was chiefly concerned with undergraduates.

In his first year in the department, Canning offered quarter-length courses in Elementary Accounting, Introduction to Statistics, Insurance, Intermediate Accounting, Business Administration, and Advanced Accounting.[35] The course description for Intermediate Accounting was as follows:

[31] 'Coach Canning Gives Analysis of Play on Line' (1921). Also see 'Canning to Give Football Lecture' (1921).

[32] Interview with Eliot Jones (1887–1971), 12 January 1965. Having once been a poor farm boy, Canning favoured athletics much more than most other faculty members.

[33] Canning judged the propriety of each jumper's technique and measured the precise height of the bar. He did not rely on a tape measure, but, as if he were an engineer, he verified the angles as well. Interviews with Edward G. Nelson, 8 June 1965, and with Burrel Leonard, 20 April 1995, and a letter from Thomas N. Canning to the author, dated 8 December 1994. (Leonard was a student of Canning's and was tapped by him to teach accounting systems and taxation in the Stanford economics department.) Maurice Moonitz recalls seeing Canning, probably in the 1930s, 'as an official at a California–Stanford track meet. He took his task very seriously, and kept the boys in line at the starting blocks.' Letter from Moonitz to William R. Smith, dated 2 April 1971.

[34] Interview with A. C. Whitaker, 12 January 1965.

[35] Unlike other accounting teachers, Canning used the term 'advanced' to describe the character of what was to be covered in a course. In a later review of a book entitled *Advanced Accounting*, he complained that 'None of the book is advanced in the sense of showing avenues to the professional literature or of opening vistas to the future advancement of knowledge' (1942, p. 312).

15

The principles of accounting common to all systems of accounts in acquisitive enterprise, developed by discussion of the information needed by the various interested persons, e.g., the stockholder, the director, the manager, the creditor, etc. Problems illustrative of theory of accountancy and problems of interpreting financial statements constitute a major portion of the work. (*Register for 1919–20*, p. 137)

From the beginning, as was evident from the description for his Advanced Accounting course, Canning was interested in two kinds of students: '(1) those who intend to become professional accountants; [and] (2) those who have chosen a future occupation and desire a knowledge of its accounting problems' (*Register for 1919–20*, p. 138). He saw one of his missions as being the attraction of qualified candidates to the public accounting profession, and from 1921 to 1929 he served as an examiner for the California State Board of Accountancy.[36]

In the intersessions (i.e., the short term between the spring semester and summer session) of 1920 and 1921, Canning had taught at the University of California at Berkeley, where he came to know Henry Rand Hatfield (the professor of accounting) and, through Hatfield, probably also John F. Forbes, a prominent San Francisco practitioner who had been giving courses in auditing and cost accounting at Berkeley since 1913. Forbes was a progressive and activist member of the State Board of Accountancy: he was a member of the State Board from 1909 to 1951, and he was its president from 1914 to 1945.[37] Hatfield and Forbes had appointed themselves as 'an unofficial committee of two' to do something about the low standard of the accounting profession in California (Forbes, 1944, p. 135; Moonitz, 1986, p. 13). It seems likely that they had much to do with inspiring Canning to become an examiner for the State Board and develop a program of accounting courses at Stanford to elevate the quality of entrants into the profession, as Hatfield was doing at Berkeley.

Steadily, Canning built a complete accounting curriculum within the economics department, with courses introduced in the following years:

1921–2   Accountancy of Industrial Management (dropped after one year)
          Interpretation of Accounting Reports ('A discussion of the balance sheet and of the income and expense statement from the points of view of the commercial creditor (chiefly the banker) and of the bondholder', *Register for 1921–22*, p. 145)
          Seminar in Accountancy
          Introduction to Auditing

[36] Canning's standards proved to be too idiosyncratic for the state board. The board was under pressure to pass more men, and it was felt that California should grade its own papers, and not rely solely on the grading system supplied by the American Institute of Accountants (AIA). Thus, Canning graded the candidates' papers on behalf of the board. But Canning's views on what were correct answers were not shared by several leading practitioners. Umpires were required to arbitrate the many differences between the solutions approved by the AIA and those acceptable to Canning. Two of the umpires, Scott Dunham and De Witt Alexander, who were San Francisco practitioners, tended to pass candidates who had been passed by the AIA and fail candidates whom Canning would have passed. In the event, Canning was fired. Interview with DeWitt Alexander, 11 December 1964.

[37] Information supplied by the Board of Accountancy of the State of California. Also see Cashion (1984, p. 5).

16

1922–3   Federal Tax Procedure
1923–4   Introduction to Cost Accounting (to become Cost Analysis in 1926–7)
1924–5   Special Work in Accounting (dropped after one year)
1925–6   Accounting Problems ('Methods appropriate for recording and reporting
         divers [*sic*] classes of transaction to which anyone is likely to be a party but
         which constitute the principal business of few persons. Such transactions
         as those between corporation and underwriter, principal and broker,
         bankrupt and referee and trustee in bankruptcy, trustee and beneficiary,
         insurer and insured (following a loss), etc., will be discussed. Liberal use
         will be made of problems set in recent examinations for Certified Public
         Accountants', *Register for 1925–26*, p. 189)
         Elementary Theory of Accounts (dropped after one year)
         Accounting Reports (an additional course under that title)
         Consolidated Reports

In 1922–3, after Whitaker stopped offering the Valuation course, Canning took
over its contents under the heading of Advanced Accounting, with the following
description:

> The valuation of fixed assets of private enterprises, and the distribution among accounting
> periods of costs and losses incurred in connection with investment in fixed assets. Special
> emphasis will be given to valuation for purposes of purchase and sale of a business, and
> purposes of corporate combination or reorganization. (*Register for 1922–23*, p. 164)

Canning gradually spun off several of the lower level courses to assistants in
instruction, but he retained Advanced Accounting, Accounting Reports, and the
Seminar for himself.[38]

In 1925, at the end of his sixth year at Stanford, Canning was promoted to associate
professor, and in the following year he installed a Division of Accountancy in the
economics department. It offered a four-year course of studies leading to the degree
of Bachelor of Arts in Economics and Accountancy, which could be followed by
a fifth year of studies culminating in the degree of Master of Arts in Economics
and Accountancy. (Such a degree title, combining economics and accountancy, was
probably without precedent in the U.S.A.) Canning's program contemplated five
years of university study for aspiring public accountants. 'He felt that the profession
wasn't demanding enough of its members, and that no-one really could prepare
himself adequately as a professional accountant in four years of college'.[39]

Canning noted that:

---

[38]   In 1926–7, Valuation reappeared, taught by Canning, and Advanced Accounting disappeared from
the *Register*. Perhaps a matter of turf was at issue. It may be that Canning's promotion in 1925
strengthened his claim to the Valuation course.

[39]   Interview with Edward G. Nelson, 8 June 1965. Canning's belief that five years of university study
should be expected of those who would become professional accountants anticipated by more than
four decades the policy adopted in 1969 by Council of the American Institute of Certified Public
Accountants that at least five years of university study should be the standard education requirement for Certified Public Accountants. Since then, forty-five states, the District of Columbia, Guam
and Puerto Rico have approved laws or regulations requiring 150 semester hours (i.e., five years) of
study for future CPAs.

17

The present stage of university training for accountancy . . . is still far from satisfactory. To judge by published curricula, relatively too much emphasis is given to routine account-ing procedure and too little to the substantive problems with which the student will have to deal as a principal when he is ten years out of school. Too little attention seems to be given also to training in those fundamental subjects that, in the academic world at least, are often supposed to lie quite outside the subject of accountancy.

Professional curricula that include as required work enough mathematics to enable the student to read critically the best of modern statistical publications are seldom found. Very few appreciate the fact that the subject matter with which the accountant deals bristles with unsolved, and largely undiscerned, problems that require for their solution a better foundation in mathematics than any but few accountants possess. (1929b, p. 329)

He also wrote that: 'To judge both by the writings and by the procedure of accountants, one must conclude that a fuller knowledge of law would often lead to material betterments in their classifications and valuations, and would also cause them to be more cautious about unqualified certification' (1929b, pp. 329–30). Some years later, Canning gave voice to his complaint of the rudimentary know-ledge of accounting possessed by practical people and even by accountants:

Accountancy has been called the language of enterprise. If it is, most business men, engineers, and economists are illiterate in that language. Some confess that accounting is a mystery to them; many others profess a knowledge of the subject but are none the less ignorant of it. Many others, including some accountants, know a great deal *of* accounting, in the way in which an assiduously trained parrot may know a great deal of English, without knowing much *about* accounting. (1933b, p. 65)

The program of studies in the Division of Accountancy reflected Canning's view that the study of accounting should be structured on the three pillars of mathem-atics, law and economics[40]:

Nature and Purpose.—The Division of Accountancy is created to administer a profes-sional training course in Accountancy. The course attempts to organize the existing facili-ties of instruction in the University in such a way that the body of knowledge necessary to the competent practice of accounting can be most readily acquired. That body of know-ledge includes: (1) a sound foundation in general mathematics and statistical method; (2) a ready and full command of certain commercial branches of private law; and (3) a real understanding of the conduct of men in their business relations and of the public problems arising from economic behavior. To this substantive knowledge must be added modes of procedure adequate for the highly specialized statistical work that constitutes the principal work of the accountants' calling. (*Register for 1926–27*, p. 346)

The first and second years' studies included Elements of Accounts (expanded from one to two quarters, with a concomitant dropping of Intermediate Accounting), Cost Analysis, Elementary Economics, Introduction to Political Science, and three

---

[40] Canning traced his early belief in the importance of studying economic theory to 'an extemporan-eous address [by Professor David Friday] to a class in elementary accounting of which I was a member [in which] he said in effect that the professional public accountant can lay no more secure foundation for the theory and practice of his profession than by acquiring a thorough familiarity with general economic theory' (1929a, p. 1). Friday (1876–1945), who was on the University of Michigan economics faculty, had been one of William A. Paton's teachers. As will be seen below, in this same article (1929a) Canning seriously questioned his article of faith that traditional economic theory was useful to the professional accountant.

18

to four courses in mathematics and statistical method. In the third year, students would take courses in Public Finance, Taxation, Corporation Finance, Accountancy of Investment (a course that Whitaker had been teaching for some years and which, one supposes, was modelled on Charles E. Sprague's book of the same name), Valuation, Federal Tax Procedure, Money and Banking, and Foreign Exchange. When, in the spring quarter of 1927, Canning revived the Valuation course once taught by Whitaker, he gave it the following description:

> The valuation of operating assets, of the liabilities, and of the proprietary interests in private enterprises; the relating of anticipated outlay costs of operation to the problem of present valuation. Emphasis is given to the theories of depreciation, depletion, and obsolescence of assets, and to the valuation of goodwill. (*Register for 1926–27*, p. 343)[41]

Fourth-year courses included Principles of Economics, Public Utilities, Auditing, Capital and Income, and either Business Law or Contracts and Agency. The course with the intriguing title, Capital and Income, was offered for the first time in the spring quarter of 1927 and was, of course, taught by Canning. The course description was as follows: 'A critical review of the economists', the lawyers', and the accountants' views of the nature of capital and income. Based on Irving Fisher's *The Nature of Capital and Income*' (p. 344).

In the master's year, the students' program would include (a) four courses in the law school curriculum (Bills and Notes, Bankruptcy, Private Corporations, and Municipal Corporations) and (b) any advanced accounting courses not already taken. Applicants for the degree were also expected to take an oral examination and submit a 'creditable thesis' (pp. 344–5). While it was reported that, in 1926, 'at least sixty [colleges and universities] accept accounting as a major towards a bachelor's degree and thirty allow it as a major for a master's degree' (Allen, 1927, p. 163), Stanford's broad interdisciplinary base was unique.

Also in 1926–7, the two Accounting Reports courses were retitled and restructured, one focusing on financial issues and the other on internal management, with the following descriptions:

> **Financial Reports.**—A discussion of the character of reports necessary to a proper control of the finances of private enterprises; corporate issues; dividend policy; borrower-depositor relations with banks; trade credit policy; etc. The statistical analysis of financial statements will be the mode of procedure.
> **Operating Reports.**—A discussion of the character of reports essential to the proper management of a concern with respect to internal operations; particularly the problems of inventories, of manufacturing and of purchasing, of labor turnover, and of budgetary control. (*Register for 1926–27*, p. 345)

By 1927–9, Canning was himself offering Cost Analysis, Valuation, Capital and Income, Accounting Problems, Financial Reports, and the Seminar in Accounting. One could easily appreciate how this ambitious teaching program would distract Canning from the timely completion of his doctoral thesis. (See below for a discussion of Canning's thesis work.)

---

[41]   In 1931, the Valuation course was expanded to cover two quarters, and, beginning in 1933, Canning imposed a calculus prerequisite on students taking the course.

19

Jackson and Robbins become accounting instructors

J. Hugh Jackson (1891–1962), who had joined the fledgling Graduate School of Business in 1926 from the Harvard Business School,[42] offered a new course, Auditing and Accounting Procedure, in the spring quarter of 1927. Jackson, who held a Harvard MBA and was (unlike Canning) a CPA, was a protégé of George O. May's and had spent several years at Price, Waterhouse & Co. in New York, giving instruction to younger staff and conducting research. In 1923, he published a book entitled *Audit Working Papers: Their Preparation and Content.* He was an active member of the American Association of University Instructors in Accounting (AAUIA), predecessor of the American Accounting Association. From 1924 to 1927 he was the association's vice-president, and in 1928–9 he served as its president.

Jackson, the practical man with an ambition to run organizations, and Canning, the rigorous theorist and a loner, were not easy colleagues.[43] As Canning saw it, Jackson was interested in the accounting process, while Canning was interested in why accounting functions as it does.[44] One departmental colleague said that Canning was 'very much the intellectual, and Jackson wasn't'.[45] Among other things, Canning and Jackson disagreed on the suitability of topics for accounting doctoral dissertations.

Carl B. Robbins (1902–74), who had received his AB, AM and PhD degrees from Stanford, joined the department as an instructor in 1927 immediately after completing an MBA at the Harvard Business School, and he gradually began to help out with some of the accounting courses. Robbins had completed a master's thesis under Canning's direction on the problem of par value, which he expanded into a book on no-par stock (1927), which in turn was accepted as his PhD dissertation in 1928. He offered Federal Tax Procedure and Operating Reports, and in 1929 he gave a new course, Elements of Cost Accounting. Robbins, who remained on the economics faculty until 1933, having risen to the rank of

---

[42] Jackson's initial appointment at Stanford was as a visiting professor from Harvard, on whose faculty he had been serving since 1923. After the year as visitor, he resigned from Harvard to remain at Stanford. From 1931 to 1956, he was dean of the Graduate School of Business. In 1931–2, Edward G. Nelson began offering the Auditing and Accounting Procedure course, as Jackson no longer had the time.

[43] Canning had little regard for the Graduate School of Business. In his view, the school was giving Stanford's financially well-off students a 'cram course' in what they would have studied as undergraduates in Canning's AB program, with the addition of two years and the concomitant expense. Interview with Burrel Leonard, 20 April 1995. (For a history of the early years of the Graduate School of Business, where it is stated that 'Stanford's economics faculty remained indifferent' toward the School at the time of its founding (p. 23), see Gleeson *et al.*, 1993, pp. 23–30, 34–5.)

[44] Interview with Thomas N. Canning, 16 October 1994.

[45] Interview with Edward S. Shaw, 7 December 1964. Shaw (1908–94) was a student of Canning's who joined the economics faculty in 1929, and for three years taught elementary accounting until, at Bernard F. Haley's suggestion, he turned his attention to money and banking, a field in which he built a large reputation. (Murray S. Wildman, who died in December 1930, had been the department's specialist in money and banking.) Interview with Edward G. Nelson, 8 June 1965.

20

associate professor in 1930, became the closest to Canning of any departmental colleague. Canning later said that he regarded Robbins as the ablest of his former students.[46]

The establishment of a Division of Accountancy within the economics department was, according to Nelson, viewed with ambivalence by Canning's colleagues. On the one hand, they admired his intellect, Whitaker above all. But, on the other, most of the faculty felt that the only accounting knowledge one needed in economics was a bit of bookkeeping, mainly to understand money and banking and business cycles.[47] Some of the economics faculty, it was said, were 'tiring' of all of Canning's accounting courses, even though they respected his judgment.[48] At that time, Stanford could not make up its mind whether the training to become a CPA belonged in the economics department or in the Graduate School of Business.[49] As Nelson wrote:

> Canning didn't have many supporters in the economics department. Accounting was not a reputable subject for academic study among the Stanford economists during the 1930s. It was taught in the economics department as a service to undergraduates, to support the study of money and banking, and in deference to Canning.[50]

Yet, in the minds of some members of the department, two factors weighed in favour of the Division of Accountancy: that it had been developed step-by-step, and not all at once; and that, while the enrolment in upper level accounting classes was small, it was composed of some of the best students in the department.

Canning as a Teacher

Canning was anything but a dramatic teacher. He talked slowly, carefully choosing his words, and developing his thoughts as he proceeded, as often as not with his back toward the class. He was not interested in whatever textbook he was using, but in applying theories of capital and price so that accounting information would yield a more rational basis for business decisions. It was said that he was often difficult to follow in the classroom, but that his best students, their intellects challenged, would seek him out for a better understanding of his ideas. He would give any amount of time to students in individual discussion, which, together with the considerable effort he would invest in the work of committees, were said to be

[16]   Letter from Canning to Irving Fisher, dated 2 November 1940.

[17]   Interview with Edward G. Nelson, 8 June 1965. Canning was hardly alone among those who taught accounting courses in American universities to be viewed with a jaundiced eye by their colleagues in economics and other discipline departments. The motivation behind Henry Rand Hatfield's famous variation on an *apologia pro vita sua*, 'An Historical Defense of Bookkeeping' (1924), was the 'implied contempt of our colleagues, who look upon accounting as an intruder, a Saul among the prophets, a pariah whose very presence detracts somewhat from the sanctity of the academic halls' (p. 241).

[48]   Interview with Eliot Jones, 12 January 1965.

[49]   Interview with Edward G. Nelson, 8 June 1965.

[50]   Letter from Edward G. Nelson to William R. Smith, dated 19 April 1971.

21

reasons why progress on his Chicago dissertation was delayed.[51] Canning would take a keen interest in his students' careers. He helped many of them find jobs, and he encouraged them to work in accounting. It was said that 'he was extraordinarily kind toward his protégés'.[52] Two of his disciples, Robbins and Nelson, stayed on to teach in the accounting program.

As Bernard F. Haley described it, the program in accounting 'was essentially a one-man show'.[53] Roy W. Jastram, who joined the economics faculty in 1936, said that nobody in the department 'gave a damn' about accounting, but they respected Canning a great deal.[54] No-one who taught in the accounting program, other than Canning, Robbins and Jackson (whose principal appointment was in the Graduate School of Business), rose above the level of assistant professor. It was said that the economics department was highly selective in making appointments to full professor, and that the salary structure was especially ungenerous at the lower levels.[55]

Walter B. McFarland, who took advanced work under Canning in the 1930s and completed his dissertation under Canning's guidance, wrote:

> Since I had reached a more mature age as a doctoral candidate, I found Professor Canning's courses to be stimulating and filled with new ideas. The undergraduates generally found them dull. No problems or paper work were assigned and the only examination was the final. Professor Canning explained the absence of problems to some of his students by saying that the only aspects of accounting definite enough to make good problems were not important enough to occupy the student's time.[56]

Robert D. Calkins, who took an AM at Stanford, became attracted to Canning in a course taken in the latter 1920s 'when I was much impressed with his approach to accounting and his tributes to Irving Fisher, who was being pooh-poohed by most economists as a nut with mathematical ability. A seminar convinced me that Canning had much to offer.' Calkins added:

> Canning was a man of complete integrity, with no trace of vanity or pompousness, and with no discernible interest in honors or ceremony. He dressed in tweedy fashion, he

---

[51] Interviews with Edward S. Shaw, 7 December 1964; with Bernard F. Haley, 5 January 1965; with Eliot Jones, 12 January 1965; and with Eugene L. Grant, 12 January 1965. Haley (1898–1993), who joined the economics faculty in 1924, had received AB and AM degree from Stanford in 1922 and 1923, respectively, during which he took Canning's insurance course. Grant (1897–1996), who came to Stanford in 1930 on the civil engineering faculty and later established a pioneering curriculum in engineering economics, sat in on Canning's Valuation course. It was said that Canning could work best with the students in the top 10 or 20 per cent of his upper-level classes. Interview with Edward G. Nelson, 8 June 1965.

[52] Interview with Edward S. Shaw, 7 December 1964.

[53] Interview with Bernard F. Haley, 5 January 1965.

[54] Interview with Roy W. Jastram, 18 January 1965.

[55] Interview with Edward G. Nelson, 8 June 1965.

[56] Letter from Walter B. McFarland to the author, dated 15 July 1965. Canning was an influential adviser on McFarland's doctoral dissertation, which was chaired by J. Hugh Jackson. McFarland (1908–83) joined the research staff of the National Association of Cost Accountants in 1946 and managed its research activity from the mid-1950s to the early 1970s, when he retired.

22

liked bridge and social engagements with interested friends, but shunned the limelight ... He gravitated to persons with challenging ideas, whose intellectual powers he could respect.[57]

Edward S. Shaw, a Stanford economics colleague who had a deep admiration for Canning, wrote,

As a student of his, mainly but not entirely at the undergraduate level, and as a friend, I found him a fine, charming and brilliant person. There was little in Economics west of Chicago to compare with him in professional skill.

Canning felt his intellectual debt to Fisher in so far as the theory of capital is concerned. He understood the potentialities of statistics and econometrics for economics and so established a close relationship here with Harold Hotelling and Holbrook Working. His concern in agricultural economics [which began to build in the 1930s] was deep, and he maintained it through friendship with Henry Schulz, Joseph Davis and Merrill Bennett at Stanford and people at the Giannini Foundation of the University of California.[58]

Even though one former student said that 'Canning was regarded by students, with little justification, as a tough teacher',[59] one of his doctoral students once said, 'Canning gave a mid-term, and the class average, as usual, was zero'.[60] Another of his students was overheard as saying that Canning was 'fantastically smart and a tough S.O.B.'[61]

Canning maintained a remoteness and a certain formality in academic and professional settings, but he could relax, enjoy stories, and play an expert hand of bridge at social gatherings. He was one of about fifteen Stanford faculty members and townspeople who belonged to a discussion group known as the Saturday Morning Club. The meetings would begin on Friday evening and continue into Saturday morning. Papers were presented and the discussion was wide-ranging. Canning's interests were broad, and he was a member of a number of interdisciplinary discussion groups over the years.[62]

Progress on His Chicago Doctorate
During his first decade at Stanford, Canning invested an enormous amount of time and creative energy in the development of the department's ambitious accounting

[57] Letter from Robert D. Calkins to the author, dated 4 October 1965. In 1929–30, Calkins (1903–92) was an assistant in instruction and taught Elements of Accounts. After leaving Stanford, he obtained a PhD from the College of William and Mary and eventually become became dean of the business schools at the University of California at Berkeley and at Columbia University and then served as president of The Brookings Institution.

[58] Letter from Edward S. Shaw to William R. Smith, dated 19 April 1971.

[59] Letter from Armen A. Alchian to William R. Smith, dated 1 May 1971. Alchian (1914–) received his AB from Stanford in 1936 and then enrolled in the PhD program.

[60] Letter from Maurice Moonitz to the author, dated 23 December 1994. Moonitz (1910–) taught accounting on the Stanford economics faculty from 1942 to 1944, while Canning was on leave. Moonitz never met Canning.

[61] Letter from Thomas N. Canning to the author, dated 8 December 1994.

[62] Interview with Joseph S. Davis (1885–1975), 28 June 1965. Davis was director of Stanford's Food Research Institute from 1921 to 1952.

23

program, and, until the arrival of Jackson in 1926 and Robbins in 1927, he and a rotating corps of assistants in instruction had offered all of the courses. Progress on his Chicago doctorate was steady but slow. During 1920–2, he took nine graduate courses at Stanford, several of which were applied to his Chicago degree. Three of the courses were in the law school: Municipal Corporations, Bills and Notes, and Private Corporations. Others were a course in the history of political theory, a reading course in German, an economics course intended for teachers of commercial subjects, a graduate seminar in the research problems of valuation, and, importantly, a pair of courses on recent economic theory and the economics of overhead costs (with grades of A and A+, respectively) given by John Maurice Clark, who was at Stanford in 1922–3, on leave from Chicago.[63] Clark's seminal *Studies in the Economics of Overhead Costs* was published in 1923.

During the summer quarter of 1924, when Canning was visiting as an assistant professor there, the Chicago economics department (probably much influenced by Clark) exempted him from the written examinations for the doctorate. In 1927, Chicago gave him credit for passing the two foreign-language examinations based on confirmations received from Stanford's departments of French and Germanics. Hence, the only remaining requirements for the degree were the dissertation and the oral examination.

The topic Canning chose for the dissertation was a critical analysis of accounting practice and the development of a model to base accountants' measurements on sound economic reasoning. As a statistical economist, he was intrigued by the wealth of empirical data provided by accounting. As he systematically constructed his accounting curriculum during the 1920s and offered an increasing number of the courses, Canning would have acquired a precious insight into the literature on accounting orthodoxy for the first part of his thesis. As noted above, the second part was profoundly influenced by Irving Fisher's *Nature of Capital and Income* (1906).

Finally, in a letter dated 20 October 1928 to Jacob Viner at Chicago, Canning submitted his 'book' (since it had already been accepted for publication by The Ronald Press Company) as his doctoral dissertation and inquired whether he could take his oral examination over the Christmas holidays, as he was coming east to read a paper at the annual meeting of the AAUIA, to be held on 27–8 December in Chicago.[64] Canning recounted the history of his book, which was to carry the title *The Economics of Accountancy: A Critical Analysis of Accounting Theory*

---

[63] Information was supplied by the Office of the Registrar, Stanford University, and is also based on the letter from Canning to Jacob Viner, dated 20 October 1928. Viner (1892–1970) was on the University of Chicago economics faculty throughout the 1920s.

[64] Canning became a member of the AAUIA in 1926. (Letter from Dorothy P. [Mrs John B.] Canning to the author, dated 28 February 1965.) J. Hugh Jackson, who joined the Stanford faculty in 1926 and was active in the AAUIA, may have played a part in Canning's decision to join, although it seems more likely that the impetus came from William A. Paton or Henry Rand Hatfield. The paper Canning read at the AAUIA annual meeting was 'Some Divergences of Accounting Theory from Economic Theory' (1929a), in which he contrasted the perspectives and approaches of the economist with those of the professional accountant (see below for further discussion of this article).

24

(1929b), and in his letter the pangs of authorship were everywhere evident. Canning was one who demanded precision in his writing.[65] He wrote to Viner as follows:

> The reading and research specifically underlying the book began in 1920. When J. M. Clark was at Stanford for a year I discussed my plans with him at some length. In the summer of 1924 when I was at Chicago, he read some 300 pages of a rough draft manuscript. In conference with him and in his written notes, he expressed a general approval. He also gave me many constructive suggestions with respect to the then contemplated writing. Later in the year I did rewrite it—with the usual multitude of alterations. I decided then to let the ms. 'rest' for a few months. After that 'mulling period' I decided that, whether it was acceptable to the [Chicago] Department or not, I could not give it my own approval. I therefore scrapped the entire writing and continued my studies with, I think, good effect. The present writing, though upon the same subject considered from nearly the same point of view as that which I discussed with Clark, is so very different in form, organization, and content that I should like to have it considered as though no preliminary writing had been submitted. Clark's going to Columbia [in 1926] makes that necessary anyway, I should suppose. Moreover, the audience addressed is a different one; and the book is to be published.

Further along in Canning's letter, the Yale economist Irving Fisher (1867–1947), his mentor by long distance, enters the picture[66]:

> I have had, already, the benefit of full critical reading by Mr. Carl B. Robbins and Miss Margaret Milliken [an instructor in statistics] of our department at Stanford. Professor Irving Fisher and Doctor Royal Meeker (who was working with Fisher this summer) have given me the benefit of full critical notes on Chapter VIII. At present Fisher is reading four other chapters (in carbon copy).

In Canning's Preface to the book, he wrote: 'I need not declare my obligation to Professor Fisher for the influence of his writings upon my thought—that obligation appears throughout the whole book' (1929b, p. iv). In his letter to Viner, he continued as follows:

> In returning Chapter VIII of my manuscript, Fisher asked permission to quote rather extensively (some ten or twelve pages) in the forthcoming revision of his *Rate of Interest.* In order to enable him to do so, I sent the unfinished ms. to the Ronald Press Company for inspection and approval. I have a contract with them which requires me to have the full copy in their hands by January 1, 1929. Since the Ronald people and I have assented to Fisher's quoting and since Fisher's copy has gone to the printer, I am no longer free to make any alterations (in the text to be printed) of Chapter VIII. You may be interested to know that Fisher accepts and adopts what he is pleased to call my constructive criticisms. In his own manuscript of the revised introduction to his book, he has even followed the suggestion, accredited to me, that his theory of income should be developed in substantially the reverse order of concepts. I shall send you, later, his comments.[67]

[65] Interview with Edward G. Nelson, 8 June 1965.

[66] Evidently, Canning met Fisher sometime in the 1920s at an annual meeting of the American Economic Association, and they engaged in a vigorous correspondence. But Fisher did not convey any views on Canning's evolving dissertation until he saw the completed manuscript. Interview with Dorothy P. (Mrs John B.) Canning, 5 December 1964. This Canning–Fisher correspondence has not survived.

[67] Fisher wrote an admiring review article of Canning's book in *The American Economic Review* (1930b). In *The Theory of Interest,* his revision of *The Rate of Interest* (1907), Fisher (1930a, pp. 507–8) quoted about 600 words from Canning's book, and, in two of the three extracts taken from the book, Canning lauded Fisher's *Nature of Capital and Income* (1906).

25

To be sure, Canning was already an associate professor at Stanford. But how much more self-confidence, indeed hubris, can a doctoral candidate exhibit? He presented the University of Chicago's economics department with a finished book: without a supervisor, without previous notice of its contents (other than to Clark, who had left), and with a deadline some two months hence for delivery of the book to the publisher.[68] Nonetheless, impressed with the work, the department accepted Canning's book as his doctoral dissertation.[69] The oral examination was successfully held on 15 December, chaired by labour economist Harry A. Millis,[70] and the Doctor of Philosophy degree was conferred on 11 June 1929, in Canning's forty-fifth year of age.

How did Canning's book, which was published later in the year (the Preface is dated 10 September 1929), come to the attention of Ronald Press, the most enterprising publisher of books in business and accounting? William A. Paton, who had written two books for Ronald Press and was regarded highly by its president, Philip J. Warner, claims the credit. Paton gave the manuscript his strong endorsement and urged Canning, ever the perfectionist, to publish it without undertaking further revisions.[71]

How did Paton come to know Canning? Jacob Viner suggests that Paton and Canning met at Chicago: 'I seem to recall that W. A. Paton, now professor emeritus at Ann Arbor, knew Canning well. Paton had some contacts with our Dept. and I associate him with Canning as seeking to marry economics with accounting, a project which in principle at least all the Department looked upon with sympathy, if not with unqualified optimism.'[72] In fact, Paton taught at Chicago during the summer of 1924, when Canning was also a visitor there, and both were attached to the School of Commerce and Administration.[73] Paton surely knew Canning by 1926, because, as editor of *The Accounting Review*, he invited him to do a book review, which was published in the December 1926 issue.

---

[68] Nelson recalls, however, that the Chicago economics faculty, evidently during Canning's visit there during the summer of 1924, 'greatly encouraged' him to move ahead with his line of research for the thesis. Interview with Edward G. Nelson, 8 June 1965.

[69] At that time, the University of Chicago required that doctoral dissertations not only be submitted and approved but also be published. Information supplied by the Department of Special Collections, Regenstein Library, University of Chicago.

[70] In 1928–9, when Canning submitted his completed dissertation, Millis was chairman of Chicago's department of economics, which probably explains why he chaired the examination committee.

[71] Letter to the author from William A. Paton (1889–1991), dated 6 August 1965. In a letter to the author dated 15 July 1965, Walter B. McFarland wrote that Paton 'once told me that "Economics of Accountancy" was published only after he [Paton] had urged very strongly that the manuscript ought to be published at that time. He expressed the opinion that in the absence of such pressure, the book would probably never have been published.' Philip J. Warner, in an interview on 26 May 1965, recalled that Paton had 'probably' recommended the Canning manuscript to Ronald.

[72] Letter from Jacob Viner to the author, dated 26 January 1965.

[73] Paton taught a course in accounting theory, and Canning offered a course on the valuation of fixed assets (*Annual Register of the University of Chicago 1923–1924*, 1924, p. 475).

26

The Economics of Accountancy earned Canning the Beta Alpha Psi Book Award for the most notable contribution to the accounting literature for the year ending 1 May 1930. Ironically, the runner-up book was J. Hugh Jackson's *Auditing Problems* (1929) (Sheldahl, 1982, p. 473). In later years, Ronald Press tried several times to persuade Canning to revise *The Economics of Accountancy*, but without success.[74]

FROM 1929 TO 1941

Developments in the Early 1930s

Stanford promoted Canning to full professor in 1930, the year after he received his doctorate and his book was published. The department had been slowly expanding: Canning was one of six full professors (including Wildman, Jones and Whitaker), and there were three associate professors (including Robbins) and two assistant professors, together with two instructors, a lecturer and seven assistants in instruction (including Calkins, Nelson and Shaw).

It was reported in 1929 that Canning 'is engaged in writing an introductory text in accounting and is assisting Carl Burton Robbins in preparing a book on certain phases of the financial problems of corporations for the Ronald Press Company'.[75] Neither of these projects achieved fruition.

Although it seems that Canning's only appearances at annual meetings of the AAUIA were in 1928 and 1930, when he read papers,[76] such was his standing that AAUIA President Howard C. Greer invited him in 1932 to serve on the newly created Council on Accounting Research, which was intended to suggest and guide research on accounting problems. Canning accepted the invitation. He and Henry Rand Hatfield were the only council members, numbering nineteen, who were not from the East or Middle West. The council never fulfilled its ambitious aims, but it was one of a series of initiatives that foreshadowed the reorganization of the AAUIA as the American Accounting Association in 1935–6 (Greer, 1932; Zeff, 1966, pp. 34–5).

Canning was actively involved in the early years of the Econometric Society, which was founded in 1930. Together with Holbrook Working, a lecturer on the Stanford economics faculty, he was in charge of the program for the society's 1934 summer meeting in Berkeley. Canning also founded the society's committee on instruction in statistics and was its chairman until 1938.[77] An article by Canning, 'A Certain Erratic Tendency in Accountants' Income Procedure', appeared in the inaugural issue of *Econometrica* (1933a), the society's journal. It was to be Canning's last article on accounting published in a journal. In addition, he had a paper on Fisher's income concept published in a conference proceedings volume (1933b), and he wrote reviews of several books on accounting in later years.

---

[74] Interview with Dorothy P. (Mrs John B.) Canning, 5 December 1964.

[75] *Annual Report of the President*, Leland Stanford Junior University (November 1929), p. 369.

[76] Also at the 1930 annual meeting, held in Cleveland, A. C. Littleton presented Canning with the Beta Alpha Psi Book Award.

[77] Interview with Holbrook Working, 12 January 1965.

27

Beginning in 1930–1, and for ten years thereafter, Canning offered a course on Index Numbers, in which he used Fisher's book of the same title. It was a course in statistics which, Nelson recalls, 'went far beyond anything that Fisher had ever done'.[78] Canning believed that statistics transcended disciplines as an important tool of analysis in doctoral research, and he was a leader in the early 1930s in securing acceptance of statistics as a minor field in the University's PhD programs.[79]

Canning's 'Some Divergences' and Two Book Reviews on Accounting
Canning's articles and book reviews were, like his book, examples of precise expression, crafted analysis and deep thinking, with the occasional appearance of a well-turned phrase. His under-appreciated article, 'Some Divergences of Accounting Theory from Economic Theory' (1929a), can be regarded, in effect, as an introductory essay to his book. In the article, he explained how Fisher, who was trained in mathematics, would appeal to Canning, who was schooled in statistics. Referring to Fisher's *Nature of Capital and Income* (1906) and *Rate of Interest* (1907), Canning wrote: 'Here is a qualitative analysis in a quantitative dress' (1929a, p. 7). In his article, Canning confessed that he had lost confidence in the usefulness to the professional accountant of mainstream economic theory—'those brands professed by the classical economists, and by Jevons, Marshall, Cannan, Taussig, Seligman, Ely, and a host of others' (p. 1). He did see hope in 'a wholly new and wholly different kind of economic theory . . . [which] exists in fragmentary form only . . . [and] consists of inquiries into the statistical relations of one real statistical series to another' (p. 7). This article was perhaps the best attempt in the accounting literature to contrast the work of the accountant with that of the economist.

Canning's book reviews were penetrating and critical. In his review of MacNeal's 1939 polemic, *Truth in Accounting*, he disparaged the author's facile reliance on 'acceptable' markets and price imputations. In the end, he counselled that 'truth may be both expensive and useless' (1939, p. 758), probably one of the early mentions of the cost of information. Three years later, on leave from Stanford, he found time to skewer Paton for the 'presence of mere number-juggling in the dress of theory' (1942, p. 313) in the author's *Advanced Accounting* (1941).

Canning did not write much on accounting in the periodical literature, but these writings repay a careful reading.

Canning's Expanding Interests in the 1930s
Canning was attracted to problems and issues of current import, and in the 1920s his concern was with upgrading the accounting profession. In the 1930s, he became preoccupied with the social and economic problems of the Depression and, eventually, of the approaching war. His strong social conscience, engaged by the severe unemployment during the Depression, caused him to become an ardent

[78]   Interview with Edward G. Nelson, 8 June 1965.

[79]   Interview with Eugene L. Grant, 12 January 1965. Canning served on the University's Academic Committee on Graduate Study in 1933–4 and again from 1935 to 1938.

28

supporter of the New Deal.[80] Indeed, during the 1930s, as one former colleague recalled,

> Canning was regarded by business circles in San Francisco as something of a radical. I do not now know what the basis of this was, but it could have been his support of social security and unemployment insurance. At any rate, [Stanford President Ray Lyman] Wilbur apparently received a number of letters complaining violently about Canning, some of which threatened to cut off financial support from the university if something were not done to keep Canning quiet.[81]

An apt summary of Canning's several areas of concern during the 1930s and in 1940–1 appears in the Memorial Resolution written by a committee of Stanford colleagues chaired by Bernard F. Haley, with Karl Brandt and Paul R. Farnsworth as the other members, shortly after Canning's death in 1962:

> One of these areas was that of fiscal policy. Professor Canning was one of the economists very early to recognize the important part to be played by government spending and an unbalanced budget in reducing the severity of [the] depression and facilitating recovery. In December 1932 he presented a paper (with E. G. Nelson, a colleague) at the annual meeting of the American Statistical Association on 'Budget Balancing versus Trade Stabilization', and followed it with an article in the *American Economic Review* (March 1934), and testimony before the U.S. Senate Committee on Finance.
>
> Second, he became actively concerned with the system of unemployment insurance and social security that was beginning to emerge at the federal and state levels. He served as a member of the Advisory Committee of the San Francisco Chamber of Commerce on Unemployment Reserves and Insurance, and as consultant to the California Joint Legislative Committee on Unemployment Insurance in 1934–35. His research program shifted to concentrate on problems of unemployment insurance and social security. He continued his consulting work in this field in succeeding years, and published several papers bearing on it.
>
> Third, when the California Medical Association became interested in health insurance about 1934, Professor Canning was called upon to serve as a member of the Advisory Board and as economic adviser to the Medical-Economic Survey carried out by a committee of the Association. This work continued in the years 1935–36.
>
> Fourth, late in the '30's, Professor Canning turned to an area of economics which was to engross his full attention for the remainder of his professional career: agricultural policy. As the Second World War became imminent, an interest which he already had in problems of agricultural labor in California led him to a concern with the national agricultural policy and the food supply in time of war. Between 1939 and 1941 he wrote a number of papers in this area, participated in two national conferences called respectively by the President and the Department of Agriculture, and served as economic consultant to the Secretary of that Department. Finally, in the spring of 1941 he took leave of

---

[80] Interview with Bernard F. Haley, 5 January 1965.

[81] Letter from W. Allen Wallis to William R. Smith, Dated 6 May 1971. Wallis (1912–98) was a member of the Stanford economics department from 1938 to 1946. He later became dean of the University of Chicago business school and president of the University of Rochester.

Joseph S. Davis, in a letter dated 6 August 1971 to William R. Smith, wrote: 'J. B. [as Canning was known by his colleagues] was a truly independent thinker, with a restless but penetrating mind ... He was always ready to break new ground, regardless of consequences. It led him occasionally into paths that some of us could not follow: I recall his activity in a Teachers' Union; a colleague recalls (as I do not) his support of Harry Bridges.' Bridges, an alleged communist, was the leader of the longshoremen's strike in May 1934 that virtually shut down the city of San Francisco.

29

absence from Stanford and moved to Washington so that he could devote full time to his work as economic adviser to the Secretary.

Carl Robbins had preceded Canning to Washington, and he was probably responsible for Canning's move there. The Memorial continues:

> During his years at Stanford previous to the war Professor Canning participated in a variety of extracurricular activities in all of which he took a leading part: the Pacific Coast Economic Association, for which he edited the *Proceedings* [during the years 1932–5] and of which he was president [in 1937]; the Social Science Research Conference of the Pacific Coast, of which he was president in 1936–37; the section on industrial relations of the Commonwealth Club of California, for which he served as chairman for many years in the '30's; and the Western Farm Economic Association.

Canning's expanding interests in the 1930s may have influenced the selection of a dissertation topic by one of his junior accounting colleagues. In 1941, Edward J. Kelly completed a thesis under Canning entitled 'A Case Study of Hospital Costs', which was an examination of the practices in three area hospitals.

The Gradual Displacement of Canning's Focus on Accounting
Inevitably, as Canning's interests and energy shifted in the 1930s, his devotion to the accounting profession began to wane. In the *Register for 1934–35*, Capital and Income, which he had taught in every year since 1926–7, no longer appeared and was not seen again.

The Master of Arts in Economics and Accountancy degree, which had been part of Canning's accounting program since 1926, disappeared from the *Register* in 1934–5, and it was not mentioned again. In fact, the degree had been granted only three times, once each in 1930, 1931 and 1932.[82] The Bachelor of Arts in Economics and Accountancy degree was awarded annually to between three and fourteen graduates from 1926–7 to 1941–2, the last year for which figures were published in the *Register*.

In 1936–7, a significant change occurred in the stated objective of the Division of Accountancy, suggesting that Canning no longer viewed the preparation of entrants into the accounting profession as his principal aim. In the *Registers* from 1926–7 to 1933–4, its objective was given as follows: 'The Division of Accountancy is created to administer a professional training course in Accountancy'. In the *Registers* for 1934–5 and 1935–6, the statement was even stronger: 'The sole object of the Division of Accountancy is to administer a course of study in certain subjects a knowledge of which is requisite to competency in professional accounting'. Beginning in the *Register for 1936–37*, however, the description reflected a diminished role for professional accounting, as follows:

> The sole object of the Division of Accountancy is to administer a program of instruction appropriate for the systematic quantitative analysis of economic relationships in private

[82] The degree recipients were, respectively, Tetsuo Hayashi, Arthur N. Lorig and Robert C. Sutro. Hayashi translated Canning's *Economics of Accountancy* into Japanese for publication in 1930, but the book never appeared.

30

enterprise ... The program is one in accountancy only in the sense that the principal *de facto* mode of quantitative analysis of economic relations is the mode adopted by accountants. Though the undergraduate program is one suited to those who intend to become responsible accountants *it does not purport to be a training course for any one professional vocation.* It is equally suited to serve the needs of those who expect subsequently to become professional students of law, economics, or business or to become fiduciaries in private enterprise (pp. 469–70; emphasis added).

Towards the end of the 1930s, by which time Canning was immersed in broader social and economic policy issues, the number of accounting courses diminished by several: the two Reports courses and the consolidations course had been dropped and, in 1939–40, the Cost Analysis and Valuation courses were combined into one. There was an attempt, however, to broaden the accounting curriculum: between 1934 and 1940, an Accounting Systems course appeared in the *Register*, taught by an assistant in instruction, although it was actually offered in only three of the six years. Yet Canning maintained an active interest in the accounting program and continued to teach his favoured courses.

Increasingly in the 1930s, Canning began to teach courses giving effect to his broadened sphere of concerns. In 1936–7, probably inspired by the Social Security Act of 1935, he developed and taught a course entitled Economic Security, dealing with voluntary and legislated programs to protect individuals from economic and social risks. Two years later, he added a companion course, American Social Insurance. He continued to offer both courses until he went on leave in 1941.

ON LEAVE FROM STANFORD, AND RETIREMENT: 1941–62

While Canning's request for a leave from Stanford in 1941 may have been induced by a desire to partipate in shaping national agricultural policy, his request may have also been prompted by displeasure over the department's decision not to continue his principal accounting colleague and disciple, Edward G. Nelson.[83] As suggested above, the departmental support for Canning's accounting program was a mark of personal respect and evidently did not extend to the careers of his junior colleagues.

After mentioning Canning's leave of absence beginning in 1941 to devote full time as an economic adviser to the Secretary of Agriculture, the authors of the Memorial Resolution continued as follows:

Thus ended his career as professor of economics and began a new career as a full-time governmental expert. In 1942 he became economic assistant to the Administrator, Agricultural Marketing Administration (U.S. Department of Agriculture), and for the next three years he continued in Washington serving in various capacities with the Department of Agriculture. In 1945, at the close of the war he moved to Berlin to serve as deputy chief of the food and agriculture branch of the economic division of the U.S. Office of Military Government. His principal duties were to serve as the U.S. representative on the Quadripartite Council concerning problems of food and agriculture in the zones of occupation.

---

[83] Letter from Robert D. Calkins to the author, dated 4 October 1965. Calkins wrote that the department's action also led to Canning's resignation from the university five years later.

31

From 1941 to 1946, Canning was an associate of Stanford's Food Research Institute, his one link with affairs in Palo Alto.[84] The Memorial continues: 'In June 1946, at his own request, he retired to emeritus status at Stanford, but he continued in Germany until December 1948 [during the airlift], when poor health necessitated his resignation from his governmental post'.

Nelson recalls that Canning suffered from chest pains in 1947, but that he nonetheless stayed on in Berlin for another year. Upon Canning's return to the San Francisco Bay area, Nelson said that 'it was exceedingly difficult for him to find a role. He had had so much experience in so many different things in American domestic economic policy, both on a state and on a national level, and in the military government in Germany, that he couldn't really bring himself to go back to teaching accounting'.[85] Moreover, as a result of several attacks of angina pectoris, his doctor had told him to take it easy. He therefore entered retirement at the age of sixty-four.

With Canning's retirement, the economics department lost no time in announcing that 'Students will not be admitted to the major in economics-accountancy after August 31, 1947' (*Register for 1946–47*, p. 515), and all references to the Division of Accountancy were dropped from the *Announcement of Courses* after 1947–8. Thereafter, some half-dozen accounting courses were offered each year by junior faculty with temporary appointments.

From 1948 onward, Canning did no professional work for publication, and he deliberately kept out of circulation.[86] He and his wife lived in their newly built home in the foothills just off the Stanford campus, and they repaired frequently to his cabin at Fallen Leaf Lake in the Sierra. Canning was a vigorous gardener, and he enjoyed fishing trips in the high country as well as deep-sea fishing. He continued to read, and he is said to have written a number of papers that he sent to officials in government, leading to a correspondence over issues that interested him. He died after a long illness, following intestinal surgery, on 4 July 1962.

CONCLUSION

Canning's book, *The Economics of Accountancy* (1929b), for which he earned a PhD at the University of Chicago in mid-career, was a seminal work. In some respects, Canning was similar to Sweeney (see Clarke, 1976) and MacNeal (see Zeff, 1982), as they wrote treatises that were highly regarded by subsequent theorists, they contributed to the accounting literature only during comparatively brief

---

[84] Nelson has suggested that Canning may have had little desire to return to Stanford during the war. According to Nelson, Ray Lyman Wilbur, Stanford's chancellor, and the Stanford board of trustees (over whom former U.S. President and Stanford alumnus Herbert C. Hoover held considerable sway) 'were not quite sure what the role of the University should be during the war. But Canning was *sure*, and he wasn't much interested in returning to a university that couldn't make up its mind. So he continued to extend his leaves.' Interview with Edward G. Nelson, 8 June 1965.

[85] Interview with Edward G. Nelson, 8 June 1965.

[86] Letter from Joseph S. Davis to William R. Smith, dated 6 August 1971.

32

periods, and they were known personally to only a few accounting academics. But neither Sweeney nor MacNeal entered academe. Canning was an academic economist *cum* statistician who installed an ambitious five-year accounting curriculum in an economics department whose other members were sceptical of this intrusion but who nonetheless greatly respected him. In the 1930s, Canning published markedly less on accounting as his interests expanded beyond accounting and towards fiscal policy and the economics of unemployment and health insurance, social security and agricultural policy. During retirement, Canning published no further work.

This article is dedicated to the memory of Ray Chambers.

REFERENCES

Accounting Research Committee, *Current Value Accounting*, Canadian Institute of Chartered Accountants, 1976.

Accounting Standards Board, *Statement of Principles for Financial Reporting*, revised exposure draft, ASB, 1999.

Accounting Standards Review Committee, *Company Accounting Standards*, ASRC, 1978.

Alexander, S. S., 'Income Measurement in a Dynamic Economy', in *Five Monographs on Business Income*, Study Group on Business Income of the American Institute of Accountants, 1950.

Allen, C. E., 'The Growth of Accounting Instruction Since 1900', *The Accounting Review*, June 1927.

American Accounting Association, Committee on Concepts and Standards for External Financial Reports, *Statement on Accounting Theory and Theory Acceptance*, AAA, 1977.

American Accounting Association, Committee to Prepare a Statement of Basic Accounting Theory, *A Statement of Basic Accounting Theory*, AAA, 1966.

Announcement of Courses, Leland Stanford Junior University, various years (from 1946–7 onward).

Annual Register of the University of Chicago 1923–1924, University of Chicago Press, 1924.

Annual Report of the President, Leland Stanford Junior University, various years.

Ashton, R. K., 'Value to the Owner: A Review and Critique', *Abacus*, March 1987.

Australian Accounting Research Foundation, 'A Comparison of Accounting Measurement Systems: An Evaluative Paper', insert to *The Chartered Accountant in Australia*, September 1975.

Ball, R., and P. Brown, 'An Empirical Evaluation of Accounting Income Numbers', *Journal of Accounting Research*, Autumn 1968.

Barton, A. D., 'Chambers' Contributions to Analytical Rigour in Accounting', *Abacus*, December 1982.

Baxter, W. T., 'Accounting Values: Sale Price Versus Replacement Cost', *Journal of Accounting Research*, Autumn 1967.

——, *Depreciation*, Sweet & Maxwell, 1971.

——, *Collected Papers on Accounting*, Arno Press, 1978.

Bedford, N. M., *Income Determination Theory: An Accounting Framework*, Addison-Wesley Publishing Company, 1965.

Bonbright, J. C., *The Valuation of Property: A Treatise on the Appraisal of Property for Different Legal Purposes*, McGraw-Hill, 1937.

'Canning to Give Football Lecture', *The Daily Palo Alto*, 2 November 1921.

Canning, J. B., 'Some Divergences of Accounting Theory from Economic Theory', *The Accounting Review*, March 1929a.

——, *The Economics of Accountancy: A Critical Analysis of Accounting Theory*, The Ronald Press Company, 1929b. (Reprinted in 1978 by Arno Press.)

33

——, 'A Certain Erratic Tendency in Accountants' Income Procedure', *Econometrica*, No. 1, 1933a.

——, 'The Income Concept and Certain of Its Implications', in J. B. Canning (ed.), *Papers and Proceedings of the Eleventh Annual Conference of the Pacific Coast Economic Association*, Edwards Brothers, 1933b.

——, review of *Truth in Accounting, Journal of the American Statistical Association*, December 1939.

——, review of *Advanced Accounting, The Journal of Political Economy*, April 1942.

Canning, J. B., and E. G. Nelson, 'The Relation of Budget Balancing to Economic Stabilization: A Suggested Federal Treasury Policy', *The American Economic Review*, March 1934.

'Canning, John Bennet', in *The National Cyclopædia of American Biography*, James T. White Company, 1968.

The Cap and Gown, The Junior Class of the University of Chicago, 1913.

Cashion, T., *The First 75 Years*, The California Society of Certified Public Accountants, 1984.

Chambers, R. J., 'Blueprint for a Theory of Accounting', *Accounting Research*, January 1955.

——, *Accounting, Evaluation and Economic Behavior*, Prentice-Hall, 1966.

——, 'Income and Capital: Fisher's Legacy', *Journal of Accounting Research*, Spring 1971.

——, 'Canning's *The Economics of Accountancy*—After 50 Years', *The Accounting Review*, October 1979.

——, *An Accounting Thesaurus: 500 Years of Accounting*, Elsevier Science, 1995.

Clark, J. M., *Studies in the Economics of Overhead Costs*, The University of Chicago Press, 1923.

Clarke, F. L., 'A Closer Look at Sweeney's Stabilized Accounting Proposals', *Accounting and Business Research*, Autumn 1976.

'Coach Canning Gives Analysis of Play on Line', *The Daily Palo Alto*, 3 November 1921.

Coats, A. W., 'The Origins of the "Chicago School(s)"?' *The Journal of Political Economy*, October 1963.

Devine, C. T., *Essays in Accounting Theory*, American Accounting Association, 1985.

Edwards, E. O., and P. W. Bell, *The Theory and Measurement of Business Income*, University of California Press, 1961.

Financial Accounting Standards Board, Statement of Financial Accounting Concepts No. 1, *Objectives of Financial Reporting by Business Enterprises*, FASB, 1978.

Fisher, I., *The Nature of Capital and Income*, Macmillan, 1906.

——, *The Rate of Interest: Its Nature, Determination and Relation to Economic Phenomena*, Macmillan, 1907.

——, *The Theory of Interest*, Macmillan, 1930a.

——, 'The Economics of Accountancy', *The American Economic Review*, December 1930b.

Forbes, J. F., 'Observations of a CPA Examiner', *The Accounting Review*, April 1944.

Gellein, O. S., 'The Conceptual Framework', in J. C. Burton, R. E. Palmer and R. S. Kay (eds), *Handbook of Accounting and Auditing*, Warren, Gorham & Lamont, 1981.

Gibson, K., 'John Bennett [sic] Canning: A Sixty Year Perspective—a Jubilee Review of "The Economics of Accountancy"', *Accounting History*, Vol. 5, No. 2, 1993.

Gleeson, R. E., S. Schlossman and D. G. Allen, 'Uncertain Ventures: The Origins of Graduate Management Education at Harvard and Stanford, 1908–1939', *Selections*, Spring 1993.

Gore, P., *The FASB Conceptual Framework Project 1973–1985: An Analysis*, Manchester University Press, 1992.

Green, D., Jr., 'A Moral to the Direct Costing Controversy?' *The Journal of Business*, July 1960.

Greer, H. C., 'A Council on Accounting Research', *The Accounting Review*, September 1932.

Gynther, R. S., 'Some "Conceptualizing" on Goodwill', *The Accounting Review*, April 1969.

Haley, B. F. (chairman), K. Brandt and P. R. Farnsworth, 'Memorial Resolution: John Bennet Canning 1884–1962', Department of Special Collections, Stanford University Libraries, [1962].

Hatfield, H. R., 'An Historical Defense of Bookkeeping', *The Journal of Accountancy*, April 1924.

34

Henderson, S., and G. Peirson, *Financial Accounting Theory: Its Nature and Development*, Longman Cheshire, 1983.

Hendriksen, E. S., *Accounting Theory*, Richard D. Irwin, 1965.

Horngren, C. T., 'William J. Vatter: Notable Contributor to Management Accounting', *Journal of Management Accounting Research*, Fall 1991.

Hunt, B. C. (ed.), *Twenty-Five Years of Accounting Responsibility, 1911–1936*, Price, Waterhouse & Co., 1936.

Inflation Accounting Committee, *Inflation Accounting*, F. E. P. Sandilands Esq., CBE (chairman), Her Majesty's Stationery Office, 1975.

Inflation Accounting Research Project, various publications, Department of Management Studies, University of Waikato, 1976–81.

Ijiri, Y., *The Foundations of Accounting Measurement*, Prentice-Hall, 1967.

Jackson, J. H., *Audit Working Papers: Their Preparation and Content*, American Institute of Accountants Foundation, 1923.

——, *Auditing Problems: A Comprehensive Study in Principles and Procedure*, The Ronald Press Company, 1929.

'John Bennett [sic] Canning Has Varied Interests', *The Daily Palo Alto*, 28 March 1921.

Kenley, W. J., and G. J. Staubus, *Objectives and Concepts of Financial Statements*, Accountancy Research Foundation, 1972.

MacNeal, K., *Truth in Accounting*, University of Pennsylvania Press, 1939.

Mattessich, R., *Accounting and Analytical Methods*, Richard D. Irwin, 1964.

Miller, M. C., and M. A. Islam, *The Definition and Recognition of Assets*, Australian Accounting Research Foundation, 1988.

Moonitz, M., *The Basic Postulates of Accounting*, American Institute of Certified Public Accountants, 1961.

——, 'Some Career Influences', *Issues in Accounting Education*, 1984.

——, *History of Accounting at Berkeley*, Professional Accounting Program, Schools of Business Administration, University of California, 1986.

Moonitz, M., and A. C. Littleton, *Significant Accounting Essays*, Prentice-Hall, 1965.

Moonitz, M., and C. C. Staehling, *Accounting: An Analysis of Its Problems*, The Foundation Press, 1950.

Morrison, L. F., 'Intangible Assets', in R. Wixon (ed.), *Accountants' Handbook*, The Ronald Press Company, 1956.

Most, K. S., *Accounting Theory*, Grid, 1977.

Myers, J. H., *Reporting of Leases in Financial Statements*, American Institute of Certified Public Accountants, 1962.

Nelson, E. G., 'That Balance-Sheet Approach', *The Accounting Review*, December 1935.

——, 'The Relation Between the Balance Sheet and the Profit and Loss Statement', *The Accounting Review*, April 1942.

Norris, H., *Accounting Theory: An Outline of Its Structure*, Sir Isaac Pitman & Sons, 1946.

Parker, R. H., and S. A. Zeff, *Milestones in the British Accounting Literature*, Garland Publishing, 1996.

Paton, W. A., 'The Significance and Treatment of Appreciation in the Accounts', in G. H. Coons (ed.), *Twentieth Annual Report of the Michigan Academy of Science*, Michigan Academy of Science, 1918.

——, *Accounting Theory—With Special Reference to the Corporate Enterprise*, The Ronald Press Company, 1922.

Paton, W. A., and A. C. Littleton, *An Introduction to Corporate Accounting Standards*, American Accounting Association, 1940.

Preinreich, G. A. D., 'Valuation and Amortization', *The Accounting Review*, September 1937.

35

'Professor Canning Managed Family Dairy In Oklahoma Before Entering High School', *The Daily Palo Alto*, 5 December 1923.

Public Sector Accounting Standards Board and the Accounting Standards Review Board, Statement of Accounting Concepts (SAC) 2, *Objective of General Purpose Financial Reporting*, Australian Accounting Research Foundation, 1990.

Register, Leland Stanford Junior University, various years (until 1946–7).

Report of the Committee of Inquiry into Inflation Accounting, I. L. M. Richardson (chairman), [N.Z.] Government Printer, 1976.

Robbins, C. B., *No-Par Stock: Legal, Financial, Economic and Accounting Aspects*, The Ronald Press Company, 1927.

Schmidt, F., *Die organische Bilanz im Rahmen der Wirtschaft*, G. A. Gloeckner, 1921.

Schumpeter, J. A., *History of Economic Analysis*, Oxford University Press, 1954.

'Seventy Enter Higher School', *The Daily Oklahoman*, 28 May 1909.

Sheldahl, T. K., *Beta Alpha Psi, From Alpha to Omega: Pursuing a Vision of Professional Education for Accountants 1919–1945*, Garland Publishing, 1982.

Smith, W. R., 'John Bennett [*sic*] Canning', *The Accounting Historian*, July 1974. (Reproduced in *The Accounting Historians Journal*, Nos 1–4, 1974.)

Solomons, D., 'Economic and Accounting Concepts of Income', *The Accounting Review*, July 1961.

——, 'Criteria for Choosing an Accounting Model', *Accounting Horizons*, March 1995.

Solomons, D., and S. A. Zeff, *Accounting Research, 1948–1958*, Garland Publishing, 1996.

Sorter, G. H., 'Review of *A Theory of Accounting to Investors*', *The Accounting Review*, January 1963.

Sorter, G. H., and C. T. Horngren, 'Asset Recognition and Economic Attributes—the Relevant Costing Approach', *The Accounting Review*, July 1962.

Sprouse, R. T., 'The Measurement of Financial Position and Income: Purpose and Procedure', in R. K. Jaedicke, Y. Ijiri and O. Nielsen (eds), *Research in Accounting Measurement*, American Accounting Association, 1966.

——, '1994 Accounting Hall of Fame Induction: Response', *The Accounting Historians Journal*, December 1994.

Sprouse, R. T., and M. Moonitz, *A Tentative Set of Broad Accounting Principles for Business Enterprises*, American Institute of Certified Public Accountants, 1962.

Staubus, G. J., *A Theory of Accounting to Investors*, University of California Press, 1961.

——, 'The Relevance of Evidence of Cash Flows', in R. R. Sterling (ed.), *Asset Valuation and Income Determination: A Consideration of the Alternatives*, Scholars Book Co., 1971.

——, *Making Accounting Decisions*, Scholars Book Company, 1977.

——, *Development of the Decision-Usefulness Theory of Accounting*, Garland Publishing, forthcoming.

Sterling, R. R., *Theory of the Measurement of Enterprise Income*, University Press of Kansas, 1970.

Storey, R. K., 'Cash Movements and Periodic Income Determination', *The Accounting Review*, July 1960.

——, *The Search for Accounting Principles*, American Institute of Certified Public Accountants, 1964.

——, *Matching Revenues with Costs*, Arno Press, 1978.

Storey, R. K., and S. Storey, *The Framework of Financial Accounting Concepts and Standards*, Financial Accounting Standards Board, 1998.

Study Group on the Objectives of Financial Statements (Trueblood Committee), *Objectives of Financial Statements*, American Institute of Certified Public Accountants, 1973.

Sweeney, H. W., 'Stabilized Appreciation', *The Accounting Review*, June 1932.

——, *Stabilized Accounting*, Harper & Brothers Publishers, 1936.

Tweedie, D., and G. Whittington, *The Debate on Inflation Accounting*, Cambridge University Press, 1984.

Vatter, W. J., *The Fund Theory of Accounting and Its Implications for Financial Reports*, University of Chicago Press, 1947.

36

——, 'Accounting and Statistics', *The Accounting Review*, October 1961.

Walker, R. G., 'The SEC's Ban on Asset Revaluations and the Disclosure of Current Values', *Abacus*, March 1992.

Watts, R. L., and J. L. Zimmerman, 'The Demand for and Supply of Accounting Theories: The Market for Excuses', *The Accounting Review*, April 1979.

Wheeler, J. T., 'Economics and Accounting', in M. Backer (ed.), *Handbook of Modern Accounting Theory*, Prentice-Hall, 1955.

Whittington, G., 'Pioneers of Income Measurement and Price-Level Accounting: A Review Article', *Accounting and Business Research*, Spring 1980.

——, 'The LSE Triumvirate and Its Contribution to Price Change Accounting', in J. R. Edwards (ed.), *Twentieth-Century Accounting Thinkers*. Routledge, 1994.

Wojdak, J. F., 'A Theoretical Foundation for Leases and Other Executory Contracts', *The Accounting Review*, July 1969.

Wright, F. K., 'Towards a General Theory of Depreciation', *Journal of Accounting Research*, Spring 1964.

Zeff, S. A., *The American Accounting Association: Its First 50 Years*, [American Accounting Association, 1966].

——, 'Truth in Accounting: The Ordeal of Kenneth MacNeal', *The Accounting Review*, July 1982.

APPENDIX

JOHN B. CANNING'S PUBLISHED WORK

Book

The Economics of Accountancy: A Critical Analysis of Accounting Theory (New York: The Ronald Press Company, 1929). A translation into Japanese was completed but never published.

Articles in Research Journals

'The Formation of Frequency Distributions', *Journal of the American Statistical Association*, June 1926, pp. 133–48.

'Some Divergences of Accounting Theory From Economic Theory', *The Accounting Review*, March 1929, pp. 1–8.

'Hatfield's Paradox', *The Accounting Review*, June 1929, pp. 111–15.

'Cost of Production and Market Price', *The Accounting Review*, September 1931, pp. 161–4.

'A Certain Erratic Tendency in Accountants' Income Procedure', *Econometrica*, [January] 1933, pp. 52–62.

(with Edward G. Nelson) 'The Relation of Budget Balancing to Economic Stabilization: A Suggested Federal Treasury Policy', *The American Economic Review*, March 1934, pp. 26–37.

'Foods for Defense', *Journal of Farm Economics*, November 1941, pp. 697–711.

'Schisms in Agricultural Policy: Rescue Programs and Managed Agricultural Progress', *Journal of Farm Economics*, May 1942, pp. 496–511.

'American Supply of Foods to Combat Areas', *The Annals of The American Academy of Political and Social Science*, January 1943, pp. 177–82.

37

'The Demand for Agricultural Commodities in the Period of Transition From War to Peace', *Journal of Farm Economics*, November 1944, pp. 709–24.

'Food and Agriculture: Long-Run Outlook and Policy', *The American Economic Review*, May 1945, pp. 405–16.

Other Articles

'The Stanford Graduate School of Business', in Proceedings of the Fourth Annual Meetings of The Pacific Economic and Commercial Conference, Seattle, Washington, 29–30 December 1925, *The Ronald Forum* (issue undated).

'The Depreciation Element in Burden Estimates', *NACA Bulletin*, 1 September 1929, sec. 1, pp. 1–14.

'Cost Accounting', in Edwin R. A. Seligman and Alvin Johnson (eds), *Encyclopaedia of the Social Sciences*, New York, Macmillan, 1931, Vol. 4, pp. 475–8.

'The Income Concept and Certain of Its Applications', in John B. Canning (ed.), *Papers and Proceedings of the Eleventh Annual Conference of the Pacific Coast Economic Association at Stanford University, California, December, 1932*, Ann Arbor, MI, Edwards Brothers, 1933, pp. 61–5.

'How Far Are Social Forces Controllable? An Economist's Point of View', *Proceedings of the Third Annual Meeting of the Social Science Research Conference of the Pacific Coast, June 1933*, pp. 8–14.

'The Securities Act of 1933', in John B. Canning (ed.), *Papers and Proceedings of the Twelfth Annual Conference of the Pacific Coast Economic Association at the University of Washington, Seattle, Washington, December, 1933*, Ann Arbor, MI, Edwards Brothers, 1934, pp. 45–9.

'De Gustibus non Disputandum Est', *Proceedings of the Seventh Annual Meeting of the Social Science Research Conference of the Pacific Coast, March 25, 26, 27, 1937*, pp. 1–12.

'A Proposed Policy for the Association', in Arthur G. Coons (ed.), *Papers and Proceedings of the Sixteenth Annual Conference of the Pacific Coast Economic Association at Pomona College, Claremont, California, December, 1937*, Ann Arbor, MI, Edwards Brothers, 1938, pp. 12–15.

Testimony on *Violations of Free Speech and Rights of Labor*, Hearings before a Subcommittee of the Committee on Education and Labor, United States Senate, Seventy-Sixth Congress, Second Session, Pursuant to S. Res. 266 (74th Congress), Part 50: California Agricultural Background, December 18–19, 1939, Washington, DC, Government Printing Office, 1940, pp. 18338–53.

'Legislatures Would Make Sorry Showing Without Lobbies', *The San Francisco Chronicle*, 3 March 1941, p. 14.

Book Reviews

Auditing, by William H. Bell and John A. Powelson, *The Accounting Review*, December 1926, pp. 89–92.

Industrial Economics, by Dexter S. Kimball, *The American Economic Review*, June 1930, pp. 263–5.

Efficiency and Scarcity Profits, by C. J. Foreman, *Journal of Political Economy*, February 1931, pp. 129–30.

38

Cause and Control of the Business Cycle, by C. E. Harwood, *The Accounting Review*, March 1933, p. 92.

The Cost Principle in Minimum Price Regulation, by Herbert F. Taggart, *Journal of Political Economy*, April 1939, pp. 279–81.

Truth in Accounting, by Kenneth MacNeal, *Journal of the American Statistical Association*, December 1939, pp. 757–8.

Advanced Accounting, by W. A. Paton, *Journal of Political Economy*, April 1942, pp. 312–13.

Sundry

Published comments as a referee on an article, in Gabriel A. D. Preinreich, 'The Practice of Depreciation', *Econometrica*, July 1939, pp. 261–4.

Unpublished Congressional Testimony

'A Brief on the Nature of the Present Depression, on the Conditions Accountable for It, and on Proposed Measures for Ending It', prepared at the request of the Committee on Finance of the United States Senate, in the 72nd Congress, February 1933.

Note: Canning edited the annual *Papers and Proceedings* of the Pacific Coast Economic Association from 1932 through 1935.

39

Accounting Historians Journal
Vol. 28, No. 2
December 2001

Stephen A. Zeff
RICE UNIVERSITY

THE WORK OF THE
SPECIAL COMMITTEE ON
RESEARCH PROGRAM

Abstract: This article begins by recounting the circumstances that led to the AICPA's decision in 1957 to appoint a special committee to recommend a stronger research program to support the process of establishing accounting principles. It then proceeds to examine in depth the committee's sometimes difficult deliberations that eventually led to a unanimous report, in which it recommended the creation of an Accounting Principles Board and an enlarged accounting research division within the Institute. In the course of the article, the author brings out the strong philosophical differences among several of the Big Eight accounting firms that had been impeding the work of the Committee on Accounting Procedure and that also intruded into the Special Committee's deliberations.

INTRODUCTION

One of the major junctures in the process of establishing accounting principles in the United States occurred in 1957-59.[1] After almost 20 years of experience with the Committee on

Acknowledgments: I am grateful to Art Wyatt, George Catlett, Chuck Horngren, Oscar Gellein, Dick Brief, Tom Dyckman, Marc Epstein and Bob Mautz for comments on earlier drafts. Mautz is the lone surviving member of the Special Committee. They are not responsible, however, for the contents of this paper.

[1]Prior to the 1970s, what is today known as "standard setting" was characterized as the establishment of accounting principles. In 1970, the Institute of Chartered Accountants in England and Wales set up the Accounting Standards Steering Committee, which began issuing Statements of Standard Accounting Practice (in succession to Recommendations on Accounting Principles). In 1972, the American Institute of Certified Public Accountants created the Financial Accounting Standards Board (in succession to the Accounting Principles Board), which began to issue Statements of Financial Accounting Standards. With the inception of these two new bodies, the term "standard setting" entered the profession's vocabulary.

Submitted April 2001
Revised August 2001
Accepted October 2001

Accounting Procedure,[2] there was increasing criticism of the committee's inability to secure agreement on the most difficult problems, including accounting for changing prices, business combinations, deferred taxes, and pensions. The leadership of the American Institute of Certified Public Accountants (Institute, AICPA) believed that a new approach was needed, one that placed more emphasis on research into the fundamentals of accounting as a means of facilitating an agreement on particulars. In December 1957, the Institute created a blue ribbon panel known as the Special Committee on Research Program in order to recommend a new approach. The Committee's report, which was issued nine months later, led to the establishment in the following year of the Accounting Principles Board (APB).

No previous study has reported on the deliberations of the Special Committee, which was composed of strong-willed leaders of the profession, including the outspoken managing partner of Arthur Andersen & Co., Leonard Spacek, who was the most vociferous critic of the Committee on Accounting Procedure. It is the objective of this article to relate the Special Committee's deliberations in a way that brings out the strong philosophical differences among the members. As standard setting for financial reporting continues to evolve, both at the national and international levels, a study of the deliberations leading to the setting up to the predecessor of the Financial Accounting Standards Board may provide readers with an understanding of the dynamics of change when moving from one regime to its successor.

The author possesses a file of the minutes of the Special Committee's meetings, together with correspondence among the members, and most of the contents of this article, including

---

[2]From 1939 to 1957, the Committee on Accounting Procedure issued 48 numbered Accounting Research Bulletins, of which eight were reports prepared by the Committee (or Subcommittee) on Terminology between 1940 and 1949. Bulletin No. 43, issued in 1953, was a restatement and revision of the previous 40 Bulletins dealing with accounting principles. In the same year, the Committee on Terminology issued a review and résumé of the eight Bulletins dealing with terminology. For all of the Bulletins and reports of the Committee on Terminology issued between 1953 and 1959, see *Accounting Research and Terminology Bulletins, Final Edition* [1961]. For all of the Bulletins issued between 1939 and 1952, see Zeff and Moonitz [1984, vol. I]. When, as will be brought out in this article, the Special Committee on Research Program recommended the establishment of an Accounting Principles Board, it was intended that the board replace both the Committee on Accounting Procedure and the Committee on Terminology. The work of the Committee on Terminology will not be treated in this article, as it was noncontroversial.

several quotations, are derived from this file.[3] This article begins with a discussion of the events and developments that collectively precipitated the creation of the committee and continues by turning to the Committee's sometimes tense deliberations and exchanges of correspondence that led to its report filed in September 1958. It ends with the appointment of the members of the new APB, which itself was not devoid of controversy.

CREATION OF THE COMMITTEE[4]

The Special Committee on Research Program was established in December 1957 as a direct consequence of a major address given two months earlier by Alvin R. Jennings, the managing partner of the Big Eight firm, Lybrand, Ross Bros. & Montgomery (LRB&M), at the Institute's annual meeting held in New Orleans. Jennings was the incoming president of the Institute. In his address, "Present-Day Challenges in Financial Reporting" [1958a], he gave voice to a growing unease among leaders in the profession with the functioning of the Committee on Accounting Procedure (CAP), which had been issuing a series of Accounting Research Bulletins since its establishment in 1938/39. In particular, he was critical of the committee for sometimes acting too quickly under pressure and of "the difficulty which exists in reversing positions previously taken" [ibid., p. 33].

Jennings expressed disappointment that the effort by the Institute's research staff to develop a "procedural method" for obtaining the views of industry spokesmen had not succeeded.[5] Some of the fault, he said, "rests largely upon a failure of industry to acknowledge in any major sense its own obligations, and a disposition to interpret leadership by the Institute as an indication of willingness to assume full responsibility" [ibid., p. 31]. For its part, the Controllers Institute of America (shortly to be

---

[3]I am immensely grateful to the late Leonard Spacek for providing me with this file in 1970, which may be the only survivng record of the Committee's minutes and correspondence. I am also grateful to Price Waterhouse and Deloitte Haskins + Sells (as they were then known) for supplying additional files of correspondence in 1981.

[4]The discussion in this section draws in part on Zeff [1972, pp. 129-171] and Zeff [1984, pp. 459-462].

[5]Curiously, the managing director of the Controllers Institute has written that, in January 1957, there were "several signs of a growing closer relationship between the two Institutes" [Haase, 1971, p. 176].

renamed the Financial Executives Institute) complained from time to time that its members were not being adequately consulted. The Institute's executive committee, however, had never appointed any industry representatives to the CAP. Its 21 members were drawn from the ranks of public accounting practitioners (including representatives from all of the major firms) and from two to four academics. All of the committee members had to be Certified Public Accountants. This was an era when leaders of the Institute regarded CPAs in industry as having "left the profession."[6]

Jennings proposed that the Institute consider setting up a small, full-time research organization whose function "generally should be to carry on continuous examination and re-examination of basic accounting assumptions and to develop authoritative statements for the guidance of both industry and our profession" [ibid., p. 32]. To Jennings, a practitioner, "Development of accounting principles should be regarded as in the nature of pure research," and it was needed to keep up with "the economic and social changes which affect accounting and financial reporting" [ibid.]. To him, staffing the research organization meant, ideally, finding "five or six Carman Bloughs"[7] [ibid., p. 33]. It should consult widely and solicit informed views from interested parties, including industry, the accounting profession, the teaching profession, and representative of regulatory bodies. The cost of the research organization should be shared "in equitable proportions" by industry and the profession. Probably his most controversial suggestion was that the basic ideas contained in the statements issued by the research organization should be presented to the Institute's Council for

---

[6]The Institute was slow to bring non-practicing members into positions of importance, let alone leadership. It was not until 1998 that its first elected chairperson came from outside of public accounting. By contrast, the Canadian Institute of Chartered Accountants and the Institute of Chartered Accountants in England and Wales named their first president from outside of public accounting in 1945 and 1968, respectively.

[7]Carman G. Blough was a onetime accounting academic, the first SEC chief accountant (1935-38), a manager and partner in Arthur Andersen & Co., an early member of the Committee on Accounting Procedure (1938-42), and the Institute's full-time director of research since 1944. As director, he supervised a small research staff, which serviced the CAP and also many other Institute committees, and, since 1947, he wrote a monthly column in *The Journal of Accountancy* in which he dispensed his wisdom and views on accounting and auditing issues of interest to practitioners of all stripes. Through his column, he acquired a towering reputation as the ultimate authority on such matters [Moonitz, 1982].

approval or rejection, and that any bulletins approved by a two-thirds majority of Council "should be considered binding upon members of our Institute" [ibid., p. 32].

Jennings had issued the challenge. He was aware of the desire by the Securities and Exchange Commission (SEC) that the CAP make progress in adopting "definite rules" [King, 1951, p. 43], and he also was sensitive to the series of hard-hitting speeches by Leonard Spacek, the managing partner of Arthur Andersen & Co., in which he charged that financial statements were misleading because they reflect "the application of anti-quated accounting principles" [1956a, p. 1] and do not reflect the "true impact of business transactions" [1956b, p. 10]. Spacek also argued that comparability was impaired by the use of alternative accounting principles, and that the profession and the Institute had abdicated their responsibility to the public by not addressing these problems.[8] In a speech made in January 1957, Spacek argued that "The profession has not ex-hibited the independence and ability which the public is en-titled to expect" [Spacek, 1957a, p. 24]. In the words of John L. Carey, the Institute's long-time executive director, Spacek ac-cused the CAP of:

> yielding to industry pressure on an important principle without public discussion. He criticized the committee also for failing to issue bulletins in the face of substan-tial internal dissent. Finally he impugned the motives of members of a special committee of the Institute ap-pointed to investigate and report on divergencies be-tween generally accepted principles of accounting and the accounting practices prescribed for railroads by the Interstate Commerce Commission [Carey, 1970, p. 77].

Spacek's criticism of the behavior of the two Institute commit-tees was reported in the press, and his criticism of railroad accounting practices triggered a Congressional hearing [*Rail-road Accounting Procedures*, 1957].

It was unheard of for a major figure in the accounting profession to direct public criticism at the profession or the Institute, and the leaders of the Institute were shocked.[9] The

---

[8]For most of Spacek's collected speeches from that period, see *A Search for Fairness* [1969, pp. 1-59]. For a further discussion of Spacek's series of critical speeches, see Carey [1970, pp. 74-80] and Previts and Merino [1998, pp. 310-311].

[9]Interview with George R. Catlett, retired partner in Arthur Andersen & Co., October 21, 1999. Catlett was a longtime close colleague of Spacek's in the home office of Arthur Andersen & Co.

Institute's executive committee, with the evident support of Carey, immediately authorized President Marquis Eaton to take the extreme step of appointing a special committee to investigate Spacek's accusations. The special committee completed its inquiry with dispatch, and in its report dated April 17, 1957, a scant six weeks after its appointment, it found that the Institute committees had not yielded to improper influences [Report of Special Committee, 1957]. If Spacek earlier had little confidence in the leadership of the Institute, by the Spring of 1957 he had become embittered toward the Institute. In a letter to the Institute, Spacek took exception to the special committee's conduct of its investigation as well as with the reasoning in its report [Spacek, 1957b].

The Institute's leadership was determined to take the report of the special committee even further. It then proposed to Council that the Institute expel Spacek from membership, but the effort failed [Spacek, 1989, pp. 242-243]. Thereupon, the Institute apparently led an unsuccessful effort to get at Spacek through the Illinois Society of Certified Public Accountants [ibid., pp. 243-244]. For his part, Spacek threatened to pull Arthur Andersen & Co. out of the Institute [ibid., p. 237]. He viewed Carey as an apologist for permissiveness on accounting principles [ibid., pp. 38-39], which he also associated with several of the Big Eight firms based in New York City. For his part, Jennings responded to Spacek's public accusations by asserting in his address that "Criticisms which suggest that the profession on any widescale basis has lost its independence . . . are baseless" [Jennings, 1958a, p. 33]. The Institute's leadership wanted to rein in Spacek, and this may have been a major factor behind Jennings' call for a new approach.

But Spacek continued his crusade. In an August 1957 speech to the American Accounting Association (AAA), he advocated establishment of a "court of accounting principles" within the Institute, which was also reported in the press. In that speech, he contended that "Our present American Institute Bulletin method is seriously lacking as to the reasoning and the criteria on which the opinions are based" [Spacek, 1957c, p. 34]. Spacek believed that the [legal] case method should be used so that "not only the accounting profession, but also industry, government, teachers, and students will know the views that prevail [on accounting principles] and why they prevail" [ibid.]. More important, he argued, "We now have no satisfactory method of challenging what are presently regarded as accepted principles of accounting" as well as determining which new principles should be adopted and which alternative principles should be eliminated [ibid.]. As criteria for making such determinations, he believed it was essential that premises and objectives be developed and agreed upon.

Another factor that might explain Jennings' proposal was the increasing belief that the AAA, a body composed primarily of accounting academics, had been stealing the Institute's thunder in establishing accounting principles [see Storey, 1964, pp. 40-52]. In 1936, 1941 and 1948, the AAA had published a series of statements of accounting principles [*Accounting and Reporting Standards*, 1957], which the SEC's chief accountant would sometimes cite as authoritative support in his speeches and in his section in the Commission's annual report to the Congress [see, e.g., Blough, 1937, p. 30; Werntz, 1946, p. 35; King, 1948, pp. 52-53; Zeff and Moonitz, 1984, vol. II, pp. 202, 252]. The AAA's 1940 monograph by Professors W. A. Paton and A. C. Littleton, *An Introduction to Corporate Accounting Standards*, which was issued as an elaboration of the 1936 statement, was widely quoted and cited by practitioners and used by accounting academics in their university courses. The AAA published a series of eight "supplementary" principles statements on specific accounting topics between 1951 and 1955, and in 1957 it issued a revision of its 1948 statement. William W. Werntz, the current chairman of the CAP, lauded the 1957 statement in an article in *The Journal of Accountancy* and contrasted the series of "integrated" AAA principles statements with the output of his own committee, which, he wrote, had "chosen to express its views only on certain aspects of accounting as the occasion presented itself" [Werntz, 1958, p. 33]. The CAP had several times decided against developing and publishing a statement of fundamental accounting principles, and instead, composed mostly of practical men, preferred to take up accounting issues as they became pressing.

In 1955 and 1956, moreover, the AAA had published three research studies on price-level changes and financial statements [Jones 1955, 1956; Mason, 1956], which attempted to get to the heart of the theoretical and practical problems of recognizing the effects of inflation in financial statements. This subject was one on which the CAP was unwilling to issue a Bulletin in the mid-1950s, once the antipathy of the SEC's accounting staff toward such reform had become known [Zeff, 1972, pp. 155-157, 165-166; and see below].

Even George O. May, the former senior partner of Price Waterhouse & Co. and the lion of the profession, expressed the belief in 1958 that the Institute had been falling behind the AAA:

> The American Accounting Association from the time of its first pronouncement has sought to relate specific provisions to a broad concept. It would seem that the Institute must successfully undertake a similar task before it can claim with reason to be either the leading authority or one of the leading authorities upon the subject [Grady, 1962b, p. 278].

One can therefore understand why Jennings placed emphasis on "pure research," by which he meant "continuous examination and re-examination of basic accounting assumptions. . ." [Jennings, 1958a, p. 32; see also Jennings, 1958b].

But perhaps the most compelling reason for a change of approach was the persistent unwillingness of the CAP to make difficult choices on controversial topics. The committee members were apparently loathe to declare that certain accounting practices that had achieved a degree of acceptance were no longer includible among "generally accepted accounting principles" (GAAP), which was the profession's code terminology for proper practice. Even though the opinions expressed in the CAP's Accounting Research Bulletins were not binding on members of the Institute[10] (which was, after all, a voluntary association of CPAs licensed by the states), the committee knew that the SEC's accounting staff was inclined to enforce compliance with its opinions. But, as Carey wrote, "except as the SEC or the New York Stock Exchange insisted on compliance, individual companies and auditors were at liberty to deviate if they chose to assume the burden of justifying their departure" [1970, p. 88]. Although housed within the Institute, the CAP was effectively a creation inspired by the SEC, whose chief accountant had made it clear in 1937 that the accounting profession should take the initiative "to develop uniformity of procedure," lest the Commission do so itself [Blough, 1938, p. 190].

In the 1940s and especially in the 1950s, it became evident that three fundamental differences among the members mili-

---

[10]Accounting Research Bulletin No. 43 [Committee on Accounting Procedure, 1953, p. 9] stated rather ominously that "the burden of justifying departure from accepted procedures, to the extent that they are evidenced in committee opinions, must be assumed by those who adopt another treatment." An almost identical *caveat*, but omitting the passage set off in commas, appeared in most of the other Bulletins.

tated against agreement within the CAP. There was a profound difference between several of the major firms over whether a desirable goal was eventual "uniformity" of practice among companies, or instead a diversity of practice that would allow company managements to choose the accounting methods that, in their view, most suit their circumstances [see Carey, 1970, p. 88]. This was the "uniformity" v. "flexibility" debate that veritably exploded into the literature in the early and middle 1960s [see, e.g., "Uniformity in Financial Accounting," 1965].[11] Arthur Andersen & Co. (AA), which had a significant client base in the regulated public utility field [Spacek, 1989, pp. 8-9], was the foremost advocate of "uniformity" [ibid., pp. 38-43; Carey, 1970, p. 127], while Price Waterhouse & Co. (PW) and Haskins & Sells (H&S) were the two leading defenders of flexibility. The latter two firms believed that the choice of accounting methods should be tailored to the circumstances of individual corporations [see, e.g., May, 1943, pp. 183, 251; Kracke, 1947; Gellein, 1957, p. 91; Powell, 1964, pp. 40-41; Bevis, 1965, pp. 21-22; Keller, 1965, p. 648].

The second fundamental difference turned on the authority that the CAP possessed to impose significant changes on accounting practice. There was a philosophical split among the major firms over the committee's proper role in "forcing" a narrowing of accounting alternatives, as opposed to a more "empirical" approach of cataloguing generally accepted practices. AA wanted there to be a strong hand to change practice,[12] while PW and H&S did not see that as being within the committee's province [see Devore, 1958, p. 122; Powell, 1964, p. 40], as will be seen below. The views of the other major firms were less diametrically opposed. This issue, together with the debate over uniformity v. flexibility, were undercurrents that periodically surfaced in the phrasing of qualified assents or dissents in several of the CAP's more controversial Bulletins.

The third fundamental difference was over the primacy of conventional historical cost versus current value accounting or general price-level accounting in the financial statements, especially as regards the measurement of depreciation expense. Views within the CAP on conventional historical cost account-

---

[11]For an editorial and four articles on the subject, see the April 1961 issue of *The Journal of Accountancy*.

[12]Spacek advocated a "court of accounting principles" because he viewed the CAP as not being up to the task [Spacek, 1957c].

ing[13] versus general price-level accounting or a form of current value accounting were disparate, and the few efforts within the committee to advance the cause of current value accounting were rebuffed by the SEC, which was an arch defender of conventional historical cost accounting in the determination of net income [see, e.g., Zeff, 1972, pp. 155-157; Walker, 1992]. Of the major firms, AA was the principal advocate of general price-level accounting or current value accounting [Spacek, 1956a; 1956b].[14] Within PW, it depended on the partner.[15] During the 1950s, Garrett T. Burns, the AA representative on the CAP from 1953 to 1959, led an effort to issue a Bulletin in favor of the upward revaluation of assets, but, in the end, a negative signal from the SEC's chief accountant scuttled his initiative.[16]

Alvin Jennings evidently believed, with Oliver Wendell Holmes the elder [1891, p. 11], that a consensus on the particulars would come more easily once they could be traced to the basic assumptions, or *"ultimata* of belief," on which they depend. In early December, the Institute's executive committee accepted Jennings' challenge and set up "a committee of the Institute to study a new approach to accounting research, as stated in the letter of invitation."[17] The letter continued: "The executive committee believes that the problem deserves and requires intensive study by a committee of distinguished members, representing so far as possible the various points of

---

[13]"Conventional historical cost accounting" is intended to describe historical cost accounting without a restatement for the changing purchasing power of the dollar.

[14]Not all AA partners favored current value. Paul K. Knight, in AA's New York office, who represented AA on the committee from 1942 to 1953, did not seem to be an advocate. Knight assented to Accounting Research Bulletin No. 33, "Depreciation and High Costs" [Committee on Accounting Procedure, 1947] and to a reaffirming letter from the CAP in 1948. Both utterances opposed departures from historical cost in the body of the financial statements.

[15]By the end of the 1940s, the retired but still very active George O. May came to believe that conventional historical cost accounting was deficient, yet John B. Inglis, PW's representative on the CAP during its busy period from 1945 to 1951, was a conventional historical coster [see Inglis, 1974, p. 111; Grady, 1978, p. 324]. May, as well as senior PW partners Paul Grady and (to a lesser extent) Percival F. Brundage, came to favor the use of general price-level adjustments, either combined with historical cost in the body of the financial statements or in a supplementary disclosure [see May, 1949, pp. 66-68; Grady, 1952; Brundage, 1951, p. 114].

[16]Minutes of the meeting of September 25-26, 1958 of the Committee on Accounting Procedure, pp. 4-5. The chief accountant at the time, Andrew Barr, placed his views on public record [see Barr and Koch, 1959, p. 182].

[17]Letter from John L. Carey to the ten invited members of the committee, dated December 11, 1957.

view of practicing accountants, and of industry, the academic world, and the investing public." This was an unprecedented breadth of membership for an Institute committee dealing with accounting principles. It acknowledged, perhaps for the first time, that representatives of industry and the investing public should have a voice in the establishment of principles. It was made clear in the letter that Institute President Jennings wished "to emphasize the fact that the scope of the committee's activity is not to be restricted to a consideration of his proposal. Rather it is hoped that the committee will make an independent approach to the basic problems to which Mr. Jennings was attempting to point out at least one possible means of solution." The suggested title of the committee was "Committee to Study a New Approach to Accounting Research."

COMPOSITION OF THE COMMITTEE

Jennings chose Weldon Powell, the senior technical partner in the New York executive office of H&S, as chairman of the committee. Powell had been serving on the Committee on Accounting Procedure since 1954. He was a member of the "gradualist" school, which favored an evolutionary change in accounting principles and methods, with considerable discretion being given to company managements to choose the methods most responsive to their circumstances [see, e.g., Powell, 1965a, 1965b]. He was highly respected for his thoughtful manner and principled views, and he was "an acknowledged authority on accounting theory" [Carey, 1970, p. 92]. The other members invited to serve, all of whom accepted, were as follows:

Andrew Barr, the SEC chief accountant.

Carman G. Blough, the Institute's director of research.

Dudley E. Browne, comptroller of Lockheed Aircraft Corporation, Burbank, California.

Arthur M. Cannon, vice president and treasurer, Standard Insurance Co., Portland, Oregon.

Marquis G. Eaton, senior partner in Eaton & Huddle, San Antonio, Texas.

Paul Grady, partner in the New York executive office of PW.

Robert K. Mautz, professor of accounting, University of Illinois.

Leonard Spacek, managing partner of AA, Chicago.

William W. Werntz, partner and member of the board of directors of Touche, Niven, Bailey & Smart, New York.

Alvin Jennings, as Institute president, was a member *ex officio* of the committee. One supposes that Barr was regarded as the representative of "the investing public" on the committee. All of the committee members were CPAs.

It was, as Carey wrote, a "high-powered committee" [1970, p. 93], composed of strong personalities. Andrew Barr had to obtain the Commission's approval to be able to serve on the committee: it was the first time that a sitting SEC chief accountant became a member of an Institute committee. Obviously, the work of the Special Committee was important to Barr and to the Commission. Both Carman Blough and William Werntz had been SEC chief accountants, and Werntz was in his second year as chairman of the Committee on Accounting Procedure.

Carman Blough, the Institute's director of research, and his small staff had been servicing the Committee on Accounting Procedure (as well as many other Institute committees) since 1944, and his name was printed on every Accounting Research Bulletin since No. 25, which was issued in April 1945. Since 1947, he had been writing a column in the monthly *Journal of Accountancy*, in which he presented his views on what constituted proper accounting and auditing practice. Blough was the profession's most respected authority on "generally accepted accounting principles" [see Carey, 1970, p. 87; Moonitz, 1982].

Dudley Browne was probably the first member from industry to serve on a high-level Institute committee, and he was there to forge a stronger link between the Institute and the Controllers Institute of America. Browne was board chairman and immediate past president of the Controllers Institute. During his presidency, Browne did much to improve relations between the two Institutes, especially on accounting principles [Haase, 1971, p. 176]. But there was still the feeling that the Controllers Institute was on the "outside" of the process by which accounting principles were established.

Arthur Cannon was a surprise choice. He had been an accounting professor at the University of Washington for some ten years prior to becoming an executive in an insurance company in Portland, Oregon. He wrote numerous articles, was an energetic and a persuasive speaker, and had been a vice-president of the AAA and president of the Washington State Society of CPAs. In addition, he had ably edited *The Accounting Review*'s book review section from 1950 to 1957, and in 1954 he launched *The Journal of Accountancy*'s lively and excellent "What to Read/Current Reading." It was in this last capacity that Cannon would have come to the attention of John L.

Carey, the Institute's powerful executive director and publisher of the *Journal*. But it was probably Perry Mason, Blough's assistant at the Institute, who recommended Cannon for the committee. Some years earlier, Cannon had spent a year at the University of California, Berkeley, in an aborted start for a Ph.D. Mason was then a professor on the Berkeley faculty, and he was impressed with Cannon.[18] At 46, Cannon was the second youngest member of the committee.

Marquis Eaton was the immediate past president of the Institute, and he was widely admired and applauded for his innovativeness and leadership in that office [Carey, 1970, pp. 294-296]. Unfortunately, he died suddenly on February 23, 1958. The executive committee did not appoint a successor.

Paul Grady was a protégé of George O. May, the doyen of the profession and former senior partner of PW [see Grady, 1962b]. Under Grady's leadership in the mid-1940s, the Institute's auditing procedures committee issued the first authoritative statement of "generally accepted auditing standards." Like Powell, Grady was a member of the "gradualist" school on accounting principles [see Grady, 1965, esp. pp. 32-34]. Grady was formerly a partner in Arthur Andersen & Co. and was the founding partner's choice as his successor. But Grady and Arthur E. Andersen had a falling out, and he was dismissed from the firm in 1942. At that time, Leonard Spacek was also a rising partner in the firm [Grady, 1978, pp. 55-56; *A Vision of Grandeur*, 1988, pp. 77, 79], and apparently subsequent relations between the two were tepid.

Robert Mautz was a prolific author on accounting and auditing and had chaired the committee that prepared the 1957 revision of the AAA's series of statements on accounting principles [see Mautz, 1957]. It was probably because of this latter role that he was named to the committee. At 42, he was the youngest member of the committee.

Leonard Spacek would have been the most controversial appointment to the committee. He had never before served on an Institute committee, and in speeches and articles he had been assailing the accounting profession and the Institute over the lack of definition of accounting principles. As noted above, the Institute had less than a year earlier convened a special

---

[18]E-mail message from Loyd Heath, dated December 20, 1999, and telephone interview with Kermit O. Hanson, July 22, 2000. During that general period at the University of Washington, Heath was a member of the accounting faculty and Hanson was the dean of the school of business administration.

investigative committee to look into allegations of improper behavior by members of two Institute committees, a charge leveled by Spacek in a speech to a chapter of the Controllers Institute. Carey reported that "A wave of indignation greeted this speech" [1970, p. 77]. But Jennings wanted Spacek on the committee so that his criticisms would be channeled toward constructive change, and also that he would become a party to whatever reform was reported out of the committee. Like Arthur E. Andersen before him, Spacek wanted nothing to do with the Institute, but Jennings, whom Spacek came to respect, persuaded him to accept the invitation.[19]

William Werntz, a lawyer, had joined the SEC's legal staff in 1935 and served as chief accountant from 1938 to 1947, when he joined the newly formed public accounting firm of Touche, Niven, Bailey & Smart, in New York, and then became a CPA.

Several of the committee members had some salient experiences in common. Barr, Grady and Powell had been classmates at the University of Illinois and had studied under Professor A. C. Littleton, who was a staunch defender of historical cost accounting and an exponent of inductively deriving theory from regularities in practice [see Littleton, 1961].[20] Mautz also was a student of A. C. Littleton's, but some 15 years later. The University of Illinois' department of accountancy has, for many years, been reputed as having one of the best bachelor's and master's programs in the country [Bedford, 1997, pp. ix, 50-51], and quite a few leaders of the accounting profession were educated there. Moreover, Barr, Blough, Cannon, Grady, Powell and Werntz had all been tapped by the AAA to serve as vice presidents, and Blough also had served as AAA president. Beginning in 1945, the AAA had a policy of electing one non-academic vice president each year in recognition of his achievements in the profession. At the time of his vice presidency, Cannon was a full-time academic. In addition, Barr, Blough and Werntz had been accounting instructors for short periods early in their careers. Finally, four of the committee members had seen service on the Committee on Accounting Procedure: Blough (1938-42), Eaton (1945-46), Powell (since 1954), and Werntz (since 1950). It is worthy of note that Blough

---

[19]Interview with George R. Catlett, October 21, 1999.

[20]Grady's and Powell's writings clearly indicate that they subscribed to Littleton's inductive approach. See, e.g., Grady [1962a, pp. 46-47] and Powell [1961, p. 29].

was involved with the committee as either a member or the principal staff liaison for all but two years of its history as the issuer of Accounting Research Bulletins.

By contrast to the inductive derivation of principles that marked Grady's and Powell's thinking, Spacek strongly believed that accounting principles should be derived deductively from "objective standards" [see Spacek, 1958b, pp. 81, 82; 1958c, p. 91] and, as will be seen, this difference of view between him and Powell would later cause friction. Spacek was the only committee member, apart from Eaton, without a university degree. A blunt-spoken Midwesterner, he did not mix well with the profession's New York establishment.

THE COMMITTEE REPLIES TO
POWELL'S QUESTIONNAIRE

In a letter dated January 9, 1958, Weldon Powell, the chairman, wrote to the other nine members of the committee to lay out the plan of work. He suggested that they do some preparatory work, by reading Jennings' address (1958a) and four recently published articles:

> Samuel J. Broad's "Applicability of Accounting Principles" [1957],
> Marquis Eaton's "Financial Reporting in a Changing Society" [1957],
> Oswald W. Knauth's "An Executive Looks at Accountancy" [1957],
> and
> May's "Generally Accepted Principles of Accounting" [1958].

He also distributed the typescript of Leonard Spacek's "accounting court" address of August 1957 [Spacek, 1957c].

In order to learn how professional bodies in different fields carried out research, Powell then asked several of the committee members to "direct inquiries to a few other organizations interested in research" and report back on their experience. The organizations were the American Enterprise Institute (on which Barr was to report), the American Accounting Association (Cannon), the National Bureau of Economic Research (Grady), and the Practicing Law Institute (Werntz). Powell said he would prepare a report on the National Industrial Conference Board. (In the event, only a few of these reports were completed and circularized to the committee.)

Powell called on Blough to "summarize for us the history of

the Committee on Accounting Procedure — its genesis, its accomplishments, its shortcomings, its present position, and so on." He also asked the members to consider whether the committee should canvass the views of accountants, businessmen, lawyers, educators, people in government, labor leaders, and others. He said that Perry Mason (a former academic), who was the Institute's associate director of research, would service the committee. Finally, he said he would propound a list of questions "to find out the extent to which there is a consensus, or lack of it, among us on some of the fundamental issues involved in the development and application of accounting principles."

In a second letter written the following day, Powell asked the members to give their views on the following 13 questions by February 1, which are reproduced below, *verbatim*, from his letter:

1. To what extent do you think that accounting is essentially utilitarian in nature?
2. How important do you think it is that there be uniformity of accounting principles among business corporations?
3. Do you think that it is practicable to enforce uniformity of accounting principles among business corporations?
4. Do you consider uniformity of accounting principles among business corporations to be more important or less important than consistency in the application of accounting principles by each of such corporations?
5. To what extent do you believe that adequate disclosure by each business corporation of the accounting principles followed by it is an acceptable substitute for uniformity among business corporations?
6. If you favor the promotion of uniformity among business corporations, what agency or combination of agencies do you think should have the primary responsibility for it? (Some possibilities are state governments, through uniform statutes, the SEC, the Internal Revenue Service, the courts, an organization of stock exchanges, an organization sponsored by corporate managements, an organization of professional accountants, an organization of educators, and an organization including representatives of some of these groups and of labor unions and the public.)

7. Do you think that [an] organized effort to develop accounting principles should confine itself to broad postulates, or that it should comprehend something more?

8. To what extent do you believe that the provisions of law and the requirements of regulatory authority should affect ordinary accounting and reporting?

9. Do you think that we should concern ourselves with the development of accounting principles for public business corporations only or for other persons [i.e., entities] as well?

10. What, if any, features of the organization and work of the present committee on accounting procedure trouble you?

11. Do you consider the proposal of the President, as outlined in his article in the Journal of Accountancy for January 1958 [Jennings, 1958a], to be practicable?

12. What, if any, alternative proposal do you have to suggest?

13. What other points, if any, would you like to have the committee consider at this time?

This was indeed a comprehensive set of questions, but only two dealt with Jennings' "research organization" proposal. Five of the 13 questions dealt with the simmering controversy over "uniformity" versus "flexibility" (or "diversity") of accounting principles, on which Powell, Grady, Browne and Spacek held strong views.

In a memo dated February 7, 1958, Carman Blough replied to Powell's request that he discuss the accomplishments and shortcomings of the Committee on Accounting Procedure. Blough recited four criticisms that had been made of the committee's performance (rather than undertaking to criticize the committee himself), which I summarize below:

1. That the committee is too slow to produce results. Implicit in his discussion was the fact that his small research department was servicing too many Institute committees to provide sufficient staff support. A contributing factor, he said, was the size of the committee, but a smaller committee would necessarily include fewer representatives of the smaller firms and individual practitioners. Blough wrote, "It must be seriously questioned whether the rank and file of the profession would accept the recommendations of a small group of large firm representatives."

2. That the "caliber of members on the committee has been . . . deteriorating." Committee members, he said, have been known to "feel compelled to go back to their firms for instructions before taking a position on a matter . . . [meaning that] partners who do not have the advantage of the discussions that take place in the committee meetings tend to make the decisions." Partly, he believed that this reflected the fact that, "since the committee first started on its present basis, most firms have developed procedures for clearing technical questions within their own organizations which were not common then." Also, it was "hard to keep a firm's top policy man on the committee indefinitely. . . ."

3. That "The charge has been made [that] client influences are felt, in the considerations of the committee, more than they should be." He believed, however, that, "While it has been clear, from time to time, that a position supported by some member of the committee was one which was being followed by an important client of his firm, it has usually been impossible to assert that it did not represent his independent considered judgment. Very seldom has it seemed that a procedure was being defended to satisfy an important client."

4. That "too many members of the committee are too reactionary in their attitudes." But, he added, "that when a man has had enough experience and background to justify his membership on the committee, he has reached an age when it is only natural to look at new ideas pretty carefully before supporting them. . . . Accordingly, established procedures are given a strong benefit of doubt."

Blough concluded by saying that "Possibly the greatest objection to the work of the committee grows out of the tendency of a good many CPAs to object to anything which prevents them from adopting any procedure they consider appropriate in the circumstances."

The members' replies to Powell's 13 questions were interesting. On question 10, concerning features of the present operation of the Committee on Accounting Procedure that trouble them, Perry Mason summarized the responses as follows (with the principal advocate of the position indicated in brackets):

> Bulletins are too brief [Barr, Grady]. The committee is too large [Grady, Powell]. The calibre of the membership has deteriorated [Cannon]. The staff may be inadequate [Grady, Werntz]. The committee settles only important specific problems and does not concern itself

with pure theory or research [Mautz]. The committee is too slow [Powell]. The committee does not work closely enough with other groups [Powell]. The committee does not do enough to guide opinion in controversial matters [Powell]. The committee is biased [Spacek]. The committee compromises too much [Spacek]. It is difficult to get members with interest and time [Werntz] [from Mason's memo to the committee dated March 3, 1958].

Barr and Grady both complained that the Bulletins did not give the reasoning in support of the conclusions. Oddly, Browne did not respond to this question, and Blough let his lengthy memorandum on the effectiveness of the Committee on Accounting Procedure be his reply.

On Question 11, the committee reacted to Jennings' proposal. Five members thought the suggestion that the Institute's Council should approve, or could veto, the research organization's pronouncements was impracticable. Several members liked the heavier emphasis on research, but they were concerned that the proposed research organization would lose touch with practical issues. In general, the committee was ambivalent toward the proposal.

In Question 7, Powell broached the evocative term, "broad postulates." (A concise summary of the evolution of the term "postulate" in the accounting literature, to which George O. May made a significant contribution, is given in an appendix.) Paul Grady, a close colleague of May's, was a partisan of the postulates approach. In his reply to Question 12, on alternatives to Jennings' proposal, he argued for (1) "a qualified group" that would identify and explain "the broad postulates or premises of determining business income," (2) a "research staff to carry out accounting research projects," and (3) an Institute committee to prepare "bulletins on accounting practice which flow from the research projects or arise from other demonstrated needs of the profession."[21] Of course, Spacek had been speaking publicly in favor of the need for the profession to establish the "premises" and "objectives" of financial reporting. In reply to Question 7, virtually all of the members favored initial attention to broad postulates or, in the case of Spacek, to "objective standards," and that a study of their implications for principles or practices should follow.

---

[21]With this three-part recommendation, Grady came close to anticipating the principal outlines of the Special Committee's final report.

The replies to Powell's Questions 2-6 on uniformity revealed the substratum of philosophical division that was, as
suggested above, impeding the work of the Committee on Accounting Procedure. The representative of the Controllers Institute on the Special Committee, Dudley Browne, was implacably
opposed to uniformity. In reply to Question 2, he wrote, "I
regard uniformity as a device designed to reduce accounting
from a profession to a clerical process," and he said "I am
inclined to favor adequate disclosure over uniformity" in reply
to Question 5. Eight years later, Browne declared:

> I maintain that divergent [accounting] practices are
> both the outgrowth and reflection of our economic sys-
> tem and that the effort to eliminate or reduce them is
> not a service either to our accounting system or to the
> economic system it serves. Such goals of restricting
> [management] choice and seeking uniformity are more
> rightfully concepts of totalitarian worlds [Browne,
> 1966, p. 42].[22]

Apart from Browne, Powell was the least won over by an
argument for uniformity. He saw uniformity as "desirable but
not essential." He added: "As a practical matter it is elusive. It is
not a panacea. There probably should be more than one right
way of doing any number of things, and business men should
have the opportunity of experimenting with different approaches to their problems." The very fact that he asked, in
Question 4, whether uniformity of accounting principles was
more or less important than consistency in the application of
accounting principles suggested his low regard for the former.
Blough pointedly replied: "These are not alternatives." After
suggesting that "the trend within a company is often more important than its comparison with other companies," he added:
"However, that is no reason for failing to get as much comparability as practicable." Cannon replied, "Uniformity encompasses
consistency. The one makes data comparable between different
businesses; and the other makes data comparable from year to
year." Mautz replied: "Consistency in application is a prerequisite to uniformity of principles. It is not a substitute for uniformity. They are about equally important." Werntz wrote, "In

---

[22]In his article, Browne interpreted principles as meaning "rules of action,"
or practices. As to fundamental principles, he wrote: "We can of course expect
general agreement and uniformity in the broad and basic principles such as
honesty, for example, or full and frank disclosure" [1966, p. 41].

broad general areas uniformity is more important. As to detailed practices, consistency is more important."

Powell's was clearly a minority position. He replied that "Consistency from year to year is very important. . . . Business enterprises vary from one to another in a number of respects anyway, and it has never troubled me that there are some differences in accounting." Even Grady, who replied that it is "very important to have consistency," added: "I favor more uniformity so long as we do not indulge in misrepresentation."[23]

On the subject of whether adequate disclosure of the accounting principles followed would be an acceptable substitute for uniformity among business corporations (Question 5), Cannon and Mautz said "no." Most of the others believed that disclosure was adequate until greater uniformity was achieved. SEC Chief Accountant Barr and two of his predecessors in that position (Blough and Werntz) made it clear, as Barr said, that "Disclosure of an unsound practice is not substitute for the adoption of sound principles,"[24] a view that Spacek espoused as well. Spacek counseled that "The accountant should have the right to criticize a generally accepted accounting principle in his certificate, if he will take responsibility for supporting his opinion" — a practice that his firm had already adopted for price-level depreciation [see Zeff, 1992, pp. 457-459; Accounting Research Division, 1963, pp. 211-217].

Hence, based on the replies to most of Powell's questions, there was a considerable difference of views on both the points of substance and approach. The first five of Powell's questions dealt with the attributes of good accounting, rather than directly addressing the mission given to the Special Committee, namely, consideration of "a new approach to accounting research." Powell and a few others on the committee were initially of the view that perhaps the Special Committee should actually propose the norms of sound accounting, including the

---

[23]Seven years later, Grady set forth a list of "basic concepts to which accepted accounting principles are oriented," which included a concept entitled "diversity in accounting among independent entities." Although he said that this concept does not imperil the objective to "narrow the areas of difference in accounting" and to promote greater comparability in financial statements, he concluded that "It does, however, place the objective within realistic limits which fall considerably short of uniformity" [Grady, 1965, p. 35].

[24]This was a restatement of the SEC's long-standing administrative policy on financial statements, which was announced by the Commission in Accounting Series Release No. 4, issued in April 1938 (when Blough was the chief accountant).

broad postulates. Nonetheless, the full range of questions posed by Powell was a useful beginning to the committee's work, because it focused the members' attention on the important issues.

THE COMMITTEE'S FIRST MEETING

The Special Committee's first meeting was held on March 23-24, 1958, in New York City. All of the members of the committee, plus Mason, were in attendance. Jennings and Carey met with the committee at lunch. The minutes of the meeting were not really a record of the discussions but instead consisted of a summary of the suggestions that were broached, without attribution to any members by name. Fortunately, the author is in possession of a confidential internal memorandum written on April 8, 1958 by one of the committee members, which reviews the proceedings in greater detail.

As the committee had not been given a formal name, it was agreed that it would be called the Special Committee on Research Program.

Powell asked the members to comment on the written answers to his questionnaire, most of which had been distributed prior to the meeting. Several members criticized Browne's categorical rejection of uniformity.

At an early point in the meeting, the committee came to the belief that the Committee on Accounting Procedure should be reorganized so that its members would be the most capable and talented men from the profession. The practice of balancing the committee geographically, and having one representative from all of the big firms, would be abandoned. Views differed according to whether the reorganized entity would continue to be the Committee on Accounting Procedure or would become a review board or an accounting court. But there was general agreement that the process for establishing accounting principles should remain within the profession and under the control of the Institute.

When discussing the issues that the new entity should address, Spacek reiterated his credo that the accounting principles adopted had to be fair to various segments of the public, including stockholders, management, consumers, and labor [see Spacek, 1957c, p. 37]. Mason disputed how it could be determined that an accounting principle was fair to all of these groups. Cannon intoned that George Meany, president of the AFL-CIO, had criticized the use of accelerated depreciation in financial statements, and had argued that depreciation should represent the fair cost of using up property from the point of view of labor, as well as stockholders and consumers.[25]

Grady then proposed George O. May's postulates for consideration, and Barr recommended that the broad postulates should include the principles enunciated by the AAA committees in prior years. There seemed to be general agreement that the Committee on Accounting Procedure had not done enough to "narrow areas of difference and inconsistency in accounting practices," a principal objective that the committee had itself enunciated.[26] Powell surprised some of the members by venturing the view that he would not support an Accounting Research Bulletin that would change accounting procedures unless he knew his clients were in favor of the change. A dispute soon developed over deferred tax accounting, bringing out the difference in views between three of the Big Eight firms over the propriety of deferred tax accounting as well as the acceptability of alternative methods. Spacek, who favored deferred tax accounting and a greater degree of uniformity, said there was only one answer. Grady and Powell, whose firms believed that a required use of deferred tax accounting was unjustifiable and were reluctant to force uniformity, believed you could sign an unqualified audit report either with or without deferred tax accounting. Barr said that, in his book, the auditor could not sign both reports.

There followed a discussion of how long a period of experimentation should be allowed before a Bulletin designating one of two alternative accounting methods as preferable would secure industry acceptance. A few members believed that the SEC would not wait for industry to acquiesce, because it had the power to prescribe accounting practices under the securities acts.[27]

---

[25]This reference to Meany's view on corporate depreciation allowances also appeared in an article by Spacek in the May-June 1958 issue of the *Harvard Business Review* [Spacek, 1958b, p. 80].

[26]It seems that the earliest expression of this objective was in Accounting Research Bulletin No. 43, *Restatement and Revision of Accounting Research Bulletins* [Committee on Accounting Procedure, 1953, p. 8]. This passage seems likely to have been drafted by Carman Blough, the committee's research director and a former SEC chief accountant.

[27]Until this point, the rendering of the proceedings during the committee's first meeting is based on the aforementioned confidential internal memorandum written by one of the members of the Special Committee.

The minutes of the meeting reproduced a series of "suggestions" made by members of the committee for the new research program. Among them was the following, which doubtless was urged by Spacek:

> There should be a "right way" to handle any given transaction, by reference to a basic principle. It was suggested that a showing that a given principle was fair to management, to the stockholder, to labor, and to the consumer would constitute an objective standard for the establishment of accounting principles.

Powell regarded the committee's first meeting as exploratory. In a communication to the Institute's Council in April, he conceptualized the direction in which the committee was headed, and he reported that agreement had been reached on several points:

> We think the Institute should take a firm lead in the development and promulgation of accounting principles, and we believe a change in the present approach to this matter is needed. We think the research program should be a planned one. Possibly the first step could be the determination of the basic principles or postulates upon which accounting procedures are based, as a framework of reference for the solution of detailed problems; next might come the preparation of a fairly broad set of coordinated but not detailed principles, similar to the statements of the American Accounting Association; and finally could follow a consideration of more detailed matters, such as those covered by the present accounting research bulletins, but in relation to the basic broad principles. . . .
>
> We are in agreement . . . that any new approach should provide for greater staff participation in research, more effort to ascertain and lead public opinion in uncertain and controversial areas, and closer attention to means of obtaining general acceptance of pronouncements on accounting matters, than there has been in the past.

Powell's concern that the acceptance by industry of any major changes in the choices of accounting principles or practices is made clear at the end of the foregoing quotation. He was certainly not one who believed that such changes, including especially a move toward uniformity, could be forced.

Spacek was elated after the committee's first meeting. In a speech the following month, he said, "This committee, in my

opinion, is making excellent progress towards its objectives"
[1958a, p. 67].

THE COMMITTEE'S SECOND MEETING

The second meeting was held in Chicago, on May 12-13,
1958. All of the members attended. Jennings and Carey, who
had lunch with the committee at the first meeting, were not
present. The quotations in this section are drawn from the minutes of the meeting.

At the beginning of the second meeting, the committee approved two important amendments to the minutes of the first
meeting. Both dealt with the sensitive issue of promoting uniformity. The summary minutes of the March meeting, which
had been drafted by Mason and probably overseen by Blough,
reported, among a series of suggestions made by one or more
members, that "The research program should be more than fact
finding. It should include conclusions and recommendations
which could result in the enforcement of uniform standards."
The second sentence was amended to read: "It should include
conclusions and recommendations directed toward the
strengthening of accounting principles or standards." It was
also stated in the minutes from the first meeting that "It is not
possible to achieve complete uniformity and comparability in
accounting and reporting, but much improvement can be
made." The second clause in the sentence was amended to read:
"but it is desirable to narrow the areas of difference." Except
for these amendments, the March minutes were written to reflect Secretary Mason's view, as edited by Chairman Powell, of
the emerging consensus of the committee's agreement on the
shape of the new program.

At this second meeting, this emerging consensus began to
look very much as it would in the committee's final report.
Contrary to Jennings' suggestion in his 1957 address [1958a]
that the cost of a new research organization should be shared
by industry and the profession, the committee decided that
"The research organization is [to be] kept within the framework
of the American Institute. Outside accounting organizations
would not participate directly but would be consulted and kept
informed of all research activities."

Two types of publication were envisioned:

Tentative, informative, thoroughly developed and
documented studies, including conclusions reached,
would be prepared by the research group and be issued

on its own authority. The purpose of these studies is to expose ideas for comment, help to mold opinion, and pave the way for more formal and more authoritative statements of generally accepted accounting principles.

The second type would be "Authoritative statements of generally accepted accounting principles, similar in standing to the present accounting research bulletins, and based upon studies made by the research group, [which] would be issued by a special 'Board' set up for that purpose." These statements were to be "based principally upon the publications of the research group." Indeed, the committee agreed that "An immediate project would be the preparation of a statement of basic postulates and standards on which all other pronouncements would be based."

Previously, the literature available to Institute members had consisted, in the main, of articles by practitioners and academics arguing one or another side of a controversial accounting issue, which were published in *The Journal of Accountancy* or *The Accounting Review*, as well as the series of monographs and principles statements published by the American Accounting Association. In addition, the Institute's research staff had, between 1940 and 1953, published a series of short papers on controversial accounting topics [see Zeff and Moonitz, 1984, vol. II].[28] With this proposal, the Special Committee sought to stimulate the production of a series of research studies that would synthesize the best of the literature and thus promote a broader understanding and agreement on accounting principles among the Institute membership.

Several names were suggested for the "Board": Accounting Procedures Board, Board on Accounting Principles, and Board on Generally Accepted Accounting Principles. The last of these three received the most support. The term "board" was apparently intended to increase the authority and standing, beyond just committee status, of the body issuing pronouncements. The board would be "somewhat smaller" than the Committee on Accounting Procedure and would be elected by the Institute membership or by Council, rather than appointed by the president. In the selection of board members, the committee agreed

---

[28]This recitation omits an occasional monograph or book as well as the "official" literature composed of Accounting Research Bulletins and the SEC's Accounting Series Releases.

that "Emphasis would be placed upon competence rather than representation of particular groups or geographic areas."

The committee agreed that "Only a very few seasoned and widely accepted pronouncements would be adopted by the membership of the Institute (or the Council) and thereby would become mandatory upon the members." In fact, only in 1918 and 1934 did the Institute membership ever vote to approve or disapprove any accounting rules or principles [Zeff, 1972, pp. 115-116, 125], and the six rules or principles approved in 1934 were repeated in Accounting Research Bulletin No. 1 [Committee on Accounting Procedure, 1939] as well as in chapter 1 of Accounting Research Bulletin No. 43 [Committee on Accounting Procedure, 1953]; four of the six continue to be applicable today. None of the contents of any other Accounting Research Bulletins were ever submitted either to Council or to the Institute's membership for approval.

"The general goal," the Special Committee agreed, "should be to make the expression of generally accepted accounting principles more complete, to continue to narrow the areas of difference, and to increase the authority and acceptance of the pronouncements."

Importantly, the committee added that "All recommendations should be founded on a statement of basic postulates and standards, but attempts should be made to keep the results flexible and not freeze accounting procedures into a set of rigid rules." Thus, the concern about limiting companies' freedom of action was clearly expressed. It is not clear from the minutes whether the "postulates" were to be normative or descriptive, and it is likely that the issue was not raised. The addition of "standards" makes the foundation appear to be more yielding than if "postulates" were used alone.

An appendix to the minutes supplied details of the new organization. It is not known whether the contents of the appendix were actually discussed and agreed in the committee meeting or were interpolated by Chairman Powell and Perry Mason. The appendix provided for a board membership of 18, compared with 21 serving on the Committee on Accounting Procedure, and they all were to be members of the Institute, and therefore CPAs. It was stated in the body of the minutes that a proposal that pronouncements be approved by a simple majority, instead of by the current two-thirds, was defeated. While it was not stated in the appendix whether all of the Big Eight firms would be represented on the board, it was probably assumed that they would, and a requirement of a two-thirds majority would prevent the Big Eight firms' representatives, were they to be in agreement, from being outvoted by the other ten members. The board members were to be selected for staggered three-year terms "on basis of competence, primarily, rather than representation of particular groups or geographical areas." They would select their own chairman. They would be elected by the Institute membership or by Council rather than be appointed by the president.

The appendix called for an accounting research staff composed of a director, three to five senior members and three junior members, plus two secretaries — representing a massive increase over the staff support for the Committee on Accounting Procedure. Further, the committee decided "Contact with accounting practice would be maintained through the use of advisory committees which would work closely with the research staff." The committee consensus was that an advisory committee should not have veto power over the publication of a research study, but that the director should make the final decision.[29]

It was also stated in the body of the minutes that "it would not be appropriate for the director of the research program to edit a column in The Journal of Accountancy, as is now done by the Director of Research." There was only one Carman Blough.

The committee agreed that the accounting research staff would not be concerned with issues relating to auditing or managerial (or cost) accounting. The scope of its research activities would be the same as that for the Committee on Accounting Procedure.

The committee considered the possible use of public hearings, or of board meetings that might be attended by representatives of outside groups, but they believed that, "while expressions of opinions of non-members of the Board should be welcomed and solicited, they should be restricted to written memoranda." "It was pointed out," the minutes went on, "that publication of research studies in advance of the preparation of statements by the Board would do much to take care of the problem of informing and securing the cooperation of outside groups."

---

[29]The issue of whether to publish a research study actually arose four years later, when the director authorized publication of the research study on broad accounting principles in the face of opposition by a number of prominent members of the advisory committees on the postulates and principles studies [see Zeff, 1972, pp. 175-178].

Therefore, at its second meeting, the committee seemed to make substantial progress toward developing a reform plan.

POWELL DRAFTS THE COMMITTEE'S REPORT, AND SPACEK OBJECTS

After two meetings, Powell believed that the members were in sufficient agreement that only one more meeting, scheduled for August 1, would be needed to put the finishing touches on its report. So he set about preparing a tentative draft report, dated July 9, 1958, which he exposed to President Alvin Jennings and Executive Director John Carey for comment prior to sending it, as modified by their comments, to the other members of the committee.

In Perry Mason's letter covering the draft, dated July 11, he cited the principal differences between Powell's draft and the plan developed at the committee's meeting in May. At Carey's suggestion, Powell decided that "Commission" would replace "Board" for the name of the new entity that was to issue the authoritative statements of generally accepted accounting principles, and that a steering committee, to be known as the Board of Managers, would supplant the Institute's executive committee as the body to oversee the financial administration of the research organization. The Board of Managers would be composed of Carey and four members chosen by Council. Powell also decided that the Commission's chairman would be chosen by the Institute's executive committee, and not by the Commission itself. Also, the director of accounting research would be selected by the Board of Managers instead of by Council. In addition, Powell risked treading on sensitive toes by allowing some of his philosophical views to seep into the draft (as will be seen).

After reading Powell's draft report, Leonard Spacek erupted. As noted above, he harbored a deep distrust of Carey and of the three firms that had been providing much of the Institute's leadership — PW, H&S and LRB&M — and he sent Powell a bluntly worded, six-page letter of criticism. In his letter, dated July 17, 1958, Spacek accused Powell of having omitted and misrepresented substantive views on which the committee had agreed, and he berated Powell for having sought Jennings' and Carey's views, for, he said, they were not members of the committee. In his reply to Spacek, dated July 22, Powell wrote that "the July 9 draft reflects the substance of the conclusions reached at the two meetings of our Committee, as I understand them. I did not knowingly include anything substantive that was not discussed, or omit or misrepresent anything substantive that was discussed." Jennings, who had been sent a copy of Spacek's letter, himself replied that, as Institute president, he was a member *ex officio* of every Institute committee, but he had scrupulously attempted not to influence the deliberations or report of the committee [letter, August 19, 1958]. Even though he respected Jennings, Spacek wanted the committee to be as free as possible of the taint of the Institute establishment, although he was well aware that Powell (H&S) and Paul Grady (PW) were senior partners of two of the most influential firms in Institute affairs.

In his letter of July 17, Spacek also criticized Powell for not emphasizing the centrality of postulates or "objective standards" in the new program. In his draft report, Powell had written:

> The general purpose of the Institute in the field of financial accounting should be to advance the written expression of what constitutes generally accepted accounting principles, for the guidance of its members and of others. This means something more than a survey of existing practice. It means inquiry to determine acceptable practice, and effort to narrow the areas of difference and inconsistency in practice.[30]

To Spacek, that sounded more like description than prescription. He reminded Powell that, at its March meeting, the committee had decided that "There should be a 'right way' to handle any given transaction, by reference to a basic principle." In fact, the committee had not made such a decision: it was merely minuted as a "suggestion," but Spacek believed that it was fundamental to the process of developing sound accounting. Powell's passage on narrowing the areas of difference and inconsistency in practice agreed almost *verbatim* with a passage in Accounting Research Bulletin No. 43 [Committee on Accounting Procedure, 1953, p. 8]. As such, it probably sounded to Spacek as a continuation of the *ancien régime*. It is interest-

---

[30]The phrase, "narrow the areas of difference and inconsistency in practice," was code terminology. As noted above, this wording appeared in the introduction to Accounting Research Bulletin No. 43 [Committee on Accounting Procedure, 1953, p. 8], and it can be traced to Accounting Research Bulletin No. 1 [Committee on Accounting Procedure, 1939, p. 2]. For many years, the SEC's chief accountant had been adjuring the Committee on Accounting Procedure to follow this course. See Pines [1965, p. 748].

ing to note that, in the committee's final report, Powell's "acceptable practice" was replaced by "appropriate practice."

The next paragraph in Powell's draft, reflecting his philosophical leaning, was as follows:

> In accomplishing this purpose, reliance should be placed on persuasion rather than on compulsion. The Institute cannot impose accounting principles by fiat. At the same time, it can, and it should make every effort to lead in the thinking on unsettled and controversial issues.

Spacek objected that the committee had not said that "reliance should be placed on persuasion rather than on compulsion." In reply to Spacek, Powell wrote, "Maybe the Committee did not say it, but, as I remember the discussion, we meant it. If we did not, we can change it." In fact, the committee eventually approved this wording for inclusion in its final report. A review of the minutes for the March meeting shows that, following Spacek's espousal of the need for an "objective standard for the establishment of accounting principles," it was stated that "There appeared, however, to be differences of opinion [within the committee] as to how far the elimination of alternative practices could be carried." Another of the "suggestions" minuted during the meeting was that "The research program should be more than fact finding. It should include conclusions and recommendations which could result in the enforcement of uniform standards." The source of this point was probably also Spacek.

Powell had stated in an early section of his draft report that:

> Thought should be given at the beginning and from time to time thereafter to the forward planning of the accounting research program and related activities, to the end that accounting principles are developed on a coherent and consistent basis and pronouncements are made in an orderly and timely manner. This does not mean the detailed codification of accounting principles. It does mean the study of the postulates, few in number, upon which accounting practices are based, followed by the formulation of a fairly broad set of coordinated but not detailed principles, as a framework of reference for the solution of detailed problems. The consideration, then, of detailed matters, such as those covered by the present accounting research bulletins, should be undertaken in relation to the postu-

lates and broad principles previously expressed. Institute pronouncements should have reasonable flexibility, and should avoid rigidity.

Spacek complained that Powell had omitted any reference in his draft to "objective standards" (Spacek's preferred term), and he suspected that Powell's description of the operation of the Commission sounded as if it were to behave like the old Committee on Accounting Procedure, in which the members advocated accounting practices without regard to a governing set of objectives or basic norms. The phrase "upon which accounting practices are based" probably grated at Spacek, because it would have implied to him that the postulates would be inferred, or inductively derived, from established practice (in the Littletonian sense), rather than prescribed on the basis of "objective standards." That phrase was not repeated in the committee's final report. Spacek would also have bridled at the juxtaposition of "reasonable flexibility" and "rigidity," as if the proponents of uniformity favored actual rigidity [see Spacek, 1958c, pp. 85-86]. The term "rigidity" did not appear in the committee's final report.

The March meeting of the committee had apparently been regarded as exploratory and not as the occasion for defining the terms of a reform proposal. Under the heading, "Goal of the Research Program," in the minutes drafted by Perry Mason, all of the nine enumerated statements of view were characterized as "suggestions," not as agreed positions. Spacek probably recalled the points that he made during the meeting, in his typically forceful manner, without recalling whether disagreement, or contrasting views, had been expressed, and he was convinced that the statements of view in the minutes corresponding with his own views had been agreed. (He also complained in his letter of July 17 that the minutes had not represented the views of the committee. Whether, at the May meeting, he had proposed amendments to the minutes of the March meeting that failed to secure committee support is not known.) Had Spacek not suspected the Institute's leaders of a Machiavellian plot, namely, that they were determined to preserve the status quo under the flag of reform, his bill of exceptions to Powell's draft report could probably have been resolved through amicable correspondence and without vituperation. But Spacek's accusatory manner was to vent his disagreements with those who ran the profession, and this was no exception.

Apparently, none of the other committee members commented in writing on Powell's draft. Spacek's letter, which detailed many concerns in addition to those mentioned above, was sharply worded, and Powell, ever the gentleman, felt injured by the tone of his remarks. Spacek intended no personal affront; it was in his nature to speak and write bluntly. His reaction to the draft was undoubtedly colored by his distrust of the Institute and its leadership. Another factor would have been the tense relationship between his firm and several others in the Big Eight, including Powell's, arising from Arthur Andersen & Co.'s crusade to persuade the Committee on Accounting Procedure (CAP) to revise its Bulletin 44, issued in 1954, which stated that income tax allocation was not required when companies used the declining-balance method of depreciation for income tax purposes and the straight-line method for financial accounting purposes. Arthur Andersen & Co. favored income tax allocation when such differences arose [see, e.g., Spacek, 1956a, p. 6; Spacek, 1956b, p. 12], and, due mainly to the efforts of Garrett T. Burns, the firm's representative on the CAP, Bulletin 44 was finally revised in July 1958, requiring income tax allocation when different depreciation methods are used (as above). Neither H&S nor PW liked income tax allocation, and Powell was then serving on the CAP. Powell and the PW representative on the CAP filed a qualified assent, which read more like a dissent, in which they disagreed with the requirement for income tax allocation [Committee on Accounting Procedure, 1958, pp. 5-A]. As has been noted above, H&S and PW were advocates of permissiveness, while AA was not.

THE COMMITTEE'S FINAL MEETING

The committee's third and final meeting was held on August 1, 1958, in New York City. All of the members but Carman Blough, who was ill, were in attendance. Although it was an all-day meeting, the three double-spaced pages of minutes revealed very little of the tenor of the discussion, virtually all of which was devoted to the points in Powell's July 9th draft of the final report. A number of minor amendments were made to the minutes of the May meeting.

The committee decided that it would not itself undertake to set forth the postulates or principles of accounting. Instead, the minutes stated that:

> The majority of the committee felt that, while the report should contain a statement of the basic considerations and philosophy underlying the need for a revision of the Institute's research program, [the com-

mittee's] principal function would be to present a plan for an organization which would accomplish the desired improvement in research activities and would result in defining and determining generally accepted accounting principles.

It seems likely that Spacek constituted the minority.

The committee disapproved of the use of a Board of Managers, as suggested by Carey, and it decided to recommend that the new research program be financed through efforts of the members of the accounting profession, and not from outside the profession. Most of the other changes were said to be of an editorial nature.

SUBSEQUENT EXCHANGES OF CORRESPONDENCE

Four days after the August 1st meeting, Perry Mason sent the committee members a rewritten draft of the final report (dated August 5), which was attached to the minutes of the meeting. The section at the outset of the report, entitled "Basic considerations," was modified and amplified. It was there that the philosophical differences over flexibility v. uniformity rose to the surface. Following the meeting, the committee members proceeded to exchange correspondence on various points in the draft with which they were at odds, and they reflected as well on decisions taken at the meeting. From this subsequent exchange of letters, it becomes clear that the committee had voted, evidently by a narrow majority, to delete a sensitive passage, "This [i.e., the development of accounting principles on a coherent and consistent basis] does not mean the detailed codification of accounting principles," from Powell's earlier draft. Grady, Powell and Blough, in correspondence, expressed regret at the committee's decision and recommended that its substance be restored [letters dated August 6, 7 and 12, respectively]. Barr believed that the sentence probably would fit better in the new draft than the old, but he did not press the matter [letter dated August 15]. Mautz said he would not object to the reinstatement of the sentence [letter dated August 15]. Cannon was willing to see it reinstated, but he felt that the point had been made adequately elsewhere in the draft [letter dated August 11]. Spacek, who had been the strongest proponent of the deletion during the committee meeting, defended the committee's decision [letter dated August 13], and Werntz agreed with him [letter dated August 15]. The deleted sentence was not restored. But a new paragraph in the August 5th draft, which survived into the final report, probably covered the same ground:

> Rules or other guides for the application of accounting principles in specific situations, then, should be developed in relation to the postulates and principles previously expressed. Statements of these probably should be comparable as to subject matter with the present accounting research bulletins. They should have reasonable flexibility.

The members continued to trade suggestions on the name of the entity to succeed the Committee on Accounting Procedure (and the Committee on Terminology). Paul Grady wrote to the committee members that he disliked the title, "Commission on Generally Accepted Accounting Principles," which the committee had just affirmed at its meeting. He said that "the word 'Commission' has a strong governmental regulatory connotation which I believe should be avoided" [letter dated August 6]. He related that "one of the principal criticisms which I have heard from businessmen in relation to Accounting Research Bulletins is that the Institute seems to be setting itself up as a regulatory body from which there is no appeal." He said that "the public relations aspect of this matter is important and that 'Board' sounds somewhat less regulatory in character than 'Commission'." Grady's suggestion of board instead of commission met with general approval, although Spacek, always suspicious of Grady's (and Powell's) motives, reminded his colleagues that the accounting profession "has regulatory aspects in its operation," although he was indifferent as between "board" and "commission" [letter dated August 13].

Grady said he favored "Accounting Research Board," thus continuing to place emphasis on "research," as had Alvin Jennings in his December 1957 address [1958a], and perhaps because he was serving on a body with the title, Special Committee on Research Program. In rapid order, Powell, Blough and Browne wrote that they agreed with Grady's preferred title [letter from Powell dated August 7; letter from Mason dated August 12, conveying Blough's view; and letter dated August 12 from Browne]. Spacek disagreed with "Accounting Research Board," as he argued that research was only one part of the responsibilities of the new board, which, he said, was to provide adequate leadership in the development of generally accepted accounting principles [letter dated August 13]. In a letter dated August 18, Werntz said he was also not happy with "Accounting Research Board," "as I do not like the connotation of 'Research' in the title." He preferred "Board on Accounting Principles," adding: "I think it is unnecessary to include the words 'generally accepted' since 'generally accepted' really comes about from the action of others" [letter dated August 18]. Blough (modifying his view) and Cannon agreed with Werntz's preference [letters from Mason dated August 19 and from Cannon dated August 20]. As the tide began to turn from "research" to "principles" in the title of the new board, Powell wrote that he did not think that the term "generally accepted accounting principles" had to appear in the new board's title so long as the board's pronouncements were characterized as "statements on generally accepted accounting principles" [letter dated August 15]. To some members, it was important that the name or published utterances of the new board be linked explicitly to the standard wording in the auditor's opinion.

Following the exchange of views, the committee's final report was revised under Powell's direction, and it was dispatched to the Institute's Council in September.[31] The final report gave Accounting Principles Board as the name of the new entity, and it is likely that Powell, Mason or Carey had made the selection. Reflecting Powell's strong preference, the final report referred to the new board's pronouncements as "statements on generally accepted accounting principles."[32] The draft also affirmed that, unlike the CAP (whose members were chosen from year to year by the Institute president), the members of the new board would be nominated by the executive committee and elected by Council. Blough later wrote, "It is anticipated that this will give the board even greater stature than was accorded the committee on accounting procedure" [1960, p. 8].

One minor crisis was averted at the eleventh hour. In a letter to Powell dated August 15, Spacek gave notice that he wanted to attach a "comment" to the report, and he submitted a preliminary draft of the comment. He believed strongly that he

---

[31]The report was published in *The Journal of Accountancy* two months later [1958].

[32]Powell's choice of preposition was apparently deliberate. Had the statements been "of generally accepted accounting principles," they would have arguably possessed a more fundamental character. The comparable preposition for auditing pronouncements (adopted by the Institute in 1973) has also been "on": Statements on Auditing Standards. The term "generally accepted auditing standards" refers to the fundamental norms that were developed in the mid-1940s and subsequently approved by the Institute's membership in 1948.

should speak out on two issues that troubled him. Although, in the proposed comment, he gave "wholehearted support to the [committee's] report," he felt it necessary to emphasize that the "objective standards [a term that was not used in the report] or postulates" must give rise to generally accepted accounting principles that require companies to show "as profit only the economic gain after preservation of beginning capital and that show the extent to which the capital is subject to prior obligations. . . . " This was a clear reference to his firm's publicly known view that general price changes must be explicitly factored into the derivation of net income [Spacek, 1956a; 1956b; Zeff, 1992, pp. 457-459]. He also wanted to state that accounting principles should "clearly recognize the reporting needs of the various segments of our society," another position that he and his firm had advanced publicly [Spacek, 1957c]. Second, he would charge the members of the new board to make "objective decisions with respect to generally accepted accounting principles on the basis of established postulates or standards without being biased because of decisions already made in their own practice." He was greatly concerned that the new board would continue as had the CAP, some of whose members, he believed, had sacrificed principle for expediency, by countenancing questionable practices supposedly to defend the interests of major clients. He said that he had less confidence than did his colleagues on the Special Committee that the members of the new board would "subordinate their prior views to the objective standards or postulates."

None of the other members of the committee would have liked the idea of Spacek's writing such a comment, and Cannon succeeded in persuading him not to do so. In a letter to Spacek dated August 28, Cannon argued that his point concerning profit being based on economic gain goes beyond the charge to the committee, which was to propose a new organization, not to settle in advance the problems that might come before it. Cannon also argued that the section on "Basic considerations" in the committee's draft report dealt with his anxiety over the meaning of accounting principles. Finally, in regard to Spacek's concern over the objectivity of the future members of the new board, Cannon wrote, "that's a risk anyone takes when he sets up an organization," and that "we have to assume that the motives of others are no less honorable than our own. . . . " After discussing Cannon's arguments with him by telephone, Spacek wrote Powell that he wished to withdraw his concurring comment [letter dated September 5].

ESTABLISHMENT OF THE
ACCOUNTING PRINCIPLES BOARD

The report of the Special Committee on Research Program marked a major turning point in the Institute's role in establishing generally accepted accounting principles. The committee succeeded in bridging significant philosophical differences among several of the major public accounting firms and their strong-willed leaders, and its report held out the promise of reinvigorating the process of establishing accounting principles. *The Journal of Accountancy*, which is published by the Institute, hailed the report and made clear "that the inspiration for it came from within the profession, rather than from outside pressure" ["Accounting Research and Accounting Principles," 1958, p. 28]. The Institute's Council adopted the report in April 1959, and the Accounting Principles Board (APB) was launched on September 1, 1959,[33] almost one year after the special committee submitted its report. Paul Grady wrote that "Accounting firms responded with generous pledges of almost one million dollars to support the newly augmented research program" [1972, p. 18].

The Institute's executive committee selected Weldon Powell to be chairman of the board. But, in a controversial move, it decided that all of the Big Eight accounting firms, apart from Powell's firm, would be represented on the board by their national managing partner, not a technical partner. Carey recalled that the reasons for this action were "both to emphasize its authority (prestige) and to speed up decision-making" [letter to the author dated July 2, 1970].[34] George O. May, who was being kept apprised of developments by Paul Grady, wrote to Institute President Louis H. Penney to criticize that decision. May argued that "the Board would operate more effectively if members chosen from the very large field were sources rather than channels of opinion."[35]

---

[33]The Committee on Accounting Procedure and the Committee on Terminology went out of existence on August 31, 1959.

[34]Carey's second reason alluded to an experience of the CAP, when some partners serving on the committee were known to seek advice from their firm's executive office prior to casting their vote.

[35]May observed that neither he nor Walter A. Staub, Samuel J. Broad and other chairmen of the Committee on Accounting Procedure were the executive head of their firm. Letter from May to Penney, dated April 2, 1959, in the George O. May collection at Price Waterhouse & Co., New York City.

Penney elaborated on the executive committee's expectation for the APB as follows:

> It is not intended that this Board will be a working committee in the sense that the Committee on Accounting Procedure has been. As we visualize the program, the Board is to be largely a policy making organization and in addition it will from time to time very likely have to make decisions regarding the selection of certain courses of action from two or more alternatives. Some of those decisions may be difficult. For that reason the Executive Committee approved the theory of selecting for the Board some of the executive heads of some of the better organized accounting firms because those individuals, generally speaking, have broad accounting experience and are accustomed to making decisions on the basis of facts submitted to them by responsible technicians [letter from Penney to Hassel Tippit, dated April 3, 1959].

The executive committee's conception of the role of the APB as a senatorial body would most certainly not have been the one envisioned by the members of the Special Committee. Nor was it an accurate forecast of the actual role of the APB. Paul Grady has written that the executive committee's decision "was a sad error in judgment, which I strongly opposed at the time" [letter from Grady to the author dated September 28, 1970]. In the end, the managing partners of seven other Big Eight firms were invited to serve on the APB,[36] but two of the firms, Peat, Marwick, Mitchell & Co. and Arthur Andersen & Co., declined to do so. They both replied that their senior technical partner, John Peoples and Russell Morrison, respectively, should represent their firm on the new board. Peat Marwick's Managing Partner William M. Black replied that his existing obligations prevented him from freeing the time to serve on the board [letter from Black to Penney, dated March 27, 1959]. AA's Managing Partner Leonard Spacek replied that Morrison was "better qualified than I," and, furthermore, he wanted to continue to speak out publicly on the deficiencies in accounting principles and practices. He also said that "it would be inappropriate for me to serve on the Board, particularly in view of my reservations as to the entire program, which I wanted to voice [in a comment appended to the Special Committee's report] but

---

[36]As noted above, Weldon Powell, the senior technical partner at Haskins & Sells, had already accepted the appointment as APB chairman.

finally agreed to withdraw in the interest of showing solidarity" [letter from Spacek to Penney, dated March 27, 1959]. But the executive committee continued to insist that Black and Spacek should represent their firms. Consequently, during 1959-60, the APB's first year, it had 18 members, including representatives from only six of the Big Eight firms.

The following year, Institute President J. S. Seidman, a partner in a middle-sized New York City firm, persuaded Spacek to join the APB [letter from George R. Catlett to the author dated November 29, 2000]. Peat Marwick's Black, not wishing to be the lone holdout, also joined the board [letter from Black to the author dated October 19, 1970]. Thereupon, the size of the board was increased from 18 to 21 to accommodate them.

Also in 1960, the Institute appointed Maurice Moonitz, an accounting professor at the University of California, Berkeley, as the first director of accounting research. His unit was deliberately called "the accounting research division," in order to assure that, unlike Blough's research department, it would not be commandeered by other committees of the Institute.

The program of accounting research and the work of the APB, as a result of the Special Committee's report, were thus ready to begin in earnest.

REFERENCES

Accounting and Reporting Standards for Corporate Financial Statements and Preceding Statements and Supplements (1957), (Madison, WI: American Accounting Association).

"Accounting Research and Accounting Principles" (1958), Editorial in *The Journal of Accountancy*, Vol. 106, No. 4, December: 27-28.

Accounting Research and Terminology Bulletins, Final Edition (1961) (New York: American Institute of Certified Public Accountants).

Accounting Research Division, staff of (1963), *Reporting the Financial Effects of Price-Level Changes*, Accounting Research Study No. 6 (New York: American Institute of Certified Public Accountants).

Barr, A. and Koch, E.C. (1959), "Accounting and the S.E.C.," *The George Washington Law Review*, Vol. 28, No. 1, October: 176-193.

Bedford, N.M. (1997), *A History of Accountancy at the University of Illinois at Urbana-Champaign* (Champaign, IL: Center for International Education and Research in Accounting).

Bevis, H.W. (1965), *Corporate Financial Reporting in a Competitive Economy* (New York: The Macmillan Company).

Blough, C.G. (1937), "The Need for Accounting Principles," *The Accounting Review*, Vol. 12, No. 1, March: 30-37.

Blough, C.G. (1938), Remarks in *The American Institute of Accountants (1887-1937): Fiftieth Anniversary Celebration 1937* (American Institute of Accountants): 188-204.

Blough, C.G. (1960), "Accounting Research for Better Financial Reporting," in *Proceedings of the Twenty-Second Annual Institute on Accounting, May 19 and 20, 1960* (Ohio State University Publications, College of Commerce Conference Series, Number C-137).

Broad, S.J. (1957), "Applicability of Accounting Principles," *The Journal of Accountancy*, Vol. 104, No. 3, September: 31-37.

Browne, D.E. (1966), "Cost of Imposing Uniform Accounting Practices," *Financial Executive*, Vol. 34, No. 3, March: 38, 41-42, 44.

Brundage, P.F. (1951), "Roadblocks in the Path of Accounting," *Harvard Business Review*, Vol. 29, No. 5, September: 110-119.

Buckley, J.W., Kircher, P. and Mathews, R. (1968), "Methodology in Accounting Theory," *The Accounting Review*, Vol. 43, No. 2, April: 274-283.

Carey, J.L. (1970), *The Rise of the Accounting Profession: To Responsibility and Authority, 1937-1969* (New York: American Institute of Certified Public Accountants).

Chambers, R.J. (1963), "Why Bother with Postulates?" *Journal of Accounting Research*, Vol. 1, No. 1, Spring: 3-15.

Committee on Accounting Procedure (1939), "General Introduction and Rules Formerly Adopted," Accounting Research Bulletin No. 1 (New York: American Institute of Accountants).

Committee on Accounting Procedure (1940), "Reports of the Committee on Terminology," Accounting Research Bulletin No. 7 (Special) (New York: American Institute of Accountants).

Committee on Accounting Procedure (1947), "Depreciation and High Costs," Accounting Research Bulletin No. 33 (New York: American Institute of Accountants).

Committee on Accounting Procedure (1948), Letter to members of the Institute reaffirming Accounting Research Bulletin No. 33, dated October 14 (American Institute of Accountants).

Committee on Accounting Procedure (1953), *Restatement and Revision of Accounting Research Bulletins*, Accounting Research Bulletin No. 43 (New York: American Institute of Accountants).

Committee on Accounting Procedure (1954), "Declining-balance Depreciation," Accounting Research Bulletin No. 44 (New York: American Institute of Accountants).

Committee on Accounting Procedure (1958), "Declining-balance Depreciation." Accounting Research Bulletin No. 44 (Revised) (New York: American Institute of Certified Public Accountants).

Devore, M.M. (1959), "Accounting Principles—Their Nature and Their Origin," in *Selected Papers 1958* (Haskins & Sells, 1959): 109-125.

Eaton, M. (1957), "Financial Reporting in a Changing Society," *The Journal of Accountancy*, Vol. 104, No. 2, August: 25-31.

Gellein, O.S. (1957), "What's New in Accounting," *1957 Conference of Accountants: Accounting Papers* (The University of Tulsa).

Gilman, S. (1939), *Accounting Concepts of Profit* (New York: The Ronald Press Company).

Gordon, M.J. (1964), "Postulates, Principles and Research in Accounting," *The Accounting Review*, Vol. 39, No. 2, April: 251-263.

Grady, P. (1952), "A Proposal for the Adoption of Standards of Disclosure for Changing Price Levels," *The Journal of Accountancy*, Vol. 94, No. 5, November: 565-569.

Grady, P. (1962a), "The Quest for Accounting Principles," *The Journal of Accountancy*, Vol. 113, No. 5, May: 45-50.

Grady, P. (editor) (1962b), *Memoirs and Accounting Thought of George O. May* (New York: The Ronald Press Company).

Grady, P. (1965), *Inventory of Generally Accepted Accounting Principles for Business Enterprises* (New York: American Institute of Certified Public Accountants).

Grady, P. (1972), "Development of Accounting Principles—A Review of the Past Fifty Years," *The Florida Certified Public Accountant*, Vol. 11, No. 2, January: 14-23.

Grady, P. (1978), *Written Contributions of Selected Accounting Practitioners: Volume 2, Paul Grady* (Center for International Education and Research in Accounting, University of Illinois at Urbana-Champaign).

Haase, P. (1971), *Financial Executives Institute: The First Forty Years* (New York: Financial Executives Institute).

Holmes, O.W. (1891), *The Autocrat of the Breakfast-Table* (Boston: Houghton Mifflin and Company).

Inglis, J.B. (1974), *My Life and Times* (Privately printed).

Jennings, A.R. (1958a), "Present-Day Challenges in Financial Reporting," *The Journal of Accountancy*, Vol. 105, No. 1, January: 28-34.

Jennings, A.R. (1958b), "Accounting Research," *The Accounting Review*, Vol. 33, No. 4, October: 547-554.

Jones, R.C. (1955), *Price Level Changes and Financial Statements: Case Studies of Four Companies* (American Accounting Association).

Jones, R.C. (1956), *Effects of Price Level Changes on Business Income, Capital, and Taxes* (American Accounting Association).

Keller, T.F. (1965), "Uniformity Versus Flexibility: A Review of the Rhetoric," in "Uniformity in Financial Accounting" (see below): 637-651.

King, E.C. (1948), "Generally Accepted Accounting Principles," in Alfred R. Roberts (editor), *Selected Papers of Earle C. King* (New York: Arno Press): 44-47.

King, E.C. (1951), "What are Accounting Principles?" in Alfred R. Roberts (editor), *Selected Papers of Earle C. King* (New York: Arno Press): 21-43.

Knauth, O.W. (1957), "An Executive Looks at Accountancy," *The Journal of Accountancy*, Vol. 103, No. 1, January: 29-32.

Kohler, E.L. (1952), *A Dictionary for Accountants* (New York: Prentice-Hall, Inc.).

Kracke, E.A. (1947), "Restoration of Fixed Asset Values to the Balance Sheet: Third Negative," *The Accounting Review*, Vol. 22, No. 2, April: 208-210.

Littleton, A.C. (1961), *Essays on Accountancy* (Urbana, IL: University of Illinois Press).

Mason, P. (1956), *Price-Level Changes and Financial Statements: Basic Concepts and Methods* (American Accounting Association).

Mautz, R.K. (1957), "The 1957 Statement of Accounting and Reporting Standards," *The Accounting Review*, Vol. 32, No. 4, October: 547-553.

May, G.O. (1937), "Principles of Accounting," *The Journal of Accountancy*, Vol. 64, No. 6, December: 423-425.

May, G.O. (1943), *Financial Accounting, A Distillation of Experience* (New York: The Macmillan Company, 1943).

May, G.O. (1948), "Postulates of Income Accounting," *The Journal of Accountancy*, Vol. 86, No. 2, August: 107-111.

May, G.O. (1949), *Business Income and Price Levels—An Accounting Study* (New York: Study Group on Business Income).

May, G.O. (1958), "Generally Accepted Principles of Accounting," *The Journal of Accountancy*, Vol. 105, No. 1, January: 23-27.

Moonitz, M. (1961), *The Basic Postulates of Accounting* (New York: American Institute of Certified Public Accountants).

Moonitz, M. (1982), "Memorial: Carman George Blough 1895-1981," *The Accounting Review*, Vol. 57, No. 1, January: 147-160.

Paton, W.A. (1922), *Accounting Theory—With Special Reference to the Corporate Enterprise* (New York: The Ronald Press Company).

Paton, W.A. and Littleton, A.C. (1940), *An Introduction to Corporate Accounting Standards* (American Accounting Association).

Pines, J.A. (1965), "The Securities and Exchange Commission and Accounting Principles," in "Uniformity in Financial Accounting" (see below): 727-751.

Powell, W. (1961), "Report on the Accounting Research Activities of the American Institute of Certified Public Accountants," *The Accounting Review*, Vol. 36, No. 1, January: 26-31.

Powell, W. (1964), "The Development of Accounting Principles," *The Journal of Accountancy*, Vol. 118, No. 3, September: 37-43.

Powell, W. (1965a), "Putting Uniformity in Financial Accounting into Perspective," in "Uniformity in Financial Accounting" (see below): 674-689.

Powell, W. (1965b), "'Inventory of Generally Accepted Accounting Principles'," *The Journal of Accountancy*, Vol. 119, No. 3, March: 29-35.

Previts, G.J. and Merino, B.D. (1998), *A History of Accountancy in the United States: The Cultural Significance of Accounting* (Columbus: Ohio State University Press).

Railroad Accounting Procedures (1957), Hearings before a subcommittee of the Committee on Government Operations, House of Representatives, Eighty-fifth Congress, First Session, April 30, May 1, 2, and 3, 1957 (Washington: United States Government Printing Office).

Report of Special Committee Investigating Certain Phases of Work of the Committee on Accounting Procedure and the Committee on Relations with the Interstate Commerce Commission (1957), in *A Search for Fairness* (below): 469-487.

Report of the Study Group on Business Income (1952), *Changing Concepts of Business Income* (New York: The Macmillan Company).

Report to Council of the Special Committee on Research Program (1958), *The Journal of Accountancy*, Vol. 106, No. 6, December: 62-68.

A Search for Fairness in Financial Reporting to the Public, 1956-1969 (1969) (Chicago: Arthur Andersen & Co.).

Securities and Exchange Commission (1938), "Administrative Policy on Financial Statements," Accounting Series Release No. 4 (Washington, DC: SEC).

Spacek, L. (1956a), "Accounting Has Failed to Prevent Major Misrepresentations," in *A Search for Fairness* (above): 1-7.

Spacek, L. (1956b), "The Elusive Truth of Business Profits," in *A Search for Fairness* (above): 9-15.

Spacek, L. (1957a), "Professional Accountants and Their Public Responsibility, in *A Search for Fairness* (above): 17-26.

Spacek, L. (1957b), Letter to the AICPA, in *A Search for Fairness* (above): 488-489.

Spacek, L. (1957c), "The Need for an Accounting Court," in *A Search for Fairness* (above): 27-38.

Spacek, L. (1958a), "The Impact of Inflation on Accounting," in *A Search for Fairness* (above): 61-67.

Spacek, L. (1958b),"Challenge to Public Accounting," in *A Search for Fairness* (above): 71-83.

Spacek, L. (1958c), "Can We Define Generally Accepted Accounting Principles?" in *A Search for Fairness* (above): 85-95

Spacek, L. (1989), *The Growth of Arthur Andersen & Co. 1928-1973: An Oral History* (New York: Garland Publishing, Inc.).

Storey, R.K. (1964), *The Search for Accounting Principles: Today's Problems in Perspective* (New York: American Institute of Certified Public Accountants).

"Uniformity in Financial Accounting" (1965), *Law and Contemporary Problems,* Vol. 30, No. 4, Autumn.

Vatter, W.J. (1963), "Postulates and Principles," *Journal of Accounting Research,* Vol. 1, No. 2, Autumn: 179-197.

A Vision of Grandeur (1988) (Chicago: Arthur Andersen & Co.).

Walker, R.G. (1992), "The SEC's Ban on Upward Asset Revaluations and the Disclosure of Current Values," *Abacus,* Vol. 28, No. 1, March: 3-35.

Werntz, W.W. (1946), "Trends in Accounting," *The Journal of Accountancy,* Vol. 81, No. 1, January: 34-41.

Werntz, W.W. (1958), "Accounting in Transition," *The Journal of Accountancy,* Vol. 105, No. 2, February: 33-36.

Zeff, S.A. (1972), *Forging Accounting Principles in Five Countries: A History and an Analysis of Trends* (Champaign, IL: Stipes Publishing Co.).

Zeff, S.A. (1984), "Some Junctures in the Evolution of the Process of Establishing Accounting Principles in the U.S.A.: 1917-1972," *The Accounting Review,* Vol. 59, No. 3, July: 447-468.

Zeff, S.A. (1992), "Arthur Andersen & Co. and the Two-Part Opinion in the Auditor's Report: 1946-1962," *Contemporary Accounting Research,* Vol. 8, No. 2, Spring: 443-467.

Zeff, S.A. and Moonitz, M. (1984), *Sourcebook on Accounting Principles and Auditing Procedures 1917-1953* (New York: Garland Publishing, Inc.).

APPENDIX

A Concise Summary of the Evolution of the Term "Postulate" in the Accounting Literature

The term "postulate" was not frequently used in the accounting literature in the 1950s, but, as is well known, Maurice Moonitz's Accounting Research Study No. 1, published in 1961 under the aegis of the Accounting Principles Board, was entitled *The Basic Postulates of Accounting* [1961]. During the 1960s, numerous authors discussed the "postulates" approach to developing accounting principles [see, e.g., Chambers, 1963, Vatter, 1963; Gordon, 1964; Buckley et al., 1968], and it might therefore be instructive to explore the provenance of this term in the accounting literature. Paton [1922, p. 472] entitled a chapter "The Basic Postulates of Accounting," in which he enumerated seven "underlying propositions upon which accounting is based." Paton's use of the term was carried forward in the "tentative statement of accounting principles" issued by the American Accounting Association's executive committee, of which Paton was a member, in 1936. The executive committee used the term "postulates" to describe "certain basic propositions of accounting which embody standards of adequacy and reasonableness in the presentation of corporate financial statements."[37] What the AAA committee called postulates, however, were in reality what it regarded as statements of proper practice.

George O. May continued the use of "postulates" but with a very different meaning. In 1937, May, who was to become chairman of the Institute's Committee on Terminology, argued that the term "principles" should be defined, quoting a dictionary definition, as "A general law or rule adopted or professed as a guide to action; a settled ground or basis of conduct or practice. . . ." He rejected its definition as "A fundamental truth or proposition on which many others depend. . . ." [ibid., p. 423]. Three years later, his terminology committee said: "Initially, accounting rules are mere postulates derived from experience and reason. Only after they have proved useful, and become generally accepted, do they become principles of accounting" [Committee on Accounting Procedure, 1940, p. 60; see also May, 1943, p. 38]. To May, therefore, postulates were principles (in reality, practices) that had not yet won general acceptance. But in the late 1940s he redefined postulates as working assumptions or guiding propositions. In a monograph written for the Study Group on Business Income, May identified two "postulates or canons of income accounting" [May, 1949, p. 23] which fell somewhere between "the foundation on which accounting concepts of income rest" and "problems of a conceptual character encountered in the determination of business income" [ibid., p. 21]. His two postulates were "the going concern concept" and "that the income statement of a year should be regarded as a part of a continuous and integrated series" [ibid.]. Three years later, in the Study Group's report, which May largely drafted, it was stated that "Income accounting necessarily rests on a framework of postulates and assumptions; these are accepted and acceptable as being useful, not as demonstrable truths; their usefulness is always open to reconsideration" [Report of the Study Group on Business Income, 1952, p. 19; see also May, 1948]. Three postulates were cited: monetary, permanence (i.e., going concern), and realization. The monetary postulate was "that fluctuations in the value of the monetary unit, which is the accounting symbol, may properly be ignored" [Report of the Study Group on Business Income, p. 20].

Eric L. Kohler, in the first edition of his *A Dictionary for Accountants*, gave the following definition of postulate: "Any of a series of axioms or assumptions constituting the supposed basis of a system of thought or an organized field of endeavor" [1952, p. 323]. He also wrote that "If a principle is accepted without evidence of proof, it may be called an *axiom, assumption,* or *postulate*" [ibid., p. 335]. Finally, in 1957, Oswald W. Knauth, a distinguished company executive and

---

[37]Although the AAA committee used the term "postulates" only once, Gilman [1939, chap. 14] referred to all 20 of the committee's propositions as postulates.

public servant who had been associated with May in the original drafting of the 1952 Study Group report [1952, p. v], reiterated the three postulates from the report in an article published in *The Journal of Accountancy*. Knauth's article was one of those that Powell asked the committee members to read.

Available online at www.sciencedirect.com

ELSEVIER   Journal of Accounting and Public Policy 22 (2003) 1–18

Journal of
Accounting
and
Public Policy

www.elsevier.com/locate/jaccpubpol

Du Pont's early policy on the rotation of audit firms

Stephen A. Zeff *

Jesse H. Jones Graduate School of Management, Rice University, 6100 Main St., P.O. Box 2932, Houston, TX 77252-2932, USA

Abstract

E.I. du Pont de Nemours & Company adopted a policy from 1910 onward of rotating its external audit firm every year, and later every several years, until the 1950s, when it finally consented to appoint a permanent auditor. This practice of audit firm rotation was exceptional, if not unique, among U.S. companies. It is the purpose of this article to review this policy and to present evidence of the company's reasons for its adoption and, in the end, the decision to appoint a permanent auditor.
© 2003 Elsevier Science Inc. All rights reserved.

1. Introduction

An issue that has come to the fore in the wake of the collapse of Enron has been whether companies should be required to rotate their external audit firms after specified periods of time. Prior to Enron, the topic had been discussed occasionally within the U.S. accounting profession, but the policy recommendation had always been not to impose such a requirement (see, e.g., Commission on Auditors' Responsibilities, 1978, pp. 108–109; Division for CPA Firms, 1992). But, following Enron, mandatory audit firm rotation was advocated in Congressional testimony by Arthur Levitt, Jr., former chairman of the Securities and Exchange Commission (SEC); former SEC chief accountant Lynn E. Turner; and Charles A. Bowsher on behalf of the Public

---

* Tel.: +1-713-348-6066; fax: +1-713-348-6296.
  E-mail address: sazeff@rice.edu (S.A. Zeff).

0278-4254/03/$ - see front matter © 2003 Elsevier Science Inc. All rights reserved.
doi:10.1016/S0278-4254(02)00083-2

Oversight Board, which he chaired; among others. [1] Audit firm rotation would be imposed by the Truth and Accountability in Accounting Act of 2002, introduced on March 14, 2002 by Rep. John D. Dingell (Democrat, Michigan) and others. [2] Many state and local government agencies in the U.S. adhere to audit firm rotation. The practice is required by law in several other countries. [3] The chairman of the Australian Securities & Investments Commission has embraced the "principle" of audit firm rotation, and a Treasury select committee in the U.K. has recommended that the government require mandatory auditor and audit firm rotation. [4]

The principal argument for mandatory rotation of the audit firm is that it would contribute to enhanced auditor independence vis-à-vis the client company, and the principal argument raised against mandatory rotation is the higher cost and the substantial risks confronting the audit firm during the initial year of an audit engagement. [5]

The almost universal practice of U.S. publicly traded companies has been to reappoint their external audit firm as an almost unquestioned practice at shareholder meetings. Only where significant differences arise between the company and the audit firm over accounting or auditing issues does one see the replacement of one audit firm by another.

Yet one major U.S. enterprise, E.I. du Pont de Nemours & Company ("Du Pont"), systematically rotated its external audit firm between 1910 and 1954. [6] Indeed, from 1911 to 1928, with only one exception, Du Pont changed its audit firm every year. Haskins & Sells and Price, Waterhouse & Co. held the majority

---

[1] The prepared remarks by these three individuals were made in hearings before the U.S. Senate Committee on Banking, Housing, and Urban Affairs on February 12 and 26 and March 19, 2002, respectively. Bowsher said he was conveying the view of the Public Oversight Board.

[2] H.R. 3970, 107th Congress, 2nd Session.

[3] Italy currently has a statutory requirement for audit firm rotation every nine years, and Austria recently approved a law that requires audit firm rotation by the end of six years. In 1989, Spain adopted legislation mandating audit firm rotation by the end of nine years, but the legislation was repealed in 1997, one year before it would have had a practical effect. Greece requires audit firm rotation every six years for public sector entities, and beginning in March 2002 the Singaporean central bank has required that banks incorporated in Singapore change their audit firms at least every five years.

[4] See Knott (2002), Mackintosh (2002, pp. 5–6), and Perry (2002). David Knott is chairman and Ian Mackintosh was then the chief accountant of the Australian Securities & Investments Commission.

[5] For a discussion of the international debate and experience as well as a recitation of the arguments for and against mandatory rotation, see Catanach and Walker (1999, pp. 43–48). Also see the recent report of the Institute of Chartered Accountants in England and Wales (Mandatory Rotation of Audit Firms, 2002).

[6] Du Pont published its first annual report carrying an audit firm's certificate for the year 1910.

of the appointments during this period. The roster of Du Pont audit firms for the fiscal years 1910 to the present is as follows: [7]

1910   Price, Waterhouse & Company
1911   The Audit Company of New York
1912   Haskins & Sells
1913   The Audit Company of New York
1914   Haskins & Sells
1915   The Audit Company of New York
1916   Haskins & Sells
1917   The Audit Company of New York
1918–19 Haskins & Sells
1920   Ernst & Ernst
1921   Price, Waterhouse & Co.
1922   Haskins & Sells
1923   Price, Waterhouse & Co.
1924   Haskins & Sells
1925   Price, Waterhouse & Co.
1926   Haskins & Sells
1927   Price, Waterhouse & Co.
1928–29 Peat, Marwick, Mitchell & Co.
1930–38 Price, Waterhouse & Co.
1939–42 Haskins & Sells
1943–45 Arthur Andersen & Co.
1946–53 Lybrand, Ross Bros. & Montgomery
Since 1954 Price, Waterhouse & Co. [8]

2. Du Pont's reason for audit firm rotation becomes evident

2.1. Exchange of letters in 1922

Du Pont says nothing in its annual reports about this policy of rotating the external audit firm. [9] But internal correspondence throws light on the reason

---

[7] Price, Waterhouse & Co. and Lybrand Ross Bros. & Montgomery are today part of PricewaterhouseCoopers; Haskins & Sells is part of Deloitte & Touche; Ernst & Ernst is part of Ernst & Young; and Peat, Marwick, Mitchell & Co. is part of KPMG. The Audit Company of New York, a corporation, was acquired in 1932 by R.G. Rankin & Co., which in 1955 merged with Price Waterhouse & Co. (Partner Retires, 1958). It was said to be "the single most significant merger in PW's history," because of the important clients it brought to the firm (Allen and McDermott, 1993, p. 117).

[8] In 1951, the firm removed the comma from its name.

[9] One reason for omitting mention of this matter is that, until the 1940s or 1950s, it was the president, not the board of directors or the stockholders, who appointed the external audit firm.

for the policy. In a letter to Irénée du Pont, the company President, dated June 23, 1922, Frank G. Tallman, a director, a member of the executive committee, and a longtime member of the upper management of Du Pont, wrote as follows: [10]

> Referring to the matter of policy of changing auditors each year, I state this has been done in the past largely because Mr. P.S. du Pont favored it and because the basic principle governing having auditors at all seems to indicate that the proper result would be more fully obtained by changing auditors annually.
>
> If I have the correct idea of the purpose of an annual audit it is that we may have:
>
> (a) a certificate of reliable, capable, independent, and disinterested accountants that our books are correct, that they have been properly kept, and that the balance sheet and profit and loss account fairly set forth the financial position of the Company;
> (b) this to be attached to the annual report for the information and benefit of all stockholders, bankers, investors, and others interested in the true condition of the Company.
>
> In order to secure the foregoing result it would seem that the auditors should be entirely separate and divorced from any immediately preceding connection with our Company. Auditors as I see it are "check-ups", such as National Bank examiners; Directors appointed to count over and report on securities in the custody of our Treasurer; checking up magazine stocks; counting cash and going over accounts of our branch offices; requests from chartered accountants to depositors in and borrowers from banks as to the condition of their accounts and collateral on any certain date, etc., etc.
>
> If I am correct in the foregoing our annual audit should be made by chartered public accountants who did not make the previous annual

---

[10] Accession 1662, Box 7, Folder C-44 in the Du Pont Archive, Hagley Museum and Library. These materials have been quoted by courtesy of the Hagley Museum and Library. All of the letters cited below are also in this holding. Tallman wrote on Du Pont stationery bearing the title of vice-president, but, according to Chandler and Salsbury (1971, p. 429), he was one of several "valued old hands" who were retired from line administration and the executive committee in 1919. Pierre S. du Pont, mentioned in Tallman's letter, relinquished the Du Pont presidency in 1919 and was succeeded by Irénée du Pont. In 1919, Irénée du Pont designated Tallman as the company officer who was to engage the external auditor each year.

audit and who have not been connected in any way with us during the year to be audited, on tax matters or otherwise.

In the same letter, Tallman explained why an exception was made in 1919, when Haskins & Sells was retained for a second year. He wrote that, after conferring with Irénée du Pont, "I made an arrangement with Haskins & Sells, who were our auditors for the preceding year, the main reason being that there was expected to be so much difficulty and so large an amount of work connected with closing up war work and accounts, that it seemed best to waive the desirability of a different auditor in order to partially relieve the great congestion in work of our accounting department at that time." The annual rotation of audit firms resumed in 1920.

Tallman's letter was precipitated by one dated June 16 from the Comptroller, James B. Eliason, addressed to Walter S. Carpenter, Jr., [11] the Treasurer, in which, among other things, Eliason questioned the wisdom of the annual rotation policy:

> While I hold no brief for Messrs. Price, Waterhouse & Company, and fully recognize that there are a number of other auditing concerns in this country who undoubtedly can serve us in an equally satisfactory and efficient manner, and whose reputation and standing are equal to that of Price, Waterhouse & Company, I wish to express my conviction that the Company's policy of changing auditors each year is without any particular merit and is expensive. A new auditing concern, for instance for 1922, would be obliged to cover to a considerable extent the same ground which has already been covered by Price, Waterhouse & Company in their work for 1921 and they would be without the knowledge of where to go and how to acquire information which Price, Waterhouse & Company, by reason of their familiarity gained during the last audit, would be in a position to get without any lost motion.

> It should also be remembered that Price, Waterhouse & Company are at present, and will undoubtedly be throughout the balance of this year, associated with us on our tax problems, and that there is some advantage to us in having the same people who are working on our tax problems also auditing our accounts, as since the accounts and the tax problems are inseparable, I cannot help but

---

[11] Carpenter went on to become the President of the company in 1940. Carpenter thus became the first President of the company who was not himself a du Pont (apart from Hamilton M. Barksdale, who was acting President in 1912–13), yet his brother, R.R.M. Carpenter, was married to the youngest sister of the brothers Pierre, Irénée and Lammot du Pont.

feel that some embarrassment would result from having others making the audit for 1922.

Carpenter, in a brief letter to Irénée du Pont dated June 17, said that "I heartily subscribe" to Eliason's view, and he added, "The importance of the Price, Waterhouse association from the standpoint of Government taxes is difficult to exaggerate." In his reply, dated June 23, Tallman conceded that Price, Waterhouse & Co. had been the auditor of United States Steel Corporation since its organization in 1901, and that "some large companies have continuous audits for which it would seem to be desirable to have the same auditors year after year." Yet he said that he was not in agreement with the views of the Comptroller or Treasurer, but that they "may wish to put both sides of the matter before the Finance Committee."

Irénée du Pont settled the matter in a letter to Carpenter dated June 29:

> It seems to me that without having the least mis-trust of you or Mr. Eliason, that good auditing should require a firm who could not be criticized by reason of any other connection with the Treasurer's Department, and as Price, Waterhouse & Co. are engaged as experts by the Treasurer's Dept., they should not be used at the present time for that reason also.

The reason given by Irénée Du Pont raises interesting questions about the scope of non-audit services that an audit firm should render to an audit client.

3. Du Pont modifies its policy of rotating its audit firm

3.1. Eliason's skepticism toward annual rotation secures favor

F.G. Tallman made a decision in 1928 to experiment with the same audit firm (Peat, Marwick, Mitchell & Co.) in consecutive years. In a letter dated April 28, 1928 to Lammot du Pont, who had become President in 1926, he wrote, "If there is any virtue in a diversification of auditors we ought to discover something at the end of this year." The result of the experiment must have been positive, because, with the support of J.B. Eliason, Price, Waterhouse & Co. ("PW") was retained as the company's auditor for nine consecutive years, from 1930 to 1938. In a letter to F.G. Tallman dated March 6, 1931, Lammot du Pont wrote, "It is my recollection that, from the standpoint of efficiency and intelligent handling, Price-Waterhouse & Company are the first choice of our Treasurer's Office. I see no reason why we should not retain Price, Waterhouse & Company for another year." Eliason, who as Comptroller had opposed the policy of annually rotating the audit firm, had become

Treasurer in June 1930 and thus was in a position to exert greater influence. Lammot du Pont wrote a similar letter to Tallman on March 7, 1932, leading to a further reappointment of PW.

3.2. Du Pont resumes rotation after PW's long tenure

In 1939, after PW had completed its ninth consecutive year as Du Pont's auditor, the company decided to change auditors. However, PW was concerned over a "misperception" at the coincidence of being rotated off the Du Pont audit in 1939, shortly after the auditing scandal erupted at McKesson & Robbins, whose audit firm was none other than PW (Allen and McDermott, 1993, p. 146). Even though J.B. Eliason was still the Du Pont Treasurer, the views of the du Pont family continued to support the policy of audit firm rotation, and apparently nine years for one audit firm was regarded as too much of a departure from the rotation policy. In a letter to Alfred P. Sloan, Jr., the Chairman of General Motors Corporation (in which Du Pont held a substantial investment), dated February 16, 1939, Lammot du Pont, still the President, wrote as follows, in which he cited

> five objectives to be accomplished by an audit by independent public accountants.
>
> (a) Check the accuracy of the accounting work done.
> (b) Criticise and improve accounting practices in accordance with general accounting practice.
> (c) Discover any error which is in the rank and file of management.
> (d) Discover any irregularity in the higher personnel.
> (e) Prevent or expose collusion among officers.

Items (a) and (c), he said, fall within the province of the internal audit, items (b) and (d) "will be covered by any independent auditor of good reputation," and item (e) "is the only one to be affected by the selection of the independent auditor." He added: "of course, the question involves the collusion of the *Auditor* with the Officers as well as among the Officers themselves." Evidently, the policy of rotating audit firms betrayed a generalized suspicion of plots and conspiracies. Perhaps the du Pont family (and certain old hands) were not entirely comfortable with third-party professionals in their midst.

W.S. Carpenter, now arguing in favor of the need to obtain a fresh perspective, said he supported occasional auditor rotation. In a letter dated March 28, 1938 to Donaldson Brown, the Vice Chairman of the board of General Motors, Carpenter, then a Du Pont Vice President and Chairman of the powerful finance committee, expressed the following view:

An audit of accounts involving hundreds of millions of dollars should not be too easy and comfortable. I would rather see it vigorous and aggressive, not merely for the purpose of trying to stir up trouble or to make a show of activity, but rather for the purpose of re-examining at all times what is being done to see that the best practices known in the profession at all times are being employed.

Accountancy as we know is not an exact science. There are many things in accountancy which cannot be adjudged right or wrong. It is quite natural that, as the years pass, the work of the various accounting firms becomes more or less formalized. They accept certain practices as being correct or incorrect, whereas, in fact, that is probably not true. It seems to me, for that reason, that occasionally we should have a rotation in order that the practices which we have been following, perhaps for years, are re-examined periodically from the viewpoint of a somewhat different philosophy. The effect of this also on our organization I think is good.

We have been going on for many years with the same auditors [PW]. I see the same faces down here year after year until I, in fact, get them confused with our own organization. I do not question their honesty, but I do question somewhat their capacity for constantly, aggressively, opening and reopening questions about theories and practices which we are following.

The public audit is an expensive procedure and is in a way a troublesome one from the standpoint of the organization, but for all of this expense and trouble I believe we should endeavor to get in return something which is beneficial to us besides a mere check on our accounts to determine that no fraud exists. I believe the best way of doing this is by occasionally getting a review and re-examination of our practices.

Carpenter's strong view in favor of occasional audit firm rotation in 1938 may seem to be at variance from the perfunctory view he expressed in 1922, but in 1922 the discussion was over changing the audit firm each year, not every several years. Also, in 1922 his motivation may have been to lend support to the opinion held by his Comptroller, J.B. Eliason. Carpenter's advocacy of occasional audit firm rotation was so marked that his biographer, when discussing Carpenter's position on rotation in 1938, has written: "At Walter's urging the company changed auditors three times in the next decade before his retirement [as President in 1948]" (Cheape, 1995, p. 90). As noted above, Carpenter became President in 1940.

In 1939, PW was succeeded as auditors by Haskins & Sells, which in turn were replaced in 1943 by Arthur Andersen & Co. Andersen served until 1946, when Lybrand, Ross Bros. & Montgomery became the auditors. Reflecting Carpenter's view, Du Pont thus reverted to a policy of rotating auditors over a shorter span of years than in the case of PW during the 1930s.

4. Issues raised by Du Pont's auditors in the 1940s

One might have supposed that a reason for Du Pont's policy of rotating its audit firm was to escape unpleasant disagreements with the auditor. There is no evidence that this was the case. In 1929, Peat, Marwick, Mitchell & Co., concluding the first of its two years as Du Pont's audit firm, did not ostensibly qualify its opinion published in Du Pont's annual report, [12] yet it recommended in a separate report to the company that the single surplus account shown in its balance sheet be segregated by source, including a designation of the portion attributable to undistributed earnings. [13] Even though Du Pont did not accept the recommendation, the firm was reappointed for a second year. As will be brought out in the next section, Arthur Andersen & Co. qualified its opinion in all three of its years as Du Pont auditor during the 1940s, yet its term as auditor did not seem to be affected.

4.1. Arthur Andersen & Co. qualifies its opinion, and Du Pont replies

The foregoing roster of Du Pont's audit firms over the years indicates that two firms served after PW in shorter multi-year engagements between 1939 and 1945: Haskins & Sells and Arthur Andersen & Co. Of the two, the Arthur Andersen ("AA") engagement was the more confrontational. In Du Pont's

---

[12] At least, no explicit qualification was signified. Yet the firm's opinion was curiously equivocal. It said only that "the attached Consolidated Balance Sheet, Income and Surplus Accounts have been prepared [from the books and accounts] and, in our opinion, present the consolidated financial position at December 31st, 1928, and the results of the operations for the year." Identical wording was used in the audit report given the following year. The firm did not use a qualitative adverb, such as "correctly" or "properly," whose inclusion in auditors' opinions of the day was common (see Himmelblau, 1927, pp. 47–48). In the firm's opinion on the financial statements for 1928 and 1929 of General Electric Company, another major Peat, Marwick client, it stated that the financial statements "correctly record" the results of the operations and the condition of its affairs. Peat, Marwick's audit reports for Du Pont and General Electric were both issued from its New York City office, at 40 Exchange Place. One supposes that the firm would have developed common criteria for major audits based in the same office.

[13] Although Peat, Marwick's separate report has not survived, Walter Carpenter replied to the firm, in a letter dated May 24, 1929, in which he defended the company's practice with respect to surplus.

annual report for 1943, the first year for which AA was the auditor, the firm qualified its report. AA disagreed with Du Pont's practice of not allocating the balance in its combined surplus account to earned surplus, paid-in surplus, and surplus arising from revaluation of assets, and in this respect it took a stronger position than did Peat, Marwick, Mitchell & Co. in 1929. In an internal memorandum to Du Pont, the firm showed how the allocation should be performed. But Du Pont was unconvinced. In a three-page statement appearing immediately after AA's audit report, Du Pont's committee on audit, composed of members of the board of directors who did not occupy a position in the company's active management, rejected the grounds for AA's exception. The committee contended that any such allocation would be arbitrary and very likely inaccurate; furthermore, the committee said that a segregation of surplus by source was irrelevant for determining the availability of dividends under the Delaware corporation law. Since the inception of the Securities and Exchange Commission in 1934, it has been rare for the auditor of a U.S. company to qualify its opinion (other than for uncertainties), but it has been rarer still for a U.S. company to respond publicly to such an exception. (AA's audit report and Du Pont's reply are reproduced in an appendix.)

So unusual was this event that *The Journal of Accountancy* reprinted both the auditor's report and the company's reply, and, in an editorial in the same issue, the *Journal* praised the two parties for providing a full disclosure of their irreconcilable differences (When Accountant and Client Disagree, 1944). Leonard Spacek, then a partner in AA's Chicago office, later recalled that "it was great publicity," showing that the firm stood on principle (Spacek, 1989, p. 62). [14]

AA also took exception for the same reason in the 1944 and 1945 annual reports. The audit committee's statement was not repeated, but in the 1944 report (as in its predecessor) the Chairman of the board and the President, in their letter to the stockholders, said that the company could not accept the auditor's view. One might suppose that Du Pont would not have reappointed AA after the clash of views exhibited in the 1943 annual report, but in fact AA remained the auditor for two more years and, as noted, did not back down from its stated belief that the combined surplus should be apportioned into three classes.

4.2. Lybrands also qualifies its opinion, but on another matter

In 1946, Lybrand, Ross Bros. & Montgomery ("Lybrands") became the Du Pont auditor, and it continued to serve for a total of eight years. In Du Pont's

---

[14] In his oral history, Spacek (1989, pp. 60–63) confused Du Pont's use of the equity method of accounting for its investment in General Motors with the dispute over the allocation of the combined surplus.

1946 annual report, Lybrands referred in its opinion to the issue regarding the combined surplus but said that it lacked "a definitive and authoritative basis upon which to predicate retrospective allocations of the various charges and credits which have been made to surplus since incorporation of the Company," and it did not qualify its opinion on the financial statements. In the 1947 annual report, Lybrands did qualify its opinion, because the company had made a charge against net income for "excessive construction costs" occasioned by the postwar inflation. The extra charge was 17% of Du Pont's net income. Du Pont was one of several prominent manufacturing corporations to make such a supplemental charge for rising costs (see Blough, 1947; Notable Deviations from Accounting Principles, 1948). Provisions such as this, which excited controversy within the accounting profession, were disapproved by the Committee on Accounting Procedure (Depreciation and High Costs, 1948) and by the Securities and Exchange Commission (Blough, 1949, p. 65). After the SEC acted to disallow the practice, Du Pont chose to record "accelerated depreciation" on historical cost in 1948.

It is curious that none of Du Pont's auditors publicly took exception to its location of Reserve for Depreciation and Obsolescence on the liabilities side of the balance sheet, rather than as a subtraction from Plants and Properties on the asset side. The company explained, "Our depreciation and obsolescence reserve is much more in the nature of a contingency reserve to provide for obsolescence than an indication of reduction in the value of our plants." [15] The company cited an article in the accounting literature as support for its aberrant practice (Simon, 1959), although its practice antedated the article by decades.

Lybrands continued as Du Pont's audit firm through 1953, a tenure of eight years. One supposes, therefore, that Crawford H. Greenewalt, who succeeded Walter Carpenter as President in 1948, did not share Carpenter's view about the frequency with which audit firms should be rotated.

5. Price, Waterhouse & Co. becomes Du Pont's permanent auditor

Du Pont's policy of rotating audit firms ostensibly continued in 1954, when PW once again became its auditor. Yet, as one retired PW audit partner recalled, the firm was determined to persuade Du Pont to abandon its rotation policy and retain PW as its permanent auditor. [16] Several years later, PW

---

[15] Letter to the author from H.W. Evans, Treasurer, dated July 30, 1965.

[16] Written transcript of the interview by Kathleen McDermott of Robert Hampton, III, May 31, 1989, p. 51, included in the PricewaterhouseCoopers Archive, housed in the Rare Book and Manuscript Library, Columbia University. Hampton was a manager in the firm's research department from 1953 to 1961.

achieved its goal. The history of PW commissioned by the firm briefly recounts the episode as follows:

> When PW once again had the opportunity to serve as auditors [of Du Pont], Paul Grady became deeply involved in the engagement, and the Philadelphia office "put a lot of power on that job, into trying to keep Du Pont happy." The increased scale and complexity of Du Pont's worldwide operations, the fact that very few auditing firms could handle such work, and the tremendous effort made by PW and Grady's "ministrations" convinced Du Pont to end its rotation policy and to remain permanently with PW (Allen and McDermott, 1993, p. 146). [17]

It is not known when Du Pont resolved to retain PW on a permanent basis, but the decision is likely to have been taken by 1960, when Paul Grady retired from the firm. A review of PW's audit reports on Du Pont's financial statements for the three decades following 1954 reveals that they all contained unqualified opinions.

For its part, Du Pont's senior management was no longer dominated by a du Pont. In January 1948, Lammot du Pont had resigned as board Chairman and was succeeded by Walter Carpenter, who thereupon resigned as President. The board chairmanship carried little authority and was largely a ceremonial position (Cheape, 1995, p. 229). Succeeding Carpenter as President, as noted above, was Crawford Greenewalt, a distinguished scientist and previously a company vice president. Greenewalt was married to Irénée du Pont's daughter. Yet, even though both Carpenter and Greenewalt were within, or on the edge, of the du Pont family, 1948 marked the first year in which a du Pont was neither Chairman nor President, although a clutch of du Ponts continued on the company's board, which numbered more than 30 members. The du Pont oligarchy was receding into the background and perhaps with it the sway of the du Ponts' concern about protecting against collusion among officers and even with the external auditor.

6. Conclusion

Du Pont's policy of rotating audit firms, initially each year and then every several years, was instituted so as to assure a disinterestedness on the part of the auditor. Pierre S. du Pont was said to favor this policy, but his reasons are not on the record. Irénée du Pont held the view that Du Pont's audit firm

---

[17] Paul Grady, the senior technical partner in PW's executive office in New York City, was one of the acknowledged leaders of the accounting profession.

should not be rendering other expert services to the Treasurer's Department. Lammot du Pont believed that the annual audit should be conducted by a firm that had no involvement with the company during the immediately preceding year. He seemed especially concerned to prevent or expose any collusion among officers, and even the external auditor was not above suspicion. Another argument, advanced by Walter S. Carpenter, Jr., was that audit firm rotation provided the company with a fresh perspective. By the 1950s, however, the du Ponts and Carpenter no longer held a senior management position in the company. Following the reappointment of Price Waterhouse & Co. as auditor in 1954, the firm succeeded in persuading Du Pont to allow it to remain as the permanent auditor, especially in view of the increasing size and complexity of the company and its extensive overseas operations. [18]

The unique Du Pont experience with audit firm rotation teaches a lesson today in view of questions that have been raised about the celebrated instances of unduly congenial relations between auditors and client companies that have been exposed in the media. One can almost argue that, in some of these audit engagements, a state of virtual *de facto* collusion seemed to exist between the auditor and the company. If that is so, one can reflect on Du Pont's concern of more than a half century ago that decisive steps must be taken when setting the terms of the audit engagement to assure that the auditor will assume a truly independent posture, which is not compromised by its partners developing overly familiar ties with company officers or board members. Whether the rotation of the partners assigned to the audit engagement will achieve the same result remains to be seen.

Acknowledgments

The author expresses gratitude for the assistance provided by staff members at the Hagley Museum and Library (especially Reference Archivist Marjorie G. McNinch), Wilmington, Delaware, and by the staff of the Rare Book and Manuscript Library, Columbia University. He appreciates the comments of Marc J. Epstein, Wanda A. Wallace, Alfred D. Chandler, Jr., and the anonymous reviewers on earlier drafts.

---

[18] PW was clearly the dominant U.S. audit firm during the early to middle 1960s. The earliest compilation of rankings by size of the Big Eight public accounting firms in the United States, drawing on data for 1964, placed PW well ahead of the other seven firms. In 1964, PW audited 136 of the 639 industrial, merchandising, transportation and utility companies in the *Fortune* list. The second firm, Haskins & Sells, audited 87 of the companies, followed by Peat Marwick, with 84. The advantage in favor of PW was also decisive when one examines the aggregate revenues of its client companies ($79.3 billion versus $59.5 for Haskins & Sells and $46.0 for Lybrands). See Zeff and Fossum (1967, p. 302).

Appendix A

AUDITOR'S OPINION AND COMMITTEE ON AUDIT RESPONSE

67 Wall Street
New York

To the Board of Directors,

E. I. DU PONT DE NEMOURS & COMPANY.

We have examined the consolidated balance sheet of E. I. du Pont de Nemours & Company and its wholly owned subsidiary companies as of December 31, 1943, and the statements of consolidated income and surplus for the year ended that date, have reviewed the system of internal control and the accounting procedures of the companies and, without making a detailed audit of the transactions, have examined or tested accounting records of the companies and other supporting evidence, by methods and to the extent we deemed appropriate. Our examination was made in accordance with generally accepted auditing standards applicable in the circumstances and included all procedures which we considered necessary; it was not practicable to confirm all receivables from United States Government departments and as to those not confirmed we have satisfied ourselves by means of other auditing procedures.

The company maintains a combined surplus account which includes earned surplus, paid-in surplus, and surplus arising from revaluation of assets. In our opinion the respective amounts of these different classes of surplus should be stated separately.

With the exception stated in the preceding paragraph, in our opinion, the accompanying consolidated balance sheet and related statements of consolidated income and surplus present fairly the financial position of E. I. du Pont de Nemours & Company and its wholly owned subsidiary companies at December 31, 1943, and the results of their operations for the year ended that date, in conformity with generally accepted accounting principles applied on a basis consistent with that of the preceding year.

ARTHUR ANDERSEN & CO.

New York, N. Y.
February 21, 1944

Statement by Committee on Audit Concerning Exception Stated in Certificate of Arthur Andersen & Co. with Respect to Surplus Account

In their Certificate, the Public Accountants, Arthur Andersen & Co., have qualified their opinion with respect to the company's financial statements at December 31, 1943, for the reason that in their opinion the respective amounts of earned surplus, paid-in surplus, and surplus arising from revaluation of assets should be stated separately.

An analysis by Arthur Andersen & Co. of the Consolidated Surplus at December 31, 1942, sets forth the allocation of the component items as follows:

Paid-in Surplus	$ 39,895,458
Unrealized appreciation of investments, less amount capitalized through stock dividends........	126,456,462
Earned Surplus	137,141,377
	$303,493,297

With respect to the foregoing Arthur Andersen & Co. have advised as follows:

"The segregation of the surplus account which we submitted to the company was prepared on the basis of the considerations outlined below.

"Paid-in surplus credits represent the excess of consideration (cash or other assets) received upon the original issues of securities over the par value thereof and the excess of consideration received in 1933 (cash and preferred stock of Remington Arms Company, Inc.) over the cost of treasury stock issued therefor. Paid-in surplus charges represent premiums paid upon redemption of debenture stock and amounts transferred to $4.50 no par cumulative preferred stock account to increase the stated value of such stock to $100 per share. These transactions are clearly of a capital nature and accordingly in our opinion are proper paid-in surplus items.

"Unrealized appreciation of investments consists of the amounts of the write-ups of investments in General Motors Corporation common stock and Canadian Industries, Ltd. common stock, less the portion of a dividend paid in du Pont common stock in 1925 which was charged against the write-up in 1925 in accordance with a resolution of the Board of Directors. In our opinion the balance of unrealized appreciation should not be combined with either paid-in surplus or earned surplus, but should be classified in the balance sheet in a separate category.

"Earned surplus consists of the net income (together with direct surplus adjustments of income) of the company since inception, October 1, 1915, and of its subsidiaries since the respective dates of acquisition; less dividends paid in cash or equivalent and in du Pont common stock (other than the stock dividend referred to above), discount on debenture stock issued, and the write-off of part of the excess of the amount recorded for the assets acquired from The Grasselli Chemical Company (approximately market price at the time of the du Pont common stock issued therefor) over the net book value of such assets. At the time of the stock dividends and the discount on debenture stock, which in the segregation were charged to earned surplus, the balance in the company's surplus account consisted only of earned surplus. The write-off of the Grasselli goodwill was reflected in part by elimination of a capital surplus balance which arose in the Grasselli acquisition; the remainder was applied as a reduction of earned surplus, there being no other class of surplus (other than unrealized appreciation) available at the time.

"In our opinion the facts surrounding each item are adequate to determine its character and segregation in accordance with generally accepted accounting principles."

The Surplus Account dates from the organization of the present company in 1915. Over the years there have been many surplus adjustments, and several stock dividends declared, generally without attempt at the time to earmark such items as falling within any particular class of surplus. Moreover, our observation has been that there does not exist sufficient uniformity or consistency of opinion among accountants with respect to the definition of the several classes into which it is suggested that surplus be divided or to the procedure which should be followed in the treatment of many specific items to enable the company to make any segregation of the Surplus Account which would not be subject to question as to its accuracy.

The amounts allocated to the respective classes of surplus by Arthur Andersen & Co. differed from those shown in a similar analysis attempted by another firm of independent public accountants who a number of years ago examined the company's accounts and certified to its financial statements.

The Committee on Audit cannot accept the opinion of Arthur Andersen & Co. as being conclusive for the reason that it believes that certain of the items comprising the Surplus Account are not susceptible of such a segregation except on the basis of arbitrary assumptions or interpretation and that the company can have no assurance that at some later date the accuracy of the segregation may not be questioned and if found inaccurate the company might not be deemed to have published erroneous information which had served to mislead the stockholders and the investing public.

The company has been advised by counsel for years that, from the standpoint of dividend payments, the law of Delaware recognizes no distinction either in the status or in the availability of any separate parts of surplus. If in the future such a segregation should be required by statute or ruling of some official body, no doubt such action would be accompanied by such instructions as to procedure as will relieve the Directors from the responsibility of making an arbitrary segregation.

The company has consistently maintained the practice of describing in its annual reports the various changes in the Surplus Account as they occur, and we are of the opinion that such practice discloses the material facts.

COMMITTEE ON AUDIT

ELWYN EVANS, *Chairman*

NOTE—The Committee on Audit is composed of members of the Board of Directors none of whom hold any position in the active management of the company.

References

Allen, D.R., McDermott, K., 1993. Accounting for Success: A History of Price Waterhouse in America 1890–1990. Harvard Business School Press, Cambridge, MA.

Blough, C.G., 1947. Replacement and excess construction costs. Current accounting problems. The Journal of Accountancy 84 (4), 333–336.

Blough, C.G., 1949. Recent developments in accounting for depreciation on replacement cost. Current accounting problems. The Journal of Accountancy 87 (1), 65–66.

Catanach Jr., A.H., Walker, P.L., 1999. The international debate over mandatory auditor rotation: A conceptual research framework. Journal of International Accounting, Auditing & Taxation 8 (1), 43–66.

Chandler Jr., A.D., Salsbury, S., 1971. Pierre S. du Pont and the Making of the Modern Corporation. Harper & Row, New York.

Cheape, C.W., 1995. Strictly Business: Walter Carpenter at Du Pont and General Motors. The Johns Hopkins University Press, Baltimore, MD.

Commission on Auditors' Responsibilities, 1978. Report, Conclusions, and Recommendations. Commission on Auditors' Responsibilities, New York.

Depreciation and High Costs, 1948. Accounting Research Bulletin No. 33. American Institute of Accountants, New York.

Division for CPA Firms, 1992. Statement of Position Regarding Mandatory Rotation of Audit Firms of Publicly Held Companies. American Institute of Certified Public Accountants, New York.

Himmelblau, D., 1927. Auditors' Certificates. The Ronald Press Company, New York.

Knott, D., 2002. Protecting the investor: The regulator and audit, address to the CPA Congress 2002 Conference, Perth, WA, Australia. Australian Securities & Investments Commission, May 15.

Mackintosh, I., 2002. Auditors and Audit Committees—A Regulator's View. Australian Securities & Investments Commission, May 28.

Mandatory Rotation of Audit Firms, 2002. The Institute of Chartered Accountants in England and Wales, London.

Notable Deviations from Accounting Principles, 1948. Editorial. The Journal of Accountancy 85 (5), 362–363.

Partner Retires, 1958. The Price Waterhouse Review 3 (4), 68.

Perry, M., 2002. Parliamentary Push for Auditor Rotation. www.AccountancyAge.com, July 23.

Simon, S., 1959. The right side of accumulated depreciation. The Accounting Review 34 (1), 97–105.

Spacek, L., 1989. The Growth of Arthur Andersen & Co. 1928–1973: An Oral History. Garland Publishing, Inc., New York.

When Accountant and Client Disagree, 1944. Editorial. The Journal of Accountancy 77 (4), 267.

Zeff, S.A., Fossum, R.L., 1967. An analysis of large audit clients. The Accounting Review 42 (2), 298–320.

Accounting, Business & Financial History 13:2 July 2003 171–206

'The apotheosis of holding company accounting': Unilever's financial reporting innovations from the 1920s to the 1940s

Kees Camfferman and Stephen A. Zeff

Abstract

The annual reports of Unilever were widely hailed in the 1940s as outstanding examples of holding company accounting. The accounts did indeed contain many new and innovative features, including segment reporting of sales turnover. This contrasts with the frequently negative assessments of the company's reporting before World War II, and the fact that the company was on record as a relatively late adopter of consolidated statements. In this paper, Unilever's reporting practices from the 1920s to the 1940s are analysed. We argue that the reporting changes of the 1940s had clear antecedents in the 1920s and 1930s, when they emerged in conjunction with the transformation of Unilever from a family-dominated enterprise into a professionally managed organisation. We also argue that, in order to evaluate properly Unilever's pre-war reporting practices, one needs to take into consideration the nature of Unilever as a complex federation of companies, rather than a unitary organisation, and to examine the chairman's address at the annual general meetings. The speeches by Francis D'Arcy Cooper, in particular, contained important disclosures not found in the annual reports.

By the early 1940s, Unilever's commitment to improve its financial reporting was sufficiently developed for its officials, in particular Geoffrey Heyworth and P.M. Rees, to play important roles in the drafting of the English Institute's Recommendations on Accounting Principles and in the deliberations of the Company Law Amendment Committee whose report led to the Companies Act 1947. We therefore conclude that Unilever should be ranked with such companies as Dunlop Rubber among the key actors in the modernisation of British financial reporting during the 1930s and 1940s.

Keywords: Unilever; Lever Brothers; financial reporting; Companies Acts; holding company reporting; segment reporting; voluntary disclosure

Kees Camfferman, Department of Economics and Business Administration, Vrije Universiteit, De Boelelaan 1105, 1081 HV Amsterdam, Netherlands (tel: +31 20 444 6076; fax: +31 20 444 6005; e-mail: ccamfferman@feweb.vu.nl). Stephen A. Zeff, Jesse H. Jones Graduate School of Management, Rice University, 6100 Main Street, Houston, TX 77005, USA (tel. +1713 348 6066; fax: +1713 348 5251; e-mail: sazeff@rice.edu).

Accounting, Business & Financial History
ISSN 0958-5206 print/ISSN 1466-4275 online © 2003 Taylor & Francis Ltd
http://www.tandf.co.uk/journals
DOI: 10.1080/0958520032000084987

Introduction

Zeff *et al.* (1992: 75–6) stated that Lever Brothers and Unilever were in the forefront of publicly traded companies in the world to report a breakdown of sales turnover by product line and geographical area in its annual report to shareholders. Beginning in its 1945 annual report, the company introduced a supplementary disclosure of sales turnover (i.e. revenues) for nine product lines and for transport services for both the 1944 and 1945 financial years. Beginning two years later, the company presented and discussed a breakdown of its sales turnover for 1946 and 1947 by six major geographical regions, and it included a characterization, but without figures, of the profitability in a number of the sub-regions and countries. This latter narrative, consuming six pages in the directors' report, anticipated by more than 20 years the US Securities and Exchange Commission's (SEC) requirement for a Management's Discussion and Analysis of Operations (MD&A). These voluntary disclosures came at a time when the company was listed in London and Amsterdam, but was contemplating a listing in New York.[1] In this paper, we show that Lever Brothers reported segment information even as early as in the 1920s and continuing well into the 1930s. We also show that, by 1945, the company was able to explain further improvements to its financial reporting in terms of an explicit financial reporting strategy, with the objective of providing shareholders and others with an array of financial information beyond what was required by Great Britain's out of date companies legislation.

It is our objective in this paper to discuss the evolution of the company's financial reporting strategy from the 1920s to the 1940s. We believe that such a study is justified, not only because of the importance of Unilever as one of the largest enterprises of the period and because of the remarkable quality of its financial reporting, but also because Unilever's financial reporting developed in close interaction with the process of modernisation of British financial reporting culminating in the Companies Act 1947. Because of this, we conclude that Unilever should be recognised as a key player during the period of accounting reform in the 1940s.

This paper is organised as follows. We start with a brief section on the formation of Unilever. The main body of the paper consists of two sections describing the development of Unilever's financial reporting, the first covering the 1920s and 1930s and the second the period of World War II and the immediate post-war years. To keep the paper within limits, we focus our discussion on the twin 'group accounting' issues of consolidation and segment reporting, which we believe did most to establish Unilever's reputation as a financial reporting pioneer during the 1940s. To be sure, the 1940s also saw a number of other important changes, for instance concerning tax accounting and inflation-adjusted profits, but we touch upon these only in passing. We open both historical sections with short biographical sketches of the three most influential figures in this story – Francis D'Arcy Cooper, Geoffrey Heyworth and P.M. Rees. All three played important roles in Unilever's financial reporting, and through these individuals, Unilever's financial reporting was linked up with contemporary developments in the wider accounting world.

The period covered in this paper ends in the 1940s. By that time, the consolidation and segment reporting policies in Unilever's annual report had matured to the point where they were continued at that level until well into the 1960s. Moreover, the sustained movement for company law reform in Great Britain had culminated in new legislation, so that any subsequent changes in Unilever's financial reporting would have to be analysed in the light of the demands arising in the post-reform environment.

Formation of Unilever

In the 1930s Unilever was a mammoth enterprise with a complex web of corporate relationships extending throughout the world, embracing more than 200 companies. Its operating companies produced and marketed a wide range of oil- and fat-based products, particularly soap and margarine. Unilever came into existence following successive mergers in 1927 and 1929 (Wilson, 1954; Chandler, 1990: 378–89; Fieldhouse, 1978: Ch. 2). In 1927, two predominantly Dutch groups with extensive international networks in margarine and related oil- and fat-based products, Jurgens and Van den Bergh's, merged. The resulting group was organised into two holding companies, one Dutch and the other British: N.V. Margarine Unie and Margarine Union Limited, respectively. The two companies' boards of directors were identical, with members of the Dutch founding families predominating, as before. Shareholders' rights were apportioned by means of a dividend equalisation agreement, and the two companies issued identical annual reports, in English and Dutch, except for issues relating to local company and tax law.

Two years later, the two holding companies merged with the British group Lever Brothers Limited to form Unilever, in what Chandler has called the largest international merger to occur prior to World War II (1990: 382). Lever Brothers had been formed in 1885, and it was incorporated as a private company in 1890. It had been taken public in 1894 even though, until the 1920s, it continued to be dominated by its founder, William H. Lever, later the first Lord Leverhulme. Lever Brothers had expanded its worldwide operations both by takeovers and internal growth, and it maintained an especially large operating presence in the British Empire and the United States. Margarine Union/Unie and its predecessors had a large complementary presence on the European continent, particularly in central and eastern Europe.

As with Margarine Union/Unie, Unilever was composed of two holding companies: Unilever Limited, in Great Britain, and Unilever N.V., in the Netherlands.[2] The two companies had identical boards of directors, except that the chairman of each company was the vice-chairman of the other. The balance of voting power on the boards was almost equally divided between the British and Dutch interests. Unilever also adopted a dividend equalisation agreement between the two holding companies. For all practical purposes, the two companies acted as one. In most years, the board chairman's address to the shareholders for each company was the same but for the language.

Apart from the two holding companies, most of the operating companies that were combined into Unilever retained their corporate identities, and some of them, notably Lever Brothers, had their own stock market listing and outside shareholders or debenture holders, and therefore they continued to publish separate accounts. This was already a feature of Lever Brothers before the merger, as Fieldhouse has written:

> Of greater practical importance [than the move of headquarters to London], how-ever, were the first steps taken during and after 1923 towards rationalisation of the multifarious industrial and other enterprises founded or acquired by Lever. To this point almost all had retained their legal identity and autonomy, each with its own board, management, factories, sales force and so on. In many respects all these survived until the 1930s for Lever had developed a strong dislike in his later years of what he called 'scrambling eggs' and this bolstered the natural aversion of the management of associated companies to losing their independent existence.
>
> (1978: 34)

Much the same could be said for the companies combined into Margarine Unie/Union, and it remained a characteristic of Unilever throughout most of the 1930s.

Following the 1929 merger, Unilever's principal head office was in London, where the chief executive officers of both of the holding companies were based. A secondary head office was in Rotterdam, where the operations of the Dutch holding company were centred. During World War II, however, contact between the operating wings of the two holding companies was severed, as the Rotterdam office, the seat of N.V., and its continental subsidiaries found themselves in German-occupied Europe. The two companies issued their own annual reports for the financial years 1939 through 1944. For this period, our paper is concerned almost entirely with the annual reports of Limited, because all of the interesting developments in Unilever's financial reporting during the war occurred in Britain and were adopted after the war by N.V.

The changes in Unilever's financial reporting discussed in this paper began to appear during the company's transition from control by its founders and their fam-ilies to the ascendancy of professional management (see Chandler, 1990: 378–89). By the time that Unilever was formed in 1929, the predecessor companies had already, to varying degrees, introduced non-family members at the highest ranks. Yet a degree of family control continued in evidence until well into the 1930s (see Sluyterman and Winkelman, 1993). Three individuals from the first generation of professional managers and technical specialists who succeeded the founding fami-lies also played leadership roles in Unilever's financial reporting between the 1920s and 1940s. They were: Francis D'Arcy Cooper, Geoffrey Heyworth, and P.M. Rees. Each of these was also to some extent involved in the work of major committees that had an important influence on the course of British financial reporting, and so provided a link between Unilever's reporting and these wider developments. Cooper will be introduced at the start of the section on the 1920s and the 1930s, and Heyworth and Rees at the start of the section on the 1940s.

Unilever's financial reporting during the 1920s and 1930s

Francis D'Arcy Cooper (1882–1941) and the Greene Committee

Francis D'Arcy Cooper joined the board of Lever Brothers in 1923. 'Probably because his father was an accountant before him', it was reported in the Unilever house organ, '[Cooper] began business by entering accountancy; he was not specially drawn to the profession, indeed he disliked arithmetic!' (Knox, 1976: 222). He was a nephew of the founder of Cooper Brothers & Co. (Edwards, 1984: 781), which was one of the leading firms of chartered accountants in the UK. He himself became a partner in Cooper Brothers in 1910 and, following the war, became its senior partner. One of the firm's largest audit clients was Lever Brothers, and the autocratic Leverhulme came to acquire great respect for Cooper's sagacity as well as for his reputation in the financial community. Cooper's success in persuading the banks to provide Lever Brothers with desperately needed finance enabled the company to stave off liquidation following Leverhulme's ill-advised purchase of the Niger Co. in 1920 (Edwards, 1984: 781–2). Cooper was gradually given a greater role in the shaping of company policy until, in 1923, he resigned from Cooper Brothers to become vice-chairman of Lever Brothers (Edwards, 1984: 782; Wilson, 1977: 131). He was named chairman following Leverhulme's death in 1925.

Cooper did much to place the financial and operating management of Lever Brothers on a rational plane. After the formation of Unilever, Cooper became a director of Unilever and he also retained his position as chairman of Lever Brothers – which was, following the merger, one of the largest operating subsidiaries in the Unilever organisation. As Fieldhouse (1978: 39) has written, 'Since Cooper held undisputed control over the largest single unit in Unilever, was accepted as an outstanding businessman, and, perhaps most important, was neutral as between the Van den Berghs, Hartogs and the rest, he was well placed to assert his position as effective head of the federal enterprise'.[3] Cooper played a key role in imposing unity of direction on Unilever, culminating in the major reorganisation of 1937. This cleared away much of the remaining organisational diversity inherited from the predecessor companies and, among other things, marked the disappearance of the remaining elements of family control over Unilever. A serious illness slowed him in 1939, and he died in December 1941.[4]

In July 1925, Cooper gave evidence to the Greene Committee on Company Law Amendment. He was the only chairman of a large industrial group to appear before the Greene Committee (Bircher, 1991: 62), and he was asked in particular for his opinion on accounting and reporting by holding companies. In his written and oral testimony, he considered two possible approaches and found both to be wanting. First, Cooper stated his opinion that consolidated balance sheets would convey no meaningful information:[5]

> The incorporation in a statement purporting to be the balance sheet of a holding Company of the assets and liabilities of other legal entities, would not, in my opinion, be a true statement of the position of the holding Company, nor would it be a true statement of the position of each of the subsidiary entities. It would be a conglomeration of figures, futile as an aid to any person desirous of understanding the true position, and, so far as it was taken literally, misleading.
>
> (*Minutes of Evidence*, 1925: ix)

Second, Cooper rejected the publication of separate accounts of subsidiaries as a possible alternative approach to holding company reporting, mainly on the ground that this would cause unacceptable competitive damage. Asked whether the shareholders would not want to know 'the way in which the subsidiaries stand and which branch of the business is profitable and which is not', Cooper answered: 'I think they are not entitled to know that' (*Minutes of Evidence*, 1925: para. 3777).

In the end, the Greene Committee did not recommend the required publication of consolidated accounts nor any disclosures concerning the operations of subsidiaries. Subsequent commentators have concluded that, on the subject of holding company accounting, the Committee was strongly influenced by Cooper's testimony (Kitchen, 1972: 126; Edwards and Webb, 1984: 40). Mainly as a result of this testimony, Cooper has been characterised as a conservative (Bircher, 1991: 62), as 'not constructive' (quoted in Kitchen, 1972: 129), one who resisted reform (Edwards, 1989: 237), and as a manager who evinced 'paternalism, and possibly disdain, for actual shareholders' (Bircher, 1991: 78).

Cooper's position in 1925 therefore appears to be an unlikely starting point for the development of Unilever into a paragon of holding company reporting. Yet we will show that, under Cooper's direction, Lever Brothers and subsequently Unilever experimented with novel forms of holding company reporting, including especially the provision of sales and profits by product line and geographical region. Hence, Cooper's reputation of disdain for shareholders and unwillingness to innovate in financial reporting requires some revision.

Outline of changes in reporting practice

The development of Unilever's reporting practices during the 1930s is difficult to summarise because of the complexity of the Unilever organisation. Apart from the identical annual reports of the two Unilever holding companies (in Dutch and English), several subsidiaries published their own annual reports, not always by the use of similar accounting policies and in comparable formats. Moreover, Cooper's speeches, as chairman, at annual general meetings, were frequently used to disclose important financial information not found in the printed annual reports. Taken together, these several sources yield an image of a gradual, sometimes halting, but on balance a significant expansion of the range of published financial disclosures during the 1920s and 1930s.

The main facts relating to the development of holding company accounting in the annual reports can be summarised as follows.

Prior to the formation of Unilever in 1929, Lever Brothers did not publish consolidated financial statements. Among the Dutch predecessors of Unilever, Van den Bergh's and one of its subsidiaries apparently included consolidated balance sheets in loan prospectuses in 1925 or 1926 ('Van den Bergh's Fabrieken', *De Kroniek*, 1926: 105). However, neither did so in its annual report. Following the merger in 1927 between Jurgens and Van den Bergh's, the combined entity, Margarine Union/Unie included a 'consolidated balance sheet' in its first (1928) annual report. In reality, however, this was merely a balance sheet with combined figures for the British and Dutch holding companies. The two companies' operating subsidiaries were omitted from the statement. The following year, after the creation of Unilever, a combined profit and loss account was added to the combined balance sheet in the holding companies' annual report. Again, these were incorrectly described as 'consolidated'. In 1931, the presentation of combined financial statements was suspended owing to the volatile currency fluctuations between the Netherlands and Britain.

In 1934, Unilever added a 'consolidated statement of working capital' to its annual report, and this time all subsidiaries were included in the consolidated figures.[6] In the 1937 report, this was expanded to become a 'consolidated overview', by inclusion of consolidated data on issued share capital, long-term receivables and loans, pension funds and pension contributions, and investments in and depreciation of fixed assets. In the 1939 annual report, publication of this overview was suspended. Prior to World War II, none of the major subsidiaries published consolidated statements in their own annual reports.

In the absence of consolidation, there were other initiatives to provide more information on the unconsolidated subsidiaries. From 1927 onwards, the Lever Brothers annual report mentioned the rate of return on total book value for the subsidiaries carried on the balance sheet. The audit report referred to this figure as well. Beginning in 1932, Unilever included a 'statement of profits' (subsequently called a 'consolidated statement of profits'). This statement opened with consolidated net profit (i.e. the combined net profit of the holding companies and the subsidiaries, less the minority interest therein), which was then reconciled to the holding company profit and the profit appropriation. This statement might be seen as an approximation of the equity method of accounting, at least as far as the income statement is concerned. In the balance sheet, subsidiaries remained at cost throughout the pre-war period.

The absence of consolidated statements was also to some extent compensated for by the inclusion in the annual report, from 1929 to 1936, of summary balance sheets and profit and loss accounts, including net profit, for six major subsidiaries.[7] The usefulness of this feature was significantly reduced, however, when it became clear in the 1932 report that most stocks of raw material had been transferred to specially created subsidiaries. The six companies for which separate information was given were thus largely reduced to holding companies themselves.

As indicated above, important financial information was also provided in the chairman's speeches at annual general meetings.[8] At the 1926 Lever Brothers meeting, Cooper volunteered the total (consolidated) sales turnover figure for 1925 in pounds sterling (and tonnage of product), which was an exceptional disclosure in the 1920s. He reported the total sales figure for every year thereafter until 1937, when Lever Brothers was amalgamated into Lever Brothers & Unilever, Limited. Moreover, from 1927 to 1931 Cooper used his chairman's address at Lever Brothers to report the breakdown of profit in pounds sterling by eight or more product lines and by up to eight geographical regions. An illustrative excerpt from these speeches is reproduced in Appendix A. In 1930, moreover, sales turnover was given for two regions. The public reporting of sales and profit breakdowns was without precedent at the time.

Comparable disclosures were not given at the annual shareholder meetings of other Unilever subsidiaries and affiliated companies during the 1930s, nor, until 1938, at the annual meetings of the two holding companies. However, in 1938 and 1939, Cooper, as chairman of Unilever, reported the global sales turnover for the group as a whole. In 1938, he also gave a breakdown of turnover for several product lines, as well as a breakdown of tonnage for products sold, accompanied by the aggregate tonnage for all products sold. In 1939, he provided particulars on the sales turnover and profitability of certain product lines and geographical regions, if only expressed in round figures and sometimes in relative rather than absolute figures. Some figures were given in physical quantities (e.g. in metric tons of soap or margarine) instead of in monetary amounts. Cooper also attempted a kind of value-added statement, showing how much of the aggregate sales turnover of approximately £200 million (itself a disclosure that was rarely supplied by companies) accrued to employees, shareholders, and the suppliers of goods and other services.

During the war, no chairman's speeches were given. Only in the 1940 report was total sales turnover (excluding operations on the continent) reported in a section of the annual report entitled 'Review of the Company's Trading'. Thereafter, no total sales turnover or segment information was supplied again until 1945.

Evaluation: contemporary practices and press reactions

The main impression from the previous summary is that, while Unilever stopped short of publishing full consolidated statements before World War II, there were significant steps taken in that direction as well as important disclosures of information relevant to holding companies.

During the 1930s, some other companies were publishing consolidated statements. Blommaert (1995: 122–3) found that 11 Dutch listed companies, out of some 500, published such statements prior to 1940, and Bircher (1991: 189–93) reported that nine out of the 40 largest UK holding companies (by market capitalisation) included a consolidated balance sheet and/or profit and loss account in their 1938 or 1939 accounts.[9] It was well known, of course, that Dunlop Rubber Company Limited published a full set of consolidated statements beginning in 1933 (see de Paula, 1948, Ch. V). Unilever was therefore clearly not among the first to publish consolidated statements. Moreover, its first 'consolidated' balance sheets were no more than combined statements of the two holding companies. This mislabelling of combined statements as consolidated statements could perhaps be explained by the lack of a literature on consolidated statements, apart from the publication of Gilbert Garnsey's celebrated 1922 lecture on the subject (Garnsey, 1923; see Kitchen, 1972).[10] Yet Garnsey was a partner in Price, Waterhouse & Co., one of the joint auditors of Margarine Union/Unie and Unilever. Moreover, another Price, Waterhouse partner, A. Lowes Dickinson, was an avowed advocate of preparing consolidated statements. During his years in the US, Dickinson played an important role in encouraging his firm's major client, United States Steel Corporation, to publish consolidated statements for 1902, thus setting an important standard of American practice (DeMond, 1951: 60; Allen and McDermott, 1993: 32–3).[11]

In evaluating Unilever's progress towards the adoption of consolidated reporting, there is no need to assume a lack of precedents or a lack of knowledge of the subject. Moreover, the subject of consolidation was repeatedly brought to the company's attention by the financial press, which subjected the company to a steady stream of criticism for failing to produce consolidated statements. However, the press was not insensitive to the problems faced by Unilever, nor did it fail to notice such improvements as did take place. Press comments on Unilever's reporting therefore show a curious mixture of criticism and praise, as if the financial press was unsure of what might reasonably be expected from a company of this extraordinary size and complexity.

A good example of these mixed feelings is provided by *The Economist*. In 1929, it characterised Lever Brothers as having a 'tradition of Olympian reticence' ('Lever Brothers', 13 April 1929). Commenting on the balance sheet items relating to associated companies, it observed in the same article: 'It is unwise to hazard an interpretation of movements in these enormous items, whose composition is wrapped up in permanent obscurity; like the capitalisation of the company in which ordinary shares represent only 4 per cent. of the whole, they are part of the Lever tradition.' Yet, the same article conceded that the disclosure of the average rate of return on subsidiaries was a part of the report 'which other companies might be encouraged to copy'. The year before, the paper had adopted a tone of praise and encouragement: 'On the whole, the directors are to be commended for their continued efforts to introduce greater clarity into the company's accounts. We would urge them not to be weary in well-doing, but to take an even bolder step next year, and publish a combined balance sheet incorporating the accounts of the subsidiary companies' ('Lever Brothers', *The Economist*, 7 April 1928: 699). Commenting on the first annual report of Margarine Unie/Union, *The Economist* called it 'a pattern of lucid exposition' ('Margarine Union', 27 April 1929: 936). Yet in 1932 it wrote that 'A year's Unilever accounts are a symphony of which the investor hears only the concluding bars. From Greenland's icy mountains to Afric's sunny fountains its subsidiaries, sub-subsidiaries and sub-sub-subsidiaries extend, and all that shareholders can conclude from the published reports is that trading profits have been satisfactorily maintained...' ('Unilever Accounts', 16 April 1932). On the adoption of a consolidated statement of working capital in the 1934 report, it wrote: 'Shareholders will heartily congratulate the directors on their decision, for none of the world's great holding concerns has hitherto excelled the Unilever group in the issue of annual statements calculated to make Oliver Twists of shareholders' ('Unilever – First Results', 6 April 1935: 799).

Finally, after having complained for about a decade about the absence of consolidated statements,[12] *The Economist* showed itself very understanding when, in the 1937 report, Unilever stopped short of a full consolidated balance sheet:

> The major introduction is a consolidated statement of earnings, assets and liabilities. The directors have not, however, attempted to give a consolidated balance sheet, which, if based merely on the conversion of currency book values into sterling, would be misleading. In any case, the sterling figures must be regarded as approximate, and further, the reserves and undistributed profits held by subsidiary and allied companies, while considerable, could only be computed – and then arbitrarily – by a complete revaluation of over 400 manufacturing units. Armed with a consolidated earnings statement, full particulars of working capital, and long-term claims and liabilities, together with the free reserves of the parent companies, most investors will consider that they have ample and strictly relevant information for

assessing the position of the group... Although a complete consolidated balance sheet is not presented – in our view rightly – it is possible to infer from the available figures that the approximate book valuation placed on the interests in subsidiary and allied concerns, is equivalent to £114 1/2 millions.

('Unilever Group Results', 30 April 1938: 242[13])

Criticism and praise can also be found elsewhere in the financial press. The absence of consolidated financial statements was frequently pointed out as a major defect both in Britain and the Netherlands.[14] But it was also noted that Unilever was searching for alternatives or substitutes. Lever Brothers' disclosure of the rate of return on subsidiaries was called 'the most useful substitute for a combined balance sheet which we have seen' (*The Accountant*, 'Finance and Commerce–Audited Yield from Subsidiaries', 28 April 1934: 605). Another favourable comment on this feature appeared in *The Times* ('City Notes – An Admirable Example', 15 April 1930: 23): 'If other companies were to follow this admirable example of giving the average return earned on book values they would go far to satisfy reasonable criticisms of the inadequacy of public company accounts'.

Similarly, the disclosures provided by Cooper in his various speeches were favourably commented upon. *The Times* wrote that Cooper had given 'A very informative speech, which might well be imitated by other company chairmen ...' ('Lever Meeting', 2 May 1930: 22; on the same speech, see *De Telegraaf* 'Lever Bros', 3 May 1930). *The Economist* observed that the speeches held 'by the chairmen of the various Unilever companies ... have thrown a flood of light on the trading position' ('A Unilever Survey', 5 May 1934: 987).

However, the amount of comment on these disclosures appears relatively small in the light of their novelty. We now know that these disclosures were unprecedented and not to be seen in the reports and accounts and even the chairman's addresses of other companies until the 1960s.[15] Cooper's addresses dealt at some length with the economic and business conditions in various parts of the world and represented an even earlier anticipation of the SEC's Management's Discussion and Analysis than did the company's 1947 annual report, mentioned above.

Internal background of reporting changes

If it is true that in the 1920s and 1930s Unilever was making credible attempts to improve its reporting as a holding company, it may be asked how the decisions to do so were taken within the company. Unfortunately, the available archival materials contain only limited information about the formulation of reporting policy.[16] In general, it is clear that the Special Committee (in effect, the executive committee of the board of directors) took a decided interest in financial reporting. In 1932 it decided that it would henceforth approve the draft annual reports of all public companies in the group.[17] During the 1930s, it regularly planned the year-end cash and profit positions of these public companies.[18] Despite this interest in financial reporting, few traces of the accounting changes outlined above were found. Some information is, however, available on the adoption of a consolidated statement of working capital in the 1934 annual report. This change was suggested in a brief memorandum from the chief accountant, P.M. Rees, together with a proposal to include comparative figures and to exclude shillings, pence and cents. This memorandum gave no reason why consolidated information should be considered at that time, but the move appears to have been prompted by demands from shareholders.[19] This memorandum does include a short comment: 'It will be noted that this does not purport to be a Consolidated Balance Sheet which we have always contended and still contend would only be a misleading document to submit.'[20] One can infer from this remark that Cooper's rejection of consolidated balance sheets in his testimony before the Greene Committee in 1925 was not an indication of unwillingness to inform shareholders, but instead derived from a lasting conviction about the usefulness of consolidated results, a view that was shared by others at the top of the Unilever organisation. Interestingly, it also appears that, unlike the conjecture made by some press commentators, technical difficulties were not an important factor in Unilever's decision not to provide a consolidated balance sheet.

Based on the available evidence, we hypothesise that the initiatives to improve financial reporting during this period came predominantly from the UK side of Unilever (i.e., Lever Brothers), and that Cooper, in particular, played the pre-eminent role.

Neither of the two Dutch predecessor companies with a history of public financial reporting (Jurgens and Van den Bergh's) had displayed a notable tendency towards expanding its financial disclosures prior to their merger. Jurgens in fact had a rather negative reputation in this regard. In 1925, the Van Oss brothers, who were crusading journalists writing in the weekly magazine *Haagsche Post*, accused Jurgens of gross manipulation in its accounts and of reporting fictitious profits. A revaluation of subsidiaries was the main object of criticism. The episode attracted considerable notice, and it drew attention to the financial reporting by holding companies at a time when the reform of companies legislation was believed to be imminent in the Netherlands. The price of Jurgens' stock fell sharply, and a shareholder brought a lawsuit against the *Haagsche Post* for the loss sustained by the panic selling of the company's shares. For its part, Jurgens issued a categorical denial but in effect refused to provide any details to enable a substantiation of the charges. In the end, the affair had no effect on the reform of Dutch companies legislation (Zeff *et al.*, 1992: 42–3; Camfferman, 1995: 176). Looking back, the newspaper *De Telegraaf* characterised the reporting policies of Margarine Unie as follow:

> [T]he limited publicity that had characterised the Jurgens concern was continued by Margarine Unie. This should not in itself cause surprise. Since the leaders of the Jurgens concern were now joined by the Van den Berghs as directors of the new enterprise, and since the latter, as partners in a family firm, did not attach much value to openness either, it was natural that the new Margarine Unie was little inclined to be very communicative towards the public. In a few instances, the company had necessarily given some additional information to the public, for instance

in order to ensure the success of a share offering. But in general it has adopted the Jurgens policy as its own.
('Het Unileverconcern biedt weerstand in de crisis', *De Telegraaf*, 16 April 1933)

If family control was an important factor, it could be pointed out that Lever Brothers under the chairmanship of William Lever should not have been keen on publishing information either. To be sure, the annual reports of Lever Brothers prior to the mid-1920s did not contain remarkable disclosures, yet even Leverhulme could occasionally publish surprising information. As early as the 1921 annual meeting, he displayed a pie-chart showing how the company's turnover was divided into the cost of raw materials, labour costs, interest, other costs and profits.[21] Moreover, with the succession of Cooper to the chairmanship in 1925, it can plausibly be argued that by then, and certainly by 1930, Lever Brothers was rather ahead of the two Dutch companies in the transition from family control to professional management.

Cooper's mark on Lever Brothers' financial reporting policy becomes evident from the surprising disclosures in his annual meeting speeches.[22] From 1931 to 1937, Cooper functioned as chairman of both Lever Brothers Limited and of Unilever Limited. Curiously, while his addresses to the Lever Brothers annual general meeting contained the important disclosures discussed above, his parallel addresses as Unilever chairman did not contain any such disclosures of sales figures or profit segmentation. Following the 1937 amalgamation, however, Cooper transferred the model of his Lever Brothers addresses to Unilever and thus began to disclose the sales figure for the group as a whole plus selected segment information. The fact that Cooper persisted in providing the global turnover and segment information for Unilever following the amalgamation underscored his personal commitment to this innovative disclosure of financial information.[23]

As to Cooper's views on segment reporting, the only recorded statement we have found is his assertion to the Greene Committee that shareholders 'are not entitled to know' how subsidiaries stand or which branch of the business is profitable and which not (*Minutes of Evidence*, 1925: para. 3777). In the light of the fact that, from 1927 onwards, he was providing this type of information to his shareholders, it is likely that before the Greene Committee he was primarily opposing claims of entitlement to this information on the part of shareholders, rather than denying its usefulness or his willingness to disclose at his own discretion. We can therefore only offer some speculations about his motives. The demand for segment reporting, a type of deconsolidation reporting, did not emerge until the 1960s, when conglomerate enterprises in large number began to be created in the UK and the US.[24] With Lever Brothers, it was the other way round. Already a conglomerate in the 1920s, but before consolidated statements had become a way of life, the company pioneered in the provision of segmental financial information. Cooper may have believed that the dissemination of consolidated statements went in the wrong direction. To convey an understanding of a conglomerate, one had to provide breakdowns by product lines or geographical regions, not consolidate across the entire diversified enterprise.

It is not clear why Cooper chose different models for his two addresses prior to 1938. The reason can hardly have been a difference in the availability of information between the Lever Brothers companies and the other parts of the group. A 1932 memorandum describing the tasks of Unilever's Head Office Administration (i.e. Chief Accountant's Department) lists as one of the principal routine duties 'to prepare the Weekly White List, which shows the estimated profit of the concern, in trades and countries'.[25] Although, for reasons of cost-cutting, it was proposed to prepare these lists on a monthly basis, there can be little doubt that, throughout the 1930s and across the entire Unilever organisation and not just within Lever Brothers, extensive resources were expended to supply management on a regular basis with the kind of statistics that Cooper quoted in his annual addresses. A possible explanation of the difference in financial disclosure as between Cooper's two annual addresses might be that some members of the Unilever board, particularly from the Dutch side, did not share his view on the disclosure of total sales turnover and the breakdown of profit information. However, because there was considerable overlap in the membership of the Lever Brothers and Unilever boards, the significance of this argument is difficult to assess.

Unilever's financial reporting during the 1940s

As in the previous section, we start our discussion with biographical sketches of two individuals who had a decisive influence on Unilever's financial reporting during this period and who ensured the involvement of Unilever with general developments in accounting.

Percy Montague Rees (1883–1970) and the Recommendations on Accounting Principles

P.M. Rees qualified as a member of the Institute of Chartered Accountants in England and Wales (English Institute) in 1905. In 1908, the firm in which he was employed became one of the auditors of Jurgens' accounts on the continent. Wilson has written that 'the growing complications of accountancy for the vast new [Jurgens] enterprises demanded the appointment of a professional accountant. The responsibility was assigned to a chartered accountant from England, Frank Hague – for the science of accountancy was further advanced in England than it was on the Continent' (1954: vol. II, 54). In 1923, Rees joined Jurgens as chief accountant in succession to Hague.

In 1927, after the merger between Jurgens and Van den Bergh's, Rees became the chief accountant of Margarine Union, and two years later he was named one of the two chief accountants, together with R. Norman Locking, of the newly created Unilever. Upon the death of Locking in 1931, the chief accountant who had served in that capacity for Lever Brothers and then Unilever since 1921, Rees became the sole chief accountant, retaining that post until his retirement in 1948.

In July 1942, Rees was selected as a charter member of the English Institute's newly created Taxation and Financial Relations (TFR) Committee which came to be the drafting committee of the Institute's path-breaking series of Recommendations on Accounting Principles (see Zeff, 1972: 7–20; Bircher, 1991: 232–42). The committee was set up 'to consider matters affecting taxation and the financial relationship of the business community with the Inland Revenue and other Government Departments' (Zeff, 1972: 8). At its first meeting, the TFR Committee asked for Council's permission to prepare drafts of guidance statements on accounting principles. The permission was granted, and these drafts, following an elaborate internal consultation process and eventual approval by Council, became known as Recommendations on Accounting Principles. The TFR Committee was aware that a revision of company law, including the norms for the presentation of financial statements, was in the offing, and it wished to issue guidance that might influence the Board of Trade committee that would propose the new legislation. In doing so, the Recommendations became the first attempt by the accounting profession in Britain at giving authoritative guidance on accounting principles.

Apart from Rees, the other non-practising member of the newly established committee was F.R.M. de Paula, who, as company comptroller, had persuaded the directors of Dunlop Rubber Company Limited to publish a consolidated balance sheet as early as 1933. De Paula had, through articles, speeches and a textbook on auditing, established a reputation as an innovative thinker. Although Rees' views had not appeared in print, it is likely that the Institute's Council was aware that, with Rees and de Paula, they were appointing two kindred spirits to the TFR Committee.[26] In 1954, when de Paula died, Rees wrote:

> I first met [de Paula] some fifty years ago when we had both just started in practice in friendly rivalry with great hopes and few clients and we both kept body and soul together by tuition for the examinations. After spending roughly half our professional lives in practice, we each took up appointments in industry where, by continual collaboration, we shared the ambition of making published accounts simpler and more informative.
>
> (1954: 670)

Bircher has written that 'the final output in the form of the [Institute] Recommendations owes much to the generative ferment in the drafting sub-subcommittee of [K.A.] Layton-Bennett, Rees and de Paula' (1991: 239). 'In the early days of the committee', Rees wrote, 'I worked with [de Paula] in the preparation of the first drafts of the original Institute Recommendations' (*The Accountant*, 18 December 1954: 670).[27]

The TFR Committee and its subcommittees fulfilled their responsibilities with alacrity, and, in less than two years, eight Recommendations were published. Recommendation 7, issued in February 1944, was entitled, 'Disclosures of the financial position and results of subsidiary companies in the accounts of holding companies'. It recommended that companies publish a consolidated balance sheet and profit and loss account.

For two years, Rees served as committee chairman, and he retired from the committee in 1953, having rarely missed a meeting in 11 years. In 1944, Rees became only the second non-practising member to be chosen to the English

Institute's Council, following de Paula, who had been named to the Council the preceding year. Rees retired from the Council in 1956 at age 73.

Geoffrey Heyworth (1894–1974) and the Cohen Committee

Geoffrey Heyworth joined Lever Brothers in 1912 as a clerk and spent a short period in the accounts department. He then obtained considerable business experience with the company's Canadian subsidiary, and, upon his return to Britain in 1924, he became involved with the company's export trade. In 1925, he became the Sales Controller of Lever Brothers' home soap trade, based at Port Sunlight, near Liverpool. He became a director of Unilever in 1931, when it swelled to more than 200 operating companies. Heyworth was charged with sorting out the many and assorted soap companies resulting from Lord Leverhulme's practised habit of buying competitors' businesses. Sir David Orr, who served as Unilever chairman from 1972 to 1984, has written:

> This left a disparate collection of companies still competing amongst themselves and jealous of their individual identities. The job of rationalizing this group of independent companies was a delicate one. Regional strengths had to be maintained, order instilled, and managers appraised and appointed in accordance with business needs. Heyworth's programme of reorganization [consummated in 1937] was a pioneering move for those times and a model for the future.
>
> (1986: 405)

Heyworth succeeded Cooper as chairman of Unilever Limited in 1941 upon the latter's death. Orr has written,

> Heyworth established an international reputation as an expert in the field of professional management. This included not only technical and production skills but also accounting, distribution, marketing, and personnel management. His speeches dealing with these topics at the Unilever annual general meetings became management textbooks.
>
> (1986: 405)

It was said that 'few men did more than he to strengthen public confidence in business' (Obituary in *The Times*, 17 June 1974).

Heyworth retired as chairman in 1960, and in 1948 he was knighted by the Queen. He was created the first Baron Heyworth in 1955 (see also Zinkin, 1985). From 1943 to 1945, Heyworth served as the only representative from industry on the Cohen Committee on Company Law Amendment. The Committee, chaired by Mr Justice Cohen, was appointed by the Board of Trade with a view towards modernising companies legislation. As with the TFR Committee, the Cohen Committee was purposely composed of progressive thinkers, as it was believed that a major reform of company law was long overdue (Bircher, 1991: 129–39). Heyworth was a member of the Cohen Committee's Sub-Committee on Accounts, which was responsible for developing the recommendations on accounting (Bircher, 1991: 243–4).

In the end, 'Much of the contents of the first eight Recommendations eventually found expression in the 1945 Report of the Cohen Committee and in the revised Companies Act itself' (Zeff, 1972: 16). One of the major Cohen Committee recommendations was in line with the Institute's Recommendation 7 on consolidated statements (*Report of the Committee on Company Law Amendment*, 1945: 72-6), and a corresponding provision was included in the Companies Act 1947. The new act was silent, however, on the disclosure of sales turnover or on segment reporting, both of which were not made a public issue in the UK until the 1960s.

The 1939 to 1944 Reports and Accounts

The developments during the period 1939–44 were characterised, at first, by a reduction in the information content of Limited's annual report and accounts because of the inevitable interruptions provoked by the wartime hostilities. From 1942 onwards, the paper shortage and difficulties in communicating with subsidiaries in occupied territories continued and even became more severe, yet, because the company apparently learned to cope, the amount and scope of information in its annual reports began a steady expansion.[28]

There can be little doubt that the publication of full consolidated statements in the 1943 report (as opposed to fragmentary consolidated data or combined balance sheets of the holding companies, as had been done before the war) was the single most important development in Unilever's financial reporting during the war, not least because it went against the long-held belief within Unilever that consolidated balance sheets would be misleading. But initially, that is from 1939 to 1941, the war caused a reduction rather than an expansion of consolidated information. In Unilever's 1939 report, it was stated:[29]

> A further consequence of the war is that it has not been possible to prepare the Consolidated Statement of the two Companies, which in previous years has been attached to the published Accounts, and in view of the Equalisation Agreement [between the two holding companies] the publication of the Consolidated figures of LIMITED alone would only be misleading.
>
> (Lever Bros & Unilever Annual Report for 1939: 2)

Nevertheless, some consolidated figures were included in the 'review of trading', the most notable being the consolidated sales figure for Limited and its subsidiaries. Apart from these, the 1939 report retained the pre-war Statement of Consolidated Profits, which showed the consolidated profits (after deduction of minority interests) and the amounts retained by subsidiaries. The years 1940 and 1941 saw little further change except for some smaller details added to the Statement of Consolidated Profit, mainly in regard to War Damage Contributions, staff pensions, and taxation. On War Damage Contributions and taxation, the changes foreshadowed the solutions that were adopted subsequently in Recommendations on Accounting Principles 2 and 3, issued by the English Institute's Council in 1942 and 1943, respectively.[30]

Formally, the Recommendations began to play a role in the 1942 annual report. In a May 1943 memorandum, Rees brought to the attention of the Special Committee that 'the Council of the Institute of Chartered Accountants have issued recently certain recommendations as regards the form of Published Accounts. These recommendations have since been adopted by the larger companies, and it has to be decided whether we shall do the same in all our published accounts.'[31] Given that the first two Recommendations had been issued as recently as December 1942, Rees may have overstated his case somewhat when he suggested that there had already been widespread adoption. Nevertheless, the adoption of the Institute's series of Recommendations as a matter of principle was agreed, with the lone exception, based on a proposal by Rees, concerning the presentation of income tax recoverable from dividends.[32]

The 1942 report arguably marked the beginning of Unilever's second and, this time, definitive adoption of consolidated reporting. The Statement of Consolidated Profit in the 1942 report begins to look like a proper consolidated profit and loss statement, because of the following changes:

- minority interests were separately shown, so that the statement opened with 'aggregate profits' of the group as a whole;
- (consolidated) items for depreciation and debenture interest were separately shown;
- profit appropriation items such as balances carried forward and proposed dividends (which previously constituted about half of the statement) were no longer shown in the statements.

At first sight, it looks as if these changes were made as a deliberate first step towards the publication of a consolidated balance sheet in the 1943 report. In that report, the first to contain a consolidated balance sheet of Limited and its subsidiaries, the directors revealed that 'preparations were made a year ago to have comparative figures available [to be shown in the consolidated balance sheet]'. The apparent meaning of this is that, sometime during the preparation of the 1942 report (which was published in September 1943), the decision had been made to move towards a full set of consolidated financial statements. However, in a lengthy August 1943 memorandum discussing all major changes in the 1942 report, Rees made no mention of consolidated balance sheets. As to the consolidated profit statement, he observed that 'so far as can be foreseen, it embraces such recommendations as have been or will be made by the Institute of Chartered Accountants and covers points which will be suggested by them in their evidence before the Cohen Committee'.[33] Given that Recommendation 7, which was approved by the English Institute's Council in February 1944, as well as the English Institute's submission of evidence before the Cohen Committee, came out strongly in favour of consolidated accounts, the absence of a reference to a consolidated balance sheet in Rees's memorandum is somewhat surprising. It is true that Recommendation 7 noted the limitations of a consolidated balance sheet, and observed that aggregate profits might be stated even if 'for any reason the publication of a complete Consolidated Balance Sheet is impracticable or inappropriate'. Similarly, the Institute's evidence argued that companies should be permitted to provide information equivalent to consolidated accounts in another format (Bircher, 1991: 264). Therefore, Rees may have intended to make use of these escape clauses. In addition, in August 1943 he may still have expected that the case for consolidated balance sheets would be made less forcefully in Recommendation 7. In any case, a decision evidently was made shortly afterwards, but not necessarily prior to the publication of the 1942 report, to prepare and issue a consolidated balance sheet in the 1943 report. One can only speculate that this may have followed from the realisation that the adopted policy of following the Recommendations would not have been very credible if the company had opted out on this important issue. The 1943 report contained a separate page of Consolidated Accounts, consisting of the already familiar Statement of Profits and a new consolidated balance sheet. The directors, in their report, made it clear that Unilever was still a rather reluctant convert, and cautioned readers as follows:

> The Consolidated Balance Sheet must be read with certain qualifications in mind. The first of these is that, as the Directors have stated on previous occasions, they consider a submission of a statement which consolidates the balance sheets of a group of companies comprised in a world-wide undertaking, involving the conversion of various currencies into one common currency, may tend to be misleading and the Consolidated Balance Sheets now presented must serve as a general guide and no more to the position of the LIMITED Group as a whole so as to show the main trends in the employment of the Company's resources.[34]

The 1943 report did not merely include a consolidated balance sheet, it also complied in other respects with Recommendation 7, for instance by indicating the nature and measure of 'controlling interest' and describing the procedure to handle different year-ends.[35] *The Economist* ('Unilever Accounts', 1944) devoted extensive attention to Unilever's 1943 report because of its wider implications:

> The publication of a consolidated balance sheet by Lever Brothers and Unilever, Limited, marks another milestone on the road towards informative accounts … . If, realising these limitations [of consolidated accounts for a company like Unilever], as they do, the board of Lever Brothers and Unilever, Limited, think it worth while, even under some pressure from public opinion, to publish a consolidated balance sheet, the arguments against publication of similar figures by less complex groups are reduced to vanishing point – that is unless they are frankly based on a belief in obscurity for its own sake. It may be of significance that the chairman of the company is a member of the Cohen Committee.

Unilever's 1944 annual report did not reflect any significant changes in regard to its consolidation policy. Even though the war had ended by October 1945, when the 1944 report was issued, N.V. was still not capable of preparing its 1944 figures. Hence, Unilever's consolidation included Limited and its subsidiaries only. In the 1944 report, the directors did not repeat the extensive cautionary remarks on the limitations of a consolidated balance sheet.

As regard N.V., there is little to say about its financial reporting during the war. As it was cut off from Britain and was under separate management, N.V. did not participate in the developments described above. Between 1939 and 1944, N.V. did not report any consolidated information, and the directors' reports from 1939 to

1943 were terse and dealt mainly with dividends. The 1944 report, which was published shortly after liberation of the Netherlands, reflected some important differences. The balance sheet showed clear signs of a more modern layout, along the lines already followed by Limited (e.g. a separate heading for 'current'). The directors' report was also more extensive, but that was mainly because of the need to discuss the complex process of undoing contractual and other legal changes imposed by the occupation authorities and of sorting out the resulting claims.

The 1945 report

Unilever's 1944 annual report had already been well received, even though, because of the wartime paper shortage, it was compressed into four fold-out pages. Nonetheless, *The Economist* ('Unilever Problems', 27 October 1945) wrote, 'Subject to this all-important limitation [the non-inclusion of N.V.], the accounts are excellent both in material and in presentation'.

Unilever's 1945 annual report was released in November 1946. Expanded to 16 pages, it included a detailed consolidated balance sheet and profit and loss account, and, for the first time, separate sets of notes to both statements. The report also included a schedule of capital expenditures and depreciation as well as a note and accompanying diagram depicting the organisational structure of the two holding companies. In the report, Unilever's management unveiled its Statement H, which reported the comparative sales turnover for 1945 for ten groups of products and services, together with the metric tons for five of these groups, and accompanied by comparative information for 1944.[36] It also displayed a breakdown of total turnover by (1) sales to third parties, (2) the value of production for the Ministry of Food and the West Africa Produce Control Board, and (3) the supplies of marketable goods and services within the organisation. (Statement H is reproduced as Appendix B to this paper.) To our knowledge, no company anywhere in the world published a tabular summary, or any reporting on a regular basis, of monetary segment information prior to 1945.[37] In fact, even the disclosure of sales turnover in financial statements was a practice that was virtually unknown outside of North America in the 1940s.

This package of information was hailed in the financial press as a reporting breakthrough. *The Economist* called Unilever's 1945 financial statements 'the apotheosis of holding company accounting' and 'an accounting *tour de force*' ('Lever and Unilever Accounts', 23 November 1946). *The Times* opined that Unilever's 1945 report was 'truly formidable' ('Unilever New Accounts', 22 November 1946). *The Investor's Chronicle* wrote that '[Geoffrey Heyworth's] selection [on the Cohen Committee] was a tribute to the efforts which the Unilever group has always made to present a lucid and comprehensive statement of its affairs, and this time the accounts give effect to the Committee's report wherever practicable' ('Unilever Documentary', 23 November 1946). *Het Financieele Dagblad* (The Financial Daily) of Amsterdam became almost lyrical:

> Apparently, after realising that shareholders need to be given better information, the joint board of the Dutch and English Unilever have made a very laudable, and,

in our opinion, for the time being, in all respects a successful attempt – one that is unique among international approaches to publicity in the business world – to give us a clearer, better-arranged and more detailed report than has been usual until now anywhere in the world. We have the fullest praise for this approach. Confidence in [Unilever] shares will, through this openness (which the company plans to expand), undoubtedly further increase.

('Unilever-publiciteit–Heeft ongeëvenaard niveau van perfectie bereikt',
21 November 1946)

Perhaps the greatest praise came from *The Statist*, which said that the 1945 report was 'one of the outstanding company documents of the year, and may indeed fairly be said to make new history in industrial finance records' ('Lever Brothers & Unilever', 23 November 1946). Most of the commentators may have judged Unilever's 1945 accounts against the standard set by the Cohen Committee report and failed to grasp the significance of the disclosure of segment turnover, which went well beyond the Committee's recommendations. *The Financial Times* ('Unilever Dividend Policy', 22 November 1949) was an exception, calling Statement H '[a]n excellent table', and reproduced it in full.

Factors leading up to the 1945 annual report

It is interesting to attempt to trace the evolution of the thinking about segment reporting in the post-Cooper Unilever organisation. In December 1943, Cooper's successor, Heyworth, discussed the issue during the hearings of the Cohen Committee. Several witnesses before the Committee 'favored requiring that both sales and profit figures be broken-down by major product activities' (Hein, 1978: 269). One of these was Hargreaves Parkinson, the editor of *The Financial News* and former city editor of *The Economist*. In discussing the issue with Parkinson, Heyworth argued that statutory requirements would be ineffective given that 'the various subsidiary companies might make agreements with each other for equalising profits and so on' (*Minutes of Evidence taken before the Company Law Amendment Committee*, 1943, para. 2704). Although he added, rather implausibly for the chairman of one of the largest conglomerates in Britain, that he did 'not know what the technique would be' for equalising profits 'and so on', it seems safe to assume that his views would have carried sufficient weight to prevent the Committee, had it been so inclined, from recommending mandatory segment disclosures. But, just as Cooper had started to provide segment information to his shareholders a few years after he had argued before the Greene Committee that they were not entitled to it, so Heyworth committed himself to segment reporting within five months after the publication of the Cohen Committee report.

In 1945, plans for important changes in disclosure were clearly developing, even though their implementation had to be delayed for practical reasons. During discussion in the Special Committee of the 'Review by the Chairman' to be included in the 1944 annual report, the following was minuted:

it was appreciated that this year it would not be practicable to include turnover figures in the review, but it was stressed that these should be mentioned next year, based on the formula laid down some time ago under which inter-company sales of marketable products would be included. Mr Heyworth referred to the project of publishing the review separately from the accounts when paper supplies are adequate. He said it was proposed to present the facts in more dramatic form, incorporating illustrations and if desirable graphical representations, bearing in mind the necessity for some basic continuity in the form which would enable it to be adapted [sic] more or less consistently from year to year, and it was hoped conditions would permit of adopting this new form for the 1945 accounts.

(Special Committee Minutes, 17 September 1945 (E.1325), item 176, 'Limited Annual Report & Accounts, Year 1944')

Despite these reservations, Heyworth devoted a significant portion of his chairman's address at the company's annual general meeting (AGM) in October 1945 to his board's strategic plan for enhancing shareholders' understanding of Unilever's state of affairs and the results of its operations.[38] It was an address that was remarkable for the amount of thoughtful attention that he and his board had been giving to the question of how best to render an account to shareholders. Heyworth gave notice that his company was contemplating a more transparent approach for reporting to shareholders, including some kind of breakdown of figures according to 'each of our main industries region by region'. The following extract from his address enables one to appreciate the care and attention that Unilever proposed to dedicate towards providing shareholders with greater transparency:

Now to [discuss] the material to be issued prior to the [annual general meeting in 1946].

PRESENTATION OF ACCOUNTS

First, the accounts. Their purpose is to record the most accurate picture that is possible of the state of the company's affairs at the end of the year and of the results of the year's operations. For many years we have sought ways and means of doing this by simplifying the capital structure wherever this has been possible and by increasing the amount and quality of the detail given. Because of the magnitude and complexity of our operations it is not easy to do this and at the same time preserve clarity; in other words we have to balance the advantages of extra detail against the need of preserving a well defined outline. This problem is under continuous study, in which the board not only have the advice of a very capable and imaginative accountancy staff of their own, but call freely upon the wider experience of the professional auditors of the company. I think it can be said that we have a record of solid and progressive achievement in the presentation of our accounts. We have already adopted – some of it many years ago – most of the accountancy practice recommended in the recent Cohen Report and the remaining recommendations are already included in the improvements being studied for adoption next year.

The directors' report we regard as an integral part of the balance sheets and profit and loss accounts, explaining their contents and freeing them from detail that would obscure their broad impression.

It is the board's intention that the presentation of the accounts shall be progressively developed not only to reflect changes in the company's affairs, but to give the shareholders the clearest possible picture of the company's position that can be given in figures. In giving practical expression to this idea, we shall hesitate neither to invent new techniques nor to copy from others.

REVIEW OF TRADING OPERATIONS

Now to turn to the first section of the proposed review. This will deal with trading operations. The probability is that this can best be done by taking each of our main industries region by region; omnibus figures of sales turnover in currency will not be appropriate; we never think of our operations in that way ourselves; we think of tons of raw materials, cases or tons of soap, pounds or tons of margarine, and so on. We hope to make a first but necessarily modest attempt at presenting material of this kind to you next year.

('Mr Geoffrey Heyworth on Improvement of Methods', *The Statist*, 3 November 1945)

The Economist ('Lever Brothers' Information', 3 November 1945), *The Investor's Chronicle* ('Informative Chairmen', 3 November 1945), and *The Accountant* (10 November 1945) cited this last paragraph as a key part of Heyworth's address.

We have already noted the favourable press reaction to Unilever's 1943 and 1944 annual reports. Heyworth's announcement at the 1945 AGM of yet more reporting changes heightened expectations even further. *The Economist* observed:

Lever Brothers and Unilever already hold high place – if not the highest – in the technical excellence of their directors' reports and accounts. In many respects they have already achieved Cohen Report standards, and next year's reports will include improvements, which are now being studied, to meet the remaining recommendations of the Report. But Mr Geoffrey Heyworth's speech at this week's meeting contemplates an extension of the range of factual information far beyond the presentation of an admirable set of accounts and explanatory directors' report, and equally beyond the directors' obligations towards the shareholders.

('Lever Brothers' Information', 3 November 1945)

Unilever's plan for providing a breakdown by product line was discussed in the board's Special Committee. Initially, the breakdown of information by product lines was to be in physical quantities, but thought was already being given to a disclosure of sales turnover, but at the aggregate level. The first mention of a possible disclosure of sales turnover in the minutes of the Special Committee was a few months later, in February 1946, when 'Mr Rees reported that Accounts Department were preparing a preliminary draft of the information it was proposed to shew in the Company's 1945 Accounts. They required, however, a ruling on one or two points and the following were agreed', which included the following point:

b) Consolidated turnover
Mr Rees tabled a memorandum shewing the formula it was proposed to adopt in determining items for the purpose of calculating the Consolidated Turnover. It was agreed to make this split on the basis of whether it would be practicable for

a separate undertaking to manufacture the products in question or to carry out the services rendered.

(Special Committee Minutes of 19 February 1946 (U.63), item 56,
'Published Accounts 1945')

The memorandum discussed how to include internal sales and services in total turnover. About 17 categories of intermediate products and services were identified for possible inclusion, in addition to the value of sales to third parties.[39] At this stage, apparently, disclosing aggregate sales turnover was already decided, but disclosing segmented turnover information was not, nor was it discussed. The discussion was confined to what internal sales should be included in the turnover figure. This was in line with Heyworth's October 1945 AGM address in which he promised information about physical quantities rather than monetary segment information.

The next, and also the last, reference in the 1946 minutes to segment reporting was for the meeting of 6 August, at which a preprint of the 1945 annual report (series U, supp. doc. 6464) was discussed:

Accounts Department were asked to prepare a re-draft incorporating suggested amendments to the form and wording, particular attention being paid to the definition and logical sequence of the groups contained in Statement 8 as it was considered desirable to establish a form which could be adopted as a framework for future accounts and white sheet statements.

(Minutes of 6 August 1946 (U.77), item 153, 'Annual Report & Accounts 1945')

Statement 8 was the draft version of what would become Statement H in the 1945 annual report. This draft contained less information than the final statement: amounts in pounds sterling were not to be given for all product categories (again, still in keeping with Heyworth's October 1945 address). Nor was there a breakdown of third-party, government-controlled, and internal sales. The total turnover figure given in Statement 8 was therefore not shown as the result of an addition but as a free-standing figure.

Statement 8 was apparently given close attention by the Special Committee. This can be seen from the reference in the minutes that the members wanted something that could be used in future reports and in the 'white sheets' (the monthly summary financial reports provided to the board of directors). It can, perhaps, also be seen from the fair amount of editorial comment scribbled on the draft included with the minutes.

Interestingly, one item of information was eliminated at a later stage (the scribblings do not indicate this elimination). The draft included wages as a percentage of sales turnover, which was not included in the published version. The total amount of wages was not, in fact, shown anywhere in the 1945 annual report.

The final decision to approve of the reporting of £-amounts for all product categories and for the one service category must have been made by the full board, and it would certainly have had Heyworth's support.

Statement H remained virtually unchanged in the 1946 and 1947 annual reports. These two reports extended to 24 pages, in comparison with 16 for the

1945 report. They contained a lengthier directors' report, more expansive notes to the financial statements, a 'highlights' summary of the more salient points in the accounts, and, for the first time, a 10-year summary of capital employed and profits distributed and retained. Also for the first time, the auditors' report covered the consolidated statements. Unilever's annual reporting continued to garner praise. *The Economist* termed the 1946 report as 'accounting elegance' ('Unilever and World Trade', 23 August 1947: 337).

The 1946 report replicated the form and presentation of the 1945 report. P.M. Rees forwarded a copy of the 1946 annual report to F.M. Wilkinson, the assistant secretary in the English Institute who managed the work of the TFR Committee. Wilkinson, a crusty conservative, pronounced as follows:

> If I may say so, [the Report and Accounts] seem to do three things very effectively: they give the ignorant the figures they really need; they give the inquisitive the information as to how those figures are arrived at, and they give accountants a terrible headache.
>
> (letter from Wilkinson to Rees, dated 18 August 1947)

The 1947 report: geographical breakdown of turnover

In the 1947 report, Unilever fulfilled Heyworth's promise in his 1945 address to shareholders, that information would be supplied 'region by region'. As noted above, Unilever had presented profitability information, and some sales turnover information, both by product lines and geographical regions in the 1920s and 1930s. Yet the 1947 report went much further. It contained comparative sales turnover figures for all four regions (Western Europe, North and South America, Africa/Middle East/Australasia (excluding the United Africa Company), and the Orient, and a separate report of turnover for the United Africa Company. These disclosures appeared in the directors' report and were accompanied by an extensive discussion of trends and prospects on a country-by-country basis within the regions. This disclosure was another example of Unilever going beyond the recommendations of the Cohen Committee report and, indeed, the best practice anywhere in the world.

What was Unilever's motivation for disclosing a geographical breakdown of sales turnover? It is not improbable that the company's hand had been forced by *Fortune* magazine, which ran a three-part article on Unilever in its December 1947 and January and February 1948 issues (Burck, 1947; 1948a; 1948b). *Fortune* had approached the company in the spring of 1947 about the article project, and Unilever promised its co-operation, for it saw the article as a good public relations vehicle.[40] But Unilever placed clear limits on its cooperation, especially when *Fortune* requested 'some detailed information of turnover in individual countries or groups of countries' (Special Committee minutes of 26 November 1947 (U.106), item 138, 'Fortune'). At that stage, the company was not prepared to disclose these confidential figures even to its shareholders, let alone to financial journalists. Undeterred, the magazine reported its own estimates of Unilever's sales turnover by regions, comparing 1946 with 1937 (Burck, 1947: 213; Burck,

1948b: 80). This disclosure may have prompted the belief within Unilever that there was little point in hiding its own figures on geographical turnover, even though *Fortune*'s estimates appeared to be reasonable. The minutes of the Special Committee do not report the underlying reasons, but they do show that, by May 1948, a decision had been taken to include a geographical breakdown of turnover (Minutes of 26 May 1948 (U.123), item 62, 'Annual Report & Accounts 1947'). But Unilever's predilection to be informative to shareholders shone through. Many companies, confronted with the same situation, would not have disclosed their own figures.

Unilever's 1947 report, as with its two immediate predecessors, drew praise. *The Times*'s city editor said that the report 'once again depicts the company's year with a precision and clarity which few other companies can rival' and placed emphasis on the company's 'admirable example by publishing figures for its annual turnover' ('Unilever in 1947', 4 August 1948). *The Accountant*, for its part, endorsed *The Times*'s assessment ('Precision and Clarity', 28 August 1948). *The Economist*, which by 1948 had run out of superlatives, referred simply to the 'riches of information' contained in the report ('Unilever in Perspective', 7 August 1948).

Statement H was retained in Unilever's annual report until 1964, after which the breakdown of sales turnover by product and service lines was reported in a different format. The sales turnover apportioned by region was retained in the directors' report until 1961, and in following years it was presented in another format.

Reasons for Unilever's Financial Reporting Innovations in the 1940s

As might be expected in the light of our argument that Unilever was closely involved with general developments in financial reporting, the factors that help explain Unilever's innovative financial reporting in the 1940s have their counterparts in the general movement towards modernization of financial reporting, symbolised by the Companies Act 1947. That Act is seen on the one hand as a break with the past and an expression of a new social ethos, forged by World War II. On the other hand, it has been argued that the Act was essentially the culmination of attempts at moderate reform that had started well before World War II (see Maltby, 2000). In the case of Unilever, one finds a similar combination of pragmatic continuity and more idealistic innovation.

Above all, it should be mentioned that Unilever's segment disclosures in its annual reports beginning in 1945 were an extension of Francis D'Arcy Cooper's financial reporting practices and policy in the 1930s. During the 1930s, Cooper, the chairman of Lever Brothers as well as of Unilever, regularly presented segment breakdowns of sales turnover and profits in his annual speech to the shareholders of Lever Brothers. We have speculated that his failure to present similar information at the annual meetings of Unilever's shareholders might have been due to a measure of opposition or ambivalence towards disclosing such information from some of the family members of Unilever's board of directors. When selecting a vehicle for informing shareholders of the trends in segmental operations, he chose the one that was most under his control: the chairman's speech.

Geoffrey Heyworth was, like Cooper, a professional manager. He evidently shared Cooper's view that shareholders should, as far as practicable, be fully apprised of the results of Unilever's far-flung and widely diversified operations. In his address to the annual meeting in October 1945, quoted at length above, Heyworth said, 'It is the board's intention that the presentation of accounts shall be progressively developed not only to reflect changes in the company's affairs, but to give the shareholders the clearest possible picture of the company's position that can be given in figures'. Segmental breakdowns that Cooper related in his chairman's speech in the 1930s could, by the mid-1940s, with a less hidebound board of directors, be incorporated into Unilever's annual report. From the early 1930s to the middle of the 1940s, the percentage of family members serving on the Unilever board gradually declined from 45 to 30 per cent.

In these financial reporting initiatives, Heyworth was surely supported by Paul Rijkens, who, in 1937, had become the first outside manager to become chairman of Unilever N.V. After Cooper's death in 1941, he and Heyworth became the joint chairmen of Unilever until Rijkens' retirement in 1955. Rijkens spent the war-years in London and must therefore have had close knowledge of the reporting innovations planned and carried out during those years. While we have no direct evidence of the hand he played in these developments, it seems certain that he was at least supportive of them. He was known in general as a progressive spirit, and as a firm believer in a wider social responsibility of companies that is often associated with the Companies Act 1947 (see Maltby, 2000: 3–5). He professed accounting to be one of his hobbies (Rijkens, 1965: 15), and he was, following World War II, named chairman of a special committee in the Netherlands to propose improvements in company financial reporting. The committee's recommendations were truly forward looking (see Zeff *et al.*, 1992: 94–112).[41]

Moreover, as Unilever's progressive management found ways and means of rationalising the complex web of Unilever's multi-faceted operations via the development of internal reports on the sales volume and profitability of product lines and geographical areas, these same reporting methods commended themselves for use in communicating with shareholders (see Wilson, 1954: vol. II, 309–16).

In general, it may be said that the Unilever management during these years were genuinely committed to openness and the improvement of its financial reporting, and that this was one of the main drivers of change in its reporting policy. While the strength of this commitment is rather unique for this period, it did not mean that Unilever's management shaped its financial reporting without an eye on the company's specific interests. This is shown by occasional modifications in underlying legal relationships and the sequencing of transactions in order to avoid certain undesired reporting consequences.[42]

Other factors were also at work. Unilever's management was aware that the company's dominant position in its markets had scarred its reputation for fair dealing. *Fortune* wrote:

> But the parent company does not share this good will [that its products enjoy], and the name Unilever rings few bells except cracked ones. People who know a little about it denounce it as a monopoly not only where it is powerful but where it

doesn't amount to beans. The Czechs still identify it with its German subsidiaries, and Britain's Socialists tend to think of it as an example of corporate iniquity that needs to be watched and curbed. And almost anyone who knows anything tangible about it, friend or foe, from Capetown to Oslo or from Shanghai to Vancouver, alludes to it as the 'Octopus'.

(Burck, 1947: 88)

The forthrightness of Unilever's annual report to shareholders was seen by *Fortune* and others as one element in the company's public relations programme in the 1940s. As early as 1942, the Special Committee had decided under the heading of 'Public Relations' that 'it would be essential in the post-war world to take a positive rather than a negative line as regards the many important questions affecting industry in general, and our own in particular'.[43] The Board of Trade's announcement in June 1943 of the appointment of Heyworth to the Committee on Company Law Amendment would have been a very good example of this stance. For his part, P.M. Rees, Unilever's chief accountant, was an active member during the 1940s of a committee of the English Institute that was intent on recommending improvements in company financial reporting.

All of these considerations – a continuation in a more integral format of Cooper's forthcoming financial disclosure policy, especially as management came to devise new and more effective internal reporting; the freer hand given to Heyworth resulting from the change in composition of Unilever's board of directors; and management's need to burnish the company's image as a corporate citizen – help explain the appearance of the notable financial reporting innovations in Unilever's annual reports in the 1940s.

Conclusions

We have documented how Unilever emerged after World War II with a reputation as a leader in the modernisation of company financial reporting in Britain. Not only was the company an early adopter in the middle 1940s of the recommendations of the Cohen Committee on Company Law Amendment, it also went considerably beyond them by providing extensive voluntary disclosures. Preeminent among these disclosures, which were without precedent in Britain and elsewhere, was a breakdown of sales turnover by product line and geographical region. Even Unilever's disclosure of company-wide sales turnover was highly unusual at the time in Britain.

In contrast, before the war Unilever and its subsidiaries were frequently criticized in the financial press for their uninformative reporting. In the historical literature, the company is portrayed as a retarding factor in the modernisation of financial reporting, mainly because of the testimony of Francis D'Arcy Cooper, the chairman of Lever Brothers, before the Greene Committee on Company Law Amendment in 1925. Yet during the 1930s, Unilever's annual report began to evolve towards consolidated financial reporting. More important still, Cooper himself provided important and innovative financial disclosures in his speeches to annual general meetings such as total sales volume and profits for selected segments. In our view, this trend towards expansive reporting showed that Cooper's opposition to consolidated reporting in his testimony to the Greene Committee was not mere conservatism, but followed from the belief that there were more effective ways of giving insight into a large and diversified group of companies.

During and after the war, this trend continued with the adoption of full consolidation in 1942 and 1943 and the provision of systematic segment information in the annual report from 1945 onwards. By 1945, it became clear that the breakdown of sales turnover and profitability by product line and geographical region emerged as part of a coherent policy of reporting to shareholders. Yet, because of a strong contrast in terms of size, number of pages and quality of printing between the 1944 and 1945 annual reports, it looks at first sight as if a sudden change of attitude occurred around that time. In fact, as shown in this paper, the 1945 report was the culmination of a long, gradual trend towards improved reporting, obscured by the wartime paper shortage. We have shown how this trend coincided with the accession of professional managers to top positions in the firm, starting with D'Arcy Cooper himself and continuing with Geoffrey Heyworth and Paul Rijkens.

The significance of these findings to the literature on financial reporting history lies not merely in a rehabilitation of the image of Cooper and of Unilever, even though, as the largest industrial enterprise in Britain during the 1930s, its financial reporting has a certain intrinsic interest. The findings also testify to the influence of Unilever during the period of financial reporting reform in Britain during the 1940s, centring on developments leading to the Companies Act 1947. In this respect, this study addresses Bircher's (1991: 295) call to supplement his analysis of the origins of that Act with research into the relationship between accounting practice and the developing ideas about best practice.

Through the participation of Heyworth in the Cohen Committee and Rees in the TFR Committee, there was a close interaction between the development of practice at Unilever and the evolving normative ideas on accounting. By anticipating or promptly adopting the recommendations of both committees, Unilever gave them added credibility and, as was clearly appreciated by the financial press at the time, denied other companies the excuse that these recommendations might be impracticable. At the same time, it is very likely that Heyworth and Rees made sure that the recommendations reflected their own views on how financial reporting ought to develop.

Altogether, we conclude that our findings justify the recognition of Unilever as a key player during the period of financial accounting reform in the 1940s.

Acknowledgements

We express our thanks to the archivists and staff of the Unilever archives in Rotterdam and at Unilever House, London, for allowing access to the relevant archival materials and for helpful assistance. We also thank participants at the 2001 ABFH Conference at Cardiff University and the ARCA research seminars at the Vrije Universiteit, Amsterdam, and two anonymous reviewers for helpful comments on earlier versions of this paper.

Notes

1 Unilever did not list its shares on the New York Stock Exchange until 1961.

2 In 1937 the names of the two holding companies were changed to Lever Brothers & Unilever Limited, and Lever Brothers & Unilever N.V., respectively. We will, however, refer to the joint companies as Unilever.

3 The family-controlled Hartog firm was a large Dutch producer of margarine, which was acquired by Margarine Unie in 1929.

4 In June 1941 he had been made a baronet in the King's Birthday Honours.

5 In a letter to *The Times* dated 3 June 1925, Cooper stated the essence of his objection to consolidated balance sheets: 'I see no useful purpose in producing an amalgamated balance sheet which would be neither fish, flesh, fowl, nor good red herring. On the contrary, in my opinion it could only do harm.' Cooper's objection applied not only to the consolidated balance sheet as a replacement for the holding company balance sheet, but also to consolidated balance sheets published as additional information (*Minutes of Evidence*, 1925: para. 3770).

6 The statement included the two holding companies and all 'subsidiary and allied companies' in which 50 per cent or over of the ordinary capital was held, either directly or indirectly.

7 It is evident from these summary statements that the several companies' accounting policies were rather diverse, which would presumably have been an impediment to consolidation. For example, one company carried its fixed assets at 1 guilder, while others were recording depreciation.

8 The following comments are based on the reproductions of these speeches in *The Times* and *The Economist* of the period.

9 To illustrate the current accounting practices for dealing with holding companies, Garnsey and Robson (1936) reproduced in Appendix II the published accounts of a number of major British, American, Canadian and Swedish companies for the financial year 1934. Unilever Limited and N.V. are included in the appendix.

10 In the Netherlands, the subject of consolidations was occasionally discussed from the mid-1920s onwards. It was first given systematic treatment in 1929, when J.J.M.H. Nijst published his *Leerboek der Accountancy* (see Camfferman, 1997: 251).

11 Walker (1978: 140–52) doubts that Dickinson was himself responsible for U.S. Steel's decision to use consolidated statements, although he acknowledges that Dickinson was a staunch advocate of such financial reporting.

12 See also the following articles in *The Economist*: 'The Unilever Colossus', 11 June 1932: 1300–1; 'Lever and Unilever', 15 April 1933: 817–18; 'Unilever Finance', 22 April 1933: 867–8; 'Lever and Unilever', 14 April 1934: 828; and 'Lever Brothers' Report', 3 April 1937: 26–7.

13 The main reason why *The Economist* thought Unilever was right not to present a consolidated balance sheet was because N.V. was faced with severe restrictions on converting earnings in Germany into sterling or guilders. In 1939, it wrote: 'The group, however, still controls over 400 manufacturing subsidiaries in almost every country of the world. ... This fact goes far to justify the directors' practice of providing only a limited range of consolidated figures for the twin Lever companies and their subsidiary and allied companies' ('Lever Brothers and Unilever', 29 April 1939: 257). It appears that in the case of Unilever, unlike the Royal Mail Group, cross-holdings were not so prevalent or complicated as to prevent consolidation (see Green and Moss, 1982: 97).

14 Persistently negative comments on the reporting quality of Unilever and its Dutch predecessors appear in *De Kroniek*, a pioneering journal in the field of financial analysis edited by Dr Alexander Sternheim. See also Nijst (1932: 5), who characterised Unilever's omission of a consolidated balance sheet as 'a major defect'. The weekly *Haagsche Post*, however, drew attention to the 'technical impossibility to prepare a consolidated balance sheet for the more than 400 industrial businesses involved' ('Notities over de beurs- en zakenwereld', 7 May 1938: 24).

15   We reviewed the 1937 speeches by the chairmen of the 40 largest UK holding companies listed by Bircher (1991: 190–1), in so far as these could be retrieved from *The Times* and *The Economist*. In none of the speeches did we find a sales figure, nor did we find any considerable amount of quantified information on the results of operations. ICI, a company known for progressive financial reporting, was, by 1930, already organised into some ten product group-ings (Chandler, 1990: 361), and, as far as he British Empire was concerned, had a comparable geographical spread as Unilever. In the 1930s, ICI's chairman included in his annual speeches to shareholders an extensive narrative discussion of the company's operations by country (but by not product line), yet he did not report any figures on the sales volume and profitability of segment operations.

16   Archival sources consulted consist mainly of the Minutes of the Special Committee, preserved in the Unilever Historical Archives, London. The Minutes are organised by subject. Matters relating to financial reporting are contained in series E (*General Matters*), series J (*Minutes of the Special Committee meeting with the Treasury*) and, starting in January 1944, series U (*Minutes of the Special Committee with Accounts, Finance, Legal & Taxation Department*). The Special Committee Minutes, including supporting documents, do contain extensive information on the background of policy decisions. Nevertheless, with respect to financial reporting the coverage is patchy and not consistent from year to year. The minutes of the boards of directors do not help to fill in these gaps, because they contain merely the formal resolutions of the boards.

17   Special Committee Minutes, 18 March 1932 (E.55), item 124 'Balance sheets of public com-panies'. In subsequent years, these annual reports do indeed regularly come up for discussion.

18   For example, Special Committee Minutes, 1 July 1935 (E.368), item 144, 'Unilever Limited – Profit position 1935' and 14 November 1935 (J.209), item 330, 'Prospective cash position'.

19   See the draft communiqué to be published with the 1934 accounts. Special Committee Minutes, Series E, supporting document 1342, 'Dates of publication for accounts', P.M. R[ees], 1 January 1935.

20   Special Committee Minutes, Series E, supported document 1338 'Published Accounts', P.M.R[ees]., 19 December 1934. The Minutes (31 December 1934) give no other information than that 'it was felt that the proposed alterations were desirable and should be given effect to in the next accounts which are published'.

21   This idea may have suggested itself to Leverhulme as president of the Institute of Cost and Works Accounts, a post he filled from 1919 until his death in 1925. See Loft (1990: 68–70).

22   No archival evidence was found that, during the 1930s, drafts of these speeches were regularly discussed by the Special Committee. It is likely that drafts were discussed by the board of directors as a whole, but this fact is not reported in the board's minutes.

23   Cooper's commitment to accountability was evidenced by his practice, during most of the 1930s, of announcing a global profit forecast in his speech to the annual general meeting, and in the following year's speech he compared the annual result to the forecast. As noted above, profit forecasts were regularly prepared for management purposes. See also Special Committee Minutes, 15 October 1931 (J. 12), item 83, 'Profit Estimates'.

24   Hein (1978: 269) reports that 'Some witnesses [before the Cohen Committee on Company Law Amendment, in 1943–5] also favored requiring that both sales and profit figures be broken-down by major product activities', but the committee did not refer to the reporting of such information in its recommendations.

25   Special Committee Minutes, Series E, supporting document 63 'Head Office Administration'.

26   See Kitchen and Parker (1994) for a short biography of de Paula. No publications by Rees from the 1930s are known to us. In later years, he would bring examples of progressive financial

reporting to the attention of the editor of *The Accountant* so that they might be given greater prominence (see *The Accountant*, 20 July 1946: 35, and 6 September 1947: 155).

27   In fact, Rees submitted a memorandum to the subcommittee of the TFR Committee that was charged with drafting the Recommendations, in which he proposed topics under broad headings that the subcommittee should consider taking up (Bircher, 1991: 236–7).

28   Our estimate of the total number of words in the narrative sections of Unilever Limited's annual reports for 1939 to 1944, encompassing the directors' report and the chairman's review (or 'review of trading'), is as follows: 1939, 4,000 words; 1940, 2,250; 1941, 2,650; 1942, 3,750; 1943, 3,750; and 1944, 3,500. By contrast, in the 1945 and 1946 annual reports, in which the notes to the consolidated accounts appeared as such for the first time, the total number of words, including the notes, was 7,350 and 11,200, respectively. Prior to the 1945 report, the notes to the consolidated accounts were incorporated in the directors' report.

29   The Equalisation Agreement refers to the dividend equalisation agreement mentioned above, by which the dividends per share paid by N.V. and Limited had to be equal. Hence, partially consolidated statements would have shown neither the common pool of assets from which dividends of both holding companies had to be paid nor the potential claims by N.V.'s shareholders against these assets.

30   Rees had previously brought up these items for discussion in March 1941, more than a year prior to the formation of the Taxation and Financial Relations Committee, and also before the Council of the English Institute issued its August 1941 circular letter on war damage contributions (Zeff, 1972: 14). Rees gave no other justification for these changes than their topicality (e.g., 'the high rates of tax now prevailing'). Special Committee Minutes, Series E, supporting document 4418, 'Special features in published accounts', P.M.R[ees]., 21 March 1941.

31   Special Committee Minutes, Series E, supporting document 5246 'Annual Accounts 1942', P.M.R[ees], 5 May 1943.

32   Special Committee Minutes, 12 May 1943 (E.1162), item 66, 'Annual Accounts 1942'. The issue of income tax deductible from dividends was covered in Recommendation 4 (March 1943), and the position taken there was one that F.R.M. de Paula had advocated at least since 1929 (De Paula, 1948: 266–70).

33   Special Committee Minutes, Series E, supporting document 5322, 'Limited Provisional Results 1942', P.M.R[ees], 19 August 1943.

34   It is interesting to note that the directors no longer mention their fear, expressed in the 1939 report, that consolidation without including N.V. would be misleading because of the dividend equalisation agreement. That agreement was still in force, and the only change in circumstances was that, from 1941 onwards, Limited was informed about N.V.'s profits, showing that N.V. was capable of paying at least its preference dividends.

35   The only obvious element of non-compliance was that the results of unconsolidated subsidiaries were not shown separately (Recommendation 7, para. 63(a)).

36   Statement H was not covered by the report of the joint auditors, Cooper Brothers & Co. and Price, Waterhouse & Co.

37   A possible exception occurred in Sweden. The Swedish Companies Act of 1944 included a requirement to segment 'intäkt' ('revenues') by activity if the activities are essentially independent of each other (see Nilsson, 1995: 228–9). An exemption was available if the company would be commercially damaged by the presentation of such information. Sven-Arne Nilsson has advised the authors by e-mail that 'revenues' at that time was understood to mean gross profits rather than gross sales revenues. In regard to compliance, Hanner (1964) reports that some segmentation of 'revenues' was being reported. Of 88 larger (mainly listed) companies that were selected as being 'best practice' companies in 1951, two disclosed four gross profit segments, 10 disclosed three segments, and 22 disclosed two segments. The remaining 54 disclosed only one segment, which presumably means that they did not segment at all. Similar figures apply for 1961 and 1964.

In the US, the Procter & Gamble Company, which was one of Unilever's major competitors, published separate balance sheets for its English and Canadian subsidiaries, and for its 'Defense U.S.A.' subsidiary, for the years 1941 to 1946, because it was thought 'advisable' to exclude them from the consolidation during the war (see the first page of the President's Report in the 1941 annual report). Following the war, in the company's annual report for 1947, these subsidiaries were once again consolidated and their separate balance-sheet figures were no longer reported.

38   Drafts of the speech were prepared by the secretary of the board, L.V. Fildes. Special Committee Minutes, 23 October 1945 (E.1332), item 201, 'Annual General Meeting – Chairman's Speech'.

39   The memorandum was included as supporting document 6277 (series U), an undated, 1-page note by Rees.

40   *Fortune* had earlier approached Unilever about an article in the summer of 1940, but the Special Committee had decided that 'under present circumstances such an article was not desirable'. However, the Special Committee did instruct Heyworth to see the London representative of *Fortune*, from which it may be inferred that it was interested in this type of publicity. Special Committee Minutes, 3 September 1940 (E.938), 'Fortune'.

41   For more information on Rijkens, see Lichtenauer (1979).

42   For example, in October 1945, Rees pointed out that Van den Bergh & Jurgens (Ltd) held 51 per cent of Home & Colonial Stores. To avoid a consolidation, he proposed to transfer some of the shares to Associated Enterprises, Ltd (which was apparently not a subsidiary) (Special Committee Minutes, 2 October 1945 (U.38), item 83).

43   Special Committee Minutes, 2 December 1942 (E.1126), item 191, 'Public Relations'.

References

Allen, D.G. and McDermott, K. (1993) *Accounting for Success: A History of Price Waterhouse in America 1890–1990*, Boston: Harvard Business School Press.

Bircher, P. (1991) *From the Companies Act of 1929 to the Companies Act of 1948*, New York/London: Garland Publishing.

Blommaert, J.M.J. (1995) *Consolideren en informeren, Een onderzoek naar de informatieve waarde van de geconsolideerde jaarrekening*, Houten: Educatieve Partners Nederland.

Burck, G. (1947) 'The World of Unilever', *Fortune*, 36: 86ff.

Burck, G. (1948a) 'Unilever's Africa', *Fortune*, 37: 57ff.

Burck, G. (1948b) 'Unilever III/The Conversion', *Fortune*, 37: 75ff.

Camfferman, K. (1995) 'The history of financial reporting in the Netherlands', in Walton, P. (ed.), *European Financial Reporting, A History*, London: Academic Press: 169–87.

Camfferman, K. (1997) *Voluntary Annual Report Disclosure by Listed Dutch Companies, 1945–1983*, New York: Garland Publishing.

Chandler, A.D. (1990) *Scale and Scope, The Dynamics of Industrial Capitalism*, Cambridge, MA: Harvard University Press.

De Paula, F.R.M. (1948) *Developments in Accounting*, London: Pitman & Sons.

DeMond, C.W. (1951) *Price, Waterhouse & Co. in America: A History of a Public Accounting Firm*, New York: privately printed.

Edwards, J.R. (1984) 'Cooper, Sir Francis D'Arcy', in Jeremy, D.J. (ed.) *Dictionary of Business Biography*, London: Butterworths, vol. 1, pp. 781–5.

Edwards, J.R. (1984) 'The Development of Group Accounting in the United kingdom to 1933'. *The Accounting Historiain Journal*, 11(1): 31–61.

Edwards, J.R. (1989) *A History of Financial Accounting*, London: Routledge.

Fieldhouse, D.K. (1978) *Unilever Overseas, The Anatomy of a Multinational*, London: Croom Helm.

Garnsey, G. (1923) *Holding Companies and Their Published Accounts*, London: Gee & Co.

Garnsey, G. and Robson, T.B. (1936) *Holding Companies and Their Published Accounts*, 3rd edn, London: Gee & Co.

Green, E. and Moss, M. (1982) *A Business of National Importance, The Royal Mail Shipping Group, 1902–1937*, London: Methuen.

Hanner, P. (1964) *Årsredovisningen i praktiken II Större svenska aktiebolags & årsredovisningar 1951–1962*, Stockholm: FFI Norstedts.

Hein, L. (1978) *The British Companies Acts and the Practice of Accountancy 1844–1962*, New York: Arno Press.

Kitchen, J. (1972) 'The accounts of British holding company groups: development and attitudes to disclosure in the early years', *Accounting and Business Research*, 2 Spring: 114–36.

Kitchen, J. and Parker, R.H. (1994) 'Frederick Rudolph Mackley de Paula (1882–1954)', in Edwards, J.R. (ed.), *Twentieth Century Accounting Thinkers*, London: Routledge: 225–51.

Knox, A.M. (1976) *Coming Clean, A Postscript after Retirement from Unilever*, London: Heinemann.

Lichtenauer, W.F. (1979) 'Rijkens, Paul Carl', in Charité, J. (ed.) *Biografisch woordenboek van Nederland*, vol. 1, Den Haag: Martinus Nijhoff. pp. 518–19.

Loft, A. (1990) *Coming into the Light: A Study of the Development of a Professional Association for Cost Accountants in Britain in the Wake of the First World War*, London: Chartered Institute of Management Accountants.

Maltby, J. (2000) 'Was the Companies Act 1947 a response to a national crisis?', *Accounting History*, 5(2): 31–60.

Minutes of Evidence taken before the Company Law Amendment Committee appointed by the Board of Trade (1943) HM Government.

Minutes of Evidence taken before the Departmental Committee appointed by the Board of Trade to Consider and Report what Amendments are Desirable in the Companies Acts, 1908 and 1917 (1925) HM Government.

Nijst, J.J.M.H. (1932) 'Rondom het laatste jaarverslag der Unilever', *De Bedrijfseconoom*, 10: 1–10.

Nilsson, S.-A. (1995) 'The history of financial reporting in Sweden', in Walton, P. (ed.) *European Financial Reporting: A History*, London: Academic Press: 221–39.

Orr, D. (1986) 'Heyworth, Geoffrey', in Blake, L. and Nichols, C.S. (eds) *Dictionary of National Biography 1971–1980*, Oxford: Oxford University Press: pp. 405–6.

Rees, P.M. (1954) 'Obituary-Frederic Rudolph, Mackley de Paula, C.B.E., F.C.A.' *The Accountant*, 131(4174): 669–70.

Report of the Committee on Company Law Amendment (1945) Cmd. 6659, HM Government.

Rijkens, P. (1965) *Handel en Wandel: Nagelaten gedenkschriften 1888–1965*, Rotterdam: Ad. Donker.

Sluyterman, K.E. and Winkelman, H.J.M. (1993) 'The Dutch family firm confronted with Chandler's dynamics of industrial capitalism, 1890–1940', *Business History*, 35: 152–83.

Walker, R.G. (1978) *Consolidated Statements*, New York: Arno Press.

Wilson, C. (1954) *The History of Unilever, A Study in Economic Growth and Social Change*, London: Cassel & Co.

Wilson, C. (1977) 'Management and policy in large-scale enterprise: Lever Brothers and Unilever, 1918–1938', in Supple, B. (ed.) *Essays in British Business History*, Oxford: Clarendon Press.

Zeff, S.A. (1972) *Forging Accounting Principles in Five Countries, A History and an Analysis of Trends*, Champaign, IL: Stipes Publishing Co.

Zeff, S.A., Van der Wel, F. and **Camfferman, K.** (1992) *Company Financial Reporting, A Historical and Comparative Study of the Dutch Regulatory Process*, Amsterdam: North-Holland.

Zinkin, M. (1985) 'Geoffrey Heyworth', in Jeremy, D.J. (ed.) *Dictionary of Business Biography*, London: Butterworths, 3: pp. 192–7.

Appendix A: Except from Speech by Francis D'Arcy Cooper to the Annual General Meeting of Lever Brothers Ltd, 1 May 1930 (from *The Times*, 2 May 1930: 23)

I now come to our business overseas, which continues to expand. Profits for the Continent of Europe show an increase from £216,813 to £350,699, Holland, France and Belgium having done particularly well.

Australasia shows a decline in profits this year, being £275,304, against £241,099, including £18,993 earned by our Pacific Plantations, against £43,981 for the previous year. Owing to the financial position in Australia and the low price of copra this drop was anticipated, and I do not suppose that we shall show any great improvement for the current year; but the businesses themselves are very sound, and I am sure it is only a temporary decrease in the results.

India and China have given us £202,091, against £218,587.

The United States of America, South America, the Philippine Islands, and the Dominion of Canada have provided £988,370, against £710,536, and I would again like to refer to the astonishing progress that we are making in the United States, not only in profits but also in sales turnover. Our turnover in the U.S.A. in 1914 was £187,923, as aganst £8,036,127 last year, and in Canada £997,216 against £1,785,538, and we must again render a tribute of admiration to Mr Countway and Mr. Tyler, the respective presidents of our American and Canadian interests.

Our trade in Africa continues to be difficult, and our profits this year, which amounted to £152,047, as compared with £179,291 in 1928, show a decrease.

The results of the overseas figures taken in total have been satisfactory because they have been maintained at exactly the same percentages – namely,

32 per cent – of the profits of the company, as last year. If the export trade, the Niger Company and Candles Limited were included, the total profits drawn from overseas would amount to £2,637,913, or 42 per cent of the profits of the company.

Owing to the fact that last year our interests in West Africa were transferred to the United Africa Company, Limited, the figures for our 1929 turnover are not comparable with those for 1928, but if you exclude the West African figures our turnover was £68,771,126 as against £66,241,066, and our tonnage shows an increase of over 40,000 tons.

The prospects for 1930 seem to me to be favourable, and glycerine prices have now become stabilized. We sold during 1929 the whole of our glycerine output for that year, and I believe the stocks in Europe and American are considerably less than they were 12 months ago. I therefore anticipate that our aggregate results for 1930 will not be disappointing.

STATEMENT H TURNOVER OF PRINCIPAL COMMODITIES OF LIMITED AND N.V. GROUPS

(Excluding subsidiary companies not consolidated)

Supplies of marketable products – for use as raw materials – and services by one industry to other industries within the organization are included in order to provide a proper ratio of turnover to capital employed and profits earned. The amounts stated represent the full cost to any unit within the organization of products which, although manufactured or processed by another concern unit, are marketable in their then condition in the normal course of trade.

In the case of production in the United Kingdom for the ministry of Food and produce purchased for the West African Produce Control Board, a value has been included based on the Government controlled price.

	1944		1945	
	Metric tons	£	Metric Tons	£
Margarine, Edible Oils and Fats	517,000	42,065,000	594,000	50,188,000
Other foods for human consumption		22,792,000		25,196,000
Other Vegetable and Animal Oils and Fats	1,343,000	79,430,000	1,511,000	90,820,000
Animal Feeding Stuffs	1,039,000	12,306,000	1,187,000	14,416,000
Soap and Other Detergents	864,000	60,846,000	864,000	61,023,000
Toilet Preparations, including Perfumes		5,767,000		6,259,000
Miscellaneous manufactures, including Glycerine		9,235,000		8,922,000
Produce (mainly tropical produce handled by the United Africa Group)	871,000	16,322,000	855,000	18,063,000
Merchandise (mainly handled by the United Africa Group)		27,243,000		28,205,000
Services (including Ocean, River and Road Transport)		4,633,000		4,256,000
Total Value		£280,639,000		£307,348,000

Represented by:	£	£
(a) Sales to Third Parties	164,732,000	182,269,000
(b) Value of Production for the Ministry of Food or produce purchased for the West African Produce Control Board	60,961,000	65,773,000
(c) Supplies of marketable products and services within the organization	54,946,000	59,306,000
	£280,639,000	£307,348,000

Expressed as percentages of the above total values:

Direct taxation on profits	£12,815,180 or 4.17%
Amount distributed as dividend (net) to shareholders of LIMITED and N.V. and outside shareholders of their subsidiary companies	£5,045,942 or 1.64%
Profit retained within the organisation	£3,945,630 or 1.28%

As explained in the Directors' Report, §(3), figures of the N.V. Group for 1944 are not comparable.

Accounting Horizons
Vol. 17, No. 3
September 2003
pp. 189–205
Submitted: January 2003
Accepted: April 2003
Corresponding author: Stephen A. Zeff

How the U.S. Accounting Profession Got Where It Is Today: Part I

Stephen A. Zeff

Synopsis: Few would deny that the U.S. accounting profession is in a very troubled state. The aim of this two-part article is to explain how and why the profession evolved and changed during the 20th century, with particular emphasis on the last three decades. It is my hope that this article will illuminate the origins and consequences of these changes that collectively brought the profession to its current condition.

This paper reviews, examines, and interprets the events and developments in the evolution of the U.S. accounting profession during the 20th century, so that one can judge "how we got where we are today." While other historical works study the evolution of the U.S. accounting profession,[1] this paper examines two issues: (1) the challenges and

Stephen A. Zeff is a Professor at Rice University.

The author expresses his appreciation to several accounting academics and to more than a dozen active and retired senior partners of major accounting firms for their comments on earlier drafts. He also appreciates the suggestions of the anonymous reviewers.

Editors note: Professor Zeff agreed to have this lengthy but very important article published in two parts. Splitting an article of this nature is judgmental and unavoidably somewhat arbitrary. We both believe that your appetite will be whetted for Part II, forthcoming in December 2003, beginning as it does with Professor Zeff's discussion of "A Gradual Degeneration of Professional Values." The complete set of references will appear at the end of Part II.

---

[1] Interested readers should consult Previts and Merino (1998), which paints on a much broader canvas than this paper. While their book treats a number of the developments in the evolution of the U.S. profession, it does not provide as extensive a discussion of the subject taken up in this paper. An article that traces the evolution of the Big Eight firms, focusing heavily on published data on their internal growth as well as their growth through mergers, is Wootton and Wolk (1992). Miranti (1990) has also written a valuable work on the development of the profession, but it extends only to 1940.

crises that faced the accounting profession and the big accounting firms, especially beginning in the mid-1960s, and (2) how the value shifts inside the big firms combined with changes in the earnings pressures on their corporate clients to create a climate in which serious confrontations between auditors and clients were destined to occur. From available evidence, auditors in recent years seem to be more susceptible to accommodation and compromise on questionable accounting practices, when compared with their more stolid posture on such matters in earlier years.

INTRODUCTION

The paucity of available evidence about actual changes occurring within the big firms, especially from the 1970s onward, poses a major difficulty in conducting this kind of research. Without statistical analysis, the court cases, regulatory investigations, and press reports of alleged audit failures can be dismissed by leaders of the profession as isolated instances, not representative of the general way in which the big firms fulfill their professional obligations. Of necessity, I relied on letters from those who do know, on public expressions of concern by leaders of the profession and by regulators, and on the writings by close students of the profession. I formed interpretations and conclusions based on the available evidence, and I welcome comments and reactions from readers.

Three major sections comprise this paper. The first section surveys the evolution of the profession prior to the 1940s, essentially a period of groundbreaking and early development. The second section, covering the 1940s, the 1950s, and the first half of the 1960s, displays the profession at the height of its reputation and influence. The third section, beginning in the mid-1960s, treats the scandals, court cases, the profession's loss of its accounting standard setter and the impact of that loss on the vitality of professional discourse, Congressional criticism, pressures from government to alter the competitive climate of the profession, the burgeoning consulting services, and, in the end, the transformation of the big firms from organizations strongly imbued with professional values to ones that strongly pursue goals associated with commercial and business success. This reshaping of the firms as engines of growth, profitability, and global reach in turn placed added pressure on audit partners, already under pressure to generate fees and to placate clients. Such circumstances exert a severe strain on auditor independence. At the same time, top executives in publicly traded companies found themselves under greatly increased pressure for revenue and earnings performance, which they transmitted first to their accounting staff and eventually to their external auditors. The confluence of these developments inevitably led to the confrontations mentioned above.

PRIOR TO THE 1940s: SETTING THE STAGE

The U.S. accounting profession emerged during the last quarter of the 19th century, the first major accounting body being the American Association of Public Accountants, the lineal predecessor of the American Institute of Certified Public Accountants, established in 1887.[2] New York State passed the first law, in 1896, to recognize the qualification known as Certified Public Accountant, which, as Carey writes, "marked the beginning of an *accredited* profession of accounting in the United States" (Carey 1969, 44).

Scottish and English Chartered Accountants, who settled in the United States during the last quarter of the 19th century to report on British interests, performed much of the early auditing work. These pioneers from Britain included Edwin Guthrie, Arthur Young, James T. Anyon, John B. Niven, Ernest Reckitt, George Wilkinson, Arthur Lowes Dickinson, and George O. May. Americans who formed important accounting firms in the late 1890s and during the first two decades of the next century included Alwin C. Ernst, Charles Waldo Haskins, Elijah Watt Sells, Robert H. Montgomery, and Arthur E. Andersen.

Prior to the 1930s, no laws or regulations obliged corporations to have their financial statements audited. Quite a few companies had done so, however, for more than a decade, including United States Steel Corporation, E. I. duPont de Nemours & Company, General Motors Corporation, Eastman Kodak Company, and International Business Machines Corporation.

Early Professional Services and Ethical Norms

In 1913, following approval of the Sixteenth Amendment to the Constitution, Congress passed the first Revenue Act, which, coupled with "[r]ising tax rates, during and after the war, and the increasing complexities of the tax laws and regulations added enormously to the demand for accountants." (Carey 1969, 146, and 67–71, 213–215; also see Sommerfeld and Easton 1987, 169–170). Previously, many companies had never kept adequate accounting records, and, as a result of the Revenue Acts of 1913 and 1918, many company executives came to appreciate the importance of recording depreciation, because it was deductible for tax purposes. The Bureau of Internal Revenue's famous Bulletin "F," *Depreciation and Obsolescence*, appeared in 1920 (Grant and Norton 1955, 208–211). Accountants responded eagerly to meet the burgeoning demand for their services. In 1924, the newly instituted Board of Tax Appeals authorized both lawyers and CPAs to practice before it, which represented a strong endorsement of the standing of CPAs to conduct tax practice (Carey 1969, 222–224).

---

[2] For an extensive treatment of this period, see Miranti (1990), Previts and Merino (1998, Chapters 5 and 6), and Carey (1969).

From the earliest days of the profession, accounting firms rendered consulting services. By the 1910s, they included the installation of factory cost systems, studies of organizational efficiency, investigations in connection with possible investments in other businesses, and an array of other services to management, which, as Carey writes, "were often rendered in conjunction with audits." (Carey 1969, 146). But accounting, auditing, and taxation constituted the solid core of the firms' services.

In 1922, the American Institute of Accountants, now known as the American Institute of Certified Public Accountants (AICPA), banned certain forms of self-promotion by accounting firms. The following year, A. C. Ernst and two of his partners in Ernst & Ernst, by then a national firm, were accused of violating the Institute's rules against soliciting and advertising, and all three promptly resigned their Institute membership. Even after his firm no longer engaged in those practices, A. C. Ernst never rejoined the Institute (Carey 1969, 233–234).

Federal agencies sought the advice of the organized accounting profession because of its growing reputation. In 1917, at the request of the Federal Trade Commission (FTC) and the Federal Reserve Board, the Institute supplied a technical memorandum for publication by the Board as a bulletin on auditing procedures. The FTC sought to promote uniform accounting, while the Board wanted to apprise commercial bankers of the importance of securing audited financial statements from their borrowers. Despite the title of the bulletin, "Uniform Accounting," it actually dealt with recommended auditing procedures and the format of the balance sheet and profit and loss statement. This represented the first authoritative guidance on auditing procedures published in the U.S. In 1929, at the request of the Federal Reserve Board, the memorandum was revised by the Institute and published anew (Carey 1969, 129–135, 159–160; Previts and Merino 1998, 229–234, 250–251; Zeff 1972, 113–115, 118–119).

Audit work developed apace in the 1920s, as an increasing number of listed companies issued audited financial statements. By 1926, more than 90 percent of industrial companies listed on the New York Exchange were audited (May 1926, 322), even though the Exchange did not require audited statements by newly listed companies until 1933 (Rappaport 1963, 39–40). Yet the Exchange had informally encouraged companies to publish audited financial statements "for some years" before then (Staub 1942, 14–15).[3]

Initial Accounting Principles and Auditing Procedures, and the SEC

In 1930, following on the heels of the 1929 stock market crash, the New York Stock Exchange sought out the Institute for advice on the policies it should adopt with respect to the financial statements of its listed

---

[3] The great increase in the frequency of appearance of audit reports occurred between 1920 and 1928 (Hawkins 1962, 364).

corporations. After three years of deliberations, a blue ribbon committee of the Institute provided the Exchange with a philosophy and a framework for dealing with the accounts of listed companies. The committee proposed a set of "five broad principles" of accounting that it regarded "as so generally accepted that they should be followed by all listed companies" (Carey 1969, 177). These, together with a sixth, were officially approved in 1934 by a vote of the Institute's membership. The committee also recommended a standard form of the auditor's report. The committee's work quickly established the Institute as a body of stature in the field of corporate financial reporting. The leader of the Institute's committee was George O. May, the senior partner of Price, Waterhouse & Co. (Carey 1969, 174–180).

In June 1932, *Fortune* magazine, the trumpet of American capitalism, acknowledged the growing importance of the accounting profession by devoting a major article to a profile of the largest firms (Certified Public Accountants, 1932).

Early in his first term, President Franklin D. Roosevelt signed into law two major pieces of reform legislation, the Securities Act of 1933 and the Securities Exchange Act of 1934, the second of which created the Securities and Exchange Commission. These Acts, as implemented by the SEC, required all new and continuing registrants to have their financial statements audited by independent CPAs, thus highlighting the importance of the accounting profession and generating an increased demand for its services. A government takeover of the auditing of publicly traded companies was averted, as Col. Arthur H. Carter, the senior partner of Haskins & Sells and the president of the New York State Society of Certified Public Accountants, succeeded in persuading the Senate Committee on Banking and Currency, during the hearings on the proposed Securities Act, not to assign the external audit function to a government agency, but instead to allow it to be done by firms in the private sector (Carey 1969, 186–187; Wiesen 1978).

In 1935, the SEC appointed a chief accountant, Carman G. Blough, who promptly began to work closely with the Institute and the American Accounting Association (the organization of academic accountants), and other accounting experts, to identify the norms of proper accounting and auditing practice. In 1937–38, Blough succeeded in persuading the Institute to empower the Institute's Committee on Accounting Procedure to approve and publish bulletins constituting "substantial authoritative support" for accounting principles, known as Accounting Research Bulletins (Zeff 1972, 132–138; Seligman 1982, 197–201).

In 1939, the Institute established a similar standing committee to promulgate a series of bulletins on auditing procedures, a step precipitated by the gigantic McKesson & Robbins auditing scandal, which led to a widely reported SEC investigation, greatly embarrassing the profession (Carey 1970, 22–38). The editor of the Institute's *Journal of Accountancy* wrote in February 1939, "Like a torrent of cold water the wave of publicity raised by the McKesson & Robbins case has shocked the accountancy profession into breathlessness" (The McKesson & Robbins Case 1939, 65).[4] McKesson & Robbins had grossly inflated its receivables and merchandise inventory, and its auditor, Price, Waterhouse & Co., had neither confirmed the receivables nor verified the existence of the inventory. Neither of these tests was a required auditing practice at the time. In response, a special committee formed by the Institute promptly issued a bulletin requiring that both of these tests become standard auditing procedures.

The organized profession consolidated into one national body in 1936, as the Institute merged with its rival, the American Society of Certified Public Accountants. Thus, for the first time since 1921, when the Society was formed, the organized accounting profession became united (Carey 1969, Chapter 19).

The decade of the 1930s ended with the organized profession, represented by the Institute, poised to be the principal source of authoritative pronouncements on both accounting and auditing that the SEC would require for use by SEC registrants and their auditors. The professional and academic literature thus became the place where improvements in accounting and auditing norms could be discussed and debated.

The end of the 1930s marked the close of a major chapter in the profession's history. In a similar vein, John L. Carey, in his landmark history of the Institute from 1896 to 1969, identified 1936/37 as the turning point between his two volumes, subtitled "From Technician to Professional" (1969) and "To Responsibility and Authority" (1970).

1940s TO THE MID-1960s: THE PROFESSION AT ITS PEAK

From the 1940s to the mid-1960s, accounting, auditing, and the accounting profession in the United States reached the height of their standing and reputation. Throughout this period, the SEC relied on committees of the Institute for "generally accepted accounting principles" (GAAP) and the auditing procedures that accounting firms were to adopt in their engagements. Nowhere else in the world did the organized accounting profession possess such a large degree of influence in setting the norms of professional practice.

Moreover, in 1947, the Institute's Committee on Auditing Procedure recommended a set of "generally accepted auditing standards," which the Institute's membership approved at an annual meeting in September 1948. These standards, as distinct from procedures, dealt with the auditor's professional qualities and the exercise of judgment in the conduct of the audit engagement (Carey 1970, 147–150). Once again, the organized profession set the terms governing the performance of its flagship service, the external audit.

---

[4] For more on the McKesson & Robbins scandal, see McCarten (1939), Shaplen (1955), and Keats (1964).

At the top of its form, the Institute held well-attended annual meetings, which addressed both policy and technical issues in plenary sessions and roundtables, and distributed the papers widely in volumes of proceedings.

By 1950, all of the states and territories had enacted CPA laws, with all jurisdictions but one adopting the Institute's Uniform CPA Examination. Accounting courses were offered in nearly all major universities, and a large American literature on accounting and auditing had come into existence (Accounting at the Half-Century Mark 1951).

In 1940, the American Accounting Association published *An Introduction to Corporate Accounting Standards*, by Professors W. A. Paton and A. C. Littleton, which both the Association and the Institute distributed as a dividend to its members (Zeff 1966, 57). This monograph, which provided an elegant rationale for the conventional accounting model, profoundly influenced accounting thought, education, and practice for decades thereafter. (See Sterling 1967, 340–343; Ijiri 1980, 620–622.)

In 1943, George O. May, the doyen of the accounting profession, wrote an important treatise, *Financial Accounting: A Distillation of Experience*, and from 1947 to 1952 he directed a major study sponsored by the Institute and the Rockefeller Foundation on the appropriateness of different concepts of business income during periods of substantial change in price levels, a subject of great importance during the postwar inflation (Study Group on Business Income 1952).

CPAs Emerge as Prominent Public Figures

From the late 1930s through the 1960s, CPAs served in important government positions, gave testimony before Congressional committees, and served as expert witnesses in court cases, in rate regulation hearings, and before federal wage tribunals. From 1938 to 1941, Eric L. Kohler was comptroller of the Tennessee Valley Authority; from 1948 to 1951, he served as controller of the post-World War II Economic Cooperation Administration, known as the Marshall Plan. In 1942, Norris Poulson became the first CPA elected to Congress; his election in 1953 as mayor of Los Angeles made him the first CPA to head a major city.[5] In 1948 and again in 1954, former President Herbert C. Hoover tapped Paul Grady, a Price Waterhouse audit partner, to chair a task force to study government lending agencies under the auspices of the first and second Commissions on Reorganization of the Executive Branch of Government, known as the Hoover Commissions. In 1949, Donald C. Cook, also a lawyer, became the first CPA to be named to the SEC; he served as chairman of the Commission in 1952–53. Three days after Cook joined the Commission, Edward T. McCormick, another CPA, became a

---

[5] Abraham Beame became comptroller of New York City in 1969 and mayor in 1973.

Commissioner.[6] McCormick left the SEC in 1951 to become chairman of the New York Curb Exchange, renamed the American Stock Exchange two years later. In 1953, T. Coleman Andrews became the first CPA to serve as Commissioner of Internal Revenue, and in 1954 Joseph Campbell became Comptroller General of the U.S., the first CPA to head the General Accounting Office.

In 1959, when Christopher Del Sesto won election as governor of Rhode Island, he became the first CPA to serve as governor of a state. Two leading accounting practitioners, Percival F. Brundage and Maurice H. Stans, became successive directors of the Bureau of the Budget, appointed by President Dwight D. Eisenhower, and in 1969 President Richard M. Nixon named Stans as his Secretary of Commerce. Members of the accounting profession were coming to the fore in public affairs because of the increasing respect accorded to the profession (see Carey 1970, 382–384).

Movement into Information-Based Services

Following the Second World War, the major accounting firms began to develop capabilities in new information-based services, gradually expanding beyond their traditional services of accounting, auditing, taxation, and systems design and installation. They chose to describe this new line as "management services," "management advisory services," or "administrative services." It began with punched card and punched tape systems, followed by the introduction in the mid-1950s of electronic computers for business applications, which in turn led to the development of computerized information systems and computer modeling. Operations research and electronic data processing were among the early pillars of this broadened scope of activity. Some firms, such as Arthur Andersen & Co., Peat, Marwick, Mitchell & Co. and Touche, Niven, Bailey & Smart, invested heavily in these new services (Glickauf 1971; Wise 1982, 48–49; Swanson 1972, 39–40).

In the mid-1950s, Arthur Andersen & Co. designed and installed the first business application of a computer, a payroll system at General Electric Company's Appliance Park facility in Kentucky. As the firm wrote, "This was a milestone event in the development of computers for business use as well as in the development of our administrative services practice, and it marked the beginning of a dramatic firm-wide growth in our practice" (*The First Sixty Years 1913–1973* 1974, 67). (Also see *A Vision of Grandeur* 1988, 95–98.) From the inception of Andersen's administrative services division in 1942, its staff grew to 400 in 1965, and nearly tripled to 1,150 by January 1970 (Glickauf 1971, 113, 175). By 1969, the division's

---

[6] Both Cook and McCormick had been SEC staff members before being named to the Commission. In 1969, James J. Needham became the first CPA firm partner to be appointed to the Commission.

gross fees accounted for "roughly one-fourth of the firm's business" (Williams 1971, vi).

In 1965, after 30 years of controversy and a protracted battle with the legal profession, CPAs secured Congressional recognition of their status to represent tax clients before the Treasury Department (Carey 1970, Chapter 9). The position of CPAs in tax practice was now secure.

Accounting Principles Become Controversial

Also in the mid-1950s, Leonard Spacek, the outspoken managing partner of Arthur Andersen & Co., began publicly criticizing the probity of the Institute's committee that issued pronouncements on GAAP. The Institute sensibly channeled Spacek's criticisms toward constructive change by appointing him to a blue ribbon committee to recommend a better approach (see Zeff 2001). The committee proposed a new body, the Accounting Principles Board, and charged it to undertake basic and applied research as well as issue pronouncements on GAAP. The Institute promptly accepted and implemented the committee's recommendation in 1959, and during the 1960s, especially in 1966–67, the APB earned some credit for narrowing the areas of difference in a number of controversial areas of GAAP.

During the 1960s, as the APB became active in addressing controversial areas, leading partners of the Big Eight firms—each of whom had a vote on the APB—began to speak at public forums and write articles and even books on the major accounting principles issues of the day. From the 1930s to the 1970s, *The Journal of Accountancy* regularly contained articles dealing with accounting and auditing issues of interest to the profession, as did *The Accounting Review* from the 1930s to the 1960s. Journals published by a number of state CPA societies also carried the dialogue, and several universities, including Ohio State, Tulsa, and the City University of New York, held annual conferences or sponsored lecture series to air controversial professional issues.

Beginning in the mid-1950s, Arthur Andersen & Co. prepared reprints of partners' speeches and booklets expressing the firm's views on accounting principles, and distributed them to a wide audience of academics, practitioners, and companies. From 1962 to 1967, the investment banking house of Hayden Stone sponsored an annual Accounting Forum, featuring major accounting practitioners speaking on accounting principles at well-attended one-day programs held at New York University. And starting in 1968, the Institute co-sponsored a series of Seaview Symposia, at which representatives of the preparers, auditors, and users of financial statements debated major issues of the day. The decade of the 1960s was marked by a vibrant dialogue on accounting principles, with active participation both by partners in the big firms and by accounting academics (see Zeff 1986).

This was a time when audit partners were, except in rare instances of substandard performance, assured of tenure until they retired, and they expected their firm to back them with its full resources when they stood up to their clients over questionable accounting practices. Partnership in one of the big accounting firms was seen as the pinnacle of one's career, it being almost unknown for partners to leave their firms to take positions in industry. The idea of a "marketing" campaign for new clients did not exist. If a partner secured a new client, he was praised, but the rewards doled out to partners recognized the quality of audit service to one's clients.

The corporate merger movement of the 1960s that led to the formation of conglomerates and multinationals focused attention on a sensitive accounting issue, segment reporting, and called forth a demand for the international comparability of financial statements. Numerous high-profile mergers heightened the pressure on top corporate executives to deliver improved earnings performance—either to defend against takeovers or to engineer takeovers—thus prompting the corporate sector to begin opposing constraints on their freedom of choice of accounting methods, especially any limits on the use of "pooling of interests" accounting for business combinations.

Early in the 1960s, the business press took notice of the much higher profile of the accounting profession. While comparatively little had been written in the press about accounting and the profession in previous decades, this coverage mushroomed in the 1960s, especially when the APB moved into controversial territory—accounting for the investment tax credit, leases, pensions, income tax allocation, convertible debt, extraordinary items, and business combinations and goodwill. The decade began with a major, two-part article in the November and December 1960 issues of *Fortune*, "The Auditors Have Arrived." Written by T. A. Wise, the article began as follows:

> It is a curious and noteworthy fact that the tremendous growth of the U.S. accounting profession in the postwar years has taken place almost unnoticed by most Americans.

This was the article that coined, or at least popularized, the term, "the Big Eight," referring to the eight largest public accounting firms. Special interest magazines such as *Business Week*[7] and *Forbes*, and even the more general *Time* and *Newsweek*, as well as *The Wall Street Journal*, *The New York Times*, and newspapers across the country, began covering accounting principles issues, as they became news of interest to more than accountants. During the 1968–70 debate over "pooling of interests" and goodwill, the Financial Executives Institute flooded the nation's press with criticisms of the APB's draft pronouncements. Articles on accounting principles also began appearing in the likes of the *Harvard Business Review* and *California Management Review*.

In 1963, after issuing its second Opinion, the APB suffered a stunning reversal. In its Opinion, the board narrowly voted to require that the investment tax

---

[7] A good example is "A Matter of Principle Splits CPAs" (1963).

credit be deferred for accounting purposes rather than be taken immediately into income. Immediately afterward, pressure from several major accounting firms, whose partners voted against the Opinion, and from an important segment of industry, as well as from the Department of the Treasury (behind the scenes), led the SEC to reject the APB's single permissible treatment. Instead, the SEC allowed registrants either to defer the credit or to take it immediately into income. This rebuff by the SEC forced the APB to concede the acceptability of both treatments in Opinion No. 4, issued two years later. In 1967, the board once more tried to gain acceptance for its preferred treatment of the credit, but it was again defeated by the Treasury, this time in the open. Political lobbying by powerful interest groups against objectionable draft standards began afflicting the APB in the early and mid-1960s. (See Zeff 1972, 178–180, 201, 202; Moonitz 1966; Zeff 1978.)

MID-1960s TO THE PRESENT—THE PROFESSION BEGINS A DESCENT UNDER STRESS

All was not rosy as the three decades from the 1940s through the 1960s came to a close. Threatening clouds began to form over the accounting profession in the middle and latter 1960s. Financial scandals burst on the scene, raising questions about the performance of auditors. Trailing in the wake of the scandals, auditors found themselves as defendants in a number of highly publicized lawsuits. And the accounting profession lost its prized authority to pronounce on "generally accepted accounting principles" (GAAP) to an independent body, with unfortunate ramifications for the vitality of professional discourse.

Scandals, Lawsuits, and Criticism of the Profession

The collapse of Westec (1965) and National Student Marketing (1969), which were notorious practitioners of what Abraham J. Briloff, an acerbic critic of unprincipled accounting, called "dirty pooling" (Briloff 1967, 1970), as well as the bankruptcies of Penn Central and Four Seasons Nursing Centers (both in 1970), visited huge losses on investors and raised questions about the performance of their auditors. The Westec case eventually animated a serious concern that its auditor's independence was compromised by rendering certain consulting services to the audit client.[8]

During the second half of the 1960s, criticism of the accounting profession was on the rise. John L. Carey, the Institute's administrative vice president, said in 1967 that "the accounting profession is going through a most unusual and difficult period. On some days it seems as though we

---

[8] This charge was made both by Briloff (1972, 292–293) and by the Commission on Auditors' Responsibilities (1978, 102).

were being attacked from all sides." He was concerned over "a feeling that CPAs are not quite the stalwart protectors of investors and creditors that the public had assumed they were" (Carey 1967, 15). It was, he said, a time of rising expectations of auditors (Carey 1967, 18). Carey's colleague at the Institute, Leonard M. Savoie, a former research and education partner in Price Waterhouse (PW) and, since 1967, the Institute's executive vice-president, bluntly criticized the "opinion shopping" that was beginning to pit firm against firm:

> competition to obtain a client for the lowest fee or to obtain or retain a client at the expense of technical standards is debilitating. It will weaken and, if unchecked, destroy the profession. Competition for a client based on accounting principles must be stopped. (Savoie 1968, 112)

The second half of the 1960s witnessed a series of important federal court decisions: *Fischer v. Kletz* (1967), also known as the Yale Express case; *Escott v. BarChris* (1968); and *United States v. Simon* (1969), also known as the Continental Vending case (see Isbell 1970), triggered a "litigation explosion" against auditors in the 1970s (Jaenicke 1977, 1). After decades of comparative calm, the profession was coming under attack by the plaintiff's bar. "By the mid-1970s," Jaenicke (1977, 1) wrote, "hundreds of suits were filed against auditors."

In a speech given in 1970, John C. (Sandy) Burton, an accounting and finance professor at Columbia Business School, took a dim view of developments in the profession:

> In recent years, there is little evidence that the "public" in public accounting has been emphasized. In its zeal to protect itself from liability, the profession has given every impression of attempting to avoid responsibility. In the professional literature pains have been taken to assert what the auditor does *not* do, and to indicate that auditors attest only to the general acceptability, rather than the desirability, of management's choice of accounting principles.
>
> It is not at all surprising that articles critical of the accounting profession are beginning to appear more and more frequently in the business press. (Burton 1971, 49)

Tribulations of the Accounting Principles Board

In the mid-1960s, under pressure from the SEC and from the Big Eight firms and at a time when the accelerated pace of corporate merger activity focused increased attention on the earnings measure, the APB began to issue longer and more prescriptive Opinions. Several of these pronouncements attracted significant numbers of dissenting votes from board members. In two instances (on interperiod tax allocation in 1967 and on business combinations/goodwill in 1970), a board member from a Big Eight firm infuriated his colleagues in the majority by rescinding his vote on a contentious Opinion after the board had, in a final vote, approved a position that had secured a bare two-thirds majority. In 1967, the reversal occurred after the Opinion in 1967 was printed and ready for distribution. In both instances, the board met in emergency session to rescue the pronouncement. Thus was the intensity of pressure on board members, probably brought, directly or indirectly, by a firm's important clients.

Burton alluded to complicity by audit firms in helping their clients escape the adverse effects of the APB's pronouncements: "By writing precise rules, . . . [the APB] has made it possible for people to observe the letter and avoid the spirit, with the blessing (and often the assistance) of their auditors" (Burton 1971, 50), a state of affairs that continues today.

Although the APB received praise from some quarters for "narrowing the areas of difference" on such contested subjects as pensions and interperiod tax allocation, other Opinions, especially Opinion No. 15 issued in 1969 on earnings per share, were criticized by leading accounting professionals for being laden with detailed rules. Ernest L. Hicks (1969, 60), a technical partner in Arthur Young & Company, complained that "much of the difficulty the Board has experienced resulted when it yielded to pressure to move too fast, with less than an adequate exposure of the issues." No less an exalted figure than Professor *Emeritus* William A. Paton, who served for 11 years on the old Committee on Accounting Procedure, reviled Opinion No. 15 as an illustration of "obscurity and unnecessary detail." He also criticized the board for its "dictatorial tendencies" in recent Opinions (Paton 1971, 42), a view echoed by retired PW senior technical partner Paul Grady, who had served as the Institute's director of accounting research in 1963–64 (Grady 1971, 24). PW executive office partner A. Carl Tietjen derided the APB for issuing "cookbooks" (Tietjen 1970, 10), as Hicks (1969, 60) did earlier. George R. Catlett, senior technical partner of Arthur Andersen & Co. and a longtime APB member, contended that the APB, like its predecessor, "has been so busy 'putting out fires' and dealing with a large and ever-increasing backlog of current problems that it has never established an adequate basis upon which to build" (Catlett 1969, 62).

Also, the ferocity with which Corporate America lobbied against APB proposals that limited companies' flexibility in matters of accounting choice, most notably between 1968 and 1970 on business combinations and goodwill as the conglomerate merger craze was losing steam, led to a widespread loss of confidence in the board's effectiveness after the board issued a highly compromised Opinion No. 16, with six dissenting votes. The press followed every step in the board's tortured deliberations with relish (Zeff 1972, 212–216; Olson 1982, 3).[9] Critics from both inside and outside the profession inveighed against the organized profession's body charged with establishing the norms of proper accounting practice.

In August 1970, the APB finally issued its two hotly contested Opinions, Nos. 16 and 17, on accounting for business combinations and goodwill; the two Opinions were regarded more as the result of intense lobbying by industry than the product of sound thinking and analysis. The Big Eight accounting firms themselves differed profoundly and even emotionally over the best solution, partly fueled by their clients' preponderant views. So strong were the firms' reactions to the pressurized process in which these two Opinions were developed that three of the Big Eight notified the Institute in November 1970 that they had lost confidence in the APB.[10] The three firms recoiled at the powerful intrusion of self-interested lobbying and lamented the board's lack of agreement on the objectives of financial statements.

In August 1970, the American Accounting Association (AAA) became involved by appointing a special committee to inquire into the formulation of accounting principles. Acting swiftly, the committee urged the Institute and other interested bodies to cooperate with the AAA to convene a Commission of Inquiry to develop a better alternative to the APB. The Association's Executive Committee promptly endorsed its report (Report of the Committee on Establishment of an Accounting Commission 1971).

The Profession Loses Its Accounting Standard Setter

Declining to share the standard-setting stage with the AAA, the Institute itself appointed a Study Group to recommend a better way of establishing accounting principles. This Study Group, chaired by Francis M. Wheat, a former SEC Commissioner, recommended the establishment of the Financial Accounting Standards Board (FASB), which was to be an independent body, not a committee of the Institute. The Institute's Council promptly endorsed the Wheat recommendation in its entirety, thereby, for the first time, ceding the authority for setting accounting standards to a body outside the province of the organized accounting profession. Members of the FASB would hold full-time appointments, be supported by a large research staff, and could count on financial support

---

[9] For further discussion, see Chatov (1975, Chapters 13 and 14), Brooks (1973, Chapter 7), Seligman (1982, 417–430) and *Conglomerate Mergers and Acquisitions: Opinion & Analysis* (1970).

[10] The firms were Arthur Andersen & Co., Touche Ross & Co., and Arthur Young & Company (Zeff 1972, 224–225). Also see the letters from Harvey E. Kapnick, Robert M. Trueblood, and Ralph E. Kent in the attachments to AICPA President Marshall S. Armstrong's letter dated December 21, 1970 to Those Invited to Conference on Establishment of Accounting Principles.

to be provided by a newly established, broad-based Financial Accounting Foundation (FAF) (Report of the Study on Establishment of Accounting Principles 1972). This sea change disenfranchised the Big Eight firms from representation on the standard-setting body. As will be seen, this repositioning of the big firms from the center to the margin of standard setting soon served to dampen their interest in actively participating in the public dialogue on accounting principles, which should be a *sine qua non* of professional discourse.

But the Institute did not surrender all of its influence over the new standard setter. The FAF's bylaws provided that four of the seven board members must be CPAs with experience in public practice and that the Institute's board of directors would be the sole elector of the FAF's trustees. Yet, in 1977, the FAF's trustees repealed both of these provisions (*Status Report No. 50* 1977, 1).

In 1974, less than a year after the APB passed the standard-setting baton to the FASB, Leonard M. Savoie (1974, 64), the Institute's principal spokesman on APB matters from 1967 to 1972, expressed his disappointment with the handover and the recent behavior of the big firms:

> In abandoning its rule-making function the AICPA has lost its most conspicuous source of prestige and good public relations potential. At the same time, it has extricated itself from the center of dissent and turmoil caused by recalcitrant accounting firms that were more interested in pushing their own views than in working within the institutional structure and reaching a consensus.

Even while the Wheat Study Group deliberated, the APB suffered another setback, again on the investment tax credit. In November 1971, when the Congress was about to enact a new form of the investment tax credit, the board, in its third such try, approved an exposure draft that required the deferral method, but the Treasury opposed it, as did the same large segment of industry as before. The opponents succeeded in persuading Congress to insert a provision in the eventual legislation that taxpayer corporations could use any method of accounting for the credit in their financial statements filed with the SEC. This denouement confirmed the inability of the Institute's standard-setting body to counter the self-serving forces arrayed against some of its more controversial Opinions (see Zeff 1972, 219–221). Three other setbacks occurred during 1971, when powerful industry pressures thwarted the APB from acting on accounting for marketable securities, leases, and oil and gas exploration (Zeff 1978, 14).

The FASB's relations with the SEC during its first five years were anything but smooth. From 1972 to 1976, during Sandy Burton's term as SEC Chief Accountant, the Commission issued 70 Accounting Series

Releases (more than a third of which dealt with financial reporting), compared with 126 from 1937 to 1972.[11] Arthur Andersen unsuccessfully challenged the propriety of one of the SEC's Releases in court (Our Firm Files Petition with SEC 1976; Arthur Andersen is Set Back in Bid to Bar SEC Rulings 1976). An activist Chief Accountant, Burton surprised the FASB by declaring that, while the FASB was to take the lead on matters of accounting measurement, financial disclosures properly fell within the province of the SEC (Burton 1974). Additionally, Burton criticized the FASB's 1974 exposure draft recommending general price-level accounting, and two years later he pressed ahead with his own solution, a requirement that some 1,300 large registrants report replacement cost data in a supplementary disclosure. Burton's initiative forced the FASB to issue its own standard, Statement No. 33, on the disclosure of current cost and constant dollar information.

In 1978, the SEC again rebuffed the FASB, this time on accounting for oil and gas exploration. Under intense political pressure from small oil and gas exploration companies, with assistance from members of Congress, the SEC rejected FASB Statement No. 19's required use of "successful efforts" costing and instead proposed a kind of current value accounting for oil and gas reserves. The SEC's decision took the FASB aback, yet the SEC made it clear that the oil and gas issue was a unique case and did not "represent any change in the Commission's basic policy of looking to the FASB for the initiative in establishing and improving accounting standards" (*Securities and Exchange Commission Report to Congress on the Accounting Profession and the Commission's Oversight Role* 1979, 50). (Also see Gorton 1991; Miller et al. 1998, 125–127.)[12]

An Important Implication of the Loss of the Profession's Standard Setter

It was not long into the FASB's tenure that the Big Eight firms began withdrawing from an active dialogue over accounting principles and standards, perhaps in the belief that their task had become one of persuading the FASB of their views and no longer persuading either academics or their brethren in the profession. Indeed, this was also a time when many accounting academics

---

[11] John R. Evans, an SEC Commissioner from 1973 to 1983, argues that "the Commission was virtually forced to become more active [in the early 1970s] because of investor losses in companies, which had been able to exaggerate reported earnings and conceal financial problems, and because of permissive accounting standards and lax auditing procedures." He then cited several major corporate failures, including Penn Central and Equity Funding, and added: "Questions were raised as to why accountants charged with performing an independent audit of these companies had failed to detect or report on the developing problems. Some questioned whether accountants had participated actively with management in a fraud" (Evans 1984, 159). Also see Orben (1984, 142–143).

[12] For a fuller discussion of these standard-setting issues, see Miller et al. (1998, Chapter 5).

seemed to abandon interest in accounting policy issues as well. Another reason for audit partners' withdrawing from this public dialogue was the increasing proliferation, complexity, and technical detail in the FASB's pronouncements.

By the mid-1980s, speeches by Big Eight audit firm partners taking positions on controversial accounting issues had almost disappeared from the scene, and only a few audit partners in, at most, three of the Big Eight firms[13] continued to write articles intermittently on such topics. Moreover, in 1982 the *Journal of Accountancy*, the Institute's journal, announced that it was encouraging the submission of "practical" articles, code language for the avoidance of controversy (see Zeff 1986). As the audit market became more competitive, one inferred that the firms did not wish to give prominence to their views on controversial issues, lest it might offend important clients, who might seek an audit firm with more accommodating views. Opinion shopping, which began to occur in the 1960s, continued into the 1970s and 1980s, as companies actively sought out more client-friendly audit firms.

More Scandals, and Attacks from Congress

In 1973, the sudden collapse of Equity Funding, coming on the heels of the Stirling Homex bankruptcy a year earlier,[14] jarred the accounting profession. (See Report of the Special Committee on Equity Funding 1975; Seidler et al. 1977.) As the Institute's executive director later wrote, "The huge losses by investors in [Equity Funding's] securities, closely following a series of other business failures, dealt a shattering blow to the credibility of independent auditors" (Olson 1982, 87–88). Propelled by these embarrassments, the Institute in 1974 appointed a Commission on Auditors' Responsibilities, headed by former SEC Chairman Manuel F. Cohen. These celebrated collapses, coupled with the discovery of illegal and improper payments by major corporations that were not disclosed in their financial statements, prompted two Congressional committees to level criticism at the accounting profession and at the private-sector setting of accounting standards.[15] The profession thus came under its first broad attack in the Congress.

Rep. John E. Moss, Democrat from California, chaired his subcommittee's investigation of federal regulatory agencies. The subcommittee's report recommended that the SEC play a direct role in setting accounting

---

[13] This included several partners from Arthur Andersen's Accounting Principles Group; Dennis R. Beresford of Ernst & Whinney until 1987, when he became FASB chairman; and Dale L. Gerboth of Arthur Young/Ernst & Young until 1990, when he retired.

[14] For the SEC's report on its investigation into the matters of Penn Central, National Student Marketing Corporation, and Stirling Homex, all of which were clients of the same audit firm, see its Accounting Series Release No. 173 (July 2, 1975).

[15] See an extract from a 1977 speech by Rep. Moss in Olson (1982, 39) and the comments by Senators Metcalf and Charles H. Percy, Republican from Illinois, and Rep. Moss in *Accounting and Auditing Practices and Procedures* (1977, 3, 10, 14). Also see Nelligan (1980, 111).

and auditing standards (*Federal Regulation and Regulatory Reform* 1976, 51–53) and thus remove this authority from the private sector. On the Senate side, a subcommittee headed by Sen. Lee Metcalf, Democrat from Montana, launched a major investigation of the accounting profession. His subcommittee's 1,760-page staff study, *The Accounting Establishment* (1976), consisted of an extensive factual examination of the Big Eight firms, the Institute, and the FASB, accompanied by a number of highly controversial conclusions and recommendations. Wallace E. Olson, the Institute's full-time chief executive, characterized the staff study as "almost as damaging to the profession as the Japanese attack on Pearl Harbor was to the U.S. Navy in 1941" (Olson 1982, 43).

Two of the staff study's conclusions were that the Big Eight firms lacked independence from their clients and that they dominated both the Institute and the process of setting of accounting standards. The study also asserted that the Big Eight firms, through their influence on the FASB, did the bidding of their corporate clients (*The Accounting Establishment* 1976, 1–24). Almost mirroring the course taken by the Moss subcommittee, the Metcalf subcommittee's staff study recommended that the federal government set accounting and auditing standards for publicly traded corporations (*The Accounting Establishment* 1976, 20–24). Although both subcommittees held hearings and issued reports, they produced no legislation.[16] Nonetheless, the two subcommittees' lengthy and well-publicized investigations, which finally concluded in 1979, put the accounting profession on the defensive.

In April 1977, both the Institute and the FASB responded at length to the Metcalf staff study's findings and recommendations. The Institute issued a 40-page booklet, *The Institute Responds . . .* in which it countered the arguments in the Metcalf staff study. To the charge that the Big Eight firms compromised their independence when they advocated positions that were favorable to their clients, the Institute asserted that, by doing so, "they are not tools of their clients" (*The Institute Responds . . .* 1977, 32). Yet, a scant six years later, Touche Ross & Co. issued a booklet, *Employers. Accounting for Pensions* (1983, 3), in which it offered to help clients prepare "an effective and persuasive response" to the FASB by which the firm would "assist your company in evaluating the effects, developing empirical supporting evidence, and identifying the economic consequences of the positions your company supports and rejects." Thus, as the competition for the favor of clients intensified in the 1980s, at least one of the Big Eight firms—Touche Ross—was willing to become a blind advocate for its clients. In its 44-page reply, the FASB defended the integrity, independence, and objectivity of its process (FASB 1977).

---

[16] Rep. Moss retired from the House on December 31, 1978. Sen. Metcalf died suddenly in January 1978, and the work of his subcommittee was carried on by Sen. Thomas F. Eagleton, Democrat from Missouri, in his own subcommittee until 1979, when interest in the subject lapsed. See Olson (1982, Chapter 3).

Under the Gun, the Institute Reforms

The unwanted public attention led the Institute to adopt a hurried reform in September 1977: creation of a Division for CPA Firms, composed of an SEC Practice Section and a Private Companies Practice Section. Wm. R. Gregory, the Institute's board chairman in 1979–80, explained the move as follows:

> Council created the division for CPA firms without seeking a vote of the membership because it believed that Congress would enact new legislation to regulate the profession if immediate steps were not then taken to bolster the profession's system of self-regulation. That perception was borne out by the introduction by the Congressman Moss on June 16, 1978 of H.R. 13175, which provided for a new federal statutory regulatory organization under the oversight of the SEC, to be known as the National Organization of Securities and Exchange Commission Accountancy. (Gregory 1980, 3)

The body proposed in Rep. Moss's bill, which died in committee at the end of 1978, foreshadowed in a striking number of respects the Public Company Accounting Oversight Board, established by the Sarbanes-Oxley Act of 2002.

The Institute also installed a Public Oversight Board (POB), composed of distinguished public servants, to oversee the activities of the SEC Practice Section, including the setting and enforcing of quality control standards and a newly established peer review process. The SEC, which had ordered several major firms to undergo peer reviews because of alleged audit deficiencies in early and middle 1970s, welcomed the Institute's new section and the POB (*Securities and Exchange Commission Report to Congress on the Accounting Profession and the Commission's Oversight Role* 1978, 15–27). But pressure from Congress had clearly precipitated the Institute's restructuring.

Intrusions of Federal Antitrust Bodies That Fundamentally Altered the Professional Climate

During the 1970s and 1980s, the Institute also felt unrelenting pressure from the Department of Justice and the Federal Trade Commission (FTC) over portions of its Code of Professional Ethics alleged to be in restraint of trade. In 1972, the Institute gave in to Justice by removing the ban on competitive bidding from its code of ethics. By 1979, Justice and the FTC compelled the Institute to drop its rules prohibiting direct, uninvited solicitation and advertising that is purely informational (see Bialkin 1987, 105–106). Many Institute members strongly opposed these forced concessions. During the 1980s, the FTC also pressed the Institute to remove its ban on contingent fees and commissions. In the end, the two bodies reached a compromise: to allow the receipt of commissions only from nonattest clients (Chenok 2000, 106). These amendments to the Institute's code of ethics, particularly on competitive bidding and direct, uninvited solicitation, profoundly changed the climate in which audit firms conducted their affairs. Competition among firms came to be signified more in the idiom of commerce—the aggressive pursuit of profit—thus, placing strains on professional values.

Whether because of the changes in the code of ethics or because of changing conditions in the practice of public accounting, allegations began to surface that competition among firms for clients was becoming more intense and vicious. In an article in *Barron's*, an editor who had long been a close observer of the accounting profession wrote as follows:

> What's happened, essentially, is that the nation's top accounting firms—some big, some smaller—are locked in a fierce battle marked by vigorous price cutting. Some blame a growth-at-any-cost syndrome they say has afflicted some of the profession's top firms. Others contend that it's an inevitable consequence of a slowing in chargeable hours as the pickings for new clients get slimmer. (Anreder 1979, 9)

The Institute's Commission on Auditors' Responsibilities also pointedly remarked, "The practice of accepting an audit engagement with the expectation of offsetting early losses or lower revenues with fees to be charged in future audits is a threat to the independence of the auditor" (The Commission on Auditors' Responsibilities 1978, xxx).

The elimination of the Institute's bans on competitive bidding, uninvited solicitation, and advertising, coupled with the apparent topping out of the audit market, all fundamentally changed the character of CPAs' relations with clients. Eli Mason, the managing partner of a medium-sized CPA firm in New York City who had long been a vocal critic of the big firms and the Institute, complained in 1985 that the practice of accounting was no longer a profession, but an industry: "Today, the media describes public accounting as an industry, seldom as a profession—and it does have all the earmarks of an industry including cut-throat competition, 'low-balling,' cheap advertising, and open solicitation by one CPA of another CPA's clients." Mason blamed the FTC and the Justice Department for creating this "unprofessional and undignified atmosphere" (Mason 1985, 732; also see Mason 1994).

Arthur W. Bowman, the editor of *Public Accounting Report*, documented some of the deep cuts in audit fees that companies negotiated in the early 1980s, which pitted the major accounting firms against one another in the sharply competitive bidding process. He reported tenders of between 25 and 50 percent under the previous year's audit fee charged by a company's current audit firm (Bowman 1985, 705–713). (Also see Berton 1985a; Berton 1985c; Berton 1985d, 12.) In a disquieting remark, he said, "If [companies] can get an audit for 0 dollars, they'd get them" (Bowman 1985, 720). Indeed, in 1991, Norman Lipshie, the president of the New York State Society of Certified Public Accountants, was quoted as saying,

"I've seen three recent instances where Big Six firms were bidding zero to do audits" (Brenner 1991). (Following two mega-mergers in 1989, creating Ernst & Young and Deloitte & Touche, the Big Eight became the Big Six.)

In an interview in 1984, incoming Peat Marwick deputy chairman and chief operating partner Robert W. Beecher complained that other firms' practice of cutting fees "has dangerous implications" (An Interview with Our New Management Team 1984, 5). Price competition between audit firms existed in earlier years, but the firms sold quality as well as price. Clients prized audit quality, before they began to view the audit as a commodity. Leonard Spacek, the architect of the modern firm of Arthur Andersen & Co., wrote in 1984, reflecting the values of an earlier era:

> The competition [today] is in fees only. We always had such competition, but to offset it a firm can strengthen itself by the energetic position it takes to make it a leader . . . outstanding service is equally an offset, and both characteristics are prime offsets to price. I know because I practiced it for 20 years—saying publicly that we were the highest priced firm, but the higher price was more than matched by quality. Prospective clients seek these qualities to prove they risk the most thorough accounting tests.[17]

The heightened competitive climate in which the firms operated seemed to haunt partners' conduct in audit engagements. A gradual development within the Big Eight firms during the 1980s was a significant shift in the posture of audit partners toward their clients, probably spurred by their perceived pressure to retain valued clients. In previous years, partners conveyed a firm position on the propriety of any borderline accounting and disclosure practices adopted by the client, but increasingly in the 1980s partners would be seen huddling with the firm's technical specialists to find any means—perhaps restructuring a major vehicle, reconfiguring a transaction, or straining to rationalize the application of a suitable analogy—to enable the firm to approve the accounting treatment sought by the client. The "accommodation" or "negotiation" mentality fostered by this important shift in focus may have led many audit partners to incline toward compromise rather than invoke their principles even in routine discussions with clients. More will be said about this development later.

Management Advisory Services Come under SEC Fire

Consulting, then still known as management advisory services (MAS), increasingly became an issue in the 1970s. In 1969, *Business Week* reported the following anti-establishment view:

---

[17] Letter to the author dated December 20, 1984.

"Some firms," says an unnamed senior partner of a big New York accounting firm, "say they draw the line against consulting that involves them in management decision making. But don't let anybody fool you. We take on any job." (Accountants Turn Tougher 1969, 124)

The term "scope of services" entered the profession's vocabulary, referring to the range of consulting services that an audit firm could render without surrendering its objectivity or independence. In the SEC's 1978 annual report to Congress submitted at the request of the Senate's Metcalf subcommittee, Chairman Harold M. Williams wrote as follows:

Another important issue requiring immediate attention is the question of the appropriate range of services—other than the performance of the audit itself—which accounting firms should be permitted to offer to their audit clients . . .

In considering this issue, it will be necessary to resolve three basic questions:

- Are there situations in which the magnitude of the potential fees from management advisory services are so large as to affect adversely an auditor's objectivity in conducting an audit?
- Are there some services that are so unrelated to the normal expertise and experience of auditors that it is inconsistent with the concept of being an auditing professional for auditors to perform those services?
- Are there, conversely, some services so closely linked to the accounting function that, for the auditor to perform those services for his client means that, the auditor will, in conducting the audit, be in a position of reviewing his own work? (*Report to Congress* 1978, 12)

Even though these three policy questions were raised at the threshold of the era of the giant diversified services firms, they are still being raised today.

In June 1978, the SEC issued Accounting Series Release (ASR) No. 250, which mandated the disclosure in a company's proxy statement of the percentage relationship to audit fees of (1) aggregate nonaudit fees, and (2) the fee for each specific nonaudit service. A year later, the SEC promulgated ASR No. 264, "Scope of Services by Independent Accountants," a strongly worded document that was issued "without prior warning or discussion with the AICPA" (Olson 1982, 218). The Release had an unmistakable target:

the growing array of nonaudit services offered by some independent public accountants—and the growing importance of management advisory services to the revenues, profits, and competitive position of accounting firms—are a cause for legitimate concern as to the impact of these activities on auditor independence, objectivity, and professionalism.

The Release was intended to "sensitize the profession and its clients to the potential effects on the independence of accountants of performance of non-audit services for audit clients." Mark Stevens, a close student of the profession, wrote that it "also cautioned the CPAs to avoid supplanting client management's role, to be cautious of accepting engagements that involve an audit of their own work (such as a review of internal controls installed by the auditor's MAS arm), and that client audit committees should gauge the relative merits of the firm's auditor providing nonaudit services" (Stevens 1981, 210–211). The Release had a chilling effect on the profession, as the firms expected companies to pull back from drawing on such services from their audit firm. The Release was couched in such categorical language that Chairman Williams felt it necessary to assure the profession in a speech that the Commission did not intend to prohibit any particular kind of MAS engagement (Williams 1980, 422).

Reacting to Release Nos. 250 and 264, Harvey E. Kapnick, the chairman and chief executive of Arthur Andersen, proposed to his partners in 1979 that the firm be split into two related firms: auditing and consulting. He reported on his private discussions with SEC Chairman Williams, who, he said, would soon require all of the big firms to make such a split. Kapnick's proposal shocked his partners, and it met with stiff resistance. Although Kapnick did not accept the views of the SEC, he believed that this was the principled action to take before the SEC acted unilaterally. The heated controversy generated by his proposal led him to take premature retirement from the firm several weeks later (*A Vision of Grandeur* 1988, 150–151).[18]

In the end, however, both SEC Release Nos. 250 and 264 were rescinded by the Commission in 1981/82, reflecting the new federal policy of deregulation under President Ronald Reagan. Nonetheless, the Commission averred in ASR No. 296 (1981) that "its views [expressed in ASR No. 264] are unchanged."Because the Institute opposed both Releases, one supposes that it welcomed President Reagan's selection as SEC Chairman, John S. R. Shad, in May 1981.

The profession went on the offense by arguing that auditors rendering management advisory services to an audit client actually had a deeper knowledge of the client from an audit standpoint. John C. (Sandy) Burton, the immediate past SEC Chief Accountant, adopted this view and believed that the "scope of services" issue was mainly one of perception by those who do not possess an understanding of the audit process (Burton 1980, 51).

---

[18] Also see Stevens (1991, 112–115) and "The Palace Revolt at Arthur Andersen" (1979). It was Kapnick who promoted an unprecedented openness of, and scrutiny over, his firm's operations. In 1973, under his leadership, Arthur Andersen became the first firm to issue an annual report (see Bows 1973), and in 1977 it was the first firm to publish audited financial statements. In 1974, Kapnick established a Public Review Board, composed of prominent outsiders, to review and report publicly on the firm's operations.

Yet, in 1979 the Public Oversight Board released a major study on *Scope of Services by CPA Firms*, in which it said:

> there is enough concern about the scope of services in responsible quarters so that the question cannot be dismissed as a "nonproblem." The Board believes that there is potential danger to the public interest and to the profession in the unlimited expansion of MAS to audit clients, and some moderating principles and procedures are needed. (Public Oversight Board 1979, 56)

The board concluded, however, that "at this time no rules should be imposed to prohibit specific services on the grounds that they are or may be incompatible with the profession of public accounting, might impair the image of the profession, or do not involve accounting or auditing related skills" (Public Oversight Board 1979, 5). In its second year of operation, the POB was not prepared to take on the profession.

Accounting Horizons
Vol. 17, No. 4
December 2003
pp. 267–286
Submitted: January 2003
Accepted: April 2003
Corresponding author: Stephen A. Zeff

How the U.S. Accounting Profession Got Where It Is Today: Part II

Stephen A. Zeff

A Gradual Degeneration of Professional Values

By 1980, a deterioration in professional values appears to have set in. At the Institute's annual meeting in October, outgoing Board Chairman Wm. R. Gregory, a practitioner from Tacoma, Washington, vividly warned members of the increasingly fractious climate in the profession:

> It seems that the effects of the phenomenal growth in the profession and competitive pressures have created in some CPAs attitudes that are intensely commercial and nearly devoid of the high-principled conduct that we have come to expect of a true professional. It is sad that we seem to have become a breed of highly skilled technicians and businessmen, but have subordinated courtesy, mutual respect, self-restraint, and fairness for a quest for firm growth and a preoccupation with the bottom line.[1]

Stephen A. Zeff is a Professor at Rice University.

Professor Zeff expresses his appreciation to several accounting academics and to more than a dozen active and retired senior partners of major accounting firms for their comments on earlier drafts. He also appreciates the suggestions of the anonymous reviewers.

Editor's note: This concluding part of Professor Zeff's sobering account of how the U.S. accounting profession fared in the 20th century addresses how the forces encountered in earlier times affected the professional nature of accounting firms for some 20 years beginning in the early 1980s. Sadly, accounting "industry" replaced accounting "profession" in many circles. Part I appears in *Accounting Horizons,* September 2003.

---

[1] Gregory's speech was given at the annual business meeting on October 6, 1980. The transcript of his speech was kindly supplied by the Institute.

In 1982, Max Block, a CPA and the former longtime editor of *The New York Certified Public Accountant,* lamented that "accounting profession" was "a term that has lost some of its relevance" (Block 1982, 165). Among other things, he remarked that "Some of the major firms do not refer to themselves as Certified Public Accountants or Accountants and Auditors," not even on their letterheads (Block 1982, 176). However, this was not news. Six years earlier, only two of the Big Eight firms, all of which wrote letters to the Metcalf subcommittee that were photocopied in *The Accounting Establishment* (1976), used stationery identifying the sender as accountants or auditors.[2] The other firms provided no identification of the sender at all, just the name and address of the firm. Block (1982, 176) added, "This [practice] undoubtedly eliminated the service limitation implicit in such titles."

This professional climate evidently worsened in the following years. In May 1985, the Institute's Special Committee on Standards of Professional Conduct for Certified Public Accountants, headed by George D. Anderson, the Institute's 1980–81 board chairman, all but pressed the panic button in its interim report to Council:

> There has been an erosion of self-restraint, conservatism, and adherence to basic professional values at a pace and to an extent that is unprecedented in [the] profession's history. . . . We believe the profession is on the brink of a crisis of confidence in its ability to serve the public interest. (Special Committee 1985, 3–4)

The Special Committee was appointed in October 1983; in May 1986, when submitting its final report, the Committee reiterated its somber assessment: "The competitive environment has placed pressure on the traditional commitment to professionalism in the practice of public accounting" (*Restructuring Professional Standards* 1986, 6). The Committee added that "Many observers are concerned . . . that the long-term consequence for the profession of uncontrolled expansion of [non-attest] services will be a diminished faith in the auditor's independence. This issue cannot be left to the marketplace alone for resolution" (*Restructuring Professional Standards* 1986, 43). In a carefully crafted sentence, the Committee proposed standards of conduct to "impose a measure of self-restraint and self-regulation by calling upon AICPA members to use their judgment in applying broad standards to determine what is consistent with professional conduct in the provision of nonattest services" (*Restructuring Professional Standards* 1986, 43). Like the Public Oversight Board in 1979, the Special Committee did not undertake to proscribe any specific non-attest services. It is noteworthy that only three of the Special Committee's 15 members were partners in Big Eight firms, none of them in their

---

[2] The stationery of both Haskins & Sells and Peat, Marwick, Mitchell & Co. identified them as Certified Public Accountants.

firm's executive office. George Anderson, the Committee's chairman, was the managing partner of a local accounting firm in Helena, Montana.

Bernard Z. Lee, a member of the Special Committee, the Institute's 1983–84 board chairman and CEO of the major accounting firm of Seidman & Seidman, in Houston, a self-described "hawk" on the subject, was quoted as saying (prophetically):

> The profession is changing and change is necessary, but we need to approach it with caution and there needs to be reasonable limitation on what services we should be providing as a profession. There's a perception by our critics, Congress for one, that we may be sacrificing our objectivity if not our independence. If we do not limit the scope of services, then someone will do it for us. (Weinstein 1987, 50)

Other changes in the big firms signaled their further removal from the mainstream professional dialogue. By the mid-1980s, all of the Big Eight firms' house organs that occasionally contained technical articles on accounting and auditing either closed down or became entirely nontechnical. Following the decision by Lybrand, Ross Bros. & Montgomery to do so in 1973, four Big Eight firms discontinued their house organs between 1981 and 1984, and the remaining two firms' house organs soon became nondescript magazines with no affinity to the accounting profession. Ernst & Ernst's house organ never contained technical articles. Between 1971 and 1973, four Big Eight firms began to publish a series of widely distributed booklets expressing their views on controversial accounting issues, but all of these series terminated, as if on cue, in 1979. Beginning in the 1970s, most of the firms began issuing newsletters that mainly described and reported current developments, yet some still contained the firm's views on technical issues. But by the mid-1980s all of the firms' newsletters had become entirely factual (Zeff 1986, 133–138), evidently steering clear of the espousal of controversial views on matters of accounting principle. Even the state societies of CPAs began discontinuing their journals or replacing them with bland magazines having little, if any, professional content.[3]

In 1985, Ralph E. Walters, a senior audit partner in Touche Ross & Co. and a former FASB member, wrote, "The dual concerns of Congressional oversight and the litigious environment have made CPAs nervous about criticizing the status quo. Some even consider it dangerous. So, controversial articles on accounting/professional matters are not in style."[4] Dale L. Gerboth, an audit partner in Arthur Young, observed in 1985:

---

[3] The leading exception has been *The CPA Journal* published by the New York State Society of Certified Public Accountants. *The Ohio CPA Journal* finally succumbed in 2002.

[4] The stationery of both Haskins & Sells and Peat, Marwick, Mitchell & Co. identified them as Certified Public Accountants.

Written articles don't even do much any more to enhance a firm's professional reputation. The business community already perceives all of the large firms as highly competent in accounting and auditing. Even the most brilliant article will not add significantly to that perception. Firms now try to differentiate themselves in other ways, primarily by stressing their commitment to client service ("We take business *personally*").[5]

Even the Big Eight firms' written submissions to the FASB were perceived to be of a lower standard in the 1980s than in the 1970s. In 1985, FASB Vice Chairman Robert T. Sprouse wrote that the quality of letters of comment from the Big Eight firms had, in recent years, deteriorated in terms of their "comprehensiveness, thoughtfulness, and clarity of the constructive recommendations they contained." The most likely explanation for this drop in quality, he said, was "that past experience has made the accounting firms reluctant to take clear positions that may prove to be offensive to some of their current and prospective clients."[6]

Others also sounded foreboding notes. Donald J. Kirk, the FASB chairman and a former audit partner of Price Waterhouse, wrote as follows in 1984:

My major concern is whether the profession will continue to operate in a way that protects its [auditing] franchise and ensures credible financial statements. . . . It is essential . . . that the additional services offered by accounting firms don't detract from the firms' major responsibility of auditing financial statements or impinge on their independence. (Kirk 1984, 29)

In its 1985–86 annual report, the Public Oversight Board warned that the appearance of independence could be endangered:

the Board is of the opinion that the continuous expansion of consulting services may be perceived as impairing auditor independence and thus adversely affect the value of the audit function in the long run. *(Annual Report 1985–1986* 1986, 16)

Implications of Firms' Big Move into Consulting Services

The growth of consulting services in the Big Eight firms from the mid-1970s onward was palpable: "consulting fees as a percentage of total gross firm fees had increased from a range of 5 percent to 19 percent in 1977, to a range of 11 percent to 28 percent in 1984" (Previts 1985, 134). Even by 1978, six of the Big Eight firms placed in the top 10 U.S. consulting firms in terms of gross billings for consulting services (Hayes 1979, D 1). By 1983, Arthur Andersen

---

[5] Letter to the author dated February 8, 1985.
[6] Letter to the author dated May 9, 1985.

& Co. was number one in the list of the top U.S. consulting firms (Previts 1985, 154). By 1990, fees from consulting vaulted to 44 percent of total gross fees for Arthur Andersen/Andersen Consulting and ranged from 20 to 25 percent of total gross fees for the other Big Six firms. (See Exhibit 1.) The relative contribution of fees for tax services to total gross fees rose by about five percentage points from 1975 to 1990 (Zeff 1992, 265).

The experience in Price Waterhouse (PW), one of the Big Eight firms that was, with Haskins & Sells, previously among the least aggressive in expanding into consulting services, epitomizes the drive toward consulting in the second half of the 1970s and even more so in the 1980s:

> Long a secondary focus within PW, consulting became an important line of business during the 1980s. The MAS Department posted significant gains during the late 1970s and early 1980s: partners increased from 33 in 1975 to 71 in 1980, and to 108 by 1985; staff increased in even greater proportions, from 337 to 1,300 (8.2 percent to 18 percent

EXHIBIT 1   Breakdown of Gross Fees According to
Accounting and Auditing, Tax, and Management Consulting

	Percentage of Gross Fees *Accounting and Auditing/Tax/Management Consulting*			
	1975	1990	2000	
Arthur Andersen & Co.	66/18/16	35/21/44		Arthur Andersen & Co./Andersen Consulting
		48/38/14	43/31/26	Arthur Andersen & Co.
Price Waterhouse & Co.	76/16/8	51/26/23		
			33/18/49	Pricewater-houseCoopers
Coopers & Lybrand	69/19/12	56/19/25		
Peat Marwick Mitchell	68/21/11	53/27/20	45/38/17	KPMG
Ernst & Ernst	73/17/10			
		53/25/22	44/30/26	Ernst & Young
Arthur Young & Company	69/17/14			
Haskins & Sells	74/15/11			
		57/23/20	31/20/49	Deloitte & Touche
Touche Ross & Co.	62/24/14			

Sources: 1975: *The Accounting Establishment* (1976, 30).

       1990: *International Accounting Bulletin,* Issue No. 84 (March 1991, 13) and the firms' annual reports for 1990 to the SEC Practice Section of the AICPA's Division for CPA Firms.

       2000: The firms' annual reports for 2000 to the SEC Practice Section of the AICPA's Division for CPA Firms.

of the total firm personnel) in the same period. In addition, the consulting practice's contribution to profit doubled, from 6.8 percent to 13.3 percent. Its dependency on work from audit clients declined at the same time, from 64 percent in 1975 to 26 percent by 1985, largely as a result of a rising volume of work from government organizations. The composition of MAS also changed. By 1988, only one out of four consultants were CPAs, compared with one out of two in 1974. In 1980, a milestone for the MAS Department was reached when one of its non-CPA partners, Paul Goodstat, began to serve on the [firm's] Policy Board. Symbolic of all of these developments was the 1984 decision to rename this practice area Management Consulting Services. (Allen and McDermott 1993, 235)

In sum: "By 1986, PW had evolved to the point where its mission was to become nothing less than a 'full-service business advisory firm'" (Allen and McDermott 1993, 233).

These developments were likely duplicated in the other Big Eight firms, where, through hiring or the takeover of boutique consulting firms, non-CPAs increasingly were brought into the firm's consulting practice (see, e.g., Berton 1985d, 12), and senior consulting partners began to play active roles at the top levels of the firm's overall management hierarchy. By the 1990s, non-CPAs were well represented in the top management of the Big Six firms.

What forces drove the accounting profession in the 1970s and 1980s? Following their aggressive expansion overseas in the 1950s and 1960s, in order to serve their globally expanding clients, the major audit firms apparently concluded in the early 1970s that the audit market was becoming largely saturated. To compensate, the firms aggressively broadened the scale and scope of their consulting practices. In addition to tax-compliance services, tax consulting also expanded. The distribution of the major firms' gross fees shifted markedly from accounting and auditing to tax and consulting services, a portent of further developments to occur in the 1990s and after.

In the 1970s and increasingly into the 1980s, consulting in the Big Eight firms commanded a much larger share of their gross fees. Moreover, in most firms the margins from consulting were believed to exceed those from the audit engagements, especially when competitive bidding often drove down the gross audit fees. While the firms, as profit-seeking enterprises, had always been run as businesses, professional values were nonetheless paramount. But the incessant drive in the 1970s and especially in the 1980s to widen the scope and scale of lucrative consulting services, coupled with the development of the firms' strategic plans, as businesses, to promote growth, greater profitability and global reach, launched them as emerging

---

[7] For a financial journalist's view in 1978 of the increasing competitiveness of the Big Eight firms, see Bernstein (1978).

international behemoths.[7] They formed integrated international firms and became truly worldwide enterprises, ready to serve their multinational clients in services across the board and around the globe. Examples were Touche Ross International in 1972, Peat Marwick International and Deloitte Haskins & Sells International in 1978, Ernst & Whinney International in 1979, and the Price Waterhouse World Firm in 1982.[8]

In the midst of the corporate merger wave of the 1980s, the firms themselves focused on forming combinations. In 1984, an attempt by Price Waterhouse and Deloitte Haskins & Sells to unite failed to materialize (see Allen and McDermott 1993, 228–229). In 1986, Peat Marwick and the European-dominated firm KMG merged to form KPMG (Cypert 1991). In mega-mergers during 1989, Ernst & Whinney and Arthur Young combined to become Ernst & Young, and Deloitte Haskins & Sells joined with Touche Ross to create Deloitte & Touche (Stevens 1991, Chapter 5). Also in 1989, Price Waterhouse and Arthur Andersen held merger talks that failed to unite the firms (Allen and McDermott 1993, 246–248). In 1997–98, Ernst & Young entered into merger talks with KPMG that ended without result. Finally, in 1998, Price Waterhouse merged with Coopers & Lybrand to form PricewaterhouseCoopers, creating the Big Five.[9]

An important element in the firms' drive toward profitability and growth—business aims, not professional aims—involved placing pressure on partners to generate more revenue by securing new audit clients and retaining existing ones, and, for audit and tax partners in particular, to cross-sell consulting and other attest services. The consequences of not meeting "income targets," where such existed, were various, including, at the extreme, dismissal from the firm. This is hardly a climate compatible with audit partners believing they should (or could) stand up to clients on questionable accounting and disclosure treatments. Indeed, in 1984, Ralph Walters, the senior partner at Touche Ross, said that the big firms, in their push toward growth and profitability, were reluctant to lose a client over a matter of principle (Walters 1984, S/9).

Evidence of the effects of this pressure has been reported in the press and elsewhere. Mark Stevens writes that, beginning in 1984–85, the newly elected CEOs of Deloitte Haskins & Sells and Touche Ross abruptly challenged the maxim, "Once a partner, always a partner." Deloitte CEO J. Michael Cook's "ultimate goal was to change Deloitte's self-image from that of a professional firm that happened to be in business (the traditional view among the giant CPA firms) to a business that happened to market professional services" (Stevens 1991, 170). "Cook knew all too well," Stevens wrote, "that if he was going to create a leaner, meaner, more businesslike firm, he would have to take the

---

[8] Arthur Andersen was always run as a worldwide firm, based in Chicago, but in 1978, it set up Arthur Andersen & Co., Société Coopérative in Geneva, Switzerland to coordinate its worldwide organization.

[9] For a historical review of the merger activity of major U.S. accounting firms, see Wootton et al. (2003).

painful step of pruning back the partnership, in part by pressuring those who couldn't cut the mustard to take early retirement. . . . Until that time partnership had been more of a coronation than a job" (Stevens 1991, 172). Underperforming partners were dismissed. Stevens added, "[Cook] awarded the biggest bonuses and highest salaries to those who proved themselves capable of graduating from being 'auditors' auditor' to being business advisers" (Stevens 1991, 174–175). Edward A. Kangas, the CEO at Touche Ross, adopted a similar strategy, "handing out pink slips to mediocre performers" (Stevens 1991, 208) and to those who did not generate minimum fee levels.

To be sure, firms dismissed underperforming client partners or reassigned them to nonclient tasks in earlier years, but typically because they failed to adhere to professional and technical standards, not because of a failure to bring in sufficient business. But now, because of the heightened pressure placed on them in their firms, including enhanced legal exposure and the need to keep current with increasingly complex and intricate accounting and auditing standards, as well as the growing disparity between their salaries and those in industry, more audit partners left their firms and headed for financial positions in enterprise.

The arrival of a profoundly altered competitive climate in the practice of public accounting was underscored in a remark attributed to Michael Cook in 1985: "Five years ago if a client of another firm came to me and complained about the service, I'd immediately warn the other firm's chief executive. . . . Today I try to take away his client" (Berton 1985d, 1). The press quoted a close observer of the accounting profession as saying at the time, "Today almost anything that makes money goes" (Berton 1985d, 1).

Peat Marwick evidently followed this route as well (Stevens 1991, 173). It was reported in 1985 that Peat Marwick and Grant Thornton & Co. dismissed partners for failing to meet marketing targets (Berton 1985d, 1). In 1985, Ralph Walters of Touche Ross wrote:

> The major firms are on a growth treadmill that inevitably will stop, but each manager is determined to keep it moving ever faster during his regime. This has required diversification into many "information-based" services. The aggregate effect of these diversifications is to change the balance of the professional mindset—moving farther from an audit mentality and toward a consulting mentality. The diversified service draws the firms increasingly into competition with other disciplines that have few or no professional/competitive constraints, and our traditional professional standards of conduct are a competitive handicap.[10]

Beginning in the 1970s, there was an increasing tendency to specialize by type of expertise or class of industry (Allen and McDermott 1993, 192–194), yet an attempt by the Institute to recognize the former through

---

[10] Letter to the author dated February 1, 1985.

a formal accreditation process met with stiff resistance (Chenok 2000, 13–16). Arthur R. Wyatt, an FASB member at the time and a former Arthur Andersen partner and a former chairman of the Institute's Accounting Standards Executive Committee, wrote in 1985: "[m]y experience has been that as one becomes more of an industry specialist he tends to become somewhat of an apologist for the industry."[11]

Impact of S&L and Bank Failures: The Dingell Hearings

The failure of many banks and savings and loan institutions during the 1980s raised troubling questions about the propriety of accounting and auditing. In addition, three notorious cases of alleged auditor fraud—E.S.M. Government Securities (Sack and Tangreti 1987), Wedtech Corp. (Traub 1990), and ZZZZ Best—embarrassed the accounting profession. A major source of pressure on the FASB and on audit firms surfaced when regulators in the banking and thrift industries advocated the use of deceptive accounting practices in order to "rescue" failing institutions in the name of the "public interest."[12] Donald J. Kirk, the FASB chairman from 1978 to 1986, was quoted in a 1990 article as saying that "[The regulators] created equity out of thin air, with incredible rationalizations" (Gerth 1990, D5). The same article reported that the AICPA joined with the regulators in lobbying the FASB to be responsive to the industry's problems. In a paraphrase, Kirk said that "the incident showed that the accountants' institute was too sympathetic to the industry, which was a big client for many accounting firms" (Gerth 1990, D5). The commercial banking sector also played with "regulatory accounting practices" (RAP), which departed from GAAP. Set by bank regulatory agencies, RAP allowed banks to ignore losses on bad loans or, at the most, amortize the losses over five- to ten-year periods.

In February 1985, Rep. John D. Dingell, Democrat from Michigan and chairman of the Subcommittee on Oversight and Investigations of the House Committee on Energy and Commerce, reacting to the accounting issues attending numerous bank, thrift, and corporate failures, launched three years of hearings into the adequacy of the accounting profession's self-regulatory system. His first two witnesses were Professors Robert Chatov and Abraham J. Briloff, who had been relied upon heavily by the Metcalf subcommittee's staff in 1976. They stated their opposition to the practice by audit firms of rendering any consulting services to their audit clients *(SEC and Corporate Audits (Part* 1) 1985, 31, 143; Briloff 1987). The year 1985 also saw the formation of the National Commission on Fraudulent Financial Reporting, known as the Treadway Commission. Jointly sponsored by the Institute and four other accounting bodies, the Commission

---

[11] Letter to the author dated March 4, 1985.
[12] See Berton (1985b), Simonetti and Andrews (1987), Arnold (1988), and Revsine (1991).

was charged "to identify causal factors that can lead to fraudulent financial reporting and steps to reduce its incidence" *(Report of the National Commission . . . 1987, 1)*. The Commission issued 49 sweeping recommendations in its final report published in 1987. Philip B. Chenok, the Institute's full-time president at the time, later observed that most of the recommendations "were subsequently implemented either through congressional legislation, regulatory action, or by the profession itself" (Chenok 2000, 29). Yet in 1992, Donald H. Chapin, a former audit partner of Arthur Young and then a senior executive in the General Accounting Office, pronounced that, "All in all the Treadway inspired work is turning out to be disappointing, and, I think counterproductive" (Chapin 1992, 18).[13]

Industry Raises the Ante

During the 1980s, financial reporting norms came under stress as (1) industry regulators increasingly viewed them as a means of achieving "public interest" goals like those mentioned above for banks and thrifts, and (2) companies and trade associations ratcheted up their lobbying of the FASB for preparer-friendly standards. A reinvigorated merger movement, coupled with the onset of pervasive restructurings, placed increased revenue and earnings pressure on CEOs, whether as engineers of attempted takeovers or as defenders against such takeovers. To the audit firms, the merger movement also portended a loss of clients, as only one of the audit firms of two merger partners would be appointed the auditor of the merged entity.[14] It was also a decade marked by an increased emphasis on analysts' earnings forecasts, adding to the pressure on CEOs to achieve earnings targets. Stevens (1985, 224) found evidence of this latter strain of earnings pressure on management as early as the mid-1980s, with the consequent insistence that the company's accountants manage the earnings to meet the forecast: "Do whatever the hell you have to do and do it quickly and discreetly" (paraphrased by Stevens).

One consequence of these pressures was a drive by companies to secure their auditor's approval for creative accounting techniques, especially in the recognition of revenue. Another involved a series of attempts by bodies representing preparers to diminish the FASB's ability to issue rigorous standards. In 1985, the Financial Executives Institute issued a white paper,

---

[13] In a memo to the author dated January 23, 2003, Chapin clarified what he meant by "counterproductive," as follows: "The Treadway Commission made a number of good recommendations in 1987, but the implementation steps for the most important of them did not go far enough and left the door open to continuing fraudulent reporting. I expressed the view in 1992 that implementation was counterproductive because many people were satisfied with the minimal implementation that had been done and that stopped the momentum for needed improvements."

[14] For discussion of this issue in the context of Price Waterhouse, see Allen and McDermott (1993, 227). The restructurings did, however, spawn new business, as "some firms, like Deloitte, Haskins & Sells and Touche Ross, began to emphasize consulting for investment bankers in mergers, reorganizations, and bankruptcies" (Allen and McDermott 1993, 227).

demanding that the trustees of the Financial Accounting Foundation (FAF) reconstitute the FASB with a larger representation of ex-financial executives, as a result of which the FAF's trustees appointed a second preparer to the Board (Miller et al. 1998, 179–180). Three years later, after Arthur R. Wyatt resigned from the Board because, he said, preparers were interfering in the Board's work *(Users and Abusers* 1987, 13; Berton 1987), a task force of The Business Roundtable, a body composed of CEOs of some 200 of the largest U.S. corporations and banks, proposed the creation of a new oversight body. It "would be given the power to add or delete projects from the FASB's agenda or to reject any of the Board's standards after they had been passed" (Miller et al. 1998, 182).[15] A representative from the preparer community was to be included on the body. SEC Chairman David S. Ruder summarily rejected the proposal, which put an end to the episode (Ruder 1989, 11–14; Van Riper 1994, 135–140).

Nonetheless, in 1990 the FAF trustees approved a stiffening of the FASB's required voting majority from 4–3 to 5–2, a move driven by corporate interests to slow down the Board (Van Riper 1994, 160–165; Miller et al. 1998, 182). These thrusts by Corporate America in the 1980s served notice that it was monitoring the work of the FASB closely and would intervene if necessary. Another assault on the FASB occurred in 1996, this time by the Financial Executives Institute, which sought to bring the Board under the control of the preparer community. It was repulsed by SEC Chairman Arthur Levitt, who countered by securing the appointment of four representatives of the public interest to the FAF board of trustees (Miller et al. 1998, 186–192; Zeff 1998b, 535–537; Levitt 2002, 111–115).

Impact of Heightened Client Pressure on Auditors

As preparers became more assertive and aggressive, audit firm partners seemed to recede into the shadows, evidently reflecting the growing pressure from their clients. In two major articles published in 1988 and 1991, Arthur Wyatt provided his own perspective as a former FASB member and as a principal in the Accounting Principles Group of Arthur Andersen, a Big Six firm that continued to express its own views forthrightly. In 1988, he wrote, "Too often the Emerging Issues Task Force (EITF) is used [by audit firm partners] more as a forum to argue a specific client's fact situation than as a forum to achieve a professionally oriented solution . . . " and "Unfortunately, the auditor today is often a participant in aggressively seeking loopholes [on behalf of corporate clients]" (Wyatt 1988, 24). Wyatt wrote in 1991:

---

[15] Some of the flavor of CEOs' criticisms of the standards that the FASB proposed to issue during the 1980s and 1990s may be appreciated by a reading of the stream of letters from Thomas A. Murphy, the retired CEO of General Motors, to Donald J. Kirk and Dennis R. Beresford, the successive chairmen of the FASB (see Bricker and Previts 2002).

Attesters [i.e., audit firm partners] . . . no longer really bring their own views to the Board, but rather too frequently present a synthesized version of their client's views. It has become commonplace for the Board to receive a response letter from an accounting firm at or near the end of the exposure period indicating its response will be delayed because the firm has not yet completed a survey of its clients. . . . Many attesters seem to have lost their ability and/or willingness to present their own views, leaving cynics to speculate that attesters are unwilling to incur potential disfavor with one or more of their clients by taking a position on controversial issues. (Wyatt 1991, 113)[16]

The Public Oversight Board agreed. In its 1993 special report, *In the Public Interest,* it expressed concern over the following scenario:

allowing the views of major clients to bias a firm's ostensibly independent response to FASB discussion memoranda, invitations to comment, and exposure drafts, or to influence a firm to not take a contentious and complex issue to the Emerging Issues Task Force because of concern about getting the "wrong" answer. (Public Oversight Board 1993, 45)

The dialogue by leading practitioners over accounting standards, so vibrant in the 1960s, had largely died out by the end of the 1980s, in part a victim of the growing commercialism of the profession.[17] When the FASB came under attack in 1990, including continued pressure from The Business Roundtable, John C. Burton and Robert J. Sack, both former chief accountants at the SEC,[18] wrote, "The public accounting firms, the traditional base of support for the Board, are strangely silent" (Burton and Sack 1990, 117). In a reference to the increasingly competitive environment in which the big accounting firms found themselves at the end of the 1980s, Van Riper (1994, 162) wrote, "the need to please clients and hold on to audit engagements was greater than it had been in more than a half a century." By the outset of the 1990s, evidently, any ostensible leadership among the Big Six firms for supporting the public interest in sound standard setting had largely disappeared.

In the latter 1980s, some of the big firms began distancing themselves from the term "accounting," as they expanded the horizons of the information services that CPAs might render. Writing with Gary John Previts in 1987, Arthur Andersen partner Robert Mednick argued that the emergence of new information technology "has placed a significant premium on the information-gathering, analyzing and evaluating skills of the CPA and has

---

[16] This author observed the same behavior during his four years of service on the Financial Accounting Standards Advisory Council (1988–1991).

[17] For a historical perspective, see Wyatt (1989).

[18] Sack was Chief Accountant of the SEC's Enforcement Division, while Burton was Chief Accountant of the Commission.

led us to conclude that there will be a gradual recognition of today's CPA as tomorrow's 'independent information professional'" (Mednick and Previts 1987, 232).

One leader of the profession went so far as to recommend that CPAs give up their exclusive franchise to conduct audits. A. Marvin Strait, a former Institute board chairman and the managing partner in a small accounting firm in Colorado Springs, Colorado, argued that, as "information professionals," CPAs need to free themselves from the constraints that state boards of accountancy place on their non-attest services. He recommended that CPAs give up the licensed monopoly accorded them under state law, that the AICPA replace the state boards as the body that examines and certifies candidates for the CPA designation, and that the state boards confine their regulation to "the CPA's work in services with a third-party interest and attest engagement, and compilations where there has been third-party reliance" (Strait 1993, 186).

The SEC and Others Voice Concerns about Auditor Conduct

During the Reagan and senior Bush administrations, the SEC seemed to adopt a less outwardly confrontational posture toward the accounting profession about the possible conflict of consulting services with auditor independence. Nonetheless, during the 1980s and apparently continuing into the 1990s, the SEC balked at allowing audit firms to engage in "business relationships" with their audit clients even if they were not material to either party (Mednick 1990, 92–93). The SEC also declined to adopt the view of the Big Six firms that the appearance of independence should be judged "from the perspective of a *reasonable and prudent person* who possesses both *knowledge and experience*" (*The Public Accounting Profession: Meeting the Needs of a Changing World* 1991, 22). Citing the U.S. Supreme Court's unanimous decision in *United States v. Arthur Young*, 465 U.S. 805 (1984), the SEC's staff instead placed emphasis on the perspective of the "investing public" (*Staff Report on Auditor Independence* 1994, 16) or of a "reasonable investor" (SEC Staff Analysis [of the AICPA White Paper], 1997, 1; Zeff 1998b, 537–539).[19] Adding to many voices, the SEC's accounting staff quoted the following passage from Chief Justice Warren Burger's opinion in the Arthur Young case, in which he said that the independent public accountant performs a "'public watchdog' function [that] demands that the accountant maintain total independence from the client at all times and requires complete fidelity to the public trust" (p. 818 of the court opinion). This debate between the big firms and the SEC's staff may continue, but the Supreme Court has spoken clearly and definitively.

---

[19] In 1994, SEC Chief Accountant Walter P. Schuetze (1994, 70) reported that his office had rejected a similar petition in 1992 from the chairman of a special committee of the AICPA.

The growth and profitability mentality that drove the big firms in the 1980s showed no sign of abating in the 1990s. In his 1991 book, *The Big Six,* Mark Stevens wrote prophetically:

> Beyond the issue of size, the firms must face a more serious question: What, exactly, do they want to be? For generations, the Big Eight were proud of their role as audit professionals. . . . The fact that they were well paid (but not wealthy) partners in collegial practices that stressed caution, prudence and a disdain for the trappings of commercial businesses was a matter of pride.
>
> Today, just the opposite is true. Anything that smacks of this traditional attitude is dismissed as a relic of the past. . . .
>
> As the firms become more intimately involved with their clients through their consulting practices, as they think of themselves more and more as consultants who happen to do audits just to get a foot in the door and as they continue to reward salesmanship and marketing over technical proficiency, they are clearly headed toward a day of reckoning—a day when the firms, or Congress acting for them, will force the issue and demand that they decide whether they want to retain the licensed privilege of auditing the corporate community by spinning off the MAS practices, or whether they want to join in the open competition of management consulting by ejecting the audit practices. (Stevens 1991, 250–251)

In 1994, the SEC's Office of the Chief Accountant expressed concern over this trend when it said, "the staff is mindful of the potential impact of MAS on auditors' independence, in the light of the increasing role of non-audit personnel who are not bound by the accounting profession's Code of Ethics at the top management levels of the firms . . . " *(Staff Report on Auditor Independence* 1994, 34). The Public Oversight Board in its 1993 special report, *In the Public Interest,* wrote that "Attacks on the accounting profession from a variety of sources [have] suggested a significant public concern with the profession's performance" (Public Oversight Board 1993, 1),[20] and it recommended several measures that the firms could take to reassure the public of their objectivity, independence and professionalism (Public Oversight Board 1993, 43–46).

Donald H. Chapin, the former Arthur Young audit partner mentioned earlier, provided a depressing outlook for the accounting profession in 1992, when he addressed an annual conference of the New York State Society of

---

[20] Much of the "attack," one supposes, arose from the audit failures and the improper financial practices relating to the "savings and loan crisis," mentioned by the Kirk Panel (Advisory Panel on Auditor Independence 1994, 4). One such "attack" may have been the author's article in a Dutch journal, "The Decline in Professionalism" (Zeff 1992), which is cited by the Board on page 45. In fact, the Board invited the author to meet with it in June 1992, while it was in the process of preparing its special report. An earlier article by the author, "Does the CPA Belong to a Profession?" (Zeff 1987), may also have given leaders of the accounting profession some pause.

CPAs as Assistant Comptroller General, Accounting and Financial Management, of the U.S. General Accounting Office. He raised the specter of possible action by Congress to regulate the profession, and he warned the profession against continuing to close the expectation gap by reducing expectations. He said, "Expectations [of auditors] are so unbelievably low that some are questioning whether there is a role for a private sector profession" (Chapin 1992, 16). He said, "We have been told that some firms are offering audits—their exclusive franchise—at big discounts to attract clients for their more lucrative consulting services. Some say the profession's traditional function has been downgraded to a loss leader" (Chapin 1992, 18). Ominously, he added, "I believe that it is very important for the profession to come up with a plan for reform which deals with survival issues. One of these issues is facilitating recognition of the public interest. How to free the profession to take on this role involves separating auditors from management control" (Chapin 1992, 22).

In 1994, SEC Chief Accountant Walter P. Schuetze, a former FASB member and former executive office partner of KPMG Peat Marwick, complained of "situations in which auditors are not standing up to their clients on financial accounting and reporting issues when their clients take a position that is, at best, not supported in the accounting literature or, at worst, directly contrary to existing accounting pronouncements" (Schuetze 1994, 70). He offered several recent examples in dealing with registrants ("of which there are more") and said, "in these cases, it is again clear that the auditors' actions are not individual engagement partners acting on their own, but that the actions are undertaken with the knowledge of the national offices of the firms" (Schuetze 1994, 72–73). Schuetze's criticism of auditor conduct, voiced at an AICPA conference, was so searing that it prompted the Public Oversight Board to appoint an Advisory Panel on Auditor Independence, headed by Donald J. Kirk, to inquire into his allegations.

The Kirk Panel on Auditor Independence

The Kirk Panel, as the Advisory Panel came to be called, referred to a "growing cynicism at the SEC about the performance of the public accounting profession" (Advisory Panel on Auditor Independence 1994, 5). It observed further that "Mergers, acquisitions and restructurings in corporate America have severely aggravated competition among the Big 6 for larger clients" (Advisory Panel on Auditor Independence 1994, 5). It then pointed out the heightened interest by the corporate community in influencing the accounting standard-setting process and its strong desire that financial managers have a larger hand, vis-à-vis the external auditor, in making the judgments about a company's accounting policies and disclosure practices. The Panel added, "Financial managers aggressively control audit activity and costs and are in a position to orchestrate meetings of the external auditor with the audit committee and the full board of directors" (Advisory Panel on Auditor Independence 1994, 6).

The Kirk Panel attested to the growing magnitude of consulting fees in relation to audit fees in the Big Six firms:

> Five of the top seven consulting firms in the United States and six of the top seven consulting firms worldwide are reported to be Big Six firms. Some of the firms now think of themselves not as accounting and auditing firms but as multi-line professional service firms. Marketing materials and advertising present the firms to the world as business consulting organizations, not as auditors. (Advisory Panel on Auditor Independence 1994, 6)[21]

By the second half of the 1990s, all of the big firms described themselves in this way.

The Kirk Panel strongly counseled the Big Six firms against writing joint letters to the FASB on proposed standards, especially when it is known that their senior partners have been conferring with The Business Roundtable. The example given by the Panel was the firms' collaboration on the employee stock option issue, which, the Panel said, "cannot help but create the impression that those senior partners and the firms they represent have responded both to peer pressure and to pressure from organized business groups that include the firms' major clients" (Advisory Panel on Auditor Independence 1994, 25). Indeed, in 1994, when former Andersen senior technical partner Arthur R. Wyatt learned that the firm's Professional Standards Group (PSG)[22] favored expensing the cost of employee stock options but was overruled by the firm's top management, perhaps because of client pressures, he said that the PSG would never reacquire its authority in the firm (McRoberts 2002, 17). Andersen joined with the other Big Six firms in a united front to oppose expensing. In a famous line, SEC Chief Accountant Walter Schuetze said, "It also appears to me, and other outside observers, that CPAs may have become cheerleaders for their clients on the issue of accounting for stock options issued to employees" (Schuetze 1994, 74).

Tensions over Compensation, Litigation, and Scope of Services

Conversations with retired partners of some of the big firms suggest that a tension in some of the firms arose from the anguish felt by audit partners that

---

[21] In 1997–98, when Ernst & Young and KPMG as well as Price Waterhouse and Coopers & Lybrand were talking merger, the press releases announcing their merger plans made not a single mention of "audit" or "auditing." The term "assurance services," under which audit is subsumed, was mentioned once. "The firms style themselves as 'professional services organizations,' and they vaunt the 'capabilities,' 'synergies,' 'presence' and 'global strength' combining to produce a 'powerful consulting resource'—'to provide our clients with the highest level of satisfaction'" (Zeff 1998a). Nothing was said in the press releases about the firms' ability to deliver an audit with objectivity, independence, and professionalism.

[22] The PSG was formerly known as the Accounting Principles Group.

their rising salaries were subsidized by the larger margins brought in by their partners in consulting. This circumstance, a likely factor in driving Andersen Consulting apart from Arthur Andersen, may have impelled the audit partners to become even more aggressive in marketing consulting and other attest services to their clients, while doing what was necessary to retain their big clients, in order to be able to hold their heads high in the firm.

Because the big firms were greatly concerned about the continuing threat of litigation, they and the Institute launched a major offensive to gain Congressional approval, eventually over President Bill Clinton's veto, of the Private Securities Litigation Reform Act of 1995. This law made it much more difficult to secure several, as opposed to joint, liability of auditors (Cook et al. 1992; Chenok 2000, 68–70). *The Economist* has since reported, "Because auditors felt safer after these changes, says John Coffee [Columbia University law professor], companies got away with more aggressive accounting in the late 1990s." In the same article, Lynn E. Turner, the SEC Chief Accountant from 1998 to 2001, said that, following the 1995 Act, "audit firms started doing less work" (Revenge of the Nerds 2003).

Furthermore, by the 1990s, Robert K. Elliott, the chairman of the Institute's Special Committee on Assurance Services, stated that "the warning signs are clear that the marketplace for audit services is saturated" *(The CPA Journal* Symposium on the Future of Assurance Services 1996, 16). The previous year, his Special Committee said, "Over the past six years inflation-adjusted accounting and auditing revenues have been flat for the 60 largest firms," at a time at which Gross Domestic Product had risen by 28 percent in real terms (Elliott 1995, 1–2). The Special Committee was established in 1994 "to develop new opportunities for the accounting profession to provide value-added assurance services" (Elliott 1995, 1). It defined *assurance services,* a new term, as "services that improve the quality of information or its context for decision makers through the application of independent professional judgment" (Elliott 1995, 2).[23] These services went well beyond the traditional financial audit function, known as *attestation,* which implies a retrospective checking up on the client. The committee charted the future implications of assurance services: "Existing services can be expanded, additional services can be provided for current users, and new services can be provided to new groups of users" (Elliott 1995, 2).

The Inevitable Clash of Two Forces

As suggested above, during the 1990s the big firms expanded into global, multidisciplinary professional services firms that also happened to conduct audits. Whether by intention of the firms' top management or through inadvertence, the firms' audit partners began to focus much

---

[23] This passage is taken from Elliott's report to the October 1995 meeting of AICPA Council, page 34 of the transcript. The author is grateful to the Institute for supplying the transcript.

more on bringing in business and keeping clients content. In a speech in June 1996, SEC Chairman Arthur Levitt said, "I'm deeply concerned that 'independence' and 'objectivity' are increasingly regarded by some [in the accounting profession] as quaint notions. . . . I caution the [accounting] industry, if I may borrow a Biblical phrase, not to 'gain the whole world, and lose [its] own soul'" (Levitt 1996). Levitt later alleged that some audit partners were compensated for the selling of nonaudit services, which he regarded as antithetical to a posture of independence from the client (Levitt 2002, 116, 139).[24]

All the while, the 1990s were a decade in which CEOs felt increasing pressures for revenue and earnings performance. With improvements in information-processing technology coupled with expanding coverage in the press, the consensus earnings forecasts of securities analysts assumed much greater prominence. During the high-tech bubble of the 1990s, earnings forecasts, including the whisper forecasts prior to the SEC's Regulation FD, began to drive the markets. They thus came to command the attention of top corporate executives who, increasingly, received earnings-based bonuses and gargantuan grants of stock options whose values were themselves believed by executives to be driven by reported earnings.[25] Furthermore, as Alan Greenspan has pointed out, "The sharp fall [in recent years] in dividend payout ratios and yields has dramatically shifted the focus of stock price evaluation toward earnings. Unlike cash dividends, whose value is unambiguous, there is no unambiguously 'correct' value of earnings" (Greenspan 2002, 3). This is where the convenient ambiguity of the accounting measure of earnings enters the picture. The self-interest of CEOs and other top executives was transparent. They wanted higher earnings, at least as high as the forecasts to which they found themselves held hostage by the press. If they failed to "make the forecast," then they feared that their stock price, and thus their compensation, would take a tumble. In August 2000, the Public Oversight Board's Panel on Audit Effectiveness (the O'Malley Panel) characterized this poisoned climate as follows:

> The growth in equity values over the past decade has introduced extreme pressures on management to achieve earnings, revenue, or other targets. These pressures are exacerbated by the unforgiving nature

---

[24] In December 2002, the SEC said, "Some accounting firms offer their professionals cash bonuses and other financial incentives to sell products or services, other than audit, review, or attest services to audit clients. We view such incentive programs as inconsistent with the independence and objectivity of external auditors that is necessary for them to maintain, both in fact and in appearance" (Securities and Exchange Commission 2002, Part IIE).

[25] It has been reported that "The top five executive officers of the 1,500 largest U.S. companies take about 30% of all options issued every year. . . . From 1992 to the peak of the market in 2000, this corporate elite saw a 1,000% increase in the paper value of their unexercised options, to a collective $80 billion. Over the same period, the Standard & Poor's 500-stock index rose 350%, which means execs gained nearly three times as much as the shareholders they serve" (Bernstein 2002).

of the equity markets as securities valuations are drastically adjusted downward whenever companies fail to meet "street" expectations. Pressures are further magnified because management's compensation often is based in large part on achieving earnings or other financial goals or stock-price increases. These pressures on management, in turn, translate into pressures on how auditors conduct audits and in their relationship with audit clients. (The Panel on Audit Effectiveness 2000, 2–3)

The accumulated testimony about the change in character of the big firms in the 1980s and 1990s suggests the evolution toward a climate in which audit partners felt less than secure in resisting clients' insistent arguments that marginal or even illicit accounting interpretations be applied in their financial statements. In the increasingly business-dominated climate of the big audit firms, one can raise serious questions about whether audit engagement partners, and indeed the firms themselves, were steadfastly resisting these pressures. Former SEC Chairman Levitt expresses an even stronger view: "More and more, it became clear [in the 1990s] that the auditors didn't want to do anything to rock the boat with clients, potentially jeopardizing their chief source of income" (Levitt 2002, 116). The clash of the client pressures against the internal pressures on modern-day audit partners strikes this author as a recipe for disaster.

Former SEC Chairman Levitt points out that the share of big accounting firms' revenues derived from consulting rose from one-third in 1993 to 51 percent in 1999 (Levitt 2002, 8); Exhibit 1 provides a breakdown by firms. Yet, as Philip B. Chenok, the full-time president of the Institute from 1980 to 1995, said, the rendering of consulting services in itself may not be the real issue. Nevertheless, it certainly creates large questions about auditor independence in the minds of investors, journalists, jurists, and others outside the accounting profession. Chenok recalled that, when he was a partner in a large accounting firm in the 1960s and 1970s, "I was more concerned with the ability of audit partners to stand up to tough clients than I was with large consulting fees affecting their judgment. If anything is going to make an auditor bend the rules, it is the intimidation factor—the inability of an individual auditor to withstand pressure from an aggressive client" (Chenok 2000, 85–86). In the last ten to 15 years, however, the "intimidation factor" has become vastly more menacing. At the same time, the foundational change in the climate within the big firms toward growth, profitability and global reach—business, not professional values—and the consequent pressure placed on audit partners to contribute toward achieving these goals, may well have weakened the backbone of auditors who do not want to endanger their careers. As the 21st century begins unfolding, this is where we are today.

CONCLUSION

A series of defining events and decisions have brought the accounting profession to where it is today:

- The actions taken by the Federal Trade Commission and the Department of Justice to force the profession to repeal its bans against competitive bidding and direct, uninvited solicitation of clients.
- The increasing degree of sharp competitiveness for audit clients by the big firms, accompanied by the burgeoning growth in tax and consulting services to compensate for declining profits in a saturated audit market.
- The gradual withdrawal of the big firms from active participation in the dialogue over accounting principles, partly stimulated by their exclusion from the standard-setting process when the FASB replaced the APB in 1973.
- The transformation of professional firms that happened to be businesses into businesses that happened to render professional services. The audit mentality at the top management of the firms was replaced by a consulting mentality, including a headlong drive for growth, profitability and global reach—business, not professional values.
- The consequent weakening of audit partners' will to take a stand against clients' questionable accounting practices, as their risk of doing so would fall squarely on their shoulders, and not be diversified throughout the firm, as in earlier decades.

At the same time as audit partners were given these *perverse* incentives by their firm's top management, their clients were becoming ever more driven by their own set of *perverse* incentives: bonuses based on earnings, and stock options with values linked to the price of the company's stock (and therefore, it was believed, to earnings). To maximize their mounting compensation, CEOs began to take every advantage of the subjective judgments implicit in accounting choices, thus placing immense pressure on audit engagement partners—themselves under pressure to keep clients content—to accede to accounting practices arguably beyond the realm of acceptability.

The magnitude and range of consulting services rendered by the big firms in recent times has played an important part in this drama. The dramatic growth in these services has fueled the increasingly widespread *perception* of auditors' lack of independence from their clients. In my view, however, the root cause of the questionable decisions attributable to audit firms in recent years has been the purely financial incentives given to audit partners by their firms, exacerbated by other aspects of the firms' reward system, such as promotions and other such intangible benefits conferred on a partner for maintaining good relations with clients. That reward system for audit partners can be changed only by the leadership in their firms.

REFERENCES

Accountants Turn Tougher. 1969. *Business Week* (October 18): 124–125, 128, 130.

Accounting and Auditing Practices and Procedures. 1977. Hearings before the Subcommittee on Reports, Accounting and Management of the Committee on Governmental Affairs, United States Senate, 95th Congress, 1st Session. Washington, D.C.: Government Printing Office.

Accounting at the Half-Century Mark. 1951. Editorial. *The Journal of Accountancy* 91 (January): 65–66.

The Accounting Establishment. 1976. A staff study prepared by the Subcommittee on Reports, Accounting, and Management of the Committee on Government Operations, United States Senate, 94th Congress, 2nd Session. Washington, D.C.: Government Printing Office.

Advisory Panel on Auditor Independence. 1994. *Strengthening the Professionalism of the Independent Auditor.* Stamford, CT: Public Oversight Board.

Allen, D. G., and K. McDermott. 1993. *Accounting for Success: A History of Price Waterhouse in America 1890–1990.* Boston, MA: Harvard Business School Press.

An Interview with Our New Management Team. 1984. *World* (Peat Marwick house organ) 18 (4): 3–5.

Annual Report 1985–1986. 1986. New York, NY: Public Oversight Board.

Anreder, S. S. 1979. Profit or Loss? Price-cutting is hitting accountants in the bottom line. *Barron's* (March 12): 9, 18, 20, 31.

Arnold, J. L. 1988. *Proceedings of the October 8, 1987 Roundtable Discussion on Generally Accepted Accounting Principles and Regulatory Accounting Practices.* Los Angeles, CA: School of Accounting, University of Southern California.

Arthur Andersen is Set Back in Bid to Bar SEC Rulings. 1976. *Wall Street Journal* (September 7): 13.

Bernstein, A. 2002. Options: Middle managers will take the hit. *Business Week* (December 9): 120.

Bernstein, P. W. 1978. Competition comes to accounting. *Fortune* 98 (July 17): 88–92, 94, 96.

Berton, L. 1985a. Audit fees fall as CPA firms jockey for bids. *Wall Street Journal* (January 28): 31.

———. 1985b. Legerdemain: Accounting at thrifts provokes controversy as gimmickry mounts. *Wall Street Journal* (March 21): 1, 21.

———. 1985c. Peat Marwick departures indicate firm's chief isn't leading merely a routine efficiency drive. *Wall Street Journal* (March 21): 4.

———. 1985d. Total war: CPA firms diversify, cut fees, steal clients in battle for business. *Wall Street Journal* (September 20): 1,12.

———. 1987. Wyatt quits FASB; some cite his views. *Wall Street Journal* (August 4): 32.

Bialkin, K. J. 1987. Government antitrust enforcement and the rules of conduct. *Journal of Accountancy* 163 (May): 105–109.

Block, M. 1982. Is there more than one accounting profession (U.S.A.)? In *Annual Accounting Review,* Volume 4, edited by S. Weinstein and M. A. Walker, 163–195. Chur, Switzerland: Harwood Academic Publishers.

Bowman, A. W. 1985. Statement reproduced in *SEC and Corporate Audits (Part 1),* Hearings before the Subcommittee on Oversight and Investigations of the Committee on Energy and Commerce, House of Representatives, 99th Congress, 1st Session, March 6, 1985: 700–719. Washington, D.C.: Government Printing Office.

Bows, A. J. 1973. Arthur Andersen opens its books. *The Arthur Andersen Chronicle* 33 (September): 54–59.

Brenner, L. 1991. See no evil: Why do accountants keep giving their stamp of approval to unsound companies? *Newsday* (February 10).

Bricker, R. J., and G. J. Previts, eds. 2002. *The Murphy-Kirk-Beresford Correspondence 1982–1996.* Oxford, Kidlington, U.K.: JAI/Elsevier Science.

Briloff, A. J. 1967. Dirty pooling. *The Accounting Review* 42 (July): 489–496.

———. 1970. Accounting practices and the merger movement. *Notre Dame Lawyer* 45 (Summer): 604–628.

———. 1972. *Unaccountable Accounting.* New York, NY: Harper & Row.

———. 1987. Do management services endanger independence and objectivity? *The CPA Journal* 57 (August): 22–24, 26–27, 29.

Brooks, J. 1973. *The Go-Go Years: When Prices Went Topless.* New York, NY: Ballantine Books.

Burton, J. C. 1971. An educator views the public accounting profession. *The Journal of Accountancy* 132 (September): 47–53.

———. 1974. Elephants, flexibility and the Financial Accounting Standards Board. *The Business Lawyer* 29 (March): 151–154.

———. 1980. A critical look at professionalism and scope of services. *The Journal of Accountancy* 149 (April): 48–56.

———, and R. J. Sack. 1990. Standard setting process in trouble (again). Editorial. *Accounting Horizons* 4 (December): 117–120.

Carey, J. L. 1967. The new pressures on the CPA. In *Ernst & Ernst Symposium for Educators,* Ernst & Ernst, 11–22. [n.p.]

———. 1969. *The Rise of the Accounting Profession: From Technician to Professional 1896–1936.* New York, NY: American Institute of Certified Public Accountants.

———. 1970. *The Rise of the Accounting Profession: To Responsibility and Authority 1937–1969.* New York, NY: American Institute of Certified Public Accountants.

Catlett, G. R. 1969. Better objectives needed to improve accounting principles. *The Journal of Accountancy* 128 (October): 62–65.

Certified Public Accountants. 1932. *Fortune* 5 (June): 62–66, 95–96, 98, 101–102.

Chapin, D. H. 1992. Changing the image of the CPA. *The CPA Journal* 92 (December): 16–18,20,22,24.

Chatov, R. 1975. *Corporate Financial Reporting: Public or Private Control?* New York, NY: The Free Press.

Chenok, P. B. 2000. *Foundations for the Future: The AICPA from 1980 to 1995.* With A. Snyder. Stamford, CT: JAI Press Inc.

The Commission on Auditors' Responsibilities. 1978. *Report, Conclusions, and Recommendations.* New York, NY: The Commission on Auditors' Responsibilities.

Conglomerate Mergers and Acquisitions: Opinion & Analysis. 1970. *St. John's Law Review* 44 (Spring, Special Edition).

Cook, J. M., E. M. Freedman, R. J. Groves, J. C. Madonna, S. F. O'Malley, and L. A. Weinbach. 1992. The liability crisis in the United States: Impact on the accounting profession. *Journal of Accountancy* 174 (November): 18–23.

The CPA Journal Symposium on the Future of Assurance Services. 1996. *The CPA Journal* 66 (May): 14ff.

Cypert, S. A. 1991. *Following the Money: The Inside Story of Accounting's First Mega-Merger.* New York, NY: AMACOM, a division of American Management Association.

Depreciation and Obsolescence. 1920. Bulletin "F." Washington, D.C.: Government Printing Office.

Elliott, R. K. 1995. Professional growth through new assurance services. Report of the Chairman of the AICPA Special Committee on Assurance Services to AICPA Council (October).

Employers' Accounting for Pensions. 1983. New York, NY: Touche Ross & Co.

Evans, J. R. 1984. An evaluation of SEC accounting policies and regulation. In *The SEC and Accounting: The First 50 Years,* edited by R. H. Mundheim and N. E. Leech, 155–167. Amsterdam, The Netherlands: North-Holland.

Federal Regulation and Regulatory Reform. 1976. Report by the Subcommittee on Oversight and Investigations of the Committee on Interstate and Foreign Commerce, House of Representatives, 94th Congress, 2nd Session. Washington, D.C.: Government Printing Office.

Financial Accounting Standards Board (FASB). 1977. *Statement of Position.* Stamford, CT: FASB (April 14).

The First Sixty Years 1913–1973. 1974. Chicago, IL: Arthur Andersen & Co.

Gerth, J. 1990. The savings debacle: How safeguards failed—A blend of tragedy and farce. *The New York Times* (July 3): D1, D5.

Glickauf, J. S. 1971. *Footsteps Toward Professionalism: The Development of an Administrative Services Practice over the Past Twenty-Five Years.* Chicago, IL: Arthur Andersen & Co.

Gorton, D. E. 1991. The SEC decision not to support SFAS No. 19: A case study of the effect of lobbying on standard setting. *Accounting Horizons* 5 (March): 29–41.

Grady, P. 1971. Research in accounting principles. Letter. *The Journal of Accountancy* 131 (April): 24,26.

Grant, E. L., and P. T. Norton, Jr. 1955. *Depreciation.* New York, NY: The Ronald Press Company.

Greenspan, A. 2002. Corporate Governance, a speech delivered at the Stern School of Business, New York University, March 26. Available at: http://www.federal-reserve.gov/boarddocs/speeches/2002.

Gregory, W. R. 1980. Letter to AICPA members attending the special meeting on July 11, 1980. *The CPA Letter* 60 (July): 3–6.

Hawkins, D. F. 1962. *Corporate Financial Disclosure, 1900–1933: A Study of Management Inertia within a Rapidly Changing Environment.* New York, NY: Garland Publishing, 1986.

Hayes, T. C. 1979. Accountants under scrutiny: Consulting jobs called risk to independence. *The New York Times* (June 25): D1, D4.

Hicks, E. L. 1969. APB: The first 3600 days. *The Journal of Accountancy* 128 (September): 56–60.

Ijiri, Y. 1980. An introduction to corporate accounting standards: A review. *The Accounting Review* 55 (October): 620–628.

The Institute Responds . . . 1977. American Institute of Certified Public Accountants (April). [n.p.]

Isbell, D. B. 1970. Continental Vending case: Lessons for the profession. *Journal of Accountancy* 130 (August): 33–40.

Jaenicke, H. R. 1977. *The Effect of Litigation on Independent Auditors.* New York, NY: The Commission on Auditors' Responsibilities.

Keats, C. 1964. *Magnificent Masquerade: The Strange Case of Dr. Coster and Mr. Musica.* New York, NY: Funk & Wagnalls.

Kirk, D. J. 1984. Where is public accounting headed? *World* (Peat Marwick house organ) 18 (4): 29, 31.

Levitt, A. 1996. The guardians of financial truth. Speech delivered at the Financial Reporting Institute, University of Southern California, Los Angeles, CA, June 6. Available at: http://www.sec.gov/news/speech/speecharchive/1996/spch106.txt.

———. 2002. *Take on the Street.* With P. Dwyer. New York, NY: Pantheon Books.

Mason, E. 1985. Statement reproduced in *SEC and Corporate Audits (Part 1),* Hearings before the Subcommittee on Oversight and Investigations of the Committee on Energy and Commerce, House of Representatives, 99th Congress, 1st Session, March 6, 730–760. Washington, D.C.: Government Printing Office.

———. 1994. Public accounting-No longer a profession? *The CPA Journal* 64 (July): 34–37.

A Matter of Principle Splits CPAs. 1963. *Business Week* (January 26): 50, 55–57, 60.

May, G. 0.1926. Corporate publicity and the auditor. *The Journal of Accountancy* 62 (November): 321–326.

————. 1943. *Financial Accounting: A Distillation of Experience*. New York, NY: Macmillan.

McCarten, J. 1939. The greatest accountant in the world. *The New Yorker* 15 (December 16): 86–95.

The McKesson & Robbins Case. 1939. Editorial. *The Journal of Accountancy* 67 (February): 65.

McRoberts, F. 2002. The fall of Andersen. *Chicago Tribune* (September 1): 1, 16, 17.

Mednick, R. 1990. Independence: Let's get back to basics. *Journal of Accountancy* 169 (January): 86–88, 90, 92–93.

————, and G. J. Previts. 1987. The scope of CPA services: A view of the future from the perspective of a century of progress. *Journal of Accountancy* 163 (May): 220ff.

Miller, P. B. W., R. J. Redding, and P. R. Bahnson. 1998. *The FASB: The People, the Process, and the Politics*. Fourth edition. Burr Ridge, IL: Irwin/McGraw-Hill.

Miranti, P., Jr. 1990. *Accountancy Comes of Age: The Development of an American Profession, 1886–1940*. Chapel Hill, NC: The University of North Carolina Press.

Moonitz, M. 1966. Some reflections on the investment credit experience. *Journal of Accounting Research* 4 (Spring): 47–61.

Nelligan, J. L. 1980. Regulation and the accounting profession: The Congressional view. In *Regulation and the Accounting Profession*, edited by J. W. Buckley and J. F. Weston, 109–122. Belmont, CA: Lifetime Learning Publications.

Olson, W. E. 1982. *The Accounting Profession, Years of Trial: 1969–1980*. New York, NY: American Institute of Certified Public Accountants.

Orben, R. A. 1984. An evaluation of the SEC's performance-A product of leadership. In *The SEC and Accounting: The First 50 Years*, edited by R. H. Mundheim and N. E. Leech, 141–148. Amsterdam, The Netherlands: North-Holland.

Our Firm Files Petition with SEC. 1976. *Executive News Briefs* (of Arthur Andersen & Co.) 4 (June): 1–4.

The Palace Revolt at Arthur Andersen. 1979. *Business Week* (October 29): 52.

The Panel on Audit Effectiveness. 2000. *Report and Recommendations*. Stamford, CT: Public Oversight Board.

Paton, W. A. 1971. Earmarks of a profession—and the APB. *The Journal of Accountancy* 131 (January): 37–45.

————, and A. C. Littleton. 1940. *An Introduction to Corporate Accounting Standards*. American Accounting Association. [n.p.]

Previts, G. J. 1985. *The Scope of CPA Services*. New York, NY: John Wiley & Sons.

————, and B. D. Merino. 1998. *A History of Accountancy in the United States: The Cultural Significance of Accounting*. Columbus, OH: Ohio State University Press.

The Public Accounting Profession: Meeting the Needs of a Changing World. 1991. Arthur Andersen & Co., Coopers & Lybrand, Deloitte & Touche, Ernst & Young, KPMG Peat Marwick and Price Waterhouse. [n.p.]

Public Oversight Board (POB). 1979. *Scope of Services by CPA Firms*. New York, NY: POB.

————. 1993. *In the Public Interest*. A special report. Stamford, CT: POB.

Rappaport, L. H. 1963. Forces influencing accounting: The stock exchanges. *1963 Conference of Accountants: Accounting Papers*, 33–43. The University of Tulsa. [n.p.]

Report of the Committee on Establishment of an Accounting Commission. 1971. *The Accounting Review* 46 (July): 609–616.

Report of the National Commission on Fraudulent Financial Reporting. 1987. National Commission on Fraudulent Financial Reporting. [n.p.]

Report of the Special Committee on Equity Funding. 1975. New York, NY: American Institute of Certified Public Accountants.

Report of the Study on Establishment of Accounting Principles. 1972. *Establishing Financial Accounting Standards*. New York, NY: American Institute of Certified Public Accountants.

Report to Congress on the Accounting Profession and the Commission's Oversight Role. 1978. July 1. Washington, D.C.: Securities and Exchange Commission.

Restructuring Professional Standards to Achieve Professional Excellence in a Changing Environment. 1986. Report of the Special Committee on Standards of Professional Conduct for Certified Public Accountants. New York, NY: American Institute of Certified Public Accountants.

Revenge of the Nerds. 2003. *The Economist* (May 31): 68, 73.

Revsine, L. 1991. The selective financial misrepresentation hypothesis. *Accounting Horizons* 5 (December): 16–27.

Ruder, D. S. 1989. Private sector accounting standards: The SEC's oversight role. Typescript speech before the AICPA Sixteenth National Conference on Current SEC Developments, Washington, D.C., January 10.

Sack, R. J., and R. Tangreti. 1987. ESM: Implications for the profession. *Journal of Accountancy* 163 (April): 94–100.

Savoie, L. M. 1968. The professional goals of the Institute. In *Leonard M. Savoie: Words from the Past, Thoughts for Today*, edited by D. E. Tidrick, 111–114. New York, NY: Garland Publishing, 1995.

———. 1974. A view of the accounting profession and accounting education from a professional accountant in industry. In *Leonard M. Savoie: Words from the Past, Thoughts for Today*, edited by D. E. Tidrick, 57–66. New York, NY: Garland Publishing, 1995.

Schuetze, W. P. 1994. A mountain or a molehill? *Accounting Horizons* 8 (March): 69–75.

SEC and Corporate Audits (Part 1). 1985. Hearings before the Subcommittee on Oversight and Investigations of the Committee on Energy and Commerce, House of Representatives, 99th Congress, 1st Session, February 20. Washington, D.C.: Government Printing Office.

SEC Staff Analysis [of the AICPA White Paper]. 1997. Prepared by the Office of the Chief Accountant. December. Washington, D.C.: Securities and Exchange Commission.

Securities and Exchange Commission (SEC). 2002. *Strengthening the Commission's Requirements Regarding Auditor Independence*. Release Nos. 33-8154, 34-46934; 35-27610; IC-25838; IA-2088, FR-64. December 2. [Washington, D.C.: Securities and Exchange Commission.]

Securities and Exchange Commission Report to Congress on the Accounting Profession and the Commission's Oversight Role. 1978. Washington, D.C.: Securities and Exchange Commission.

Securities and Exchange Commission Report to Congress on the Accounting Profession and the Commission's Oversight Role. 1979. Prepared for the Subcommittee on Governmental Efficiency and the District of Columbia of the Committee on Governmental Affairs, United States Senate, by the Securities and Exchange Commission (96th Congress, 1st Session). Washington, D.C.: Government Printing Office.

Seidler, L. J., F. Andrews, and M. J. Epstein. 1977. *The Equity Funding Papers: The Anatomy of a Fraud*. Santa Barbara, CA: Wiley/Hamilton.

Seligman, J. 1982. *The Transformation of Wall Street: A History of the Securities and Exchange Commission and Modern Corporate Finance*. Boston, MA: Houghton Mifflin.

Shaplen, R. 1955. Annals of crime: The metamorphosis of Philip Musica. *The New Yorker* 31 (October 22): 49–81, (October 29): 39–79.

Simonetti, G., Jr., and A. R. Andrews. 1987. "RAP-man"—It's devouring GAAP. *Review* (of Price Waterhouse) 31 (3): 55–58.

Sommerfeld, R. M., and J. E. Easton. 1987. The CPA's tax practice today—And how it got that way. *Journal of Accountancy* 163 (May): 166–172, 174–176, 178–179.

Special Committee on Standards of Professional Conduct for CPAs. 1985. Interim Report to Council for Discussion at Break-Out Session. Typescript dated May 16. New York, NY: American Institute of Certified Public Accountants.

Staff Report on Auditor Independence. 1994. Prepared by the Office of the Chief Accountant. Securities and Exchange Commission. March. [n.p.]

Status Report No. 50. 1977. Stamford, CT: Financial Accounting Standards Board.

Staub, W. A. 1942. *Auditing Developments during the Present Century.* Cambridge, MA: Harvard University Press.

Sterling, R. R. 1967. Conservatism: The fundamental principle of valuation in traditional accounting. *Abacus* 3 (December): 329–352.

Stevens, M. 1981. *The Big Eight.* New York, NY: Macmillan.

———. 1985. *The Accounting Wars.* New York, NY: Macmillan.

———. 1991. *The Big Six: The Selling Out of America's Top Accounting Firms.* New York, NY: Simon & Schuster.

Strait, A. M. 1993. A call for change. *Research in Accounting Regulation* 7: 183–186.

Study Group on Business Income. 1952. *Changing Concepts of Business Income.* New York, NY: Macmillan.

Swanson, T. 1972. *Touche Ross: A Biography.* Touche Ross & Co. [n.p.]

Tietjen, A. C. 1970. Financial reporting responsibilities. *The Price Waterhouse Review* 15 (Spring): 6–15.

Traub, J. 1990. *Too Good to be True: The Outlandish Story of Wedtech.* New York, NY: Doubleday.

Users and Abusers: Here's The Bottom Line on the Accounting Profession. 1987. Interview with Arthur R. Wyatt. *Barron's* (September 14): 13ff.

Van Riper, R. 1994. *Setting Standards for Financial Reporting: FASB and the Struggle for Control of a Critical Process.* Westport, CT: Quorum Books.

A Vision of Grandeur. 1988. Arthur Andersen & Co., S.C. [n.p.]

Walters, R. E. 1984. Looking Back in Sorrow. *International Accounting Bulletin* Special Report (January): S/6–S/9.

Weinstein, G. W. 1987. *The Bottom Line—Inside Accounting Today.* New York, NY: NAL Books/New American Library.

Wiesen, J. 1978. *The Securities Acts and Independent Auditors: What Did Congress Intend?* New York, NY: American Institute of Certified Public Accountants.

Williams, H. M. 1980. The 1980s: The future of the accounting profession. In *The Development of SEC Accounting,* edited by G. J. Previts, 418–427. Reading, MA: Addison-Wesley Publishing Company, 1981.

Williams, P. D. 1971. In *Footsteps Toward Professionalism: The Development of an Administrative Services Practice over the Past Twenty-five Years,* edited by J. S. Glickauf, v–vi. Chicago, IL: Arthur Andersen & Co.

Wise, T. A. 1960. The auditors have arrived. *Fortune* 62 (November): 151ff., (December): 144ff.

———. 1982. *Peat, Marwick, Mitchell & Co. 85 Years.* Peat, Marwick, Mitchell & Co. [n.p.]

Wootton, C. W., and C. M. Wolk. 1992. The development of "The Big Eight" accounting firms in the United States, 1900 to 1990. *The Accounting Historians Journal* 19 (June): 1–27.

———, and C. Normand. 2003. An historical perspective on mergers and acquisitions by major US accounting firms. *Accounting History* 8 (May): 25–60.

Wyatt, A. R. 1988. *Professionalism in standard-setting.* The CPA Journal 58 (July): 20ff.

———. 1989. Accounting standards and the professional auditor. *Accounting Horizons* 3 (June): 96–102.

———. 1991. Accounting standard setting at a crossroads. *Accounting Horizons* 5 (September): 110–114.'

Zeff, S. A. 1966. *The American Accounting Association: Its First 50 Years*. American Accounting Association. [n.p.]

———. 1972. *Forging Accounting Principles in Five Countries: A History and an Analysis of Trends*. Champaign, IL: Stipes Publishing Co.

———. 1978. The rise of "economic consequences." *Stanford Lectures in Accounting 1978*, 11–19. Stanford, CA: Graduate School of Business, Stanford University.

———. 1986. Big Eight firms and the accounting literature: The falloff in advocacy writing. *Journal of Accounting, Auditing & Finance* (new series, 1) (Spring): 131–154.

———. 1987. Does the CPA belong to a profession? *Accounting Horizons* 1 (June): 65–68.

———. 1992. The decline of professionalism. *De Accountant* (The Netherlands) 98 (January): 264–267.

———. 1998a. Whither the independent audit? *Chartered Accountants Journal* 77 (February): 41.

———. 1998b. Independence and standard setting. *Critical Perspectives on Accounting* 9 (October): 535–543.

———. 2001. The work of the Special Committee on Research Program. *The Accounting Historians Journal* 28 (December): 141–186.

The Primacy of "Present Fairly" in the Auditor's Report[*]

Stephen A. Zeff
Rice University

ABSTRACT

In this paper, the author examines the historical evolution in the United States of the use of the term "present fairly" in the auditor's report, as well as the experience and arguments in the United States and Canada regarding the use of a "two-part" opinion in the report. He then develops an argument for the adoption of a "two-part" opinion, decoupling "present fairly" from conformity with generally accepted accounting principles, which would place primary emphasis on "present fairly".

Keywords   Auditing standards; Auditor's report; Present fairly

LA PRÉSÉANCE DE LA FORMULE « DONNE UNE IMAGE FIDÈLE » DANS LE RAPPORT DU VÉRIFICATEUR

RÉSUMÉ

L'auteur examine l'évolution, au fil du temps, de l'usage de la formule « donne une image fidèle » (« *present fairly* ») dans le rapport du vérificateur aux États-Unis, ainsi que l'expérience du Canada et des États-Unis et les arguments qui y sont invoqués pour justifier l'expression d'une « opinion en deux parties » dans le rapport. Il élabore ensuite une argumentation légitimant l'adoption d'une telle opinion distinguant l'« image fidèle » de la conformité aux PCGR, ce qui donnerait préséance à l'« image fidèle ».

---

* This paper was given as the Emanuel Saxe Lecture, Baruch College, City University of New York, on April 10, 2006. The author is grateful to the following commentators on earlier versions of the paper: Andy Bailey, Denny Beresford, Doug Carmichael, Bala Dharan, Michael Granof, Dan Guy, Jonathan Hayward, Bob Herz, Bill Kinney, Peter Knutson, Chris Nobes, Hugo Nurnberg, Larry Revsine, and Brian Rountree. The author is solely responsible for what remains.

One of the hottest issues in accounting today is "principles versus rules", but it goes back a long way. I have in my files a letter in which the top partner in one of the major U.S. public accounting firms wrote me as follows:

> I suspect that the greatest single difficulty at the present time is that we have forgotten what the word "principle" means. Many of the accounting controversies today and in the recent past actually deal with rather detailed accounting treatments and methods.

The author of these words was Herman W. Bevis, the senior partner of Price Waterhouse and a former member of the Accounting Principles Board (APB). He wrote them to me in a letter dated May 5, 1967. Leading figures in the accounting profession later complained about *APB Opinion No. 15*, issued in 1969, on earnings per share being a "cookbook" of rules (see Zeff, 2003: 197). "Principles versus rules" is hardly a new issue in this country.

What I wish to do in this paper is to draw on history to propose an important change in the opinion that the auditor gives on a company's financial statements. I wish to refocus the "principles versus rules" controversy from the role and performance of the standard setter to the role and performance of the external auditor. My proposal is to decouple the two elements in the phrase "present fairly in conformity with generally accepted accounting principles", to "present fairly and were prepared in conformity with generally accepted accounting principles", thus obliging the external auditor to give two opinions, not just one. The first opinion, on a matter of principle, is whether the financial statements "present fairly". The second opinion, on a matter of conformity with the practices specified in accounting standards and other authoritative pronouncements, is conformity with generally accepted accounting principles (GAAP).

The focus of my paper is primarily the audit environment in North America.

I will first delve into some history and then indicate how the issue of giving a separate opinion on "present fairly" is a live one today. I will conclude with my argument.

A BIT OF HISTORY

Origin of "Present Fairly"

The origin in the United States of the term "present fairly" in the standard form of the auditor's report may be traced to the report of a special committee set up in 1932 by the American Institute of Accountants (AIA). After engaging in correspondence with the New York Stock Exchange (NYSE), the special committee recommended the "modern" form of the auditor's report, whose opinion paragraph included the wording "fairly present, in accordance with accepted principles of accounting" (AIA, 1934: 31). Walter A. Staub, the senior partner of Lybrand, Ross Bros. & Montgomery and one of the six signatories of the special committee's letter to the NYSE of December 21, 1933, in which it recommended the format of the auditor's report, wrote in 1942 that the committee meant that the auditor should give separate opinions on "fairly present" and "in accordance with accepted principles of accounting" (Staub, 1942: 75). Perhaps the comma between "fairly present" and "in accordance with accepted principles of accounting" was intended to signify a disengagement of the two elements into two separate opinions.

Note should be taken of the somewhat embarrassing origin of "fairly". The term "fairly . . . present" was an innovation put forward in January 1933 by Richard Whitney, the president of the New York Stock Exchange (AIA, 1934: 16). Five years later, Whitney pleaded guilty to two counts of grand larceny, was expelled from the NYSE, and was sentenced to a term of 5 to 10 years in Sing Sing prison.[1]

George O. May, the chair of the Institute's special committee, made it clear that "principles of accounting" was intended to mean norms of accepted usage, and not the rules, conventions, or methods that are applications of the principles (May, 1937: 423–4).[2] The special committee believed the principles were few in number. The term "generally accepted accounting principles" was used for the first time in an Institute publication in 1936 (AIA, 1936: 1). The idea was that accounting principles had to secure acceptance by more than just a few companies—thus the term "generally". "Accepted" was preferred over "acceptable" as setting a more objective standard.[3] This was before the Institute authorized a committee to develop a body of accounting principles on a programmatic basis in order to guide judgements. Despite the intention to limit "accounting principles" to norms of accepted usage, in 1949 the authors of the leading auditing textbook said that "generally accepted accounting principles" had come to mean rules, conventions, and doctrines (Montgomery, Lenhart, and Jennings, 1949: 66).

By 1937, it was reported that the special committee's recommended format was being used in substance by the auditors of more than 95 percent of the corporations, other than railroads, listed on the New York Stock Exchange (The auditor's report, 1937: 246–7).

In 1939, the AIA's Committee on Auditing Procedure altered the wording of the opinion paragraph to: "present fairly . . . , in conformity with

---

[1] For Whitney's downfall, see "Richard Whitney," Wikipedia (http://en.wikipedia.org/wiki/ Richard_Whitney) and Seligman (2003: 169).

[2] For further discussion, see Storey (1964: 11) and AIA (1934: 4–14).

[3] Letter from Samuel J. Broad to the author, dated January 3, 1966. Broad was chair of the AIA committee that drafted the 1936 report, *Examination of Financial Statements by Independent Public Accountants* (AIA, 1936).

generally accepted accounting principles" (Committee on Auditing Procedure, 1939). Andrew Barr, who was on the accounting staff of the Securities and Exchange Commission (SEC) in 1939, subsequently said that he was "fairly certain that SEC staff urged including 'generally' to strengthen the [auditor's] certificate".[4] This wording has, but for a recent change to indicate the country of origin for GAAP (for example, U.S. GAAP or Canadian GAAP), remained essentially the same in all the years since then.[5] Again, the comma, mentioned above, appeared. The comma continued to appear in the same format recommended in *Statement on Auditing Standards (SAS) No. 2* (Auditing Standards Executive Committee [AudSEC], 1974: para. 7). The comma was removed in 1988, in *SAS No. 58* (Auditing Standards Board [ASB], 1988a: para. 8). After conferring with several of those who took part in the development of *SAS No. 58*, I have concluded, with some surprise, that there was no awareness that the deletion of the comma was a substantive issue.[6]

But this was not the end of the "comma affair". Four years later, in *SAS No. 69* (ASB, 1992), which superseded and reaffirmed *SAS No. 5* (AudSEC, 1975) (see below), the comma suddenly reappeared in the rendering of the standard form of the auditor's opinion (ASB, 1992: para. 1). Evidently, punctuation was not a strong suit at the Auditing Standards Board.

The comma finally disappeared from auditing statements in 2000, when *SAS No. 93* was issued (ASB, 2000: para. 3).

What practice do the Big 4 audit firms follow? In a casual sample of 75 annual reports for 2004 issued by U.S. companies, I found that Deloitte, Ernst & Young, and KPMG, with a few exceptions, insert the comma, while PricewaterhouseCoopers, also with a few exceptions, omits the comma. Evidently, there is a "comma crisis" in the profession!

"Present Fairly": The Upside

In 1952, Eric L. Kohler wrote in *A Dictionary for Accountants* that "present fairly" meant that the presentation of the financial statements "conforms to overall tests of truth, justness, equity, and candor" (1952: 177).

---

[4] Letter from Andrew Barr to the author, dated September 3, 1987. The term "generally accepted accounting principles" appeared for the first time in an SEC annual report in 1939 (SEC, 1940: 47–8, 118).

[5] The decision to specify the country of origin was made in *SAS No. 93* (Auditing Standards Board [ASB], 2000: para. 3).

[6] Carelessness about the comma was evident before then. In *The Independent Auditor's Reporting Standards in Three Nations* (Accountants International Study Group [AISG], 1969), a cooperative venture among the professional accounting bodies in the United States, the United Kingdom, and Canada, the comma was omitted from the standard form of the U.S. auditor's report given in paragraph 26. This AISG booklet was prepared by staff of the American Institute of Certified Public Accountants (AICPA).

In 1961, R. K. Mautz and Hussein A. Sharaf, in their classic work *The Philosophy of Auditing* (1961: 169), wrote:

> [T]he determination of accounting propriety is ultimately a matter of audit judgment. Although the auditor borrows generally accepted accounting principles from the field of accounting, he does so with full recognition that he may have to reject their application in some cases. To the extent that they are satisfactory in bringing about a realistic portrayal of the facts of business activity and conditions he is grateful to them; to the extent that they fail, he must draw upon his knowledge of their goals and develop solutions which his experience and judgment tell him are constructively useful.

In 1969, Judge Henry J. Friendly of the U.S. Court of Appeals for the Second Circuit ruled in the *Continental Vending* case (*United States v. Simon*, 1969) that the auditor's judgement about what is called for by GAAP does not necessarily mean that the financial statements "present fairly". In effect, he regarded "present fairly" and "in conformity with GAAP" as separate opinions. His ruling is still valid law today (Mano, Mouritsen, and Pace, 2006: 60).[7]

In February 1975, John C. (Sandy) Burton, the SEC chief accountant, sided with those who believe that " 'fairly' adds something significant to the auditor's representation beyond attesting to conformity with generally accepted accounting principles" (1975: 28). He said that the SEC "for many years has taken the position that fairness connotes something beyond conformity with generally accepted accounting principles" (32).

In 1975, SEC commissioner Al Sommer made the point even more emphatically: "The increased concern with the fairness of financial statements poses an opportunity to move away from the rigidities of generally accepted accounting principles and other deterrents to meaningful financial disclosure" (1976: 23).

"Present Fairly": The Downside

"Present fairly" has had an uncertain career. In 1972, probably influenced by the *Continental Vending* decision, the Institute's Committee on Auditing Procedure recommended deletion of "fairly" from the auditor's report, but in the end it withdrew the recommendation.[8]

In 1974, Douglas Carmichael, the Institute's director of auditing standards, contended that a two-part opinion "might be as chaotic as using

---

[7] For a recent application of *United States v. Simon*, see the decision reported in the case of *United States of America v. Bernard J. Ebbers* in the Court of Appeals for the Second Circuit, dated July 28, 2006.

[8] See Carmichael and Winters (1982: 14–5). For the Committee on Auditing Procedure's proposed format of the auditor's report, see Aranoff (1975: 31–2).

fairness alone. The state of confusion would be blatantly apparent in auditor's reports" (1974: 85). He concluded that "the essential meaning of the auditor's opinion that financial statements are fairly presented in conformity with GAAP is that the accounting principles a company uses are appropriate for the circumstances to which they are applied" (86).

In July 1975, the Auditing Standards Executive Committee issued *SAS No. 5*, also a reaction to *Continental Vending* , which said that the auditor should apply "fairness" within the framework of GAAP. "Without that framework", *SAS No. 5* went on, "the auditor would have no uniform standard for judging the presentation of financial position, results of operations, and changes in financial position in financial statements" (AudSEC, 1975: para. 3). To the untutored reader, this advice seems to suggest that "present fairly" adds little, if anything, beyond conformity with GAAP. In February 1975, Sandy Burton pointed out that he was instructed by the SEC Commissioners to advise AudSEC, "We believe that it is apparent from court cases and other sources that 'present fairly' cannot be defined by simple references to generally accepted accounting principles" (Burton, 1975: 34). Hence, AudSEC instead referred to "the framework" of GAAP, which was not much different.

In 1978, the American Institute of Certified Public Accountants (AICPA) Commission on Auditors' Responsibilities recommended, with the full support of its founding chair, former SEC chair Manuel F. Cohen, that "present fairly" be deleted from the auditor's report because fairness "is not a property that can be objectively measured by the auditor" (Commission on Auditors' Responsibilities, 1978: 13, 14). Two years later, the Auditing Standards Board proposed the deletion of "fairly" from the auditor's report because "the word is subjective and is interpreted differently by different users of the auditor's report" (ASB, 1980: 6). Finally, after reading the letters of comment and reconsidering, the board decided not to delete "fairly" (Carmichael and Winters, 1982: 18). Carmichael was the research director of the Commission and was the AICPA's Vice-President, Auditing at the time of these deliberations on "fairly".

"Present Fairly" Versus "Not Misleading"

Since at least 1938, the SEC has held financial statements to the standard of being not "misleading", a term that would appeal more to lawyers than would "fair presentation". The term "misleading" is cited in the SEC's *Accounting Series Release No. 4* (SEC, 1938), in rule 4-01(a) of the SEC's *Regulation S-X*, and in rule 203 under the AICPA's *Code of Professional Ethics*, now known as the *Code of Professional Conduct*, which took effect on March 1, 1973 (AICPA, 1972: 22). The latter obliges the auditor, in "unusual circumstances", to countenance a departure in the financial statements "from an accounting principle promulgated by bodies designated by Council to establish such principles" (such as the Financial Accounting Standards Board [FASB]) where the use of the principle would have caused the financial statements to be "misleading". Interestingly, the first draft of rule 203 referred to "fair presentation" instead of to "misleading" (Revised text, 1972: 9, 11). Sandy Burton said that rule 203 "seems to indicate that a fairness test should be applied, at least on a negative basis" (Burton, 1975: 34). And Judge Friendly, in the *Continental Vending* decision, seemed to use "fair presentation" and "not materially false and misleading" as rough equivalents.

It strikes me that "fair presentation" means that the financial statements meet a positive standard of informativeness. By contrast, "not misleading" connotes that readers have not been led astray. The object of financial reporting is to convey useful financial information, not merely to avoid a deception. R. J. Chambers once wrote that "if accounting is to be related to choices, it requires 'leading information,' not 'not misleading information' " (1982: 53). I agree with Chambers that "not misleading" is not a phrase equivalent in substance and connotation to "fair presentation".

Mautz and Sharaf (1961: 169, footnote omitted) have written:

> An approach sometimes followed is one that finds acceptable any [accounting] method that is "not misleading". Such a negative attitude should not be condoned and certainly does not satisfy the concept of accounting propriety. Surely the auditor should insist upon something more constructive than the mere absence of injury; unless a practice actually aids and furthers understanding, it should be held deficient.

SHOULD THE AUDITOR GIVE ONE OR TWO OPINIONS? THE RECORD SO FAR

As mentioned above, Walter Staub believed in 1942 that his special committee's recommended form of the auditor's report implied the giving of separate opinions on "fairly present" and "in accordance with accepted principles of accounting". Whether auditors in the 1930s believed that they were to give separate opinions is not known.

Arthur Andersen & Co. Adopts the Two-Part Opinion

In 1946, the upstart Chicago-based accounting firm of Arthur Andersen & Co., whose lead partners—Arthur Andersen himself and Leonard Spacek—believed that the firm should stand up for what it believed, decided that the firm could no longer countenance giving an opinion that clients' financial statements "present fairly" when they used accounting

---

⁹ This section on Arthur Andersen & Co.'s two-part opinion is based on Zeff (1992).

principles or applications thereof that were, in its judgement, not appropriate, even if they were "generally accepted".[9] The firm therefore decoupled its single opinion into two, on "present fairly" and on "in conformity with generally accepted accounting principles". To do so, it added three words (shown here in italics) in the opinion paragraph of its auditor's report: "present fairly *and were prepared* in conformity with generally accepted accounting principles". The firm continued to use the two-part opinion in its auditor's report until 1962.

The firm had two levels of concern about GAAP. First, some generally accepted practices were not appropriate in the circumstances or were not believed to be proper accounting. Examples at that time were full costing versus successful-efforts costing in oil and gas exploration and the propriety of deferred tax accounting when companies adopted full costing in their financial statements but successful-efforts costing for tax purposes. Today, one could cite last-in, first-out (LIFO) versus first-in, first-out (FIFO), the use of accelerated versus straight-line depreciation methods, whether the capital lease or operating lease method should be adopted for long-term, noncancelable leases—if bright lines do not appear in the standard, as with *International Accounting Standard (IAS) No. 17 Revised* (International Accounting Standards Committee [IASC], 1997)—whether the conversion of bonds into stock should be accounted for at historical cost or at the market value of the issued shares, whether the proper treatment of marketable securities should be as "available for sale" or "trading", and by what method the cash received from installment sales should be recognized as revenue. Andersen believed that it was the professional responsibility of an audit firm to assess the propriety of the manner in which clients applied accounting principles, and not just to accept any application that was generally accepted. It believed that some applications of GAAP did not "present fairly" in all circumstances.

It is interesting to speculate whether such an interpretation of the audit firm's responsibility, by overriding the unquestioning adherence to GAAP rules, would have prevented any of the accounting and auditing scandals we have witnessed in the last number of years.

Second, Andersen believed that some non-GAAP did "present fairly". The best illustration of this was the firm's advocacy of depreciation based on general price-level restatements or current valuations of fixed assets, especially for its public utility clients, because of the importance of calculating a fair rate of return. In the 1950s and 1960s, the firm used its auditor's report to comment favorably on the "fair presentation" of these departures from GAAP (see below).

What did the SEC think of Andersen's two-part opinion? As far as is known, none of the three chief accountants between 1946 and 1962—William W. Werntz, Earle C. King, and Andrew Barr—objected to it. They did insist that GAAP be followed, but the firm's opinion on "present fairly" was its own decision.

In 1958, Carman G. Blough, a former SEC chief accountant who was then the AICPA's director of research, criticized Andersen's two-part opinion, arguing that "present fairly" should be judged within the framework of GAAP and should not be decided by each auditor "for himself " (1958a: 76). In this respect, Blough anticipated *SAS No. 5*, issued 18 years later. Another prominent accountant, Maurice E. Peloubet, a former president of both the New York State Society of Certified Public Accountants and the New Jersey Society of Certified Public Accountants, as well as a former member of the AIA's Committees on Auditing Procedure and Accounting Procedure, disagreed with Blough. He argued that, where there are choices within GAAP, it is incumbent on the auditor to decide whether the methods chosen by the client are appropriate in the circumstances. If not, the auditor should qualify his opinion on fairness. Otherwise, Peloubet said, "why bother about 'present fairly'?" (1958: 73).

Arthur Andersen's 16-year experiment with the two-part opinion represented a pioneering attempt to communicate the firm's judgement on the propriety of the accounting norms used in its clients' financial statements, and thus to infuse more meaning into the auditor's report.

Why did Arthur Andersen revert to the single opinion in 1962? The reasons were several, but one was singled out by Leonard Spacek: "We could not get our clients to prepare statements according to our view and be out of step with other companies".[10]

By the second half of the 1970s, Arthur Andersen's position on "present fairly" had changed. It wrote, " 'Fairness' in the presentation of financial data is a desirable objective, but the goal should be an *authoritative adoption* of 'fair' standards and principles on behalf of the profession [that is, by the standard-setter] and not the *personal definition* of 'fairness' by thousands of auditors" (Arthur Andersen & Co., 1977: 39).

Alexander Grant & Company Also Supports the Two-Part Opinion

Alexander Grant & Company, another major accounting firm based in Chicago, signified its support of the two-part opinion in its submission to the Accounting Objectives Study Group, known as the Trueblood Committee, in 1972.[11] Charles Werner, who testified at the Study Group's public hearing on behalf of the partners of the firm, said, "we believe that more is expected of us as professionals than simply compliance with a rulebook." He asked, "isn't the concept of fairness in presentation as

---

[10] Letter from Leonard Spacek to the author, dated June 8, 1986.
[11] The firm's suggested auditor's opinion was reproduced in Rosenfield and Lorensen (1974: 80).

clear to the professional accountant as honesty and decency are to the public?" (Werner, 1972: 1.59). There is no sign, however, that the firm actually used the two-part opinion in its audit engagements.

Canada Adopts the Two-Part Opinion

It was not only Arthur Andersen that broke the mold. From 1967 (some would say even earlier) to 1976, the Canadian Institute of Chartered Accountants (CICA) required the auditor to give two opinions, on "present fairly" and on conformity with GAAP.[12] It seems that there was no clear rationale behind the adoption of the two-part opinion. The decision to move to a single opinion in 1976 was, in part, because one major audit firm allowed a client to use an accounting practice, the discounting of deferred tax, without noting that it was a departure from GAAP. The practice had little support in Canada and caused a furor within the profession. Another reason for the change was that the regulatory authorities declared the *CICA Handbook* to be the authoritative source of GAAP. It was therefore decided that the *CICA Handbook*, not each auditor, should be the arbiter of GAAP. But the CICA's decision in 1976 to change to a single opinion said that "the auditor must exercise his professional judgment as to the appropriateness of the selection and application of [accounting] principles to the particular circumstances of an enterprise" (CICA, 1977: section 5400.13, "The Auditor's Standard Report"), which led one commentator to exclaim, "In effect, we still have a two-part opinion!" (Johnston, 1979: 53). In effect, the CICA had seemed to exempt only non-GAAP from the opinion on "fairness".

Contemporary Signs of Interest in the Primacy of "Present Fairly"

Sarbanes-Oxley Act (2002)

In the Sarbanes-Oxley Act of 2002, the term "fairly present" in connection with corporate financial reporting entered federal legislation for the first time, in reference to the certification by the chief executive officer (CEO) and the chief financial officer (CFO) of their company's annual and quarterly reports, including the financial statements. Section 302(a)(3) mandates that these corporate officers certify that "the financial statements, and other information included in the report, fairly present in all material respects the financial condition and results of operations of the issuer". "Fairly present" stands as the lone criterion of propriety, without any reference to conformity with GAAP. Lynn Turner, who helped draft that provision, has said that he and the Senate Banking Committee's staff, who managed the

---

[12] See Zeff (1992: 444–7) and Eckel (1973).

drafting of the bill, wanted to preserve the spirit of the *Continental Vending* decision, which elevated "present fairly" to a position of primacy in the auditor's report. Especially in the light of recent accounting scandals, they believed strongly that preparers should not be allowed to hide behind GAAP (Turner, 2005).

If preparers should not be allowed to hide behind GAAP in this certification, should they be allowed to take refuge in GAAP when their auditors opine on whether their financial statements "present fairly"?

IAS No. 1 (2003)

IAS No. 1, "Presentation of Financial Statements", issued in 1997 by the International Accounting Standards Committee and revised in 2003 by the International Accounting Standards Board (IASB), expresses a preference to treat "fair presentation" as an overriding concept and not, as in the United States, as coextensive with GAAP. To be sure, the IASB counsels, "In virtually all circumstances, a fair presentation is achieved by compliance with applicable [IASB standards]" (IASB, 2003: paras. 13, 15, 17, 18). Above all, the purport of the revised standard is that "fair presentation" means adhering to the objective of financial statements and the definitions in its conceptual framework.

U.S. Comptroller General's Address (2004)

On August 10, 2004, at the American Accounting Association's annual meeting in Orlando, U.S. Comptroller General David M. Walker, a former partner in Arthur Andersen & Co., argued in a plenary address that auditors should give two opinions: one on "present fairly" and one on conformity with GAAP.[13]

Public Company Accounting Oversight Board Meeting (2005)

The Public Company Accounting Oversight Board held a 25-minute discussion of the following question at the October 5, 2005 meeting of its Standing Advisory Group:

> B4. Would a requirement for the auditor to express separate opinions on whether the financial statements (1) present fairly and (2) are in conformity with GAAP improve the quality of audits or audit reports? If so, how? (Office of the Chief Auditor, 2005: 10)

---

[13] The Government Accountability Office (GAO) kindly supplied the slides for Walker's address. The GAO, then the General Accounting Office, took a similar position for a short period in the early 1970s. See Rosenfield and Lorensen (1974: 80).

Views were expressed on both sides during the meeting.

These recent developments suggest that the subject of this paper continues to be a live one in accounting and regulatory circles. It is now my intention to develop the argument.

SHOULD THE AUDITOR GIVE ONE OR TWO OPINIONS? THE ARGUMENT

A Possible Framework

Expectations rose for auditors in the 1960s and 1970s, and they have risen again since the beginning of the 1990s. Fair value accounting has become a riveting issue not only in standard-setting circles but also for SEC chair Richard C. Breeden, if only because of the failure of historical cost accounting to reveal massive unrealized losses in mortgage portfolios until after many savings and loans associations had entered bankruptcy. Breeden convened a conference entitled "Relevance in Financial Reporting: Moving Toward Market Value Accounting" on November 15, 1991, the first conference on accounting standards ever hosted by the SEC, a body that has, with few exceptions, always championed historical cost accounting.[14] During the 1990s, issues such as accounting for marketable securities and other financial instruments, employee stock options, and business combinations have sidelined historical cost accounting in favor of a wider use of fair values. Concerns have also been expressed at the SEC and elsewhere about the absence, in large measure, of intangibles from company balance sheets, which, for many companies, may be the bulk of their total asset values. On April 11–12, 1996, SEC commissioner Steven M. H. Wallman convened an SEC symposium on "Financial Accounting and Reporting of Intangible Assets", which addressed the omission of many intangibles from company balance sheets. One sees good evidence, therefore, that the SEC has begun to question the propriety of long-standing GAAP.

There has been a growing belief that a company's financial statements should reflect the economic substance of transactions, also characterized as economic reality. In a leading financial accounting textbook, Lawrence Revsine, Daniel Collins, and Bruce Johnson state that U.S. financial reports are "intended to reflect the underlying economic events and activities of the reporting entity" (2002: 943). Yet in the United States some believe that the "political" compromises made in the setting of accounting standards have led to a significant diminution of the meaningfulness of financial statements. In his last month as SEC chief accountant, in October 2005, Donald Nicolaisen, a former partner in PricewaterhouseCoopers, said in an open

---

[14] For a report on the conference, see Atchley (1991).

meeting, "If I were to opine on a set of financial statements with my own views, there are few that I would find to be other than misleading" (Nicolaisen, 2005). He blamed this circumstance on compromised accounting standards. Is this where GAAP has brought us?

The financial press often cites "present fairly" as a benchmark that it believes is implied by the wording of the standard form of the auditor's report.[15]

In 1950, a partner in a Big 8 firm who was president of the New York State Society of Certified Public Accountants wrote that "[a]ccounts are 'fair' if they are impartial, equitable" (Cochrane, 1950: 458), but that characterization is an anachronism in this day and age. In 1977, a leading Canadian author wrote, "To 'present fairly in accordance with GAAP' is to apply GAAP intelligently, judiciously and appropriately to the fact situation covered by the financial statements" (Anderson, 1977: 485). That is also a period piece. Today, there is an overriding concern that the financial statements reflect economic reality or, otherwise put, the economic substance of the transactions. GAAP, detailed and compromised as it is, will not necessarily reflect this reality. In some major areas, such as accounting for leases and pensions, it is far from economic reality. Paul Miller and Paul Bahnson recently wrote, "We feel so strongly about FASB's erroneous premise that compliance with GAAP automatically yields useful financial reports that we're producing three more columns that show how today's GAAP is too compromised, flexible and outdated to produce what the capital markets need" (2005: 14).

My premise is that principles should supplant, or at least supplement, rules in the conduct of the audit, just as they are being proposed to govern the setting of accounting standards. It should not be enough that the auditor's opinion reflects little more than a ticking off of the company's accounting methods against the rules of GAAP, even as challenging as that assignment is today. To serve the readers of financial statements and make the opinion paragraph of the auditor's report meaningful and not just a boilerplate, the auditor should be expected to treat "present fairly" as a substantive issue, and not as a "rubber stamp" of GAAP. Toward this end, I think that shareholders and the market would be served by decoupling the auditor's opinion into whether the financial statements "present fairly" and whether they are in conformity with GAAP. I realize that myriad legal questions could well be raised about such a change, but that must be the subject of another paper, written by a legal specialist. I will content myself here with recommending that serious consideration be given to decoupling the auditor's opinion into two.

The SEC's *Regulation S-X* should not be an obstacle to a two-part opinion, because the current version of its rule 2-02(c), on the opinion to

---

[15] For example, see "Why Everybody's Jumping on the Accountants These Days" (1977) and Worthy (1984).

be expressed in the auditor's report, says, in a rather open-ended manner, that the report is to state clearly "the opinion of the accountant in respect of the financial statements covered by the report and the accounting principles and practices reflected therein" (PricewaterhouseCoopers, 2005: vol. 1).[16] Nothing is said about "present fairly" or conformity with GAAP.

Now, how would it work? There are three variations:

- a "fairness" opinion on a company's choice to depart from GAAP;
- a "fairness" opinion on a company's choice of one method from among two or more alternatively accepted methods in the application of GAAP, where the auditor assesses whether the company's choice is appropriate in the circumstances;
- a "fairness" opinion on the superiority of a non-GAAP accounting method over a GAAP method used by a company.

First Variation

We have had considerable experience in the United States with the first of these variations. Between the 1950s and the 1990s, three public utilities, a colliery, and a property development company integrated either general price-level (GPL) restatements or current valuations into their basic financial statements, which the AIA's Committee on Accounting Procedure had said should appear, if at all, in supplementary schedules (1953: ch. 9A, para. 17). Beginning in the middle 1950s and into the 1960s, the public utilities that so reported were Indiana Telephone Corporation, Iowa-Illinois Gas and Electric, and Sacramento Municipal Utility District (SMUD); the fourth company was Ayrshire Collieries. The motives of the public utilities were to raise their rate base and to reduce their reported net income (by means of the extra depreciation expense). For the three public utilities and the coal mining company, Arthur Andersen and a small audit firm (between 1954 and 1963 for Indiana Telephone, and Andersen afterward) managed to accommodate this adoption of non-GAAP measurement methods because they believed in their merit.

Iowa-Illinois, SMUD, and Ayrshire inserted into their traditional financial statements an additional depreciation charge based either on GPL restatements or on current valuations. The audit firms affirmed in their report that the financial statements "present fairly" in conformity with GAAP. They also said in their reports that income reflecting a depreciation charge based on GPL restatements or current valuations was "a fairer statement", "a fair statement", or "is more fairly presented", respectively, than GAAP income, based on the methodology adopted

---

[16] In previous versions, *Regulation S-X* referred to the auditor's "certificate".

and disclosed by the company.[17] Arthur Andersen audited all three companies.

Indiana Telephone divided its financial statements into columns A and B. Column A displayed traditional historical cost figures, while column B showed the corresponding GPL restated figures. The auditor said that the figures in column A "present fairly" in conformity with GAAP. Carman Blough, in one of his monthly columns in the *Journal of Accountancy*, regarded Indiana Telephone's column B as being in line with what the Committee on Accounting Procedure had in mind as "supplementary", but he took exception to the small audit firm's opinion contained in the company's 1956 report that the figures in column B "more fairly reflect the economic truth of the operation of the corporation" (1958b: 49–50). In subsequent years, up to 1963, the small audit firm said that Indiana Telephone's financial statement figures displayed in column B "were more fairly presented" or "more fairly present". From 1964 to 1976, when Arthur Andersen was Indiana Telephone's auditor, it continued to give the same opinion as the small audit firm on column B ("more fairly present").

These unusual opinions given by the audit firms were reproduced in *Accounting Research Study No. 6* issued by the AICPA in 1963 (Staff of the Accounting Research Division, 1963: appendix D). Indiana Telephone, Iowa-Illinois, and Ayrshire were subject to the SEC and therefore had to display the extra depreciation charge below the derivation of income, as a surplus appropriation, in their filings with the SEC.[18]

The property development company was The Rouse Company, which, between 1976 and 1994, presented a current-value balance sheet based on valuations supplied by an appraisal firm. The SEC accepted the current-value balance sheet in lieu of the supplementary disclosures mandated in *Accounting Series Release No. 190* (Palmon and Seidler, 1978: 781). Rouse's audit firm, Peat Marwick (succeeded by KPMG), said in its opinion in every year that the historical cost-based financial statements "present fairly" in conformity with GAAP, but that the current-value balance sheet was "presented fairly" in accordance with the methodology set forth in an explanatory note.

Not all auditors followed this path. In its 1979 annual report, Days Inns of America also presented a current-value balance sheet, based on an appraiser's valuation, but its audit firm, Price Waterhouse, went no further than to say that it provided "relevant information about assets and liabilities of the Company which is not provided by the historical cost financial statements". It declined to say that the current-value balance sheet "presents fairly". In its 1977 annual report, Iowa Beef Processors

---

[17] For a discussion of Andersen's opinion on Ayrshire, see "Price-Level Depreciation in Annual Statements" (1959: 18). Also see Zeff (1992: 457–9).

[18] For Indiana Telephone, see the letter from Pierre F. Goodrich (1959), the company's president.

presented a full set of current-value financial statements in addition to its traditional financial statements. After saying that the current-value statements differed significantly from GAAP, Touche Ross, its audit firm, opined only that the current-value statements "are a reasonable and appropriate presentation of the information set forth therein on the basis indicated in Note 1".

Somehow, corporate financial reporting was not thrown into chaos because of these announced departures from GAAP measures, and three audit firms had the courage to give their opinion on the "fairness" of the information provided by the departures.

Second Variation

As will be seen, the second variation is not as much of a challenge as the third. Let us say that a company selling products on the installment plan were to use the instalment method, not the cost-recovery method, of recognizing revenues. Suppose, too, that the audit firm believes that the cost-recovery method is appropriate and that (as many believe) the installment method is not. If the company were adamant in its adoption of the installment method, which is allowed under GAAP, the auditor could well opt to say, if the difference were material, that the financial statements do not "present fairly" even though they are in conformity with GAAP. That would be a useful bit of information for shareholders and the market.

If a company engaged in oil and gas exploration were to use full costing, while the auditor believed, in line with the FASB in *Statement of Financial Accounting Standards (SFAS) No. 19* (1977), that successful-efforts costing is the appropriate method, the auditor should be obliged to say that the financial statements do not "present fairly" even though a GAAP method was used.

If a construction company were to use the percentage-of-completion method for recognizing revenues in circumstances where the auditor believes that the estimates of total cash eventually to be received and the total construction cost eventually to be incurred were not sufficiently foreseeable to justify the use of this method, the auditor would be obliged to state that, although the financial statements were prepared in conformity with GAAP (though some might contest that assertion), they do not "present fairly".

In other areas of GAAP where optional methods are admissible, the auditor should be expected to opine whether the company has made the appropriate selection so as to "present fairly". If *SFAS No. 13* (FASB, 1976) on leases were modified to be similar to *IAS No. 17 Revised* (IASC, 1997b), which I think is likely, thus removing the bright lines, the auditor would be under an obligation to determine whether, as a lessee, the company should treat long-term, noncancelable leases as operating leases or as capital leases. If the company were to adopt the treatment with which the auditor disagrees, the auditor should qualify "present fairly", even though the company's method falls within the options allowed under GAAP.

Therefore, the second variation would oblige the audit firm to qualify "present fairly" if it were to disagree with the company *in principle* over a GAAP method used, or if it were to disagree with the company on the use of a GAAP method in the light of the particular circumstances in which it is being used. Examples of such circumstances would be a significant difference of view between the auditor and the company over the estimates of key variables (for example, the discount rate, estimated future cash flows, or fair values).

I believe that these qualifications of "present fairly" would be important information to shareholders and the market, and I agree with Arthur Andersen of the 1940s that one of the hallmarks of professionalism is for an auditor to give an opinion on whether a company's financial statements "present fairly", and not hide behind GAAP, or allow the company to hide behind GAAP.

The second variation is somewhat analogous to the attempt by SEC chief accountant Sandy Burton, in *Accounting Series Release No. 177* (SEC, 1975), supplemented by the SEC's *Staff Accounting Bulletin No. 14* (SEC's Office of the Chief Accountant and Division of Corporation Finance, 1977), to oblige the auditor to comment on whether a company's change in accounting "principle", other than a change mandated by a new standard, is "preferable in the circumstances". Because the SEC release dealt with interim reports, it did not explicitly raise the issue of the auditor's opinion on the "fairness" of the financial statements.[19] Revsine has written, however, that "the method that is chosen should 'present fairly' the financial condition of the firm" (1980: 80). In the context of this paper, the issue facing the auditor should be the appropriateness of a GAAP method, and the question should not arise only when the company changes from one method to another. If the method is, in the auditor's view, inappropriate and the difference is material, "fairness" is called into question.

The second variation also would reflect a strict application of *SAS No. 69* (ASB, 1992), which states that the auditor's opinion on "present fairly" in conformity with GAAP should be based on a judgement concerning five attributes, one of which is that "the accounting principles are appropriate in the circumstances" (ASB, 1992: para. 4(b)). This variation also implements

---

[19] "Preferability letters" are still required to be filed by the auditor with the SEC. Since 1971, under APB *Opinion No. 20* (1971: para. 17), the entity has been required to explain why a newly adopted accounting principle is preferable. The FASB's *SFAS No. 154* (2005: para. 17(a)) reaffirmed this requirement.

the advice of Maurice Peloubet (1958) and Douglas Carmichael (1974), cited above.

Third Variation

The third variation presents the greatest challenge: whether the auditor believes that a non-GAAP method is superior to the GAAP method adopted by the company on a particular measurement or disclosure issue. This is somewhat the inverse of the first variation, where both the auditor and the company believe that the GAAP method is inferior to a non-GAAP method, and therefore unacceptable. Here, the auditor may believe that the use of historical cost accounting for certain assets or liabilities is inadequate to "present fairly" and that fair value accounting should be used instead, perhaps with the unrealized gains and losses to be taken directly into income. Or the auditor may believe that the omission of certain intangible assets from the balance sheet means that the financial statements do not "present fairly".

Other examples could be cited. Does the auditor regard the recording of non-GAAP accretion or fair value for growing stands of timber as the proper accounting method for a forest products company? Does the auditor believe that non-GAAP proportional consolidation, not the equity method of accounting, should be used to reflect joint ventures? Should the implicit discount on an issuance of convertible securities be recorded instead of the GAAP method of crediting the entire proceeds to the bonds payable account? The options to U.S. GAAP in all three of these circumstances are prescribed as GAAP in Canada or under International Financial Reporting Standards, or both.

Such a difference of opinion will truly test the relationship between the auditor and the company, but professionalism—doing what society expects of a professional—must govern the engagement.

CONCLUSION

My argument is that the time has arrived, in the light of the heightened expectations for financial reporting, to give serious consideration to decoupling the auditor's opinion into two: whether the financial statements "present fairly", and whether they are in conformity with GAAP. I believe that this reform, which is hardly without precedent in North America, would provide shareholders and the market with useful information.

The question raised in the early 1970s, when *SAS No. 5* (AudSEC, 1975) was being drafted, was, what framework should the auditor use when making "fairness" judgements? The answer then was that the framework should be GAAP. Today, the framework that should be used is the FASB's conceptual framework for business entities, which was completed in 1984. The auditor should call on the conceptual framework to make such judgements.

A problem that I see as being an obstacle to acceptance of the argument in this paper is the absence of evidence that auditors, including the major audit firms, actually invest in *thinking in depth* about accounting principles and their applications and, indeed, about the conceptual framework. There was a time, before the 1980s, when partners in audit firms would give speeches in public forums, write articles, and even write books, in which they debated accounting principles and their applications. It was also a time when their firms issued booklets in which they took reasoned positions on accounting issues facing the Accounting Principles Board or the Financial Accounting Standards Board. They actively engaged in advocacy of their views. One does not see this behavior today and, with rare exceptions, it has not been in evidence for more than 20 years. I have written about the demise of this intellectual discourse and how its absence detracts from professionalism in our field (Zeff, 1986). Do partners and their firms even think about these issues any more? Do they have beliefs about what is "right" and "wrong" about accounting principles and their applications? There is little outward sign that they do. If accounting is to be regarded as a "profession", it would fall within a very shallow definition of the term. For this reason, putting questions of enhanced legal exposure aside, I am pessimistic that we will see a disposition on the part of audit firms to pronounce on "fairness" other than as being coextensive with rule-laden GAAP.

There is, however, a ray of hope. *SAS No. 90* (ASB, 1999), which amended paragraph 7 of *SAS No. 61* (ASB, 1988b), stated, "In each SEC engagement, the auditor should discuss with the audit committee the auditor's judgments about the quality, not just the acceptability, of the entity's accounting principles applied in its financial reporting. . . . The discussion should also include items that have a significant impact on the representational faithfulness, verifiability, and neutrality of the accounting information included in the financial statements" (ASB, 1999: para. 11, footnote omitted). These three qualitative characteristics were drawn from the FASB's conceptual framework. This provision was reinforced by section 204 of the Sarbanes-Oxley Act (2002) and the SEC's rule adopted thereunder.[20] I am informed that these discussions between the auditor and the audit committee are in reality "fairness" discussions and, under section 204, the auditor is required to inform the audit committee of the treatment that he or she prefers. When there are material, unresolved disagreements with management over the

---

[20] See section II(F)(6)(G) of the SEC's adopting release (SEC, 2003) and paragraph 210.2-07, which is the rule itself.

accounting principles and their applications adopted by the entity, the next step should, in my view, be a qualification of "present fairly" in the auditor's report.

REFERENCES

Accountants International Study Group (AISG). 1969. *The independent auditor's reporting standards in three nations.* AISG.

Accounting Principles Board (APB). 1969. *Opinion No. 15: Earnings per share.* New York: American Institute of Certified Public Accountants.

Accounting Principles Board (APB). 1971. *Opinion No. 20: Accounting changes.* New York: American Institute of Certified Public Accountants.

American Institute of Accountants (AIA). 1934. *Audits of corporate accounts 1932–1934.* New York: AIA.

American Institute of Accountants (AIA). 1936. *Examination of financial statements by independent public accountants.* New York: AIA.

American Institute of Certified Public Accountants (AICPA). 1972. *Restatement of the code of professional ethics.* New York: AICPA.

Anderson, R. J. 1977. *The external audit.* Toronto: Pitman Publishing.

Aranoff, T. D. 1975. The auditor's standard report. A background paper prepared for the Commission on Auditors' Responsibilities. Unpublished.

Arthur Andersen & Co. 1977. *The public interest in public accounting: The challenges of a changing role.* Chicago: Arthur Andersen & Co.

Atchley, K. 1991. SEC presses for market value. *World Accounting Report*, December: 1–2.

Auditing Standards Board (ASB). 1980. *Proposed statement on auditing standards: The auditor's standard report.* New York: American Institute of Certified Public Accountants.

Auditing Standards Board (ASB). 1988a. *Statement on Auditing Standards No. 58: Reports on audited financial statements.* New York: American Institute of Certified Public Accountants.

Auditing Standards Board (ASB). 1988b. *Statement on Auditing Standards No. 61: Communication with audit committees.* New York: American Institute of Certified Public Accountants.

Auditing Standards Board (ASB). 1992. *Statement on Auditing Standards No. 69: The meaning of* present fairly in conformity with generally accepted accounting principles *in the independent auditor's report.* New York: American Institute of Certified Public Accountants.

Auditing Standards Board (ASB). 1999. *Statement on Auditing Standards No. 90: Audit committee communications.* New York: American Institute of Certified Public Accountants.

Auditing Standards Board (ASB). 2000. *Statement on Auditing Standards No. 93: Omnibus statement on auditing standards—2000.* New York: American Institute of Certified Public Accountants.

Auditing Standards Executive Committee (AudSEC). 1974. *Statement on Auditing Standards No. 2: Reports on audited financial statements.* New York: American Institute of Certified Public Accountants.

Auditing Standards Executive Committee (AudSEC). 1975. *Statement on Auditing Standards No. 5: The meaning of "present fairly in conformity with generally accepted accounting principles" in the independent auditor's report.* New York: American Institute of Certified Public Accountants.

The auditor's report (editorial). 1937. *Journal of Accountancy* 63 (4): 246–8.

Barr, A. 1987. Letter to author. September 3.

Bevis, H. W. 1967. Letter to author. May 5.

Blough, C. G. 1958a. Implications of "present fairly" in the auditor's report. *Journal of Accountancy* 105 (3): 76–7.

Blough, C. G. 1958b. An instance of price-level adjustment of depreciation. *Journal of Accountancy* 105 (1): 49–50.

Broad, S. J. 1966. Letter to author. January 3.

Burton, J. C. 1975. Fair presentation: Another view. In *The Emanuel Saxe Distinguished Lectures in Accounting 1974–1975*, 27–39. New York: Baruch College, City University of New York.

Canadian Institute of Chartered Accountants (CICA). 1977. *CICA handbook*. Toronto: CICA.

Carmichael, D. R. 1974. What does the independent auditor's opinion really mean? *Journal of Accountancy* 137 (5): 83–7.

Carmichael, D. R., and A. J. Winters. 1982. The evolution of audit reporting. In *Auditing Symposium VI*, eds. D. R. Nichols and H. F. Stettler, 1–20. Lawrence, KS: School of Business, University of Kansas.

Chambers, R. J. 1982. Comments of the seventh participant: The TIMS initiative of 1962. In *The Accounting Postulates and Principles Controversy of the 1960s*, ed. S. A. Zeff. New York: Garland Publishing.

Cochrane, G. 1950. The auditor's report: Its evolution in the U.S.A. *The Accountant* 123 (3959): 448–60.

Commission on Auditors' Responsibilities. 1978. *Report, conclusions, and recommendations*. Commission on Auditors' Responsibilities.

Committee on Accounting Procedure. 1953. *Accounting Research Bulletin No. 43: Restatement and revision of Accounting Research Bulletins*. New York: American Institute of Accountants.

Committee on Auditing Procedure. 1939. *Statement on Auditing Procedure No. 1: Extensions of auditing procedure*. New York: American Institute of Accountants.

Eckel, L. G. 1973. The two-part opinion. *CAmagazine* 105 (5): 40–2.

Financial Accounting Standards Board (FASB). 1976. *Statement of Financial Accounting Standards No. 13: Accounting for leases*. Stamford, CT: FASB.

Financial Accounting Standards Board (FASB). 1977. *Statement of Financial Accounting Standards No. 19: Financial accounting and reporting by oil and gas producing companies*. Stamford, CT: FASB.

Financial Accounting Standards Board (FASB). 2005. *Statement of Financial Accounting Standards No. 154: Accounting changes and error corrections*. Norwalk, CT: FASB.

Goodrich, P. F. 1959. Letter. *Journal of Accountancy* 108 (6): 23–4.

International Accounting Standards Board (IASB). 2003. *International Accounting Standard No. 1: Presentation of financial statements*. In *Improvements to International Accounting Standards*. London: IASB.

International Accounting Standards Committee (IASC). 1997a. *International Accounting Standard No. 1: Presentation of financial statements*. London: IASC.

International Accounting Standards Committee (IASC). 1997b. *International Accounting Standard No. 17 Revised: Leases*. London: IASC.

Johnston, D. J. 1979. Fairness & the one-part opinion. *CAmagazine* 112 (2): 46–54.

Kohler, E. L. 1952. *A dictionary for accountants*. New York: Prentice Hall.

Mano, R. M., M. Mouritsen, and R. Pace. 2006. Principles-based accounting. *CPA Journal* 76 (2): 60–3.

Mautz, R. K., and H. A. Sharaf. 1961. *The philosophy of auditing*. American Accounting Association.

May, G. O. 1937. Principles of accounting. *Journal of Accountancy* 64 (6): 423–5.

Miller, P. B. W., and P. R. Bahnson. 2005. PEAP: Proof that FASB has faulty premise on 203. *Accounting Today* 19 (14): 14–5.

Montgomery, R. H., N. J. Lenhart, and A. R. Jennings. 1949. *Montgomery's auditing*. New York: The Ronald Press Company.

Nicolaisen, D. 2005. Remarks made during a meeting on October 5, 2005 of the Standing Advisor Group of the Public Company Accounting Oversight Board. Available online at http://www.pcaobus.org/News_and_Events/Webcasts.aspx#32.

Office of the Chief Auditor, Public Company Accounting Oversight Board (PCAOB). 2005. A paper for the Standing Advisory Group meeting on October 5–6, 2005. Unpublished.

Palmon, D., and L. J. Seidler. 1978. Current value reporting of real estate companies and a possible example of market inefficiency. *The Accounting Review* 53 (3): 776–90.

Peloubet, M. E. 1958. Letter reproduced in Carman G. Blough, More about "present fairly" in the auditor's report. *Journal of Accountancy* 105 (5): 73–7.

Price-level depreciation in annual statements. 1959. *Journal of Accountancy* 108 (3): 16, 18.

PricewaterhouseCoopers. 2005. *SEC*. PricewaterhouseCoopers.

Revised text of the proposed Code restatement as approved by Council. 1972. *CPA* (June): 9–12.

Revsine, L. 1980. The preferability dilemma. *Journal of Accountancy* 144 (3): 80–9.

Revsine, L., D. W. Collins, and W. B. Johnson. 2002. *Financial reporting & analysis*. Upper Saddle River, NJ: Prentice Hall.

Richard Whitney. Wikipedia. http://en.wikipedia.org/wiki/Richard_Whitney.

Rosenfield, P., and L. Lorensen. 1974. Auditors' responsibilities and the audit report. *Journal of Accountancy* 138 (3): 73–83.

Sarbanes-Oxley Act of 2002. 2002. Pub. L. no. 107-204, 116 Stat. 745.

Securities and Exchange Commission (SEC). 1938. *Accounting Series Release No. 4: Administrative policy on financial statements*. Washington, DC: SEC.

Securities and Exchange Commission (SEC). 1940. *Fifth annual report of the Securities and Exchange Commission, fiscal year ended June 30, 1939*. Washington, DC: United States Government Printing Office.

Securities and Exchange Commission (SEC). 1975. *Accounting Series Release No. 177: Notice of adoption of amendments to Form 10-Q and Regulation S-X regarding interim financial reporting*. Washington, DC: SEC.

Securities and Exchange Commission (SEC). 1976. *Accounting Series Release No. 190: Amendments to Regulation S-X requiring disclosure of certain replacement cost data*. Washington, DC: SEC.

Securities and Exchange Commission (SEC). 2003. *Release No. 33-8183: Strengthening the Commission's requirements regarding auditor independence*. Washington, DC: SEC. Available online at http://www.sec.gov/rules/final/33-8183 .htm.

Securities and Exchange Commission's Office of the Chief Accountant and Division of Corporation Finance. 1977. *Staff Accounting Bulletin No. 14: Revisions to SAB No. 6 regarding reporting requirements for accounting changes*. Washington, DC: SEC.

Seligman, J. 2003. *The transformation of Wall Street: A history of the Securities and Exchange Commission and modern corporate finance*. New York: Aspen Publishers.

Sommer, A. A., Jr. 1976. Keep your eye on the donut. An address to the National Association of Accountants, New York City, March 18, 1975. Extract reproduced in *Before the Securities and Exchange Commission: Request for action by Commission with respect to certain rules and pronouncements relating to accounting principles*. Chicago: Arthur Andersen & Co.

Staff of the Accounting Research Division. 1963. *Reporting the financial effects of price-level changes*. New York: American Institute of Certified Public Accountants.

Staub, W. A. 1942. *Auditing developments during the present century*. Cambridge, MA: Harvard University Press.

Storey, R. K. 1964. *The search for accounting principles*. New York: American Institute of Certified Public Accountants.

Turner, L. E. 2005. Remarks made during a meeting on October 5, 2005 of the Standing Advisory Group of the Public Company Accounting Oversight Board. Available online at http://www.pcaobus.org/News_and_Events/Webcasts.aspx#32.

United States v. Simon (*Continental Vending* case). 1969. 425 F. 2d 796 (1969), certiorari denied, 397 U.S. 1006 (1970).

United States of America v. Bernard J. Ebbers (Court of Appeals, Second Circuit, July 28, 2006).

Werner, C. 1972. *Public hearing of the Accounting Objectives Study Group*. Transcript of proceedings held on May 15, 16, and 17, 1972 in New York.

Why everybody's jumping on the accountants these days. 1977. *Forbes*, March 15. Available online at http://www.forbes.com/free_forbes/1977/0315/037.html.

Worthy, F. S. 1984. Manipulating profits: How it's done. *Fortune*, June 25, 50–4.

Zeff, S. A. 1986. Big eight firms and the accounting literature: The falloff in advocacy writing. *Journal of Accounting, Auditing and Finance* 1 (2) new series: 131–54.

Zeff, S. A. 1992. Arthur Andersen & Co. and the two-part opinion in the auditor's report: 1946–1962. *Contemporary Accounting Research* 8 (2): 443–67.

Zeff, S. A. 2003. How the U.S. accounting profession got where it is today: Part I. *Accounting Horizons* 17 (3): 189–205.

Accounting Historians Journal
Vol. 34, No. 1
June 2007
pp. 1-23

Stephen A. Zeff
RICE UNIVERSITY

THE SEC PREEMPTS THE ACCOUNTING PRINCIPLES BOARD IN 1965: THE CLASSIFICATION OF THE DEFERRED TAX CREDIT RELATING TO INSTALLMENT SALES

Abstract: In 1959, the Accounting Principles Board (APB) replaced the Committee on Accounting Procedure because the latter was unable to deal forthrightly with a series of important issues. But during the APB's first half-dozen years, its record of achievement was no more impressive than its predecessor's. The chairman of the Securities and Exchange Commission (SEC), Manuel F. Cohen, criticized the APB's slow pace and unwillingness to tackle difficult issues. This article discusses the circumstances attending the SEC's issuance of an *Accounting Series Release* in late 1965 to demonstrate forcefully to the APB that, when it is unable to carry out its responsibility to "narrow the areas of difference" in accounting practice, the SEC is prepared to step in and do so itself. In this sense, the article deals with the tensions between the private and public sectors in the establishment of accounting principles in the U.S. during the mid-1960s. The article makes extensive use of primary resource materials in the author's personal archive, which have not been used previously in published work.

INTRODUCTION

In 1959, the American Institute of Certified Public Account ants (Institute, AICPA) appointed a new body, the Accounting Principles Board (APB), to succeed the Committee on Accounting Procedure (CAP). The APB had been charged to do a better job than its predecessor in raising the standard of accounting practice [see Zeff, 2001]. But the APB got off to a slow and uncertain start. In an embarrassing decision made in early 1962, it rejected the recommendations of a research study it had commissioned on broad accounting principles and shelved the

Acknowledgments: The author is grateful to Hugo Nurnberg, Sundaresh Ramnath, and an anonymous reviewer for comments on an earlier draft, as well as to Bill Coxsey and Travis Holt for services provided.

study [see Moonitz, 1974, pp. 17-20]. In early 1963, the APB was rebuffed by the Securities and Exchange Commission (SEC) on the investment tax credit [see Moonitz, 1966]. Finally, in 1964-1966, the APB seemed poised to right its course. Foremost among the reasons for this turn of events were (1) the decision by the Institute's executive committee to abandon its policy of appointing only the strong-willed managing partners of the Big Eight accounting firms to the board, and (2) the decision by the new board chairman, Clifford V. Heimbucher, a past president of the Institute and a partner in a small San Francisco CPA firm, to organize the board's work more effectively [Carey, 1970, pp. 130-132]. These were administrative improvements of considerable importance.

But there was a third reason – the increasing public pressure from the activist chairman of the SEC, Manuel F. Cohen. In a series of speeches, he urged the APB to make the difficult decisions so as to "narrow the areas of difference and inconsistency in practice," which the CAP had set as one of its objectives in 1953, and which had been laid down as an objective for the APB by the Institute's Special Committee on Research Program in 1958 ["Report to Council of the Special Committee   ,".1958, pp. 62-63].

In 1965, the APB was drafting an *Opinion* on the status of the CAP's *Accounting Research Bulletins.* In its exposure draft, it proposed to classify the deferred tax credit as a current liability when it relates to installment sales receivables shown as a current asset. Then the board recanted its position, greatly annoying one of its supporters, Arthur Andersen & Co. (AA). In late 1965, AA petitioned the SEC to require its classification as a current liability, thus overruling the APB. Manuel Cohen seized upon the petition as an opportunity to lecture a delegation from the APB at a specially called meeting of the Commission and then to issue an *Accounting Series Release* on the deferred tax classification as requested by AA. It was unprecedented for the SEC to issue a rule on accounting recognition, measurement, or classification in an area in which the accounting profession had declined to act after having initially undertaken to do so.[1] This action by the SEC has been little noticed in the literature

---

[1] To be sure, the SEC's accounting staff had exerted its influence on the CAP and the APB in other ways. The only comparable confrontation between the standard setter and the SEC on income tax allocation occurred in 1945, when the SEC issued *Accounting Series Release No. 53* [SEC, 1945] in order to limit the applicability of *ARB No. 23* [CAP, 1944].

[cf. see Pines, 1965, pp. 739-740; Defliese, 1974, p. 39], and there is some evidence to suggest that the SEC's release was a factor contributing to the APB's greater inclination to address difficult questions head-on in 1966-1967, especially on pensions and income tax allocation. In its later years, however, the APB foundered once again, in particular on accounting for business combinations [see Chatov, 1975, chap. 14; Seligman, 2003, pp. 418-430]. In 1973, the APB was succeeded by the independent Financial Accounting Standards Board. It is the purpose of this paper to examine in some depth this unique intervention by the SEC in the process by which the profession established accounting principles in the mid-1960s.

BACKGROUND

When the APB was established in 1959, the Institute's executive committee, probably at the behest of President Louis H. Penney, decided that only managing partners would be invited to represent the Big Eight firms on the board.[2] The executive committee apparently believed that the board would be making broad policy decisions based on technical support from its research staff, and that the managing partners were the most suited to making such executive decisions. But it quickly became evident that the board could not avoid immersing itself in highly technical issues. It also became clear that a number of the managing partners were not technical specialists, did not always read their agenda materials prior to the meetings, were typically men of strong conviction, and, thus, did not work easily together during the board's early years. Also, the board exhausted itself in lengthy debates leading up to *Opinion Nos. 2* and *4* [APB, 1962, 1964] on the investment tax credit, on which a total of 11 members dissented and a further nine filed qualified assents. Further, the board expended considerable time and energy on the controversial research study on accounting principles [Sprouse and Moonitz, 1962] and on a recommendation to Council on the authority that the board should be given to make changes in "generally accepted accounting principles" (GAAP) [Zeff, 1972, pp. 180-182].

By 1964, it became clear to the Institute's executive committee that its policy on managing partners had been a mistake,

---

[2] The lone exception was Weldon Powell, the senior technical partner of Haskins & Sells. Powell had chaired the special committee that called for establishment of the APB and the new accounting research division to provide the board with technical support.

and it proceeded to appoint the Big Eight firms' senior technical partners as the terms of their firms' managing partners expired [see Zeff, 1972, p. 193]. (It was always the Institute's unstated policy to have one representative on the board from each Big Eight firm.) By 1966, all but one of the managing partners of the Big Eight firms had departed the board. The lone exception was John W. Queenan, who had succeeded Weldon Powell as the representative of Haskins & Sells in 1963. But Queenan had served on the CAP from 1949 to 1954 and was strongly interested in technical accounting issues.

When Heimbucher became chairman of the board in 1964, he established subject-area subcommittees to study and draft *Opinions*. Previously, the board itself had done the drafting *in plenum*. Also, he arranged for an administrative staff to circularize exposure drafts and to read and analyze the letters of comment, thus freeing up time for the accounting research staff to concentrate on research. In addition, he set up a planning committee to set priorities and target dates for the board's agenda of projects. Finally, he allowed board members to bring an adviser to board meetings [see Heimbucher, 1966].

All the while, the board was being criticized in the financial press, in speeches by Leonard Spacek, the outspoken and feisty managing partner of AA, and by SEC Chairman Cohen. The issue coming in for the greatest attention was over "uniformity" v. "flexibility" when companies made choices of accounting principles, including the consequent diversity of accounting practice. Spacek spoke in favor of greater uniformity, while several other large firms, such as Price Waterhouse & Co. and Haskins & Sells, defended flexibility in the choice of accounting principles.[3] The SEC was on record for many years as favoring greater uniformity, and, in a speech in late 1964, Cohen [1964, p. 12] became more insistent that decisive progress be made in that direction. He said that "an immediate and pressing objective is to eliminate the use of alternative accounting principles underlying financial statements not justified by differing circumstances." During its first 5½ years, by the end of 1964, the APB had issued only five *Opinions*, and none had had the effect of narrowing accepted practice.[4]

---

[3] See the symposium, "Uniformity in Financial Accounting" [1965], for papers by Spacek, Weldon Powell, J. Arnold Pines (of the SEC staff), and others. For the Price Waterhouse view, see Bevis [1965] and Grady [1965, pp. 32-34].

It was not for lack of trying, however. In *Opinion No. 2* [APB, 1962], a divided board tried mightily to limit to one the number of ways to account for the investment tax credit. But the SEC was lobbied into allowing an alternative

WHY THE CLASSIFICATION OF THE DEFERRED TAX CREDIT BECAME IMPORTANT TO SPACEK AND ANDERSEN IN 1965

It was in this roiling environment that Leonard Spacek and AA became concerned about the diversity of practice allowed for treating the deferred tax credit arising from retailers' use of the installment method for recognizing gross income for income tax purposes coincident with recording sales revenue for financial reporting purposes as soon as an installment sale was made. Retailers, especially the department stores and mail-order houses, were the industry most significantly marked by this diversity of practice. The majority of companies had been classifying the deferred tax credit as a noncurrent liability. A few were displaying it as a current liability. Some companies had deducted the deferred tax credit from the installment receivables [see Hicks, 1966, p. 130].

Norman O. Olson [1966, p. 60], a partner in AA's executive office, explained why the deferred tax credit was becoming of increasing importance to companies in the retail industry. Referring to the divergence in practice between its classification as current or noncurrent, he wrote:

> The effect of this divergence in practice was assuming greatly increased significance by 1965, and it was likely to increase even further. With the expanded use of revolving credit plans and various other installment payment plans by merchandising companies and with the relatively recent regulations of the Internal Revenue Service permitting sales under revolving credit plans to be treated as installment sales for income tax purposes, many companies were accumulating an increasingly large amount of deferred income taxes on installment sales.

Olson added that the classification of deferred tax "has a significant effect on the determination of a company's working capital and the credit rating it receives."

The classification of the deferred tax credit became an important issue to Spacek and AA in early 1965, when the president of one of its major retail clients, Montgomery Ward & Co., Incorporated (MW) complained about having to show its credit

---

method, and, in *Opinion No. 4* [APB, 1964], the board reluctantly conceded defeat. This rebuff of the board by the SEC provoked considerable comment in the press.

as a current liability in its 1964-1965 financial statements (fiscal year ending on February 3, 1965). In line with a position which it had recently announced, AA [1962, pp. 66-67] insisted that MW classify its deferred tax credit as a current liability. The current portion of the deferred tax credit balance in its balance sheet dated February 3, 1965 was $3.9m, which represented 1.8% of its total current liabilities excluding the credit, but the president surely knew in early 1965 that this percentage would increase steeply in the years ahead. (It did indeed rise to 6.5% by February 2, 1966 and to 9.7% a year later.) Sears, Roebuck and Co., a much larger retail company, also based in Chicago, and audited by Touche, Ross, Bailey & Smart, had been displaying its deferred tax credit as noncurrent. The balance of Sears' deferred tax credit on January 31, 1965, the end of its fiscal year, was $454m, equal to *one-third* of its total current liabilities on that date. MW's president wanted to know why his company should be penalized for carrying the credit as a current liability while most other major retailers were not. Spacek agreed that his company should not be penalized, and he offered him a deal. If MW would agree to show the credit as a current liability in its 1964-1965 financial statements, and if Spacek could not get the APB to call for a uniform classification of the credit as a current liability by the end of 1965, he would approve of MW's adoption of noncurrent treatment in its 1965-1966 financial statements. MW's president agreed to the deal.[6]

SPACEK'S EFFORT TO PERSUADE THE APB
TO ACT ON DEFERRED TAXES

Previously, the CAP had dealt with the tax effect of a timing difference between reporting accelerated depreciation for income tax purposes and recording straight-line depreciation expense for financial reporting purposes (*Accounting Research*

---

[5] Neither MW nor Sears disclosed the current portion of its deferred tax credit, that is, the portion relating to installment receivables shown as current assets, in their 1965 year-end annual reports. Yet both companies had to break down their deferred tax credit account into its current and noncurrent components in their February 2, 1966/January 31, 1966 balance sheets, owing to the dictum in *Accounting Series Release No. 102* [SEC, 1965] (see below). They were also obliged to give, which they did, the comparative current/noncurrent breakdown for the previous year's balance sheet. As will be seen, the SEC release dealt with the classification of the deferred tax credit only in relation to installment receivables shown as current assets.

[6] This anecdote is recounted in interviews with George R. Catlett, September 3, 1970 and May 3, 1978.

Bulletin [ARB] No. 44 Revised) [CAP, 1958]. It had recommended that, except in special circumstances, such differences should be accounted for as deferred taxes. The CAP announced in 1959 that the deferred tax credit account relating to the depreciation differential should be shown in the balance sheet as a liability or deferred credit, not as part of equity capital [CAP, 1959]. As far back as 1944, the CAP had recommended that a provision should be made for the estimated tax to be paid on installment sales which were deferred for income tax purposes (*ARB No. 23*, final paragraph) [CAP, 1944]. The CAP reaffirmed this position in paragraph 18 of Chapter 10B of *ARB No. 43* [CAP, 1953]. But the CAP did not say how to classify the deferred tax credit account. In the retail field, as indicated, there was a lack of agreement whether the deferred tax credit should be shown as a current or noncurrent liability when the installment sales receivable was shown as a current asset.

During 1964-1965, the APB was deliberating a pronouncement, which became *Opinion No. 6* issued in October 1965, in which it was to announce which of the CAP's *Accounting Research Bulletins* should be continued without amendment and which should either be revised or be withdrawn entirely.[7] All of the board members, as well as Andrew Barr, the SEC chief accountant, were invited by Chairman Heimbucher to give their views on which of the *ARBs* should be retained, in their original form or as amended. In a letter dated May 26, 1965, Leonard Spacek, who was in his last year of service on the board, replied that the definition of current liabilities in *ARB No. 43*, Chapter 3A, paragraph 7 [CAP, 1953] should be amended to include deferred taxes to the extent that they relate to current assets, such as the current portion of installment sales receivable. It was expected that much of the impact of this amendment would be on retailers.[8] On June 4, 1965, Andrew Barr replied at length to

---

[7] The board's review of the *ARBs* became necessary after the AICPA Council decided in October 1964 that any departures in company financial statements from accounting principles accepted in the board's *Opinions* and in the *ARBs* had to be disclosed either in the footnotes or in the auditor's report, effective with financial statements for fiscal periods beginning after December 31, 1965. The board, therefore, had to determine which of the contents of the *ARBs*, with or without amendment, were to serve as this benchmark.

[8] The references to board correspondence and board minutes are drawn from files that AA generously allowed the author to copy during the summers of 1982 and 1983 in the firm's Chicago executive office, at the invitation of Arthur R. Wyatt. Documents have been obtained from other sources as well. Researchers interested in pursuing the issue raised in this article are invited to inspect copies of the related documents in the author's personal archive.

Heimbucher's invitation, and, among other things, stated that "Paragraph 7 [of *ARB No. 43*, Chapter 3A] should be expanded to specifically state that liabilities maturing in the time period of the operating cycle should be included in current liabilities, such as liabilities related to installment receivables and deferred income taxes on installment sales."

Spacek sought the view of Anson Herrick, a retired San Francisco practitioner who, as a member of the CAP in the 1940s, had drafted *ARB No. 30*, "Current Assets and Current Liabilities – Working Capital" [CAP, 1947], which served as the basis for Chapter 3A of *ARB No. 43*. Herrick replied that he supported the proposed classification of the deferred tax credit as a current liability in such circumstances. He said that "[the classification] is completely consistent with the cycle theory which I originated."[9]

In 1953, no less an authority than Carman G. Blough, the Institute's director of research, who attended the meetings of the CAP, had opined that the deferred tax credit relating to installment receivables should be shown as a current liability in line with *ARB No. 30* [Blough, 1953, p. 347].

SEC Chairman Cohen [1966, p. 59] was later to say that, in 1965, "no fewer than four different reporting methods were used by companies for which the [deferred tax] item was of considerable importance. ... Significantly, each method carried the opinion of an independent public accountant reporting that the financial statements had been prepared in accordance with generally accepted accounting principles." Clearly, a uniform approach was lacking.[10]

At its meeting on June 21-23, 1965, the APB unanimously approved Spacek's proposed amendment of paragraph 7, and it was duly included in the board's exposure draft that was issued in July ["Exposure Draft of Tentative Opinion.. ,".1965].[11] The draft was widely circulated, including a special mailing to the presidents of the some 1,300 companies listed on the New York Stock Exchange. The pertinent passage in the exposure draft appeared in paragraph 13. In that paragraph, it was stated that the AICPA's accounting research division will conduct a research study on current assets and liabilities, and that, "[p]ending completion of this study, and publication of a Board Opinion

---

[9]letter from Herrick to Spacek, dated June 17, 1965

[10]This matter was also discussed at length by Rappaport [1972, pp. 3-7 to 3-10].

[11]AICPA – APB, minutes of meeting, June 21-23, 1965, p. 1

thereon," the following paragraph was to be added to Chapter 3A (p. 58):

> 10. Whenever it is appropriate to record deferred income taxes, such deferred taxes should be classified as a current liability in the balance sheet to the extent that they are related to current assets which give rise to the tax deferment.

As can be seen, the proposed change was solely one of balance-sheet classification, and it was to be reconsidered once the board could review the research study on current assets and liabilities. The provision did not pretend to impose tax allocation accounting (today known as deferred tax accounting) where it had otherwise not been recommended by the CAP or the APB. Indeed, the APB was then considering whether to pronounce in favor or against tax allocation generally, and two of the Big Eight firms (Price Waterhouse & Co. and Haskins & Sells) had already registered antipathy, or at least profound skepticism, toward any tax allocation at all. AA was the Big Eight firm that was the strongest advocate of tax allocation.

During the board's June meeting, George R. Catlett succeeded Spacek as AA's representative on the board. He later recalled that board member Ira Schur of S.D. Leidesdorf & Co., a middle-sized firm based in New York City, said that his firm had been trying to persuade City Stores, one of its clients, to reclassify its deferred tax liability relating to installment receivables as current but had been unable to do so because of the noncurrent classification used by most other companies in the industry. He also recalled that board member Donald J. Bevis of Touche, Ross, Bailey & Smart said that he had always favored the current classification for the deferred tax credit relating to installment sales.[12] Touche, Ross, the auditor of Sears, was then the predominant Big Eight firm with major clients in retail trade – department stores, mail-order houses, etc. [see Zeff and Fossum, 1967, p. 317].

Key commentators on the exposure draft expressed reservations or outright opposition to paragraph 13 on the current classification. The Panel on Accounting Principles of the Financial Executives Institute argued that the paragraph prejudged the research study on current assets and liabilities still under way

---

[12]internal AA memorandum from George R. Catlett to partners R.I. Jones, W.J. Mueller, J.J. Brice, and J.W. Boyle, dated July 1, 1965

by the board's research staff.[13] Awaiting the results of research has always been an easy argument to make against unwelcome changes in accounting principles. The Retail Committee on Accounting Principles of the National Retail Merchants Association (NRMA), representing 15 major department stores and mail-order houses (including MW, Sears, and City Stores), objected to the reclassification. It argued that only income taxes payable during the current year should be shown as current: "The deferred income taxes of retailers arising out of the installment method of tax accounting are, in effect, a long-term obligation which is not payable until the outstanding receivables are liquidated – a very remote possibility in a going business."[14]

Of the 15 companies represented on the NRMA's accounting principles committee (apart from MW and Sears), five had balances in their deferred tax credit account relating to installment receivables that were equal to or exceeded 15% of their total current liabilities, excluding the credit, at the end of their 1964-1965 fiscal years: J.C. Penney Company, Inc. (16.8%), Broadway-Hale Stores, Inc. (18.8%), May Department Stores Company (20.3%), Miller & Rhoads, Inc. (48.9%), and Rich's Inc. (50.6%) . Five of the other companies disclosed that they had balances of less than 15%, while no information is available for the remaining three companies.[15]

One reason why retail companies objected to the current classification of the deferred tax credit was that it did not represent a current claim on liquid assets and, thus, would give a misleading impression of a retailer's ability to meet its financial obligations. It would also place such companies in an awkward position because of the working capital requirements stipulated in their bond indentures.[16]

In correspondence among board members following issuance of the exposure draft, the two Big Eight firms that were known to be unsympathetic toward tax allocation, mentioned

---

[13]letter from J.R. Janssen, chairman of the Panel, to Richard C. Lytle (APB administrative director), dated September 15, 1965

[14]letter from K.S. Axelson, chairman of the committee, to Richard C. Lytle, dated September 15, 1965

[15]These percentages were developed from ProQuest's Historical Annual Reports service and from *Moody's Industrials* for the year 1966. Because of the unavailability of the other three companies' annual reports and their omission from *Moody's Industrials*, it was impossible to determine how much of the balances in their deferred tax credit account, if any, was attributable to installment receivables.

[16]letter from Malise L. Graham, of the New York law firm of Faulkner, Dawkins & Sullivan, to William D. Hall, a partner of AA, dated March 30, 1966

above, made known their disagreement with paragraph 13. In retrospect, it is surprising that they assented to the provision during the June meeting of the board. Board member Herman W. Bevis, the senior partner of Price Waterhouse, recommended that the paragraph be deleted, as it was not clear, he said, whether the deferred tax credit was a liability at all, even though it must be shown on the liability side of the balance sheet. He believed that it was, in essence, only a contingency.[17] Bevis said he had canvassed his partners for their views, and it seems likely that his partners had in turn canvassed the views of their retail clients. Haskins & Sells submitted a memorandum in which it also opposed the provision, as it believed that the amount might never fall due. The firm said that the balance in the deferred tax credit account might constantly grow and, thus, may never mature as an amount to be paid. The firm conceded that it would be more theoretically defensible to classify the deferred tax as a current liability if it were expected to mature within one year from the balance sheet date. The firm also argued that the board's proposed reclassification goes beyond prevailing practice. Furthermore, it said, any such recommendation should await completion of the research studies on current assets and liabilities and on tax allocation accounting.[18] Letters submitted by the board members from Ernst & Ernst (E&E) and Lybrand, Ross Bros. & Montgomery (LRB&M), which were two of the other Big Eight firms, did not mention the proposed reclassification in paragraph 13.[19]

At the board's next meeting, on September 16-17, 1965, it reversed its unanimous approval of paragraph 13. The board voted 14-2 to delete the provision on the classification of deferred tax "on the condition that a subcommittee would be appointed to consider the subject."[20] It was the only item in the exposure draft that the board deleted in its entirety [Lytle, 1965, p. 72]. George Catlett "objected strenuously to deferring this question" [Olson, 1966, p. 61]. Richard C. Lytle [1965, p. 72], the board's administrative director, gave the following reasons for the board's action:

---

[17]letter from Herman W. Bevis to Reed K. Storey (AICPA director of accounting research), dated August 9, 1965

[18]memorandum attached to the letter from Oscar S. Gellein to Richard C. Lytle, dated September 10, 1965

[19]letters from Hassel Tippit (E&E) to Richard C. Lytle, dated July 20, 1965, and from Philip L. Defliese (LRB&M) to members of the APB, dated September 13, 1965

[20]AICPA – APB, minutes of meeting, September 16-17, 1965, p. 4.

Unlike other changes proposed in the exposure draft, this paragraph was directed to a matter not specifically covered in the ARBs and its inclusion would have been consistent with what appears to be the more predominant accepted practice currently.

He added that it could have "important implications with regard to the broad area of accounting for income taxes," a subject on which a research study was being completed (which had been in preparation since 1961). One major question, he said, was "whether deferred income taxes are a 'deferred credit' or a 'liability'." This last point, which had been debated for years, was probably significant in crippling the effort to classify the deferred tax, if only in defined circumstances, as a current liability. In its *Executive Letter* to partners and managers, Price Waterhouse said: "The APB decided to omit the [reclassification] requirement from Opinion No. 6 largely because it was out of context with an opinion having the avowed purpose of revising existing pronouncements in order to 'obviate conflicts between present accepted practice and provisions of outstanding Bulletins'" ["Special Bulletin...," 1965, p. 4].

AA's Catlett was convinced that the reversal was a clear result of client pressure brought on the firms, whose board representatives had not realized in June how large the impact of the reclassification might be on their clients' balance sheets.[21] Not surprisingly, the paragraph had met with considerable opposition from retail industry commentators on the exposure draft, including a number of major companies, such as Broadway-Hale Stores, Sears, Spiegel, and MW, which wrote separate letters apart from the letter from the NRMA.[22] Many of those opposing the paragraph on classifying deferred tax criticized the precedent of linking an item on the liability side of the balance sheet with one or more classes of assets; instead, they believed that the deferred tax should be classified according to when it will be liquidated. Others questioned whether the deferred tax would ever actually be paid, and, thus, they saw no ground for requiring that it reduce working capital. Some said that the reclassification went beyond the scope of the pronouncement, which was to determine which pre-existing positions in the ARBs were to be regarded as still in force. *Opinion No. 6,* "Status of Accounting Research Bulletins," was published in October

---

[21] interview with George R. Catlett, May 3, 1978

[22] These separate letters were in the batches of comment letters conveyed to the board by Richard Lytle.

1965 and reproduced in the November issue of the *Journal of Accountancy.*

AA PETITIONS THE SEC

On October 1, 1965, two weeks after the board meeting at which paragraph 13 was deleted, AA petitioned the SEC to issue an *Accounting Series Release (ASR)* that would classify the deferred tax arising from current assets such as installment sales receivable as a current liability. AA knew, of course, that SEC Chief Accountant Andrew Barr had advised the APB that he favored such a classification. And, as mentioned above, SEC Chairman Cohen had been railing against the diversity in accounting practice. The firm had reason to believe that the SEC might be sympathetic to its cause. Yet it privately harbored doubts that the SEC would act favorably on its petition.[23]

As was the SEC's practice in such matters, AA's petition was held in confidence, except that Barr notified Richard Lytle, at the board, that AA had filed the petition. Barr inquired if the board might be able to act on the deferred classification by November 15, which was viewed as the deadline for the SEC to publish a proposed accounting rule that, after a 30-day exposure period, could be adopted in time to apply to financial statements ending on or before December 31. At Lytle's request, and with the acquiescence of Barr, AA provided the APB with a copy of the petition for confidential circulation to the board members. The board's planning subcommittee met on October 22. It concluded that the subject was too complex for the board to be able to act on the matter by the end of 1965.

Contrary to what some might have expected, namely, that AA would publicize its petition to vaunt the role it was playing to achieve greater uniformity in financial reporting, the firm rarely mentioned its authorship of the petition in its publications, and only well after the event.[24] Chief Accountant Barr had advised AA that the Commission would prefer that the firm not publicize the petition until it was acted upon, and the firm complied.[25]

---

[23]interview with George R. Catlett, September 3, 1970

[24]The only two mentions the author has found are in Olson [1966, p. 61] and AA [1969, p. 67]. Spacek did not mention the petition in his speeches. The author can find no other mentions in the literature of AA being the source of the petition. Cohen [1966, p. 59] said that "a leading accounting firm" had petitioned the SEC but did not name the firm.

[25] interviews with George R. Catlett, September 3, 1970 and May 3, 1978

THE SEC CONFERS WITH A DELEGATION
FROM THE APB

In November 1965, the SEC invited the APB to send a delegation to meet with the five members of the Commission to discuss the AA petition. The four members of the APB's planning committee, composed of Chairman Clifford Heimbucher, Herman Bevis (Price Waterhouse and APB vice chairman), John Queenan (Haskins & Sells), and Frank T. Weston (Arthur Young & Company), accompanied by two senior staff members, attended the conference. All four of the APB members in attendance were practitioners who were held in high regard for their serious dedication to the development of accounting principles. The hour-long meeting was held in the SEC's offices in Washington on November 22. SEC Chairman Cohen presided, and Chief Accountant Barr attended.[26] It was one of the rare occasions on which the Commission met formally with members of the APB, and it was rarer still for such a meeting to be recorded on a stenographic transcript.[27] In his prepared remarks, Cohen made it known that the Commission's staff had "as early as August, 1950 recommended to a committee of the American Institute of Accountants to take a firm position" (p. 3) in the matter of the classification of deferred tax in such cases. He added: "The increasing incidence of these practices and the growing significance of the amounts involved convince us that the petition is right in urging us to act now rather than to tolerate further delay which your procedures would seem to require" (p. 3).

Cohen quoted from the AA petition as follows:

> Some companies which have heretofore included the deferred taxes in current liabilities have changed the classification to noncurrent liabilities. Other companies (some of which are our clients) are now taking the position that they will change the classification to noncurrent at the end of the current fiscal year if other companies are permitted to continue the noncurrent classification. This represents a retrogression in ac-

---

[26]"In the Matter of Conference with Representatives of the Accounting Principles Board re: Arthur Andersen & Co. Petition," Official Transcript of Proceedings before the Securities and Exchange Commission, Washington, D.C., November 22, 1965 (ACE-Federal Reporters, Inc, Official Reporters). Quotations from this transcript will be indicated by page number.

[27]On December 21, 1962, following issuance of the board's controversial *Opinion No. 2* [APB, 1962] on the investment tax credit, a delegation from the board met in Washington with four SEC Commissioners and several SEC staff members, but, as far as is known, no transcript was prepared.

counting which occurs when such alternative practices exist.

Cohen stated that the SEC's staff had already drafted a proposed release that would effectuate the AA petition, but that, before issuing the release, the Commission wanted to have the benefit of hearing the comments of the APB's delegation. And then he bluntly expressed his unhappiness with the board's performance and issued a thinly veiled threat (pp. 4-5):

> ... before we hear your comments I do want to take this opportunity to observe that this Commission, as you know, has been quite patient with the efforts of the ac-counting profession to solve a number of accounting matters as to which questionable alternative solutions have been accepted for some time. I am sure you are aware that, we and important persons in other parts of Washington, hear and receive many complaints that the profession seems unable to come to grips with the problems and to adopt solutions, even though extensive studies have been made and published.
>
> As you know, we have certain statutory responsi-bilities. It has been suggested strongly that if you can-not or will not move with reasonable dispatch to cope with these issues, we should. Now, while our patience has not been exhausted and we believe that coopera-tion with the Board has been most helpful and should continue, I wish to make the point that we do have a responsibility and that we do have to account for it.

In reply, Heimbucher stated that the board's decision to drop the paragraph on deferred tax from *Opinion No. 6* [APB, 1965] was that it had become controversial and that the pro-nouncement had to be issued with dispatch. He added that "some of those who voted to remove it from the bulletin at that time did so on the condition that a committee of the Board be appointed immediately to deal forthwith with this question" (p. 8). He said that he expected a three-man committee to report in time for the board's next meeting, in December, "and it is our earnest belief that we will be able to reach a conclusion on this during 1966, allowing for all of our exposure requirements, which take two or three months, and then a final ballot on the draft" (p. 9). Heimbucher hoped to persuade the SEC not to issue its release. Cohen then reminded the board members that the issue concerning the Commission is a larger one, namely, that "the profession finds great difficulty in arriving at solutions to problems which, albeit difficult, nevertheless appear to be subject to solution" (p. 10).

Herman Bevis pointed out that "these questions are far more difficult and far more complex than those you can state in rather simple form, and I myself believe, and I think you would agree, that what we are looking for is not just any solution which can't stand up in trial very long. We are looking for sound solutions" (p. 11). Cohen replied that he shared Bevis' view, but "as I pointed out this problem was addressed with a certain amount of conviction by our Chief Accountant 15 years ago, and I would think anyone would agree that is a reasonable period within which to find a solution" (p. 11).

John Queenan emphasized that the APB's program of research studies was now coming to the stage where the board will become more active in issuing *Opinions*. On the matter of income tax allocation, he said that he was one of those who did not consider it as a liability. To have approved the deferred tax as a current liability in some cases would, he said, have prejudged the outcome of the research study on tax allocation accounting that was still in preparation. Queenan also doubted that it was as urgent a matter as AA had argued, as he believed that the predominant practice was to show the deferred tax "outside of current [liabilities]" and that there are relatively few companies showing it as current. Hence, he implied, there would be few occasions for switchovers.

Chairman Cohen said he had no reason to question that the board could resolve the issue in 1966, but "I don't know how your resolution will come out...." (p. 18). It was clear to everyone that the Commission had made up its mind on the matter.

Herman Bevis, who was no more sympathetic with the current liability classification than was Queenan, proceeded to argue a point that could be described as *reductio ad absurdum*. He cited Spiegel Co., which showed $120m of long-term debt and only $30m of noncurrent assets. He then proposed that, if the deferred tax associated with installment receivables (a current asset) should be shown as a current liability, "it immediately raises the question of whether 90 of the 120 million of the long-term debt shouldn't also go up there, because it has to apply to something on the current asset side"[28] (p. 19). Chairman Cohen dismissed the argument peremptorily, as if everything

---

[28]This same point was made by a number of commentators on the exposure draft.

on the right side of the balance sheet should be linked to everything on the left side. This strained argument by Bevis could
not have given Cohen confidence in the board's ability to solve
the deferred tax problem. Then Bevis argued that most of the
companies that show the deferred tax as a noncurrent item are
the ones where the amount is the most significant, while those
that show it as a current liability claim only small amounts, as
if to suggest that the issue is not all that important. Amused at
Bevis' analysis, Chairman Cohen interjected, "May I partially in
jest – I hope it will be so understood – say that I draw from what
has been said that where the amount is not material and really
can't affect the current ratio very much they assign it to the current section, but where it is material and could affect the current
ratio it is assigned elsewhere. Is that too unfair a suggestion?"
(pp. 21-22). Bevis was not able to disagree with this reconstruc-
tion of his argument as an opportunity for manipulation.

Cohen then ventured the view that the Commission's draft
release, being an interpretation of existing requirements, could
be issued forthwith, without any prior exposure. He said he
was interested in issuing the release in time to affect financial
statements for the year ending December 31, 1965. Cohen also
expressed exasperation with the board's process: "there ought to
be an end to all the studies and all the committees that review
the work of prior committees, and someone ought to decide
something" (p. 25).

In the course of the discussion, Heimbucher and Weston
said they would classify deferred tax as a liability, while Queenan and Bevis had taken the other side. These matched pairs
could not have filled Chairman Cohen with confidence that the
board would successfully resolve the issue, even in 1966.

At the end of the meeting, Heimbucher and Weston urged
the Commission not to act in a way that would reflect unfavorably on the standing of the board, and Cohen expressed sym
pathy with their view. In fact, in a speech delivered eight days
later, he was reassuring on this point. Cohen [1965, p. 11] said:

> We are now considering some limited action of our
> own [on accounting] – action which is not designed to
> undermine the efforts of the leaders of the profession
> but rather to emphasize to the entire profession the
> urgency of immediate and effective support of those
> who are seeking sound procedures to obviate unjustified
> differences in the treatment and presentation of similar
> problems.

THE SEC ISSUES *ACCOUNTING SERIES RELEASE NO. 102*

On December 7, 1965, the day before the next APB meeting, the SEC issued *Accounting Series Release No. 102,* "Balance Sheet Classification of Deferred Income Taxes Arising from Installment Sales."[29] In the release, the Commission said: "Where installment receivables are classified as current assets in accordance with the operating cycle practice [citing *ARB No. 43,* Chapter 3A], the related liabilities or credit items maturing or expiring in the time period of the operating cycle, including the deferred income taxes on installment sales, should be classified as current liabilities." The SEC made no mention in the release of AA's petition or of the fact that the matter had been under study by the APB.

Although AA had asked in its petition that the rule take effect for fiscal years beginning after December 31, 1965, the SEC opted for a much faster implementation. The rule would apply to fiscal years *ending on or after* December 31, 1965. Catlett had informed Chief Accountant Barr of his firm's "deal" with MW, and he told Barr that if the SEC's rule were not to take effect until 1966 fiscal-year reports, MW and others in the small minority of retailers who were classifying the deferred tax liability as current would all switch to noncurrent in their 1965 reports. Catlett believed that this argument may have been a factor in the SEC's decision to accelerate the effective date.[30]

THE AFTERMATH OF *ACCOUNTING SERIES RELEASE NO. 102*

At the outset of the meeting of the APB on December 8-10, 1965, Chairman Heimbucher handed out confidential copies of the transcript of the meeting with the SEC and said that, at the time of the meeting with the SEC, the members of the APB's delegation were "certain" that the Commission would proceed to issue its draft release.[31] Heimbucher then quoted from SEC Chairman Cohen's remarks during the meeting that the board is taking much too long to solve the problems before it. Heimbucher was trying to impress on the members that, if the board

---

[29]Publication of the release was reported in "SEC Acts to Make Concerns More Uniform in Handling of Assets-Liabilities Accounts," *Wall Street Journal,* December 8, 1965, and in "SEC Prods Accountants," *Business Week,* January 15, 1966, p. 102.

[30]interview with George R. Catlett, dated May 3, 1978

[31]AICPA – APB, minutes of meeting, December 8-10, 1965, p. 2

did not begin to act more expeditiously, others, such as the SEC, would fill the void. Following the board's three-day meeting, George Catlett reported to his partners that he detected more of a sense of urgency about achieving constructive and effective progress than had ever existed since the board's inception. Not surprisingly, he said he noticed a degree of resentment toward AA on the part of some members, yet the salient point was that the impact on board members of the encounter with the SEC was palpable.[32]

Two members of the APB's research staff recalled that an effect of *Accounting Series Release No. 102* was that the board became more careful to include in exposure drafts only those views for which there was strong support.[33]

At a later point in the board's meeting, some members thought it would be desirable for the board to state publicly that it was not in conflict with the SEC over *Accounting Series Release No. 102*. The board therefore voted to authorize the administrative director to publish a statement in the *Journal of Accountancy* ["SEC Issues Opinion...," 1966] that it was "in substantial agreement with the position of the SEC." Yet the informal vote to do so was 11-5, a bare two-thirds majority.[34] The statement appeared in the January 1966 issue. While there apparently were only a few board members who disagreed in principle with the position espoused in the SEC's release, other board members had procedural concerns, including the belief that the board should not express a view on the classification question until the research study on current assets and liabilities, and perhaps also that on income tax allocation, were completed.

In April 1966, Kenneth S. Axelson, the financial vice president of J.C. Penney Company and chairman of NRMA's accounting principles committee, attacked *Accounting Series Release No. 102* in a letter to the *Journal of Accountancy*. He said that the NRMA had petitioned the SEC to delay the effective date of the release by three months, but that its petition was denied [Axelson, 1966, p. 27].[35]

---

[32]memorandum by George R. Catlett to his partners in AA, dated December 15, 1965

[33]interview with Reed K. Storey and Paul Rosenfield, August 1970

[34]AICPA – APB, minutes of meeting, December 8-10, 1965, p. 9

[35]Perhaps because of a belief that the retail industry should be better represented on the APB, the Institute's executive committee appointed Axelson to the board in 1968.

In May 1966, Leonard Spacek [1966, p. 381] said in a speech that "the SEC came to the rescue of professional accountants … while the accounting profession remained in an immobile state of indecision." On the other hand, Herman Bevis [1966] criticized the SEC's release as supporting uniformity of method over genuine comparability in financial reporting.[36]

By coincidence, in early December 1965, AA published a 42-page booklet, *Establishing Accounting Principles – A Crisis in Decision Making*, in which it criticized the APB for its ineffectiveness in narrowing the areas of difference in accounting practice. Copies of the booklet were distributed at the APB's meeting on December 8. AA [1965, p. 28] argued in the booklet that the APB should take steps "to deal with current problems on a timely basis and carry out its responsibilities in a truly professional manner." AA called for the establishment of a U.S. Court of Accounting Appeals in order to promote the uniformity of accounting practices prescribed by U.S. federal regulatory agencies, including the SEC [see "Accounting Court…," 1966]. At the board's meeting, Chairman Heimbucher took the time to quote from SEC Chairman Cohen's strong remarks during the hearing as well as from AA's charge to the APB to improve its effectiveness. The minutes of the board meeting reported that "Mr. Heimbucher stated that he quoted from these documents to emphasize the necessity for action on the part of the Board in dealing with accounting principles and to stress that, if the Board does not, other groups will assume the responsibility."[37]

George Catlett, who was a member of the APB from 1965 to 1971, said that the SEC's release was the event that prompted the board to begin taking difficult decisions on matters that would change prevailing practice, and to begin paying more attention to the SEC than to their clients.[38]

For his part, SEC Chairman Cohen [1966, p. 59] sent a strong message to the APB in a speech in May 1966. He said that *Accounting Series Release No. 102* was an example that "Stronger leadership by the Commission is one avenue being followed" in moving toward the goal of uniformity in accounting practice. He added:

> Although Accounting Series Release No. 102 was used to resolve one problem of uniformity, I do not be-

---

[36]See also the searing criticism of the release by Theodore Herz [1966], one of Bevis' partners.

[37]AICPA – APB, minutes of meeting, December 8-10, 1965, p. 3

[38]interviews with George R. Catlett, September 3, 1970 and May 3, 1978

lieve it will be necessary for us to use that device with great frequency—although the option is always open to us. The extent to which action on our part is required will depend in large measure on the vigor and determination of the Accounting Principles Board. . .

In December 1967, the APB issued *Opinion No. 11*, "Accounting for Income Taxes," which, in paragraph 57, explicitly adopted the SEC's position in *Accounting Series Release No. 102*. The APB really had little option but to do so. Three board members dissented, saying that this treatment "would contribute to a lack of understanding of working capital, because of the commingling of contingent items with items which are expected to be realized or discharged during the normal operating cycle of the business."[39] The *Opinion* passed by the barest two-thirds majority, 14-6.

REFERENCES

"Accounting Court of Appeals Proposed for Discussion" (1966), *Journal of Accountancy*, Vol. 121, No. 1: 8, 10.

Accounting Principles Board (APB) (1962), "Accounting for the 'Investment Credit'," *Opinion No. 2* (New York: American Institute of Certified Public Accountants).

Accounting Principles Board (APB) (1964), "Accounting for the 'Investment Credit'," *Opinion No. 4* (New York: American Institute of Certified Public Accountants).

Accounting Principles Board (APB) (1965), "Status of Accounting Research Bulletins," *Opinion No. 6* (New York: American Institute of Certified Public Accountants).

Accounting Principles Board (APB) (1967), "Accounting for Income Taxes," *Opinion No. 11* (New York: American Institute of Certified Public Accountants).

Arthur Andersen & Co. (1962), *Accounting and Reporting Problems of the Accounting Profession*, 2nd edn. (Chicago: Arthur Andersen & Co.).

Arthur Andersen & Co. (1965), *Establishing Accounting Principles – A Crisis in Decision Making* (Chicago: Arthur Andersen & Co.).

Arthur Andersen & Co. (1969), *Accounting and Reporting Problems of the Accounting Profession*, 3rd edn. (Chicago: Arthur Andersen & Co.).

Axelson, K.S. (1966), "NRMA Views on SEC Accounting Release No. 102" (Letters), *Journal of Accountancy*, Vol. 121, No. 4: 27, 29-30, 32.

Bevis, H.W. (1965), *Corporate Financial Reporting in a Competitive Economy* (New York: Macmillan).

Bevis, H.W. (1966), "Progress and Poverty in Accounting Thought," *Journal of Accountancy*, Vol. 122, No. 1: 34-40.

---

[39]The dissenting board members were John P. Biegler of Price Waterhouse, Sidney Davidson of the University of Chicago, and John Queenan of Haskins & Sells. All three members also dissented to the overall requirement for income tax allocation.

Blough, C.G. (1953), "Tax Provision for Uncollected Profit on Installment Accounts Receivable," *Journal of Accountancy*, Vol. 96, No. 3: 346-348.

Carey, J.L. (1970), *The Rise of the Accounting Profession: To Responsibility and Authority 1937-1969* (New York: American Institute of Certified Public Accountants).

Chatov, R. (1975), *Corporate Financial Reporting: Public or Private Control?* (New York: The Free Press/Macmillan).

Cohen, M.F. (1964), "Address before the Investment Bankers Association of America," Hollywood, FL, December 1 (typescript).

Cohen, M.F. (1965), "Address before the Investment Bankers Association of America," Hollywood, FL, November 30 (typescript).

Cohen, M.F. (1966), "Analysts, Accountants and the SEC – Necessary Joint Efforts," *Journal of Accountancy*, Vol. 122, No. 2: 57-62.

Committee on Accounting Procedure (1944), "Accounting for Income Taxes," *Accounting Research Bulletin No. 23* (New York: American Institute of Accountants).

Committee on Accounting Procedure (1947), "Current Assets and Current Liabilities – Working Capital," *Accounting Research Bulletin No. 30* (New York: American Institute of Accountants).

Committee on Accounting Procedure (1953), "Restatement and Revision of Accounting Research Bulletins," *Accounting Research Bulletin No. 43* (New York: American Institute of Accountants).

Committee on Accounting Procedure (1958), "Declining-balance Depreciation," *Accounting Research Bulletin No. 44 Revised* (New York: American Institute of Certified Public Accountants, July).

Committee on Accounting Procedure (1959), "Letter to the Members of the American Institute of Certified Public Accountants," dated April 15, in *Accounting Research and Terminology Bulletins – Final Edition* (New York: American Institute of Certified Public Accountants, 1961).

Defliese, P.L. (1974), "The Search for Standards: U.S. and Abroad" (colloquy), in Burns, T.J. (ed.), *Accounting in Transition: Oral Histories of Recent U.S. Experience* (Columbus, OH: College of Administrative Science, Ohio State University): 16-46.

"Exposure Draft of Tentative Opinion: Status of Accounting Research Bulletins" (1965), *Journal of Accountancy*, Vol. 120, No. 2: 57-60.

Grady, P.F. (1965), *Inventory of Generally Accepted Accounting Principles for Business Enterprises* (New York: American Institute of Certified Public Accountants).

Heimbucher, C.V. (1966), "Current Developments at the Accounting Principles Board," *Journal of Accountancy*, Vol. 121, No. 2: 47-48.

Herz, T. (1966), "SEC Accounting Series Release No. 102" (Letters), *Financial Executive*, Vol. 34, No. 3: 6, 8.

Hicks, E.L. (1966), "Accounting Series Release No. 102," *The New York Certified Public Accountant*, Vol. 36, No. 2: 130-131.

Lytle, R.C. (1965), "APB Revises Exposure Draft in Issuing Opinion No. 6," *Journal of Accountancy*, Vol. 120, No. 6: 71-73.

Moonitz, M. (1966), "Some Reflections on the Investment Credit Experience," *Journal of Accounting Research*, Vol. 4, No. 1: 47-61.

Moonitz, M. (1974), *Obtaining Agreement on Standards in the Accounting Profession* (Sarasota, FL: American Accounting Association).

Olson, N.O. (1966), "Establishing Accounting Principles and the Role of Research," in *In Pursuit of Professional Goals* (Chicago: Arthur Andersen & Co., 1973): 53-65.

"Opinion No. 6 – Status of Accounting Research Bulletins" (1965), *Journal of Accountancy*, Vol. 120, No. 5: 54-58.

Pines, J.A. (1965), "The Securities and Exchange Commission and Accounting Principles," *Law and Contemporary Problems*, Vol. 30, No. 4: 727-751.

Rappaport, L.H. (1972), *SEC Accounting Practice and Procedure*, 3rd edn. (New York: The Ronald Press Company).

"Report to Council of the Special Committee on Research Program" (1958), *Journal of Accountancy*, Vol. 106, No. 6: 62-68.

"SEC Issues Opinion on Deferred Income Taxes" (News Report) (1966), *Journal of Accountancy*, Vol. 121, No. 1: 8.

Securities and Exchange Commission (1945), "In the Matter of 'Charges in Lieu of Taxes': Statement of the Commission's Opinion Regarding 'Charges in Lieu of Income Taxes' and 'Provisions for Income Taxes' in the Profit and Loss Statement," *Accounting Series Release No. 53* (Washington, DC: Securities and Exchange Commission).

Securities and Exchange Commission (1965), "Balance Sheet Classification of Deferred Income Taxes Arising from Installment Sales," *Accounting Series Release No. 102* (Washington, DC: Securities and Exchange Commission).

Seligman, J. (2003), *The Transformation of Wall Street: A History of the Securities and Exchange Commission and Modern Corporate Finance*, 3rd edn. (New York: Aspen Publishers).

Spacek, L. (1966), "Burdens Placed on the Investor by Questionable Accounting Practices" in *A Search for Fairness in Financial Reporting to the Public* (Chicago: Arthur Andersen & Co., 1969): 377-386.

"Special Bulletin (Disclosure of Departures from Opinions of APB) and APB Opinion No. 6 (Status of Accounting Research Bulletins)" (1965), *Executive Letter* (Price Waterhouse & Co.), November 18.

Sprouse, R.T. and Moonitz, M. (1962), *A Tentative Set of Broad Accounting Principles for Business Enterprises* (New York: American Institute of Certified Public Accountants).

"Uniformity in Financial Accounting" (1965), *Law and Contemporary Problems*, Vol. 30, No. 4.

Zeff, S.A. (1972), *Forging Accounting Principles in Five Countries: A History and an Analysis of Trends* (Champaign, IL: Stipes Publishing).

Zeff, S.A. (2001), "The Work of the Special Committee on Research Program," *Accounting Historians Journal*, Vol. 28, No. 2: 141-186.

Zeff, S.A. and Fossum, R.L. (1967), "An Analysis of Large Audit Clients," *Accounting Review*, Vol. 42, No. 2: 298-320.

The SEC Rules Historical Cost Accounting
1934 to the 1970s

*Stephen A. Zeff**

Abstract—From its founding in 1934 until 1972 the SEC, and especially its Chief Accountant, disapproved of most upward revaluations and general price-level restatements of fixed assets as well as depreciation charges based thereon. This article is a historical study of the evolution of the SEC's policy on upward revaluations and restatements of non-financial assets. It treats episodes prior to 1972 when the private-sector bodies that established accounting principles sought to gain a degree of acceptance for such revaluations and restatements but were consistently rebuffed by the SEC. The SEC reversed its policy on upward revaluations during the period from 1972 to the end of the 1970s. Throughout the article, the author endeavours to explain the factors that influenced the successive positions taken by the SEC.

It is well known that the United States has long been a bastion of predominantly historical cost accounting for inventories and fixed assets. Not so well known, however, is the fact that the US insistence on the use of historical cost accounting has emanated from the Securities and Exchange Commission (SEC) and has not always been a tenet held and advocated by leaders of the accountancy profession. It is the aim of this paper to trace the SEC's powerful influence over the predominance of historical cost accounting in the US from its founding in 1934 until the 1970s.

1. EARLY EVOLUTION OF THE SEC'S POSITION ON HISTORICAL COST

The SEC came into existence on 2 July 1934 and was charged with administering the Securities Act of 1933 and the Securities Exchange Act of 1934,

---

* The author is the Herbert S. Autrey Professor of Accounting, Rice University, Houston, Texas, USA. Correspondence address: Jesse H. Jones Graduate School of Management, Rice University—MS 531, PO Box 2932, Houston, TX 77252-2932, USA. E-mail: sazeff@ rice.edu. This paper is an outgrowth of the author's presentation at the Information for Better Markets conference, sponsored by the Institute of Chartered Accountants in England and Wales and held in London on December 18–19, 2006. The author is grateful to Kees Camfferman, Todd Johnson, seminar participants at Cardiff Business School, and an anonymous reviewer for useful comments on earlier drafts.

the second of which established the SEC.[1] This legislation empowered the SEC to set the rules and regulations to govern the reporting, accounting and disclosure of financial information by companies whose securities were quoted on any national securities exchange, including the contents of prospectuses and periodic filings with the Commission. The SEC created the position of Chief Accountant in the autumn of 1935, and after a short search it named Carman G. Blough, a Certified Public Accountant and former academic and Wisconsin government employee who had joined the Commission's registration division in 1934, to the position on 1 December 1935 (Chatov, 1975:103; Cooper, 1980:22). He remained as Chief Accountant until May 1938, when he left the Commission. From 1944 to 1961, he served as the full-time Director of Research of the American Institute of Accountants (AIA, Institute).[2]

The person who effectively cemented the SEC's policy to insist upon historical accounting was Robert E. Healy (pronounced Haley). Prior to becoming one of the five founding SEC Commissioners in 1934, Healy had been Chief Counsel of the Federal Trade Commission (FTC) from 1928 to 1934 and directed the FTC's six-year, Congressionally mandated investigation into the market manipulations by public utility holding companies, with heavy emphasis on their use of dubious accounting practices during the 1920s. In the end, the record of the investigation accumulated to 95 volumes.

Healy had been a justice on the Vermont Supreme Court, and President Calvin Coolidge, a Vermonter himself, selected his fellow Republican to direct the FTC's mammoth investigation. Joel Seligman, the SEC's historian, has written, 'The experience radicalised the conservative Healy. Shocked to find that "you can capitalise in some States practically everything except the furnace ashes in the basement", he became an uncompromising advocate of accounting and public utility reform' (2003:108).

Healy was livid at the asset value write-ups that public utilities had been booking. It was not only the write-ups themselves, 'however arrived at' (as he said), that incensed him as much as the utilities' follow-on accounting practices. He complained of 'write-ups used to create income or to relieve the income accounts of important charges' (1938:1), which would be debited to the capital surplus account that had been credited with the write-ups. Dividends would sometimes be paid against this unrealised appreciation, and 'Very often unamortised debt discount was charged against a capital surplus so created, thus increasing the reported earnings of the company in future years' (Healy, 1939:4). He was driven to the conclusion that all upward departures from historical cost were veritably heinous. In testimony

---

[1] The Federal Trade Commission administered the Securities Act of 1933 from June 1933 until 1 September 1934, when this authority was transferred to the SEC.

[2] For a discussion of the role of the Chief Accountant in relation to the establishment of accounting principles, see the Appendix [to this paper].

to a Congressional committee in April 1934, he said, 'I think the proper function of accounting is to make a historical record of events as they happen' (*Stock Exchange Practices*, 1934:7606).[3] Later in the 1930s he wrote, 'I think the purpose of accounting is to account—not to present opinions of value' (1938:6).

Remarking on Healy's influence within the SEC, Carman Blough wrote as follows, 30 years later:

'One of the first members of the newly formed SEC to be appointed was a former General Counsel for the Federal Trade Commission who had been in charge of that Commission's very comprehensive investigation of the public utility holding companies. During that study the flagrant write-up policies of the holding companies and their subsidiaries and the havoc they caused when the crash came in 1929 and 1930 kept impressing themselves on the chief investigator to the point that their evil became almost an obsession with him. . . . So strong were his convictions and so convincing were his arguments against write-ups that all of the other members of the Commission were persuaded to take a positive stand against them from the very first case in which the question arose.' (1967:10).

Homer Kripke, a distinguished legal scholar who was an SEC attorney in 1939–44, has written,

'Healy's strong views dominated the Commission in the 1930s and 1940s when it was still struggling to undo the effects of the indiscriminate departures from [historical] cost in the 1920s. They influenced a whole generation of SEC accountants, the seniors of whom had served during his incumbency, until the retirement of Andrew Barr as Chief Accountant in 1972. It would be unfair to attribute the SEC's position *solely* to Healy, since the position continued for over a quarter of a century after his death. His position became that of other commissioners and a long succession of staff members because it suited their needs to emphasise objectivity at the expense of other potential attributes of an accounting system.' (1979:182)

Healy served on the SEC from 1934 until his death in November 1946. His record of service as a Commissioner was the longest in the SEC's history. Blough's immediate three successors as Chief Accountant—William W. Werntz (1938–47), Earle C. King (1947–56), and Andrew Barr (1956–72)—all had joined the Commission's accounting staff in the 1930s. Healy and like-minded Commissioners succeeded in instilling in them an aversion to

---

[3] This passage was quoted, slightly amiss, in de Bedts (1964:93).

upward departures from historical cost if they had not already held that view. In fact, Barr had studied under A. C. Littleton, at the University of Illinois, who was the intellectual leader of the historical cost school.

In a comprehensive study of write-ups, R.G. Walker found that, in the SEC's first several years, its staff discouraged write-ups, and the Commission rejected asset appraisals that were devoid of adequate supporting evidence, not so much because of the revaluation practice *per se* (1992:10–15).[4] In some cases, notably *Northern States Power Company*, a divided Commission (with Healy in the minority) allowed appraisals if there was sufficient disclosure of the procedure used (Healy, 1938:2–3). Around 1937/38, however, the SEC and its accounting staff began to take a more unequivocal stance against write-ups and by the 1940s were actively banning them. Walker wrote, 'It appears that the SEC had virtually eliminated write-ups from the accounting practices of its registrants by the mid-1940s' (1992:22). By 1970, Kripke would write, 'In effect the SEC has made it an exercise in futility for practicing accountants or anyone else to argue for revision of valuation methods in balance sheets or income statements' (1970:1189).

In 1936, the SEC received some academic support for its historical cost position when the American Accounting Association's executive committee, led by Association President Eric L. Kohler, published 'A tentative statement of accounting principles affecting corporate reports', which strongly endorsed 'original cost' for physical assets. The committee said, 'If values other than unamortised [historical] costs are to be quoted they should be expressed in financial statements only as collateral notations for informative purposes' (1936:189). The committee was explicitly critical of revaluations and the use of adjustments for 'ordinary' changes in price levels. It is likely that the Association's executive committee was also recoiling from the indiscriminate asset write-ups in the 1920s.

Not surprisingly, SEC Chief Accountant Blough said in 1937 that he agreed with the Association's tentative statement (1937:30). Four years later, the Association published an important monograph written by two members of its 1936 executive committee, William A. Paton and A. C. Littleton, which contained an elegant conceptual rationale for the use of historical cost accounting. Yet in their final chapter, entitled 'Interpretation', the authors (chiefly Paton) objectively discussed the pros and cons of replacement cost accounting and 'common dollar' accounting. As to the latter, they said, 'At the most what is needed is a special report supplementing the usual periodic statements and designed to trace the main effects of general price movements upon the affairs of the enterprise' (1940:141), which was a heady proposal at that time. Of the two authors of the monograph, Littleton, at the University

---

[4] Reflecting mainly on the Commission's early years, Barr and Koch (1959:181–2) have written, 'A review of the informal cases involving appraisals shows that the Commission usually effected the elimination of the appraisal'.

of Illinois, was, throughout his career, an arch historical coster. Paton, at the University of Michigan, was a 'value' man.[5] The historical cost portion of this monograph became a standard text used in university accounting curricula and was widely read by practitioners as well.

2. DEVELOPMENTS IN THE 1940s AND 1950s: THE SEC'S POSITION HARDENS

2.1. Write-ups

In the context of the SEC's stiffening position on asset write-ups, the US body that established accounting principles (as standard setting was then known), the AIA's part-time Committee on Accounting Procedure, which was composed of 18 practitioners in accountancy firms and three academics, began addressing the question itself. In its *Accounting Research Bulletin (ARB) No. 5*, 'Depreciation on appreciation', issued in April 1940, the committee said, in less than categorical terms, 'Appreciation [on fixed assets] normally should not be reflected on the books of account of corporations' (461). It added, however, that, where such appreciation has been recorded, 'income should be charged with depreciation computed on the new and higher figures' (461). The editor of *The Journal of Accountancy* said that the topic of the *Bulletin* 'has proved to be a particularly thorny subject' ('Two new Research Bulletins', 1940:427). In fact, there were four dissenters. Noteworthy among them was William Paton, who wrote that depreciation on appreciation should not be a determinant of net income 'except in cases where the appraisal is a feature of formal or quasi-reorganization' (467). The *Bulletin* contained only an inconclusive discussion of the pros and cons of allowing asset write-ups by means of a quasi-reorganisation.

The term 'quasi-reorganisation' refers to an accounting procedure by which a company in severe financial straits, with a deficit in retained earnings, could avoid the expensive process of a legal reorganisation by eliminating the deficit and writing down its net asset values to levels that are justified in the light of its economic prospects, as if the company were engaging in a fresh start. Thereby, the company would have the prospect of declaring dividends in future years. Today, we would use the term 'impairment loss' as the rough equivalent of the write-down in the net assets, although the procedure to be used in a quasi-reorganisation is much more elaborate and may require approval by the shareholders (see SEC, 1941; Davis and Largay, 1995).

By the middle of the 1940s, the committee began looking for ways to gain acceptance for upward departures from historical cost. In 1945, the

---

[5] Letter from Paton to the author, dated 24 February 1979.

committee unanimously resolved to elaborate on *ARB No. 5*. The committee's proposal, made in the form of a resolution in October 1945, was intended to open the door to the acceptability of an 'upward' quasi-reorganisation when 'supported by convincing evidence and [when] effected with due formality' ('Annual Report', 1946:104).[6] The argument was made that, since a company could liquidate itself and come into existence afresh by recognising contemporary current costs, whether higher or lower, in its balance sheet, why should it not be possible to establish a new basis of accountability without actually liquidating and relaunching the company? This may have been a tactic to 'blind-side' the SEC, which had accepted a 'downward' quasi-reorganisation. The committee intended to draft an *Accounting Research Bulletin* to reflect this unanimous view. Yet, the following year, the committee reported that it had decided to postpone the preparation of a formal *Bulletin* ('Annual Report', 1947:109). The reason was that SEC Chief Accountant William Werntz had publicly made known his antipathy to using the quasi-reorganisation to record a write-up of assets (1945:386–7). Instead, the committee was content to write a letter to the AIA's executive committee dated 20 October 1945, saying

> '. . . a new cost may and should be recognised whenever a new basis of corporate accountability is established by reorganisation or quasi-reorganisation if the carrying value of assets on the books has ceased to be representative of their value.'[7] (the letter was reproduced in Research Department, 1950:390)

Five years later, in 1950, the committee returned to the question, following the high post-war inflation. It decided, again unanimously, to draft a *Bulletin* to recommend quasi-reorganisation accounting that would allow write-ups. But the SEC scotched the initiative yet again by advising the committee that it would not accept financial statements with write-ups of the kind envisaged in the proposed *Bulletin*. Hence, the *Bulletin* was never issued (see Zeff, 1972:156–7).

When SEC Chief Accountants criticised upward departures from historical cost, it was customary that they raised the spectre of the indiscriminate write-up practices of the 1920s, as if it were a nightmare that should not be experienced again.

It was apparently of no moment to the SEC's Chief Accountant that an 'upward' quasi-reorganisation had won the support of two of the intellectual

---

[6] An 'upward' quasi-reorganisation might be labelled today as an 'enhancement gain' as the opposite number of an impairment loss.

[7] It is not clear what authority such a letter would possess, although it may be assumed that the SEC's accounting staff knew of it. In effect, by sending the letter instead of issuing an *Accounting Research Bulletin*, the Committee was registering its view without 'officially' proposing a practice to be followed.

leaders of the profession. The *doyen* of the accountancy profession, George O. May, a retired partner of Price, Waterhouse & Co. and a member and a former vice-chairman of the Committee, had given support to such a procedure in a major book (1943:99). William Paton, who was a member of the Committee from 1939 to 1950, had been writing since 1940 that there was an urgent need to allow an 'upward' quasi-reorganisation in order to correct for historical costs that were out of line with current economic realities (see Zeff, 1979:115, 122–6).

Between these two ill-fated attempts to issue a *Bulletin* in favour of 'upward' quasi-reorganisations, which were crushed by explicit opposition from the SEC, the Committee faced the question of accounting for the effects of the high post-war inflation on depreciation. In 1947, several major companies, including United States Steel, DuPont, Allied Chemical & Dye, and Sears Roebuck, opted to record depreciation at replacement cost in their financial statements. Industry was concerned that companies with a sizable depreciation charge were significantly overstating their reported earnings. Such earnings reports, companies believed, would be a stimulus for encouraging labour unions, which had been prevented from pursuing negotiations over wages during the war, to press for significant wage increases and pension benefits. Also, major companies sought a way of defending themselves against public criticisms that they were profiteering at the public's expense (see Smith, 1955:172, 363–5, Appendix B; *Depreciation Policy When Price Levels Change*, 1948). Finally, industry hoped that the use of replacement cost depreciation in their financial statements might persuade Congress to give them comparable relief from being taxed on capital. But SEC Chief Accountant Earle King, as could be predicted, immediately objected to these upward departures from historical cost (1947a:22), which prompted US Steel instead to adopt accelerated historical cost depreciation on its post-war expenditures for property, plant and equipment, which, as it happens, produced financial results that were not all that different from the use of replacement cost depreciation (see McMullen, 1949; Blough, 1947). King was content with this tactical shift adopted by US Steel (1950:43). Congress, like the SEC, preferred the objectivity of historical cost, and in 1954 it struck a compromise by introducing two new methods of accelerated depreciation on historical cost into the income tax law.

Because of the suddenness of the decision of these major companies in 1947 to adopt replacement cost depreciation in the determination of earnings, the Committee had to act quickly to express its view as soon as possible. After the rebuff administered by the SEC two years earlier to the Committee's attempt to sanction write-ups under the head of quasi-reorganisations, it is likely that some Committee members who favoured the use of replacement cost depreciation would have voted against it because of expected opposition of the SEC. Therefore, it is difficult to know whether all of the Committee members were voting their genuinely held views. The

Committee reacted quickly by publishing a statement in the October 1947 issue of *The Journal of Accountancy* (Committee on Accounting Procedure, 1947). The Committee re-issued this statement as *Accounting Research Bulletin No. 33*, entitled 'Depreciation and high costs', dated December 1947. The Committee's decision, which was taken with one qualified assent and one abstention,[8] was that any depreciation in excess of normal historical cost depreciation for the year should be recorded 'below the line', meaning as an appropriation of net income or surplus and not as a deduction in arriving at net income. It said that 'consideration of radical changes in accepted accounting procedure should not be undertaken, at least until a stable price level would make it practicable for business as a whole to make the change at the same time'. Of course, by the time a stable price level were to be achieved, the opponents of an upward departure from historical cost depreciation could dismiss the issue as no longer urgent. SEC Chief Accountant King, who had attended the Committee's meeting, publicly lauded the Committee's statement (1947b:127–8).[9]

In October 1948, the Committee, stung by criticisms made of *ARB No. 33* at the Institute's annual meeting the previous month,[10] reaffirmed its position on replacement cost depreciation in a letter to Institute members (Committee on Accounting Procedure, 1948). But by then the vote attracted four dissenters—the chairman who was the senior technical partner at Peat Marwick (Samuel J. Broad), two well-known partners from middle-sized firms (Maurice E. Peloubet and C. Oliver Wellington, a former chairman of the Committee), and an accounting professor (Paton). These four disagreed with the Committee's view that 'no basic change in the accounting treatment of depreciation of plant and equipment is practicable or desirable under present [inflationary] conditions' (1948:381). This was the first time in the Committee's history that its chairman had registered a dissent. But, as always, the SEC won the day. In the same issue of *The Journal of Accountancy* in which the Committee's letter was reproduced, the editor defended the Committee's position at length in an editorial ('Institute Committee', 1948).

During the 1940s, the American Accounting Association twice published revisions of its 1936 'principles' statement, in 1941 and 1948 ('Accounting principles', 1941; 'Accounting concepts and standards',

---

[8] The abstaining party was William Paton, who wrote to the author on 6 December 1971 that he left the Committee's meeting room in despair during the discussion prior to taking the vote.

[9] King wrote, '[Assistant Chief Accountant Andrew] Barr and I were present at the meeting at which this release was decided upon and it was strongly advocated by us'. Letter from Earle C. King to The Commission, dated 22 October 1947 (in the author's files).

[10] Prominent among those who criticised *ARB No. 33* during the annual meeting was George O. May, who had been privately counselling U.S. Steel on the wording of the disclosures relating to its replacement cost depreciation charge, with which he agreed. Another critic, who spoke on the floor of the annual meeting, was William Blackie, a CPA, who was vice president of Caterpillar Tractor Co. See Blackie (1948). Interview with Carman Blough, January 1967. See also Papworth (1948:383–4).

1948). Both reaffirmed the 'cost principle'. As in 1936, they were critical of revaluations, and they said that the country's experience with changing price levels did not warrant making adjustments for such changes. Again, as in 1936, they relegated values other than historical cost to supplementary disclosures. In its 1941 *Annual Report*, the SEC applauded the 1941 revision (SEC, 1942:198; see also Werntz, 1941:315). In its 1948 Annual Report, the SEC mentioned the 1948 revision in a favourable light (SEC, 1949:112).

For its part, the SEC took a step in 1950 towards making permanent its requirement that historical cost be used in registrants' financial statements. It announced a general revision of its *Regulation S-X*, which governs the contents of financial reports filed with the Commission and until then had dealt chiefly with matters of disclosure and display. The proposed revision incorporated a number of substantive accounting policy positions that had been dealt with during the 1940s in *Accounting Series Releases*. These included a new provision that said, 'Except as otherwise specifically provided, accounting for all assets shall be based on cost' ('Security [sic] and Exchange Commission', 1950:160). The effect of this new provision would change an ad hoc position of the Commission on the use of historical cost to one that was set in stone. So strong was the negative reaction within the accountancy profession to many of the SEC's proposed changes in *Regulation S-X*, which included a rare expression of opposition from the assembled members at an annual meeting of the American Accounting Association (Zeff, 1966:64–5), that the SEC in 1951 withdrew the provisions dealing with accounting principles in the proposed revision of *Regulation S-X* in return for an assurance that the Committee on Accounting Procedure would, among other things, codify its series of *Bulletins* (Zeff, 1972:158–9).[11] Yet the SEC achieved its objective by another means: the revised *Regulation S-X* included a provision that in effect incorporated the *Accounting Series Releases* in the regulation (see Barr, 1979:51).

In 1953, the Committee issued *Accounting Research Bulletin No. 43*, which was a restatement and revision of the Committee's previous *Bulletins* dealing with accounting principles and procedure. This was the codification sought by the SEC. Chapter 9A of the *Bulletin* was a reaffirmation of *ARB No. 33*, but six of the 20 Committee members dissented, which was one vote short of defeating the reaffirmation. The dissenters included senior partners of Peat Marwick and Price Waterhouse, three well-known partners of middle-sized firms, and an academic. The Committee felt obliged to state in Chapter 9B of *ARB No. 43* that, in cases where upward revaluations in depreciable assets had

---

[11] Chief Accountant King had earlier recommended that the Committee on Accounting Procedure publish a comprehensive statement of accounting principles (1948).

been recorded, the subsequent depreciation should be computed on the written-up amounts.

In the late 1940s and into the 1950s, there was disagreement within and among the largest accountancy firms on the propriety of using replacement cost depreciation. Evidently, Peat Marwick was opposed, but senior partners in Price Waterhouse and Arthur Andersen were at odds within their respective firms on the contentious subject.[12]

From 1954 to 1958, consecutive subcommittees of the Committee on Accounting Procedure laboured to develop a *Bulletin* that would allow the upward revaluation of assets, using the analogy of a quasi-reorganisation. Curiously, these efforts had been encouraged by a suggestion from SEC Chairman J. Sinclair Armstrong that it would be helpful to have an authoritative statement of the circumstances in which upward departures from historical cost might be justified (see Armstrong, 1956:159–60). Yet in 1958, by which time Armstrong was no longer on the Commission, the SEC's accounting staff signified to the committee that there was no need for such a general statement. Thereupon, the committee removed the project from its agenda.[13]

2.2. General Price-Level Accounting

Since the late 1940s, interest had been growing in the use of general price-level adjustments applied to historical cost, rather than the use of current cost, to reflect the impact of the increase in prices on financial statements.[14] Perhaps a reason for this different tack, in the minds of some, was the hope that the SEC might view it as less open to objection than the use of current cost. In 1952, the report of the Study Group on Business Income, which

---

[12] Two successive senior technical partners at Peat Marwick, Samuel Broad and John Peoples, dissented from the Committee on Accounting Procedure's letter reaffirming *ARB No. 33* and Chapter 9A in *ARB No. 43*, respectively. In Price, Waterhouse (PW), John B. Inglis, who gave US Steel a qualified report in 1947 because of its use of replacement cost depreciation, voted in favour, but the redoubtable George O. May, by then retired but very much an active thinker and writer, and his protégé in the firm, Paul Grady, together with several other senior PW partners were opposed. In Arthur Andersen, Paul K. Knight, a partner in the firm's New York office and a member of the committee, was in favour, while Leonard Spacek and the partners in the Chicago home office were opposed. The academic who opposed Chapter 9A was C. Aubrey Smith, of the University of Texas, who had spent the summer of 1935 in the SEC's registration division. From outward appearances, the leading partners in Ernst & Ernst, Haskins & Sells, and Lybrand, Ross Bros. & Montgomery were in favour of the position adopted in *ARB No. 33* and in Chapter 9A of *ARB No. 43*.

[13] Report of the Committee on Accounting Procedure, dated 30 September 1958 (in the author's files). As it happened, the Committee chairman at that time was former SEC Chief Accountant Werntz, by then a partner in a major accountancy firm.

[14] An early indication of this interest was the publication in April 1949 by the AIA's Research Department of a memorandum entitled 'An inquiry into the reliability of index numbers', which was originally intended 'for use as background material for consideration by the committee on accounting procedure in its deliberations as to the feasibility of using index numbers for adjustment of depreciation and/or property carrying values' (Research Department, 1949:312 ftn 1).

was engineered by George O. May, recommended that 'corporations whose ownership is widely distributed should be encouraged to furnish [supplementary] information that will facilitate the determination of income measured in units of approximately equal purchasing power', subject to audit where practicable (1952:105).[15] SEC Chief Accountant King, who was a member of the broadly constituted Study Group, strongly dissented from this recommendation (1952:122–3). The Study Group's report provided encouragement for the emerging interest, stimulated by the earlier writings of Henry W. Sweeney (1936) and William Paton (1941), in general price-level (GPL)-restated financial information to deal with the recent run-up of inflation.

Beginning in 1953/54, under the aggressive leadership of Leonard Spacek, Arthur Andersen & Co., which had a large client base in the public utility industry, was an outspoken advocate of current cost accounting or, alternatively, the use of GPL indices to restate historical cost depreciation.[16] Indeed, in March 1954 the firm boldly petitioned the SEC to require companies to state in an audited footnote the amount by which net income failed to reflect GPL-restated depreciation of plant and property.[17] In May 1954, the SEC denied the firm's petition, saying as follows:

'The Commission has concluded that [the firm's proposal] is not in accordance with sound and generally accepted accounting principles, that it does not have substantial authoritative support, and that its adoption is not necessary or appropriate in the public interest or for the protection of investors or consumers to carry out the provisions of the statutes administered by the Commission.'[18]

A more categorical denial could hardly be imagined. In the 1950s and 1960s, Spacek's activism led his firm to support the efforts of several of its public utility clients to record GPL-restated depreciation or current cost-adjusted depreciation in their financial statements, one client also doing a

---

[15] The Study Group was sponsored by the Institute and was financed jointly by it and the Rockefeller Foundation. It was composed of businessmen, lawyers, economists, statisticians, and others, as well as accountants.

[16] In the UK, GPL accounting became known as Current Purchasing Power (CPP) accounting. GPL accounting was not regarded by theorists as a departure from historical cost accounting but instead as an adaptation of historical cost accounting to inflationary conditions.

[17] The petition was transmitted in a letter to the Commission on 24 March 1954 and was signed by Leonard Spacek on behalf of the firm. Curiously, the SEC, when reporting on the petition in its next *Annual Report*, erroneously referred to the petition as calling for 'economic depreciation (based on replacement at current prices)' (SEC, 1955:107). Perhaps Chief Accountant King did not fully appreciate the difference between GPL-restatements and replacement cost adjustments.

[18] Letter from Orval L. DuBois, Secretary, Securities and Exchange Commission, to Leonard Spacek, dated 28 May, 1954. The firm's petition, as well as the letter from DuBois, is in the author's files. The term 'substantial authoritative support' has been used by the SEC since 1938 as the criterion for sound accounting practice. See the SEC's *Accounting Series Release No. 4* (1938), which continues to be in effect today.

GPLrestatement of its fixed assets in the balance sheet (see Randall, 1974; Staff of the Accounting Research Division, 1963:194–9, 211–17). The companies' motivation was to show a reduced net income in the light of a larger investment base following the post-war inflation, so that this lower rate of return on assets would support their argument to regulators for higher energy rates to consumers. Yet those of its clients that were SEC registrants were required to relocate the depreciation charge 'below the line' in their filings with the Commission (Zeff, 1992:457–9; Goodrich, 1969). The SEC insisted that a company's reported earnings must reflect depreciation based on conventional historical cost.

Apart from its work with audit clients, Andersen issued a series of publications from 1959 onwards in which it advocated one or another form of price-level depreciation, price-level accounting, and eventually 'value accounting' (*Memorandum on Price-Level Depreciation*, 1959; *Accounting and Reporting Problems of the Accounting Profession*, 1969:5–16; *Objectives of Financial Statements*, 1972).

Also during the 1950s, the American Accounting Association, the organisation of accounting academics, took up the cause of GPL-restated financial reporting. In 1951, an Association committee, which included a leading practitioner (Maurice H. Stans, of Alexander Grant & Company), recommended that companies include comprehensive GPL-restated financial statements as supplementary information to their primary statements ('Price level changes and financial statements', 1951). In 1955–56, the Association published three monographs that explained and illustrated GPL-restated financial statements and argued their merits (Mason, 1955; Jones, 1955; Jones, 1956).

In 1957, the Association committee charged with revising its 'principles' statements turned a corner, departing from the Association's three previous 'principles' statements on whether to provide GPL-restated information. The committee, chaired by Robert K. Mautz of the University of Illinois, recommended that investors *should be* furnished with supplementary data 'to reflect the effect of price changes in the specific assets held by the enterprise during the period, to show the effect upon the enterprise of movements in the general price level, or to achieve both purposes' (Committee on Accounting Concepts and Standards, 1957:544). After having indicated its positive view on the Association's three previous 'principles' statement, the SEC was conspicuously silent in its *Annual Reports* about whether it endorsed the Association's most recent statement. Chief Accountant Barr would write in 1959, begrudgingly, that the SEC 'probably would not object to the inclusion of such [GPL-restated] statements as supplementary material in a filing with the Commission' (Barr and Koch, 1959:182).

During the 1960s, the Accounting Principles Board (APB), which had succeeded the Committee on Accounting Procedure in 1959, became interested in GPL-restatements. In 1963, the APB sponsored the publication of a research study that explained and illustrated GPL-restated financial statements (Staff of the Accounting Research Division, 1963). In an APB research study published in 1965 and written by Paul Grady, a senior partner in Price Waterhouse, he carried forward the views of his late mentor, George O. May, by advocating a supplementary reporting of the financial effects of price-level changes (1965:370).

By the end of the 1960s, the APB added tempered support for GPL-restated financial statements as supplements to the primary statements. In 1969, the APB unanimously approved a non-binding *Statement* to call for the supplementary disclosure of GPL-restated statements. Initially, the subcommittee that began in 1966 to draft the pronouncement understood that the board intended to issue it as a mandatory *Opinion*. Miller and Redding report that the pronouncement became a *Statement* when the board found that it was unable to secure a two-thirds majority for GPL-restatements as a required practice (1986:91).[19] Had the APB issued an *Opinion*, the SEC would not have enforced compliance with it. Indeed, at the board's August 1967 meeting, LeRoy Layton, the chairman of the subcommittee, informed the board that SEC Chief Accountant Andrew Barr 'was generally not in favour of the positions taken in the draft Opinion principally because of the problems associated with (a) parallel statement presentation, (b) continued restatement of previous financial statements as general price indices change, which he believes would be baffling to readers and might be used as an excuse for "appraisal accounting" by some persons, and (c) possible legal implications'.[20] In the event, few companies adopted the APB's recommendation.

As noted earlier, the periodic intervention of the SEC Chief Accountant on certain drafts of the Committee on Accounting Procedure and the APB, which occurred also on issues other than the ones that are germane to this article, raises a question whether Committee and APB members were voting their genuine beliefs or were bowing to the inevitable, namely, the position espoused, or known to be held, by the Chief Accountant.[21]

2.3. Further on Upward Departures from Historical Cost

Those who might have hoped at the outset of the 1960s that the newly formed APB could open the door, if only slightly, to upward departures

---

[19] Sidney Davidson, who was a member of the APB at that time, has confirmed this reason for the change from an *Opinion* to a *Statement*. Telephone conversation with Davidson on 31 December 2006.

[20] Accounting Principles Board, Minutes of meeting—16–18 August 1967, p.10 (in the author's files).

[21] In 1972, Charles T. Horngren, an academic and a member of the APB, argued: 'The SEC (top management) has used decentralisation with a master's touch. Its lower-level management (APB) does an enormous amount of work for no salary and has just enough freedom to want to continue the arrangement. . . . the Board has been unjustifiably criticised for timidity or vacillation on several occasions when the basic explanation for the Board's behavior has been no assurance of support from the SEC' (1972:39).

from historical cost accounting were rudely taken aback by the APB's peremptory rejection of its research study on accounting principles, today known as a conceptual framework document, which was published in 1962. The two academic authors of the study, Robert T. Sprouse and Maurice Moonitz, advocated the use of net realisable values or, alternatively, current replacement cost to measure merchandise inventory and the use of current replacement cost to measure plant and equipment (1962:27–34). The research study was received coolly, to say the least, by the members of the APB and by the advisory committee on the project. Indeed, three members of the advisory committee, former SEC Chief Accountants Blough and Werntz and the sitting Chief Accountant, Barr, totally rejected the authors' recommendations.[22] Barr minced no words when he wrote, 'indiscriminate application of the [recommended] principles could result in false and misleading financial statements and might tend to undermine the confidence of the public in all published financial statements' (Sprouse and Moonitz, 1962:60). For its part, the APB discarded the research study and declined to consider it again ('Statement', 1962).

In 1963, Arthur R. Wyatt wrote an accounting research study on business combinations for the APB in which, among other things, he recommended a 'fair-value pooling' concept. This meant that, for business combinations effected by an issue of shares and where the constituents were of approximately equal size, the assets of both constituents should be restated at their fair values, up or down (1963:107). He insisted that this approach was 'applicable *only* when the facts of the transaction indicate clearly that the resultant entity is, in effect, a new enterprise' (107). Yet Chief Accountant Barr likened Wyatt's 'fair-value pooling' concept for business combinations to the upward quasi-reorganisations to which the SEC had objected some years ago (1965:24). Barr was ever on guard for what he regarded as 'upward' quasi-reorganisations in new guise.

In APB *Opinion No. 6*, issued in 1965, whose purpose was to declare the status of the previously issued *Accounting Research Bulletins* from No. 43 onwards, it was stated that, with respect to Chapters 9A and 9B of *ARB No. 43*, 'property, plant and equipment should not be written up by an entity to reflect appraisal, market or current values which are above cost to the entity' but that 'Whenever appreciation has been recorded on the books, income should be charged with depreciation computed on the written up amounts' (APB, 1965:42). One of the APB members, Sidney Davidson, of the University of Chicago and a former student of Paton's, qualified his assent to the board's view that fixed assets should not be written up to

---

[22] Blough was then a member of the APB, and Werntz, a partner in the firm of Lybrand, Ross Bros. & Montgomery, had been the last chairman of the Committee on Accounting Procedure. Barr had been expressly authorised by the Commission to accept the invitation to serve on the advisory committee, which was an unprecedented instance of a Chief Accountant serving on an Institute committee.

reflect current costs 'but only because he feels current measurement techniques are inadequate for such restatement. When adequate measurement methods are developed, he believes that both the reporting of operations in the income statement and the valuation of plant in the balance sheet would be improved through the use of current rather than acquisition costs' (42).

In 1966, an American Accounting Association committee produced *A Statement of Basic Accounting Theory* (Committee to Prepare a Statement of Basic Accounting Theory, 1966). Among other things, it recommended that both historical and current costs be reported in the body of companies' financial statements (30–1, Appendix B). The author recalls a gathering during the Association's 1966 annual meeting, at which the committee presented its recommendations. During the meeting, SEC Chief Accountant Barr stated that the SEC would not accept such financial statements.

A possible reason why US companies may not have been greatly concerned over the impact on earnings of historical cost accounting during times of rising prices was the availability of last-in, first-out (LIFO) accounting for inventories as well as the use by a considerable number of companies of one or both of the accelerated methods of depreciation for financial reporting purposes following enactment of the Internal Revenue Code of 1954.

3. COPING WITH THE INFLATION OF THE 1970s— THE SEC RECANTS ON CURRENT COST/VALUE

A major changing of the guard within the SEC occurred in 1972. Andrew Barr, the last of the Chief Accountants who had joined the SEC's accounting staff in the 1930s, retired. Instead of tapping A. Clarence Sampson, Barr's deputy whom he had intended to succeed him, SEC Chairman William J. Casey decided that he wanted to look outside the Commission for the next Chief Accountant.[23] He chose an activist, John C. (Sandy) Burton, an accounting and finance professor at Columbia University who had studied accounting at Haverford College with Philip W. Bell. It was Bell, together with Edgar O. Edwards, who wrote a highly influential book in 1961, *The Theory and the Measurement of Business Income*, in which they explained and advocated the use of current cost accounting. Burton was already on record as favouring a change in the traditional accounting model that would better depict economic reality (1971:50). Burton, at age 39, had not been an accountant during the 1930s and thus would not have been haunted, like his predecessors, by tales of the write-ups during the 1920s.

US inflation was high throughout the 1970s, and one of the earliest exposure drafts issued by the newly established Financial Accounting Standards Board (FASB), which succeeded the APB in July 1973, was entitled

---

[23] Interview with A. Clarence Sampson, conducted by Ernest Ten Eyck, 7 July 2005 (SEC Historical Society, at http://www.sechistorical.org/museum/oralhistories/index.php#sampson).

'Financial reporting in units of general purchasing power' (1974). Prior to the issue of the exposure draft, the FASB had published a discussion memorandum and held a public hearing on the subject. The recommendation in the draft was that companies' conventional financial statements should include a comprehensive GPL-restatement of their statements. Almost immediately, SEC Chief Accountant Burton derided the FASB's 'Units of general purchasing power' proposal as 'PuPU accounting' (1975:70). He argued that GPL-restated financial statements would not provide investors with any better information than conventional statements. He observed that 'the impact of inflation falls with dramatic unevenness on various sectors of the economy and various parts of firms'. He added, 'It is essential that rapid movement take place in the direction of replacement cost accounting so that investors can perceive the effects of inflation on the activities of business enterprise' (70). Coming from the SEC, this was indeed a revolutionary call for reform.

Burton meant what he said. In August 1975, the SEC announced a proposed revision to *Regulation S-X* to require that a defined set of large companies make footnote disclosure of replacement cost information for cost of sales, inventories, depreciation, and productive capacity (SEC, 1975; 'SEC proposes', 1975). The proposal, affecting about 1,000 of the country's largest non-financial corporations, went into effect in March 1976, when the SEC issued *Accounting Series Release (ASR) No. 190*, thereby rebuffing the FASB, which had opted for GPL-restatements (SEC, 1976; 'SEC adopts', 1976). The SEC stated in the release that 'it did not and does not view its [1975] proposal as competitive with that of the FASB', because companies could adopt GPL-restatements in conjunction with historical costs or replacement costs. But Leonard M. Savoie, a former AICPA executive vice-president, wrote, 'I do not know of anyone who agrees with the Commission on that, and the FASB deferred action on its exposure draft' (1979:231). The SEC clearly had taken the initiative for dealing with the effects of inflation out of the FASB's hands. Although the required replacement cost information was not to be reflected in the body of the financial statements and did not have to be subject to audit, this was nonetheless a historic deviation from the SEC's defence of the primacy of historical cost accounting. Charles Horngren, a close student of the US accounting standard-setting process, attested to the pivotal role played by the Chief Accountant:

> 'As chief accountant, John C. Burton persuaded the SEC to mandate fair values. . . . strong influential leaders can make a difference, especially if they are at points of leverage in the process. And timing counts too. For example, as chief accountant of the SEC, Andrew Barr had a well-known aversion to upward departures from historical costs. If Barr were sitting in Burton's chair in 1976, I wonder if the replacement cost requirements would have been issued.' (Horngren, 1986:38)

Under Burton's leadership, the SEC performed a role in the US similar to that played by the Sandilands Committee in the UK in 1975, when the latter suddenly refocused the field of debate from Current Purchasing Power accounting, which had been recommended by the Accounting Standards Steering Committee in a provisional standard, to current cost accounting (see Tweedie and Whittington, 1984, ch. 5).

In 1979, the FASB recovered its lost ground. It issued *Statement of Financial Accounting Standards (SFAS) No. 33* (1979b), which called for the supplementary disclosure of both current cost and GPL-restated data, dubbing the latter as 'constant dollar accounting', which, like the SEC release, applied only to very large corporations. Accordingly, in October 1979, the SEC issued *Accounting Series Release No. 271* to delete the disclosure requirements set out in *ASR No. 190* once the FASB's *SFAS No. 33* were to take effect. Although an FASB standard now governed practice, it had been much influenced by the SEC's powerful intervention.

Later in the 1970s, the SEC took a further step away from its long embrace of historical cost accounting by calling for the required use of current value information for proven reserves in the body of the financial statements of oil and gas producers.[24] The issue arose in the aftermath of the Arab Oil Embargo of the United States and other Western nations in 1973. Congress enacted the Energy Policy and Conservation Act (EPCA) of 1975, which directed the SEC, after receiving formal advice from the FASB, to eliminate the diversity of accounting practice used in oil and gas production. Until then, some producers would capitalise only the costs incurred in successful production, while expensing the costs associated with failed attempts at discovering oil or gas deposits. This method, used mainly by the large, vertically integrated oil and gas companies, is known as 'successful efforts costing'. Other producers would capitalise all of the costs associated with oil and gas exploration. This method, used mainly by the smaller companies, is known as 'full costing'.

In 1977, the FASB issued *SFAS No. 19*, which, by a 4–3 vote, recommended that only the 'successful efforts costing' method be permitted. In reaching its conclusion, the board was under considerable pressure from small and medium-sized oil and gas companies not to require the use of 'successful efforts costing' (Staubus, 2003: 185–6; Van Riper, 1994, ch.4). As required by the EPCA, the SEC held public hearings, covering 12 days and accumulating 2,700 pages of transcript, with all five members of the Commission in attendance. Furthermore, there was intense pressure brought on the SEC from the smaller oil and gas companies, much of which was transmitted through members of Congress and federal departments, such as Justice and Energy. They used all of their lobbying might to defend

---

[24] For a full and authoritative treatment of this oil and gas accounting episode, see Gorton (1991).

against the imposition of 'successful efforts costing', which, they believed, would make their earnings trend much more volatile. For one of the few times in the SEC's history, all of the Commissioners—who rarely are versed in accounting—personally became immersed in an accounting issue.[25] Not being schooled in accounting, the Commissioners had no allegiance to historical cost accounting, and they believed that, for the oil and gas industry, it was market values, not historical costs, that were relevant to investors. Indeed, this view was pressed on them numerous times during the hearings. It helped that the Chairman, Harold M. Williams, although trained as a lawyer, had been formerly a business school dean and a board director of a major oil and gas company. The Commissioners also believed, as did their accounting staff, that neither 'successful efforts costing' nor 'full costing' was demonstrably superior to the other. Accordingly, in August 1978, the SEC issued *Accounting Series Release No. 253*, which said that steps should be taken to develop and implement 'reserve recognition accounting' (RRA), a variant of current value accounting, for required use in the body of oil and gas companies' financial statements. Under RRA, the unrealised holding gains and losses in value of proven oil and gas reserves were to be taken to earnings. For the first time since the founding of the SEC in 1934, the Commission required a class of registrants to depart from historical cost accounting in the body of their financial statements. Times had indeed changed, and by then the memories of the flagrant write-ups of the 1920s had faded.

The SEC said that, in the interim, until RRA is ready for implementation, oil and gas companies may continue using either 'successful efforts costing' or 'full costing'. Thereupon, the FASB felt it had no option but to issue *SFAS No. 25* to suspend the effective date for the requirement in *SFAS No. 19* to use 'successful efforts costing' (1979a). Following the issue of the SEC's release, the major oil and gas companies began to bring pressure on the SEC not to require the use of current values for their proven oil and gas reserves because of its impact on the public's perception of their profitability at a time of steadily rising petrol prices and constricted supply. The Organisation of the Petroleum Exporting Countries (OPEC) was raising the price of crude each quarter, and the major refining and marketing companies were already being denounced in the media for their escalating profits. In the end, in February 1981, the SEC reconsidered its requirement that RRA be used in the body of producers' financial statements and instead announced its support of a move by the FASB to develop a comprehensive footnote disclosure that would reflect the principles implicit in RRA. The FASB issued that guidance in *SFAS No. 69*, issued in November 1982.

---

[25] An earlier such hearing was on 22 November 1965, when the Commissioners met with a delegation from the APB to discuss the classification of the deferred tax credit, which led to the issue of *Accounting Series Release No. 102* (SEC, 1965). For a discussion of this episode, see Zeff (2007).

But the precedent had been set. In 1978, for the first time, the SEC had announced as a matter of policy that historical cost accounting was not always to be preferred over the use of current values in the body of companies' financial statements.

4. CONCLUSION

One can see from the foregoing analysis that the SEC established and restated its position time and again on the primacy of conventional historical cost accounting during its first 38 years (that is, until 1972), even when the Committee on Accounting Procedure or the Accounting Principles Board was disposed to approve upward adjustments in one manner or another from conventional historical cost. This posture of the SEC explains the deeply held attachment to historical cost accounting that one associates with US financial reporting during much of the 20th century. The year 1972 marked the arrival of a Chief Accountant who was unencumbered by memories of the indiscriminate write-ups of the 1920s and, moreover, had been tutored in the merits of current cost accounting. Owing to his proactive influence, the SEC approved the required use by more than one thousand large companies of supplementary replacement cost disclosures during the inflationary 1970s. The SEC took one major step further when, during an intense period of controversy over accounting for oil and gas exploration in the second half of the 1970s, it called for the integration of current values into the body of companies' financial statements as a better solution than arbitrating the supremacy of 'full cost costing' in relation to 'successful efforts costing'. In the 1970s, the SEC had entered a new era in the regulation of company financial reporting. The record of the SEC's numerous and powerful intrusions into the process of establishing proper accounting practice for inventories and fixed assets does much to call into question whether the United States truly has had a private-sector process for establishing 'generally accepted accounting principles'.

APPENDIX

The Role of the SEC Chief Accountant in Relation to the Bodies That Establish Accounting Principles

The Chief Accountant is the principal adviser to the Commission on accounting and auditing matters. From 1937 to 1982, the Commission issued *Accounting Series Releases* to express its view on accounting and auditing matters and to report on enforcement actions taken by the Commission. The Office of the Chief Accountant, together with the Division of Corporation Finance, which oversees corporate disclosure of important information to the investing public, have, since 1975, issued *Staff Accounting Bulletins* to convey their interpretations and practices in administering the disclosure requirements of the federal securities acts.

While the SEC has stated that it looks to the private sector for leadership in the establishment of accounting principles, all parties know that the ultimate authority to establish those principles rests with the SEC, which, in most instances, usually means the Office of the Chief Accountant.

The American Institute of Accountants, at the urging of the Chief Accountant (Blough, 1967: 5–7), enlarged its Committee on Accounting Procedure in 1938–39 and invested it with authority to issue *Accounting Research Bulletins (ARBs)*, setting out its opinion on proper accounting practice, which came to be known as 'generally accepted accounting principles' (GAAP). Unless the Chief Accountant were to make known his disagreement with an *ARB* or with the authoritative pronouncements of its successor bodies, it may be assumed that the SEC expects all publicly traded companies, known as registrants, to comply with them. As is made evident in this article, the Chief Accountant occasionally attended meetings of the committee, and he and his staff communicated on a regular basis, in writing and orally, with members of the committee and its research staff.

The Accounting Principles Board (APB), which succeeded the Committee on Accounting Procedure in 1959, was a senior technical committee of the American Institute of Certified Public Accountants, which adopted its new name in 1957. Its authoritative recommendations on GAAP were called Opinions. In addition, it issued several Statements that constituted non-binding advice. The SEC Chief Accountant and his staff maintained frequent contact with the APB and its staff but did not attend its meetings.

The Financial Accounting Standards Board (FASB), an independent standard-setting body overseen by a board of trustees, succeeded the APB in 1973. Its authoritative recommendations on GAAP are known as *Statements of Financial Accounting Standards*. As with the FASB's two predecessors, the SEC Chief Accountant and his staff have been in regular contact with the FASB and its staff. Some or all of the SEC Commissioners meet periodically with some or all of the FASB members, together with their respective staffs, and the Chief Accountant participates in meetings of the FASB's Emerging Issues Task Force and attends and speaks at the quarterly meetings of the FASB's advisory council.

REFERENCES

'Accounting concepts and standards underlying corporate financial statements: 1948 revision' (1948). *The Accounting Review*, 23 (4): 339–44.

Accounting Principles Board. (1965). 'Status of Accounting Research Bulletins'. *Opinion No. 6*. New York: American Institute of Certified Public Accountants.

Accounting Principles Board (1969). 'Financial statements restated for general price-level changes'. *Statement No. 3*. New York: American Institute of Certified Public Accountants.

'Accounting principles underlying corporate financial statements' (1941). *The Accounting Review*, 16 (2): 133–9.

Arthur Andersen & Co. (1959). *Memorandum on Price-Level Depreciation*. Chicago: Arthur Andersen & Co.

Arthur Andersen & Co. (1969). *Accounting and Reporting Problems of the Accounting Profession*. 3d edition. Arthur Andersen & Co.

Arthur Andersen & Co. (1972). *Objectives of Financial Statements for Business Enterprises*. Arthur Andersen & Co.

'Annual Report of the Committee on Accounting Procedure' (1946). *Yearbook/ American Institute of Accountants 1944–45*. New York: American Institute of Accountants.

'Annual Report of the Committee on Accounting Procedure' (1947). *Yearbook/ American Institute of Accountants 1945–1946*. New York: American Institute of Accountants.

Armstrong, J.S. (1956). 'Corporate accounting standards under federal securities laws'. *The Ohio Certified Public Accountant*, 15: 155–60.

Barr, A. (1965). 'The influence of government agencies on accounting principles with particular reference to the Securities and Exchange Commission'. *The International Journal of Accounting Education and Research*, 1 (1): 15–33.

Barr, A. (1979). 'Relations between the development of accounting principles and the activities of the SEC', in W. Cooper and Y. Ijiri (eds), *Eric Louis Kohler: Accounting's Man of Principles*, 41–61. Reston, VA: Reston Publishing.

Barr, A. and Koch, E.C. (1959). 'Accounting and the S.E.C.' *The George Washington Law Review*, 28 (1): 176–93.

Blackie, W. (1948). 'What is accounting accounting for—Now?' *N.A.C.A. Bulletin*, 29 (21), section 1: 1349–78.

Blough, C.G. (1937). 'The need for accounting principles'. *The Accounting Review*, 12 (1): 30–7.

Blough, C.G. (1947). 'Replacement and excess construction costs', *The Journal of Accountancy*, 84 (4): 333–6.

Blough, C.G. (1967). 'Development of accounting principles in the United States'. In *Berkeley Symposium on the Foundations of Financial Accounting*, 1–14. Berkeley: Schools of Business Administration, University of California.

Burton, J.C. (1971). 'An educator views the public accounting profession'. *The Journal of Accountancy*, 132 (3): 47–53.

Burton, J.C. (1975). 'Financial reporting in an age of inflation'. *Journal of Accountancy*, 139 (2): 68–71.

Chatov, R. (1975). *Corporate Financial Reporting: Public or Private Control?* New York: The Free Press/Macmillan.

Committee on Accounting Concepts and Standards (1957). 'Accounting and reporting standards for corporate financial statements, 1957 revision'. *The Accounting Review*, Vol. 32 (4): 536–46.

Committee on Accounting Procedure (1940). 'Depreciation on appreciation'. *Accounting Research Bulletin No. 5. The Journal of Accountancy*, 69 (6): 461–7.

Committee on Accounting Procedure (1947). 'Appropriation, not charges, recommended to cover inflated replacement cost'. *The Journal of Accountancy*, 84 (4): 289–90.

Committee on Accounting Procedure (1948). 'Institute committee rejects change in basis for depreciation charges'. *The Journal of Accountancy*, 86 (5): 380–1.

Committee on Accounting Procedure (1953). 'Restatement and revision of Accounting Research Bulletins'. *Accounting Research Bulletin No. 43*. New York: American Institute of Accountants.

Committee to Prepare a Statement of Basic Accounting Theory (1966). *A Statement of Basic Accounting Theory*. American Accounting Association.

Cooper, W.D. (1980). 'Carman G. Blough: A study of selected contributions to the accounting profession'. PhD dissertation completed at the University of Arkansas. Published as *Carman G. Blough: Selected Contributions in Accounting*. Atlanta: Georgia State University Press, 1982.

Davis, M.L. and Largay, J.A. III (1995). 'Quasi reorganization: Fresh or false start'. *Journal of Accountancy*, 180 (1): 79–84.

De Bedts, R.F. (1964). *The New Deal's SEC: The Formative Years*. New York: Columbia University Press.

Depreciation Policy When Price Levels Change (1948). New York: Controllership Foundation.

Edwards, E.O. and Bell, P.W. (1961). *The Theory and Measurement of Business Income*. Berkeley, CA: University of California Press.

Financial Accounting Standards Board (1974). 'Financial Reporting in Units of General Purchasing Power'. *Exposure Draft*, December 31. Stamford, CT: Financial Accounting Standards Board.

Financial Accounting Standards Board (1977). 'Financial accounting and reporting by oil and gas producing companies'. *Statement of Financial Accounting Standards No. 19*. Stamford, CT: Financial Accounting Standards Board.

Financial Accounting Standards Board (1979a). 'Suspension of Certain Accounting Requirements for Oil and Gas Producing Companies, an amendment of FASB Statement No. 19'. *Statement of Financial Accounting Standards No. 25*. Stamford, CT: Financial Accounting Standards Board.

Financial Accounting Standards Board (1979b). 'Financial reporting for changing prices'. *Statement of Financial Accounting Standards No. 33*. Stamford, CT: Financial Accounting Standards Board.

Financial Accounting Standards Board (1982). 'Disclosures about oil and gas producing activities, an amendment of FASB Statements 19, 25, 33, and 39'. *Statement of Financial Accounting Standards No. 69*. Stamford, CT: Financial Accounting Standards Board.

Goodrich, P.F. (1969). Letter. *The Journal of Accountancy*, 128 (6): 23–4.

Gorton, D.E. (1991). 'The SEC decision not to support SFAS 19: A case study of the effect of lobbying on standard setting'. *Accounting Horizons*, 5 (1): 29–41.

Grady, P. (1965). *Inventory of Generally Accepted Accounting Principles for Business Enterprises*. New York: American Institute of Certified Public Accountants.

Healy, R.E. (1938). 'The next step in accounting'. *The Accounting Review*, 13 (1): 1–9.

Healy, R.E. (1939). 'Address before the Harvard Business School Alumni Association at its Ninth Annual Special Meeting, at Baker Library, Harvard Business School, Boston'. Typescript, 16 June.

Horngren, C.T. (1972). 'Accounting principles: Private or public sector?' *Journal of Accountancy*, 133 (5): 37–41.

Horngren, C.T. (1986). 'Institutional alternatives for regulating financial reporting'. In R.H. Mundheim and N.E. Leech (eds), *The SEC and Accounting: The First 50 Years*, 29–51. Amsterdam: North-Holland.

'Institute committee holds to depreciation on cost' (1948). Editorial. *The Journal of Accountancy*, 86 (5):353–4.

Jones, R.C. (1955). *Price Level Changes and Financial Statements: Case Studies of Four Companies*. American Accounting Association.

Jones, R.C. (1956). *Effects of Price Level Changes on Business Income, Capital, and Taxes*. American Accounting Association.

King, E.C. (1947a). 'Footnotes to financial statements'. *Virginia Accountant*, 1: 9–22.

King, E.C. (1947b). 'Some current accounting problems'. Reproduced in A.R. Roberts (ed), *Selected Papers of Earle C. King*, 123–31. New York: Arno Press, 1980.

King. E.C. (1948). 'Need for definitive statement of accounting principles'. *The Journal of Accountancy*, 86 (5): 369.

King, E.C. (1950). 'Current accounting problems'. *The Accounting Review*, 25 (1): 35–44.

Kripke, H. (1970). 'The SEC, the accountants, some myths and some realities'. *New York University Law Review*, 45 (6): 1151–1205.

Kripke, H. (1979). *The SEC and Corporate Disclosure: Regulation in Search of a Purpose*. New York: Law & Business, Inc./Harcourt Brace Jovanovich, Publishers.

Mason, P. (1955). *Price-Level Changes and Financial Statements: Basic Concepts and Methods*. American Accounting Association.

May, G.O. (1943). *Financial Accounting: A Distillation of Experience*. New York: Macmillan.

McMullen, S.Y. (1949). 'Depreciation and high costs: The emerging pattern'. *The Journal of Accountancy*, 88 (4): 302–10.

Miller, P.B.W. and Redding, R. (1986). *The FASB: The People, the Process, & the Politics*. Homewood, IL: Irwin.

Papworth, W.S. (1948). 'A summary of papers from the Institute's 1947–48 annual meeting'. *The Journal of Accountancy*, 86 (5): 382–8.

Paton, W.A. (1941) *Advanced Accounting*. New York: Macmillan.

Paton, W.A. and Littleton, A.C. (1940). *An Introduction to Corporate Accounting Standards*. American Accounting Association.

'Price level changes and financial statements' (1951). Supplementary Statement No. 2. *The Accounting Review*, 26 (4): 468–74.

Randall, R.F. (1974). 'Finally—Inflation accounting?' *Management Accounting*, 56 (5): 57–9.

Research Department (1949). 'An inquiry into the reliability of index numbers'. *The Journal of Accountancy*, 87 (4): 312–19.

Research Department (1950). 'Departures from the cost basis'. *The Journal of Accountancy*, 89 (5): 388–91.

Savoie, L.M. (1979). 'Some views of current activities of the Securities and Exchange Commission'. In D.E. Tidrick (ed), *Leonard M. Savoie: Words from the Past, Thoughts for Today*. New York: Garland Publishing, 1995.

'SEC adopts disclosure rules for replacement costs' (1976). *Journal of Accountancy*, 141 (5): 11.

'SEC proposes replacement cost disclosure' (1975). *Journal of Accountancy*, 140 (4): 22.

Securities and Exchange Commission (1938). 'Administrative policy on financial statements'. *Accounting Series Release No. 4* (April 25). Washington: Securities and Exchange Commission.

Securities and Exchange Commission (1941). 'Procedure in quasi-reorganization'. *Accounting Series Release No. 25* (May 29). Washington: Securities and Exchange Commission.

Securities and Exchange Commission (1942). *Seventh Annual Report of the Securities and Exchange Commission, Fiscal Year Ended June 30, 1941*. Washington: United States Government Printing Office.

Securities and Exchange Commission (1949). *14th Annual Report, Securities and Exchange Commission, 1948, Fiscal Year Ended June 30*. Washington: United States Government Printing Office.

Securities and Exchange Commission (1955). *20th Annual Report, Securities and Exchange Commission, 1954, Fiscal Year Ended June 30*. Washington: United States Government Printing Office.

Securities and Exchange Commission (1965). 'Balance Sheet Classification of Deferred Income Taxes Arising from Installment Sales'. *Accounting Series Release No. 102* (December 7). Washington: Securities and Exchange Commission.

Securities and Exchange Commission (1975). 'Notice of proposed amendments to Regulation S-X to require disclosure of certain replacement cost data in notes to financial statements (S7-579)'. Securities Act Release No. 5608/August 21; Securities Exchange Act Release No. 11608. Washington: Securities and Exchange Commission.

Securities and Exchange Commission (1976). 'Notice of adoption of amendments to Regulation S-X requiring disclosure of certain replacement cost data'. *Accounting Series Release No. 190* (March 23). Washington: Securities and Exchange Commission.

Securities and Exchange Commission (1978). 'Adoption of requirements for financial accounting and reporting practices for oil and gas producing activities'. *Accounting Series Release No. 253* (August 31). Washington: Securities and Exchange Commission.

Securities and Exchange Commission (1979). 'Deletion of requirement to disclose replacement cost information'. *Accounting Series Release No. 271* (October 23). Washington: Securities and Exchange Commission.

Securities and Exchange Commission (1981). 'Financial reporting by oil and gas producers'. *Accounting Series Release No. 289* (February 26). Washington: Securities and Exchange Commission.

'Security and Exchange Commission proposes to revise its Regulation S-X which governs financial statements filed with it'. (1950). *The Journal of Accountancy*, 90 (2): 158–65.

Seligman, J. (2003). *The Transformation of Wall Street: A History of the Securities and Exchange Commission and Modern Corporate Finance.* 3d edition. New York: Aspen Publishers.

Smith, R.L. (1955). 'A case analysis of external accounting influence over managerial decisions'. Doctoral dissertation done at the Harvard Business School (August).

Sprouse, R.T. and Moonitz, M. (1962). *A Tentative Set of Broad Accounting Principles for Business Enterprises.* New York: American Institute of Certified Public Accountants.

Staff of the Accounting Research Division (1963). *Reporting the Financial Effects of Price-Level Changes.* New York: American Institute of Certified Public Accountants.

'Statement by the Accounting Principles Board' (1962). New York: American Institute of Certified Public Accountants, April 13.

Staubus, G.J. (2003). 'An accountant's education'. *The Accounting Historians Journal*, 30 (1): 155–96.

Stock Exchange Practices (1934). Hearings before the Committee on Banking and Currency, United States Senate, 73d Congress, 2d Session, on S.Res. 84, S.Res. 56, and S.Res. 97, Part 16: National Securities Exchange Act (continued), March 23 to April 5. Washington: United States Government Printing Office.

Study Group on Business Income (1952). *Changing Concepts of Business Income.* New York: Macmillan.

Sweeney, H.W. (1936) *Stabilized Accounting.* New York: Harper & Brothers.

'A tentative statement of accounting principles affecting corporate reports' (1936). *The Accounting Review*, 11 (2): 187–91.

Tweedie, D. and Whittington, G. (1984). *The Debate on Inflation Accounting.* Cambridge: Cambridge University Press.

'Two new Research Bulletins' (1940). Editorial. *The Journal of Accountancy*, 69 (6): 427–8.

Van Riper, R. (1994). *Setting Standards for Financial Reporting: FASB and the Struggle for Control of a Critical Process*. Westport, CT: Quorum Books.

Walker, R.G. (1992). 'The SEC's ban on upward asset revaluations and the disclosure of current values'. *Abacus*, 28 (1): 3–35.

Werntz, W.W. (1941). 'Progress in accounting'. *The Journal of Accountancy*, 72 (4): 315–23.

Werntz, W.W. (1945). 'Corporate consolidations, reorganizations and mergers'. *The New York Certified Public Accountant*, 15 (7): 379–87.

Wyatt, A.R. (1963). *A Critical Study of Accounting for Business Combinations*. New York: American Institute of Certified Public Accountants.

Zeff, S.A. (1966). *The American Accounting Association, Its First 50 Years*. American Accounting Association.

Zeff, S.A (1972). *Forging Accounting Principles in Five Countries: A History and an Analysis of Trends*. Champaign, IL: Stipes Publishing Company.

Zeff, S.A. (1979). 'Paton on the effects of changing prices on accounting, 1915–55'. In S.A. Zeff, J. Demski, and N. Dopuch (eds), *Essays in Honor of William A. Paton: Pioneer Accounting Theorist*, 91–137. Ann Arbor, MI: Graduate School of Business Administration, The University of Michigan.

Zeff, S.A. (1992). 'Arthur Andersen & Co. and the two-part opinion in the auditor's report: 1946–1962'. *Contemporary Accounting Research*, 8 (2): 443–67.

Zeff, S.A. (2007). 'The SEC preempts the Accounting Principles Board in 1965: The classification of the deferred tax credit relating to installment sales'. *The Accounting Historians Journal*, 34 (1): 1–23.

Appendix
Publications

BOOKS AND MONOGRAPHS

Uses of Accounting for Small Business, Bureau of Business Research, University of Michigan, 1962, 67 pp.

(editor with T.F. Keller) *Financial Accounting Theory: Issues and Controversies*, McGraw-Hill Book Company, 1964, 456 pp.

The American Accounting Association—Its First Fifty Years, AAA, 1966, 96 pp.; reprinted by AAA in 1991.

(editor with A. Rappaport and P.A. Firmin) *Public Reporting by Conglomerates*, Prentice-Hall, Inc., 1968, 156 pp.

(editor) *Business Schools and the Challenge of International Business*, Tulane Graduate School of Business Administration, 1968, 292 pp.

(editor with T.F. Keller) *Financial Accounting Theory II: Issues and Controversies*, McGraw-Hill Book Company, 1969, 458 pp.

Forging Accounting Principles in Five Countries: A History and an Analysis of Trends, Stipes Publishing Co., 1972, 332 pp.; Chapter IV, Canada, reprinted in Murphy (ed.), *A History of Canadian Accounting Thought and Practice*, Garland Publishing, 1993.

Forging Accounting Principles in Australia, Australian Society of Accountants, 1973, 67 pp.; reprinted in Parker (ed.), *Accounting in Australia: Historical Essays*, Garland Publishing, 1990.

(editor with T.F. Keller) *Financial Accounting Theory I: Issues and Controversies*, McGraw-Hill Book Company, second edition, 1973, 622 pp.

(editor and author of introductory essay) *Asset Appreciation, Business Income and Price-Level Accounting: 1918–1935*, Arno Press, 1976.

(editor) *Selected Dickinson Lectures in Accounting 1936–1952*, Arno Press, 1978.

A Critical Examination of the Orientation Postulate in Accounting, with Particular Attention to Its Historical Development, Arno Press, 1978 (doctoral dissertation).

(editor with J. Demski and N. Dopuch) *Essays in Honor of William A. Paton: Pioneer Accounting Theorist*, Division of Research, Graduate School of Business Administration, The University of Michigan, 1979, 217 pp.

Forging Accounting Principles in New Zealand, Victoria University Press, 1979, 88 pp.

(editor) *Accounting Principles Through the Years: The Views of Professional and Academic Leaders, 1938–1954*, Garland Publishing, 1982, 475 pp.

(compiler and editor) *The Accounting Postulates and Principles Controversy of the 1960s*, Garland Publishing, 1982, 574 pp.

(editor with M. Moonitz) *Sourcebook on Accounting Principles and Auditing Procedures: 1917–1953*, Garland Publishing, 1985, 1,104 pp. (2 vols.).

(editor with T.F. Keller) *Financial Accounting Theory: Issues and Controversies*, McGraw-Hill Book Company, third edition, 1985, 660 pp.

(editor) *The U.S. Accounting Profession in the 1890s and Early 1900s*, Garland Publishing, 1988, 585 pp.

(with F. van der Wel and K. Camfferman) *Company Financial Reporting: A Historical and Comparative Study of the Dutch Regulatory Process*, North-Holland, 1992, 410 pp.

(with B.G. Dharan) *Readings and Notes on Financial Accounting: Issues and Controversies*, McGraw-Hill Book Company, fourth edition, 1994, 782 pp.

(editor with D. Solomons) *Accounting Research, 1948–1958, Volume 1: Selected Articles on Accounting History*, Garland Publishing, 1996; and *Accounting Research, 1948–1958, Volume 2: Selected Articles on Accounting Theory*, Garland Publishing, 1996; 510 pp.

(compiler and author of introductory notes, with R.H. Parker) *Milestones in the British Accounting Literature*, Garland Publishing, 1996, 418 pp.

(with B.G. Dharan), *Readings & Notes on Financial Accounting: Issues and Controversies* and *Instructor's Manual*, The McGraw-Hill Companies, fifth edition, 1997, 671 and 139 pp.

Henry Rand Hatfield: Humanist, Scholar, and Accounting Educator, JAI Press Inc./Elsevier, 2000, 515 pp.

(with K. Camfferman) *Financial Reporting and Global Capital Markets: A History of the International Accounting Standards Committee 1973–2000*, Oxford University Press, 2007, 676 pp.

(editor) *Principles before Standards: The ICAEW's 'N Series' of Recommendations on Accounting Principles 1942–1969*, Institute of Chartered Accountants in England and Wales, 2009, 189 pp.

CHAPTER IN A BOOK

"Political Lobbying on Accounting Standards—National and International Experience," Chapter 9 in the 9th edition of Nobes and Parker, *Comparative International Accounting* (UK: FT Prentice Hall, 2006); revised as Chapter 10 in the 10th edition published in 2008, further revised as Chapter 11 in the 11th edition to be published in 2010.

COLLECTED WORKS

Accounting Standards Setting: Theory and Practice (Beijing: Public Finance and Economics Publisher, 2005)—14 articles in English, which were translated into Chinese on the initiative of the Ministry of Finance.

LECTURES

A Perspective on the US Public/Private-Sector Approach to Standard Setting and Financial Reporting, University of Limburg, 1994, 38 pp.

Academic and Professional Accounting Journals: Whence, Why and Whither?, 1996 Coopers & Lybrand Lecture, The University of Wales, Aberystwyth, 38 pp.

MAJOR REPORTS

(draftsman) "Business Administration" (pp. 35–70), in *The Professional School and World Affairs*, published by the University of New Mexico Press for Education and World Affairs, 1968.

(principal draftsman) Report of the AAA Committee on Accounting History, *The Accounting Review*, Supplement to Vol. XLV, 1970.

(draftsman, with eight others) *Statement on Accounting Theory and Theory Acceptance*, American Accounting Association, 1977, 61 pp.

(co-author, as member of the Research Committee) *Auditing into the Twenty-first Century*, The Institute of Chartered Accountants of Scotland, 1993, 63 pp.

MAJOR ARTICLES

"Standard Costs in Financial Statements—Theory and Practice," *N.A.A. Bulletin*, April 1959; reprinted in Anton and Firmin (eds.), *Contemporary Issues in Cost Accounting: A Discipline in Transition* (Houghton Mifflin, 1966, 1972), and in Parker (ed.), *Accountancy: A Sourcebook of Readings* (Pitman, 1971).

"Legal Dividend Sources: A National Survey and Critique," *The New York Certified Public Accountant*, November and December 1961.

"Replacement Cost: Member of the Family, Welcome Guest, or Intruder?," *The Accounting Review*, October 1962; reprinted in Dean and Wells (eds.), *Current Cost Accounting: Identifying the Issues* (ICRA/University of Sydney, 1978, 1979).

"Episodes in the Progression of Price-Level Accounting in the United States," *The Accountants' Magazine*, April 1964; reprinted in *Illinois CPA*, Autumn 1964, in Langhout (ed.), *Aspects of Accounting and Auditing*, vol. 1 (Balkema, 1965), and in Chatfield (ed.), *Contemporary Studies in the Evolution of Accounting Thought* (Dickenson, 1968).

(with W.D. Maxwell) "Holding Gains on Fixed Assets—A Demurrer," *The Accounting Review*, January 1965.

(with R.L. Fossum) "An Analysis of Large Audit Clients," *The Accounting Review*, April 1967.

"El Proceso de Desarrollo de Principios Contables en México," *Dirección y Control*, febrero de 1971.

"Forging Accounting Principles in Canada," *Canadian Chartered Accountant*, May and June 1971.

"1926 to 1971 Chronology of Significant Developments in the Establishment of Accounting Principles in the United States," in Rappaport and Revsine (eds.), *Corporate Financial Reporting: The Issues, the Objectives and Some New Proposals* (Commerce Clearing House, Inc., 1972); reprinted in Zeff and Keller (see above), 1973; reprinted with updatings in *Journal of Accounting Research*, Spring 1972, and in Burns (ed.), *Accounting in Transition: Oral Histories of Recent U.S. Experience* (The Ohio State University, 1974); reprinted with further updatings in Parker and Lee (eds.), *The Evolution of Corporate Financial Reporting* (Thomas Nelson and Sons Limited, 1979).

"Forging Accounting Principles in New Zealand," *The Accountants' Journal*, June 1977.

"The Rise of 'Economic Consequences'," *Stanford Lectures in Accounting 1978*, Graduate School of Business, Stanford University, [1979]; abridged version published in *Journal of Accountancy*, December 1978. The former was reprinted in Zeff and Keller 1985 (see above under Books) and in Zeff and Dharan 1994 (see above under Books). The latter was reprinted in Pound (ed.), *The Development of Accounting Principles—A Study of Diversity*, AFM Exploratory Series No. 6 (Armidale, NSW, Australia: University of New England, 1979); in Bloom and Elgers (eds.), *Accounting Theory & Policy: A Reader* (Harcourt, Brace Jovanovich, 1981, 1987); in McCullers and Schroeder, *Accounting Theory: Text and Readings* (Wiley, 1982; with Clark, 1987; in Schroeder and Clark, 1995), in Burns and Hendrickson (eds.), *The Accounting Sampler* (McGraw-Hill, 1986); in Anderson (ed.), *Readings in Canadian Financial Reporting* (Clarence Byrd, 1988); in Bloom & Elgers (eds.), *Foundations of Accounting Theory and Policy: A Reader* (Dryden, 1995); in Jones, Romano and Ratnatunga (eds.), *Accounting Theory: A Contemporary Review* (Sydney: Harcourt Brace, 1995); and in Zeff and Dharan 1997 (see above under Books).

"Paton on the Effects of Changing Prices on Accounting, 1916–55," in Zeff, Demski and Dopuch (see above under Books).

"Evolución de la Teoría Contable. La Investigación Empírica," *Administración de Empresas* (Argentina), abril de 1982; reprinted in *Contaduría Universidad de Antioquia*, marzo de 1985, and in *Revista de Investigación Contable TEUKEN*, IV trimestre de 1988.

"Truth in Accounting: The Ordeal of Kenneth MacNeal," *The Accounting Review*, July 1982; reprinted in Edwards (ed.), *Twentieth-Century Accounting Thinkers* (London: Routledge, 1994), and in Edwards (ed.), *The History of Accounting: Critical Perspectives on Business and Management* (London: Routledge, 2000).

"Towards A Fundamental Rethinking of the Role of the 'Intermediate' Course in the Accounting Curriculum," in Jensen (ed.), *The Impact of Rule-Making on Intermediate Financial Accounting Textbooks* (The Ohio State University, 1983).

(with S.-E. Johansson) "The Curious Accounting Treatment of the Swedish Government Loan to Uddeholm," *The Accounting Review*, April 1984; reprinted in Zeff and Keller 1985 (see above under Books).

(with T.R. Dyckman) "Two Decades of the *Journal of Accounting Research*," *Journal of Accounting Research*, Spring 1984.

"Some Junctures in the Evolution of the Process of Establishing Accounting Principles in the U.S.A.: 1917–1972," *The Accounting Review*, July 1984; reprinted in *The Accountants Digest*, June 1985, and in Bloom and Elgers (eds.), *Issues in Accounting Policy: A Reader* (Dryden, 1995).

"Big Eight Firms and the Accounting Literature: The Falloff in Advocacy Writing," *Journal of Accounting, Auditing & Finance*, Spring 1986.

"Leaders of the Accounting Profession: 14 Who Made a Difference," *Journal of Accountancy*, May 1987.

"Recent Trends in Accounting Education and Research in the USA: Some Implications for UK Academics," *The British Accounting Review*, June 1989.

"Arthur Andersen & Co. and the Two-Part Opinion in the Auditor's Report: 1946–1962," *Contemporary Accounting Research*, Spring 1992.

"The Politics of Accounting Standards," *Economia Aziendale*, August 1993.

"The Regulation of Financial Reporting: Historical Developments and Policy Recommendations," *De Accountant*, November 1993; reprinted in Walton (ed.), *Country Studies in International Accounting—Europe* (Elgar, 1996).

(with K. Camfferman) "The Contributions of Theodore Limperg Jr (1879–1961) to Dutch Accounting and Auditing," in Edwards (ed.), *Twentieth-Century Accounting Thinkers* (London: Routledge, 1994).

"A Perspective on the U.S. Public/Private-Sector Approach to the Regulation of Financial Reporting," *Accounting Horizons*, March 1995; reprinted in Zeff and Dharan 1997 (see above under Books); reprinted in French translation in *Revue Française de Comptabilité*, March and April 1995 and in *Mélanges en l'Honneur du Professeur Jean-Claude Scheid* (Ordre des Experts Comptables, February 2005); reprinted in Spanish translation in *Contaduría Universidad de Antioquia*, marzo-septiembre de 1995; for earlier version, see same title under Lectures, above.

"A Study of Academic Research Journals in Accounting," *Accounting Horizons*, September 1996; adapted and updated from *Academic and Professional Accounting Journals: Whence, Why and Whither?* (see Lectures, above).

"The U.S. Senate Votes on Accounting for Employee Stock Options" in Zeff and Dharan 1997 (see above under Books); reprinted with a new introduction as "Playing the Congressional Card on Employee Stock Options: A Fearful Escalation in the Impact of Economic Consequences Lobbying on Standard Setting," in Cooke and Nobes (eds.),*The Development of Accounting in an International Context: A Festschrift in Honour of R. H. Parker* (London: Routledge, 1997).

"The Early Years of the Association of University Teachers of Accounting: 1947–1959," *The British Accounting Review*, June 1997 (Special Issue).

"The Coming Confrontation on International Accounting Standards," *The Irish Accounting Review*, Autumn 1998; posted on the database of PricewaterhouseCoopers' global corporate reporting group, December 1998; also in Spanish: "Normas Internacionales de Contabilidad—Confrontación Futura," *Accountability: Desarrollo, Productividad, Interdisciplinariedad* (Colombia), enero-febrero de 1999; "Confrontación Futura sobre Normas Internacionales de Contabilidad," *InterAméricA* (journal of the Asociación Interamericana de Contabilidad), abril-junio de 1999, and in *Enciclopedia de Contabilidad* (Bogotá: Panamericana Editorial, 2002), capítulo 22; extracts published as "The SEC: Rampant Speculation but What Happens Next?" in *Accounting & Business* (UK), February 1999; modified version published as "The IASC's Core Standards: What Will the SEC Do?," *The Journal of Financial Statement Analysis*, Fall 1998.

(with W. Buijink and K. Camfferman) "'True and Fair' in the Netherlands: *inzicht* or *getrouw beeld*?," *The European Accounting Review*, Vol. 8, No. 3 (1999).

"The Evolution of the Conceptual Framework for Business Enterprises in the United States," *The Accounting Historians Journal*, December 1999; reprinted in Fleischman (ed.), *Accounting History* (Sage Publications, 2005); published in Spanish translation as "La Evolución del Marco Conceptual para las Empresas Mercantiles en Estados Unidos," *Revista Española de Financiación y Contabilidad*, No. 100 (Extraordinario 1999) and, with a slight revision, in Tua (coordinador), *El Marco Conceptual para la Información Financiera: Análisis y Comentarios* (Madrid: Asociación Española de Contabilidad y Administración de Empresas, 2000), and in *Revista Legis del Contador* (Colombia), octubre-diciembre de 2000.

"John B. Canning: A View of His Academic Career," *Abacus*, February 2000.

(with G. Whittington) "Mathews, Gynther and Chambers: Three Pioneering Australian Theorists," *Accounting and Business Research*, Summer 2001.

"The Work of the Special Committee on Research Program," *The Accounting Historians Journal*, December 2001.

"'Political' Lobbying on Proposed Standards: A Challenge to the IASB," *Accounting Horizons*, March 2002; also in *Indian Accounting Review*, December 2002; reprinted in Nobes (ed.), *Developments in the International Harmonization of Accounting* (Elgar, 2004).

"Du Pont's Early Policy on the Rotation of Audit Firms," *Journal of Accounting and Public Policy*, January/February 2003.

(with K. Camfferman) "'The Apotheosis of Holding Company Accounting': Unilever's Financial Reporting Innovations from the 1920s to the 1940s," *Accounting, Business & Financial History*, July 2003.

"How the U.S. Accounting Profession Got Where It Is Today: Part I," *Accounting Horizons*, September 2003; "How the U.S. Accounting Profession Got Where It Is Today: Part II," *Accounting Horizons*, December 2003; the "Conclusion" section was reproduced in *CA Magazine* (Scotland), July 2004.

"The Evolution of U.S. GAAP: The Political Forces Behind Professional Standards," *The CPA Journal*, January and February 2005; earlier version posted on Deloitte's IAS PLUS Website, July 2004; also posted in Japanese translation on Website of Akira Yokoyama, CPA, Tokyo (http://www.hi-ho.ne.jp/yokoyama-a/usgaap.htm).

"The Primacy of 'Present Fairly' in the Auditor's Report," *Accounting Perspectives*, Vol. 6, No. 1 (2007); posted in the Emanuel Saxe Digital Media Library and on the Emanuel Saxe Lecture Series website.

"The SEC Preempts the Accounting Principles Board in 1965: The Classification of the Deferred Tax Credit Relating to Installment Sales," *The Accounting Historians Journal*, June 2007.

"The SEC Rules Historical Cost Accounting: 1934 to the 1970s," *Accounting and Business Research*, International Accounting Policy Forum Issue (2007).

"Some Obstacles to Global Financial Reporting Comparability and Convergence at a High Level of Quality," *The British Accounting Review*, December 2007.

"IFRS Developments in the USA and EU, and Some Implications for Australia," *Australian Accounting Review*, December 2008. Also delivered as the Ken Spencer Memorial Lecture, on May 28 2008 in Sydney, Australia, and posted at http://www.frc.gov.au/reports/other/ken_spencer_2008.asp, the website of the Australian Government's Financial Reporting Council.

(with C. Nobes) "Auditors' Affirmations of Company Compliance with IFRS around the World: An Exploratory Study," *Accounting Perspectives*, Vol. 7, No. 4 (2008).

"The Contribution of the Harvard Business School to Management Control, 1908–1980," *Journal of Management Accounting Research*, 2008 special issue.

(with K. Camfferman) "The Formation and Early Years of the Union Européenne des Experts Comptables, Economiques et Financiers (UEC), 1951–1963—or: How the Dutch Tried to Bring Down the UEC," *Accounting, Business & Financial History*, November 2009.